www.ingramcontent.com/pod-product-compliance
Lightning Source LLC
LaVergne TN
LVHW080900300926
849162LV00003B/493

Championing Civil Rights in the Digital Era

Adrian David Cheok
https://orcid.org/0000-0001-6316-2339

Nanjing University of Information Science and Technology, China

IGI Global
Scientific Publishing
Publishing Tomorrow's Research Today

Vice President of Editorial — Melissa Wagner
Director of Acquisitions — Mikaela Felty
Director of Book Development — Jocelynn Hessler
Production Manager — Mike Brehm
Cover Design — Jose Rosado

Published in the United States of America by
IGI Global Scientific Publishing
701 East Chocolate Avenue
Hershey, PA, 17033, USA
Tel: 717-533-8845 | Fax: 717-533-7115
Website: https://www.igi-global.com E-mail: cust@igi-global.com

Library of Congress Cataloging-in-Publication Data

LCCN: (CIP Data Pending)
ISBN13: 9798369339206
Isbn13Softcover: 9798369351048
EISBN13: 9798369339213

British Cataloguing in Publication Data
A Cataloguing in Publication record for this book is available from the British Library.

Dedicated to my forever beloved children Nikola and Angelina (Boo Boops).

Table of Contents

Detailed Table of Contents

This chapter examines the complex relationship between artificial intelligence (AI) and civil rights, highlighting how algorithmic systems can both enhance opportunities and intensify inequalities. While AI offers advancements in efficiency, healthcare, and public services, it also risks perpetuating bias, eroding privacy, and undermining democratic freedoms if left unchecked. The discussion emphasizes the need to balance innovation with rights protection by embedding fairness, accountability, and transparency into AI design and governance. Strategies include legal reforms, technological safeguards, participatory governance, and international collaboration. The chapter concludes with a call for a multi-stakeholder roadmap to ensure that AI development respects justice, equality, and human dignity in the digital era.

The issue regarding freedom of expression and content moderation is one of the vast issues in digital times. This chapter examines the various policy contexts that deal with this challenge in the digital platforms. It looks at the conflict between safeguarding civil liberties and guarding against the propagation of dangerous information, i.e., hate speech, misinformation, and hate speech. The chapter looks at national and international regulations, regulations specific to platforms and developing legal standards. It further examines the effect played by the privately owned technology companies in determining online discourse by using moderation methods and algorithmic filtering. Essential issues of transparency, accountability and protection of marginalized voice are addressed. The chapter contains some case studies which illustrate the practice of governments and platforms balancing this situation. It concludes with policy proposals that enhance integrity of democracy, freedom of speech and responsible moderation in digital areas.

The evolution of the state surveillance apparatus in India, particularly through the integration of novel technologies such as Facial Recognition Technology (FRT) and Artificial Intelligence (AI), has significantly transformed national security and law enforcement strategies. While these advancements enhance the state's capacity for counter-terrorism and crime prevention, they also raise critical privacy and human rights concerns. The paper analyses the existing legal framework governing surveillance in India, focusing on the implications of AI-driven FRT. Key concerns are categorised into three areas: (a) security vulnerabilities, (b) inaccuracies, biases, and lack of transparency in FRT systems, and (c) the potential misuse of surveillance powers by the state. The paper is not technical in nature; instead, it critically analyses existing laws and proposes policy recommendations and regulatory mechanisms to balance national security imperatives with the protection of individual privacy rights in a democratic society.

This chapter explores the transformative potential of digital technologies in advancing inclusive education for all learners, particularly those from marginalized or underserved communities. In an increasingly digital world, integrating inclusive principles into educational technologies and pedagogical design is not only necessary but also urgent. Connected for All examines how digital tools can break down traditional barriers to learning, promote equitable access, and support diverse educational needs, including those of learners with disabilities, language differences, and socio-economic disadvantages. Through practical examples, case studies, and evidence-based strategies, this work demonstrates how educators, policymakers, and technology developers can collaborate to ensure that no learner is left behind. It also addresses the challenges, such as the digital divide, lack of accessibility standards, and educator readiness, that must be overcome to make digital inclusion a reality.

In the contemporary era, technological progress has led to a heightened emphasis not only on distinguishing between private and public spheres but also on identifying elements that may inadvertently enter the public domain but nonetheless contribute to privacy concerns. This study aims to examine the complex interplay between privacy rights and dignity in the context of widespread technological progress. This article explores the notion of human dignity, which is presented as a major subject that emphasizes the importance of people and their right to autonomy and respect. The study assesses the intricate interplay between privacy, governance, and societal values by drawing from philosophical viewpoints, legal frameworks, and case studies. This study highlights the pressing need for strong norms and ethical standards to safeguard privacy and promote democratic principles in the digital era, as it seeks to comprehend India's stance on privacy rights and concerns related to mass surveillance programs.

Freedom of speech and expression is the cornerstone of a democracy. Humor as an expression of free speech is well protected under its ambit. In India, Article 19(1)(a) of the Indian Constitution guarantees the fundamental right to freedom of speech and expression. However, this right is also subject to certain reasonable restrictions under Article 19(2). Even though there is ample jurisprudence existing on freedom of speech and expression in India, the protection of humor and its different forms in the digital age has been rarely explored comprehensively. This chapter first aims to study the jurisprudential foundations of freedom of speech and expression and evolution of humor as a form of speech. Second, the relationship between humor as free speech in India and law in the digital age is analyzed through the framework of free speech regulations and various judicial precedents. Finally, the chapter highlights

Preface

Civil rights protections in the United States have always evolved in tight orbit around the prevailing political constellation. Today, that constellation is once again centred on Donald J. Trump, who—after an interlude of partisan realignment—returned to the White House on 20 January 2025 as the 47 th president of the Republic. The White House His renewed incumbency, emerging in a post pandemic landscape dominated by artificial intelligence platforms, algorithmic governance, and hyper polarised online discourse, creates an unprecedented laboratory for re examining the trajectory of American civil rights.

OVERVIEW OF THE SUBJECT MATTER

Championing Civil Rights in the Digital Era interrogates the complex interplay among legislation, executive directives, court rulings, administrative discretion, and digitally amplified public opinion from 2016 through the dawn of Trump's second presidency. Rather than cataloguing events chronologically, the book adopts a thematic, data driven lens that traces how power is exercised, contested, and reconfigured across five core domains—voting access, criminal justice reform, LGBTQ+ equality, immigration enforcement, and affirmative action policy. At each analytical juncture, digital infrastructures—social media virality, predictive policing algorithms, voter file analytics, and deep fakes—serve both as accelerants of change and as new battlegrounds for civil rights advocacy.

WHERE THE TOPIC FITS IN THE WORLD TODAY

The world of 2025 is mediated by code as much as by courts. Generative AI news feeds, biometric border controls, and real time sentiment dashboards shape not merely how citizens interpret policy, but also how policymakers anticipate backlash and craft messaging. The reinstatement of a Trump administration—bolstered by an expanded conservative judiciary and a newly assertive coalition of digital native activists—intensifies debates about the durability of long-standing norms:

A. Legislative flux is accelerated by executive rule makings propagated almost instantly through official social media accounts.
B. Judicial interpretations travel faster and more widely via livestreamed hearings, creating quasi crowdsourced legitimacy—or delegitimacy—within hours.
C. Grass roots mobilisation now occurs on encrypted group chats, DAOs, and algorithmically curated micro networks, challenging classical First Amendment assumptions about public squares.
D. Understanding civil rights in this moment therefore demands both doctrinal analysis and a literacy in the computational substrates that deliver those doctrines to lived experience.

TARGET AUDIENCE

The book is purpose built for a constellation of readers whose professional or civic lives intersect with civil rights questions:

A. Scholars and students in political science, constitutional law, sociology, and data science, who require an integrated framework marrying doctrinal exegesis with computational evidence.
B. Legal practitioners, judges, and policymakers seeking empirically grounded context to inform litigation strategies, statutory drafting, and regulatory oversight.
C. Civil rights organisations and investigative journalists intent on moving beyond anecdote to statistically defensible claims about disparate impact and systemic bias.
D. Informed citizens eager to parse sensational headlines and algorithmically filtered feeds in favour of historically contextualised, peer reviewed knowledge.
E. Importance of the Contributed Studies

ORGANIZATION OF THE BOOK

Chapter 1: Civil Rights in the Age of AI Challenges and Strategies examines the complex relationship between artificial intelligence (AI) and civil rights, highlighting how algorithmic systems can both enhance opportunities and intensify inequalities. While AI offers advancements in efficiency, healthcare, and public services, it also risks perpetuating bias, eroding privacy, and undermining democratic freedoms if left unchecked. The discussion emphasizes the need to balance innovation with rights protection by embedding fairness, accountability, and transparency into AI design and governance. Strategies include legal reforms, technological safeguards, participatory governance, and international collaboration. The chapter concludes with a call for a multi-stakeholder roadmap to ensure that AI development respects justice, equality, and human dignity in the digital era.

Chapter 2: Balancing Freedom of Expression and Moderation: Policy Frameworks in Digital Spaces examines the various policy contexts that deal with this challenge in the digital platforms. It looks at the conflict between safeguarding civil liberties and guarding against the propagation of dangerous information, i.e., hate speech, misinformation, and hate speech. The chapter looks at national and international regulations, regulations specific to platforms and developing legal standards. It further examines the effect played by the privately owned technology companies in determining online discourse by using moderation methods and algorithmic filtering. Essential issues of transparency, accountability and protection of marginalized voice are addressed. The chapter contains some case studies which illustrate the practice of governments and platforms balancing this situation. It concludes with policy proposals that enhance integrity of democracy, freedom of speech and responsible moderation in digital areas.

Chapter 3: A Legal Analysis on Navigating Facial Recognition Technology in India's State Surveillance Framework explores the evolution of the state surveillance apparatus in India, particularly through the integration of novel technologies such as Facial Recognition Technology (FRT) and Artificial Intelligence (AI), has significantly transformed national security and law enforcement strategies. While these advancements enhance the state's capacity for counter-terrorism and crime prevention, they also raise critical privacy and human rights concerns. The paper analyses the existing legal framework governing surveillance in India, focusing on the implications of AI-driven FRT. Key concerns are categorised into three areas: (a) security vulnerabilities, (b) inaccuracies, biases, and lack of transparency in FRT systems, and (c) the potential misuse of surveillance powers by the state. The paper is not technical in nature; instead, it critically analyses existing laws and proposes policy recommendations and regulatory mechanisms to balance national security imperatives with the protection of individual privacy rights in a democratic society.

Chapter 4: Connected for All Championing Inclusive Education in the Digital Era explores the transformative potential of digital technologies in advancing inclusive education for all learners, particularly those from marginalized or underserved communities. In an increasingly digital world, integrating inclusive principles into educational technologies and pedagogical design is not only necessary but also urgent. Connected for All examines how digital tools can break down traditional barriers to learning, promote equitable access, and support diverse educational needs, including those of learners with disabilities, language differences, and socio-economic disadvantages. Through practical examples, case studies, and evidence-based strategies, this work demonstrates how educators, policymakers, and technology developers can collaborate to ensure that no learner is left behind. It also addresses the challenges, such as the digital divide, lack of accessibility standards, and educator readiness, that must be overcome to make digital inclusion a reality.

Chapter 5: Digital Activism and Social Movements: Exploring the Role of Digital Platforms in Mobilizing and Empowering Civil Rights Movements examines the shift from traditional collective action to connective action, emphasizing more flexible and personalized ways of engagement. It discusses how digital platforms enable individuals to express dissent, build solidarity, and advocate for their rights. It also addresses the risks and contradictions associated with online activism. The chapter concludes by presenting a framework that highlights key areas, including global visibility, marginalized voices, and independent spaces, where digital civil rights movements are making a meaningful impact. Ultimately, digital platforms serve as powerful spaces for negotiating and advancing civil rights in the digital age.

Chapter 6: Digital Dissent and Grassroots Mobilization: The Reconfiguration of Civil Rights Activism in the Age of Social Media explores movements like #BlackLivesMatter, #DalitLivesMatter, and anti-CAA protests to examine how digital tools foster participation while also exposing activists to surveillance, censorship, and algorithmic bias. Integrating perspectives from cyberfeminism and digital sociology, it advocates a rights-based framework for digital justice, emphasizing the need for legal protections and inclusive digital citizenship in the face of rising digital authoritarianism.

Chapter 7: Safeguarding Prisoner's Human Rights in the Age of Surveillance and AI: Digital Shackles evaluates the impact of AI surveillance on privacy, autonomy, and the ethical, legal, and psychological effects on prisoners. Continuous monitoring increases anxiety, stress, and diminishes control. It also examines human rights issues when AI influences parole, recidivism, and behavior predictions, noting the criticism of AI for racial and socio-economic biases. The study compares the approaches of the US, China, UK, and EU, highlighting rapid adoption in the US and China with privacy violations and discrimination. The EU and UK maintain more reserved approaches, emphasizing privacy. The paper recommends ethical AI usage in prisons, advocating for transparency, accountability, audits, and international collaboration to ensure responsible implementation and respect for prisoner rights.

Chapter 8: Empowering Water and Sanitation Rights Through Digital Justice Legal Reform and Inclusive Governance examines how digital justice, legal reform, and inclusive governance can be harnessed to advance equitable access to water and sanitation as essential human rights. It draws upon international legal instruments such as the ICESCR and the UN Watercourses Convention to explore how digital technologies, regulatory innovation, and smart infrastructure can support rights-based water and sanitation systems. Emphasis is placed on the intersection of environmental justice, digital inclusion, and legal empowerment in addressing systemic inequalities that affect marginalized populations. The chapter highlights how data-driven governance and public-private collaboration can improve transparency, accountability, and accessibility in service delivery. By framing water and sanitation access within the evolving discourse on civil rights in the digital era, the chapter advocates for forward-looking, interdisciplinary strategies that integrate law, technology, and sustainable development to build inclusive and resilient infrastructure.

Chapter 9: From Hashtags to Human Rights: Digital Advocacy and Constitutional Engagement in India and Nepal provides a critical argument on the relationship between digital advocacy and constitutional engagement in India and Nepal in regard to redefining citizen participation in the digital space, rights discourse, and accountability to the people and democracy. It talks about the development of digital civic activism protests of Nirbhaya, CAA-NRC demonstrations, and the Enough is Enough movement, pointing out the revolutionary contribution of hashtags and internet mobilizations. The chapter offers a comparative constitutional overview of legal safeguards of digital expression, judicial involvement, regulatory schemes and surveillance. It provides analysis of such issues as algorithmic censorship, digital divides, state interventions, promoting emergence of inclusive, rights-based practices in digital governance.

Chapter 10: Guardians of the Self: Rethinking Privacy and Data Sovereignty in the Digital Age discusses into the evolving concept of privacy rights and the emerging discourse on data sovereignty in the digital age. As individuals generate vast amounts of personal data through everyday digital interactions—often unknowingly—the ownership, control, and ethical use of that data have become central to civil liberties. The chapter critically examines how mass data collection, algorithmic profiling, and pervasive surveillance by both corporations and governments challenge the traditional boundaries of privacy. It highlights global regulatory efforts such as the GDPR, India's Digital Personal Data Protection Act, and emerging data localization mandates as attempts to restore agency to data subjects. However, these efforts are often undermined by techno-legal loopholes, cross-border data flows, and asymmetries of power between data collectors and individuals. Through real-world examples such as the Facebook-Cambridge Analytica scandal and Aadhaar-linked surveillance concerns, the chapter explores the tension between innovation, state control, and personal autonomy.

Chapter 11: Impact of Artificial Intelligence on Civil Liberties: Delving into the Ethical and Civil Rights Concerns Arising from AI Advancements critically examines the growing influence of artificial intelligence (AI) on civil liberties, exploring how algorithmic systems—while promising efficiency and innovation—pose significant risks to foundational rights such as privacy, due process, equality, and freedom of expression. As AI becomes embedded in policing, employment, healthcare, education, and social services, it increasingly mediates decisions that shape civic life and democratic participation. The chapter questions the moral and legal dilemmas of opaque algorithms, biased and unregulated data, and unmoderated surveillance, and how such technology can help to drive structural inequalities and cover up responsibility. Based on case law studies across various jurisdictions and multidisciplinary approach combining law, ethics, and technology; it puts forward a version of AI governance framework based on civil rights.

According to **Chapter 12: Law and Civil Rights in an Age of Artificial Intelligence,** as artificial intelligence (AI) has become an important part of modern society, it has created challenges for civil rights law. These challenges have created a variety of concerns regarding civil liberties, privacy, due process, and inequalities. AI has been integrated into various government agencies and private sectors to enhance safety, security, and efficiency. AI is quickly altering society, bringing unexpected advancements across various fields. The widespread nature of AI, from its application in government services to its deployment in private industries, requires a complete assessment of its effect on individual rights and liberties.

Chapter 13: Legal Frameworks for Privacy and Digital Freedoms critically analyzes the legal foundations of privacy and freedom of expression in the digital age, positioning them as central to democratic legitimacy and institutional accountability. It explores the normative evolution of digital rights across jurisdictions, the jurisdictional tensions in cross-border enforcement and the systemic inequalities that hinder access to redress. By integrating comparative constitutional analysis with global governance frameworks, the chapter argues for a rights-based and inclusive model of digital regulation. It concludes by emphasizing the need for global legal standards that advance justice, transparency and institutional equity in digital governance, aligning with broader development goals.

According to **Chapter 14: Right to Internet Access vs. National Security Concerns: Addressing the Complex Questions of the Digital Era**, the globe has made tremendous progress over the last few decades. The scientific and technological advancements have provided immense possibilities and opportunities to the world through the latest digitalization process. The present century is even termed as the digital era. Internet access is the most crucial element for the maximum utilization of digital technologies. Accordingly, the concept of digital rights evolved and identified the right to Internet access as the most essential digital right. However, several countries have not implemented this right as part of their human rights framework due to a lack of an international covenant or treaty. Besides, many countries violate the right to Internet access through many mechanisms, claiming national security grounds. In 2024, almost 300 Internet shutdowns happened across the globe, violating people's fundamental rights. From this perspective, this chapter examines the relevance of Internet access and critically evaluates the national security defensive mechanism.

According to **Chapter 15: Technocracy: The Rule of Expertise in a Modern World**, Technocracy—governance by technical experts—has emerged as a response to today's complex challenges, including climate change, rapid technological shifts, and social inequality. Rooted in the belief that expert knowledge can lead to more effective policy decisions, technocratic systems prioritize data, evidence, and efficiency over political ideology. Case studies show that such systems can deliver strong results, especially in areas like public health and environmental policy. However, technocracy faces criticism for being elitist, disconnected from public needs, and lacking transparency. To create a balanced model, it's essential to integrate ethical values, enhance accountability, and foster meaningful public participation. A reimagined technocracy must not only rely on experts but also engage citizens in decision-making. By blending technical expertise with democratic ideals, societies can work toward more inclusive, sustainable, and effective governance.

According to **Chapter 16: Upholding the Rights of Visually Impaired Individuals in a Digitally Driven World** The number of visually impaired individuals is increasing day by day; as per the previous reports of the World Health Organization (WHO), more than 2.2 individuals are now visually impaired, and sadly, this number is increasing rapidly. Due to low vision, such individuals face numerous challenges, whether it's related to education or employment. In most cases even their basic rights are neglected, making them backward in this digital era. This chapter proposes how digital assistive and modern artificial intelligence technologies can be used to uphold their rights in this era. The ideas can be implemented on the basis of a conceptual model that focuses on their important rights, probable policymaking, and measures to ensure transparency. This framework will ensure that the rights of visually impaired individuals are fulfilled and that they can spend their lives independently.

According to **Chapter 17: Unravelling Digital Ethics: Dark Patterns and Algorithm Bias** The present era can be categorised as digital not just because of the availability of digital space and platforms but because people are gearing up for these platforms by using them in their daily lives. It cannot be denied that digitalisation has made our lives immensely easier in many ways than one could have ever thought of. However, the negative aspects of the same cannot be denied. The emergence of new technology daily is posing severe concerns amongst the people at large as these digital algorithms, deceptive designs, and machine learning are few of the by-products of this era where the proliferation of online platforms and algorithmic decision-making has revolutionised the way individuals interact, consume information and make decisions. The present chapter conceptualises digital ethics in terms of algorithm bias and dark patterns with specific reference to e-commerce platforms. It also understands user relationships through the lens of e-contracts and consent, as observed by the Indian courts through various case laws.

Chapter 18: Digital Governance, Security, and Privacy Rights in India: Exploring Evolving Political Theory and Recent Legislative Developments aims to examine the complex interplay between privacy rights and dignity in the context of widespread technological progress. This article explores the notion of human dignity, which is presented as a major subject that emphasizes the importance of people and their right to autonomy and respect. The study assesses the intricate interplay between privacy, governance, and societal values by drawing from philosophical viewpoints, legal frameworks, and case studies. This study highlights the pressing need for strong norms and ethical standards to safeguard privacy and promote democratic principles in the digital era, as it seeks to comprehend India's stance on privacy rights and concerns related to mass surveillance programs.

Chapter 19: Humor as Free Speech in the Digital Age: Evolving Legal Dimensions in India first aims to study the jurisprudential foundations of freedom of speech and expression and evolution of humor as a form of speech. Second, the relationship between humor as free speech in India and law in the digital age is analyzed through the framework of free speech regulations and various judicial precedents. Finally, the chapter highlights the socio-legal challenges and ambiguities existing in the Indian legal system on governing humor and attempts to provide some suggestions for the way forward.

CONCLUDING REFLECTIONS ON IMPACT

By entwining historical context with cutting edge data analytics, Championing Civil Rights in the Digital Era provides an evidentiary scaffold for future scholarship and advocacy. It demonstrates that civil rights progress—and regression—no longer unfolds solely in marble columned chambers but is co produced in real time by server farms, social graph algorithms, and the rhetorical economies of 280 character bursts. In doing so, the book equips its readers with the conceptual and empirical tools needed to anticipate, critique, and ultimately steer the evolving civil rights ecosystem toward greater resilience and inclusivity, even under the intensified partisan cross winds of a renewed Trump presidency.

Adrian David Cheok
School of Automation, Nanjing University of Information Science and Technology, China

Acknowledgment

Adrian David Cheok would like to thank the School of Automation, Nanjing University of Information Science and Technology for giving me the support and research time to complete this work.

Chapter 1
Civil Rights in the Age of AI:
Challenges and Strategies

Akmal Abdurakhmanov
Termez University of Economics and Service, Uzbekistan

Abdurahim Boltayev
Mamun University, Uzbekistan

Mangubek Urazmetov
https://orcid.org/0009-0004-2155-7809
Urgench State University, Uzbekistan

Munir Ahmad
https://orcid.org/0000-0003-4836-6151
Survey of Pakistan, Pakistan

ABSTRACT

This chapter examines the complex relationship between artificial intelligence (AI) and civil rights, highlighting how algorithmic systems can both enhance opportunities and intensify inequalities. While AI offers advancements in efficiency, healthcare, and public services, it also risks perpetuating bias, eroding privacy, and undermining democratic freedoms if left unchecked. The discussion emphasizes the need to balance innovation with rights protection by embedding fairness, accountability, and transparency into AI design and governance. Strategies include legal reforms, technological safeguards, participatory governance, and international collaboration. The chapter concludes with a call for a multi-stakeholder roadmap to ensure that AI development respects justice, equality, and human dignity in the digital era.

DOI: 10.4018/979-8-3693-3920-6.ch001

INTRODUCTION

Artificial intelligence (AI) has become one of the most transformative developments of the twenty-first century, altering economic systems, social interactions, and the way public and private institutions operate. From predictive policing to automated recruitment in jobs, AI is increasingly shaping how opportunities, resources, and services are distributed in our society (Berk, 2021; Montasari, 2023). While these technologies hold out a promise of efficiency and innovation, they also raise pressing questions about their compatibility with long-standing civil rights protections. As algorithmic systems are increasingly tasked with roles that were formerly the exclusive preserve of human judgment, the threats of bias, exclusion, and rights abuses are increased (Schuilenburg & Soudijn, 2023; Ugwudike, 2022).

This intersection between AI and civil rights matters so much because it reveals the tension between technological innovation and democratic accountability (Buhmann & Fieseler, 2021; Niklas & Dencik, 2021). Civil rights structures - formed over the course of decades through legal, political, and social struggle - seek to protect basic freedoms like equality, privacy, due process, and freedom of expression. However, when designed without transparency or oversight, AI systems run the risk of perpetuating historical inequalities or creating new forms of discrimination. Predictive policing can perpetuate racial profiling, credit-scoring algorithms can disempower vulnerable groups, and black-box decision-making systems can undermine the right to challenge unfair decisions (Egbert & Mann, 2021; Joseph, 2025; Sandhu & Fussey, 2021). These advances show that for civil rights in the digital age, it is not sufficient to just modify current legal tools, but it is necessary to reimagine governance mechanisms to fit with technological realities.

This chapter aims to discuss these challenges holistically, while also suggesting ways in which AI can be made to be an instrument for giving power rather than for excluding. Specifically, the talk will chart the frontiers of AI connection with civil rights - policing, employment, housing, healthcare, and access to public services - while highlighting the risk of systemic discrimination and rights erosion. Through real-life case studies of algorithm bias and misuse, the chapter seeks to anchor the debate with concrete evidence. Finally, it will explore legal, technological, and policy-based strategies for rights protection, such as algorithmic audits, transparency requirements, rights-based AI design, and inclusive governance structures. The chapter provides a roadmap for scholars, policymakers, and practitioners who are determined to ensure that the promise of AI is not achieved at the cost of justice, equality, and human dignity.

ALGORITHMIC SYSTEMS AND CIVIL RIGHTS

There are also more and more AI systems that affect individual rights and determine the chances of life for people. While these technologies might increase efficiency, scalability, and predictive precision, their use in sensitive social domains has sparked serious civil rights concerns. In particular, the use of AI in the context of policing, employment, housing, and financial access, but also healthcare and public services, evolves around the risks of discrimination, exclusion, and the dilution of due process. Each of these areas of focus exposes where algorithmic decision-making intersects with centuries-old struggles for equality and justice.

AI in Policing and Criminal Justice

The criminal justice system is among the most visible and controversial of frontiers of AI deployment, since decisions here have a direct impact on basic rights such as liberty, equality, and due process (Blount, 2024; Dempsey, Brunet, & Dubljević, 2023; Haley & Burrell, 2025). Predictive policing schemes, which use historical crime data to predict future "hotspots," have been tested or implemented in cities throughout North America, Europe, and Asia (Khan, Ali, & Alharbi, 2022; van Dijk, Nieuwbeerta, & Joudo Larsen, 2022). Proponents believe that these systems enable law enforcement agencies to better allocate resources, focus on areas with the most risk, and drive down crime by intervening before crimes happen. However, critics argue that predictive policing can be used as a tool for perpetuating existing systemic disparities. Crime data are not neutral; they trace the history of over-policing in marginalized neighborhoods where minority groups have long been under heavy surveillance. This data is then input into predictive models, which guide additional law enforcement resources to the same neighborhoods, creating a self-reinforcing loop of surveillance, suspicion, and criminalization. Instead of breaking patterns of discrimination, AI systems may hardwire them into future enforcement practices.

In addition to the experience-based risks associated with AI in policing, facial recognition technologies offer another notable example of how both promise and risk come together (Ahmed Khan & Rizvi, 2021). Researchers point to their usefulness in finding missing persons, tracking down suspects, and improving security in public places. Yet there have been plenty of peer-reviewed studies and civil rights analyses documenting significant differences in accuracy among demographic groups. Facial recognition algorithms are more accurate for lighter-skinned males, but are less successful when it comes to darker-skinned people, women, and children. The consequences of these errors are not just technical - they can lead to miscarriages of justice, unwarranted prosecutions, and a breach of the presumption of innocence. There are several cases, for example, where innocent people have been arrested and detained based on faulty facial recognition matches (Bergold & Kovera, 2024). Apart from accuracy, transparency is another big issue. Citizens, and even legislators, often don't have a legible understanding of how these tools are acquired, what data they are trained on, and under what conditions they are used. Not only that, police often use "proprietary rights" of vendors as a justification for withholding technical aspects of their cases, and this effectively means that people who are wronged by an algorithmic error are up against virtually impossible odds. Lack of transparency and accountability: This lack of transparency and accountability undermines democratic oversight and raises constitutional issues regarding due process and equal protection.

Together, predictive policing and facial recognition illustrate the extreme danger of integrating AI into the criminal justice system without proper protections in place. While these technologies hold the promise of efficiency, they can erode public trust, perpetuate racial inequalities, and undermine civil liberties if left unchecked. Their utilization highlights the importance of robust legal frameworks, algorithmic audits, and transparent redress mechanisms to ensure that AI doesn't become an instrument of injustice.

Human Resources Management Systems

The recruitment industry has been one of the biggest testbeds for AI applications, especially in the fields of recruitment and hiring. AI-powered platforms are becoming more and more popular for screening resumes, evaluating your qualifications, and even delivering automated video interviews. From an efficiency perspective, these technologies are very attractive: they can sift through thousands of applications in minutes, identify candidates with valuable skills, and save time and dollars associated with hiring. However, the data used to train these systems can inadvertently perpetuate past inequities, meaning that the push toward efficiency can come at the cost of fairness or equal opportunity (Deepa, Sekar, Malik, Kumar, & Attri, 2024; Gong, Zhao, Wang, & Lv, 2022; Madanchian, Taherdoost, & Mohamed, 2023; Votto, Valecha, Najafirad, & Rao, 2021). Data bias is a fundamental issue in training data. So, if a company historically recruited many more men than women into leadership positions, an AI trained using that data may learn to perpetuate those biases, continuing to favor male applicants for comparable roles (Vidhya, Nirmala, & Manju, 2023; Whang, Roh, Song, & Lee, 2023). This issue is not theoretical; it has been reported in the real world in cases where hiring algorithms discriminated against resumes containing terms and connections related to women, including membership in women's organizations. Far from creating meritocratic systems, AI risks automating old prejudices behind a veneer of technological neutrality.

These challenges are further exacerbated by the emergence of automated video interview platforms. Some systems claim to assess personality traits, emotional intelligence, or cultural fit from facial expressions, tone of voice, or body language. These tools run the risk of disadvantaging applicants who do not conform to narrow norms of behavior. For instance, people with disabilities, including autism spectrum conditions, speech impairments, or people with differing mobility needs, may be penalized unnecessarily. Non-native speakers (and candidates from a variety of different cultures) can be misjudged if their communication styles differ from the system's embedded norms. Furthermore, the secrecy of such determinations leaves rejected applicants with no recourse for the reasons for which they are rejected. Without transparency, there is a lack of recourse for those who may be affected, a lack of assurance for employers that they are acting in a manner consistent with anti-discrimination laws, and an inability for regulators to evaluate systemic fairness.

These issues point to larger questions around accountability in the future of work. Employers can depend on AI vendors to offer tools to accomplish their goals, but end-to-end responsibility for fairness should fall to the organizations using them. In the absence of robust regulatory frameworks and algorithmic audits, the unbridled growth of AI in hiring holds the danger of perpetuating systemic discrimination, eroding trust in hiring processes, and compromising efforts towards diversity and inclusion in the workplace.

Housing, Credit, and Financial Access

The provision of housing, credit, and financial services is a fundamental prerequisite for social mobility, participation in the economy, and equality of opportunity. More and more, these life-enhancing areas are mediated by AI-powered decision-making systems like mortgage approval algorithms, tenant screening systems, and credit-scoring models. Although these systems are often presented as neutral, objective, and efficient alternatives to human decision-making, they are profoundly influenced by the data and assumptions that are built into their construction (Kothandapani, 2025; Kshetri, 2021; Perry, Martin, & Schnare, 2023; Sadok, Sakka, & El Maknouzi, 2022).

One high-profile example is the legacy of redlining in the United States, during which minorities were systematically refused housing loans and insurance based on their location. Even though these types of practices are now illegal, the data they produced continues to inform modern algorithms. When approval systems for mortgages or rentals are based on historical data that contain patterns of exclusion, they run the risk of repeating discriminatory results. For example, applicants who come from historically disinvested neighborhoods may be rejected at a higher rate or given less favorable terms, not because of their individual financial behavior but because of structural biases introduced into the data.

Credit-scoring algorithms create other risks (Sadok et al., 2022). While they are intended to measure financial integrity, they commonly include proxies for socioeconomic status like education level, employment history, or zip code. Some new models even include non-traditional data like online buying data or social media. These variables could have the unintended consequence of disadvantaging low-income individuals, racial minorities, and immigrants who are less likely to perform the behaviors the algorithm has come to correlate with "creditworthiness." What is even more damaging is that these models are opaque. Denied applicants often have little to no insight as to why they were rejected, nor do they have clear recourse mechanisms for decision appeal or to correct errors in their profiles.

Together, these practices contribute to the perpetuation of economic inequality. These acts of denial, whether it's the refusal of credit or housing, impede the ability of individuals to accumulate wealth, secure stable living conditions, or advance socially. At a societal level, this leads not only to questions of policy, but also of civil rights: access to economic opportunity is a basic tenet in democratic societies. AI systems without robust oversight in the areas of housing and finance are at risk of becoming powerful tools for exclusion, deepening the divide between those with privilege and those who live with marginalisation.

Healthcare and Public Services

Healthcare and public service delivery are just a few examples of areas where AI can create enormous value - lowering costs, increasing efficiency, and saving lives. However, these areas also have some of the greatest stakes in terms of equity and civil rights. Examples of AI applications in healthcare include: diagnostic algorithms, predictive analytics for patient risk, and resource allocation systems that may decide eligibility for treatments or referrals to specialists. While such tools may improve clinicians' decision-making, their reliance on past and often incomplete data can result in systemic inequities (Achanta, 2025; Anshari, Hamdan, Ahmad, & Ali, 2025; Briganti & Le Moine, 2020; Sunarti et al., 2021). For example, research has found that the health risk prediction algorithms that major insurers and hospital systems use systematically underestimate the severity of illness for Black patients more than for white patients with similar clinical profiles. This was the case because people were using the algorithms that use spending on healthcare as a proxy for health needs. Since Black patients have had less access to healthcare, the lower spending was analyzed as a lower health risk, resulting in fewer referrals for advanced care. This is a stark example of how even seemingly neutral AI tools can yield discriminatory outcomes that further exacerbate the racial disparity in health outcomes.

Public services are another good example of the dangers. Governments across the world are increasingly resorting to automated decision-making systems to determine eligibility for welfare payments, child support, unemployment benefits, and the processing of immigration applications. While automation can help automate bureaucratic processes and cut costs, it also creates vulnerabilities. Incorrect input of data, flawed algorithms, or biased risk assessment models can lead to unauthorized denial of vital services to at-risk groups. Procedures are often not transparent, and opportunities for appeals are restricted, meaning that errors can be hard to identify and even harder to challenge.

The opaqueness of these systems creates important governance issues. As more and more important social safeguards rely on algorithmic decisions, people are often unable to challenge decisions that impact their livelihoods, health, and dignity. This has the potential to erode the values of fairness, transparency, and accountability that are fundamental to democratic governance. Furthermore, the fact that these systems unequally affect marginalized and low-income populations means that questions of technical accuracy are also important matters of social justice and human rights. To better illustrate how algorithmic systems intersect with civil rights across different social domains, Table 1 summarizes the opportunities and risks identified in policing, employment, housing, and financial access, as well as healthcare and public services. The table highlights not only the potential benefits of AI applications but also the structural challenges and rights-based concerns they raise.

Table 1. Algorithmic systems and civil rights across key domains

Domain	AI Applications	Potential Benefits	Civil Rights Risks	Key Concerns
Policing & Criminal Justice	Predictive policing, facial recognition	Resource allocation, crime prevention, and locating missing persons	Reinforcement of racial biases, wrongful arrests, and a lack of due process	Over-policing, transparency gaps, and weak oversight
Employment & Hiring	Resume screening, automated video interviews, predictive assessments	Faster recruitment, cost savings, and identification of skills	Gender and disability bias, cultural misinterpretation, and opacity in rejection	Discrimination in hiring, lack of explainability, and erosion of workplace diversity
Housing & Financial Access	Mortgage approval algorithms, tenant screening, and credit scoring models	Efficiency in lending, risk assessment, and broader data use	Perpetuation of redlining, socioeconomic discrimination, and opaque rejections	Restricted mobility, denial of wealth-building opportunities, systemic exclusion
Healthcare & Public Services	Diagnostic algorithms, patient risk prediction, welfare eligibility systems	Improved diagnostics, efficient resource allocation, and faster service delivery	Racial health disparities, wrongful denial of benefits, and a lack of appeal mechanisms	Deepened inequities, governance challenges, and loss of trust in public systems

By consolidating these findings, the table underscores a central theme: while AI systems promise efficiency and innovation, their unregulated use in sensitive domains risks embedding historical inequities into the very fabric of decision-making.

RISKS AND CHALLENGES OF AI DEPLOYMENT

Increasingly, AI systems are influencing decision-making in important aspects of life, so the risks these systems present to civil rights are becoming more evident. These risks are not limited to technical failures but are inextricably linked to historical inequities, institutional structures, and governance gaps. The subsections below list four key concerns - algorithmic bias, erosion of privacy, lack of due process, and attacks on freedom of expression - that together demonstrate how AI can jeopardize civil rights if left unchecked:

Algorithmic Bias and Systematic Discrimination

One of the most urgent dangers involved in using AI is its ability to replicate, perpetuate, and justify existing social injustices. At the heart of this problem are the data used to train AI systems. Datasets are seldom neutral; they are the products of processes of history, institution, and social hierarchy that tend to be heavily biased by processes of historical discrimination. And when these data are fed into algorithms, these inequities are internalized and operationalized by the system, resulting in outcomes that disproportionately disadvantage communities of color (Varona & Suárez, 2022).

A vivid example of this relationship is found in predictive policing models used in the criminal justice system. Because this surveillance system often makes use of past data on arrests and crimes, it can lead to increased policing in areas with large minority populations. Because these communities have been over-policed in the past, the cycle becomes vicious: increased police presence equals increased arrests, and more arrests feed more biased data into next year's algorithms. This feedback loop exists between people and algorithms, yet it's hard to challenge or even see as discriminatory because the outcomes of algorithms seem so objective.

The dynamics are similar in employment and education. Many automated hiring systems have been shown to discriminate against resumes that don't match the demographic profiles of the current employees, giving an advantage to male candidates or disadvantaging those with non-Western-sounding names. Also, AI-based admissions or scholarship systems trained on past data may exclude qualified students from underrepresented groups under the guise of efficiency, perpetuating exclusion. In both cases, the veneer of algorithmic neutrality provides these outcomes with some sense of legitimacy, making them less subject to public scrutiny and rendering them less susceptible to legal challenges.

Researchers have described this as the "black box" of algorithmic discrimination (Christin, 2020), the confluence of obscure technical processes and socially biased data that comes together to create unfair outcomes protected from blame. Unless specific interventions such as fairness audits, bias testing, inclusive data collection, and participatory design are implemented, AI will perpetuate or deepen rather than reduce systemic discrimination. The challenge, then, is not only technological but deeply societal, implicating questions of justice, equality, and the protection of civil rights in the digital age.

Infringement on Privacy and Data Security

AI technologies are founded on the extraction and analysis of massive amounts of personal data, which presents new and unexplored challenges for privacy and data protection. From the use of facial recognition systems in airports and shopping malls to predictive analytics based on online browsing behaviour, people are being tracked, profiled, and analyzed - almost always without their informed consent. This pervasive data surveillance not only poses a threat to individual autonomy but also transforms the nature of the relationship between the citizens, the corporate world, and the state (Lami, Mohd. Hussein, Rajamanickam, & Emmanuel, 2024; Majeed & Hwang, 2023).

One of the most worrying issues is the lack of control people have over how their data is collected, shared, and reused. For example, biometric data that is collected for seemingly harmless purposes, such as workplace security or border control, may subsequently be used for surveillance, behavioral employee monitoring, or migration tracking. Similarly, health and location data that are collected during public emergencies - such as the Covid-19 pandemic - although initially intended to control public safety, have often been stored in government or commercial databases long after the emergency has passed. Without adequate protections, these data can be used for purposes far removed from their initial intent, undermining trust in institutions while breaching rights to privacy.

In many countries, these problems are worsened by weak data protection regimes. While the European Union's General Data Protection Regulation (GDPR) has established a benchmark for data protection that much of the rest of the world is missing, citizens everywhere are at risk of unbridled surveillance and commercial exploitation (Francesca, 2019; Li, Yu, & He, 2019). In countries that lack regulatory oversight, corporations can sell or share sensitive data with third parties, and governments can rely on AI-powered surveillance systems to monitor dissent or control the population. The normalization of continual extraction of data - what some academics call “surveillance capitalism” - risks making privacy a luxury instead of a right, reserved for those with the means to protect themselves from the gaze of digital trackers.

Nonetheless, the societal implications are significant beyond individual harms. Inconsistent with the principles of democracy, in which citizens are endlessly monitored, freedom of expression is stifled, and the very fabric of civic life is sacrificed. Moreover, the eroding of privacy is not just a technical and legal question but a civil rights problem and one that requires collective action now and not later.

Accountability Gaps in Automated Decision Making

A key issue in the implementation of AI is the lack of accountability that comes with algorithms making - or at least contributing substantially to - decisions impacting people's lives (Cobbe, Lee, & Singh, 2021). Traditionally, due process helps ensure people have the right to understand, challenge, and appeal decisions that impact their rights and opportunities. But as decisions are made based on opaque proprietary algorithms, this principle is increasingly eroded. You should consider welfare benefits or unemployment benefits. Many countries now rely on machine-driven eligibility checks that can compute risk scores or identify possible fraud to determine eligibility for social services. People who are refused help often find it very difficult to get an explanation, let alone appeal a decision. Sometimes, even government officials running the programs do not necessarily know exactly how the algorithm made its decision, putting citizens in an accountability void. This also happens in financial services when loan or credit applications are denied based on scores that are determined by an unknown machine learning model. Applicants receive little information as to why they were rejected or how they might repair their status.

The accountability problem is exacerbated by the private vendor factor. Many governments and corporations outsource their AI system to third-party providers who declare "trade secret" protection for their algorithms. This excludes decision-making processes from public scrutiny, judicial review, or democratic oversight. As such, citizens can be subject to life-changing consequences - loss of benefits, denial of loans, restriction of movement - with no recourse or explanation. This loss of due process is a fundamental crisis of the legitimacy of democratic government. When no one understands or can contest decisions that impact their rights, people lose confidence in institutions, and the rule of law suffers. This challenge will not only call for technical solutions, like explainable AI, but also for legal reforms that ensure that transparency, accountability, and redress mechanisms are incorporated into all phases of algorithmic decision-making.

Restrictions on Freedom of Expression and Assembly

AI-powered surveillance and content moderation technologies also present pressing questions of freedoms of expression and assembly - rights which are critical to democratic engagement and civic life. On digital platforms, automated moderation systems are called upon to scour out harmful or illegal content in bulk. While these systems are necessary in order to combat misinformation and hate speech, they are often prone to removing lawful speech, particularly when running afoul of politically sensitive topics, satire, or minority languages. Minority communities, journalists, and activists are disproportionately impacted as their content is more likely to be misclassified and censored. The result is a shrinking of public debate in which dissenting voices have difficulty being heard.

In physical space, AI surveillance has chilling effects on civic participation. Facial recognition cameras used at protests or other public events can identify individuals in live video feeds and associate their identities with political activity. The fact that one's face is capable of being photographed and entered into government databases further dissuades people from participating in demonstrations, further undermining the right to peacefully assemble. The chilling effect is especially pronounced under authoritarian regimes where AI surveillance is wielded as a tool to suppress dissent, target activists, and crack down on democratic movements. Yet even in established democracies, indiscriminate use of AI surveillance can help normalize restrictions on protest in the name of "public safety" or "efficiency." AI systems are used in predictive policing or crowd monitoring, which may target marginalized groups and perpetuate patterns of exclusion from public life beyond the context of protests. Minority communities, for example, may end up being disproportionately surveilled, which can inhibit their ability to organize or speak out about their rights. Combined with algorithmic biases in online moderation, these dynamics constitute a double bind where marginalized groups are oppressed both online and offline, with AI technologies serving as accelerators of inequality.

Taken as a whole, these threats show how AI - in the absence of safeguards - can work to undermine the very freedoms that support democratic societies. Ensuring that freedom of expression and assembly in the digital age is protected not only necessitates technical changes to moderation systems but also robust legal protections with guarantees of public accountability, as well as clear boundaries on the use of AI-based surveillance technologies. To distill the complex risks and challenges discussed above, Table 2 categorizes the main civil rights concerns arising from AI deployment. It highlights how algorithmic bias, privacy erosion, due process gaps, and threats to free expression each manifest, why they matter, and what is at stake for democratic societies.

Table 2. Major risks and civil rights challenges of AI deployment

Risk Area	How It Manifests	Civil Rights Implications	Key Concerns
Algorithmic Bias & Systemic Discrimination	Training on historically biased datasets; biased outputs in policing, hiring, and education	Reinforces inequality, legitimizes discrimination, and limits equal opportunity	Feedback loops in policing, biased hiring tools, and exclusion of underrepresented groups
Erosion of Privacy & Data Protection	Mass collection and repurposing of personal/ biometric data; weak legal safeguards	Undermines autonomy, enables surveillance capitalism, normalizes state/corporate monitoring.	Lack of consent, repurposed crisis data, and global disparities in privacy protections
Due Process & Accountability Gaps	Automated, opaque decision-making in welfare, credit, and public services; vendor secrecy	Denial of rights without recourse, weakening of the rule of law, erosion of trust in institutions	Opaque algorithms, limited appeals, shielded by trade secrets
Threats to Freedom of Expression & Assembly	AI-driven moderation over-removing lawful speech; surveillance at protests/ public gatherings.	Chilling effect on activism, narrowing of public discourse, suppression of dissent	Protest monitoring, misclassification of minority voices, and targeting marginalized groups

By synthesizing these risks, the table emphasizes that the challenges of AI deployment are not isolated technical flaws but structural civil rights issues requiring legal safeguards, democratic oversight, and proactive design interventions.

ALGORITHMIC BIAS AND CIVIL RIGHTS IMPLICATIONS

Algorithmic systems - often sold as efficient and unbiased - have repeatedly been shown to perpetuate and magnify structural inequality. Far from being neutral, these technologies exist within historical social structures where patterns of injustice exist in the data they use and the results they produce. The civil rights implications are especially stark in the realms of facial recognition, predictive policing, and automated decision-making in welfare, credit, and employment. In each case, we see how the misuse of AI not only erodes trust but also poses real threats to equality, due process, and human dignity.

Facial Recognition Misuse and Racial Profiling

Facial recognition technologies (FRTs) have rapidly transitioned from experimental tools to ubiquitous tools of surveillance used by law enforcement agencies, border control, security providers, and even private enterprises like retailers and airlines. Yet despite their increasing prevalence, research has shown that these systems are less accurate for people with darker skin tones, women, and younger populations. Analysis of data generated by the MIT Media Lab and the National Institute of Standards and Technology (NIST) validates the significantly higher error rates for minority groups as compared with white males. The stakes of these inaccuracies are not theoretical: they've led to disparate rates of misidentification, false arrests, and months of detention. For example, there are multiple cases of people unjustly arrested under misidentifications by police facial recognition software, which directly weaken civil rights protections for liberty, equality before the law, and due process of law (Gentzel, 2024; Smith & Miller, 2022).

The harms of facial recognition do not just relate to questions of accuracy but to structural issues of surveillance and racial profiling. In communities already disproportionately policed, FRT can increase existing cycles of suspicion, stigmatization, and over-enforcement. By profiling individuals based on false matches or by allowing blanket coverage of whole populations, FRT threatens to give legitimacy to discriminatory practices in the name of technological neutrality. These tools also have chilling effects on civil liberties, in particular the freedoms to assemble and to move. If people believe that by going to a protest, attending a public demonstration, or even walking through certain parts of the city, they will be subjected to ongoing algorithmic surveillance, they might self-censor their behavior and undermine democratic participation.

Additionally, the use of FRT is often poorly regulated, and recourse opportunities are very limited. Unfortunately, many people incorrectly identified by the systems are unable to challenge their classification due to the lack of transparency about how the algorithms operate and the way in which matches are confirmed. Poor transparency contributes to power imbalances in favor of state institutions over citizens. Without strong regulatory protections, facial recognition threatens to normalize the use of discriminatory practices, inject racial bias into policing and governance systems, and undermine civil rights in the name of technological advancement.

Predictive Policing Controversies

Predictive policing systems have been one of the most controversial uses of AI in policing. These tools promise to use crime data to predict where crimes are likely to happen or who might be involved, so that police agencies can better target their resources (Alikhademi et al., 2022; Hung & Yen, 2023). However, critics caution that the datasets these models are trained on are not objective pictures of crimes but, in fact, mirror the history of policing itself. If minority neighborhoods have historically been policed at a higher rate, then patterns in the data will reflect that, flagging such communities as high-risk areas even if those areas may have been affected by a lower level of crime. This creates a positive feedback loop where biased data is used to justify further surveillance and enforcement, which perpetuates the racial and socioeconomic disparities.

Well-publicized controversies have highlighted the risks of such an approach. In Los Angeles, for instance, the LAPD came under a wave of criticism for employing predictive policing programs to disproportionately target Black and Latino communities. Similarly, Chicago's "Strategic Subject List" program, intended to identify people who would be most likely to be involved in violent crime, was shut down after public outrage and evidence that it was ineffective and discriminatory (Da-Viera, Uriostegui, Gottlieb, & Onyeka, 2024). These examples show how predictive policing often gets it wrong, both in terms of accuracy and fairness, and drives up long-standing injustices in policing.

Beyond technical restrictions, predictive policing raises tremendous civil rights concerns. The presumption of innocence, a bedrock of democratic jurisprudence, is violated when a person is treated as a risk not due to his or her own behavior but because of a correlation from an algorithm. The opacity of these systems makes the problem worse. The algorithms work as "black boxes," meaning communities have few to no avenues to analyze or question the logic behind a heightened police presence or individual risk scores. This lack of transparency deprives affected individuals of due process, undermines public trust in law enforcement, and contributes to resentment in communities already skeptical of police practices. Furthermore, the very logic of predictive policing can drive law enforcement priorities further away from addressing the underlying causes of crime (poverty, education, social services, etc.) and toward technocratic solutions that regard crime as a problem of data rather than a social problem. Not only does this have the potential to deepen systemic inequities, but it also draws focus and resources away from structural change that would better move us toward safety and justice.

Automated Decision-Making

Algorithmic bias goes beyond the realm of policing into areas important for social and economic participation, such as welfare, financial services, and employment. In welfare administration, using automated decision-making systems has been introduced to identify fraud, allocate resources, and distribute benefits. Whilst dressed up as measures of efficiency, these systems are often based on inappropriate proxies of risk that systematically penalise vulnerable groups. "A remarkable example is the system in the Netherlands called SyRI, which merged data from housing, tax, and employment records to detect possible fraud in welfare payments." In 2020, it was struck down by courts after determining that it disproportionately affected low-income and immigrant neighborhoods and infringed on rights to privacy, equality, and protection from discrimination. Similar controversies have occurred in the US, where autopilot systems have wrongly accused parents of fraud in child care benefits or incorrectly terminated unemployment insurance, rendering families without vital support.

In the financial world, algorithms for credit rating, lending, and housing access tend to replicate historical biases. Although ostensibly neutral, things like zip codes, utility bills, or consumer purchasing behaviors are often surrogates for race, class, or socioeconomic status. This leads to the rejection of loans, mortgages, or rental housing for those who are marginalized, not due to personal financial irresponsibility, but due to systemic correlations built into the data. The discretion of these decisions makes them particularly insidious: individuals are not routinely informed of the reasons they've been denied access, nor are there available channels to appeal a decision. This violates the ideals of due process and equal economic opportunity.

Employment practices are yet another important front of algorithmic bias. There is strong evidence that AI-powered recruitment tools like resume screening algorithms, video interview analyzers, and personality tests are widely used by large corporations that require an efficient way to hire people. Yet many of these tools replicate and institutionalize present biases. Amazon provides a popular example of an AI gone wrong: the machine learning algorithm it used to screen resumes was trained on historical data that was overwhelmingly male and systematically demoted resumes that contained signs of female identity, such as membership in women's organizations. Other tools have been found to penalize applicants for their accents, their physical appearance, or unspoken nonverbal behaviors during video interviews, enshrining discriminatory tendencies into the seemingly objective systems.

Because these processes are not transparent, their damage is increased. Applicants are often not told what criteria they are being assessed on and therefore have no recourse against unfair rejections or calls for accountability. In this sense, algorithmic hiring technologies not only endanger equal employment opportunity but also shroud discriminatory processes in a veil of "neutral" technological objectivity. The cumulative impact is further entrenchment of obstacles to social mobility, access to resources, and economic empowerment for marginalised groups.

In each of these areas, algorithmic bias is not just a technical defect, but a civil rights issue with significant ramifications. Whether it is racial profiling through facial recognition, discriminatory surveillance through predictive policing, or exclusion from access to welfare, credit, and employment prospects, biased AI systems risk enshrining inequality in the guise of neutrality. To overcome these challenges, it is essential to recognize the social and historical contexts in which algorithms should intervene and to implement robust safeguards to ensure that technology works in the service of justice and not against it. Table 3 synthesizes the ways algorithmic bias manifests across policing, welfare, credit, and employment. By juxtaposing mechanisms of bias, civil rights implications, and real-world examples, the table underscores how systemic discrimination is not a side effect of flawed design but a structural issue embedded in algorithmic systems.

Table 3. Algorithmic bias and civil rights implications across domains

Domain	AI Application	Mechanism of Bias	Civil Rights Implications	Real-World Example
Facial Recognition	Law enforcement, border control, retail/security	Higher error rates for darker-skinned individuals, women, and youth; disproportionate misidentification	Wrongful arrests, racial profiling, erosion of due process, and liberty	Robert Williams & Michael Oliver (U.S.)—wrongful arrests due to misidentification
Predictive Policing	Crime hotspot forecasting, risk-based individual profiling	Reliance on historically biased policing data; feedback loops targeting minority neighborhoods	Over-surveillance, violation of the presumption of innocence, and unequal treatment before the law	LAPD predictive policing criticized for targeting Black & Latino communities; Chicago's "Strategic Subject List" dismantled
Welfare Administration	Automated fraud detection, benefits allocation	Use of proxies (e.g., housing, tax, employment data) that disproportionately flag marginalized groups	Wrongful denial of benefits, privacy violations, and discrimination against low-income communities	The Netherlands' SyRI system was struck down in 2020 for violating equality and privacy rights.

continued on following page

Table 3. Continued

Domain	AI Application	Mechanism of Bias	Civil Rights Implications	Real-World Example
Credit & Financial Access	Credit scoring, mortgage approval, and rental screening	Use of socioeconomic proxies (zip code, bills, consumer data) reinforces structural inequalities	Denial of credit/ housing, restricted upward mobility, systemic exclusion	U.S. mortgage and credit models perpetuating the legacy of redlining
Employment	Resume screening, video interviews, personality assessments	Training on biased historical hiring data; penalizing gender, accents, or nonconforming traits	Employment discrimination, reduced diversity, lack of accountability in hiring	Amazon's recruitment algorithm penalized resumes referencing women's organizations

As shown in Table 3, algorithmic bias operates not in isolation but across multiple domains of social and economic life. Its consequences—ranging from wrongful arrests to denial of livelihood—highlight the urgent need for fairness audits, transparency requirements, and strong civil rights safeguards in AI deployment.

STRATEGIES FOR SAFEGUARDING CIVIL RIGHTS

The threats of artificial intelligence to civil rights are great, but they're not overwhelming. A growing body of scholarship, policy work, and advocacy indicates a variety of approaches for aligning AI technologies with democratic values and fundamental freedoms. These approaches range from legal and regulatory measures to technological safeguards, to reframing governance and policy, and from the active involvement of civil society. Together, they comprise a multi-level approach to create AI systems that are accountable, transparent, and rights-respecting.

Legal and Regulatory Responses

The most direct avenue for safeguarding civil rights in the age of AI is probably through the development of adequate legal and regulatory frameworks. Laws and regulations help by defining acceptable practices and providing redress if rights are infringed upon. A key instrument in this area is the introduction of transparency obligations, which are the obligation for organisations to reveal how algorithms operate, what type of data they use, and on what basis decisions are made. By decreasing opacity, these mandates allow individuals to understand, question, and, if needed, challenge decisions that impact their lives. This is an important change for combating the pervasive view of algorithms as neutral, objective tools.

Accountability mechanisms provide yet another key element of safeguard. Independent oversight bodies or specialized regulatory agencies can be responsible for monitoring the deployment of AI, investigating complaints, and ensuring adherence to human rights standards. Beyond enforcing legal requirements, these bodies often help to encourage accountability by making organizations aware that their systems are under scrutiny. Importantly, they provide a neutral space where individuals and civil society organisations can raise grievances and seek redress.

Globally, different jurisdictions have started to experiment with these sorts of frameworks. The European Union's proposed AI Act has been widely discussed as a landmark step, with its proposed classifications of AI systems based on risk and its demand for increased scrutiny on applications deemed high-risk (e.g., in the fields of policing, healthcare, and employment). These requirements also include mandatory risk assessments, documentation of data sources, and ongoing monitoring for compliance. In the United States, progress has been less unified, but local governments in cities such as San Francisco, Boston, and Portland have adopted bans or moratoriums on the use of facial recognition technologies in public areas. These decisions come in the wake of increasing concern over racial profiling, privacy intrusions, and even the chilling effects of surveillance. Taken together, these developments point towards the power of legal tools to not only mitigate harms but to positively shape AI systems towards better alignment with democratic values and civil rights protections.

Technological Solutions

While legal structures create external guardrails, technological innovation itself can be leveraged to promote civil rights protections. In light of these risks, there is an emerging body of tools and practices that move toward understanding, measuring, and mitigating algorithm harms. One of the most promising approaches is algorithmic audit: systematic evaluations of how models perform, including models' bias, accuracy, and fairness for various demographic groups. By revealing how systems actually work, audits bring hard evidence of discriminatory outcomes and open up options for correction before they are deployed.

Furthermore, the evolution of fairness metrics allows a more nuanced approach to AI equity. These measurements can be used to determine if different groups are consistently receiving similar outcomes, if false positives and negatives are distributed evenly, and so on, and if there are still any systemic discrepancies. By incorporating these measures into model evaluation, developers can re-engineer or retrain algorithms to make them more equitable.

Another area of innovation is privacy-preserving AI methods such as differential privacy, homomorphic encryption, and federated learning. These techniques make it possible for organizations to make use of large datasets without compromising individuals' raw personal data. For example, federated learning can allow models to be trained locally on end devices, and only aggregate updates are transferred for centralized training. In this way, the risk of surveillance, data breaches, and unauthorized use of data is minimized while still ensuring that the system remains performant.

Crucially, these technological safeguards have to be integrated throughout the AI lifecycle - from the design phase through to training and testing, and into deployment and post-deployment monitoring. Too often, fair and privacy considerations are added as an afterthought or tacked on after problems have already occurred. Implementing ethical considerations in the technical development process can help to ensure that the protections of civil rights are not sacrificed for the sake of efficiency or profit. In this way, technology can become not only a source of risk, but also a powerful engine for defending and promoting basic rights.

Governance and Policy Frameworks

Beyond specific legislation or technical solutions, it is necessary to have wider governance and policy frameworks in place to ensure that AI systems reflect inclusive and democratic values. One potential solution is to implement rights-based design principles, which place equality, privacy, accountability, and fairness as central to technological design. Rather than trying to add safeguards after a product or service has been deployed, rights-based design ensures that civil rights considerations are a central part of the innovation process. Governments can facilitate this by issuing guidelines, funding experimental projects, and providing incentives for organizations that show they comply with rights-based standards.

Participatory democracy is another pillar of good governance. AI also has significant effects for marginalized and historically disadvantaged groups, but these communities must have a meaningful voice in the policies and systems that go on to shape their lives. Citizen assemblies, community advisory boards, and multi-stakeholder forums - these are all examples of participatory governance models that can open up avenues for a range of voices to be heard. These mechanisms can ensure that the voices of those who experience the social impacts of AI are not left out of the decision-making process and that there is a pathway for communication between technical experts, policymakers, and everyday citizens.

Governance frameworks also need to consider how AI is global. Since technologies and data flows don't stop at borders, unilateral rules might not be enough to ensure civil rights are secured holistically. It is, therefore, crucial to work together on a global scale. By sharing common ethical standards, technical norms, and tools for cross-border accountability, regulatory arbitrage - in which firms shift operations to areas with less robust protections - can be minimized. Although steps towards global coordination have been taken with UNESCO's Recommendation on the Ethics of Artificial Intelligence and the OECD's Principles on AI, there is still much more work to be done to ensure consistency and enforceability. By integrating design principles of rights, participation in governance, and international cooperation, policymakers can build governance ecosystems that protect civil rights while facilitating responsible innovation.

Role of Civil Society and Advocacy

Non-governmental organizations, media outlets, and advocacy groups play an invaluable role in holding governments and corporations accountable for the social implications of AI. These actors typically form the frontline in detecting algorithmic harms, documenting incidences of discrimination, and supporting the voices of communities they affect. For example, watchdog journalism has surfaced false arrests due to faulty facial recognition systems, while activist campaigns have forced municipalities to abandon predictive policing programs proven to be biased and discriminatory policing against minority communities.

In particular, grassroots mobilization has been extremely effective in influencing policy outcomes. Civil rights advocates in the United States, for example, have waged successful lawsuits against discriminatory welfare algorithms, resulting in court decisions that acknowledge the threats to due process and equality that automated systems create. These victories underpin the important role advocacy plays in turning abstract concerns about algorithmic bias into concrete legal and policy changes.

Civil society also proactively helps by developing capacity in communities. Digital rights groups offer toolkits, trainings, and legal materials that teach people how to understand and challenge algorithmic decisions. Independent audits and evaluations of high-risk systems-which are often carried out by academic researchers in collaboration with advocacy groups-are one of the few means of uncovering risks hidden from the view of others. The combination of public pressure and expert analysis lends legitimacy to reform efforts and improves their likelihood of success.

Civil society serves as a link between the jargon of technical expertise and public debate. By breaking down complex technical issues into easily understandable language, advocates contribute to expanding public awareness of the risks and opportunities of AI, leading to more informed and inclusive conversations. In doing so, they ensure the debate about AI is not relegated to corporate boardrooms or government agencies but takes the debate to society at large. In the long term, the active engagement of civil society is essential for accountability, transparency, and ensuring that AI systems develop in a way that is consistent with democratic values and civil rights.

Taken as a whole, these strategies show how protecting civil rights in the age of AI demands a multi-stakeholder approach. Institutions provide accountability, technological solutions mitigate risks, governance reforms integrate inclusive values, and civil society provides constant monitoring. Only through a combination of these factors can societies ensure that they are realizing the benefits of AI while safeguarding the fundamental freedoms that are the bedrock of democratic life. The strategies outlined above can be consolidated into four complementary pillars, each addressing different aspects of the challenge of safeguarding civil rights in the age of AI. Table 4 provides a comparative overview of these strategies, highlighting their key mechanisms, strengths, and potential limitations. This synthesis underscores the importance of a multi-stakeholder and multi-layered approach in ensuring AI systems remain accountable, transparent, and aligned with democratic values.

Table 4. Strategies for safeguarding civil rights in AI

Strategy Domain	Key Mechanisms	Strengths	Limitations/Challenges	Illustrative Examples
Legal & Regulatory Responses	Transparency mandates, independent oversight bodies, bans/ moratoriums on high-risk systems	Establishes accountability; provides legal remedies; creates enforceable boundaries	Fragmented adoption; slow legislative processes; risk of regulatory arbitrage	EU AI Act (risk-based framework); U.S. city bans on facial recognition (San Francisco, Boston, Portland)
Technological Solutions	Algorithmic audits, fairness metrics, privacy-preserving AI (differential privacy, federated learning)	Empirical bias detection; measurable fairness; protects privacy while enabling innovation.	Requires technical expertise; can be co-opted as compliance "checklists"; limited by data quality.	Algorithmic audits by academia & NGOs; federated learning in healthcare
Governance & Policy Frameworks	Rights-based design, participatory governance (citizen assemblies, advisory boards), international collaboration	Embeds values early in design; empowers marginalized communities; addresses the global nature of AI.	Risk of tokenism in participation; international enforcement remains weak	UNESCO Recommendation on AI Ethics; OECD AI Principles
Civil Society & Advocacy	Investigative reporting, litigation, grassroots mobilization, independent audits, public education	Amplifies voices of affected groups; holds governments & corporations accountable; builds public awareness.	Limited resources; potential political pushback; uneven influence across regions	U.S. legal challenges to welfare algorithms; campaigns against predictive policing; NGO toolkits for communities

As Table 4 illustrates, no single strategy is sufficient on its own; rather, it is the interplay of legal safeguards, technological innovations, governance reforms, and civil society advocacy that creates a resilient ecosystem for protecting civil rights in the AI era.

CONCLUSION

From the accessibility of public services to the possibility of involvement in democratic processes, AI is quickly integrated into the everyday fabric of our lives, influencing decisions that shape our realities. This dual reality - the fact that AI has the potential to both increase opportunity and perpetuate inequality - highlights the urgency of finding ways to balance technological innovation with the protection of civil rights. The challenge is not just technical but essentially societal: how to ensure the power of AI is used to promote justice, equality, and human dignity, rather than to undermine them. One of the key themes that emerged from this was that there is a delicate balance to be found between innovation and rights protection. AI already shows potential to increase efficiency, facilitate breakthroughs in healthcare, and increase access to services. Yet without safeguards, these same systems can perpetuate bias, compromise privacy, and undermine democratic freedoms. Policymakers, technologists, and communities, therefore, must consider AI development through a dual mandate - innovation, but with rights-based principles integrated into each phase of design and deployment. Such a balance must make due allowance for the fact that civil rights are not impediments to development but rather the necessary preconditions for a sustainable and legitimate form of technological development.

In the long run, the future of ethical AI will be shaped by the institutionalization of effective governance frameworks. Comprehensive AI regulations and constitutional privacy protections are necessary to set clear boundaries for applications with high risk. This means that technology development should be informed by principles of fairness, transparency, and privacy protections to avoid discriminatory or exploitative results. Also of importance is the development of participatory governance models that include marginalized voices in the design and oversight of AI systems. International partnership is also going to be determinant. AI technologies are transnational and, without harmonized standards and rights protection, they can be unevenly protected and open to exploitation. Cross-border systems of accountability working in tandem with multilateral agreements on ethical AI may help prevent a "race to the bottom" in which civil rights are sacrificed for economic or security interests.

Ensuring civil rights in the age of AI needs to be a multistakeholder approach. Governments need to put in place robust regulatory frameworks and independent supervision. Technology companies must take ownership of fair auditing, transparent practices, and rights-based design. Civil society groups, academics, and the media will need to hold institutions to account and enable people to understand and challenge algorithmic decisions. International organizations and transnational networks need to facilitate cooperation and knowledge transfer, making sure that rights protections don't remain limited to areas and only relevant to a few jurisdictions, but are accessible worldwide. The roadmap forward, therefore, needs to be multi-stakeholder, multi-level, and future-focused. It should focus on making civil rights considerations a core part of the innovation processes, to have mechanisms for redress and accountability, and to build trust between citizens and institutions. In doing so, societies can unleash the transformative power of AI while ensuring that fundamental freedoms are protected.

REFERENCES

Achanta, S. V. (2025). AI in Public Services: Analysing AI-Driven Tools in Healthcare, Education, Transportation, and Safety. In *AI Driven Tools for Sustainable Public Administration* (pp. 113–152). IGI Global Scientific Publishing.

Ahmed Khan, Z., & Rizvi, A. (2021). AI Based recognition technology and criminal justice: Issues and challenges. *Turkish Journal of Computer and Mathematics Education*, *12*(14).

Alikhademi, K., Drobina, E., Prioleau, D., Richardson, B., Purves, D., & Gilbert, J. E. (2022). A review of predictive policing from the perspective of fairness. *Artificial Intelligence and Law*, *30*(1), 1–17. Advance online publication. DOI: 10.1007/s10506-021-09286-4

Anshari, M., Hamdan, M., Ahmad, N., & Ali, E. (2025). Public service delivery, artificial intelligence and the sustainable development goals: Trends, evidence and complexities. *Journal of Science and Technology Policy Management*, *16*(1), 163–181. DOI: 10.1108/JSTPM-07-2023-0123

Bergold, A. N., & Kovera, M. B. (2024). The Contribution of Facial Recognition Technology to Wrongful Arrests and Trauma. *Psychological Trauma: Theory, Research, Practice, and Policy*, *17*(Suppl 1), S225–S233. DOI: 10.1037/tra0001783 PMID: 39509226

Berk, R. A. (2021). Artificial Intelligence, Predictive Policing, and Risk Assessment for Law Enforcement. *Annual Review of Criminology*, *4*(1), 209–237. Advance online publication. DOI: 10.1146/annurev-criminol-051520-012342

Blount, K. (2024). Using artificial intelligence to prevent crime: Implications for due process and criminal justice. *AI & Society*, *39*(1), 359–368. Advance online publication. DOI: 10.1007/s00146-022-01513-z

Briganti, G., & Le Moine, O. (2020). Artificial Intelligence in Medicine: Today and Tomorrow. *Frontiers in Medicine*, *7*, 27. Advance online publication. DOI: 10.3389/fmed.2020.00027 PMID: 32118012

Buhmann, A., & Fieseler, C. (2021). Towards a deliberative framework for responsible innovation in artificial intelligence. *Technology in Society*, *64*, 101475. Advance online publication. DOI: 10.1016/j.techsoc.2020.101475

Christin, A. (2020). The ethnographer and the algorithm: Beyond the black box. *Theory and Society*, *49*(5–6), 897–918. Advance online publication. DOI: 10.1007/s11186-020-09411-3

Cobbe, J., Lee, M. S. A., & Singh, J. (2021). *Reviewable automated decision-making: A framework for accountable algorithmic systems*. In *FAccT 2021 - Proceedings of the 2021 ACM Conference on Fairness, Accountability, and Transparency*. DOI: 10.1145/3442188.3445921

DaViera, A. L., Uriostegui, M., Gottlieb, A., & Onyeka, O. (2024). Risk, race, and predictive policing: A critical race theory analysis of the strategic subject list. *American Journal of Community Psychology*, *73*(1–2), 91–103. Advance online publication. DOI: 10.1002/ajcp.12671 PMID: 37067014

Deepa, R., Sekar, S., Malik, A., Kumar, J., & Attri, R. (2024). Impact of AI-focussed technologies on social and technical competencies for HR managers – A systematic review and research agenda. *Technological Forecasting and Social Change*, *202*, 123301. Advance online publication. DOI: 10.1016/j.techfore.2024.123301

Dempsey, R. P., Brunet, J. R., & Dubljević, V. (2023). Exploring and Understanding Law Enforcement's Relationship with Technology: A Qualitative Interview Study of Police Officers in North Carolina. *Applied Sciences (Basel, Switzerland)*, *13*(6), 3887. Advance online publication. DOI: 10.3390/app13063887

Egbert, S., & Mann, M. (2021). Discrimination in predictive policing: The (dangerous) myth of impartiality and the need for STS analysis. In *Automating Crime Prevention*. Surveillance, and Military Operations., DOI: 10.1007/978-3-030-73276-9_2

Francesca, T. (2019). Comparing privacy laws: GDPR v. CCPA. Retrieved 9 June 2025, from https://futurium.ec.europa.eu/en/european-ai-alliance/open-library/comparing-privacy-laws-gdpr-v-ccpa

Gentzel, M. J. (2024). Facial profiling technology and discrimination: A new threat to civil rights in liberal democracies. *Philosophical Studies*, *181*(6–7), 1369–1392. DOI: 10.1007/s11098-024-02156-0

Gong, Y., Zhao, M., Wang, Q., & Lv, Z. (2022). Design and interactive performance of human resource management system based on artificial intelligence. *PLoS One*, *17*(1), e0262398. Advance online publication. DOI: 10.1371/journal.pone.0262398 PMID: 35089946

Haley, P., & Burrell, D. N. (2025). Using Artificial Intelligence in Law Enforcement and Policing to Improve Public Health and Safety. *Law. Economics and Society*, *1*(1), 46–p46. DOI: 10.30560/les.v1n1p46

Hung, T. W., & Yen, C. P. (2023). Predictive policing and algorithmic fairness. *Synthese*, *201*(6), 206. Advance online publication. DOI: 10.1007/s11229-023-04189-0

Joseph, J. (2025). Predicting crime or perpetuating bias? The AI dilemma. *AI & Society, 40*(4), 2319–2321. DOI: 10.1007/s00146-024-02032-9

Khan, M., Ali, A., & Alharbi, Y. (2022). Predicting and Preventing Crime: A Crime Prediction Model Using San Francisco Crime Data by Classification Techniques. *Complexity, 2022*(1), 4830411. Advance online publication. DOI: 10.1155/2022/4830411

Kothandapani, H. P. (2025). Social Implications of Algorithmic Decision-Making in Housing Finance: Examining the broader social impacts of deploying machine learning in lending decisions, including potential disparities and community effects. *Journal of Knowledge Learning and Science Technology ISSN: 2959-6386 (Online), 4*(1), 78–97. DOI: 10.60087/jklst.v4.n1.009

Kshetri, N. (2021). The Role of Artificial Intelligence in Promoting Financial Inclusion in Developing Countries. *Journal of Global Information Technology Management, 24*(1), 1–6. Advance online publication. DOI: 10.1080/1097198X.2021.1871273

Lami, B., Mohd. Hussein, S., Rajamanickam, R., & Emmanuel, G. K. (2024). The role of artificial intelligence (AI) in shaping data privacy. *International Journal of Law and Management*. doi:, H., Yu, L., & He, W. (2019). The Impact of GDPR on Global Technology Development. *Journal of Global Information Technology Management*. doi:DOI: 10.1108/IJLMA-07-2024-0242/1250516/ Li

Madanchian, M., Taherdoost, H., & Mohamed, N. (2023). *AI-Based Human Resource Management Tools and Techniques; A Systematic Literature Review*. In *Procedia Computer Science* (Vol. 229). DOI: 10.1016/j.procs.2023.12.039

Majeed, A., & Hwang, S. O. (2023). When AI Meets Information Privacy: The Adversarial Role of AI in Data Sharing Scenario. *IEEE Access : Practical Innovations, Open Solutions, 11*, 76177–76195. Advance online publication. DOI: 10.1109/ACCESS.2023.3297646

Montasari, R. (2023). The Application of Big Data Predictive Analytics and Surveillance Technologies in the Field of Policing. In *Advances in Information Security* (Vol. 101). DOI: 10.1007/978-3-031-21920-7_5

Niklas, J., & Dencik, L. (2021). What rights matter? Examining the place of social rights in the eu's artificial intelligence policy debate. *Internet Policy Review, 10*(3). Advance online publication. DOI: 10.14763/2021.3.1579

Perry, V. G., Martin, K., & Schnare, A. (2023). Algorithms for All: Can AI in the Mortgage Market Expand Access to Homeownership? *AI, 4*(4), 888–903. Advance online publication. DOI: 10.3390/ai4040045

Sadok, H., Sakka, F., & El Maknouzi, M. E. H. (2022). Artificial intelligence and bank credit analysis: A review. *Cogent Economics & Finance, 10*(1), 2023262. Advance online publication. DOI: 10.1080/23322039.2021.2023262

Sandhu, A., & Fussey, P. (2021). The 'uberization of policing'? How police negotiate and operationalise predictive policing technology. *Policing and Society, 31*(1), 66–81. Advance online publication. DOI: 10.1080/10439463.2020.1803315

Schuilenburg, M., & Soudijn, M. (2023). Big data policing: The use of big data and algorithms by the Netherlands Police. *Policing (Oxford, England), 17*, paad061. Advance online publication. DOI: 10.1093/police/paad061

Smith, M., & Miller, S. (2022). The ethical application of biometric facial recognition technology. *AI & Society, 37*(1), 167–175. DOI: 10.1007/s00146-021-01199-9 PMID: 33867693

Sunarti, S., Fadzlul Rahman, F., Naufal, M., Risky, M., Febriyanto, K., & Masnina, R. (2021). Artificial intelligence in healthcare: Opportunities and risk for future. *Gaceta Sanitaria, 35*, S67–S70. Advance online publication. DOI: 10.1016/j.gaceta.2020.12.019 PMID: 33832631

Ugwudike, P. (2022). AI audits for assessing design logics and building ethical systems: The case of predictive policing algorithms. *AI and Ethics, 2*(1), 199–208. Advance online publication. DOI: 10.1007/s43681-021-00117-5

van Dijk, J., Nieuwbeerta, P., & Joudo Larsen, J. (2022). Global Crime Patterns: An Analysis of Survey Data from 166 Countries Around the World, 2006–2019. *Journal of Quantitative Criminology, 38*(4), 793–827. Advance online publication. DOI: 10.1007/s10940-021-09501-0

Varona, D., & Suárez, J. L. (2022). *Discrimination, Bias, Fairness, and Trustworthy AI*. Applied Sciences., DOI: 10.3390/app12125826

Vidhya, G., Nirmala, D., & Manju, T. (2023). Quality challenges in Deep Learning Data Collection in perspective of Artificial Intelligence. *Journal of Information Technology and Computing, 4*(1), 46–58. Advance online publication. DOI: 10.48185/jitc.v4i1.725

Votto, A. M., Valecha, R., Najafirad, P., & Rao, H. R. (2021). Artificial Intelligence in Tactical Human Resource Management: A Systematic Literature Review. *International Journal of Information Management Data Insights, 1*(2), 100047. Advance online publication. DOI: 10.1016/j.jjimei.2021.100047

Whang, S. E., Roh, Y., Song, H., & Lee, J. G. (2023). Data collection and quality challenges in deep learning: A data-centric AI perspective. *The VLDB Journal*, *32*(4), 791–813. Advance online publication. DOI: 10.1007/s00778-022-00775-9

Chapter 2
Balancing Freedom of Expression and Moderation:
Policy Frameworks in Digital Spaces

Azamat Ali
https://orcid.org/0000-0003-2931-2166
Lovely Professional University, Punjab, India

Romica Bhat
Lovely Professional University, Punjab, India

ABSTRACT

The issue regarding freedom of expression and content moderation is one of the vast issues in digital times. This chapter examines the various policy contexts that deal with this challenge in the digital platforms. It looks at the conflict between safeguarding civil liberties and guarding against the propagation of dangerous information, i.e., hate speech, misinformation, and hate speech. The chapter looks at national and international regulations, regulations specific to platforms and developing legal standards. It further examines the effect played by the privately owned technology companies in determining online discourse by using moderation methods and algorithmic filtering. Essential issues of transparency, accountability and protection of marginalized voice are addressed. The chapter contains some case studies which illustrate the practice of governments and platforms balancing this situation. It concludes with policy proposals that enhance integrity of democracy, freedom of speech and responsible moderation in digital areas.

DOI: 10.4018/979-8-3693-3920-6.ch002

INTRODUCTION

The freedom of expression as a fundamental right is enjoyed in all democratic societies throughout the world. It gives people a chance to exchange their opinions, ideas, and beliefs without being censored and, therefore, punished (Gunatilleke, 2021). This right has acquired a different meaning and complexity in the era of the digital age. The internet via social media channels, blogs, video sharing as well as internet forums have provided an avenue in which millions of individuals are allowed to express themselves without any restriction of time. Consequently, freedom of expression has greatly increased in its nature and scope in the digital realm (Pangrazio & Sefton-Green, 2021).

The phenomenon of user-generated content is one of the qualities of the digital age. Digital platforms have also combined the generation and distribution of information, which has been traditionally limited by a selective few institutions in the control of tradition media to all communications who have access to the internet. The change has made communication more democratic and ordinary people creators, influencers and opinion leaders. Facebook, Twitter (now X), Instagram, YouTube and TikTok are excellent social media in which self-expression, political activism and cultural involvement can take place. These systems allow individuals to exchange individual experiences, communicate on societal matters, bring awareness on social inhumanities, as well as interact with our communities beyond national boundaries (Dumitrica & Hockin-Boyers, 2023).

Yet, the very platforms, where it is possible to express freely, turn into an instrument of destructive information. Hate speech, misinformation, disinformation, cyber bullying, extremism are also on the rise on the digital space. Although freedom of speech is an essential ingredient of democracy, unregulated harmful content may destroy social harmony, cause violence, and create threats to common health and safety. As an illustration, a presumptuous medical data about the COVID-19 pandemic were spread in the social media creating confusion and undesirable behaviour. In a similar fashion, online hate speech also led to marginalization of minority groups and even actual violence in the real world (Kumar & Maurya, 2024).

This has created conflict between espousing free speech and safeguarding the society against online vice. On the one hand, one has got to maintain the freedom of expression as one of the vital principles of democracy. Conversely, the governments and platforms are facing an exertion of pressure to filter harmful content. This juggling is not so simple. Censorship and spindling out the opposing views, particularly on politically-sensitive grounds, are some of the consequences that over-regulation may cause. However, little regulation can result in the distribution of unhealthy narratives over time, endangering the safety and rights of vulnerable populations (Masferrer, 2023).

Policies structures in this complicated environment are important. They provide a framework within which acceptable online speech may be defined and establish the liability that the governments and the platform have. In place of efficient policies, the digital attitudes will remain open and safe to every user. They are aimed at the preservation of civil liberties and protect against abuse and harm as well. Digital policy has become a key focus of governance in many countries and legislators are producing laws that will determine the regulation of content moderation, responsibility of the platforms, and their protection of the users. To illustrate, the Digital Services Act (DSA) in the European Union and the Information Technology (Intermediary Guidelines and Digital Media Ethics Code) Rules in India are some attempts to establish control over digital texts and at the same time do not violate fundamental rights (Guha & Matilal, 2023).

Meanwhile, tech businesses also contribute an effective force to the discourse of the digital sphere. Such platforms set their own laws on what can be permitted or deleted as content. They rely on algorithmic systems to find and filter content in most cases unmercifully of human review. Their choice may affect the people, elections and social trends. That raises serious concerns regarding transparency and accountability. Who determines what is going to get shut down or be permitted to remain? Do these decisions get made equitably and devoid of prejudice? How is it possible to appeal against the unjust removals or bans?

Moreover, policies ought to solve the problem of cross-border content. Since the digital world is global, the content published in one nation can reach a target audience in a different country. Nevertheless, standards in law differ greatly caountry-to-country. The same behavior may be considered as legal in one place and illegal in another. This generates legal and ethical contradictions in the control of the online world, content moderation, and digital rights across the world (Siapera, 2022).

THEORETICAL AND LEGAL FOUNDATIONS

Freedom of expression is at the heart of democratic societies and is guaranteed not only by the international human rights mechanism but also by national law. The freedom of speech is however not absolute. It needs to be restricted by the other rights and duties, particularly in the online age when malicious submissions could propagate even faster and further. The section investigates theoretical and legal guidance through which the societies interpret and manage the freedom of expression by considering harmful digital contents.

International Human Rights Instruments

Freedom of expression is a principle human right acclaimed at the global level in major international documents. One of the first and highly recognizable statements on this matter is the Universal Declaration of Human Rights (UDHR) that was adopted in the United Nations back in 1948 (Alfredsson & Eide, 2023).

Article 19 of the UDHR states:

"Everyone has the right to freedom of opinion and expression; this right includes freedom to hold opinions without interference and to seek, receive, and impart information and ideas through any media and regardless of frontiers."

This general language also encompasses such modern forms of media as digital media, though the existence of the internet at the time of the UDHR writing is unknown. The principles have not lost relevance and most courts and human rights organs have taken their meaning to cover online speech. The other pertinent tool is the International Covenant on Civil and Political rights (ICCPR) which was adopted in 1966. Article 19 of the ICCPR is very similar to the UDHR with additions of some qualifications. It acknowledges that the freedom of expression can be limited (Abdulai & Abdulai, 2022).

These restrictions must be:

- Provided by law,
- Necessary for respect of the rights or reputations of others, or
- Necessary for the protection of national security, public order, public health, or morals.

These restrictions bring in the relevant laws of necessity and proportionality which are standard in use in the legal capacity of validating the justification of whichever restriction is placed on speech. In 2011, the UN Human Rights Council passed a resolution affirming that "the same rights that people have offline must also be protected online." This entails the freedom of expression. The resolution highlights the need to consider human rights principles in virtual environments, which is required in the context of increased popularity of the Internet and social media (Song & Ma, 2022).

National Constitutional Protections for Free Speech

The freedom of expression by most of the democratic nations is guaranteed under constitution or their basic laws. Nevertheless, this freedom is different and limited in its degrees and boundaries just because of the cultural, legal and historical realities. At the United States, the first amendment to the constitution guarantees freedom of speech in its strongest levels. The U.S. courts are often hesitant to place any forms of restrictions, even on the speech which can be considered offensive or controversial. Though some categories of speech are not covered by protection namely incitement to violence, obscenity, defamation and so-called true threats. Otherwise, the European countries, which refer to the European Convention on Human Rights (ECHR), adopt more balanced approach. Article 10 of ECHR entitles the right of freedom of expression, so the restriction is permissible according to restrictions that are necessary in a democratic society. Hate speech, denial of the Holocaust, or incite to hatred are often restricted by the European countries especially in the countries with troubled ethnic or religious pasts (Wasiq, 2022).

Article 19(1)(a) of the Constitution of India gives the right of speech and expression of India. Article 19(2) however gives the state the power to place under its discretion, reasonable restrictions on this right on a number of grounds that include: national security, public order, decency and morality, contempt of court action, defamation, incitement to offense, and the sovereignty and integrity of India. The Indian court has been in the lead with regards to specifying the scope of free speech through the balancing of other rights and state interests (Kohli, 2022).

Legal Definitions of Harmful Content

To ensure policy and regulation considerations, the definition of a harmful content must be arrived at. The concept of harmful speech the legal system has a tendency to differentiate between certain types of harmful speech to categorize them. The major types are as follows:

- Hate Speech: Hate speech is a form of speech that tears into an individual or a group of people due to some of their attributes like race, religion, ethnicity, gender, sex, sexual orientation, or disability. A lot of states punish hate speech as it can inspire violence or discrimination. As an illustration, hate speech, particularly Nazi propaganda and Holocaust denial, are highly prohibited in Germany (Carlson, 2021).
- Misinformation and Disinformation: These are the terms which indicate false or misleading information. Disinformation includes intentionally false information sent to mislead or manipulate, whereas misinformation tends to refer to distributing false information without bad intent. In the course of the COVID-19 pandemic, governments and platforms have been responding to misinformation, which has caused a dangerous effect on people during a public health crisis (Aimeuret al., 2023).
- Promotion of Violence or Terrorism: usually, it is nationally prohibited to promote or directly encourage violence, terrorism, or criminal activities. As

an illustration, incitement to riot or murder of government officials is unlawful in majority of nations (Bassiouni, 2024).

- Obscenity and Child sexual abuse material (CSAM): The majority of countries ban obscene content and there is no tolerance to the content that deals with child sexual exploitation. Since such content is a legal issue, the digital platforms are compelled to delete them and report to the law enforcement (Rajput et al., 2024).

Such legal classifications assist in shaping rules in managing online contents. But there can be a tremendous range of interpretations and enforcement and there are concerns about overreach and selectivity.

The Role of Proportionality and Necessity

Proportionality and necessity are two important legal criteria that are applied to measure restriction of speech. The principles are enshrined in the international human rights law designing the process through which courts and policymakers can determine whether any restriction applied on the possibility of speaking is necessary (Gunatilleke, 2021).

- Necessity: A restriction should correspond to the urgent social necessity. As illustration, acts that promote violence should be eliminated to secure national peace.
- Proportionality: The restriction should be proportional to the damage being avoided. The total banning of a social media site might be termed as overboard when other less drastic solutions are able to bring the same effect.

Digital scenarios use these principles specifically because moderation of content may be by an automated system, and there is a danger of excessive removal of material. As an example, some sites can ban or remove political criticism, artistic, or satire contents due to misleading reports on them by their algorithms. This evokes the importance of human control, appeals, and transparency. The principles are useful in the implementation and oversight of the content regulation process since its possible misuse as a way to censor information and to create political domination. In various jurisdictions, courts have been an important tool in examining challenges on content restriction which they deem to be lawful, necessary and disproportionate. The legislation and policies provided through judicial review will not abuse fundamental rights and are not enforced pitilessly (Dixon, 2023).

REGULATORY APPROACHES ACROSS JURISDICTIONS

Online content control is turning out to be an essential matter across all parts of the world as governments, civil society and special administrations attempt to find a balance between good and bad content and how to control it whenever they eat. Various nations have come up with distinct legal and policy mechanisms depending on their political regime, legal heritage, and cultural principles. In this section, an overview is given of the regulatory approaches in the major jurisdictions such as the European Union (EU), India, and the United States comparatively. It speaks also about how governments and platforms should share responsibility, new trends in self-regulation and co-regulation, and how to enforce such regulations in a global digital landscape.

Comparative Overview of Regulatory Models

Online content regulation is treated differently in varied parts of the world. There are three different models that are present in the European Union, India and the United States, and these models are summarizations of the larger philosophical approach to law and politics.

European Union – Digital Services Act (DSA)

One of the most detailed regulation attempts of digital platforms is the European Union Digital Services act (DSA) of 2022. The DSA applies to each online service in every industry that links consumers and content, goods or services. It has requirements that attach determination to the reach and platform of the platform. The most massive ones are called Very Large Online Platforms (VLOPs), and they have a higher responsibility. Some of the main elements of the DSA are the transparency obligations, the takedown processes of content, the risk evaluation and the necessity to implement the systems of user redress. The DSA intention is to advance accountability without censoring the freedom of expression by proportional regulation (Nannini et al, 2025).

India Information Technology (IT) Rules, 2021

The Information Technology (Intermediary Guidelines and Digital Media Ethics Code) Rules 2021 in India created more responsibilities on social media organizations and digital news publishers. The platforms must take down illegal material at a limited time upon being notified by the authorities, fill in compliance officers based in India, and offer anything of originators in some cases. Although the Indian government claims that the regulations enhance accountability and safety, critics have expressed fears that they are having adverse effects on the right to privacy, freedom of speech and freedom of press. It has undergone some areas that courts are currently reviewing on their constitutionality (Abhishek, 2023).

United States First Amendment Principles

The United States has a different direction dictated by the First Amendment of its Constitution whereby it encourages liberal safeguards to free speech. The only situations where platforms are legally obliged to take down hate speech or false information involve direct advocacy of violence against others or another very specific set of exceptions. Section 230 of the Communications Decency Act instead provides sites with legal immunity against the content created by their users and enables them to make decisions on how to moderate the content depending on their own standards. This strategy prioritizes platform independence and the freedom of government intervention, a problem of this approach has been raised that allows the existence of potentially dangerous content and get away with it (Montalbano, 2022).

Table 1. Comparison of regulatory models in EU, India, and the U.S.

Aspect	European Union (DSA)	India (IT Rules, 2021)	United States (First Amendment, Sec. 230)
Regulatory Approach	Proactive regulation with obligations for platforms	Government-mandated rules with compliance deadlines	Minimal government control; strong free speech protection
Content Takedown	Required with clear notice and appeal mechanisms	Mandatory within 36 hours of government notice	No legal obligation unless content violates federal laws
Platform Obligations	Transparency, audits, redress mechanisms, risk assessments	Appoint compliance officers, trace originators	Platforms free to define and enforce their own policies
User Rights	Emphasis on transparency and right to appeal	Limited mechanisms for redress	Users can sue platforms but only in limited situations
Criticism	Risk of over-compliance or suppression of dissent	Potential misuse to silence dissent, vague language	Lack of accountability for harmful content

Government Responsibilities vs. Platform Obligations

Content moderation in the digital environment comprises the role of governments and corporations. Governments should draft laws to safeguard the right to free speech without causing any damage online. Meanwhile, it is the task of platforms to ensure the community guidelines, content moderation, and the assistance of a tool that can help the user report abuse (Brown & Marsden, 2023). Such a collective duty introduces pertinent issues. Are sites to be regarded as mini-regulators of speech? Are platforms enforceable by the governments to remove content? What rules can govern platforms without breaching the right of the users? The majority of democracies use the hybrid form, in which law is established by the government and the content policies by the platforms are more extensive than the law. Nonetheless, there are countries where the government is more controlling and it demands removals without enough transparency. This may cause censorship and power maltreatment (Gorwa, 2024). In order to overcome these misgivings, a number of analysts promote definite roles and boundaries. Restrictions should be motivated by governments with legal basis and their execution enforced by the platforms in a reasonable and transparent way. Both sides are supposed to be under control and responsibility.

Emerging Trends: Co-regulation and Self-regulation

New forms of regulation had been introduced in previous years. These are the co-regulation that involves governments and platforms to implement uniform content standards and the self-regulation model that involves the platforms as the leading in managing its own policy.

Co-regulation

Co-regulation is where there is both participation and industry action. Governments can specify harms (e.g. sexual abuse of children, terrorism content) and platforms accept to be regulated by codes of conduct. This model is flexible and innovative and guarantees the protection of the interest of the public. One case of co-regulation is the EU Code of Practice on Disinformation, which Google, Facebook, and Twitter companies signed the agreement to meet the standards voluntarily to address the misinformation. DSA codifies part of these practices and enacts them in the law, mixing co-regulation and binding commitments (Batura, 2024).

Self-regulation

Self-regulation gets rid of state intervention in content policies, allowing each platform to establish its own policies and implement them. This model prevails in the U.S. but is becoming scrutinized more and more. Critics state that platforms are inconsistent in their actions, they are not transparent and serve their profits rather than people. To enhance exertion of trust, certain sites have formed Oversight Boards or Transparency Reports. As an example, Meta has the Oversight Board that works with high-impact content and offers recommendations. The effect of this type of initiative remains, however, constrained by voluntary nature (Cusumano et al., 2021).

Challenges of Enforcement in Cross-border Digital Environments

The international scope of digital platforms poses one of the greatest challenges that are associated with managing online content. The content that is shared in a particular country can be viewed internationally. But the norms and laws vary largely between borders. There is lawful speech in one country which is viewed as unlawful or offensive in another. Nazi symbolism is prohibited in Germany but free speech in the United States as an example. On the same note, political opposition is free in democracies but can be punishable in an authoritarian regime. This poses conflict between national sovereignty and international networking. There is also the jurisdiction problem that leads to cross-border enforcement. The platform can be hosted in a different location than a country that requests its content to be removed because it goes against its laws. In addition to that, multinationals can lack local offices so penalties are difficult to impose (Afzal, 2024).

In response to these issues, platforms are required in some countries to appoint local compliance officers, keep grievance mechanisms and be responsive to take-down demands. Nevertheless, such actions pose specific questions regarding the fragmentation of the internet, the so-called, the splinternet, in which users in various global locations will see a different version of the internet. One of the solutions is an international cooperation. The initiatives such as the Christchurch Call to Action, introduced by governments and tech corporations in the wake of the 2019 New Zealand mosque attacks, are going to establish a shared solution to eradicate terrorist content on the internet. In the same vein, the Global Internet Forum to Counter Terrorism (GIFCT) facilitates the process of uniting efforts related to responding to the extremist content on various platforms (Thorley & Saltman, 2023). But this collaboration is on a modest level and there is still a low level of international accords. Effective governance remains to be an issue due to the non-existence of universal legal criteria of regulating contents.

PLATFORM GOVERNANCE AND PRIVATE MODERATION

The role of the private technology companies in the present-day digital environment is to regulate online speech. Meta (Facebook and Instagram), X (previously Twitter), YouTube, and Tik Tok constitute social media where the number of users runs in billions and is the primary source of news, entertainment, and gossip. People working in these companies design and implement their own regulations of which contents are allowed and which are deleted. It is called platform governance and is a type of a private regulation, which works parallel to the national and international legislation. Since such websites are privately owned they are not subjected directly to constitutional speech protection. Nonetheless, their ruling influences greatly the practice of freedom of expression in the global arena. Thus, knowledge of how the platforms oversee their content or the management of moderation policies, algorithms, and human review and transparency are essential in how these rights to digital space and democratic accountability can be assessed (Gorwa, 2024).

Content Moderation Policies of Major Platforms

Each major platform has its own Community Guidelines or Terms of Service, which define what users can and cannot post. These rules typically prohibit content that involves:

- Hate speech
- Harassment and bullying
- Misinformation (particularly around elections or public health)
- Graphic violence and terrorism content
- Nudity or sexually explicit material
- Promotion of self-harm or suicide

As an example, Meta does not allow hate speech on the grounds of the race, religion, ethnicity, gender, and sexual orientation. It also censors the content praising terrorist activity or misinformation about vaccines. Harmful or dangerous content and disinformation campaigns are highly prohibited in YouTube. X (the former Twitter), with a new owner, has eased some of its rules of moderation, but instead, it removes illegal material but marks misinformation in some situations (Madio & Quinn, 2025). These policies, though, with the aim to provide a safe online environment, are disputable in their implementation, as, more frequently, they are unevenly implemented. On the one hand, some customers say that platforms fail to prevent the spread of dangerous material, whereas, on the other hand, customers tell that platforms restrict what should not be called censorship but critical political opinions.

Algorithmic Filtering, Automated Takedowns, and Human Review

Because the magnitude of online usage is of such large proportions, moderation relies heavily on automated systems. Algorithms search posts, comments, videos, and images on possible violation of rules. It is referred to as algorithmic filtering or automated content moderation.

Such system apply an artificial intelligence (AI) and machine learning to identify words or image patterns or behaviour that can signal potentially dangerous content (Marsoof et al., 2023). For example:

- An image uploaded on Facebook that has violent content will, automatically, be flagged and taken down.
- A tweet that violates hate speech can be concealed or blocked.
- There is a possibility of demonetization of a YouTube video that contains COVID-19 misinformation or deleting it.

Rather than fighting through each piece, automated tools allow platforms to process millions of posts per day but they also make errors. When one communicates, it matters in the context and in many situations algorithm cannot tell the difference between speech with malicious intent and satire, art, journalism, or actual criticism. It results in false positive (the deletion of legal information) and false negatives (permitted harmful content to remain). Most platforms use this by maintaining both people powered reviews and automation, creating teams who review flagged content, and make the final decision. Such teams tend to have no time to think and they could be exposed to tough conditions of work. Outsourced content moderators in certain situations have to work on the distribution of violent materials and it exposes them to traumatic content over periods of time without proper support (Enarsson et al., 2022). This combination of machine assisted performance and human reasoning is necessary to carry out content moderation but is one that needs great supervision to maintain a balance of justice, precision, and reliability.

Transparency Reports and Accountability Mechanisms

To improve trust, many platforms publish **transparency reports**. These are regular documents that provide statistics on:

- The number of posts removed
- The types of violations detected
- Government requests for takedown
- Appeals and reinstatement outcomes
- Actions taken on fake accounts or bots

As an illustration, the Transparency Centre provided by Meta provides insight as to how the company implements its content policies on platforms such as Facebook and Instagram. It indicates the amount of content that it removed due to hate speech, information, or copyright infringement. YouTube also releases a Community Guidelines Enforcement Report that shows the numbers of videos removed, which countries they affect, and which methods were used to flag that content (users, or automated, or trusted flaggers). X has also published transparency data though its recent reporting has fallen over the last couple of years (Shajari & Agarwal, 2025). Some platforms have established external oversight institutions besides promoting the publication of transparency reports. The Meta Oversight Board, an independent example is a panel of experts that reviews instances where the content is deemed controversial and passes a verdict of the content. People can contest the deletion of contents to the Board, which serves as a Supreme Court Facebook and Instagram moderation. Its judgments are final and Meta has to execute them or provide reasons as to why it was unable to. Although they represent a step in the right direction, some critics hold the view that transparency reports are usually too light, and platforms are not transparent about the functioning of their algorithms and decision-making at scale. In addition, there is a dearth of liability in cases where unjust removal of content prejudices the interest of the people or speech (Marsoof et al., 2023).

Case Examples: Platform Response to Political Speech and Misinformation

Even platforms themselves are often criticized on the way they treat political content and misinformation especially in case of elections or a crisis situation. A number of high-profile examples show the strength and the lack thereof of platform governance.

U.S. Capitol Riots (January 2021)

After the storming of the U.S. Capitol, platforms clamped down on information that led to incitement. Twitter also permanently suspended the account of Donald Trump, referring to the threat of further violence. Facebook has also banned him on the social media site, two years (Bao et al., 2022). This has given rise to a debate around the world; were these platforms upholding democracy, or de-platforming a political personality?

COVID-19 Pandemic

In the case of the pandemic, measures were taken by platforms to eliminate misleading health information. YouTube has censored advertisements of unproven medicines. Facebook also marked down posts that discouraged vaccination. Although this move was applauded by numerous people, some expressed its dangers as over-moderation may suppress genuine scientific debate arising on current scientific questions (Melchior & Oliveira, 2022).

Indian Farmers' Protest (2020–2021)

At some point during the protests, forced by Indian authorities, Twitter blocked some hashtags and accounts claiming these were misinformation. Twitter acceded but reversed course and allowed some material in the name of free expression. This event demonstrates the conflict between state authorities and international platforms and the challenging dilemmas businesses have to make when they approach a politically hostile location (Raj & Suresh, 2024).

Myanmar Genocide and Facebook's Role

In Myanmar, the Rohingya Muslims minority continuously faced hate speech through the most widespread form of social media, namely, Facebook. A report by the UN on violent extremism in the digital age concluded that the site had been deployed to promote violence and Facebook itself eventually acknowledged that it had been insufficient in its efforts to curb harmful content. The case illustrated the risks of promoting hate by algorithms and outcomes of the underdeveloped moderation in conflict areas (Schissler, 2024).

IMPACTS ON DEMOCRACY AND MARGINALIZED VOICES

In Myanmar, the Rohingya Muslims minority were constantly being subjected to hate speech by the use of the most popular type of social media, that is, Facebook. A report on violent extremism concerning the digital era given by the UN decided that the site had been used to enhance violence, and Facebook itself ended up accepting that it had been very lax in its push to end abhorrent content. The case depicted the dangers of encouraging hatred through algorithms and consequences of the poorly developed censorship in areas of conflict (Schissler, 2024).

Risks of Over-Moderation and Under-Moderation

The moderation of their content is required to eliminate dangerous information on the internet. Nevertheless, applied without a great deal of care, it may result in the case of over-moderation or under-moderation, both of which are detrimental to democratic values. Over-moderation occurs when websites act so as to remove excess content including speech that is acceptable. Machine learning outfits occasionally fail to detect context and remove posts that are important in the name of discussion. They can be flagged as violation of political commentary, satire or even artistic contents. Such moderation has the potential to shut down the voices of significant discussions, particularly those that hold complicated institutions or debate prevailing narratives (Celeste et al., 2023).

To illustrate, in the case of political protests, users tend to share messages or recordings of the violence of the police, or address governmental activities. When such platforms, remove this content under the inequitable excuse of violating their policy of graphic content, they inadvertently hide information and restrict awareness on violation of human rights. On the one hand, the lack of removal of dangerous or illicit material is called under-moderation. These are hate speech, fake news and violence. Such posts become rampant and detrimental to individuals or groups when platforms are not responsive and vigilant. This issue may cause radicalization, harassment, or even physical violence in the real world (Celeste et al., 2023).

Neither over-moderation, nor under-moderation serves to develop confidence in platforms and undermine their democratic engagement support. Platforms must also find a balance that supports the protection of free speech but limits it to a minimum.

Disproportionate Impact on Minority and Dissenting Voices

Ethnic minorities, religious minorities, LGBTQ +, Native peoples, and political dissidents tend to use the digital space to raise their voices on behalf of marginalized groups. Instead, they might not get space and coverage in traditional media and this makes online spaces essential in their self-representation and activism (Schmitz et al., 2022).

Nonetheless, it has been indicated that such groups are more susceptible to being targeted by the negative contents and having their posts deleted. This has a number of reasons:

- *Algorithm discrimination:* Biased training data can be used by the system to detect discrimination when automated algorithms are used to detect an item posted by a minority group. An example is that African American Vernacular English (AAVE) or native names can be classified as an offensive word in confusion.
- *Mass Reporting Campaigns:* In rare cases, bad actors can perform coordinated strikes by mass reporting material by minority members. The problem is that platforms tend to have a reaction to volume, instead of context verification, thus making wrongful takedowns.

- *Unaware of local language, history or political circumstances:* Content moderators do not know local cultures, including history, political situations and languages. It may cause the deletion of valid or necessary content to the communities (Chan et al., 2023).

What ensues is a twofold disadvantage to marginalized users since they are both a target of online abuse more often and less safeguarded by moderation mechanisms. They are not strong in democracy and speaking out their rights.

Censorship, Digital Authoritarianism, and Suppression of Activism

In most places, the internet is being employed as a mean of controlling and censoring. One of the demands that governments make on platforms is the removal of content that criticizes governments, even though such content does not contravene any platforms policy or international law. This type of digital authoritarianism in authoritarian regimes is on the rise (Roberts & Oosterom, 2024). By way of example, in some countries such as China, Iran, and Russia, online activity is highly monitored by authorities and certain platforms are blocked off. People may be jailed because of what they say on social media. The governments of even the most democratic states have begun employing such legal mechanism as fake news legislations or national security clauses to stifle journalism and the activities of activists. The social media may bow down to such demands so as not to lose access to such huge markets. By so doing, they are collaborators of censorship. When such control is applied to organizations of movements that rely on online space to conduct protests, raise funds, or record violations it is especially perilous.

An illustration of this is the Arab Spring where Facebook and Twitter was used by activists to gain mass protests. As a reaction, certain governments blocked or introduced disinformation overload on the platforms. Videos, messages were deleted and accounts were blocked during the Hong Kong pro-democracy protests undermining the means of communication in the movement (Kwong, 2024). Online suppression is a direct influence of offline freedom in such a scenario. The upsurge of shrinking space of differences threatens the idea of democracy and reinforces dictatorship.

ROLE OF CIVIL SOCIETY AND WATCHDOG ORGANIZATIONS

As the digital censorship and bias become increasingly more concerning, civil society groups, researchers, journalists, and digital rights groups become a crucial part of keeping governments and platforms accountable (Gohdes, 2024).

These organizations work to:

- Monitor takedowns and assess whether content removal was fair
- Advocate for policy change to protect free expression and digital rights
- Support affected users by providing legal help and public platforms
- Promote transparency through research and independent audits

Examples of such organizations include:

- Access Now – Works to defend and extend the digital rights of users at risk
- Electronic Frontier Foundation (EFF) – Provides legal support and campaigns for internet freedom
- Article 19 – Focuses on promoting freedom of expression globally
- Ranking Digital Rights (RDR) – Evaluates tech companies on their respect for human rights

These organizations call to increase algorithmic moderation transparency, improve defence systems, and independent checking. They also put pressure on the platforms to put human rights into consideration when operating, more so in nations where there are fewer democratic protection measures. Moreover, the civil society engages in digital literacy and citizen education that enables the users to learn their rights, report the abuse, and contribute to creating more equitable cyberspaces (Asimakopoulos et al., 2025).

CASE STUDIES: BALANCING ACTS IN ACTION

In digital governance, the role of balance between freedom of expression and content moderation may be problematic. Internationally, various approaches have been taken by states and online media in control of non-substantive online speech, the removal of negative content, and the preservation of democratic principles. One school of thought is the need to enforce the legal aspect, and the other school of thought depends on the level of responsibility of the platform. The three cases described in this part highlight how countries and businesses have managed the problems: the NetzDG law of Germany, the Indian approach to these challenges, and platform enforcement in the U.S. elections of 2020. All the examples leave lessons on unity, tension, and the essence of safeguarding both safety and the right to say what one wants to say.

Case Study 1: Germany's NetzDG and Hate Speech Removal

Germany also boasts of strict online speech laws globally, most of which are because of its past with fascism and societal based ideologies. In 2017, Germany enacted the Network Enforcement Act (NetzDG) against the hate speech and unlawful content on the social media.

On full name: (Under NetzDG, companies based on digital platforms that have more than 2 million German users, including Facebook, Twitter (now X), and YouTube, are obliged to delete content that is clearly illegal within 24 hours after complaint). In failure to do this, companies may be fined as much as an amount of 50 million euros. The content that is deemed as not clearly illegal is to be reviewed and removed within 7 days in case it is observed as a violation (Tworek, 2021).

The law covers content that violates ten sections of the German Criminal Code, including:

- Incitement to hatred
- Public threats of violence
- Defamation of religious groups
- Holocaust denial

Impact and Criticism

NetzDG has led to faster response rate of platforms and closer collaborations with German authorities. It made it even more transparent in that it mandated firms to date reports of their content removal. Nevertheless, the law has been branded as promoting excessive compliance. To prevent fines, platforms are motivated to take borderline content off the site - even though it is not obviously illegal. Critics have said that this causes chilling effects on political speech and public discourse. And civil society organizations and free speech activists have expressed concerns that it is not the courts but private companies that are determining what can and cannot be shown. Nevertheless, NetzDG has attracted followership among other countries across the world, notably France, Austria, and Russia, but not necessarily with the democratic protection (Neudert, 2024).

Case Study 2: India's Regulatory Landscape and Challenges of Overreach

China ranks higher in internet penetration than India as India has the largest number of internet users world over. Online space in the country is vibrant yet it is highly polarized. The worries regarding the misinformation, communal violence, and online abuse were the reasons why the government came up with the Information Technology (Intermediary Guidelines and Digital Media Ethics Code) Rules, 2021 (Abhishek, 2023).

The IT Rules require social media platforms to:

- Appoint a Grievance Officer, Nodal Officer, and Chief Compliance Officer based in India
- Remove content within 36 hours of a government or court order
- Enable traceability of the originator of messages (for platforms like WhatsApp)
- Provide monthly transparency reports

Even the digital news publishers and OTT platforms are subject to the rules, and in their case, they have to adhere to a three-layer system of regulation along with self-regulation and a government appointed committee.

Impact and Criticism

Indian government maintains that such regulations enhance accountability, particularly on curbing online maltreatment and click baits. Nonetheless, the rules have been criticized by journalists, civil liberty organizations and technologists who are worried that they can be applied to quash criticism, and diminish privacy rights. These issues attract attention through a number of controversies. In 2021, Twitter, at first, did not intend to abide by the regulations, especially about the appointment of officers. The Indian government answered with actions of court statements and the visit of the police in company offices. When there were farmer protests and unrest, government demanded platforms to impose hashtags and accounts. There was a certain content that came back because of the pressure of people that reflect the clash between the right to express oneself and the desire of the government to control things (Raj & Suresh, 2024). The IT Rules have been contrary in numerous Indian courts. They have been criticized by being against constitutional provisions stated in Article 19 (freedom of speech) and Article 21 (right to privacy). The future of internet regulation in India is going to be determined by the response of the judiciary.

Case Study 3: Platform Moderation during the 2020 U.S. Elections

The content moderation was put into the test in the 2020 U.S. presidential election. Disinformation on the use of mail-in voting, counterfeited election results, and conspiracy theories move extraordinarily fast on platforms such as Facebook, Twitter, and YouTube. A number of this misinformation was boosted by political leaders such as the former President Donald Trump.

To address this, platforms took several major steps:

- Labelling misleading posts about voting or election results
- Reducing the reach of harmful content through algorithmic adjustments
- Removing false claims about voter fraud and incitement to violence
- Banning accounts that repeatedly violated policies

The account was permanently banned by Twitter following the January 6, 2021, Capitol riot, after Twitter, citing the possibility of future violence, suspending Trump account said it was taking action because of the risk of future violence. Facebook also took away his account lasts 24 months, whereas YouTube erased videos and locked the channel (Jeppesen et al., 2022).

Impact and Criticism

Some of these activities were hailed as something that had to be employed to preserve democracy and avoid actual world damage. Some of them however were regarded as political biased censorship. The move to shut down the social media accounts of a sitting president created challenging inquiries of the power of the platforms, responsibility, and governance of free speech on the internet. The American tradition is influenced by the first amendment given that the government does not regulate speech yet privately it is moderated. Nevertheless, this incident further revived the discussions of the Section 230 of the Communications Decency Act, as it grants immunity of platforms with regard to user-generated content and makes its subjects free to police themselves in the way they deem necessary. In return, legislators in both political parties have floated revision of Section 230, but with varying intentions, with some seeking to lower the potency of platforms, and others seeking greater immoderation. The controversy is still going on without a definite answer so far (Montalbano, 2022).

Table 2. Key features and impacts of case studies

Case Study	Key Regulation/ Policy	Platform Response	Impact	Criticism
Germany – NetzDG	NetzDG (2017) – 24–48 hour content removal	Faster takedowns, transparency reports	Improved response to hate speech, model for other nations	Over-removal of legal content, platforms act as private censors
India – IT Rules, 2021	Mandatory local officers, content takedown, traceability	Legal tension with platforms, compliance issues	Stronger government control, concerns about online safety	Risks to free speech and privacy, political misuse
U.S. – 2020 Elections	No federal law, platform self-regulation	Fact-checking, labelling, account suspensions (e.g., Trump)	Helped curb disinformation, raised platform accountability	Censorship concerns, calls for reform of Section 230

Lessons Learned from Government Platform Cooperation and Conflict

Case studies show opportunities and risks in the interaction between the governments and the platforms:

i. Rights should be guarded by law: Regulation, as in Germany and the NetzDG, should make it easier to clean up dangerous content. Nevertheless, it cannot lack protection that would make it avoid excesses or have legal control.
ii. Excessive government control may suppress freedom of speech: the case of India demonstrates how perilous it might be to transfer excessive authority to the authorities. Devoid of checks and balances, regulation turns out to become an instrument of censorship.
iii. Platforms require policy clarity and autonomy: The case of the U.S. election controls the ability of platforms to take action to avoid injury, as well as the shortcomings of self-regulation without external authority.
iv. Transparency and accountability is a requirement: All three instances demonstrate that the platforms should ensure that they provide transparency related to how they regulate the content, provide an appeal mechanism as well as allowing the content to be scrutinized publicly.
v. Non-exceptionalized cannot be used: Countries have diverse issues of law, culture, and politics. Moderation of such content needs to be responsive to local situations and at the same time abide by international human rights principles.

7. CONCLUSION AND POLICY RECOMMENDATIONS

Online tools have changed communication and idea sharing and allowing people to be involved in the democratic life to a great extent. Although such sites provide a chance to communicate and be included, they come with serious issues related to hate speech, misinformation, and abuse. In this chapter, the issue of freedom of expression mixed with the desired control of harmful content using regulation systems and measures implemented by platforms in moderating their content has been addressed. One of the important insights is that there is no universal answer that would suit every situation. Various nations have different patterns depending on the existence of the laws, political ideals, and social issues. NetzDG in Germany can be described as the law-based model that is strictly enforced whereas IT Rules in India is defined by the mounting government intervention which might be a danger of overreaching the law. In contrast, the United States depends on platform participant self-regulation and thus experiences concern over corporate power, as well as unequal enforcement. The delicate balance between freedom of speech and moderation imposes tensions in the event that these efforts make a legal speech dormant or facilitate the actual harm. Excessive moderation may suppress activists and minority opinion, and suppress political dissent, whereas insufficient moderation enables dangerous information and incitement to be spread. These problems are exacerbated by automation and that the moderation decisions are not transparent.

In a bid to make digital spaces veritable democratic, inclusive, and safe, the balance, rights-respecting governance is urgently necessary. The best of governments, the most important of platforms, the civil society, and users should collaborate to ensure that we can come up with a clear standard that safeguards each other in terms of safety and freedom.

An efficient content moderation must be based on three main principles:

- Transparency: Plages should be open about their policies, moderation rules and standards of decisions. They should be able to get access to appeal mechanisms as well as transparency reports on a regular basis.
- Proportionality: Procedures to be pursued against content or users should be relevant to the damage incurred. The legal and platform action ought not to be harshly punitively or an outright ban.
- Accountability: Governments and platforms need to be answerable with their choices. The role of independent mechanisms of oversight, courts and civil society organizations are very important.

Policies that can be used involve the creation of independent content oversight boards, rebalancing algorithmic fairness issues, strengthening appeal apparatus of users and digital literacy. It is also essential that cross-border cooperation can help solve problems and spread similar standards based on human rights. In summation, the key to having a just digital future is to have an inclusive and democratic policymaking process that empowers users and at the same time attains accountability on the part of both states and platforms. The freedom of expression should not only exist in principles but also in the digital practice.

REFERENCES

Abdulai, E. S., & Abdulai, E. S. (2022). Introduction: A Brief Global History of the Emergence, Evolution, Development and Proliferation of Freedom of Information—Principles Definitive of Scope and Substance. *Freedom of Information Law and Good Governance: The Curse of Corruption in Sierra Leone*, 3-25. DOI: 10.1007/978-3-030-83658-0_1

Abhishek, A. (2023). The state deputizing citizens to discipline digital news media: The case of the IT rules 2021 in India. *Digital Journalism (Abingdon, England)*, *11*(10), 1769–1787. DOI: 10.1080/21670811.2022.2134163

Afzal, J. (2024). Digital Law Enforcement Challenges and Improvement. In *Implementation of Digital Law as a Legal Tool in the Current Digital Era* (pp. 47–78). Springer Nature Singapore., DOI: 10.1007/978-981-97-7106-6_3

Aïmeur, E., Amri, S., & Brassard, G. (2023). Fake news, disinformation and misinformation in social media: A review. *Social Network Analysis and Mining*, *13*(1), 30. DOI: 10.1007/s13278-023-01028-5 PMID: 36789378

Alfredsson, G., & Eide, A. (Eds.). (2023). *The Universal Declaration of Human Rights: a common standard of achievement*. Martinus Nijhoff Publishers.

Asimakopoulos, G., Antonopoulou, H., Giotopoulos, K., & Halkiopoulos, C. (2025). Impact of information and communication technologies on democratic processes and citizen participation. *Societies (Basel, Switzerland)*, *15*(2), 40. DOI: 10.3390/soc15020040

Bao, T., Wei, L., & Yu, Y. (2022). The impact of information interventions on public opinion on social media regulation: Evidence from a survey on Twitter's Trump Ban. *Journal of Behavioral and Experimental Economics*, *101*, 101947. DOI: 10.1016/j.socec.2022.101947

Bassiouni, M. C. (Ed.). (2024). *Legal responses to international terrorism: US procedural aspects* (Vol. 4). Martinus Nijhoff Publishers.

Batura, O. (2024, August). Relationship between the DSA and the 2022 Code of Practice on Disinformation: Self-Regulation, Co-regulation or Regulation? In *Disinformation in Europe* (pp. 85-104). Nomos Verlagsgesellschaft mbH & Co. KG. DOI: 10.5771/9783748948124

Brown, I., & Marsden, C. T. (2023). *Regulating code: Good governance and better regulation in the information age*. MIT press.

Carlson, C. R. (2021). *Hate speech*. MIT Press. DOI: 10.7551/mitpress/12491.001.0001

Celeste, E., Palladino, N., Redeker, D., & Yilma, K. (2023). Platform policies versus human rights standards. In *The content governance dilemma: Digital constitutionalism, social media and the search for a global standard* (pp. 93–129). Springer International Publishing., DOI: 10.1007/978-3-031-32924-1_5

Chan, A. J., García, J. L. R., Silvestri, F., O'Donnel, C., & Palla, K. (2023). Harmonizing global voices: Culturally-aware models for enhanced content moderation. *arXiv preprint arXiv:2312.02401*. https://doi.org//arXiv.2312.02401DOI: 10.48550

Cusumano, M. A., Gawer, A., & Yoffie, D. B. (2021). Can self-regulation save digital platforms? *Industrial and Corporate Change*, *30*(5), 1259–1285. DOI: 10.1093/icc/dtab052

Dixon, R. (2023). *Responsive judicial review: democracy and dysfunction in the modern age*. Oxford University Press. DOI: 10.1093/oso/9780192865779.001.0001

Dumitrica, D., & Hockin-Boyers, H. (2023). Slideshow activism on Instagram: Constructing the political activist subject. *Information Communication and Society*, *26*(16), 3318–3336. DOI: 10.1080/1369118X.2022.2155487

Enarsson, T., Enqvist, L., & Naarttijärvi, M. (2022). Approaching the human in the loop–legal perspectives on hybrid human/algorithmic decision-making in three contexts. *Information & Communications Technology Law*, *31*(1), 123–153. DOI: 10.1080/13600834.2021.1958860

Gohdes, A. R. (2024). *Repression in the digital age: Surveillance, censorship, and the dynamics of state violence*. Oxford University Press. DOI: 10.1093/oso/9780197743577.001.0001

Gorwa, R. (2024). *The politics of platform regulation: How governments shape online content moderation*. Oxford University Press. DOI: 10.1093/oso/9780197692851.001.0001

Guha, S., & Matilal, S. (2023). Information Technology (Intermediary Guidelines and Digital Media Ethics Code) Rules, 2021-A Reassessment of the Contours and Limits. *NUJS Journal of Regulatory Studies*, *8*(2). Advance online publication. DOI: 10.69953/nurs.v8i2.288

Gunatilleke, G. (2021). Justifying limitations on the freedom of expression. *Human Rights Review (Piscataway, N.J.)*, *22*(1), 91–108. DOI: 10.1007/s12142-020-00608-8

Jeppesen, S., Giroux, H., Hoechsmann, M., Kumanyika, C., VanDyke, D., & McKee, M. (2022). *The Capitol riots: digital media, disinformation, and democracy under attack*. Routledge. DOI: 10.4324/9781003246862

Kohli, R. (2022). The Sound of Constitutional Silences: Interpretive Holism and Free Speech under Article 19 of the Indian Constitution. *Statute Law Review*, *43*(1), 68–78. DOI: 10.1093/slr/hmaa012

Kumar, A., & Maurya, M. K. (2024). Online Public Sphere and Threats of Disinformation, Extremism and Hate Speech: Reflections on Threat-Mitigation. *The Journal of Communication Inquiry*, *01968599241292623*, 01968599241292623. Advance online publication. DOI: 10.1177/01968599241292623

Kwong, Y. H. (2024). Online counter-mobilisation via social media: Exploration of pro-regime opinion leaders in Hong Kong under Chinese sovereignty. *Asia Pacific Viewpoint*, *65*(2), 202–215. DOI: 10.1111/apv.12398

Madio, L., & Quinn, M. (2025). Content moderation and advertising in social media platforms. *Journal of Economics & Management Strategy*, *34*(2), 342–369. DOI: 10.1111/jems.12602

Marsoof, A., Luco, A., Tan, H., & Joty, S. (2023). Content-filtering AI systems–limitations, challenges and regulatory approaches. *Information & Communications Technology Law*, *32*(1), 64–101. DOI: 10.1080/13600834.2022.2078395

Masferrer, A. (2023). The decline of freedom of expression and social vulnerability in Western democracy. *International Journal for the Semiotics of Law-Revue internationale de Sémiotique juridique, 36*(4), 1443-1475. DOI: 10.1007/s11196-023-09990-1

Melchior, C., & Oliveira, M. (2022). Health-related fake news on social media platforms: A systematic literature review. *New Media & Society*, *24*(6), 1500–1522. DOI: 10.1177/14614448211038762

Montalbano, K. (2022). Reimagining section 230 and content moderation: Regulating incivility on anonymous digital platforms. *Communication Law and Policy*, *27*(3-4), 187–219. DOI: 10.1080/10811680.2022.2136442

Nannini, L., Bonel, E., Bassi, D., & Maggini, M. J. (2025). Beyond phase-in: Assessing impacts on disinformation of the EU Digital Services Act. *AI and Ethics*, *5*(2), 1241–1269. DOI: 10.1007/s43681-024-00467-w

Neudert, L. M. (2024). Reclaiming Digital Sovereignty: Policy and Power Dynamics Behind Germany's NetzDG. *Journal of Information Policy*, *14*, 417–470. Advance online publication. DOI: 10.5325/jinfopoli.14.2024.0013

Pangrazio, L., & Sefton-Green, J. (2021). Digital rights, digital citizenship and digital literacy: What's the difference?. *Journal of new approaches in educational research, 10*(1), 15-27. DOI: 10.7821/naer.2021.1.616

Raj, S. J., & Suresh, A. K. (2024). The Truth Lies In-between: Mind Engineering in the 2020–2021 Indian Farmers' Protest. In *The Routledge Handbook of Language and Mind Engineering* (pp. 197-211). Routledge.

Rajput, B., & Amit, K. (2024). *Balsing/Gada Rajput (Dhrum)*. Online Child Sexual Abuse., DOI: 10.1007/978-3-031-45697-8

Roberts, T., & Oosterom, M. (2024). Digital authoritarianism: A systematic literature review. *Information Technology for Development*, •••, 1–25. DOI: 10.1080/02681102.2024.2425352

Schissler, M. (2024). Beyond Hate Speech and Misinformation: Facebook and the Rohingya Genocide in Myanmar. *Journal of Genocide Research*, •••, 1–26.

Schmitz, R. M., Coley, J. S., Thomas, C., & Ramirez, A. (2022). The cyber power of marginalized identities: Intersectional strategies of online LGBTQ+ Latinx activism. *Feminist Media Studies*, *22*(2), 271–290. DOI: 10.1080/14680777.2020.1786430

Shajari, S., & Agarwal, N. (2025). Safeguarding youtube discussions: A framework for detecting anomalous commenter and engagement behaviors. *Social Network Analysis and Mining*, *15*(1), 1–24. DOI: 10.1007/s13278-025-01470-7

Siapera, E. (2022). AI content moderation, racism and (de) coloniality. *International Journal of Bullying Prevention : an Official Publication of the International Bullying Prevention Association*, *4*(1), 55–65. DOI: 10.1007/s42380-021-00105-7

Song, L., & Ma, C. (2022). Identifying the fourth generation of human rights in digital era. *International Journal of Legal Discourse*, *7*(1), 83–111. DOI: 10.1515/ijld-2022-2065

Thorley, T. G., & Saltman, E. (2023). GIFCT tech trials: Combining behavioural signals to surface terrorist and violent extremist content online. *Studies in Conflict and Terrorism*, •••, 1–26. DOI: 10.1080/1057610X.2023.2222901

Tworek, H. J. (2021). Fighting hate with speech law: Media and German visions of democracy. *The Journal of Holocaust Research*, *35*(2), 106–122. DOI: 10.1080/25785648.2021.1899510

Wasiq, M. R. (2022). Legal Regime on Freedom of Speech and Expression with Special Reference to Sedition Law under India, the United Kingdom, and the United States Of America. *International Journal of Creative Research Thoughts (IJCRT)*. https://ssrn.com/abstract=4221059

Chapter 3
A Legal Analysis on Navigating Facial Recognition Technology in India's State Surveillance Framework

Manu Mariyan Abraham
https://orcid.org/0000-0002-2196-3645
Christ University, Bangalore, India

ABSTRACT

The evolution of the state surveillance apparatus in India, particularly through the integration of novel technologies such as Facial Recognition Technology (FRT) and Artificial Intelligence (AI), has significantly transformed national security and law enforcement strategies. While these advancements enhance the state's capacity for counter-terrorism and crime prevention, they also raise critical privacy and human rights concerns. The paper analyses the existing legal framework governing surveillance in India, focusing on the implications of AI-driven FRT. Key concerns are categorised into three areas: (a) security vulnerabilities, (b) inaccuracies, biases, and lack of transparency in FRT systems, and (c) the potential misuse of surveillance powers by the state. The paper is not technical in nature; instead, it critically analyses existing laws and proposes policy recommendations and regulatory mechanisms to balance national security imperatives with the protection of individual privacy rights in a democratic society.

DOI: 10.4018/979-8-3693-3920-6.ch003

INTRODUCTION

The state surveillance apparatus in India is an absolute necessity for the national security imperative. Governments utilise novel technologies like Facial recognition (FRT) to bolster the surveillance mechanisms (Lynch, 2024, 35). The modern surveillance apparatus, coupled with AI, has changed the landscape of counter-terrorism and law enforcement. This surge in AI-driven systems in the surveillance regime has raised several privacy concerns. Systems like FRTs without proper regulations and operational grounds could adversely affect the privacy rights of citizens of India. It is claimed that the Indian legal framework on FRTs is non-existent, and even the existing laws on surveillance do not provide reasonable protection to citizens' right to privacy (Krishnamurthy, 2021).

This paper initially aims to provide an operational and technical understanding. This paper follows a legal perspective where the researcher claims that there is a lack of procedural safeguards in the Indian surveillance legal architecture that the state and state actors can abuse. The paper examines India's existing state surveillance apparatus with a special emphasis on FRTs and the incorporation of AI systems. The paper also elucidates the laws governing state surveillance activities in India. This paper primarily focuses on analysing the legal framework surrounding FRTs in India rather than elaborating on the technical concerns that such a technology might face. Simply put, the paper seeks to address the absence of laws regulating FRTs in India, especially the use of such technology by state actors in surveillance operations. The paper does not dive further into the technological understanding of the FRTs and potential risks from a technical standpoint, except for the following brief explanation on best practices adopted worldwide.

Further, the paper examines the privacy and security concerns with respect to FRT systems in the state surveillance regime. This section classifies the aforementioned concerns into three: a) security risks, b) inaccuracy, bias and lack of transparency in FRTs, and c) potential misuse of powers/exemptions by the state with respect to surveillance through FRT. Finally, the paper suggests the best approaches to mitigating the aforementioned concerns in the last section.

The researcher follows doctrinal methodology, analysing existing laws, regulations, legal precedents and judicial decisions with respect to FRTs in India. The analysis involves perusing the letter of the law to determine the scope of the regulations, comparing best legal practices worldwide in an attempt to realise such provisions that are adaptable to Indian legal system and exploring security and privacy concerns generally encountered due to the implementation of FRTs.

FACIAL RECOGNITION SYSTEMS: TECHNICAL AND OPERATIONAL UNDERSTANDING

The proliferation of Facial recognition technology (FRT) in law enforcement and surveillance has given reasonable impetus to understanding the technical and operational foundations of the technology. The traditional CCTV surveillance mechanism was a revolution, considering the impact it had in replacing the much more conventional approach of physical surveillance. Earlier, police personnel had to picket outside the suspect's house to monitor activities, giving rise to the 'stake-out' surveillance method. The introduction of CCTV cameras allowed law enforcement to establish numerous surveillance points, some installed by the state and some by private individuals and businesses, the footage of which is retrieved by the police to assist their investigation (Ashby, 2017). Traditional cameras involve observation, capture and storage of information. It captured the real-time instances that are in its line of sight. The footage is transmitted to a limited number of display devices, like a monitor or mobile device and is subsequently stored on a hard drive or any other storage mechanism. This method allowed revisiting the footage for clarity. It also assisted in monitoring multiple places of interest at once. However, this method was not autonomous and required the involvement of human actors in cross-checking the footage to find a possible match for the perpetrator's face, as captured by the cameras, with the available database.

In contrast, FRT introduced some additional elements to the traditional methods, making them more efficient in assisting surveillance activities. The technical understanding of FRTs starts from 'face detection.' This means the identification of faces from a particular input. The input can be video footage captured by the cameras integrated into the surveillance apparatus or an image captured, which may include the suspect or persons of interest. Face detection involves several steps: (a) input – video footage or an image, (b) FRT algorithm interacts with the image or footage to find the existence of a face/s, even from a crowd, (c) the face of the person of interest/suspect is analysed to establish specific facial features with corresponding reference points. Subsequently, the FRTs employ the facial recognition element to match the face with the millions of faces in their database. This involves several steps: (a) the extracted facial features are converted into a digital format, and (b) the digital format containing the facial features is matched against similar formats in the database. The recognition algorithm would develop a face template similar to the output template from the face detection process. If a mathematical similarity is determined that is above an acceptable threshold, then the faces are considered matching and of the same person (Li and Jain 2011).

INTERSECTION OF STATE SURVEILLANCE APPARATUS AND FRTS IN INDIA

The application of Facial Recognition Technology can be found in several industries and sectors (Adjabi et al., 2020). The specific use cases differ based on the purpose or objective of employment of such a technology. Both the state and private parties utilise FRTs differently. Some of the most common use cases are Law enforcement, state surveillance and protection of the security of the state, biometric attendance and access controls (Lee and Chin 2022), FRT embedded in devices and the possibility of the usage of FRT by social media platforms storing vast amounts of images or the sale/transfer of their data to a third party that utilises FRT. The research encapsulated in this paper limits itself to critically analysing the use of FRTs by the state for purposes such as law enforcement and surveillance.

State surveillance mechanisms in India are an imperative to the national security efforts. Even though serious privacy concerns have been raised against several mechanisms and technologies used for surveillance efforts, it is not advisable to dismantle the entire surveillance apparatus in India (Bansal and Nah, 2022). FRT is one such technology that has raised privacy concerns among the public. The state surveillance apparatus in India can be identified as a combination of technologies and databases that engage in interception, monitoring, collecting, storing, and analysing communication and information conveyed through every possible medium. Monitoring organs like the Central Monitoring System (CMS) (Jain, 2020a) aims to achieve smooth and rapid interception of communications between individuals primarily through their mobile devices. On the other hand, there are interconnected databases that store information on citizens and offenders, from which relevant information is retrieved in real-time at the behest of investigating agencies. The National Intelligence Grid (NATGRID) (Jain, 2020b) and Crime and Criminal Tracking Network & Systems (CCTNS) (Press Information Bureau, 2025) are the most prominent among such databases. NATGRID connects different agencies and departments of the government and provides real-time data on individuals at the request of investigating agencies. NATGRID is exclusively used for counter terrorism purposes. While CCTNS collects and stores information on criminals and details of crimes, which can be accessed by investigating agencies and other law enforcement agencies in pursuance of prevention of a crime. NAFRS is the surveillance mechanism that utilises facial recognition to identify and match individuals with images and information on the connected database (Jain, 2020c). The introduction of AI has enhanced the capabilities of these systems. The state can now monitor and analyse individuals and identify their behavioural patterns through AI-driven facial recognition systems (Fontes et al., 2022).

LAWS CONCERNING STATE SURVEILLANCE OPERATIONS AND FRTS IN INDIA

The legal architecture that governs state surveillance activities is fragmented, with a combination of laws dealing with specific areas and matters of surveillance. The whole surveillance regime, however, stands on two laws: the Telecommunications Act of 2023 (the Telegraph Act of 1885 and subsequent rules were repealed under this Act) and the Information Technology Act of 2000. No specific laws govern the use of FRT in surveillance operations. Instead, the general provisions that empower the government to further the surveillance activities will also apply to the use of FRTs.

Section 20(2) of the Telecommunications Act of 2023 (hereinafter referred to as the Telecom Act) empowers the state to intercept any form of telecommunications on the enabling grounds, such as 'occurrence of any public emergency' or 'in the interest of public safety.' The government must also be satisfied that such an interception is in the interest of the sovereignty of the nation, security of the state, public order and several other grounds. Similar powers are granted to the state with respect to the interception of information and communication in relation to computer resources under Section 69 of the Information Technology Act of 2000 (hereinafter referred to as the IT Act).

Further, the new Digital Personal Data Protection Act (DPDPA) of 2023 (hereinafter called the DPDPA), which regulates the body corporates in processing the data of the citizens, provides similar exemptions as discussed earlier, empowering the state to engage in non-consensual processing of citizen's data (Section 17(2) of the Digital Personal Data Protection Act of 2023). Moreover, Section 7(c) of the DPDPA states that the data fiduciaries can process the personal data of individuals if it is in furtherance of the performance of any function by the state or its instrumentalities under any law on the grounds of national security and sovereignty.

The IT (Procedure and Safeguards for Interception, Monitoring and Decryption of Information) Rules, 2009 and Telecommunications (Procedures and Safeguards for Lawful Interception of Messages) Rules, 2024 provide for the authorisation and review of a surveillance order. Under Rule 3 of the IT Rules and Rule 3 of the Telecom Rules, the competent authority to authorise an order for interception is the Secretary to the Government of India in the Ministry of Home Affairs at the Union level and the Secretary in charge of the Home Department at the State and Union territory levels. Rule 22 of the IT Rules and Rule 5 of the Telecom Rules state that a review committee that consists of the same members who authorise the order shall review the surveillance directions once every 2 months.

NATURE OF CONCERNS RELATED TO FRTS

The nature of concerns with respect to facial recognition technology can be categorised into three, all of which involve a potential violation of citizens' right to privacy. Firstly, the paper analyses the security concerns related to FRT in terms of its privacy leakages and infrastructural vulnerabilities. Secondly, the potential bias and inaccuracy induced by a faulty FRT are discussed in the paper. Lastly, the concerns regarding government misuse of AI-enhanced FRT in the absence of proper safeguards are analysed in the paper. Table 1 provides a concise understanding of the nature of concerns as classified for the purpose of this research.

Table 1. Nature of concerns with respect to FRTs

Nature	Specific concerns
Security concerns related to FRT	Privacy leakages, data breaches, and hacking of embedded physical systems
Design-based Issues	Potential bias, inaccuracy, explainability of AI models, transparency, accountability and assuming responsibility.
Possible misuse of power by the State (Indian context)	Power to process non-consensual data under DPDPA, Ambiguity in the definition and understanding of exemptions for the state under different surveillance laws, and lack of procedural safeguards to protect citizens' privacy.
(Source: Author's compilation)	

Security concerns related to FRT

Security risks concerning FRTs can be at different levels. Generally, it would include privacy leakages, data breaches, hacking of embedded physical systems in the surveillance network, and several others. A recent study (Laishram et al., 2025) classifies these security risks based on various levels. At the 'camera level,' hacking is the most prominent security risk. An attack on the CCTV system could compromise the whole FRT apparatus. Every day, hackers devise novel methods of infiltration and control of CCTV systems (Vennam et al., 2021). In 2018, Kaspersky, a cybersecurity company, found around 2000 smart cameras with an open IP address on the web (Alfred, 2018). The company stated that these cameras can be easily controlled and are vulnerable to an attack. On the 'image level,' facial information and identifying factors can be obtained by attackers if the collected images or footage are not properly sanitised. This particular issue occurs in cases where the footage or images are released in public without systematically obscuring the identities of individuals in the picture, subsequently violating their privacy (Croft et al., 2021). Another concern would be the breach of face images from the databases. Facial biometrics are used worldwide for various purposes like banking (Nosrati et al., 2024), healthcare and medical records (Lei et al., 2025), face unlock on devices (Gururaj et al., 2024) and several others. A breach at the 'face detection level' would lead to irreversible damage as the biometric data cannot be changed like your credit card details. Other forms of breaches or privacy leakages are at the 'database level,' wherein the collected data would be transferred to the wrong hands.

Bias, inaccuracy and transparency of AI-driven FRTs

Although boasted to be one of the most advanced technologies in the world, facial recognition systems face several design-based issues. Potential inaccuracy is one of the prominent concerns with respect to the operational understanding of FRTs. There is a possibility of false positives and false negatives. FRTs generally operate with three datasets: the training dataset, gallery and probe images (Philips and Newton, 2002). False negatives result in the non-identification of a person whose identification metrics are available in the gallery, but the FRT could not identify and match it with the probe image.

On the other hand, false positives result in misidentification, wherein the FRT has erroneously identified and matched an individual with the probe image. During the investigation of the Easter bombings in Sri Lanka, a similar instance happened, where a student was erroneously identified as the suspect, which was corrected immediately by the authorities (Fox, 2019). Inaccuracy can also be caused by the quality of the images (Senior and Bolle 2002), often dictated by the conditions and the surroundings.

A potential bias in FRT detection and identification could also lead to inaccuracy. Bias can be caused mainly by poor and less diverse training data. Most operational biases leading to inaccuracies are based on colour and gender. A 2018 study confirmed the higher error rates in commercially available FRT systems while identifying and matching persons of colour. The error rate was found to be high in females of colour, while the error rates concerning light-skinned males were significantly lower (Buolamwin, 2018). This particular issue could be aggravated by India's multi-ethnic and diverse culture, where there are discernible differences in facial patterns and features of individuals hailing from different parts of the nation (Prasanna et al., 2013). It is also important to note that most facial recognition technology systems are developed outside India, for which the training data is not diverse enough. This would lead to further inaccuracies and bias, resulting in misidentification and wrongful accusations.

In addition to the abovementioned concerns, there are several other issues with AI-driven FRT. AI models generally suffer from problems such as transparency, accountability and explainability. Transparency requirements in the operation of surveillance mechanisms, especially FRTs, are a slippery slope. The Indian government has always tried to shelter itself under the blanket of national security for almost every matter involving surveillance (Kumar, 2005). Transparency in FRT systems would require the state to divulge specific information relating to the operation of FRTs to the public. It also involves informing the surveilled individual about the fact. Some even argue that informed consent (Parsheera, 2019) should be a mandate for FRT identification and matching. This particular opaqueness surrounding FRTs would also lead to doubts as to the use of 'sensitive' personal data such as facial features and other biometric information for purposes other than what they are intended for (Narayan, 2022).

Concerning AI-driven FRTs, accountability and explainability prove to be another obstacle. The AI models generally lack explainability, commonly touted as the *'black-box problem* (Blouin, 2023).*'* It is challenging to discern the reasons for which the AI model made a particular decision under a given circumstance. The same applies to real-world scenarios involving facial recognition, identification and matching. The difficulty in deducing the thought process (Office of General Counsel, 2024) of AI models and the basis of its actions translates to a lack of explainability. Subsequently, assigning responsibility and accountability for erroneous decisions by AI-driven FRTs would become strenuous, as it would be difficult to identify and explain the reasoning behind AI decisions. Additionally, most of the FRT systems are developed by several agencies and companies that collaborate with each other. This engagement of multiple minds and personnel in the development and deployment contributes to the difficulty in determining accountability in case of an error. Due to the absence of explainable AI models, it would also be taxing to determine whether a wrong decision was due to biased training data, system glitches, system manipulation or an error in judgment by a human agent supervising the FRT.

Concerns regarding government misuse of FRT and AI-driven surveillance mechanisms

The third point of concern is the state's potential misuse of AI-driven FRT. As mentioned earlier, Facial recognition technology is not explicitly regulated under any law. Instead, the legal framework for surveillance also governs the operation of FRTs. FRT has cabinet approval, according to the NCRB; hence, no executive order or legislation is required to approve the creation of the Automated Facial Recognition System (AFRS). Cabinet clearance does not, however, provide any legal authority for the use of face recognition technology, nor is it a statutory provision. The DPDPA regulates body corporates with respect to the collection and processing of data. At the same time, the Act gives blanket exemptions for the state to engage in processing non-consensual data under Section 7(c) and Section 17(2). Some exemptions, like 'security of the state', are not adequately defined under any law, giving arbitrary power to the executive to determine whether an offence rises to the gravity of a national security matter. National security has been identified as a legitimate state aim by the Supreme Court of India in the Puttaswamy judgment (Justice K S Puttaswamy (Retd.) v Union of India (2017) 10 SCC 1). However, the court in the Pegasus case (Manohar Lal Sharma v Union of India (2023) 11 SCC 401) also expressed concern regarding the government utilising the exemption of national security as a free pass. Further, there is a lack of procedural safeguards to protect citizens' privacy rights against the potential misuse of AI-driven surveillance mechanisms.

Moreover, it is also pertinent to note that a surveillance order is authorised by a competent authority under the IT and Telecom Rules. The members that constitute the authorising authority are from the executive branch. Similarly, the review committee constituted under the rules comprises the same individuals who essentially review their own directions. It can be argued that the review committee will comprehensively analyse the surveillance operation and determine whether it was carried out according to the directives issued during authorisation. However, the review committee does not provide for an interbranch check, weakening the instruments of checks and balances.

SUGGESTED APPROACHES

The security and design-based concerns presented in the paper can be categorised as purely technical. These issues require technical and design-based solutions, most of which are employed during the development stage and deployment of the technology. Some of the best practices developed and followed in different jurisdictions with respect to these concerns are mentioned in this section. Further, this paper primarily focuses on analysing the legal framework regulating FRTs in India rather than elaborating on the technical concerns that such a technology might face. Simply put, the paper seeks to address the absence of laws regulating FRTs in India, especially the use of such technology by state actors in surveillance operations. The paper does not dive further into the technological understanding of the FRTs and potential risks from a technical standpoint, except for the following brief explanation on best practices adopted worldwide.

Concerning the security of facial recognition technology

As mentioned earlier in the paper, security risks to an FRT system can be realised at different levels. A hacker could easily tamper with an FRT system or embedded camera to access facial data and footage from the apparatus (security risk at the 'camera level'). A commonly used technique to hide facial areas post-capture is at the post-processing stage (involving the de-identification process) (Newton et al., 2005). Recent research has suggested using privacy safeguards at the optical level (Ma et al., 2019) and sensor level (Pittaluga et al., 2016), whereby the data captured by the sensors are already sanitised and protected before transmitting to the camera's host board. Security safeguards at the 'image level' include face obfuscation (Khamis, 2022), pixelation techniques (Cammozzo, 2011) and masking methods (Hill et al., 2016). However, such privacy-preserving techniques employed at an image level to protect data from a potential attack are irreversible. Once the quality of the image is tampered with, it cannot be brought back to its original condition, affecting reusability. Techniques like face obfuscation (degrading the image to a particular level from which face identification is not possible), face de-identification (replacing the real face of the individual with an artificial or synthetic face) (Du et al., 2014), face swapping (swapping a face with someone else's) (Nirkin et al., 2019) is utilised to safeguard privacy leakages at the 'face level.' A potential risk to the databases used as the *gallery dataset* could be countered by better encryption techniques. It is also advisable to have only a handful of individuals who can access the database. An access privilege to the admins should mandate the nature of the usage of such access, requiring them to access only the data that is necessary to execute the directions at hand (Rubens, 2022).

Concerning accurate FRTs

Regarding potential inaccuracies in FRTs, recent research suggests that 3D Facial recognition systems have managed to alleviate several accuracy and reliability issues connected to the traditional 2D FRT systems, with respect to quality of the image, lighting, variance in camera positioning, changing facial expressions and several other image characteristics (Zhou and Xiao 2018). These are generally categorised as technical inaccuracies. On the other hand, there are inaccuracies caused by bias due to underrepresentation or misrepresentation within the training data. It is vital to ensure that FRT systems used for state surveillance operations are trained with datasets that are consistent with the Indian demography. The lack of diversity with respect to the availability of facial data in the training dataset hinders the establishment of a robust FRT in India.

Additionally, large-scale AI models such as FRTs in surveillance mechanisms would have difficulty providing scalable explanations for their use cases. Explainable AI models are considered the solution to the transparency issue and the *black-box problem.* Explainable AI models include sets of processes and standards that focus on providing unambiguous and clear human-understandable explanations for the decisions taken by the AI system (Hassija et al., 2024). Explainable AI would also help assign responsibility in case of an erroneous decision. Since the process of AI decision-making is discernible, it would be easier for the developers to identify and rectify the issues with the AI models in case of a technical or operational glitch that led to an error.

BEST PRACTICES IN OTHER JURISDICTIONS

The previous section briefly analysed technical and security challenges faced worldwide by FRTs in general. The technology could face similar difficulties when embedded in a surveillance apparatus as part of a state initiative. The penultimate section also mentioned the best approaches to counter and alleviate such technical obstacles. This section will explain the approaches different nations adopt in their legal framework in mitigating privacy and civil liberty issues raised by FRTs. This section solely focuses on the best regulatory measures employed by other jurisdictions in regulating the application of FRTs into their state surveillance mechanisms. Initially, this section deals with the legislations in select countries enacted to govern the FRTs exclusively.

Best practices concerning the regulation of implementation and application of FRTs

Any discussion on laws regulating the operation of FRTs splits opinions into two. Some think that requiring the developers of such technologies and systems to adopt self-regulatory measures during the development stages – while giving due consideration to ethical and privacy implications of their creations – is sufficient to address the lingering doubts (Parsheera, 2019). Others suggest a more robust and perceivable approach wherein legislation is enacted to supervise the operation of FRTs. The provisions of such a law would act as an oversight mechanism to protect citizens' rights. The initial approaches adopted by nations were aligned with the concept of self-regulation (Algorithm Watch, 2019). Self-regulatory measures involved corporations focusing on their technology's ethical and privacy implications and its potential buyers. There have been instances where corporations took such a restraint in selling their technology to law enforcement agencies with a questionable reputation in matters of surveillance (Kraus, 2019) and maintaining self-regulatory principles (Microsoft, 2018).

Nations have been alert to the rising privacy concerns regarding FRTs, starting a shift from the self-regulatory approach. Belgium has a ban in place to stop private actors from using FRTs for non-police use (Dokmanović and Cvetićanin 2023), while the law enforcement agencies are free to utilise FRTs embedded in the surveillance mechanisms (but vehemently opposed by human rights organisations). Interestingly, in 2023, China, which has pioneered in surveillance and facial recognition and has instigated the proliferation of FRTs around the globe, enacted the Cyberspace Administration of China, which places several restrictions on facial recognition, such as individuals' consent and use of non-biometric measures for the same purpose. It has restricted the use of FRTs exclusively for matters involving public safety and administrative uses, wherein the safeguards will not be applicable (Zheng, 2025). The European Union, on the other hand, has implemented stricter regulations on the use of FRTs by government agencies through the new AI Act (Satariano, 2023). The EU AI Act, through its provisions, has limited the powers of law enforcement agencies by only permitting the use of FRTs in investigating specific crimes (like trafficking, abduction or crimes punishable with more than four years of imprisonment) and in imminent threats to persons or terrorist attacks (Zulehner, 2024). Japan protects facial biometrics under the Personal Information Protection Code, requiring consent from the individual. It also requires that FRT be used through a public notice or notification to the targeted individual (Russell, 2024).

An Ideal Regulatory Framework For India Concerning Frts

The Indian surveillance framework is not comprehensive enough to govern novel technologies. Presently, such technologies are employed and used arbitrarily without any scrutiny. Technologies such as FRTs have been paramount in defining surveillance efforts in recent years. There is no denying the value of FRTs to the national security imperative. However, it is also exigent that proper safeguards are established to bridle the state's potential misuse of powers/exemptions.

Firstly, even if the national security imperative is a recognised, legitimate goal, provisions like Section 17(2) are unclear and insufficient because of its vague description and the lack of a mandate that controls officials' discretion in surveillance-related matters. Clarity in understanding the national security imperative, either through a regulation or judicial interpretation, would restrain the government from raising the national security exemption on surveillance-related issues. It would also clarify the requirements or grounds for which a particular offence/instance can be classified as a matter involving national security, the threshold for which should be clearly defined.

Secondly, an inter-branch check on the surveillance activities could help to curb arbitrariness. As mentioned earlier, the absence of clear procedural safeguards opens a door for the potential abuse of certain powers. Any form of judicial oversight could provide for an inter-branch check determining the validity of specific surveillance operations. In general, judicial oversight can be *ex-ante* (prior to the issuance of surveillance directions) or *ex-post* (review of surveillance order after the fact). Facial recognition, identification and matching, mainly when driven by AI, happen in real-time. Most of the identification and matching involved in the FRT system of state surveillance apparatus is 1:n (a known facial image at hand cross-referenced against several unknowns) in nature. This type of facial recognition is required in real time since such a piece of information could be time-sensitive. It is, thus, inadvisable to have an *ex-ante* judicial oversight in matters involving FRTs in state surveillance. In instances where a 1:1 identification paradigm (verification of an individual's identity, especially in cases of targeted delivery of benefits) is sought after, safeguards such as notice-consent and *ex-ante* oversight can be implemented. On the contrary, in cases of 1:n identification, ex-post oversight could be brought in as a procedural safeguard. Such a review, post-surveillance, could apply the proportionality test by determining whether: a) there was a legitimate state aim, b) the surveillance directive was in accordance with the law, c) the state action involving surveillance and the means employed are proportional to the expected result/goal.

Finally, another procedural safeguard can be a mandate for streamlining data collected and processed. The collation of excessive amounts of data through FRT can be attributed to the failure to streamline, prioritise, and compartmentalise to gather the necessary data pertinent to the context of that specific surveillance order. Additionally, surveillance activities entail several transactions, resulting in several requests for surveillance orders and the following documentation. The issues with few resources may be resolved with clear rules on the type of surveillance activity to be carried out and the streamlining needed to collect data.

CONCLUSION

In the Pegasus case, the Supreme Court of India stated that surveillance activities to fight terrorism, crime, and corruption are accepted standards worldwide. The state must employ every mechanism and technology at its disposal to protect its interests. The use of FRT in the state surveillance mechanism can be justified following the same argument. However, it is equally important to protect citizens' right to privacy. It is a common practice that privacy concerns are overridden in national security matters. However, firstly, it is pertinent to realise whether the state has exhausted every possible alternative to resolve such situations without violating individuals' privacy. Secondly, it must be determined whether such state action in furtherance of national security is carried out with procedural safeguards established to protect citizens' privacy and curb potential arbitrariness. Thirdly, it is also important to examine whether the means adopted by the state are proportional to the expected results.

Concerns regarding FRT systems are different in nature. There can be security risks with respect to FRT infrastructure and embedded systems that are susceptible to a potential cyber-attack. Further, bias, lack of transparency, and inaccuracy can lead to wrongful accusations, weakening the public's trust in the technology. There are also concerns with respect to the encroachment of the government in utilising FRTs, as a result of lack of proper safeguards. It is crucial to ensure that such concerns are sufficiently addressed and resolved to have an effective FRT system employed beyond the boundaries of citizens' right to privacy, undermining privacy only under specific circumstances after proper checks.

REFERENCES

Adjabi, I., Ouahabi, A., Benzaoui, A., & Taleb-Ahmed, A. (2020). Past, present, and future of face recognition: A review. *Electronics (Basel)*, *9*(8), 1188. DOI: 10.3390/electronics9081188

Alfred, N. G. (2018). Your smart camera may have been spying on you. CNET. https://www.cnet.com/home/smart-home/your-smart-camera-may-have-been-spying-on-you/ (accessed April 4, 2025).

Ashby, M. P. J. (2017). The value of CCTV surveillance cameras as an investigative tool: An empirical analysis. *European Journal on Criminal Policy and Research*, *23*(3), 441–459. DOI: 10.1007/s10610-017-9341-6

Bansal, G., & Nah, F. F.-H. (2022). Internet Privacy Concerns Revisited: Oversight from Surveillance and Right to be Forgotten as New Dimensions. *Information & Management*, *59*(3), 103618. Advance online publication. DOI: 10.1016/j.im.2022.103618

Blouin, L. (2023). AI's mysterious 'black box' problem, explained. UM-Dearborn News. https://umdearborn.edu/news/ais-mysterious-black-box-problem-explained (accessed April 2, 2025).

Buolamwin, J., & Gebru, T. (2018). Gender shades: Intersectional accuracy disparities in commercial gender classification. Proceedings of Machine Learning Research. In 2018 Conference on Fairness, Accountability and Transparency (PMLR) (pp. 77-91). https://proceedings.mlr.press/v81/buolamwini18a.html (accessed March 29, 2025).

Cammozzo, A. (2011). Face recognition and privacy enhancing techniques. In Bissett, A., Bynum, T. W., Light, A., Lauener, A., & Rogerson, S. (Eds.), *The social impact of social computing* (pp. 101–109). Sheffield University.

Croft, W. L., Sack, J., & Shi, W. (2021). Obfuscation of images via differential privacy: From facial images to general images. *Peer-to-Peer Networking and Applications*, *14*(3), 1705–1733. DOI: 10.1007/s12083-021-01091-9

Dokmanović, M., & Cvetićanin, N. (2023). Regulation of the use of facial recognition technology –limitations and challenges from a human rights perspective. *Teorija in Praksa*, *60*(3), 548–564. DOI: 10.51936/tip.60.3.548

Du, L., Yi, M., Blasch, E., & Ling, H. (2014) GARP-face: Balancing privacy protection and utility preservation in face de-identification. *IEEE International Joint Conference on Biometrics*, pp. 1-8. DOI: 10.1109/BTAS.2014.6996249

Fontes, C., Hohma, E., Corrigan, C. C., & Lütge, C. (2022). AI-powered public surveillance systems: Why we (might) need them and how we want them. *Technology in Society*, *71*, 102137. DOI: 10.1016/j.techsoc.2022.102137

Fox, J. C. (2019). Brown University student mistakenly identified as Sri Lanka bombing suspect. The Boston Globe. https://www.bostonglobe.com/metro/2019/04/28/brown-student-mistaken-identified-sri-lanka-bombings-suspect/0hP2YwyYi4qrCEdxKZCpZM/story.html (accessed April 4, 2025).

Gururaj, H. L., Soundarya, B. C., Priya, S., Shreyas, J., & Flammini, F. (2024). A comprehensive review of face recognition techniques, trends and challenges. *IEEE Access : Practical Innovations, Open Solutions*, *12*, 107903–107926. DOI: 10.1109/ACCESS.2024.3424933

Hassija, V., Chamola, V., Mahapatra, A., Singal, A., Goel, D., Huang, K., Scardapane, S., Spinelli, I., Mahmud, M., & Hussain, A. (2024). Interpreting black-box models: A review on explainable artificial intelligence. *Cognitive Computation*, *16*(1), 45–74. DOI: 10.1007/s12559-023-10179-8

Hill, S., Zhimin, Z., Saul, L. K., & Shacham, H. (2016). On the (In)effectiveness of mosaicing and blurring as tools for document redaction. *Proceedings on Privacy Enhancing Technologies. Privacy Enhancing Technologies Symposium*, *2016*(4), 403–417. DOI: 10.1515/popets-2016-0047

Jain, A. (2020a). The centralised monitoring system. Internet Freedom Foundation. https://internetfreedom.in/watch-the-watchmen-series-part-2-the-centralised-monitoring-system/ (accessed March 29, 2025).

Jain, A. (2020b). The national intelligence grid. Internet Freedom Foundation. https://internetfreedom.in/watch-the-watchmen-part-1-the-national-intelligence-grid/ (accessed March 29, 2025).

Jain, A. (2020c). The national automated facial recognition system. Internet Freedom Foundation. https://internetfreedom.in/watch-the-watchmen-series-part-4-the-national-automated-facial-recognition-system/ (accessed March 29, 2025).

Khamis, M., Farzand, H., Mumm, M., & Marky, K. (2022). Deepfakes for privacy: Investigating the effectiveness of state-of-the-art privacy-enhancing face obfuscation methods. International Conference on Advanced Visual Interfaces. ACM New York. 21:1–5.

Kraus, R. (2019). Microsoft refused to sell facial recognition tech to law enforcement. Mashable Middle East. https://me.mashable.com/tech/4207/microsoft-refused-to-sell-facial-recognition-tech-to-law-enforcement (accessed April 2, 2025).

Krishnamurthy, R. 2021. Facial recognition technology in India. Project Statecraft. https://www.projectstatecraft.org/post/facial-recognition-technology-in-india (accessed April 2, 2025).

Kumar, R. C. (2005). Human rights implications of national security laws in India: Combating terrorism while preserving civil liberties. *Denver Journal of International Law and Policy*, *33*(195), 195–222.

Laishram, L., Shaheryar, M., Lee, J. T., & Jung, S. K. (2025). Toward a privacy-preserving face recognition system: A survey of leakages and solutions. *ACM Computing Surveys*, *57*(6), 1–38. DOI: 10.1145/3673224

Lee, N., & Chin, C. (2022). Police surveillance and facial recognition: Why data privacy is an imperative for communities of color. Brookings. https://www.brookings.edu/research/police-surveillance-and-facial-recognition-why-data-privacy-is-an-imperative-for-communities-of-color/ (accessed April 1, 2025).

Lei, C., Dang, K., Song, S., Wang, Z., Chew, S. P., Bian, R., Yang, X., Guan, Z., Lopes, C. I. M. D. A., Wang, M. H., Choy, R. W. C., Hu, X., Lai, K. K. H., Chong, K. K. L., Pang, C. P., Song, X., Su, J., Ding, X., & Zhou, H. (2025). AI-assisted facial analysis in healthcare: From disease detection to comprehensive management. *Patterns (New York, N.Y.)*, *6*(2), 101175. DOI: 10.1016/j.patter.2025.101175 PMID: 40041850

Li, S. Z., & Jain, A. K. (2011). *Handbook of Face Recognition* (2nd ed.). Springer. DOI: 10.1007/978-0-85729-932-1

Lynch, N. (2024). Facial Recognition Technology in Policing and Security—Case Studies in Regulation. *Laws*, *13*(3), 35. DOI: 10.3390/laws13030035

Ma, C., Shimada, A., Uchiyama, H., Nagahara, H., & Taniguchi, R. I. (2019). Fall detection using optical level anonymous image sensing system. *Optics & Laser Technology*, *110*, 44–61. DOI: 10.1016/j.optlastec.2018.07.013

Microsoft. (2018). Six principles for developing and deploying facial recognition technology. MS Blogs. https://msblogs.thesourcemediaassets.com/sites/5/2018/12/MSFT-Principles-on-Facial-Recognition.pdf (accessed April 1, 2025).

Narayan, S., & Chandrasekhar, R. (2022). Adopting the responsible AI principles: A use case approach on facial recognition technology. Discussion paper, Niti Aayog. https://ssrn.com/abstract=4476124 (accessed March 27, 2025).

Newton, E. M., Latanya, S., & Bradley, M. (2005). Preserving privacy by de-identifying facial images. *IEEE Transactions on Knowledge and Data Engineering*, *17*(2), 232–243. DOI: 10.1109/TKDE.2005.32

Nirkin, Y., Keller, Y., & Hassner, T. (2019). Subject agnostic face swapping and reenactment. CVPR. IEEE. 7184–7193. DOI: 10.1109/ICCV.2019.00728

Nosrati, L., Bidgoli, A. M., & Javadi, H. H. S. (2024). Identifying people's faces in smart banking systems using artificial neural networks. *Int. J. Comput. Intell. Syst*, *17*(9), 9. DOI: 10.1007/s44196-023-00383-7

Office of General Counsel. (2024). AI best practices guidelines. Canada: MacEwan University. https://www.macewan.ca/c/documents/ai-best-practices-guidelines.pdf (accessed March 20, 2025).

Parsheera, S. (2019). Adoption and Regulation of Facial Recognition Technologies in India: Why and Why Not?.

Pittaluga, F., Zivkovic, A., & Koppal, S. J. (2016). Sensor-level privacy for thermal cameras. Paper presented in International Conference on Computational Photography. IEEE. DOI: 10.1109/ICCPHOT.2016.7492877

Prasanna, L., Bhosale, S., D'Souza, A., Mamatha, H., Thomas, R., & Sachin, K. (2013). Facial indices of north and south Indian adults: Reliability in stature estimation and sexual dimorphism. *Journal of Clinical and Diagnostic Research : JCDR*, *7*(8). PMID: 24086833

Press Information Bureau. (2025). Crime and criminal tracking network and system. Ministry of Home Affairs, India. https://pib.gov.in/PressReleseDetailm.aspx?PRID=2117265&reg=3&lang=1 (accessed March 29, 2025).

Rubens, P. (2022). Database security: Best practices. eSecurity Planet. https://www.esecurityplanet.com/networks/database-security-best-practices/ (accessed April 10, 2025)

Russell, A. (2024). Emerging laws and norms for AI facial recognition technology. Æther: A Journal of Strategic Airpower & Spacepower 3(2): 25.

Satariano, A. (2023). E.U. agrees on landmark artificial intelligence rules. New York Times. https://www.nytimes.com/2023/12/08/technology/eu-ai-act-regulation/ (accessed April 10, 2025)

Senior, A. W., & Bolle, R. M. (2002). Face recognition and its application. In Zhang, D. (Ed.), *Biometric Solutions* (pp. 83–97). Springer. DOI: 10.1007/978-1-4615-1053-6_4

Vennam, P., Pramod, T. C., Thippeswamy, B. M., Kim, Y. G., & Pavan Kumar, B. N. (2021). Attacks and preventive measures on video surveillance systems: A review. *Applied Sciences (Basel, Switzerland)*, *11*(12), 5571. DOI: 10.3390/app11125571

Watch, A. (2019). Ai ethics guidelines global inventory. https://algorithmwatch.org/en/project/ai-ethics-guidelines-global-inventory/ (accessed April 4, 2025).

Zheng, W. (2025). China lays down the law in facial recognition first with focus on privacy, security. https://www.herbertsmithfreehills.com/notes/data/2025-posts/china-releases-laws-to-regulate-the-use-of-facial-recognition-technology (accessed April 10, 2025)

Zhou, S., & Xiao, S. (2018). 3D face recognition: A survey. *Human-centric Computing and Information Sciences*, *8*(1), 1–27. DOI: 10.1186/s13673-018-0157-2

Zulehner, B. (2024). EU artificial intelligence act: regulating the use of facial recognition technologies in publicly accessible spaces. Stanford-Vienna European Union Law Working Paper no. 91. http://ttlf.stanford.edu (accessed April 10, 2025)

Chapter 4
Connected for All:
Championing Inclusive Education in the Digital Era

Marubini Christinah Sadiki
https://orcid.org/0009-0001-3655-9610
University of South Africa, South Africa

ABSTRACT

This chapter explores the transformative potential of digital technologies in advancing inclusive education for all learners, particularly those from marginalized or underserved communities. In an increasingly digital world, integrating inclusive principles into educational technologies and pedagogical design is not only necessary but also urgent. Connected for All examines how digital tools can break down traditional barriers to learning, promote equitable access, and support diverse educational needs, including those of learners with disabilities, language differences, and socio-economic disadvantages. Through practical examples, case studies, and evidence-based strategies, this work demonstrates how educators, policymakers, and technology developers can collaborate to ensure that no learner is left behind. It also addresses the challenges, such as the digital divide, lack of accessibility standards, and educator readiness, that must be overcome to make digital inclusion a reality.

INTRODUCTION

The 21st century has ushered in unprecedented advancements in digital technology, reshaping the way we communicate, work, and learn (Rahimi, & Oh 2024; Kalyani,2024). While this digital transformation offers immense potential for educational innovation, it also raises urgent questions about equity, access, and inclusion (Matsieli, & Mutula, 2024). As classrooms increasingly adopt digital tools

DOI: 10.4018/979-8-3693-3920-6.ch004

and platforms, there is a critical need to ensure that these technologies serve all learners especially those who have historically been marginalized due to disability, poverty, language barriers, or other systemic disadvantages (Hankerson, & Brown 2020). Inclusive education, rooted in the principle that every learner has the right to quality education within a supportive and equitable environment, must now evolve alongside technological progress (Siddiqi, 2024; Yildirimer 2024). The digital era presents both opportunities and challenges it enables personalized learning, flexible content delivery, and greater connectivity, but it can also deepen existing inequalities if not implemented with intentional inclusivity (Whalley, et al. 2021; Memon, & Memon 2025).

This chapter, *Connected for All: Championing Inclusive Education in the Digital Era*, explores how inclusive education can be effectively supported through digital innovation. It examines the policies, pedagogies, and practices needed to design digital learning environments that are accessible, engaging, and responsive to diverse learning needs (Adeshina, 2024; Ajani, & Ajani, 2025). Drawing on global trends, case studies, and emerging research, the chapter calls on educators, technologists, and policymakers to actively champion inclusion as a core value in digital education (Rahimi, & Oh, 2024). In doing so, it challenges us to move beyond access alone and toward true participation where every learner, regardless of ability or background, is not only connected but fully empowered to thrive in a digital learning landscape. Digital innovation has the potential to profoundly enhance inclusive education by making learning more accessible, personalized, flexible, and engaging (Shireesha, & Jeevan 2024; Chopra, et al 2024). It empowers both learners and educators to overcome traditional barriers, fosters collaboration, and supports the development of skills necessary for the 21st century (Adeoye, et al 2024). To fully realize this potential, deliberate efforts are required to bridge the digital divide, embed accessibility in technology design, and provide educators with the resources and training they need (Riyat, et al 2025). When these conditions are met, digital innovation becomes a powerful enabler of inclusive education that truly leaves no learner behind (Ojetunde, 2024).

Technologists and educators are co-champions of inclusion in the digital education era (Rodrigues, et al 2024; Gilleland Marchak, et al 2021). Their collaboration is essential for creating learning environments where all students, regardless of ability or background, can access, participate, and thrive (Adera, 2025). Combining innovative technology design with responsive teaching strategies, they can break down barriers and unlock the full potential of inclusive education for future generations (Parashar, et al 2025; Monica, et al 2025). Inclusive education in the digital era requires policy coherence and investment (Peruzzo, & Allan 2024). Many education systems lack clear guidelines or funding structures to support the integration of inclusive technologies in schools (Navas-Bonilla, et al 2025). The digital innovation holds transformative potential for inclusive education, realizing this vision demands intentional, inclusive design, equity-focused policies, and capacity building among educators and institutions (Ngqunguza, Seleke, & Makhoba 2024). Without this, the promise of inclusive education in the digital age risks becoming another source of exclusion (Migliarini, & Elder, 2024). The integration of inclusive principles into educational technologies is not optional it is a moral, legal, and practical imperative (Siddiqi, 2024; Zhao, Zhao, & Shi, 2024). When educational tools are designed inclusively, they benefit everyone by creating more flexible, responsive, and effective learning environments (Sharma, 2024). True digital transformation in education must be inclusive at every stage from policy and design to implementation and evaluation (Ari, et al 2022; Joseph, Onwuzulike, & Shitu 2024).

THE SIGNIFICANCE OF CHAMPIONING INCLUSIVE EDUCATION IN THE DIGITAL ERA

The significance of championing inclusive education in the digital era lies in ensuring that the rapid advancement of technology leads to greater educational equity, rather than widening existing disparities (Ngongpah, & Yetunde Oni 2025). Here are the key reasons why this is critically important:

Ensuring Equal Access to Learning Opportunities

In the digital era, education increasingly depends on technology for content delivery, communication, and assessment (Abrahams, et al 2024; Xu, Khan, & Shahzad, 2024). Without intentional inclusive practices, students with disabilities, learners from rural or low-income communities, and those with language barriers may be left behind (Hinds, Newby, & Korman, 2022; Hayvon et al 2024). Championing inclusive education ensures that digital tools and platforms are accessible to all learners, supporting their right to quality education regardless of their background or abilities (Dubey, & Pandey, 2024; Wahengbam, T., & Wahengbam, 2024).

Promoting Equity Through Technological Design

When inclusive education principles guide digital innovation, technologies are designed with diverse needs in mind from the outset (Cesaroni, et al 2024; Rice, Cantergiani, & Macias 2025). This includes implementing features like screen readers, alternative input methods, multilingual content, and customizable interfaces (García Garcinuño, & Torres-del-Rey, 2024; Phutane, et al 2023). Such designs do not only benefit students with special needs but improve learning experiences for everyone. Championing inclusion leads to more equitable and user-friendly technologies for all learners.

Empowering Marginalized Learners

Inclusive education in the digital era empowers students who have traditionally faced exclusion by giving them access to tools that enhance their independence and confidence (Karagianni, & Drigas, 2023). Assistive technologies, adaptive learning platforms, and inclusive digital curricula help remove barriers and foster self-directed learning (Strielkowski, et al 2025). This empowerment supports lifelong learning and social inclusion beyond the classroom.

Upholding Human Rights and Social Justice

Inclusive education is a fundamental human right. In a time when technology increasingly defines access to knowledge, championing inclusion is a moral imperative (Mampane, & Mampane, 2024; Mphahlele, & Korkmaz, 2023). It ensures that digital progress does not become a new form of discrimination, but a vehicle for justice, participation, and equality. Upholding these values strengthens democratic societies and inclusive economies (Oyeyipo, et al 2024; Berch, et al 2024).

Building Resilient and Future-Ready Education Systems

Crises such as the COVID-19 pandemic revealed the fragility of education systems and the urgency of digital transformation (Nurhas, et al 2022; Barreto, et al 2023). However, resilience depends not just on technology, but on inclusivity (Mbangweta, 2023; Tarricone, Mestan, & Teo 2021). Systems that champion inclusive education are better equipped to adapt, respond to diverse needs, and ensure continuity of learning for all even in emergencies(Guglielmi, et al 2021; Cvetković, et al 2024).

WHAT IS DIGITAL ERA?

The Digital Era, also known as the Information Age or Digital Age, refers to the current period in human history characterized by the widespread use and rapid advancement of digital technology, particularly computers, the internet, mobile devices, artificial intelligence (AI), and other forms of information and communication technology (ICT) (Madhusudhan, & Manasa,2024).

WHAT IS INCLUSIVE EDUCATION?

Inclusive education is an education system that includes all students and welcomes and supports them to learn, whoever they are and whatever their abilities or requirements (Resier, 2012; UNESCO, 1994). This means making sure that teaching and the curriculum, school buildings, classrooms, play areas, transport, and toilets are appropriate for all children at all levels (Shuelka, 2016). Global Partnership for Education (2018) defines inclusive education as a transformational process of constant change and improvement within schools and the wider education ecosystem to make education welcoming and participatory achievement-oriented for all students. In this study, inclusive education in this context means welcoming students with and without disabilities with effective pedagogy and resources in mainstream classrooms. Inclusive education is an educational approach that ensures all learners regardless of their abilities, disabilities, backgrounds, or differences learn together in the same environment with equal access to high-quality education, resources, and opportunities (Halawa, & Salmi, 2024). It is based on the principle that every child has a right to learn and that diversity in the classroom is a strength, not a challenge.

WHY INCLUSIVE EDUCATION RIGHTS MUST SHAPE TECHNOLOGICAL ADVANCEMENTS?

Inclusive education is a fundamental human right recognized globally, emphasizing that every learner, regardless of their abilities, background, or circumstances, deserves equitable access to quality education (Qureshi, Malkani, & Rose 2020). As technology increasingly becomes central to education, it is imperative that inclusive education rights guide the development and implementation of technological advancements (Tiwari, & Fahrudin, 2024; Hassan, 2023). Ensuring that technology aligns with these rights is not only a matter of fairness but a necessity for creating learning environments where all students can thrive (Hassan, 2023). Firstly, technology has the power to either bridge or widen educational inequalities (Chari,2024). Without deliberate consideration of inclusive rights, digital tools risk excluding learners with disabilities, those from marginalized communities, or students lacking access to resources (Hankerson, & Brown 2020). For example, educational platforms lacking accessibility features like screen readers or captioning can prevent learners with visual or hearing impairments from fully participating (Farhan, & Razmak, 2022). Centering inclusive education rights, developers and policymakers are compelled to create technologies that accommodate diverse needs, ensuring no student is left behind (Memon, & Memon, 2025; Bruce, & Williams, 2025).

Moreover, integrating inclusive rights into technological innovation promotes equity and social justice (Olawale, 2024; Sargiotis, 2024). Education is a vehicle for empowerment, and technology should enhance this by providing personalized, flexible, and adaptable learning experiences (Rane, Choudhary, & Rane 2023). When rights to inclusion shape tech design, tools can address varied learning styles, languages, and abilities, fostering an environment where differences are respected and valued (Saborío-Taylor, & Rojas-Ramírez, 2024). This approach contributes to dismantling systemic barriers and promoting lifelong learning opportunities for all (Yadav, Sharma, & Nghiem, 2025). Inclusive education rights also have a crucial role in informing ethical standards and accountability in technology (Ossiannilsson, 2025; Naruka, & Sharma, 2024). With increasing reliance on artificial intelligence and data-driven tools in education, issues such as bias, privacy, and transparency come to the forefront (Ramnani, 2024). Embedding inclusive principles ensures that technological solutions are developed and deployed responsibly, protecting learners' dignity and rights (Ossiannilsson, 2025). When inclusive education rights shape technological advancements, they encourage collaboration among stakeholders including educators, learners, technologists, and policymakers (Ari, et al 2025) . This collaborative process ensures that innovations reflect real-world needs and experiences, resulting in more effective, relevant, and sustainable educational technologies (Blankesteijn, 2024; Bjelobaba, et al 2023). Embedding inclusive education rights in the heart of technological advancement is essential for building educational systems that are just, accessible, and empowering (Bruce, & Williams, 2025; Worsley, & Bar-El, 2022). It ensures that technology acts as a catalyst for inclusion, rather than a barrier, ultimately supporting the vision of education for all.

WHAT IS THE MEANING CHAMPIONING DIGITAL, INCLUSIVE EDUCATION?

Championing digital, inclusive education" means actively advocating for, promoting, and implementing the use of digital technologies to support inclusive education where all learners, regardless of their abilities, backgrounds, or needs, can access and benefit from high-quality learning experiences (Charles-Zalakoro, 2025). Championing digital, inclusive education refers to leading efforts to ensure that digital tools and technologies are designed, adapted, and used in ways that promote full access, participation, and success for all learners in educational environments Murphy, Bratković, & Vivoda, 2025). An educational approach that ensures all learners including those with disabilities, learning differences, or from marginalized communities are welcomed, supported, and included in mainstream education settings. Many digital tools are not inherently inclusive they must be designed or adapted with accessibility in mind (Worsley, & Bar-El, 2022). There's a risk of deepening the digital divide if inclusion is not prioritized (Djatmiko, Sinaga, & Pawirosumarto, 2025). Championing this cause ensures that no learner is left behind, especially in an increasingly tech-driven world (Kaletski-Maisel, & Jowallah, 2025).

DIGITAL ERA OPPORTUNITIES IN CHAMPIONING INCLUSIVE EDUCATION?

The Digital Era presents a powerful opportunity to reimagine and transform education systems to become more inclusive, accessible, and equitable for all learners (Seegobin, 2024). As technology reshapes how knowledge is delivered and accessed, it also opens new pathways to support diverse learning needs, particularly for students with disabilities, those in remote areas, and marginalized communities (Castaño-Muñoz, et al 2025). One of the most significant opportunities lies in the use of assistive technologies, such as screen readers, voice-to-text software, and customizable digital learning platforms (Ruhela, 2025). These tools can help overcome barriers that traditionally excluded learners with visual, hearing, physical, or cognitive disabilities (Kravchenko, et al 2022). For instance, learners who are blind can access digital textbooks in Braille or audio formats, while students with dyslexia can benefit from tools that support multi-sensory reading experiences (Jinghong, & Sanmugam 2025).

Online and blended learning environments also offer flexible and individualized approaches to education (Mulenga, & Shilongo, 2025). Through adaptive learning systems, educators can tailor instruction based on a learner's pace, interests, and abilities promoting equity within the classroom (Jose, et al 2024). Additionally, real-time feedback, virtual simulations, and interactive content foster deeper engagement and support different learning styles (Vaghela, & Parsana, 2024). The Digital Era further enables global connectivity, allowing educators, learners, and families to collaborate beyond traditional boundaries(Fischer, Lundin, & Lindberg, 2020). Platforms like MOOCs, open educational resources (OER), and virtual communities of practice provide access to knowledge and inclusive teaching strategies worldwide, empowering educators to continuously develop and share best practices (Cinganotto, & Cuccurullo, 2016).

Moreover, data analytics and AI can support early identification of learning needs and monitor progress more effectively, helping teachers to intervene early and personalize support (Wang, Zou, & Xie 2024) . This technology-driven insight helps close achievement gaps and ensures no learner is overlooked. The Digital Era offers a robust toolkit for championing inclusive education provided that intentional steps are taken to bridge the digital divide, ensure accessibility, and promote inclusive design (Murphy, Bratković, & Vivoda 2025). When used thoughtfully, digital innovation becomes a powerful enabler of education for all, fostering systems where every learner can thrive. Digital innovation becomes a powerful enabler of education for all, fostering systems where every learner can thrive (Allam, Gyamfi, & AlOmar 2025).

DIGITAL ERA CHALLENGES IN CHAMPIONING INCLUSIVE EDUCATION

The Digital Era offers significant opportunities to advance inclusive education, it also presents a number of challenges that must be addressed to ensure equitable access and participation for all learners (Pittman et al 2021). Without deliberate planning, the expansion of digital learning can exacerbate existing inequalities and create new barriers, particularly for learners with disabilities and those from disadvantaged backgrounds (Ersoy, 2023). A major challenge is the digital divide the gap between those who have access to technology and the internet and those who do not (Afzal, et al 2023). Many learners, especially in rural or low-income communities, still lack reliable internet connectivity, digital devices, or even electricity (Parks, Srinivasan, & Aragon 2022; Sucipto, Zaki, & Lima 2024). This results in exclusion from digital learning environments, leaving already marginalized students further behind.

Another issue is the lack of accessible digital content and platforms. Many online learning tools are not designed with inclusivity in mind, making them difficult or impossible to use for learners with visual, hearing, or mobility impairments (Worsley, & Bar-El, 2022; Lomellini, et al 2023). For instance, videos without captions or learning management systems that are not screen reader compatible effectively exclude certain students(Leporini, Buzzi, & Hersh, 2023). Educators themselves often face challenges, such as limited training in inclusive digital pedagogy (Samarakkody, et al 2022). Many teachers are not adequately equipped to adapt digital tools to support diverse learning needs or to identify appropriate assistive technologies (Alsolami, 2022). This skills gap reduces the effectiveness of even the most advanced digital resources (Saikkonen, & Kaarakainen, 2021). Language barriers and cultural biases embedded in digital content can also marginalize learners from non-dominant linguistic or cultural backgrounds (Brown, & Laihonen 2025; Cervantes-Soon, 2025). Additionally, data privacy concerns, especially for students with special needs, must be addressed to avoid misuse or discrimination based on sensitive personal information (Stahl, & Karger, 2016; Herath, et al 2024).

INTEGRATION OF INCLUSIVE PRINCIPLES INTO EDUCATIONAL TECHNOLOGIES

Integrating inclusive principles into educational technologies is essential for ensuring that all learners regardless of ability, background, or circumstance can access, participate in, and benefit from digital learning environments (Memon, & Memon, 2025). In the context of the Digital Era, where technology increasingly shapes how education is delivered, inclusion must move beyond physical presence to full engagement and equity in learning outcomes (Kulal, et al 2024). At its core, inclusive educational technology is about designing with diversity in mind (Kaczorowski, et al 2023). This includes applying Universal Design for Learning (UDL) principles, which emphasize flexibility in content presentation, learner engagement, and expression. UDL-informed digital tools provide multiple ways for students to interact with material such as audio, video, text, or tactile formats and) to different learning preferences and needs (Roman, Collins, & Son 2024). Accessibility is a foundational aspect of inclusion. Educational platforms and software must comply with international accessibility standards (like WCAG), ensuring compatibility with assistive devices such as screen readers, magnifiers, and voice recognition tools (Barrera-Cámara, et al 2025). Features like adjustable text size, closed captions, keyboard navigation, and simplified interfaces help to reduce barriers for students with disabilities (Ntoa,et al 2024).

Moreover, inclusive edtech goes beyond disability to address linguistic, cultural, and socio-economic diversity (Lynch, Singhal, & Francis 2021). Multilingual content, culturally relevant examples, and offline access options can help reach learners who may otherwise be excluded(Jiang, Li & Leung, 2024). Technologies should be adaptable to various contexts urban or rural, well-resourced or under-resourced to prevent widening the digital divide (Katunga, 2019). Equally important is educator training in using these technologies inclusively (Charles, & Alshamsi, 2025). Teachers must be equipped not only with technical skills but also with awareness of how to support diverse learners effectively through digital means (Falloon,2020). Inclusive technology should empower educators to personalize learning, track progress, and intervene where additional support is needed (Shireesha, & Jeevan, 2024; Sambyal, 2023).

CRITICAL ROLE OF INCLUSIVE EDUCATION RIGHTS IN GUIDING TECHNOLOGICAL INNOVATION

Inclusive education rights play a vital role in shaping technological innovation by ensuring that all learners, regardless of their abilities or backgrounds, are considered in the design and implementation of new technologies (Karagianni, & Drigas 2023; Debasu, & Yitayew, 2024). At its core, inclusive education advocates for the removal of barriers to learning and full participation, promoting equity and access for all (Sebti, & Elder, 2024) . This principle, when extended to the technological landscape, guides innovators to develop tools and systems that are universally accessible and responsive to diverse learning needs (Makda, 2025; Mena-Guacas, et al 2025).

One of the key contributions of inclusive education rights is the push for Universal Design for Learning (UDL), which encourages the development of flexible technologies that accommodate a wide range of learners (Bracken, et al 2025; Smith, 2025). Technologies influenced by UDL principles such as screen readers, speech-to-text software, captioning tools, and customizable user interfaces not only support students with disabilities but enhance learning for everyone (Zaugg, 2024; Kumar, & Shubhi, 2025). These innovations are driven by the understanding that accessibility benefits a broader audience, making technology more user-friendly and effective across contexts (Shah, Gupta, & Saini, 2024; Vetrivel, et al 2024)

Moreover, inclusive education rights serve as an ethical and legal framework that compels tech developers and educational institutions to consider marginalized voices in the innovation process (Bulathwela, et al 2024; Almufareh, et al 2024). This includes students with disabilities, linguistic minorities, and those from under-resourced communities. By foregrounding equity and participation, inclusive education ensures that technological advancements do not perpetuate existing disparities but instead become tools for empowerment and social justice(Thompson, Dombrowski, & Smith 2025;Mergen, Çetin-Kılıç, & Özbilgin 2025).

INCLUSIVE EDUCATION THROUGH RIGHTS-BASED TECHNOLOGICAL DEVELOPMENT

Inclusive education is rooted in the fundamental belief that every learner, regardless of ability, socio-economic status, gender, or background, has the right to quality education in an environment that embraces diversity and promotes equity (Alisultanova, & Qu, 2025; Nguéhan, Fangwi, & Mukama 2025). As technology becomes increasingly central to education systems across the globe, it presents both opportunities and challenges in fulfilling this vision. A rights-based approach to technological development in education ensures that innovation aligns with human rights principles particularly the rights to education, participation, and non-discrimination (Fobosi, & Mkuzo, 2024; Atabey, 2024). The technological development can advance inclusive education by ensuring accessibility, promoting equity, and transforming systems for the benefit of all learners (Almufareh, et al 2024; Kulal, et al 2024).

THE FOUNDATION OF RIGHTS-BASED TECHNOLOGICAL DEVELOPMENT

Rights-based development places human dignity, participation, and equality at the core of innovation (Tarshish, & Benish, 2025). In the context of education, this means designing and implementing technology that actively supports the rights of all learners to access, participate in, and benefit from education (Wong, 2024; Vettriselvan, 2025). The United Nations Convention on the Rights of Persons with Disabilities (CRPD) and the Sustainable Development Goals (especially SDG 4) emphasize inclusive, equitable, and quality education for all (Gomez, et al 2024; Nassar, Abbas, & Al-Sify 2024). These frameworks demand that education technologies be designed to remove barriers, accommodate diverse needs, and respect the agency of learners (Mrayhi, et al 2024; Rice, Cantergiani, & Macias 2025). In practice, this means involving marginalized groups including persons with disabilities, rural learners, and linguistic minorities in the design and feedback processes of technological tools(Navas-Bonilla, et al 2025). When technological development ignores these voices, it risks reinforcing systemic inequalities (Stephens, 2024; Calzada, 2024). Conversely, a rights-based approach ensures that technological solutions are contextually relevant and accessible to those most often excluded from traditional education systems (Fernandes, 2024; Holloway, et al 2023).

TECHNOLOGY AS AN ENABLER OF INCLUSIVE PEDAGOGIES

Inclusive education requires flexible pedagogies that accommodate diverse learning styles and needs (Kaur, & Bhatia, 2024; Akintayo, et al 2024). Rights-based technological development supports this by encouraging tools grounded in Universal Design for Learning (UDL) principles (Johnsson, 2025; Bennett, 2024). UDL promotes the creation of learning environments that provide multiple means of engagement, representation, and expression ensuring that learners can access content, demonstrate knowledge, and stay motivated in ways that suit them best (Sanguinetti, 2024; Bray, et al 2024).

Examples of such technologies include screen readers, text-to-speech and speech-to-text programs, adaptive learning platforms, captioned videos, and multilingual interfaces (Millett, 2021; Orynbay, et al 2024). These tools are not just assistive devices for students with disabilities they enhance learning for all by offering choice, flexibility, and personalization (Bugaj, 2023; Karagianni, & Drigas 2023). Moreover, data-driven insights from inclusive educational technologies can help educators identify and respond to learning gaps more effectively, thereby promoting equity and continuous improvement (Chigbu, & Makapela 2025; Ajiga, et al 2025). In low-resource settings, mobile technologies and offline learning applications have also proven crucial in reaching marginalized learners (Castillo, Adam, & Haßler, 2022; Selepe, Nhase, & Okeke, 2024). Rights-based innovation in these contexts involves designing low-bandwidth, multilingual, and culturally responsive tools that accommodate the realities of underserved communities (Maspul, et al 2025).

EMPOWERMENT, PARTICIPATION, AND SOCIAL JUSTICE

Inclusive education through rights-based technology is not only about accessibility it is also about agency and empowerment (Shabir, 2025). When learners have tools that respect their individual identities and abilities, they are more likely to participate meaningfully in educational processes (Engeness, 2021). Rights-based development prioritizes participation by actively involving learners in the development and evaluation of educational technologies (Shikako, et al 2024). Participation is a core right in inclusive education and must be reflected in both policy and practice (Mangiaracina, et al 2021; Vetoniemi, & Kärnä, 2021). Technological development guided by inclusive principles invites learners, especially those with disabilities or from disadvantaged backgrounds, to co-create and evaluate educational tools (Santamaría Graff, Price, & Coomer, 2023). Their involvement ensures that the technologies developed are not only technically effective but also socially relevant and ethically grounded (Powell, et al 2022). True participation moves beyond tokenism, fostering environments where diverse voices influence decision-making and design processes (Ahmad, & Islam, 2024).

SHAPING FUTURE TECHNOLOGIES WITH INCLUSIVE EDUCATION AT THE CORE

Technology continues to evolve and redefine how societies learn, work, and interact, it becomes increasingly vital to ensure that inclusive education is not an afterthought but a foundational principle in the design and implementation of emerging technologies (Charles, & Alshamsi, 2025; Amiri, Islam, & Akter, 2025). Inclusive education emphasizes equal access, participation, and opportunity for all learners, regardless of ability, background, or circumstance (Galkienė, & Monkevičienė, 2021; Graham, et al 2023). By placing these values at the core of technological development, we can build systems that are equitable, empowering, and responsive to the diverse needs of all users (Suklabaidya, 2024; Weber-Lewerenz, & Vasiliu-Feltes, 2022).

Designing technology through an inclusive lens begins with recognizing that exclusion often results from design choices choices that fail to account for the wide spectrum of human experiences (Patrick, & Hollenbeck 2021; Sin, et al 2021). Inclusive education demands that technologies be built with accessibility, usability, and adaptability in mind from the outset (Yenduri, et al 2023; Kaimara, Deliyannis, & Oikonomou, 2022). Tools like screen readers, captioned content, speech-to-text software, and culturally responsive digital platforms are just a few examples of how inclusive values translate into practical innovation (Jatto, & Aladesusi, 2025). Such tools not only support learners with disabilities but enhance learning for everyone by offering multiple pathways for engagement and expression.

Moreover, inclusive design requires collaboration with the very communities it seeks to serve. Co-creation with learners, educators, and marginalized groups ensures that technologies reflect lived realities and respect human rights (Ahrweiler, et al 2025). This participatory approach leads to solutions that are not only technically effective but also socially just (Wikberg Nilsson, 2024). It also challenges the digital divide by advocating for affordable, multilingual, and low-bandwidth solutions that extend educational access to underserved regions (Bhagat, Mishra, & Wang 2025). Shaping future technologies with inclusive education at the core, we are not only expanding access but reimagining the purpose of innovation itself (Kauffman, et al 2022; Facer, & Selwyn, 2021). The ultimate goal is not merely to create smarter tools, but to build a more equitable world one where every learner has the opportunity to thrive in a system that values their presence, potential, and participation (Ngubane, & Makua, 2021; Allal-Chérif, Aránega, & Sánchez, 2021).

CONCLUSION

Digital innovation has the potential to profoundly enhance inclusive education by making learning more accessible, personalized, flexible, and engaging. It empowers both learners and educators to overcome traditional barriers, fosters collaboration, and supports the development of skills necessary for the 21st century. To fully realize this potential, deliberate efforts are required to bridge the digital divide, embed accessibility in technology design, and provide educators with the resources and training they need. When these conditions are met, digital innovation becomes a powerful enabler of inclusive education that truly leaves no learner behind. Championing inclusive education in the digital era is not just about fairness it's about creating smarter, more compassionate, and more sustainable education systems. It ensures that no learner is left behind as we move into an increasingly digital future. Through embedding inclusivity at the heart of technological and educational innovation, we build a world where every learner has the opportunity to thrive.

REFERENCES

Abrahams, T. O., Farayola, O. A., Kaggwa, S., Uwaoma, P. U., Hassan, A. O., & Dawodu, S. O. (2024). Cybersecurity awareness and education programs: A review of employee engagement and accountability. *Computer Science & IT Research Journal, 5*(1), 100–119. DOI: 10.51594/csitrj.v5i1.708

Adeoye, M. A., Prastikawati, E. F., & Abimbowo, Y. O. (2024). Empowering learning: Pedagogical strategies for advancing 21st century skills and quality education. *Journal of Nonformal Education, 10*(1), 10–21. DOI: 10.15294/jone.v10i1.1451

Adera, N. (2025). Innovative learning spaces and blended learning: Quest for 21st century competency teaching and learning approaches. Creating Dynamic Space in Higher Education: Modern Shifts in Policy, Competencies, and Governance, 139-174.

Adeshina, A. E. (2024). The transformative role of digital resources in teaching and learning. Open Journal of Educational Development (ISSN: 2734-2050), 5(1), 1-9.

Afzal, A., Khan, S., Daud, S., Ahmad, Z., & Butt, A. (2023). Addressing the digital divide: Access and use of technology in education. *Journal of Social Sciences Review, 3*(2), 883–895. DOI: 10.54183/jssr.v3i2.326

Ahmad, I., & Islam, M. R. (2024). Empowerment and participation: Key strategies for inclusive development. In Building Strong Communities: Ethical Approaches to Inclusive Development (pp. 47-68). Emerald Publishing Limited.

Ahrweiler, P., Späth, E., Siqueiros García, J. M., Capellas, B. L., & Wurster, D. (2025). Inclusive technology co-design for participatory AI. Participatory Artificial Intelligence in Public Social Services: From Bias to Fairness in Assessing Beneficiaries, 35-62.

Ajani, B. O., & Ajani, O. A. (2025). Leveraging Technology for Inclusive Assessment: Enablers, Barriers, and Pedagogical Strategies in Diverse Learning Environments. In Improving Academic Performance and Achievement With Inclusive Learning Practices (pp. 109-136). IGI Global Scientific Publishing.

Ajiga, D. I., Hamza, O., Eweje, A., Kokogho, E., & Odio, P. E. (2025). (Forthcoming). Data-driven strategies for enhancing student success in underserved US communities. *Journal of Educational Analytics and Equity.*

Akintayo, O. T., Eden, C. A., Ayeni, O. O., & Onyebuchi, N. C.Olateju Temitope AkintayoChima Abimbola EdenOyebola Olusola AyeniNneamaka Chisom Onyebuchi. (2024). Inclusive curriculum design: Meeting the diverse needs of students for social improvement. *International Journal of Applied Research in Social Sciences*, *6*(5), 770–784. DOI: 10.51594/ijarss.v6i5.1100

Alisultanova, A., & Qu, X. (2025). Barriers and enablers—Early years educators' understanding of inclusive education for children with autism spectrum conditions in Baku, Azerbaijan. *International Journal of Qualitative Studies in Education : QSE*, *38*(9), 1–16. DOI: 10.1080/09518398.2025.2452634

Allal-Chérif, O., Aránega, A. Y., & Sánchez, R. C. (2021). Intelligent recruitment: How to identify, select, and retain talents from around the world using artificial intelligence. *Technological Forecasting and Social Change*, *169*, 120822. DOI: 10.1016/j.techfore.2021.120822

Allam, H. M., Gyamfi, B., & AlOmar, B. (2025). Sustainable Innovation: Harnessing AI and Living Intelligence to Transform Higher Education. *Education Sciences*, *15*(4), 398. DOI: 10.3390/educsci15040398

Almufareh, M. F., Kausar, S., Humayun, M., & Tehsin, S. (2024). A conceptual model for inclusive technology: Advancing disability inclusion through artificial intelligence. *Journal of Disability Research*, *3*(1), 20230060. DOI: 10.57197/JDR-2023-0060

Alsolami, A. S. (2022). Teachers of special education and assistive technology: Teachers' perceptions of knowledge, competencies and professional development. *SAGE Open*, *12*(1), 21582440221079900. DOI: 10.1177/21582440221079900

Amiri, S. M. H., Islam, M. M., & Akter, N. (2025). Rethinking Education Policy: Pathways to Equitable and Future-Ready Learning. Available at *SSRN* 5194153. DOI: 10.2139/ssrn.5194153

Ari, R., Altinay, Z., Altinay, F., Dagli, G., & Ari, E. (2022). Sustainable management and policies: The roles of stakeholders in the practice of inclusive education in digital transformation. *Electronics (Basel)*, *11*(4), 585. DOI: 10.3390/electronics11040585

Atabey, A. (2024). Response to the Call for Contributions: artificial intelligence in education and its human rights-based use at the service of the advancement of the right to education by the UN's Special Rapporteur on the right to education.

Barrera-Cámara, R. A., Fuentes-Penna, A., & Loranca, M. B. B. (2025). Inclusion and Accessibility in Smart Education. In Revolutionizing Pedagogy Through Smart Education (pp. 79-96). IGI Global Scientific Publishing. DOI: 10.4018/979-8-3693-7793-2.ch005

Barreto, I. B., Sánchez, R. M. S., Sanchez, W. S., Jordan, O. H., & Escalante, J. D. B. (2023). The process of digital transformation in education during the COVID-19 pandemic. International Journal of Professional Business Review: Int. *J. Prof. Bus. Rev.*, *8*(9), 22.

BENNETT, K. (2024). Centering Disability in Digital Classes by Applying Disability Justice to User-Experience and Universal Design Practices. Amplifying Voices in UX: Balancing Design and User Needs in Technical Communication.

Berch, V., Lankevych, A., Naturkach, R., Bysaha, Y., & Prodan, V. (2024). The role of digital technologies in building an inclusive and transparent society: An analysis of the legal mechanisms of democratic governance. *Amazonia Investiga*, *13*(79), 177–188. DOI: 10.34069/AI/2024.79.07.14

Bhagat, K. K., Mishra, S., & Wang, T. (2025). Blended learning in Commonwealth countries: A comparative analysis of implementation and impact. *Journal of Computers in Education*, •••, 1–31. DOI: 10.1007/s40692-025-00356-z

Bjelobaba, G., Savić, A., Tošić, T., Stefanović, I., & Kocić, B. (2023). Collaborative learning supported by Blockchain Technology as a model for improving the Educational process. *Sustainability (Basel)*, *15*(6), 4780. DOI: 10.3390/su15064780

Blankesteijn, M. L. M., Houtkamp, J. J., & Bossink, B. B. A. G. (2024). Towards transformative experiential learning in science-and technology-based entrepreneurship education for sustainable technological innovation. *Journal of Innovation & Knowledge*, *9*(3), 100544. DOI: 10.1016/j.jik.2024.100544

Bracken, S., Hopkins, A., Kennett, A., Lawrence, H., Richardson, E., Wedgbury, K., & Wilson, C. T. (2025). Empowering disabled learners' voices and agency through universal design for learning. In Learner Voices, Perspectives, and Positionings (pp. 130-144). Routledge.

Bray, A., Devitt, A., Banks, J., Sanchez Fuentes, S., Sandoval, M., Riviou, K., Byrne, D., Flood, M., Reale, J., & Terrenzio, S. (2024). What next for Universal Design for Learning? A systematic literature review of technology in UDL implementations at second level. *British Journal of Educational Technology*, *55*(1), 113–138. DOI: 10.1111/bjet.13328

Brown, K. D., & Laihonen, P. (2025). Marginalisation: Non-dominant language learning and teaching from a comparative perspective. *Compare: A Journal of Comparative Education*, *55*(2), 155–173. DOI: 10.1080/03057925.2023.2234281

Bruce, A., & Williams, L. A. (2025). Access and Citizenship for Those With Disabilities: Digitally Enabled Education and AI as a Bridge to Innovative Inclusion. In Digital Citizenship and the Future of AI Engagement, Ethics, and Privacy (pp. 31-78). IGI Global Scientific Publishing.

Bugaj, C. (2023). *The new assistive tech: Make learning awesome for all!* International Society for Technology in Education.

Bulathwela, S., Pérez-Ortiz, M., Holloway, C., Cukurova, M., & Shawe-Taylor, J. (2024). Artificial intelligence alone will not democratise education: On educational inequality, techno-solutionism and inclusive tools. *Sustainability (Basel)*, *16*(2), 781. DOI: 10.3390/su16020781

Calzada, I. (2024). Artificial intelligence for social innovation: Beyond the noise of algorithms and datafication. *Sustainability (Basel)*, *16*(19), 8638. DOI: 10.3390/su16198638

Castaño-Muñoz, J., Moreno-Morilla, C., Reina-Parrado, M., & Lopez-Cobo, I. (2025). Unheard voices: Identifying aspects for an inclusive digital education through the lens of low-income contexts schools. *Education and Information Technologies*, *30*(13), 1–22. DOI: 10.1007/s10639-025-13490-z

Castillo, N. M., Adam, T., & Haßler, B. (2022). *4. Improving the Impact of Educational Technologies on Learning Within Low*. Learning, Marginalization, and Improving the Quality of Education in Low-income Countries.

Cervantes-Soon, C. G. (2025). When Silence Speaks: Power, Marginalization, and Latinx Immigrant Students in Dual Language Classrooms. *Journal of Latinos and Education*, •••, 1–20.

Cesaroni, V., Galletti, M., Pasqua, E., & Nardi, D. (2024). Towards Trustworthy AI in Inclusive Education: A Co-Creation Approach Rooted in Ecological Frameworks. In Ital-IA 2024: 4th National Conference on Artificial Intelligence, organized by CINI

Chari, S. G. (2024). Bridging Gaps, Building Futures: Tackling Socio-Economic Disparities Through Education and Technology. *London Journal of Research In Humanities and Social Sciences*, *24*(16), 1–12.

Charles, T., & Alshamsi, A. (2025). Navigating Challenges in Technology Integration for Inclusive Classrooms: Insights for Pre-Service Teachers. In Empowering Pre-Service Teachers to Enhance Inclusive Education Through Technology (pp. 87-126). IGI Global Scientific Publishing.

Charles-Zalakoro, J. L. (2025). Inclusive Education and Digital Literacy: Developing Essential Skills in the Digital Age in Selected Public Secondary Schools in Bayelsa State. International Journal of Educational Management, Rivers State University., 1(2), 266-283.

Chigbu, B. I., & Makapela, S. L. (2025). Data-Driven Leadership in Higher Education: Advancing Sustainable Development Goals and Inclusive Transformation. *Sustainability (Basel)*, *17*(7), 3116. DOI: 10.3390/su17073116

Chopra, A., Patel, H., Rajput, D. S., & Bansal, N. (2024). Empowering Inclusive Education: Leveraging AI-ML and Innovative Tech Stacks to Support Students with Learning Disabilities in Higher Education. In *Applied Assistive Technologies and Informatics for Students with Disabilities* (pp. 255–275). Springer Nature Singapore. DOI: 10.1007/978-981-97-0914-4_15

Cinganotto, L., & Cuccurullo, D. (2016). Open Educational Resources, ICT and Virtual Communities for Content and Language Integrated Learning. *Teaching English with Technology*, *16*(4), 3–11.

Cvetković, V. M., Tanasić, J., Renner, R., Rokvić, V., & Beriša, H. (2024, October). Comprehensive Risk Analysis of Emergency Medical Response Systems in Serbian Healthcare: Assessing Systemic Vulnerabilities in Disaster Preparedness and Response. In Healthcare (Vol. 12, No. 19, p. 1962). MDPI.

Debasu, H., & Yitayew, A. (2024). Examining Elements of Designing and Managing of Creating Inclusive Learning Environment: Systematic Literature Review. *International Journal of Special Education*, *39*(1), 33–43. DOI: 10.52291/ijse.2024.39.4

Djatmiko, G. H., Sinaga, O., & Pawirosumarto, S. (2025). Digital transformation and social inclusion in public services: A qualitative analysis of e-government adoption for marginalized communities in sustainable governance. *Sustainability (Basel)*, *17*(7), 2908. DOI: 10.3390/su17072908

Dubey, P., & Pandey, R. K. (2024). Inclusive Education in India: Challenges, Progress, and Future Directions. Issue 1 Int'l JL Mgmt. &. *Human.*, *7*, 2343.

Engeness, I. (2021). Developing teachers' digital identity: Towards the pedagogic design principles of digital environments to enhance students' learning in the 21st century. *European Journal of Teacher Education, 44*(1), 96–114. DOI: 10.1080/02619768.2020.1849129

Ersoy, N. S. (2023). Empowering Inclusion: Addressing Barriers in Distance Learning for Disadvantaged Groups. *Turkish Online Journal of Educational Technology-TOJET, 22*(4), 52–60.

Facer, K., & Selwyn, N. (2021). *Digital technology and the futures of education: Towards 'Non-Stupid'optimism. Futures of Education initiative*. UNESCO.

Falloon, G. (2020). From digital literacy to digital competence: The teacher digital competency (TDC) framework. *Educational Technology Research and Development, 68*(5), 2449–2472. DOI: 10.1007/s11423-020-09767-4

Farhan, W., & Razmak, J. (2022). A comparative study of an assistive e-learning interface among students with and without visual and hearing impairments. *Disability and Rehabilitation. Assistive Technology, 17*(4), 431–441. DOI: 10.1080/17483107.2020.1786733 PMID: 32627612

Fernandes, E. R. (2024). Navigating the Digital Classroom: Analyzing risks to children's data protection in educational technology.

Fischer, G., Lundin, J., & Lindberg, J. O. (2020). Rethinking and reinventing learning, education and collaboration in the digital age—From creating technologies to transforming cultures. *The International Journal of Information and Learning Technology, 37*(5), 241–252. DOI: 10.1108/IJILT-04-2020-0051

Fobosi, S. C., & Mkuzo, Z. P. (2024, June). Social Justice and Human Rights: A Case of Blended Learning in Higher Education. In *University of Fort Hare Teaching and Learning Conference (UFHTL 2023)* (pp. 4-20). Atlantis Press. DOI: 10.2991/978-94-6463-439-6_2

Galkienė, A., & Monkevičienė, O. (2021). Preconditions of transforming the educational process by applying inclusive education strategies: Theoretical background. Improving inclusive education through universal design for learning, 1-21.

García Garcinuño, Á., & Torres-del-Rey, J. (2024). Multilingual accessibility in human-screen reader interaction with web content: an exploratory study. Tradumàtica, (22), 0426-449.

Gilleland Marchak, J., Halpin, S. N., Escoffery, C., Owolabi, S., Mertens, A. C., & Wasilewski-Masker, K. (2021). Using formative evaluation to plan for electronic psychosocial screening in pediatric oncology. *Psycho-Oncology*, *30*(2), 202–211. DOI: 10.1002/pon.5550 PMID: 32931620

Gomez, L. E., Moran, M. L., Navas, P., Verdugo, M. A., Schalock, R. L., Lombardi, M., Vicente, E., Guillén, V. M., Balboni, G., Swerts, C., Al-Halabí, S., Alcedo, M. Á., Monsalve, A., & Brown, I. (2024). Using the quality of life framework to operationalize and assess the CRPD articles and the Sustainable Development Goals. *Journal of Policy and Practice in Intellectual Disabilities*, *21*(1), e12470. DOI: 10.1111/jppi.12470

Graham, L. J., Medhurst, M., Tancredi, H., Spandagou, I., & Walton, E. (2023). Fundamental concepts of inclusive education. In *Inclusive Education for the 21st century* (pp. 60–80). Routledge. DOI: 10.4324/9781003350897-5

Guglielmi, S., Jones, N., Nicolai, S., Pereznieto, P., Plank, G., Vu, N., & Mackintosh, A. (2021). *Reimagining Girls' Education: Solutions to Keep Girls Learning in Emergencies*. UNICEF.

Halawa, Y., & Salmi, H. (2024). Inclusive education strategies in improving access and quality of learning for students with special needs. Jurnal Ilmu Pendidikan dan Kearifan Lokal, 4(3), 174-189.

Hankerson, D. L., & Brown, L. X. (2020). Technology as a civil right and a move toward disability justice: Ensuring digital access for disabled students in the pandemic. *Drexel L. Rev.*, *13*, 869.

Hassan, G. (2023). Technology and the transformation of educational practices: A future perspective. International Journal of Economic, Business, Accounting [IJEBAS]. *Agriculture Management and Sharia Administration*, *3*(1), 1596–1603.

Hayvon, J. C., Cordeiro, V. J., Dunhamn, J., Strömberg Jämsvi, S., Stainbrook, J., & Singhal, N. (2024). Equality in higher education opportunities: Practitioners' perspectives from global, rural, post-colonial disability. *Journal of Praxis in Higher Education*, *6*(4), 30–47. DOI: 10.47989/kpdc518

Herath, H. M. S. S., Herath, H. M. K. K. M. B., Madhusanka, B. G. D. A., & Guruge, L. G. P. K. (2024). Data protection challenges in the processing of sensitive data. In *Data Protection: The Wake of AI and Machine Learning* (pp. 155–179). Springer Nature Switzerland. DOI: 10.1007/978-3-031-76473-8_8

Hinds, H., Newby, L. D., & Korman, H. T. (2022). *Ignored, Punished, and Underserved: Understanding and Addressing Disparities in Education Experiences and Outcomes for Black Children with Disabilities*. Bellwether.

Holloway, C., Barbareschi, G., Codina, O. V., Colton, N., Eide, A. H., Morgado-Ramirez, Z. D., & Austin, V. (2023). A human rights-based approach to assistive technology provision in global policy. In *Research Handbook on Disability Policy* (pp. 807–822). Edward Elgar Publishing. DOI: 10.4337/9781800373655.00079

Jatto, E. O., & Aladesusi, G. A. (2025). Empowering Pre-Service Teachers for Inclusive Education Through Technology: Strategies, Tools, and Innovations. In Empowering Pre-Service Teachers to Enhance Inclusive Education Through Technology (pp. 301-336). IGI Global Scientific Publishing.

Jiang, L., Li, Z., & Leung, J. S. (2024). Digital multimodal composing as translanguaging assessment in CLIL classrooms. *Learning and Instruction*, *92*, 101900. DOI: 10.1016/j.learninstruc.2024.101900

Jinghong, Z., & Sanmugam, M. (2025). Strategies for Bridging the Digital Divide in Inclusive Education Through Multisensory Learning and Emerging Technologies. Fostering Inclusive Education With AI and Emerging Technologies, 207-232.

Johnsson, C. (2025). Inclusive Human Rights Education. In *Discourses of Human Rights Education* (pp. 15–35). Springer. DOI: 10.1007/978-3-031-88615-7_2

Jose, B. C., Kumar, M., Udayabanu, T., & Nagalakshmi, M. (2024). Assessing the effectiveness of adaptive learning systems in K-12 education. [IJAITRD]. *International Journal of Advanced IT Research and Development*, *1*(1).

Joseph, O., Onwuzulike, O., & Shitu, K. (2024). Digital transformation in education: Strategies for effective implementation. *World Journal of Advanced Research and Reviews.*, *2*. Advance online publication. DOI: 10.30574/wjarr

Kaczorowski, T., McMahon, D., Gardiner-Walsh, S., & Hollingshead, A. (2023). Designing an inclusive future: Including diversity and equity with innovations in special education technology. *Teaching Exceptional Children*, *55*(5), 376–383. DOI: 10.1177/00400599221090506

Kaimara, P., Deliyannis, I., & Oikonomou, A. (2022). Content design for inclusive educational environments. In *Inclusive digital education* (pp. 97–121). Springer International Publishing. DOI: 10.1007/978-3-031-14775-3_6

Kaletski-Maisel, G., & Jowallah, R. (2025). Empowering Citizens: Preparing for the Future of Digital Literacy and AI in Education. In Digital Citizenship and the Future of AI Engagement, Ethics, and Privacy (pp. 133-150). IGI Global Scientific Publishing.

Kalyani, L. K. (2024). The role of technology in education: Enhancing learning outcomes and 21st century skills. International journal of scientific research in modern science and technology, 3(4), 05-10.

Karagianni, E., & Drigas, A. (2023). New Technologies for Inclusive Learning for Students with Special Educational Needs. *International Journal of Online & Biomedical Engineering*, *19*(5), 4–21. DOI: 10.3991/ijoe.v19i05.36417

Katunga, N. (2019). Communicating for development using social media: a case study of e-inclusion intermediaries in under-resourced communities.

Kauffman, J. M., Anastasiou, D., Hornby, G., Lopes, J., Burke, M. D., Felder, M., Ahrbeck, B., & Wiley, A. (2022). Imagining and reimagining the future of special and inclusive education. *Education Sciences*, *12*(12), 903. DOI: 10.3390/educsci12120903

Kaur, J., & Bhatia, R. (2024). Pedagogical Practices: A Promising Approach to Empower Diverse Learners in Inclusive Setup. *Shanlax International Journal of Education*, *12*(S1-June), 96–103. DOI: 10.34293/education.v12iS1-June.7222

Kravchenko, O., Koliada, N., Berezivska, L., Dikhtyarenko, S., Baida, S., & Danylevych, L. (2022). Digital barrier-free and psychosocial support for students with disabilities in distance learning environments. *International Journal of Computer Science & Network Security*, *22*(8), 15–24.

Kulal, A., Dinesh, S., Abhishek, N., & Anchan, A. (2024). Digital access and learning outcomes: A study of equity and inclusivity in distance education. *International Journal of Educational Management*, *38*(5), 1391–1423. DOI: 10.1108/IJEM-03-2024-0166

Kumar, M. V., & Shubhi, M. (2025). Remote Learning for Children with Disabilities. This work would not have been possible without the unwavering support of many individuals and institutions. We express our deepest gratitude to the contributing authors, whose expertise and dedication have shaped this volume., 43.

Leporini, B., Buzzi, M., & Hersh, M. (2023). Video conferencing tools: Comparative study of the experiences of screen reader users and the development of more inclusive design guidelines. *ACM Transactions on Accessible Computing*, *16*(1), 1–36. DOI: 10.1145/3573012

Lomellini, A., Lowenthal, P. R., Snelson, C., & Trespalacios, J. H. (2023). Higher education leaders' perspectives of accessible and inclusive online learning. In *Inclusive Online and Distance Education for Learners with Dis/abilities* (pp. 92–113). Routledge. DOI: 10.4324/9781003412076-7

Lynch, P., Singhal, N., & Francis, G. A. (2021). EdTech for learners with disabilities in primary school settings in LMICs: A systematic literature review.

Madhusudhan, H., & Manasa, C. (2024). Computing through the ages: from early devices to modern AI. Digital Evolution: Advances in Computer Science and Information Technology, 9.

Makda, F. (2025). Digital education: Mapping the landscape of virtual teaching in higher education–a bibliometric review. *Education and Information Technologies*, *30*(2), 2547–2575. DOI: 10.1007/s10639-024-12899-2

Mampane, M. R., & Mampane, N. S. (2024). Inclusive Education: Human Rights, Ethical Concerns, Challenges, and Solutions. In Handbook of Research on Inclusive and Accessible Education (pp. 104-126). IGI Global Scientific Publishing.

Mangiaracina, A., Kefallinou, A., Kyriazopoulou, M., & Watkins, A. (2021). Learners' voices in inclusive education policy debates. *Education Sciences*, *11*(10), 599. DOI: 10.3390/educsci11100599

Maspul, K., Melinda, Y., Wisudayanti, K., & Rochmah, D. F. (2025). How Can ChatGPT Empower Indonesian Classrooms? *Frontiers in Research Journal*, *1*(3), 26–26. DOI: 10.47134/frontiers.v1i3.423

Matsieli, M., & Mutula, S. (2024). COVID-19 and digital transformation in higher Education Institutions: Towards inclusive and equitable access to quality education. *Education Sciences*, *14*(8), 819. DOI: 10.3390/educsci14080819

Mbangweta, P. L. (2023). inclusive resilience: Empowering people living with disabilities in the fight against Covid-19. *Journal of Preventive and Rehabilitative Medicine*, *5*(2), 31–36.

Memon, F. N., & Memon, S. N. (2025). Digital Divide and Equity in Education: Bridging Gaps to Ensure Inclusive Learning. In Impact of Digitalization on Education and Social Sustainability (pp. 107-130). IGI Global.

Mena-Guacas, A. F., López-Catalán, L., Bernal-Bravo, C., & Ballesteros-Regaña, C. (2025). Educational transformation through emerging technologies: Critical review of scientific impact on learning. *Education Sciences*, *15*(3), 368. DOI: 10.3390/educsci15030368

Mergen, A., Çetin-Kılıç, N., & Özbilgin, M. F. (2025). Artificial Intelligence and Bias Towards Marginalised Groups: Theoretical Roots and Challenges. In AI and Diversity in a Datafied World of Work: Will the Future of Work be Inclusive? (Vol. 12, pp. 17-38). Emerald Publishing Limited.

Migliarini, V., & Elder, B. C. (2024). The future of inclusive education. In *The future of inclusive education: Intersectional perspectives* (pp. 1–21). Springer Nature Switzerland.

Millett, P. (2021). Accuracy of Speech-to-Text Captioning for Students Who are Deaf or Hard of Hearing. Journal of Educational, Pediatric & (Re) Habilitative Audiology, 25.

Monica, J. A., Malar, J. H., Arun, C., Sharmila, L., & Arif, M. (2025). Leveraging technology and universal design for inclusive and engaging learning in Indian higher education. In *Educational Philosophy and Sociological Foundation of Education* (pp. 177–212). IGI Global.

Mphahlele, R. S., & Korkmaz, Ö. (2023). Inclusive education embracing virtual reality through technology integration as part of a human rights agenda. In Shaping the Future of Online Learning: Education in the Metaverse (pp. 112-133). IGI Global. DOI: 10.4018/978-1-6684-6513-4.ch007

Mrayhi, S., Khribi, M. K., Belhadj, H., & Jemni, M. (2024). Designing future education for all: principles and frameworks. In *Envisioning the future of education through design* (pp. 147–177). Springer Nature Singapore. DOI: 10.1007/978-981-97-0076-9_7

Mulenga, R., & Shilongo, H. (2025). Hybrid and blended learning models: Innovations, challenges, and future directions in education. *Acta Pedagogia Asiana*, *4*(1), 1–13. DOI: 10.53623/apga.v4i1.495

Murphy, E., Bratković, D., & Vivoda, A. (2025). The inclusive design of a digital education programme–contribution and experiences of people with accessibility needs. In *Championing Co-production in the Design of Inclusive Practices* (pp. 101–114). Routledge. DOI: 10.4324/9781003459651-12

Naruka, V. S., & Sharma, C. (2024). Ethical Challenges and Dilemmas in Teaching Students with Special Needs in Inclusive Classrooms. Ethical Frameworks in Special Education: A Guide for Researchers, 120.

Nassar, F. S., Abbas, A. O., & Al-Sify, H. (2024). Enhancing Quality of Learning Experiences for Students with Disabilities in Higher Education Institutions in Alignment with Sustainable Development Goals. *Journal of Ecohumanism*, *3*(7), 4911–4922. DOI: 10.62754/joe.v3i7.4601

Navas-Bonilla, C. D. R., Guerra-Arango, J. A., Oviedo-Guado, D. A., & Murillo-Noriega, D. E. (2025, February). Inclusive education through technology: A systematic review of types, tools and characteristics. [). Frontiers Media SA.]. *Frontiers in Education*, *10*, 1527851. DOI: 10.3389/feduc.2025.1527851

Ngongpah, G., & Yetunde Oni, O. (2025). Exploring the Impact of Digital Technologies in Education: A Comprehensive review. Exploring the Impact of Digital Technologies in Education: A Comprehensive Review.

Ngqunguza, A., Seleke, Z., & Makhoba, T. I. (2024). Digital Transformation in Higher Education: Leadership Strategies for Ensuring Equity and Inclusion in Digital Learning Environments. [JPADA]. *Journal of Public Administration and Development Alternatives*, *9*(2), 101–114. DOI: 10.55190/JPADA.2024.329

Ngubane, N. I., & Makua, M. (2021). Intersection of Ubuntu pedagogy and social justice: Transforming South African higher education. *Transformation in Higher Education*, *6*, 113. DOI: 10.4102/the.v6i0.113

Nguéhan, S. B., Fangwi, M. L., & Mukama, E. (2025). Tracing Inclusive Education in Cameroon: A Genealogical Analysis of Policies and Practices. In Improving Academic Performance and Achievement With Inclusive Learning Practices (pp. 415-462). IGI Global Scientific Publishing. DOI: 10.4018/979-8-3373-4501-7.ch017

Ntoa, S., Margetis, G., Adami, I., Balafa, K., Antona, M., & Stephanidis, C. (2024). Digital accessibility for users with disabilities. In *Designing for usability, inclusion and sustainability in human-computer interaction* (pp. 406–460). CRC Press.

Nurhas, I., Aditya, B. R., Jacob, D. W., & Pawlowski, J. M. (2022). Understanding the challenges of rapid digital transformation: The case of COVID-19 pandemic in higher education. *Behaviour & Information Technology*, *41*(13), 2924–2940. DOI: 10.1080/0144929X.2021.1962977

Ojetunde, S. M. (2024). Left-behind learners: Exclusion-inclusion paradox of 4IR/5IR education technology. *E-Learning and Digital Media*, •••, 20427530241239407. DOI: 10.1177/20427530241239407

Olawale, B. E. (2024). Inclusive Innovations: Promoting Digital Equity and Inclusion through Technological Solutions.

Orynbay, L., Razakhova, B., Peer, P., Meden, B., & Emeršič, Ž. (2024). Recent advances in synthesis and interaction of speech, text, and vision. *Electronics (Basel), 13*(9), 1726. DOI: 10.3390/electronics13091726

Ossiannilsson, E. (2025). *The Role of Ethical Leadership in Improving Education Through Open Education, Digital Inclusion and Seamless Learning*. AI for Seamless Education.

Oyeyipo, E. J., Oyekola, I. A., Salako, O. P., & Babatunde, O. S. (2024). Understanding the Importance of Inclusive Techniques in Promoting Peace and Equal Justice. In Sustainable Development Goals (pp. 291-301). CRC Press. DOI: 10.1201/9781003468257-16

Parashar, A. K., Mannepalli, S., Manimegalai, V., Priyadharishini, B., & Muruganandham, S. (2025). Integrating Universal Design in Education Policy Through Technological Solutions: Breaking Barriers. In Global Practices in Inclusive Education Curriculum and Policy (pp. 231-260). IGI Global.

Parks, L., Srinivasan, R., & Aragon, D. C. (2022). Digital empowerment for whom? An analysis of 'Network sovereignty' in low-income, rural communities in Mexico and Tanzania. *Information Communication and Society, 25*(14), 2140–2161. DOI: 10.1080/1369118X.2021.1928264

Patrick, V. M., & Hollenbeck, C. R. (2021). Designing for all: Consumer response to inclusive design. *Journal of Consumer Psychology, 31*(2), 360–381. DOI: 10.1002/jcpy.1225

Peruzzo, F., & Allan, J. (2024). Rethinking inclusive (digital) education: Lessons from the pandemic to reconceptualise inclusion through convivial technologies. *Learning, Media and Technology, 49*(2), 244–258. DOI: 10.1080/17439884.2022.2131817

Phutane, M., Jung, C., Chen, N., & Azenkot, S. (2023, October). Speaking with My Screen Reader: Using Audio Fictions to Explore Conversational Access to Interfaces. In *Proceedings of the 25th International ACM SIGACCESS Conference on Computers and Accessibility* (pp. 1-18). DOI: 10.1145/3597638.3608404

Pittman, J., Severino, L., DeCarlo-Tecce, M. J., & Kiosoglous, C. (2021). An action research case study: Digital equity and educational inclusion during an emergent COVID-19 divide. *Journal for Multicultural Education, 15*(1), 68–84. DOI: 10.1108/JME-09-2020-0099

Powell, A. B., Ustek-Spilda, F., Lehuedé, S., & Shklovski, I. (2022). Addressing ethical gaps in 'Technology for Good': Foregrounding care and capabilities. *Big Data & Society, 9*(2), 20539517221113774. DOI: 10.1177/20539517221113774

Qureshi, S., Malkani, R., & Rose, R. (2020). Achieving inclusive and equitable quality education for all. Handbook on promoting social justice in education, 3-32.

Rahimi, R. A., & Oh, G. S. (2024). Rethinking the role of educators in the 21st century: Navigating globalization, technology, and pandemics. *Journal of Marketing Analytics*, *12*(2), 182–197. DOI: 10.1057/s41270-024-00303-4

Ramnani, S. (2024). Exploring Ethical Considerations of Artificial Intelligence in Educational Settings: An Examination of Bias, Privacy, and Accountability. [IJNRD]. *International Journal of Novel Research and Development*, *9*(2), 2456–4184.

Rane, N., Choudhary, S., & Rane, J. (2023). Education 4.0 and 5.0: Integrating artificial intelligence (AI) for personalized and adaptive learning.

Rice, M. F., Cantergiani, K., & Macias, D. (2025). A research-based conceptual framework for inclusive K-12 online, distance, and digital education. *Journal of Research on Technology in Education*, *57*(2), 482–498. DOI: 10.1080/15391523.2023.2264982

Riyat, M. K., Kakkar, A., Rana, A., & Mathur, D. (2025). Bridging the Digital Divide: Challenges and Opportunities for Sustainable EdTech in Emerging Markets. Digital Transformation for Business Sustainability and Growth in Emerging Markets, 23-51.

Rodrigues, I. B., Ioannidis, G., Kane, L. L., Hillier, L. M., Adachi, J., Heckman, G., Hirdes, J., Holroyd-Leduc, J., Jaglal, S., Kaasalainen, S., Marr, S., McArthur, C., Straus, S., Tarride, J.-E., Abbas, M., Costa, A. P., Lau, A. N., Thabane, L., & Papaioannou, A. (2024). Assessing the feasibility of an i ntegrated c ollection of education modules for fa ll and fr acture pr e vention (iCARE) for healthcare providers in long term care: A longitudinal study. *PLOS Global Public Health*, *4*(11), e0003096. DOI: 10.1371/journal.pgph.0003096 PMID: 39585819

Roman, T. A., Collins, E. E., & Son, H. (2024). Supporting Music Literacy for Students with Special Needs in the Elementary General Music Classroom: A Design Case of a Digital Tool. *TechTrends*, *68*(5), 962–972. DOI: 10.1007/s11528-024-00984-9

Ruhela, V. S. (2025). Technology-Enhanced inclusive education: Tools and Resources. Global Perspectives on Inclusive Education: Future Directions, 193.Seegobin, T. (2024). Transforming Education through the implementation of ICT pedagogical integration: A case of ICT and Non-ICT schools in South Africa (Doctoral dissertation, University of the Witwatersrand, Johannesburg).

Saborío-Taylor, S., & Rojas-Ramírez, F. (2024). Universal Design for Learning and artificial intelligence in the digital era: Fostering inclusion and autonomous learning. International Journal of Professional Development, Learners and Learning, 6(2).

Saikkonen, L., & Kaarakainen, M. T. (2021). Multivariate analysis of teachers' digital information skills-The importance of available resources. *Computers & Education*, *168*, 104206. DOI: 10.1016/j.compedu.2021.104206

Samarakkody, A., Malalgoda, C., Amaratunga, D., & Haigh, R. (2022). Barriers That Hinder Inclusive Online Education and the Good Practices in Digital Pedagogy. In *EDULEARN22 Proceedings* (pp. 8884-8891). IATED. DOI: 10.21125/edulearn.2022.2132

Sambyal, S. (2023). Technological interventions for learning enrichment/enhancement in student with diverse needs. *World Journal of Advanced Research and Reviews*, *20*(1), 946–954. DOI: 10.30574/wjarr.2023.20.1.2089

Sanguinetti, H. (2024). Exploring the Implications: The Impact of Universal Design for Learning on Student Engagement and Motivation in Diverse Classroom Environments.

Santamaría Graff, C., Price, J. F., & Coomer, M. N. (2023). Technology as a bridge to co-create inclusive and equitable learning environments for students with intersectional identities.

Sargiotis, D. (2024). Building a Cohesive, Prosperous, and Inclusive Europe: A Strategic Framework for Policy Innovation and Sustainable Development. Prosperous, and Inclusive Europe: A Strategic Framework for Policy Innovation and Sustainable Development (November 18, 2024).

Sebti, L., & Elder, B. C. (2024). "Inclusion is definitely a possibility for all": Promoting inclusive education through a critical professional development schools model. *School-University Partnerships*, *17*(3), 285–302. DOI: 10.1108/SUP-06-2023-0021

Selepe, M. A., Nhase, Z., & Okeke, C. I. (2024). How Mobile ECCE Practitioners Leverage a Variety of Learning Materials in Resource-Scarce Communities. International Journal of Learning. *Teaching and Educational Research*, *23*(9), 161–178.

Shabir, I., Parveen, A., Jabeen, S., & Jan, U. (2025). Empowerment of Students With Disabilities in Education. In Enablers, Barriers, and Challenges for Inclusive Curriculum (pp. 45-76). IGI Global Scientific Publishing. DOI: 10.4018/979-8-3373-1000-8.ch003

Shah, D., Gupta, D., & Saini, S. (2024, March). Evolving Perspectives: Exploring Accessibility and Inclusivity in Spatial UI/UX. In 2024 11th International Conference on Reliability, Infocom Technologies and Optimization (Trends and Future Directions)(ICRITO) (pp. 1-6). IEEE.

Sharma, S. (2024). Enhancing Inclusive Learning Environments: Strategies for Curriculum Adaptation and Modification. Future of Special Education in India, 109.

Shikako, K., Lai, J., Yoo, P. Y., Teachman, G., & Majnemer, A. (2024). Evidence-informed stakeholder consultations to promote rights-based approaches for children with disabilities. *Frontiers in Rehabilitation Sciences*, *5*, 1322191. DOI: 10.3389/fresc.2024.1322191 PMID: 38742042

Shireesha, M., & Jeevan, J. (2024). The Role of Artificial Intelligence in Personalized Learning: A Pathway to Inclusive Education. Library of Progress-Library Science, Information Technology & Computer, 44(3).

Siddiqi, M. M. (2024). Future of digital education: Inclusive, immersive, equitable. MediaSpace. *DME Media Journal of Communication*, *5*(01), 8–24. DOI: 10.53361/dmejc.v5i01.02

Sin, J., & Franz, L., R., Munteanu, C., & Barbosa Neves, B. (2021, May). Digital design marginalization: New perspectives on designing inclusive interfaces. In Proceedings of the 2021 CHI Conference on Human Factors in Computing Systems (pp. 1-11). DOI: 10.1145/3411764.3445180

Smith, E. (2025). An Examination of Universal Design for Learning and its Impact Potential on Support Staff Practices within. *Higher Education*.

Stahl, W. M., & Karger, J. (2016). Student Data Privacy, Digital Learning, and Special Education: Challenges at the Intersection of Policy and Practice. *Journal of Special Education Leadership*, *29*(2), 79–88.

Stephens, J. C. (2024). The dangers of masculine technological optimism: Why feminist, antiracist values are essential for social justice, economic justice, and climate justice. *Environmental Values*, *33*(1), 58–70. DOI: 10.1177/09632719231208752

Strielkowski, W., Grebennikova, V., Lisovskiy, A., Rakhimova, G., & Vasileva, T. (2025). AI-driven adaptive learning for sustainable educational transformation. *Sustainable Development (Bradford)*, *33*(2), 1921–1947. DOI: 10.1002/sd.3221

Sucipto, P. A., Zaki, A., & Lima, L. (2024). Challenges in Implementing ICT Solutions in Low-Income Schools. Al-Hijr: JIIET. *Journal International Inspire Education Technology*, *3*(3).

Suklabaidya, S. (2024). Towards inclusive societies: Leveraging IoT for community development and education.

Tarricone, P., Mestan, K., & Teo, I. (2021). Building resilient education systems: A rapid review of the education in emergencies literature.

Tarshish, N., & Benish, A. (2025). The Three Spheres of Rights-Based Practice in Social Work: Respecting, Claiming, and Changing. *Clinical Social Work Journal*, •••, 1–9. DOI: 10.1007/s10615-025-00998-7

Thompson, G., Dombrowski, L., & Smith, A. D. (2025, April). Embracing Social Justice within a Computing Curriculum to Foster Social Change. In *Proceedings of the 2025 CHI Conference on Human Factors in Computing Systems* (pp. 1-17). DOI: 10.1145/3706598.3713125

Tiwari, S. P., & Fahrudin, A. (2024). Evolving School Dynamics and Emerging Technologies in Education: Critical Success Factors.

Vaghela, V. S., & Parsana, D. F. (2024). *Teaching and Learning: Fostering Student Engagement*. Critical Thinking, and Lifelong Learning Skills.

Vetoniemi, J., & Kärnä, E. (2021). Being included experiences of social participation of pupils with special education needs in mainstream schools. *International Journal of Inclusive Education, 25*(10), 1190–1204. DOI: 10.1080/13603116.2019.1603329

Vetrivel, S. C., Sowmiya, K. C., Sabareeshwari, V., & Arun, V. P. (2024). Navigating the Digital Economy: The Crucial Role of Human-Computer Interaction. In Social Reflections of Human-Computer Interaction in Education, Management, and Economics (pp. 184-216). IGI Global.

Vettriselvan, R. (2025). Empowering Digital Education: The Future of Value-Based Learning in the Digital Era. In Empowering Value Co-Creation in the Digital Era (pp. 199-228). IGI Global Scientific Publishing.

Wahengbam, T., & Wahengbam, C. (2024). Inclusive education and integration into national education policy 2020: A comprehensive analysis.

Wang, C., Zou, J., & Xie, Z. (2024, August). AI-Powered Educational Data Analysis for Early Identification of Learning Difficulties. In The 31st International scientific and practical conference "Methodological aspects of education: achievements and prospects"(August 06–09, 2024) Rotterdam, Netherlands. International Science Group. 2024. 252 p. (p. 223).

Weber-Lewerenz, B., & Vasiliu-Feltes, I. (2022). Empowering digital innovation by diverse leadership in ICT–A roadmap to a better value system in computer algorithms. *Humanistic Management Journal, 7*(1), 117–134. DOI: 10.1007/s41463-022-00123-7

Whalley, B., France, D., Park, J., Mauchline, A., & Welsh, K. (2021). Towards flexible personalized learning and the future educational system in the fourth industrial revolution in the wake of Covid-19. *Higher Education Pedagogies, 6*(1), 79–99. DOI: 10.1080/23752696.2021.1883458

Wikberg Nilsson, Å. (2024). Young 2.0: Advancing an inclusive framework for co-creating futures with youth. *CoDesign*, *20*(2), 313–331. DOI: 10.1080/15710882.2024.2358967

Wong, J. M. S. (2024). Student experiences of agile-blended learning in emergency online education: Insights from a participatory case study. *Asian Association of Open Universities Journal*, *19*(2), 202–216. DOI: 10.1108/AAOUJ-02-2024-0017

Worsley, M., & Bar-El, D. (2022). Inclusive Making: Designing tools and experiences to promote accessibility and redefine making. *Computer Science Education*, *32*(2), 155–187. DOI: 10.1080/08993408.2020.1863705

Worsley, M., & Bar-El, D. (2022). Inclusive Making: designing tools and experiences to promote accessibility and redefine making. Computer Science Education, 32(2), 155-187. D. (2022). Inclusive Making: designing tools and experiences to promote accessibility and redefine making. *Computer Science Education*, *32*(2), 155–187. DOI: 10.1080/08993408.2020.1863705

Xu, S., Khan, K. I., & Shahzad, M. F. (2024). Examining the influence of technological self-efficacy, perceived trust, security, and electronic word of mouth on ICT usage in the education sector. *Scientific Reports*, *14*(1), 16196. DOI: 10.1038/s41598-024-66689-4 PMID: 39003300

Yadav, M., Sharma, P., & Nghiem, X. H. (2025). Impact of inclusive education and lifelong learning in higher education. In *Academic Support Services and Strategies in Higher Education* (pp. 221–250). IGI Global Scientific Publishing. DOI: 10.4018/979-8-3693-4175-9.ch009

Yenduri, G., Kaluri, R., Rajput, D. S., Lakshmanna, K., Gadekallu, T. R., Mahmud, M., & Brown, D. J. (2023). From assistive technologies to metaverse—Technologies in inclusive higher education for students with specific learning difficulties: A review. *IEEE Access : Practical Innovations, Open Solutions*, *11*, 64907–64927. DOI: 10.1109/ACCESS.2023.3289496

Yildirimer, K. S. (2024). Roadmap for Equality in Education: Problems, Solutions and Implementation Strategies. *Dinamika Ilmu*, *24*(1), 11–28. DOI: 10.21093/di.v24i1.7515

Zaugg, T. (2024). Future innovations for assistive technology and universal design for learning. Assistive technology and universal design for learning: Toolkits for inclusive instruction, 275-318.

Zhao, Y., Zhao, M., & Shi, F. (2024). Integrating moral education and educational information technology: A strategic approach to enhance rural teacher training in universities. *Journal of the Knowledge Economy*, *15*(3), 15053–15093. DOI: 10.1007/s13132-023-01693-z

Chapter 5
Digital Activism and Social Movements:
Exploring the Role of Digital Platforms in Mobilizing and Empowering Civil Rights Movements

Satyam Verma
https://orcid.org/0009-0002-0194-1198
Banaras Hindu University, India

Alok Gardia
https://orcid.org/0009-0005-6982-7203
Banaras Hindu University, India

Bipasha Das
https://orcid.org/0009-0009-9152-6756
Banaras Hindu University, India

ABSTRACT

In recent years, social and civil rights movements have undergone significant changes in their principles, organization, and support systems. Digital platforms have empowered marginalized groups by amplifying their voices, transforming how activism is organized and experienced. This chapter examines the shift from traditional collective action to connective action, emphasizing more flexible and personalized ways of engagement. It discusses how digital platforms enable individuals to express dissent, build solidarity, and advocate for their rights. It also addresses the risks and contradictions associated with online activism. The chapter

DOI: 10.4018/979-8-3693-3920-6.ch005

concludes by presenting a framework that highlights key areas, including global visibility, marginalized voices, and independent spaces, where digital civil rights movements are making a meaningful impact. Ultimately, digital platforms serve as powerful spaces for negotiating and advancing civil rights in the digital age.

INTRODUCTION

The 21st century has experienced a substantial transformation in the principles, structure, and support of social and civil rights movements. This change is primarily driven by the rapid development of digital technologies, particularly the widespread adoption of the internet and social media platforms. These virtual spaces have matured into powerful instruments for activism, enabling individuals and communities to coordinate extensively, transcend geographical boundaries, and challenge dominant narratives instantly (Earl & Kimport, 2011; Tufekci, 2017; Castells, 2015). Scholars and practitioners frequently refer to this phenomenon as digital activism, cyberactivism, or networked activism (Joyce, 2010; Bennett & Segerberg, 2012; Gerbaudo, 2012). Contrary to traditional activism, which primarily relied on in-person organization, physical venues, formal organizations, and print or broadcast media, digital activism is characterized by decentralized, real-time, user-driven participation (Tufekci, 2017; Gerbaudo, 2012; Joyce, 2010). The proliferation of platforms such as Facebook, Instagram, X (formerly Twitter), TikTok, YouTube, along with encrypted messaging applications like WhatsApp and Telegram, has fundamentally transformed the way protests are organized and publicly exhibited (Milan, 2015; Kavada, 2015; Bruns & Burgess, 2015). These platforms provide critical functionalities including immediacy, amplification, and scalability, which aid in the dissemination of protest messages, the coordination of on-the-ground activities, and the development of alternative narratives (van Dijck et al, 2018; Freelon et al., 2016a; Papacharissi, 2015).

This transformation is evident in the significant global movements that have been fostered, supported, or intensified via digital tools. Examples encompass the Arab Spring (2010–2012), #BlackLivesMatter (2013–present), #MeToo (2017–present), and the Hong Kong Protests (2019–2020). These instances demonstrate how activists utilize social media to increase awareness, coordinate demonstrations, and contest authority (Howard & Hussain, 2013; Wolfsfeld et al., 2013; Jackson et al., 2020; Gill & Orgad, 2018; Lee et al., 2021). In each case, hashtags, viral images, livestreams, and citizen journalism have played key roles in shaping public debate and gaining international support (Tufekci, 2017; Gerbaudo, 2012). This phenomenon is aptly depicted by Bennett and Segerberg's (2012) Connective Action Theory, which redefines traditional collective action (Olson, 1965) in the context of digitally interconnected public spheres. In contrast to classical collective action, which depends substantially on formal organizations and consolidated group identities, connective action highlights individualized content dissemination, peer-to-peer interaction, and dynamic, decentralized engagement. (Bennett & Segerberg, 2012). This shift has fostered robust new forms of solidarity, profound emotional connections, and lively global engagement (Yang, 2016; Fisher & Nasrin, 2021).

Digital activism has primarily empowered marginalized communities, such as Dalits, LGBTQ+ individuals, Black populations, and indigenous peoples, to circumvent traditional media channels, reclaim their narratives, and establish digital counterpublics (Joyce, 2010; Fraser, 1990; Jackson & Welles, 2015). In India, Dalit activists utilize platforms like Twitter and YouTube to reveal caste-based discrimination, oppose Brahminical dominance, and mobilize anti-caste resistance through hashtags such as #DalitLivesMatter (Paik, 2021; Soundararajan, 2019). Nonetheless, digital activism encounters challenges including authoritarian regimes implementing internet shutdowns, monitoring social media activity, and employing cyber harassment, bots, and trolls to quash dissent (Deibert, 2015; Tufekci, 2017; United Nations, n.d.). Activists face significant risks, including doxxing, algorithmic silencing, and the dissemination of misinformation, all of which threaten their safety and advocacy efforts (Roberts, 2019; Gillespie, 2018; Noble, 2018; Morozov, 2011). This chapter seeks to examine these issues by focusing on both user empowerment and potential risks. It provides a comprehensive review of the current landscape and critically examines which areas would benefit from digital activism. This chapter also highlights how digital platforms enable marginalized groups to find a voice through individual channels. Furthermore, it discusses the possible dangers associated with these platforms, helping readers grasp the current state and consequences of digital activism.

HISTORICAL TRAJECTORIES OF CIVIL RIGHTS MOVEMENTS AND DIGITAL MEDIA

The development of civil rights movements has been closely linked to advances in media technology, shaping how resistance is expressed, coordinated, and documented. Although their core goals, such as equality, justice, and systemic change, have stayed consistent, the strategies have changed significantly, shifting from traditional print media to modern digital platforms Today's digital activism marks the latest stage in a long history of mediated resistance, demonstrating how ongoing technological progress constantly transforms the methods and scope of civil rights efforts (USA History Timeline, n.d.; Goodwin, 2019; Kashak, 2024).

The roots of modern civil rights movements can be traced back to the early and mid-20th century, when marginalized groups worldwide used emerging media to challenge oppressive systems. In the anti-colonial struggles in India and the African American civil rights movement in the United States, print media such as pamphlets, underground newspapers, and flyers played a vital role in spreading counter-narratives beyond state-controlled presses (Singh et al., 2025; Goodwin, 2019). By the 1950s and 1960s, mainstream media, including radio and television, became central to activism. Leaders like Martin Luther King Jr. and organizations such as the NAACP strategically utilized televised images of brutality, as seen during the Montgomery Bus Boycott (1955) and the Selma marches (1965), to evoke public sympathy and push for policy changes, including the Civil Rights Act of 1964. Globally, televised violence against peaceful protesters played a key role in rallying international support and legislative reform (Goodwin, 2019; Kashak, 2024; Library of Congress, n.d.; USA History Timeline, n.d.). However, reliance on mainstream media placed control in the hands of editors who often resisted challenging dominant hierarchies, prompting activists to develop alternative communication networks, underground presses, community radio, and grassroots publications that laid the groundwork for participatory and decentralized media strategies. (Tufekci, 2017; Pickard, 2006).

The trajectory advanced even further with the advent of the digital revolution. The 1991 camcorder recording of Rodney King's beating marked a key turning point, sparking what scholars call "citizen documentary practice," where everyday devices became tools for recording injustice—precursors to today's mobile-driven activism (Martin, 2005). The 1990s saw the rise of the internet, transforming activism by enabling decentralized and transnational networks. A pivotal moment was the 1994 Zapatista uprising in Chiapas, Mexico, where Subcomandante Marcos and the EZLN (Zapatista Army of National Liberation) used online messages to bypass government-controlled media and foster global solidarity (Cleaver, 1998; Russell, 2001). This uprising is widely recognized as one of the first examples of "netwar," where digital communication tools were strategically employed to rally transnational support and reshape public discourse (Ronfeldt et al., 1998). At the same time, early digital activism emerged through platforms like listservs, Bulletin Board System (BBS) systems, and PeaceNet, introducing the concept of "electronic civil disobedience", a form of digital protest in which activists utilized online tools to challenge traditional power structures. These early technologies enabled transnational coordination among activists well before the rise of social media (Critical Art Ensemble, 1996; Wray, 1999). A notable example was the 1999 Seattle WTO protests, where Indymedia—autonomous, open-publishing platforms—allowed participants to share real-time, unfiltered multimedia reports, bypassing traditional gatekeepers (Pickard, 2006). This strategic use of the internet marked a shift toward what Castells (2015) described as "networks of outrage and hope," empowering grassroots groups to challenge dominant narratives and build international alliances without relying on traditional media.

With the rise of Web 2.0 and social media in the early 2000s, digital activism entered a new phase defined by interactivity, virality, and user-generated content. Platforms like Facebook, Twitter, and YouTube enabled real-time communication, decentralized coordination, and global visibility, transforming how social movements organized and mobilized (Milan, 2015; Kavada, 2015). A defining example was the Arab Spring (2010–2012), during which activists across Tunisia, Egypt, and Libya utilized social media to coordinate protests, disseminate live updates, and garner international attention. While the precise causal role of social media in regime change remains debated, scholars agree that these platforms significantly amplified activist voices and expanded civic participation (Howard & Hussain, 2013; Tufekci, 2017).

Similarly, the Spanish indignados (15-M) movement and Occupy Wall Street in the United States further illustrated the influence of digital networks in organizing mass protests. (Theocharis et al., 2014). Researchers documented how protest messages spread through scale-free Twitter networks, linking broadcasters and influential users, and revealed new patterns of public mobilization (Gerbaudo, 2012; Tufekci, 2017; Theocharis et al., 2014). After 2010, hashtag activism shifted from simple coordination to building collective identity and applying societal pressure. Movements like #BlackLivesMatter, #MeToo, #FridaysForFuture, and #DalitLivesMatter demonstrate how personal stories can coalesce into powerful, decentralized civic action, phenomena known as "connective action" (Bennett & Segerberg, 2012).

In summary, the history of civil rights movements reveals a dynamic interplay between media technologies and activism. From print pamphlets to viral Twitter threads, media have consistently shaped how civil rights movements craft narratives, gather support, and challenge authority. Although digital platforms have decentralized communication and mobilized audiences, structural power still exists, shifting from editors to algorithms. Examining digital activism through a historical lens reveals both continuity and change: activists have long utilized media to advocate for justice, and today's tools build upon that tradition. Understanding this development enables us to critically assess platform dynamics and envision more inclusive civic futures in the digital era.

THEORETICAL FRAMEWORK: FROM COLLECTIVE TO CONNECTIVE ACTION

The evolution of civil rights activism in the digital age has introduced new theoretical models that challenge traditional views of political mobilization. Previously, activism depended on collective action principles that emphasized formal organizations, hierarchical leadership, and shared identity to organize and motivate participants (Olson, 1965; Tilly & Wood, 2013; McCarthy & Zald, 1977). Movements like the U.S. Civil Rights Movement or India's anti-colonial campaigns relied on identifiable leaders and centralized messaging, often disseminated through mainstream media or institutions (Morris, 1984; Tilly & Wood, 2013). These efforts focused on structured coordination, resource sharing, and cultivating collective identities (Snow et al., 1986; Melucci, 1989). With the rise of digital platforms for organizing and amplifying protests, scholars presently suggest a shift toward what Bennett and Segerberg (2012) refer to as the 'logic of connective action,' a form of participation driven by personalized content, online networks, and decentralized coordination.

Connective action is enabled by the architecture of digital platforms, which facilitate the rapid, peer-to-peer dissemination of information and emotions across global networks. Unlike collective action, which depends on central planning and resource mobilization, connective action thrives on immediacy, emotional resonance, and algorithmic amplification (Papacharissi, 2015; Freelon et al., 2016a). While this model decentralizes control, it also reflects a broader cultural shift toward *networked individualism*, wherein individuals operate as autonomous agents connected through overlapping, fluid networks rather than as members of tightly bound, hierarchical groups (Wellman et al., 2003; Rainie & Wellman, 2012). Within this context, digital activism enables the inclusion of diverse voices and perspectives, accommodating a range of motivations while sustaining collective momentum (Mercea, 2016; Bennett & Segerberg, 2012). Participants can personalize their engagement based on individual experiences, emotional resonance, and perceived relevance of issues, often resulting in passionate and viral protest narratives (Papacharissi, 2015). This dynamic also fosters the emergence of *affective public,* emotionally charged communities formed around shared feelings such as outrage, empathy, or solidarity. Far from being merely reactive, these publics are politically generative, shaping discourse, amplifying marginalized perspectives, and spotlighting issues often neglected by mainstream media (Papacharissi, 2015).

The viral circulation of videos such as George Floyd's killing, or testimonies of survivors in #MeToo, highlights how affect plays a central role in connecting individuals and mobilizing action globally (Anderson et al., 2020; Johnson & Renderos, 2020). Furthermore, digital platforms serve as infrastructures for this new mode of activism, providing affordances such as hashtags, livestreaming, and content sharing that enable personalized messages to aggregate into powerful public discourses (Kavada, 2015; Tufekci, 2017; Joyce, 2010). While connective action may lack long-term strategic cohesion, numerous contemporary movements employ hybrid models that utilize connective action to enhance visibility and generate initial momentum, alongside collective structures to ensure sustained advocacy and engagement with institutions (Gerbaudo, 2012). This hybrid approach was exemplified by movements such as Black Lives Matter, where decentralized digital mobilization coexisted with on-the-ground organization and policy advocacy.

Figure 1. From collective action to connective action (Bennett & Segerberg, 2012)

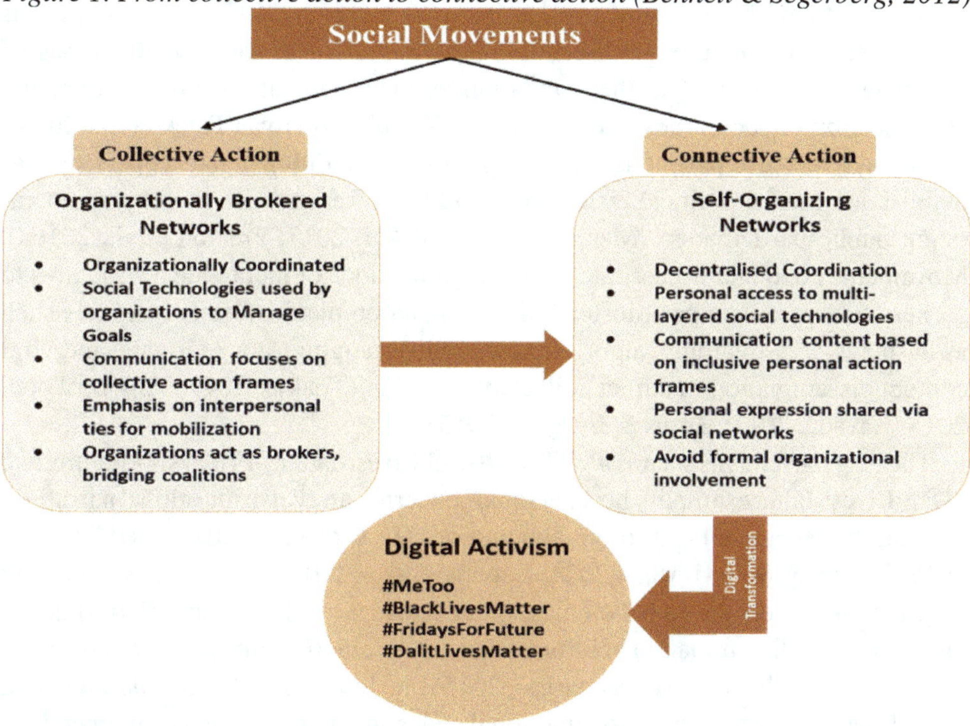

As shown in Figure 1, the shift from collective to connective action indicates a broader change in how civil rights movement is understood and practiced (Bennett & Segerberg, 2012; Papacharissi, 2015). This change does not mean traditional activism is disappearing, but instead broadens its forms (Gerbaudo, 2012; Tufekci, 2017). Understanding connective action is therefore essential for analyzing modern civil rights movements, especially those led by youth, diasporic communities, and digitally native populations Bennett & Segerberg, 2012; Freelon et al., 2016a). It challenges conventional metrics of activism, such as participation in protests or organizational affiliation, and instead emphasizes a politics rooted in presence, emotion, and interconnected visibility (Mercea, 2016; Papacharissi, 2015; Kavada, 2015). As digital platforms advance, the methods of resistance and solidarity they facilitate will likewise develop (Mendes et al., 2018; Jackson et al., 2020).

SOCIAL MEDIA AS SPACE FOR CIVIL RIGHTS ACTIVISM

In the digital age, social media platforms such as X (formerly Twitter), Facebook, Instagram, YouTube, TikTok, and WhatsApp have evolved from basic communication tools into complex socio-technical systems that support modern civil rights activism (Milan, 2015; Kavada, 2015; Bruns & Burgess, 2015). These platforms provide essential features and technological tools that enable specific types of user interactions, serving as the foundation for the mobilization, coordination, and amplification of social movements (Tilly & Wood, 2013; van Dijck et al., 2018). Digital systems also permit activists to circumvent traditional gatekeepers such as mainstream media, political institutions, and legal frameworks, thereby democratizing public participation (Mercea, 2016; Tufekci, 2017; Freelon et al., 2016a). Movements no longer necessitate formal organizations or hierarchical structures to garner widespread support; instead, they depend on platform functionalities such as hashtags, livestreaming, algorithmic visibility, tagging, story formats, and viral content dissemination to attract collective attention (Thakur, 2019; Tilly & Wood, 2013; Kavada, 2015; Bruns & Burgess, 2015).

Hashtag movements such as #MeToo, #BlackLivesMatter, #FridaysForFuture, and #DalitLivesMatter exemplify how personal concerns can evolve into global narratives that transcend regional and cultural boundaries (Jackson et al., 2020; Mendes et al., 2018; Terren & Soler-i-Martí 2021; Soundararajan, 2019). These movements are amplified not solely through their messages but also via technological platforms that facilitate rapid dissemination of information, evoke emotional responses, and enable content creation by users (Papacharissi, 2015; Freelon et al., 2016a). Consequently, digital spaces become centers of emotional engagement, fostering the emergence of affective public groups united by shared sentiments such as anger, hope, grief, and solidarity (Papacharissi, 2015). Furthermore, these platforms function as archives of resistance, preserving tweets, videos, and livestreams documenting issues including police brutality, governmental violence, systemic discrimination, and protests. These digital records may later serve as evidence in legal proceedings, inform policy debates, or function as educational and activist tools (Aouragh & Alexander, 2011; Bonilla & Rosa, 2015). In regions where traditional media are subject to censorship or control, these platforms offer alternative venues for counterpublics to form and contest mainstream narratives (Fraser, 1990; Jackson & Welles, 2015).

FROM HASHTAGS TO IMPACT: CASE ANALYSIS IN NETWORKED RESISTANCE

The emergence of networked resistance signifies a paradigm shift in the methodologies by which social movements mobilize, engage, and influence, with hashtags functioning as both discursive tools and infrastructures for mobilization (Yang, 2016; Freelon et al., 2016a). Social media platforms like X (formerly Twitter), Facebook, and Instagram enable activists to bypass traditional gatekeepers, promote transnational solidarity, and drive political and social change (Tufekci, 2017; Gerbaudo, 2012; Earl & Kimport, 2011). Analyzing a series of hashtag-based movements reveals the interactions among personal stories, emotional publics, and connective action in digital civil rights activism (Bennett & Segerberg, 2012; Papacharissi, 2015).

Case 1: Arab Spring

The Arab Spring (2010–2012) marked a significant milestone in digital-era activism, with platforms like Facebook, Twitter, and YouTube enabling youth and civil society groups to bypass government-controlled media, share footage of repression, and organize flash protests in cities (Howard & Hussain, 2013; Lotan et al., 2011; Wolfsfeld et al., 2013). Starting with Mohamed Bouazizi's self-immolation in Tunisia on December 17, 2010, and sparking uprisings across Egypt, Libya, Syria, and beyond, digital platforms became essential for turning personal grievances into mass mobilizations (Howard & Hussain, 2013; Wolfsfeld et al., 2013; Brownlee et al., 2015). In Egypt, the hashtag #Jan25 signaled the call for mass protests in Tahrir Square, while #SidiBouzid in Tunisia memorialized the town where Bouazizi's protest began. These hashtags did not just label events, but they acted as mobilizing frames (Snow et al., 1986; Melucci, 1989), emotional triggers, and dynamic records of resistance stories (Aouragh & Alexander, 2011; Lotan et al., 2011).

Various empirical studies support the strategic importance of social media. For instance, Howard and Hussain (2013), analyzing data from over 2.5 million tweets, found that social media use spiked during key protest moments, helping to spread information across borders and foster connections among Arabic-speaking communities. Similarly, Lotan et al. (2011) demonstrated that global Twitter users served as both amplifiers and interpreters, facilitating local protests to gain international attention and framing the movement around universal themes of democracy and justice. However, digital infrastructure was not the only driver of revolution. Gerbaudo (2012) argues that "emotional choreography," the affective coordination of outrage, hope, and solidarity, was just as crucial. Hashtags served as emotional rallying points, creating shared spaces that encouraged physical gatherings. Likewise, Castells (2015) describes these digital movements as "networks of outrage and hope," where networked individualism builds into collective momentum (Wellman et al., 2003; Rainie & Wellman, 2012).

Although the outcomes of the Arab Spring were mixed, Tunisia advanced toward democratic governance while Egypt experienced a military rollback following the 2013 coup (Stepan, 2012; Brownlee et al., 2015). The case illustrates how a hybrid media system enabled social media to collaborate with traditional media and grassroots activism, thereby sparking rapid political mobilization. It was not solely technology but the integration of digital and emotional infrastructure, which Gerbaudo (2012) terms the "choreography of assembly," that facilitated a wave of political transformation.

Case 2: #BlackLivesMatter

Black Lives Matter (BLM) is a powerful social movement that started in the United States in 2013, focusing on fighting systemic racism, racial violence, and anti-Black police brutality (Lebron, 2017; Freelon et al., 2016b; Morris, 1984). It was co-founded by three Black organizers, Alicia Garza, Patrisse Khan-Cullors, and Opal Tometi, as an online campaign using the hashtag #BlackLivesMatter. This campaign was launched after George Zimmerman was acquitted for the killing of Trayvon Martin, an unarmed Black teenager in Sanford, Florida, in 2012 (Lebron, 2017). What started as a simple digital hashtag quickly evolved into a decentralized yet unified global movement, transforming grief into action and identity into activism. BLM offered a digital platform for coordinated protests, connecting individual experiences of injustice with broader systemic critiques (Bonilla & Rosa, 2015; Jackson & Welles, 2015; Taylor, 2016).

The killing of George Floyd by Minneapolis police in May 2020 marked a major turning point. According to Pew Research Center, #BlackLivesMatter was mentioned roughly 47.8 million times on Twitter from May 26 to June 7, 2020 (Anderson et al., 2020), sparking protests in over 2,000 U.S. cities and more than 60 countries, making it one of the largest social movements in U.S. history (Burch et al., 2020). This shows how hashtag activism functions as digital infrastructure that supports collective action (Gerbaudo, 2012; Tufekci, 2017).

BLM's structure aligns with a connective action logic of mobilization, fueled by personalized, digitally mediated engagement rather than centralized organization (Bennett & Segerberg, 2012). It also functions as a networked counterpublic, a communicative space where Black voices challenge dominant narratives and reframe state violence as systemic oppression (Jackson & Welles, 2015). BLM not only affected media framing and public opinion but also led to tangible outcomes in policy and institutional responses, ranging from police reform proposals to corporate diversity initiatives (Freelon et al., 2016b; Bonilla & Rosa, 2015). The movement is rooted in intersectional justice, addressing gender, class, and sexuality alongside race (Crenshaw, 1991; Taylor, 2016).

Case 3 #MeToo

The #MeToo movement, although widely recognized worldwide in 2017, was originally started in 2006 by African-American activist Tarana Burke as a grassroots effort to support survivors of sexual violence, especially young women of color in underserved communities (Burke, n.d.; Burke, 2017; Gill & Orgad, 2018; Crenshaw, 1991). It gained viral attention after actress Alyssa Milano encouraged survivors to tweet "#MeToo" in response to allegations against Hollywood producer Harvey Weinstein, sparking a digital wave of disclosures and solidarity (Gill & Orgad, 2018; Banet-Weiser, 2018). Within 24 hours, the hashtag was used over 500,000 times on Twitter, and 12 million posts were created on Facebook across 85 countries (MeToo, n.d.; Mendes et al., 2018). The movement rapidly evolved into a networked feminist counterpublic, wherein personal narratives transformed into collective action through digital affordances that enabled visibility, solidarity, and emotional resonance (Mendes et al., 2018; Banet-Weiser, 2018).

In India, the #MeToo movement gained momentum in 2018 as a powerful response to sexual harassment in workplaces, with testimonies implicating prominent figures in media, academia, and politics. The movement's visibility increased after Raya Sarkar's List of Sexual Harassers in Academia (LoSHA), which named several respected academics and sparked nationwide debate. This online exposé circumvented traditional legal channels, enabling survivors to share experiences that were often silenced by institutional barriers (Gangoli, 2024; Panda, 2024). Indian #MeToo also took inspiration from earlier feminist protests such as the Pink Chaddi campaign (2009) against moral policing, the Slut Walk (2011) against victim-blaming, Pinjra Tod (2015) challenging hostel curfews, and Bekhauf Azadi (2017) advocating for women's right to public spaces (Panda, 2024). Collectively, these movements created a digital feminist legacy that emphasized bodily autonomy, public agency, and resistance against patriarchal control.

#MeToo exemplifies networked resistance through emotional storytelling, where personal trauma becomes a political tool, transforming individual pain into a collective voice (Papacharissi, 2015; Jackson et al., 2020; Johnson & Renderos, 2020). The movement's strength lay in its logic of connective action, with personalized stories shared across networks without a central organizational body (Bennett & Segerberg, 2012). However, scholars have critiqued the movement's uneven reach, structural inequalities in digital access, and limited media visibility, which meant that many marginalized voices remained unheard (Johnson & Renderos, 2020; Panda, 2024). Moreover, digital backlash, trolling, and performative allyship questioned the sustainability of the movement (Banet-Weiser, 2018). Despite these limitations, #MeToo succeeded in reshaping global discourses around sexual violence, accountability, and gender power, demonstrating how hashtags can evolve into transnational feminist movements with tangible cultural and institutional impacts (Mendes et al., 2018; Gill & Orgad, 2018).

Case 4 #FridaysForFuture

The #FridaysForFuture (FFF) movement began in August 2018, when Swedish teenager Greta Thunberg started holding weekly school strikes for climate action outside the Swedish Parliament. Her solo effort quickly sparked a global youth-led movement, motivating millions of young people to organize and join climate protests under the FFF name. By March 2019, the movement had rallied over 1.6 million youths in 133 countries, making it one of the largest and most organized youth climate movements in history (Bergmann & Ossewaarde, 2020; Fisher & Nasrin, 2021).

FFF's strength lies in its hybrid approach, which combines digital and physical activism. It utilizes platforms such as Twitter, Instagram, TikTok, and YouTube to disseminate messages, organize protests, and foster transnational solidarity. Digital tools such as hashtags, livestreams, memes, and short videos enable real-time coordination and emotional engagement (O'Brien et al., 2018; Bergmann & Ossewaarde, 2020). These features help form affective public networks driven by shared emotions, such as climate anxiety, anger, and hope (Papacharissi, 2015).

FFF's uniqueness also comes from its translocal framework. While mainly concentrating on global climate issues, its initiatives are tailored to fit the specific ecological and policy contexts of each country and region, giving the movement both a global urgency and local credibility (Wahlström et al., 2019; Terren & Soler-i-Martí 2021). The movement has prompted international organizations, including the United Nations, the European Parliament, and the Intergovernmental Panel on Climate Change (IPCC), to emphasize the importance of climate policies and sustainability goals (Wahlström et al., 2019; O'Brien et al., 2018). Importantly, the movement highlights intergenerational justice, arguing that the failure of today's political leaders violates the rights and future opportunities of younger generations (von Zabern et al., 2020).

Case 5: The Hong Kong Protests

The 2019–2020 Hong Kong protests, which initially opposed the Extradition Law Amendment Bill (ELAB), evolved into a larger pro-democracy movement characterized by digital and decentralized activism typical of the 21st century. Building on the legacy of the 2014 Umbrella Movement, these mostly youth-led protests were driven by concerns over democratic decline as China's influence increased. Protesters utilized encrypted messaging apps, anonymous forums, and real-time crowdsourced tools to coordinate their efforts without a central leader, also attempting to evade government surveillance (Li, 2025; Lee et al., 2021). Platforms like Telegram and LIHKG, a Reddit-style local forum, became essential for discussion, polling, and strategic coordination. Protesters shared flyers via AirDrop, edited protest materials on Google Docs, and utilized hashtags such as #StandWithHongKong and #BeWater to amplify global attention. A lively protest culture emerged through symbolic media, including Pepe the Frog, Lennon Walls, and creative memes, which strengthened collective identity and resilience (Frosina, 2021; Lee et al., 2021; Purbrick, 2019).

The protest strategy was based on the "Be Water" philosophy, emphasizing flexibility, mobility, and leaderlessness. This approach challenged traditional, state-centered protest policing by allowing activists to move freely across both digital and physical spaces. Protesters crowdsourced maps of police presence using tools like OpenStreetMap and HKmap.live, enabling real-time tracking to avoid arrests and coordinate their movements (Ting, 2020; Anderlini, 2019). This digital infrastructure supported a form of liquid resistance, where control flows through decentralized, temporary networks rather than hierarchical structures (Milan, 2015; Ting, 2020).

However, this digital empowerment also exposed protesters to intense surveillance and cyber repression. Chinese authorities used facial recognition, AI-assisted monitoring, and metadata analysis to track participants (Qiang, 2019; Human Rights Watch, 2019). The National Security Law passed in June 2020 criminalized online dissent with vague charges of subversion, leading to mass arrests, digital erasure of protest materials, and the forced shutdown of independent media outlets (Amnesty International, 2021). According to Amnesty International (2025), 80% of people arrested were targeted for lawful expression, with nearly 90% denied bail and held for an average of 11 months before trial.

Case 6: #DalitLivesMatter

The #DalitLivesMatter movement emerged as a digital response to caste violence in India, notably following the institutional murder of Rohith Vemula in 2016 and the Hathras rape case in 2020. Inspired by #BlackLivesMatter, it created a localized yet globally relevant platform for resistance against Brahmanical dominance and systemic neglect (Thakur, 2019;). Through platforms like Dalit Camera, Round Table India, and hashtags such as #JusticeForRohithVemula and #UnaFlogging, Dalit activists have built counterpublic digital spaces that emphasize lived experiences, political critique, and the visibility of the subaltern. Scholars describe this as the "digitisation of Dalit assertion," where youth-led, intersectional, and decentralized networks used visual storytelling, viral content, and transmedia memorialization to mobilize caste consciousness (Ahuja, 2018; Thakur, 2019; Soundararajan, 2019).

Despite its transformative potential, the #DalitLivesMatter movement faces significant structural and digital challenges. Poor internet connectivity prevents rural Dalit voices from reaching broader audiences, while online platforms are filled with caste-based abuse, including slurs, threats, cyberbullying, and social exclusion, which have caused serious psychological harm to Dalit users (Soundararajan, 2019; Singh, 2025). The spread of radical rhetoric by savarna allies, algorithmic marginalization, and internal divisions within Dalit digital spaces further weaken the likelihood of unified action (Noble, 2018; Ahuja, 2018; Thakur, 2019). This underscores both the potential and the vulnerabilities of digital activism: although social media can boost visibility, it also exposes marginalized groups to emotional damage and algorithmic suppression.

FRAMEWORK DEVELOPED FOR DIGITAL CIVIL RIGHTS ACTIVISM

Figure 2. Framework illustrating how global visibility, independent space, and marginalized voices, for action intersect to shape transformative digital civil rights activism

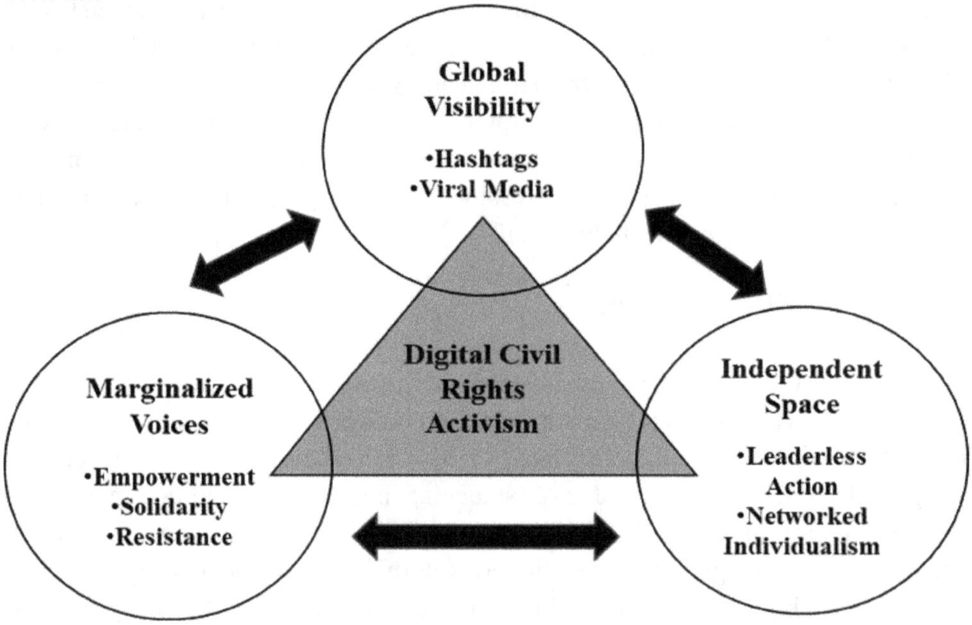

This framework, developed based on findings from empirical studies and depicted through a three-circle diagram, delineates the interconnected realms of digital civil rights activism in the modern era. It elucidates how global visibility, marginalized voices, and independent civic spaces converge within digital platforms to redefine political engagement and assert civil rights. The intersecting regions illustrate how visibility amplifies voice, how voice catalyzes autonomous action, and how action, in turn, fortifies global solidarity. At the nexus of these intersections lies a dynamic place fluid, networked, and emotionally compelling, where digital activism serves as both a form of resistance and a reimagining of democratic civic engagement.

DOUBLE-EDGED SWORD: FROM EMPOWERMENT TO EXPLOITATION

Digital activism is widely recognized as a powerful force for civil rights, providing marginalized groups with new avenues to gain visibility, engage, and resist. Campaigns such as #BlackLivesMatter, #MeToo, #FridaysForFuture, and #DalitLivesMatter exemplify the role of hashtags as both rallying cries and organizational tools, transforming individual experiences into collective political assertions. However, this optimistic outlook exposes contradictions that undermine the notion of free and open digital spaces (Gangoli, 2024; Johnson & Renderos, 2020; Terren & Soler-i-Martí, 2021)

The infrastructural function of platforms is not neutral; instead, it inherently influences the content and interactions they host. The algorithmic management of content, driven by corporate imperatives of profit, virality, and engagement, can prioritize sensationalism over substantive content and amplify misinformation or extremist materials (van Dijck et al, 2018; Gillespie, 2018; Roberts, 2019; Noble, 2018). Consequently, activists face various forms of platform censorship, shadow banning, content removal, and surveillance conducted by both state and non-state actors (Deibert, 2015; Milan, 2015). These limitations highlight a crucial paradox: while digital platforms facilitate mobilization and visibility, they also impose structural constraints that shape the scope and direction of activism (Thakur, 2019; Singh, 2025).

Another issue emerges from the platform-based approach to social justice, where activism depends on the features offered by platforms. The way people engage through likes, shares, and followers can soften radical demands into simpler stories that appeal to liberal audiences. This trend is evident in the selective visibility of specific movements. While #BlackLivesMatter receives global solidarity, caste-based activism, such as #DalitLivesMatter, struggles to gain similar traction due to platform-centric audience biases and a lack of global contextual understanding

(Paik, 2021; Thakur, 2019; Taylor, 2016). This global inequality in digital solidarity often mirrors geopolitical hierarchies and reifies the marginalization of non-Western struggles. As Srnicek (2017) argues, digital capitalism turns even dissent into data: clicks, shares, and views are collected for profit, making activism vulnerable to what Morozov (2011) calls "slacktivism," a superficial engagement lacking sustained political commitment.

Gendered and intersectional vulnerabilities are also exacerbated in digital activism. Feminist activists, especially those from marginalized communities, face disproportionate levels of online abuse, ranging from doxxing and trolling to sexualized violence and casteist slurs (Banet-Weiser, 2018). These forms of digital harassment are not simply aberrations but are structurally enabled by platform designs that prioritize engagement over safety. Women and Dalit activists in India, for instance, report severe mental health repercussions due to casteist cyberbullying, leading many to self-censor or withdraw from public digital spaces (Singh, 2025; Thakur, 2019).

Despite these conflicts, the solution is not digital disengagement. Instead, as Milan (2015) and Papacharissi (2015) note, activists need to engage with "platform politics" by understanding and strategically managing the infrastructural and algorithmic aspects of digital media. This involves creating digital security practices, expanding resistance on diverse platforms, and advocating for algorithmic transparency and platform reforms. Overall, digital activism operates on a double-edged sword. It provides tools for empowerment, visibility, and mobilization, but also exposes activists to risks like commodification, surveillance, suppression, and violence. Acknowledging these contradictions is crucial not to undermine digital activism but to establish a more critical, intersectional, and reflexive approach that challenges both techno-optimism and techno-pessimism (Dean, 2010).

EMPOWERING THE FUTURE: STRATEGIC DIRECTIONS FOR DIGITAL ACTIVISM

As digital activism evolves amid growing technological complexity and socio-political challenges, it is crucial to develop forward-thinking strategies that foster participation, amplify the voices of marginalized individuals, and safeguard democratic processes. The next stage of digital civil rights movements must proactively confront systemic issues such as digital inequality (Eubanks, 2018), algorithmic governance (Noble, 2018), surveillance capitalism (Zuboff, 2019), and state-led digital repression (Feldstein, 2021; Qiang, 2019). At the same time, movements must champion ethical technological innovation, civic digital literacy (Mihailidis & Viotty, 2017), and international solidarity frameworks that protect civil rights online (Hintz et al., 2019; Ryng et al., 2022).

1. Bridge the Digital Divide

A major obstacle to inclusive digital activism is the ongoing global and internal digital divide. Access to the internet and digital technology is still highly unequal across different regions, social classes, castes, races, and genders (Eubanks, 2018). By 2023, more than 2.6 billion people, primarily in the Global South, will still lack internet access. Even in regions with connectivity, disparities in infrastructure, cost, education, and access, particularly by gender, limit meaningful participation/ These digital gaps not only reduce engagement but also reinforce broader patterns of exclusion from civic conversations and online activism.

To empower future activists, governments should prioritize ensuring universal and affordable internet access, particularly in remote and underserved areas. Examples such as India's BharatNet and Kenya's Digital Economy Blueprint offer effective models (Government of India, n.d.; Republic of Kenya, 2019). Additionally, digital inclusion must be intersectional, overcoming linguistic, cultural, and ability-related obstacles by promoting local language content, community-led internet initiatives, and inclusive design practices (Eubanks, 2018).

2. Digital Literacy and Critical Consciousness

Digital empowerment is not just about access but also about building capacity and fostering critical consciousness. Without basic digital literacy, individuals remain vulnerable to misinformation, manipulation, and mass surveillance—issues that disproportionately affect marginalized communities, particularly those with limited access to education and media resources (UNESCO, 2021). As Mihailidis and Viotty (2017) argue, today's citizens must navigate an "algorithmically-curated spectacle," where attention is influenced by unseen platform logics. In such a landscape, media, data, and algorithmic literacy are not optional but essential for meaningful civic engagement.

Future-oriented education policies should integrate essential digital pedagogy into curricula, particularly in higher education and community learning environments. This involves educating students about algorithmic bias, content moderation politics, data ethics, and cybersecurity. Providing grassroots activists with open-source tools and secure communication methods, such as Signal and Tor, is vital for enhancing digital resilience (Hintz et al., 2019).

3. Platform Accountability and Ethical AI Governance

While social media platforms serve as primary spaces for activism, they are controlled by opaque, profit-driven algorithms that often suppress dissenting voices or spread disinformation. Research indicates that algorithmic systems on platforms such as Facebook and YouTube are designed to prioritize engagement over accuracy and ethics, thereby enabling polarization and ideological manipulation (Tufekci, 2017; Noble, 2018).

Therefore, reforming platform governance is essential. Future strategies should promote legally binding transparency standards, algorithmic audits, and participatory moderation frameworks. Civil society organizations, technologists, and policy makers need to work together to develop global accountability frameworks, such as the EU's Digital Services Act and the UN's "Code of Conduct for Information Integrity on Digital Platforms," that regulate platform conduct while protecting freedom of speech (Gorwa, 2019).

4. Protecting Digital Rights and Privacy

With the rise of digital repression tactics, such as biometric surveillance, internet shutdowns, spyware, targeted misinformation, and doxxing, the need to protect digital rights has become an urgent priority for civil society and policymakers. Authoritarian regimes are increasingly using these tools to suppress dissent, monitor activists, and criminalize online resistance (Feldstein, 2021; Qiang, 2019). At the same time, surveillance capitalism turns personal data into a commodity, raising serious ethical concerns about consent, autonomy, and control in the digital public sphere (Zuboff, 2019). To counter these threats, activists must be equipped with practical cybersecurity skills, including encryption, anonymization, and secure communication tools. Digital hygiene should be considered essential civic knowledge. Similarly, governments must implement robust data protection laws, especially in repressive or hybrid regimes where online expression is heavily monitored (Hintz et al., 2019).

Future digital activism should be founded on a rights-based digital infrastructure that safeguards civic freedoms and democratic participation. National governments must align their data governance policies with international standards, such as the General Data Protection Regulation (GDPR), and acknowledge that practices like mass surveillance, internet blackouts, and censorship violate human rights (Ryng et al., 2022). Legal protections must also extend to whistleblowers, digital journalists, and online human rights advocates to prevent the criminalization of legitimate dissent. Furthermore, international forums such as the United Nations Internet Governance Forum (IGF) must be strengthened to promote global digital rights frameworks and combat the weaponization of technology by authoritarian and non-state actors (Hintz et al., 2019).

5. Intersectional and Transnational Solidarity

The future of digital activism depends on sustainable, intersectional coalitions that connect issues, locations, and identities, rather than relying on isolated viral moments. Movements such as #BlackLivesMatter, #MeToo, #FridaysForFuture, and #DalitLivesMatter have demonstrated the power of transnational solidarity (Jackson, 2020; Mendes et al., 2019; Terren & Soler-i-Martí, 2021). However, maintaining momentum requires strategic partnerships with labor unions, student federations, educational institutions, environmental groups, indigenous communities, and international justice networks.

Intersectionality should function not only as a theoretical tool but also as a strategic organizing framework that promotes inclusivity and amplifies voices from historically silenced communities (Crenshaw, 1991). Future campaigns must be co-created with grassroots organizers and rooted in the lived experiences of those at the margins. Transnational collaboration, knowledge exchange, and mutual aid networks can help activists fight isolation and censorship in authoritarian contexts (Cammaerts, 2015; Milan, 2015).

6. *Innovative Digital Tactics and Creative Resistance*

The future of digital activism will need innovative, adaptable, and creative tactics, from Augmented Reality (AR) installations and blockchain-based whistleblowing tools to meme-driven storytelling and open-source data activism. These inventive forms of protest not only attract attention but also resist censorship more effectively. Research indicates that participatory and artistic protest strategies enhance engagement and mitigate vulnerability to government control (Cammaerts, 2015; Kaun & Uldam, 2017).

Technological innovation, when rooted in justice and inclusion, represents the next frontier of digital resistance. Civic tech tools, such as Ushahidi for crowdsourced crisis mapping and Bridgefy for decentralized communication during internet blackouts, demonstrate how people-centered technologies can empower communities (Okolloh, 2009; Wakefield, 2019). Creative digital expressions, such as memes, games, and immersive media, are particularly effective in engaging younger audiences and sustaining movements under repressive conditions (Tufekci, 2017; Kaun & Uldam, 2017). To support this growth, public policies must invest in ethical tech ecosystems, encouraging open-source infrastructure, indigenous coding initiatives, and digital artivism. Creating resilient, decentralized, and culturally rooted technologies will ensure that future digital activism remains inclusive, flexible, and ready to face new challenges.

CONCLUSION

Voices of marginalized communities have gained greater visibility in the digital era, as online platforms redefine how activism is organized and experienced. This study highlights the shift from traditional collective action to the more fluid, individualized form of engagement described by Bennett and Segerberg's (2012) Connective Action Theory. Unlike movements rooted in rigid hierarchies, today's digital activism thrives on personalization, emotional resonance, and flexible networks, allowing participants to engage on their own terms while still contributing to a larger cause. This shift from collective to connective action marks a major change in the legacy of civic rights movements. While earlier fights for justice, like the civil rights movement, relied on centralized leadership, organized groups, and face-to-face rallies, today's digital activism operates through decentralized networks, emotional connections, and algorithmic boosts.

Movements like the Arab Spring, #BlackLivesMatter #MeToo, #FridaysForFuture, the Hong Kong Protests, and #DalitLivesMatter build on the core goals of past civic struggles: equality, dignity, and rights, but they do so through new, personalized ways of engagement that transcend borders and identities. Digital platforms have empowered individuals, particularly those from marginalized communities, to shape narratives, mobilize support, and demand accountability in real-time. Yet, this transformation also brings challenges: surveillance, online harassment, platform bias, and the commodification of activism. As Milan (2015) and Papacharissi (2015) emphasize, digital activism must reckon with the politics of platforms, demanding algorithmic transparency, security, and greater digital justice. In this evolving landscape, the spirit of civic resistance endures, but in a new form, one that blends the moral force of past movements with the connective power of digital networks. Embracing this shift with critical awareness and strategic engagement is key to sustaining meaningful, inclusive, and resilient activism in the 21st century.

To conclude, the chapter presented a robust conceptual framework with the key societal domains where digital civil rights movements are effecting real change, such as global visibility, voice for marginalized, and independence. Collectively, this chapter reveals that digital platforms are not mere communication tools; they are dynamic arenas for negotiating, asserting, and expanding civil rights in the 21st century. These insights have not only highlighted the remarkable empowering potential of digital tools such as unparalleled access, extensive outreach, and deep emotional connections, but also confronted the significant challenges they pose. Ultimately, this chapter aspires to provide a rich and nuanced understanding of how digital activism is an indispensable force for advancing and safeguarding civil rights in an ever-evolving media landscape.

ACKNOWLEDGMENTS

The authors would like to acknowledge the use of language editing software, which was particularly helpful as a non-native English speaker. After using this tool, the authors reviewed and edited the content as needed and took full responsibility for the publication's content.

REFERENCES

Ahuja, A. (2018, April 23). *Digital Dalits: Is social media a game changer for Dalit politics?* The Print. https://theprint.in/opinion/dalit-history-month/digital-dalits-is-social-media-a-game-changer-for-dalit-politics/51284/

Amnesty International. (2021). *Hong Kong: In the Name of National Security.* https://www.amnesty.nl/content/uploads/2021/06/HKNSL-briefing-2021-1.pdf?x58675

Amnesty International. (2025, June 30). *Hong Kong: National Security Law analysis reveals a vast majority were unjustly arrested.* https://www.amnesty.org/en/latest/news/2025/06/hong-kong-national-security-law-analysis-shows-vast-majority-unjustly-arrested/

Anderlini, J. (2019, September 2). *Hong Kong's 'Water Revolution' Spins Out of Control.* Financial Times. https://www.ft.com/content/d1f60a3a-cd58-11e9-b018-ca4456540ea6

Anderson, M., Barthel, M., Perrin, A., & Vogels, E. A. (2020, June 10). *#BlackLivesMatter surges on Twitter after George Floyd's death.* Pew Research Centre. https://www.pewresearch.org/short-reads/2020/06/10/blacklivesmatter-surges-on-twitter-after-george-floyds-death/

Aouragh, M., & Alexander, A. (2011). The Egyptian Experience: Sense and Nonsense of the Internet Revolution. *International Journal of Communication*, *5*, 1344–1358. https://ijoc.org/index.php/ijoc/article/download/1191/610

Banet-Weiser, S. (2018). *Empowered: Popular Feminism and Popular Misogyny.* Duke University Press.

Bennett, W. L., & Segerberg, A. (2012). The Logic of Connective Action: Digital Media and the Personalization of Contentious Politics. *Information Communication and Society*, *15*(5), 739–768. DOI: 10.1080/1369118X.2012.670661

Bergmann, Z., & Ossewaarde, R. (2020). Youth climate activists meet environmental governance: Ageist depictions of the FFF movement and Greta Thunberg in German newspaper coverage. *Journal of Multicultural Discourses*, *15*(3), 267–290. DOI: 10.1080/17447143.2020.1745211

Bonilla, Y., & Rosa, J. (2015). #Ferguson: Digital protest, hashtag ethnography, and the racial politics of social media in the United States. *American Ethnologist*, *42*(1), 4–17. DOI: 10.1111/amet.12112

Brownlee, J., Masoud, T., & Reynolds, A. (2015). *The Arab Spring: Pathways of Repression and Reform*. Oxford University Press. DOI: 10.1093/acprof:oso/9780199660063.001.0001

Bruns, A., & Burgess, J. (2015). Twitter hashtags from ad hoc to calculated publics. In Rambukkana, N. (Ed.), *Hashtag publics: The power and politics of discursive networks* (pp. 13–27). Peter Lang Publishing.

Burch, A. D. S., Cai, W., Gianordoli, G., McCarthy, M., & Patel, J. K. (2020, June 13). *How Black Lives Matter Reach Every Corner of America.* The New York Times. https://www.nytimes.com/interactive/2020/06/13/us/george-floyd-protests-cities-photos.html

Burke, T. (2017, November 9). *#MeToo was started for black and brown women and girls. They're still being ignored.* The Washington Post. https://www.washingtonpost.com/news/post-nation/wp/2017/11/09/the-waitress-who-works-in-the-diner-needs-to-know-that-the-issue-of-sexual-harassment-is-about-her-too/

Burke, T. (n.d.). *History & Inception*. MeToo. https://metoomvmt.org/get-to-know-us/history-inception/

Cammaerts, B. (2015). Technologies of self-mediation: Affordances and constraints of social media for protest movements. In Uldam, J., & Vestergaard, A. (Eds.), *Civic engagement and social media: Political participation beyond protest* (pp. 97–110). Palgrave Macmillan. DOI: 10.1057/9781137434166_5

Castells, M. (2015). *Networks of outrage and hope: Social movements in the Internet age* (2nd ed.). Polity Press., https://voidnetwork.gr/wp-content/uploads/2019/11/Networks-of-Outrage-and-Hope-Social-Movements-in-the-Internet-Age-Manuel-Castells.pdf

Cleaver, H. (1998). The Zapatista effect: The internet and the rise of an alternative political fabric. *Journal of International Affairs*, *51*(2), 621–640.

Crenshaw, K. (1991). Mapping the Margins: Intersectionality, Identity Politics, and Violence against Women of Color. *Stanford Law Review*, *43*(6), 1241–1299. DOI: 10.2307/1229039

Critical Art Ensemble. (1996). *Electronic Civil Disobedience and Other Unpopular Ideas*. Autonomedia.

Dean, J. (2010). Blog Theory: Feedback and Capture in the Circuits of Drive. *Polity*.

Deibert, R. (2015). *Black Code: Surveillance, Privacy, and the Dark Side of the Internet*. Signal.

Earl, J., & Kimport, K. (2011). *Digitally enabled social change: Activism in the Internet age*. MIT Press. DOI: 10.7551/mitpress/9780262015103.001.0001

Eubanks, V. (2018). *Automating Inequality: How High-Tech Tools Profile, Police, and Punish the Poor*. St. Martin's Press.

Feldstein, S. (2021). *The Rise of Digital Repression: How Technology is Reshaping Power, Politics, and Resistance*. Oxford University Press. DOI: 10.1093/oso/9780190057497.001.0001

Fisher, D. R., & Nasrin, S. (2021). Climate activism and its effects. *Wiley Interdisciplinary Reviews: Climate Change*, *12*(2), e683. DOI: 10.1002/wcc.683

Fraser, N. (1990). Rethinking the Public Sphere: A Contribution to the Critique of Actually Existing Democracy. *Social Text*, (25/26), 56–80. DOI: 10.2307/466240

Freelon, D., McIlwain, C., & Bonilla, M. (2016a). Quantifying the Power and Consequences of Social Media Protest. *New Media & Society*, *20*(3), 990–1011. DOI: 10.1177/1461444816676646

Freelon, D., McIlwain, C., & Clark, M. (2016b). *Beyond the hashtags: #Ferguson, #Blacklivesmatter, and the online struggle for offline justice*. Center for Media and Social Impact, American University. http://dx.doi.org/DOI: 10.2139/ssrn.2747066

Frosina, S. (2021, June 8). *Digital revolution: How social media shaped the 2019 Hong Kong protests*. Italian Institute for International Political Studies. https://www.ispionline.it/en/publication/digital-revolution-how-social-media-shaped-2019-hong-kong-protests-30756

Gangoli, G. (2024). The #MeToo movement in India: Emotions and (in)justice in feminist responses. *Feminist Legal Studies*, *32*(2), 213–230. DOI: 10.1007/s10691-023-09540-x

Gerbaudo, P. (2012). *Tweets and the Streets: Social Media and Contemporary Activism*. Pluto Press. https://library.oapen.org/handle/20.500.12657/30772

Gill, R., & Orgad, S. (2018). The shifting terrain of sex and power: From the 'sexualization of culture' to #MeToo. *Sexualities, 21*(8), 1313–1324. DOI: 10.1177/1363460718794647

Gillespie, T. (2018). *Custodians of the Internet: Platforms, Content Moderation, and the Hidden Decisions That Shape Social Media*. Yale University Press.

Goodwin, S. (2019, June 26). *The civil rights movement and the media*. Oxford Bibliographies https://doi.org/DOI: 10.1093/obo/9780199756841-0231

Gorwa, R. (2019). The platform governance triangle: Conceptualising the informal regulation of online content. *Internet Policy Review, 8*(2). Advance online publication. DOI: 10.14763/2019.2.1407

Government of India. (n.d.). *BharatNet Project*. Digital Bharat Nidhi. https://usof.gov.in/en/bharatnet-project

Hintz, A., Dencik, L., & Wahl-Jorgensen, K. (2019). *Digital Citizenship in a Datafied Society*. Polity Press.

History Timeline, U. S. A. (n.d.). *The Role of Media in Shaping Civil Rights Narratives*. https://www.usahistorytimeline.com/pages/the-role-of-media-in-shaping-civil-rights-narratives-498ce6c1.php?utm_source=chatgpt.com

Howard, P. N., & Hussain, M. M. (2013). *Democracy's Fourth Wave? Digital Media and the Arab Spring*. Oxford University Press., DOI: 10.1093/acprof:oso/9780199936953.001.0001

Human Rights Watch. (2019). *China's Algorithms of Repression: Reverse Engineering a Xinjiang Police Mass Surveillance App*. https://www.hrw.org/sites/default/files/report_pdf/china0519_web.pdf

Jackson, S. J., Bailey, M., & Foucault Welles, B. (2020). *HashtagActivism: Networks of Race and Gender Justice*. MIT Press. DOI: 10.7551/mitpress/10858.001.0001

Jackson, S. J., & Welles, B. F. (2015). Hijacking #myNYPD: Social Media Dissent and Networked Counterpublics. *Journal of Communication, 65*(6), 932–952. DOI: 10.1111/jcom.12185

Johnson, R. G.III, & Renderos, H. (2020). Invisible populations and the #MeToo movement. *Public Administration Review, 80*(6), 1040–1045. DOI: 10.1111/puar.13209

Joyce, M. C. (Ed.). (2010). *Digital activism decoded: The new mechanics of change*. International Debate Education Association. https://www.opensocietyfoundations.org/uploads/e03a4445-3838-4aa6-98e0-a485ccc349f7/digiact10all.pdf

Kashak, N. D. (2024). The Evolution of Activism: From Civil Rights to Digital Advocacy. *NEWPORT INTERNATIONAL JOURNAL OF CURRENT ISSUES IN ARTS AND MANAGEMENT*, *5*(3), 18–21. DOI: 10.59298/NIJCIAM/2024/5.3.18210

Kaun, A., & Uldam, J. (2017). Digital activism: After the hype. *New Media & Society*, *20*(6), 2099–2106. DOI: 10.1177/1461444817731924

Kavada, A. (2015). Creating the collective: Social media, the Occupy Movement and its constitution as a collective actor. *Information Communication and Society*, *18*(8), 872–886. DOI: 10.1080/1369118X.2015.1043318

Lebron, C. J. (2017). *The Making of Black Lives Matter: A Brief History of an Idea*. Oxford University Press.

Lee, F. L. F., Liang, H., Cheng, E. W., Tang, G. K. Y., & Yuen, S. (2021). Affordances, movement dynamics, and a centralized digital communication platform in a networked movement. *Information Communication and Society*, *25*(12), 1699–1716. DOI: 10.1080/1369118X.2021.1877772

Li, Y.-T. (2025). Digital Organizers in Hong Kong: The Challenges of Movement Organizing Through Social Media Amid Democratic Backsliding. *Social Media + Society*, *11*(2), 20563051251337205. Advance online publication. DOI: 10.1177/20563051251337205

Library of Congress. (n.d.). *The Civil Rights Act of 1964: A Long Struggle for Freedom Civil Rights Era (1950–1963)*. https://www.loc.gov/exhibits/civil-rights-act/civil-rights-era.html

Lotan, G., Graeff, E., Ananny, M., Gaffney, D., Pearce, I., & Boyd, D. (2011). The Revolutions Were Tweeted: Information Flows During the 2011 Tunisian and Egyptian Revolutions. *International Journal of Communication*, *5*, 1375–1405. https://ijoc.org/index.php/ijoc/article/download/1246/643

Martin, B. (2005). The beating of Rodney King: The dynamics of backfire. *Critical Criminology*, *13*(3), 307–326. DOI: 10.1007/s10612-005-3186-x

McCarthy, J. D., & Zald, M. N. (1977). Resource Mobilization and Social Movements: A Partial Theory. *American Journal of Sociology*, *82*(6), 1212–1241. https://archiv.soms.ethz.ch/teaching/OppFall09/mccarthyzald77.pdf. DOI: 10.1086/226464

Melucci, A. (1989). *Nomads of the Present: Social Movements and Individual Needs in Contemporary Society*. Temple University Press.

Mendes, K., Ringrose, J., & Keller, J. (2018). #MeToo and the promise and pitfalls of challenging rape culture through digital feminist activism. *European Journal of Women's Studies*, *25*(2), 236–246. DOI: 10.1177/1350506818765318

Mercea, D. (2016). *Civic Participation in Contentious Politics: The Digital Foreshadowing of Protest*. Palgrave Macmillan., DOI: 10.1057/978-1-137-50869-0

MeToo. (n.d.). *Media Kit.* https://metoomvmt.org/stay-informed/media-kit/

Mihailidis, P., & Viotty, S. (2017). Spreadable Spectacle in Digital Culture: Civic Expression, Fake News, and the Role of Media Literacies in "Post-Fact" Society. *The American Behavioral Scientist*, *61*(4), 441–454. DOI: 10.1177/0002764217701217

Milan, S. (2015). When Algorithms Shape Collective Action: Social Media and the Dynamics of Cloud Protesting. *Social Media + Society*, *1*(2), 2056305115622481. Advance online publication. DOI: 10.1177/2056305115622481

Morozov, E. (2011). *The Net Delusion: The Dark Side of Internet Freedom*. PublicAffairs.

Morris, A. D. (1984). *The Origins of the Civil Rights Movement: Black Communities Organizing for Change*. Free Press.

Noble, S. U. (2018). *Algorithms of Oppression: How Search Engines Reinforce Racism*. New York University Press. DOI: 10.18574/nyu/9781479833641.001.0001

O'Brien, K., Selboe, E., & Hayward, B. M. (2018). Exploring youth activism on climate change: Dutiful, disruptive, and dangerous dissent. *Ecology and Society*, *23*(3), 42. DOI: 10.5751/ES-10287-230342

Okolloh, O. (2009). Ushahidi, or 'testimony': Web 2.0 tools for crowdsourcing crisis information. *Participatory Learning and Action*, *59*(1), 65–70. https://www.iied.org/sites/default/files/pdfs/migrate/G02842.pdf

Olson, M. (1965). *The Logic of Collective Action: Public Goods and the Theory of Groups*. Harvard University Press. DOI: 10.4159/9780674041660

Paik, S. (2021). Dalit feminist thought. In Fernandes, L. (Ed.), *Routledge handbook of gender in South Asia* (pp. 55–69). Routledge., DOI: 10.4324/9781003043102-6

Panda, M., & Das, D. P. (2024). #MeToo movement in India: Sexual-violence, casteism and gender bias. *Migration Letters : An International Journal of Migration Studies, 21*(S4), 1485–1494. https://migrationletters.com/index.php/ml/article/view/7563/4899

Papacharissi, Z. (2015). *Affective Publics: Sentiment, Technology, and Politics.* Oxford University Press., DOI: 10.1093/acprof:oso/9780199999736.001.0001

Pickard, V. (2006). United yet autonomous: Indymedia and the struggle to sustain a radical democratic network. *Media Culture & Society, 28*(3), 315–336. DOI: 10.1177/0163443706061685

Purbrick, M. (2019). A REPORT OF THE 2019 HONG KONG PROTESTS. *Asian Affairs, 50*(4), 465–487. DOI: 10.1080/03068374.2019.1672397

Qiang, X. (2019). The Road to Digital Unfreedom: President Xi's Surveillance State. *Journal of Democracy, 30*(1), 53–67. DOI: 10.1353/jod.2019.0004

Rainie, L., & Wellman, B. (2012). *Networked: The new social operating system.* MIT Press., DOI: 10.7551/mitpress/8358.001.0001

Republic of Kenya. (2019). *Digital Economy Blueprint: Powering Kenya's Transformation.* https://smartafrica.org/wp-content/uploads/2021/08/Kenya_Digital_Economy_2019.pdf

Roberts, S. T. (2019). *Behind the Screen: Content Moderation in the Shadows of Social Media.* Yale University Press.

Ronfeldt, D., Arquilla, J., Fuller, G., & Fuller, M. (1998). *The Zapatista "Social Netwar" in Mexico.* RAND Corporation. https://www.rand.org/content/dam/rand/pubs/monograph_reports/1998/MR994.pdf

Russell, A. (2001). The Zapatistas Online: Shifting the Discourse of Globalization. *Gazette (Leiden, Netherlands), 63*(5), 399–413. DOI: 10.1177/0016549201063005003

Ryng, J., Guicherd, G., Saman, J. A., Choudhury, P., & Kellett, A. (2022). Internet Shutdowns: A Human Rights Issue. *RUSI Journal, 167*(4–5), 50–63. DOI: 10.1080/03071847.2022.2156234

Singh, D. (2025). Dalits' encounters with casteism on social media: A thematic analysis. *Information Communication and Society, 28*(2), 335–353. DOI: 10.1080/1369118X.2025.2462244

Singh, G. K., Alam, K., & Kumar, S.Dr. Girish Kumar SinghDr. Khursheed Alam-Mr. Shailender Kumar. (2025). The Powerful Role of Print Media in India's Fight for Independence: A Study. *International Journal for Research Publication and Seminar, 16*(2), 111–122. DOI: 10.36676/jrps.v16.i2.258

Snow, D. A., Rochford, E. B., Worden, S. K., & Benford, R. D. (1986). Frame Alignment Processes, Micromobilization, and Movement Participation. *American Sociological Review, 51*(4), 464–481. DOI: 10.2307/2095581

Soundararajan, T. (2019). The Dalit Diva's guide to digital resistance. In Daniels, J., Gregory, K., & McMillan Cottom, T. (Eds.), *Digital sociologies* (pp. 231–248). Policy Press.

Srnicek, N. (2017). *Platform Capitalism.* Polity Press. https://mudancatecnologicaedinamicacapitalista.wordpress.com/wp-content/uploads/2019/02/platform-capitalism.pdf

Stepan, A. (2012). Tunisia's Transition and the Twin Tolerations. *Journal of Democracy, 23*(2), 89–103. https://www.journalofdemocracy.org/wp-content/uploads/2012/04/Stepan-23-2.pdf. DOI: 10.1353/jod.2012.0034

Taylor, K.-Y. (2016). *From #BlackLivesMatter to Black liberation.* Haymarket Books.

Terren, L., & Soler-i-Martí, R. (2021). "Glocal" and transversal engagement in youth social movements: A Twitter-based case study of Fridays For Future-Barcelona. *Frontiers in Political Science, 3*, 635822. DOI: 10.3389/fpos.2021.635822

Thakur, A. K. (2019). New Media and the Dalit Counter-public Sphere. *Television & New Media, 21*(4), 360–375. DOI: 10.1177/1527476419872133

Theocharis, Y., Lowe, W., van Deth, J. W., & García-Albacete, G. (2014). Using Twitter to mobilize protest action: Online mobilization patterns and action repertoires in the Occupy Wall Street, Indignados, and Aganaktismenoi movements. *Information Communication and Society, 18*(2), 202–220. DOI: 10.1080/1369118X.2014.948035

Tilly, C., & Wood, L. J. (2013). *Social Movements, 1768 - 2012* (3rd ed.). Routledge., DOI: 10.4324/9781315632070

Ting, T. (2020). From 'be water' to 'be fire': Nascent smart mob and networked protests in Hong Kong. *Social Movement Studies, 19*(3), 362–368. DOI: 10.1080/14742837.2020.1727736

Tufekci, Z. (2017). *Twitter and tear gas: The power and fragility of networked protest.* Yale University Press.

UNESCO. (2021). *Media and information literate citizens: think critically, click wisely!* https://unesdoc.unesco.org/ark:/48223/pf0000377068

United Nations. (n.d.). Digital space and human rights. United Nations Human Rights. https://www.ohchr.org/en/topic/digital-space-and-human-rights

van Dijck, J., Poell, T., & de Waal, M. (2018). *The Platform Society: Public Values in a Connective World.* Oxford University Press., DOI: 10.1093/oso/9780190889760.001.0001

von Zabern, L., & Tulloch, C. D. (2020). Rebel with a cause: The framing of climate change and intergenerational justice in the German press treatment of the Fridays for Future protests. *Media Culture & Society*, *43*(1), 23–47. DOI: 10.1177/0163443720960923

Wahlström, M., Kocyba, P., De Vydt, M., & de Moor, J. (Eds.). (2019). *Protest for a future: Composition, mobilization and motives of the participants in Fridays For Future climate protests on 15 March, 2019 in 13 European cities.* https://protestinstitut.eu/wp-content/uploads/2019/07/20190709_Protest-for-a-future_GCS-Descriptive-Report.pdf

Wakefield, J. (2019). Hong Kong protesters using Bluetooth Bridgefy app. https://www.bbc.com/news/technology-49565587

Wellman, B., Quan-Haase, A., Boase, J., Chen, W., Hampton, K., Díaz, I., & Miyata, K. (2003). The social affordances of the Internet for networked individualism. *Journal of Computer-Mediated Communication*, *8*(3), 0. Advance online publication. DOI: 10.1111/j.1083-6101.2003.tb00216.x

Wolfsfeld, G., Segev, E., & Sheafer, T. (2013). Social Media and the Arab Spring: Politics Comes First. *The International Journal of Press/Politics*, *18*(2), 115–137. DOI: 10.1177/1940161212471716

World Bank. (2023). *Digital Transformation Overview* https://www.worldbank.org/en/topic/digital/overview

Wray, S. (1999). On electronic civil disobedience. *Peace Review*, *11*(1), 107–111. DOI: 10.1080/10402659908426237

Yang, G. (2016). Narrative agency in hashtag activism: The case of #BlackLivesMatter. *Media and Communication*, *4*(4), 13–17. DOI: 10.17645/mac.v4i4.692

Zuboff, S. (2019). *The Age of Surveillance Capitalism: The Fight for a Human Future at the New Frontier of Power*. PublicAffairs.

KEY TERMS AND DEFINITIONS

Civil Rights Movements: Social and political campaigns aimed at achieving equality, justice, and the protection of fundamental human rights, particularly for marginalized communities.

Connective Action: A form of digital-era collective mobilization where individuals participate through personalized, digitally-mediated expressions rather than coordinated organizational structures. As proposed by Bennett and Segerberg (2012), connective action is central to understanding decentralized activism facilitated by hashtags, memes, and online communities in modern civil rights movements.

Digital Activism: The use of digital technologies—such as social media, online petitions, livestreams, and blogs—to advocate for social or political change.

Digital Empowerment: The process by which individuals and marginalized communities gain access, voice, and agency through digital tools and platforms

Global Visibility: The ability of local movements to achieve international recognition and solidarity through digital platforms. Global visibility enables grassroots struggles to garner transnational support, craft their narratives on a global scale, and exert pressure on local governments and institutions through increased international awareness.

Hashtags: Short, searchable keywords preceded by the "#" symbol that facilitate online visibility, discourse aggregation, and collective identification.

Marginalized Voices: Refers to individuals or groups historically excluded from mainstream media, political power, or societal influence.

Networked Individualism: A social pattern in which individuals operate more independently while still being connected through digital networks.

Social Media: Web-based platforms such as X (formerly Twitter), Facebook, Instagram, and YouTube, which facilitate user-generated content, interaction, and networking.

Chapter 6
Digital Dissent and Grassroots Mobilization: The Reconfiguration of Civil Rights Activism in the Age of Social Media

Sangeeta Mathur
https://orcid.org/0000-0003-1861-2868
Career Point University, Kota, India

ABSTRACT

Social media platforms have transformed civil rights activism by enabling marginalized voices through hashtags, livestreams, and digital storytelling. This chapter explores movements like #BlackLivesMatter, #DalitLivesMatter, and anti-CAA protests to examine how digital tools foster participation while also exposing activists to surveillance, censorship, and algorithmic bias. Integrating perspectives from cyberfeminism and digital sociology, it advocates a rights-based framework for digital justice, emphasizing the need for legal protections and inclusive digital citizenship in the face of rising digital authoritarianism.

1. INTRODUCTION: CIVIL RIGHTS AND THE RISE OF THE DIGITAL PROTESTOR

The advent of the digital era has radically transformed the terrain of civil rights activism, redefining how dissent is expressed, organized, and sustained. Traditional forms of resistance—physical marches, sit-ins, and community organizing—have not vanished; rather, they now coexist with or are amplified by digital mechanisms

DOI: 10.4018/979-8-3693-3920-6.ch006

such as hashtags, livestreams, and viral content. These tools allow for real-time mobilization, decentralized leadership, and global visibility—hallmarks of what scholars now identify as "networked protest" (Tufekci, 2017).

Where mid-20th-century civil rights leaders depended on church congregations, physical mailers, and local press to disseminate messages, today's digital protestors harness the power of social media to build rapid consensus and transnational solidarity. The transformation is not merely technological—it is fundamentally political. Movements like the Arab Spring, #BlackLivesMatter, #MeToo, and India's anti-CAA protests exemplify how digitally enabled activism challenges state authority, exposes structural injustice, and enables marginalized voices to bypass traditional gatekeeping institutions (Gerbaudo, 2012; Jackson, Bailey & Welles, 2020).

This digital reconfiguration of dissent reflects both continuity and change. Just as the Selma to Montgomery marches dramatized the violence of voter suppression in 1965, viral videos of police brutality now galvanize mass outrage and legislative attention within hours. From protest flyers to Instagram infographics, the medium has evolved, but the underlying objective remains—challenging systemic injustice and reasserting civil rights.

Yet the digital realm is not a utopia of free expression. It is a deeply contested space where empowerment coexists with repression. The same platforms that enable visibility also expose activists to algorithmic surveillance, online harassment, and state-sponsored disinformation campaigns. Where the FBI once infiltrated civil rights groups through COINTELPRO, contemporary governments deploy facial recognition software, geofencing, and AI-enabled social media monitoring to suppress dissent (Brunton & Nissenbaum, 2015; Deibert, 2020). The result is a paradox of visibility: protestors are more seen than ever before, yet increasingly vulnerable to digital control.

The rise of the digital protestor—an actor who navigates both physical and virtual arenas of resistance—also signifies a profound shift in the organization and philosophy of movements. Networked activism often replaces hierarchical leadership with horizontal, decentralized communities that organize through encrypted messaging and mutual aid platforms. During the 2020 George Floyd protests, for instance, activists in Minneapolis received guidance on protest safety from Palestinians in Gaza, a moment of transnational solidarity enabled entirely by digital platforms (Milner & Phillips, 2021).

This transnational exchange of tactics and narratives signals a reconfiguration of power, where globalized information flows forge new solidarities that transcend borders, languages, and ideologies. At the same time, it introduces new challenges: the commodification of protest, the dilution of messaging for algorithmic engagement, and the risk of performative activism that values aesthetics over impact.

This chapter seeks to critically examine these tensions by tracing the evolution of civil rights activism in the digital age. It interrogates how social media reshapes protest dynamics, redefines grassroots engagement, and introduces new ethical and legal dilemmas around surveillance, censorship, and accountability. By foregrounding the digital protestor as both inheritor of legacy resistance and innovator of new paradigms, this inquiry underscores the duality of digital mobilization—its radical potential and its embedded risks.

In doing so, the chapter contributes to the growing body of scholarship on digital dissent, offering a multidimensional framework to understand how civil rights are enacted, contested, and negotiated in an era of datafication, algorithmic governance, and hyper-connectivity (Cammaerts, 2015; Zuboff, 2019).

2. HASHTAGS AND HUMAN RIGHTS: MAPPING CONTEMPORARY DIGITAL MOVEMENTS

In the digital age, hashtags have become powerful tools of civil rights advocacy—shaping solidarity, mobilization, and public discourse. Movements like #BlackLivesMatter, #MeToo, #DalitLivesMatter, and #FarmersProtest use hashtags to amplify marginalized voices, archive collective memory, and influence policy. These decentralized digital signifiers bypass traditional gatekeepers, enabling real-time activism and global solidarity. Though shaped by platform algorithms and commercial interests, hashtags—when paired with offline action—remain pivotal in transforming outrage into lasting social movements and redefining the structure of civic engagement in the 21st century.

In recent years, hashtags have emerged as powerful instruments of civil rights advocacy. As illustrated in Figure 1, hashtags in the digital era function as multi-faceted tools, serving as rallying cries, frameworks for solidarity, repositories of memory, and catalysts for action.

Figure 1. The Multifunctional Role of Hashtags in Contemporary Civil Rights Movements.

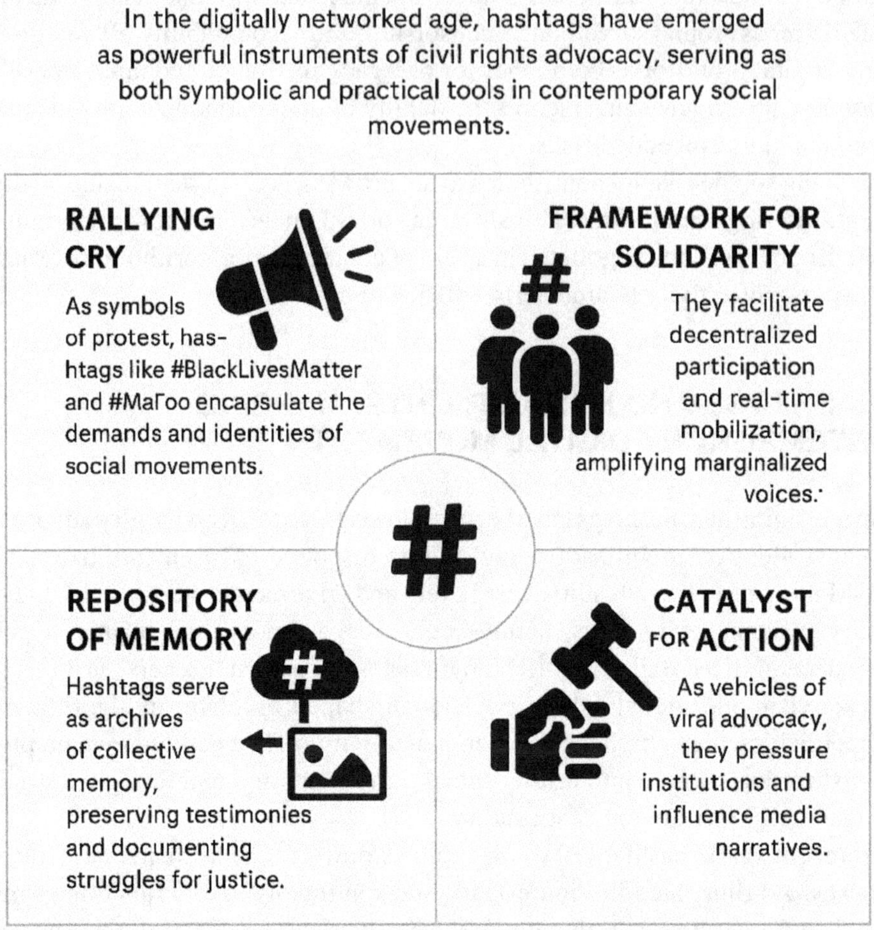

This infographic highlights four core functions of hashtags in digitally networked activism: (1) Rallying Cry – encapsulating identity and protest (e.g., #BlackLivesMatter); (2) Framework for Solidarity – enabling decentralized participation and amplifying marginalized voices; (3) Repository of Memory – archiving collective experiences and testimonies; and (4) Catalyst for Action – generating viral advocacy to pressure institutions and influence narratives

From Symbol to Structure: The Rise of Hashtag Activism

The evolution of hashtag activism reflects a broader transformation in how dissent is articulated and enacted. With the introduction of Twitter hashtags in 2007, what began as a digital convenience soon matured into a formidable tactic for socio-political engagement. In particular, hashtag activism has become a defining feature of twenty-first-century civil rights struggles, transforming individual grievances into collective calls for accountability. Hashtags function simultaneously as discursive tools and organizing frameworks, collapsing temporal and spatial barriers to protest and enabling instantaneous amplification of local injustices to global audiences.

The participatory nature of hashtags allows diverse actors—activists, scholars, survivors, artists, and ordinary citizens—to shape the discourse around human rights issues. Unlike traditional media narratives, which are often filtered through institutional biases, hashtags create a counter public sphere where suppressed or overlooked voices can gain visibility and agency.

Case Studies: How Hashtags Shape Human Rights Discourse

Several high-profile movements demonstrate the power of hashtag activism in reshaping global conversations and policy landscapes:

- *#BlackLivesMatter* began in 2013 following the acquittal of George Zimmerman in the shooting death of Trayvon Martin. It rapidly evolved into an international movement against systemic racism and police brutality. The hashtag unified protests across continents, challenged dominant racial narratives, and spurred debates on policing, equity, and justice (Freelon, McIlwain, & Clark, 2018).
- *#MeToo*, originally coined by Tarana Burke in 2006 and popularized in 2017, enabled survivors of sexual harassment and assault to share their experiences publicly. In doing so, it broke long-standing silences around gender-based violence, held high-profile perpetrators accountable, and led to policy reforms in corporate, legal, and academic spaces (Gill & Orgad, 2018).
- *#BringBackOurGirls* emerged after the 2014 kidnapping of 276 schoolgirls by Boko Haram in Nigeria. Amplified by global figures like Michelle Obama, the hashtag pressured the Nigerian government and international actors to take action. It highlighted the vulnerability of girls in conflict zones and the global neglect of African crises (Obi, 2019).
- *#FarmersProtest* in India mobilized millions in opposition to three agricultural laws introduced in 2020. Hashtags like #IStandWithFarmers were instrumental in organizing protests, debunking misinformation, and drawing international attention to rural distress. The eventual repeal of the laws illustrated the movement's influence.
- *#StandWithUkraine* surfaced during the 2022 Russian invasion, catalyzing global solidarity, humanitarian aid, and diplomatic pressure. It facilitated the rapid spread of updates, humanized conflict through firsthand accounts, and kept the crisis in international focus.

- Indigenous and caste-based hashtags such as *#DalitLivesMatter*, *#JusticeForAsifa*, and *#SaveAarey* reveal the versatility of digital activism in addressing diverse forms of marginalization—caste violence, sexual brutality, and environmental degradation. These movements, while rooted in local contexts, used digital platforms to challenge entrenched hierarchies and demand systemic change.

Digital Counter publics and the Politics of Visibility

Hashtags are integral to the formation of *networked counter publics*—digital spaces where suppressed identities and oppositional discourses flourish (Jackson et al., 2020). For communities historically denied access to mainstream platforms—women, Dalits, LGBTQ+ persons, indigenous groups—hashtag activism becomes a mode of reclaiming voice and visibility. Digital storytelling, often in the form of videos, infographics, or threads, enables participants to document lived experiences, memorialize injustices, and frame their struggles on their own terms.

Furthermore, hashtags challenge the hegemony of top-down knowledge production. Instead of relying on journalistic gatekeeping or academic framing, digital movements produce knowledge horizontally through collective participation. This democratization fosters radical empathy, blurring the boundary between observer and participant, and inviting broader publics into acts of witnessing and solidarity.

From Clicks to Change: Hashtag Activism's Real-World Impact

While some critics dismiss hashtag activism as *"slacktivism"*—symbolic participation without material engagement—it is increasingly evident that digital campaigns can drive substantial offline outcomes. Effective hashtag movements tend to exhibit several common traits: clarity of message, consistency, emotional resonance, and integration with offline organizing (Tufekci, 2017).

1. **Mobilization and Organization**: Hashtags facilitate rapid coordination. During the #FarmersProtest, for example, digital platforms were used to share protest locations, legal advice, and health alerts in real-time—bypassing both media censorship and logistical bottlenecks.
2. **Awareness and Solidarity**: They transcend geographical boundaries, attracting international attention. #BlackLivesMatter was taken up in London, Berlin, and Sydney, demonstrating the portability of local struggles to global contexts.
3. **Policy and Legal Impact**: Campaigns like #MeToo prompted institutional investigations, workplace policy overhauls, and the enactment of new laws.

This underscores that virtual protest, when strategically sustained, can reshape public policy and discourse.

4. **Cultural Shifts**: Hashtag activism influences how societies understand justice, power, and identity. For instance, the normalization of terms like "systemic racism" or "consent culture" owes much to digital movements.

Challenges and Critiques: Navigating the Limits of Hashtag Activism

Despite its successes, hashtag activism faces significant limitations. One key concern is *ephemerality*: social media trends are fleeting, and sustaining momentum requires continuous engagement. Movements risk losing focus as attention shifts or as hashtags are co-opted by opportunists and trolls.

Algorithmic bias also presents a structural barrier. Platforms may prioritize content based on virality rather than substance, inadvertently marginalizing complex or less sensational narratives. Moreover, *digital surveillance* poses a growing threat. State and corporate actors increasingly monitor hashtag activity, track participants, and deploy counter-narratives to discredit movements (Deibert, 2020).

Performative activism—where users signal virtue by sharing a hashtag without real engagement—dilutes the potency of movements. The risk of "optical allyship," where appearances substitute for action, can erode public trust and internal cohesion.

Finally, the *accessibility divide* must be acknowledged. Hashtag activism often presumes digital literacy and access to technology, sidelining those in remote or impoverished regions. This digital exclusion may reinforce existing inequalities, even within progressive movements.

Hashtag activism stands at the intersection of urgency and uncertainty. It offers unprecedented avenues for collective expression, resistance, and reform—yet it also operates within the constraints of platform capitalism, algorithmic governance, and digital surveillance. When wielded strategically and ethically, hashtags can catalyze global movements, shift policy landscapes, and humanize struggles that were once invisible.

The future of civil rights activism will depend on our ability to synthesize the speed and scale of digital tools with the depth and durability of grassroots organizing. Hashtags are not a panacea, but they are undeniably a potent force in the ongoing struggle for justice, dignity, and human rights in the 21st century.

3. DIGITAL VISIBILITY AND THE POLITICS OF PLATFORM ALGORITHMS

In today's digital landscape, visibility is power—but this power is increasingly controlled by opaque algorithmic systems optimized for engagement and profit, not equity or justice (Noble, 2018; Zuboff, 2019). As activism moves from the streets to screens, it enters an attention economy where algorithms prioritize viral, emotionally charged content, often amplifying dominant narratives while muting dissenting or marginalized voices (Tufekci, 2015; Gillespie, 2018). Movements like #BlackLivesMatter and #MeToo have benefited from algorithmic amplification, yet posts by Dalit, Indigenous, queer, or non-English-speaking activists are often demoted or censored under vague platform guidelines. With little transparency, many rely on "algorithmic folk theories" to guess how visibility works (Eslami et al., 2015), reinforcing a politics of performance over substance. In effect, algorithms act as gatekeepers of public discourse, shaping not just what is seen, but what is possible to know and contest. While digital tools offer immense potential for resistance, they also entrench structural inequities. A just digital public sphere demands algorithmic transparency, equitable platform design, and accountability mechanisms that prioritize pluralism and democratic participation over commodified attention.

How Algorithms Shape Activist Visibility

At the core of algorithmic governance is the logic of *engagement maximization*. Content that garners more likes, comments, shares, or watch time is ranked higher and shown to more users. Activists must therefore engage in *platform-specific optimization* to ensure their messages are seen (Bishop, 2019).

On *TikTok*, for instance, creators adopt trending audio tracks, visual templates, and hashtags that align with the platform's recommendation engine to increase their chances of appearing on the "For You Page." Activists speaking out on issues like climate justice, caste violence, or reproductive rights often blend education with entertainment to boost reach (Abidin, 2021). Conversely, on *Twitter/X*, movements like #BlackLivesMatter or #FarmersProtest have relied on *networked virality*—rapid retweeting, hashtag chaining, and strategic tagging—to mobilize attention. However, Twitter users also report experiences of *"shadow banning,"* where content visibility is algorithmically suppressed without formal notification (Rieder et al., 2020).

Because algorithmic processes are proprietary and non-transparent, activists frequently rely on *algorithmic folk theories*—informal beliefs about how to "game the system." These include posting at peak hours, avoiding banned terms, and interacting with trending content to improve their own post visibility (Eslami et al., 2015).

Such speculative practices reveal the power imbalance between users and platforms, where civil rights discourse is shaped by an invisible, unaccountable infrastructure.

The Double-Edged Sword of Algorithmic Mediation

The algorithmic visibility model functions as *a double-edged sword.* On the one hand, platforms can *amplify marginalized voices* and create global momentum for grassroots movements. Hashtag campaigns like #MeToo and #JusticeForAsifa reached millions through algorithm-driven amplification, sparking policy debates and public reckonings (Gill & Orgad, 2018).

On the other hand, *content moderation and algorithmic suppression* often disproportionately affect dissenting voices. Posts documenting police brutality or state violence are flagged for violating community guidelines, while misinformation, hate speech, and extremist propaganda continue to flourish. This imbalance stems from the *commercial logic* of virality: sensational content tends to generate more engagement and is therefore rewarded, regardless of accuracy or harm (Venturini, 2019).

One notable example is Facebook's internal algorithm changes in 2018, which were later shown to *boost divisive content* and downgrade content perceived as "political," including some human rights reporting (Horwitz & Seetharaman, 2021). In India, during the anti-CAA protests, several posts were *shadow-banned or de-ranked*, and activists alleged deliberate bias in content takedowns (Chakravartty & Roy, 2020).

Moreover, *algorithmic opacity* fosters suspicion and undermines activist trust. Without transparency in how content is ranked or removed, users face uncertainty about whether their declining reach is the result of user disengagement, platform punishment, or state-influenced moderation (Gillespie, 2018). This uncertainty weakens the reliability of digital platforms as spaces for free expression.

The Fragmentation of Collective Action

Algorithms not only affect visibility—they also *fragment information flows*, shaping how activists coordinate and sustain movements. Automated curation may bury important updates, prioritize trending content over urgent alerts, or send inconsistent notifications to followers. This disrupts the cohesion of digital movements, making it difficult to maintain focus, build momentum, or mobilize effectively (Margetts et al., 2015).

Furthermore, the algorithmic emphasis on *individual content performance* can distort movement goals. Activists may feel pressured to produce viral-friendly material rather than substantive political critique, leading to what some scholars call the *"performance trap"* of digital activism (Poell & van Dijck, 2018). This shift prioritizes emotional appeal and aesthetic virality over sustained engagement and policy-oriented outcomes.

Activist Adaptation and Resistance

In response to algorithmic suppression and unpredictability, activists have developed *creative strategies* to navigate, subvert, or challenge platform logics:

- **Code-switching and linguistic camouflage**: Activists use euphemisms or visual memes to evade automated moderation—for example, writing "s3xual" instead of "sexual" in sensitive discussions (Matamoros-Fernández, 2017).
- **Cross-platform coordination**: By disseminating the same message across Instagram, Telegram, YouTube, and Signal, activists reduce reliance on any single platform and diversify their visibility sources (Treré & Mattoni, 2019).
- **Community amplification**: Users create mutual-aid "boosting" networks to like, share, and repost critical content, counteracting the effects of shadow banning or algorithmic filtering.
- **Demanding algorithmic accountability**: Civil society organizations are increasingly calling for transparency in algorithm design, clear explanations of moderation policies, and *democratic oversight* of content governance (Mozilla Foundation, 2020).

These practices highlight the *agency of digital protestors*, who resist not only political oppression but also technological architectures of invisibility.

The *politics of platform algorithms* are central to understanding the dynamics of contemporary civil rights activism. In a digital environment where attention is commodified, *activist visibility* **is** *conditional*—shaped not solely by the merit of content or the urgency of cause, but by platform economics, moderation logics, and systemic biases.

While algorithms can indeed *amplify resistance*, they also risk reproducing *digital inequalities*, privileging movements that align with platform norms and suppressing those that disrupt hegemonic narratives. This paradox underscores the need to *rethink digital public spheres* as spaces not just of communication, but of *algorithmic governance*.

To ensure that platforms fulfill their democratic promise, it is essential to implement structural reforms: algorithmic transparency, participatory content policymaking, diverse representation in tech development, and independent oversight. Until such measures are adopted, the fight for civil rights online will remain precariously subject to the logics of capital and control.

Ultimately, *visibility in the digital age is not a given—it is contested, negotiated, and deeply political.* The future of activist movements depends on their ability to *reclaim agency* over the very systems that mediate their presence.

4. REPRESSION IN THE CLOUD: CENSORSHIP, SURVEILLANCE, AND STATE RESPONSE

As digital activism has surged across the globe, so too has the repressive capacity of states, evolving in tandem with the very technologies that once promised democratization and civic empowerment. In both authoritarian regimes and liberal democracies, governments have *swiftly adapted to the affordances of networked technologies*, transforming the digital sphere into a domain of control and surveillance. This convergence of state power and digital infrastructure has birthed a *new paradigm of repression in the cloud, where censorship is increasingly subtle, algorithmic, and institutionally normalized*—rarely enforced through visible coercion, but rather through platform manipulation, legal ambiguity, and psychological deterrence (Howard & Hussain, 2013; Deibert, 2020).

Unlike the overt censorship of previous eras—book burnings, media bans, or mass arrests—*contemporary digital repression is cloaked in the language of cybersecurity, public order, and national sovereignty.* It operates through the deployment of *state-sponsored surveillance technologies*, the selective enforcement of *vague digital laws*, and the strategic use of *disinformation to delegitimize protest movements.* In countries such as India, Turkey, Iran, and Egypt, for example, internet shutdowns and platform bans are frequently justified under the pretext of maintaining law and order, while in democratic societies like the United States and the UK, digital surveillance programs have been quietly expanded under counterterrorism frameworks (Feldstein, 2019; Freedom House, 2022).

The repressive toolkit is both *diverse and scalable.* On one hand, it includes *direct censorship tactics* such as blocking websites, filtering search results, or removing content from social media platforms at the request of governments. On the other, it extends to *mass surveillance operations* that track activists' communications, locations, and social networks through spyware, facial recognition, and metadata analytics (Greenwald, 2014; Marczak et al., 2021). Such monitoring is often facilitated by *commercial collaboration*, wherein tech firms provide governments with access to user data, either willingly under legal compulsion or passively through inadequate privacy protections.

One of the most insidious dimensions of digital repression is its *transnational reach.* Governments increasingly engage in *cross-border digital harassment*, targeting dissidents in exile with online threats, hacking attempts, and intimidation of family members back home. For instance, exiled journalists and human rights defenders from Saudi Arabia, China, or Iran have reported orchestrated cyber campaigns aimed at silencing their advocacy even on foreign soil (Feldstein, 2019). The proliferation of *mercenary surveillance tools*, such as Pegasus spyware, has further enabled regimes to *extend their coercive reach beyond territorial boundaries*, effectively eroding the sanctuary traditionally afforded by exile (Deibert, 2020; Citizen Lab, 2021).

These digital tactics pose *profound threats to the health of civil society*. By normalizing surveillance and criminalizing dissent, states foster an atmosphere of *paranoia and fear*, which leads to *self-censorship, disengagement, and fragmentation* of activist communities. Individuals may avoid speaking out, organizing events, or even sharing content online for fear of reprisal—thus undermining the democratic function of public discourse. More broadly, the persistent intrusion into digital spaces corrodes *the trust necessary for collective mobilization*, eroding the very foundations upon which participatory politics rest (Penney, 2017).

Digital repression also thrives on *asymmetric power dynamics*, where the state, armed with advanced cyber tools and expansive legal authority, confronts individuals and movements often lacking resources, technical expertise, or institutional protections. This *imbalance forces activists into reactive modes*, relying on circumvention tools like VPNs, encrypted messaging apps, or anonymity strategies that are themselves constantly threatened by evolving state capabilities (Tanczer et al., 2018). In some cases, even these defenses are criminalized, further narrowing the safe spaces for digital dissent.

What distinguishes this era of repression is not just its technological sophistication but its *plausible deniability and normalized legality*. Under the guise of protecting "digital sovereignty" or "information hygiene," states routinely curtail fundamental rights—freedom of expression, association, and privacy—while claiming to uphold the rule of law. This double speak masks authoritarian practices in democratic rhetoric, rendering resistance more difficult and less visible to the broader public (UNHRC, 2018).

In sum, digital repression today is *multi-pronged, transnational, and deeply institutionalized*. It not only threatens the personal safety and privacy of activists but also undermines *democratic pluralism, public accountability, and civic engagement*. To confront this architecture of repression, civil society must advocate not only for *technological safeguards* and *legal reforms*, but also for a *reimagining of digital rights as fundamental human rights*—inseparable from the broader struggle for justice, transparency, and democratic governance.

Evolving Tactics of Digital Repression

1. Surveillance and Targeting

Governments now deploy sophisticated surveillance technologies—ranging from spyware and phishing to AI-driven facial recognition and social media analytics. High-profile tools like *NSO Group's Pegasus spyware* have enabled states to infiltrate smartphones, access encrypted messages, track locations, and record conversations of journalists, activists, and opposition leaders (Marczak et al., 2021). Such surveillance extends beyond intelligence-gathering; it serves as a tool of intimidation, mapping activist networks for further targeting and discrediting movements before they escalate.

2. Content Control and Manipulation

Internet censorship has evolved beyond brute-force website blocking. States increasingly use *Domain Name System (DNS) tampering, IP blocking, throttling, and algorithmic de-ranking* to suppress dissent. More insidiously, they deploy *pro-government trolls*, coordinated disinformation campaigns, and platform manipulation to drown out oppositional voices or distort narratives (Bradshaw & Howard, 2019). During political unrest, states often issue *blanket internet shutdowns*—as seen *in India's Jammu and Kashmir, Iran, Myanmar, and Ethiopia*—effectively silencing entire regions under the guise of "public order" (Access Now, 2023).

3. Transnational Repression

Digital repression increasingly *transcends borders*. Exiled dissidents, diaspora activists, and refugee journalists face *online harassment, cyberbullying, and threats to family members* in their home countries. States outsource digital surveillance to *"hack-for-hire" outfits*, targeting critical voices globally. For instance, Chinese, Russian, and Saudi governments have all been implicated in *harassing activists abroad* using social media threats and spyware tools (Freedom House, 2022).

4. Corporate Collaboration

The role of *telecom and social media companies* in enabling surveillance cannot be ignored. Through *data sharing agreements*, acquiescence to takedown orders, or opaque moderation policies, corporations often comply with state demands. The global export of surveillance tools—driven by private-sector innovation—has created a *security-industrial complex* wherein even less technologically advanced regimes gain access to cutting-edge surveillance capacities (Zuboff, 2019).

Impacts on Activism and Civil Society

1. Self-Censorship and Psychological Distress

The looming threat of surveillance produces a *chilling effect*. Activists become cautious in their communication, avoid sensitive topics, or withdraw from online platforms altogether to shield themselves or their communities. This *self-censorship* erodes the possibility of meaningful organizing and weakens the transformative potential of digital activism (Penney, 2017).

2. Curtailing Collective Action

Digital repression disrupts coordination. Fear of monitoring and reprisal deters activists from using mainstream platforms or digital tools. In several instances, activists have reported *curtailed online activities* when family or colleagues were threatened or arrested due to their digital footprints. This fragmentation weakens trust networks and reduces the effectiveness of transnational advocacy (Deibert, 2020).

3. Marginalization of Vulnerable Groups

Repression disproportionately affects already vulnerable communities—ethnic minorities, LGBTQ+ persons, migrants, and political dissidents. They are often targeted with *surveillance, smear campaigns, and cyberviolence*, compounding their social precarity. Moreover, *digital literacy gaps* make it difficult for these groups to protect themselves effectively from technological intrusions (UN Special Rapporteur, 2021).

Strategies of Circumvention and Resistance

In response to digital repression, activists employ a range of *circumvention strategies*—though often with limited reach or sustainability:

1. Privacy and Anonymity Tools

Virtual Private Networks (VPNs), encrypted messaging apps (e.g., Signal), the *Tor browser*, and secure cloud storage tools are used to bypass censorship and evade surveillance. However, *many governments have begun blocking VPNs*, and the effectiveness of these tools depends on digital literacy and technical capacity (Rydzak, 2020).

2. Tactical Adaptation

Activists adapt by switching platforms, using *coded language*, or organizing in closed, encrypted networks. These adaptations buy time but are insufficient against well-resourced state actors with access to bulk surveillance capabilities or platform cooperation (Treré, 2019).

3. International Advocacy

Human rights organizations and civil society coalitions are increasingly *demanding accountability* through naming-and-shaming reports, digital rights campaigns, and strategic litigation. Campaigns like *#KeepItOn* by Access Now have sought to challenge internet shutdowns through global pressure and legal mechanisms.

Censorship in Democratic Regimes: A Growing Paradox

The troubling rise of digital repression is not confined to authoritarian contexts. *Liberal democracies* have also employed *draconian cybercrime laws, anti-terror legislation, and national security arguments* to crack down on dissent. In India, social media users have faced sedition charges for tweets, while protest organizers have been booked under *Unlawful Activities (Prevention) Acts (UAPA)* for digital campaigns. The *Digital Security Act in Bangladesh* and similar laws in the Philippines and Egypt show how governments use lawfare to criminalize speech under digital pretexts (Article 19, 2021).

Such repression under democratic regimes *normalizes authoritarian tactics*, legitimizing surveillance and censorship in the name of public safety or national unity. This trend, termed *"digital authoritarianism"*, underscores the danger of unregulated digital power being co-opted by political interests (Feldstein, 2019).

The shift from analog to digital protest has not simply altered the tools of resistance—it has also transformed the *technologies of repression*. In today's cloud-based battleground, *repression is quieter, more precise, and algorithmically enforced.* Governments are no longer dependent on visible crackdowns when they can de-platform, de-rank, surveil, and intimidate from behind the screen.

This asymmetry between state power and activist defenses raises fundamental questions about *freedom, privacy, and accountability* in the digital age. To protect civil liberties, robust *legal safeguards, transparency in surveillance practices, global data protection frameworks*, and an empowered civil society are essential.

The fight for civil rights must now encompass *digital rights* as an integral frontier—recognizing that *repression in the cloud* is not the exception but an increasingly entrenched global norm.

Unless confronted with strategic resistance, surveillance and censorship risk becoming *default mechanisms of statecraft*, undermining the emancipatory promise of digital activism.

5. GRASSROOTS NARRATIVES AND THE POWER OF COLLECTIVE MEMORY

In the dynamic ecosystem of digital activism, storytelling is not merely communicative—it is a radical, political act. At the core of contemporary civil rights movements lies the power of grassroots narratives, which draw from personal testimony, local realities, and embodied experience to contest dominant discourses, disrupt state-sponsored historical narratives, and expose the systemic violence of structural inequalities. These stories—raw, situated, and unapologetically subjective—function as tools of resistance and truth-making, asserting the legitimacy of marginalized voices long excluded from institutional histories (Kaun & Uldam, 2018).

The digital age has transformed how such narratives are generated, circulated, and remembered. Smartphones, livestreams, microblogs, and social media platforms have enabled individuals from historically silenced communities to become archivists of their own resistance, shifting their role from passive subjects of representation to active curators of collective memory. A tribal woman livestreaming her forced eviction, a Dalit student narrating experiences of caste discrimination, or a young protestor documenting police brutality in real time are no longer isolated instances—they are nodes in a distributed memory network, forging solidarity and visibility across borders and generations.

This shift in narrative agency is not merely symbolic; it is strategic. It allows activists to preempt erasure, correct misrepresentation, and produce counter-histories that serve as enduring repositories of struggle and resilience. Unlike top-down media accounts shaped by institutional filters, grassroots digital storytelling is polyvocal and participatory, drawing strength from its ability to reflect the heterogeneity of lived experience while linking individual pain to collective injustice (Treré, 2019).

Furthermore, these digital narratives do more than resist—they build. They serve as scaffolding for memory-based movements, creating a continuity of resistance that survives repression, co-optation, and the ephemerality of media cycles. In doing so, they sustain intergenerational solidarity, connecting the legacies of past struggles to the urgencies of the present. The invocation of B. R. Ambedkar in caste abolition campaigns, or of Rosa Parks in anti-racism protests, illustrates how historical figures and past movements are reanimated through digitally mediated storytelling to ground present-day activism in a lineage of struggle.

Yet, this emergent power is not without vulnerability. The platformization of memory renders it susceptible to deletion, distortion, and algorithmic suppression. Content moderation policies, data loss, shadow banning, and de-platforming threaten the long-term durability of these counter-narratives. Thus, the preservation of grassroots memory in volatile digital environments requires intentional archiving practices, metadata curation, and the development of decentralized, open-source infrastructures that resist erasure (Hoskins, 2018).

Ultimately, grassroots digital storytelling is the lifeblood of democratic resistance in the digital age. It reclaims the act of remembering from institutional silos, embeds justice in the terrain of everyday experience, and constructs a living, breathing archive of dissent. In amplifying the testimonies of those at the margins, it not only reshapes how we remember, but also redefines who gets to be remembered—and on whose terms.

Digital Storytelling: From Individual Testimony to Collective Mobilization

Digital platforms have democratized the means of story production and dissemination. Platforms like YouTube, Instagram, TikTok, and X (formerly Twitter) allow individuals to document and narrate experiences in real time. A tribal woman livestreaming her eviction, a Dalit student exposing casteism on campus, or a protestor capturing police brutality on camera—these are not isolated events but digital acts of testimony that bypass traditional gatekeeping institutions and reach global audiences directly (Tufekci, 2017).

This immediacy enables real-time solidarity and visibility. For example, during the Black Lives Matter (BLM) protests, viral videos of George Floyd's killing and subsequent marches forced mainstream media to engage with the movement's framing of systemic racism, rather than impose their own narrative filters (Freelon et al., 2018). Similarly, the Shaheen Bagh protest in India, led primarily by Muslim women, gained national and international recognition through digital storytelling that reclaimed both space and speech in a context of increasing communal polarization (Roy, 2020).

These narratives do more than inform—they foster empathy, personalize complex socio-political issues, and catalyze collective action. In doing so, they serve as affective tools that bridge geographical, cultural, and linguistic divides, converting passive audiences into active allies (Papacharissi, 2015).

Building Digital Archives of Dissent

As stories accumulate online, they form decentralized repositories of resistance—a form of collective memory that challenges official historiographies. Hashtags, vlogs, blogs, podcasts, and archived livestreams act as digital monuments that preserve movements and their ideological underpinnings long after the street protests have ended.

For example, movements like Standing Rock's opposition to the Dakota Access Pipeline, Hong Kong's Umbrella Movement, and India's #FarmersProtest have all used digital storytelling to capture the lived experiences of protestors, document police excesses, and preserve indigenous or grassroots knowledge systems (Costanza-Chock, 2020). These archives enable activists to learn from past tactics, avoid earlier mistakes, and sustain momentum in the face of state repression.

Crucially, these repositories offer a counter-memory to state-sanctioned forgetting or distortion. In regimes where state-controlled media dominates, digital footprints act as witnesses of truth, resisting historical amnesia and providing future generations with authentic records of dissent (Hoskins, 2018).

Collective Memory and Intergenerational Resistance

Digital storytelling plays a critical role in linking contemporary struggles with historical legacies. Collective memory—when embedded in narratives—anchors present-day demands in the unfinished projects of earlier movements. This connection not only legitimizes current activism but provides ideological continuity and emotional depth.

For instance, references to Bhagat Singh in India's anti-farm law protests or the invocation of Martin Luther King Jr. in global racial justice campaigns are not mere symbols; they are strategic alignments that revive ideological ancestors to inspire, mobilize, and educate (Yates, 2018). Through memes, quotations, and retellings, these icons are recontextualized for contemporary audiences, helping to translate older paradigms of resistance into current frameworks of struggle.

This intergenerational bridging ensures that memory does not remain static but evolves with new insights, technologies, and contexts—deepening the political consciousness of each wave of activism.

Mobilizing Resources Through Narratives

Grassroots narratives also facilitate resource mobilization. Personal stories humanize causes and inspire contributions—whether emotional, logistical, or financial. Crowdfunding for legal defenses, bail funds, or protest logistics often relies on affective storytelling to galvanize support.

Campaigns such as #JusticeForAsifa in India or the bail fund initiatives during the George Floyd protests saw unprecedented public donations, mobilized primarily through viral storytelling and peer-to-peer sharing (Cammaerts, 2015). Here, storytelling transcends awareness to become an engine of tangible support, fostering networks of care and resistance that operate beyond institutional frameworks.

The Fragility of Digital Memory

Despite their potency, grassroots narratives face persistent risks in digital ecosystems. De-platforming, algorithmic suppression, trolling, and content manipulation threaten the integrity and longevity of activist storytelling. Digital stories—especially those critical of state or corporate power—can be deleted, shadow banned, or buried under disinformation.

Moreover, the ephemeral nature of social media and the rapid pace of digital consumption often lead to memory loss unless deliberate efforts are made to preserve and curate content. The dependency on commercial platforms for memory-keeping exposes activists to corporate censorship and technological obsolescence (Treré & Mattoni, 2020).

To counteract this fragility, activists have turned to open-source archiving, blockchain documentation, and decentralized repositories. Initiatives like the *Internet Archive*, *WikiLeaks*, or decentralized tools like *IPFS* offer alternatives to fragile, profit-driven platforms, reinforcing the role of digital memory as a public good.

In the digital age, grassroots narratives are not merely stories—they are infrastructures of resistance. They memorialize suffering, honor resilience, and provide blueprints for future dissent. These narratives democratize history-making, allowing the oppressed to not only testify but also to author their place in public memory.

Yet this power must be protected. The preservation, amplification, and institutionalization of grassroots narratives are essential not only for present advocacy but also for the future of civil rights historiography. Activists, scholars, and technologists must collaborate to ensure that the digital record remains intact, accessible, and accountable.

Ultimately, in an era where disinformation and erasure threaten truth itself, the storytelling of the oppressed is an act of survival—and a roadmap for liberation.

6. DIGITAL DISOBEDIENCE: ETHICAL DIMENSIONS OF ONLINE DISSENT

As digital technologies increasingly mediate social and political life, a new mode of resistance—*digital disobedience*—has emerged as a defining feature of contemporary activism. Rooted in the intellectual tradition of civil disobedience, digital disobedience involves a spectrum of technologically enabled protest actions, such as *DDoS attacks, data leaks, website defacement, and anti-censorship tool development*, designed to challenge authority, highlight injustice, or disrupt systems of power (Jordan & Taylor, 2004).

What distinguishes digital disobedience from its analog predecessors is not merely its tools but its context. These acts are *frequently anonymous, transnational, and decentralized*, leveraging global digital infrastructures to question authority in ways that often circumvent legal jurisdictions and traditional protest ethics. This shift raises *complex normative questions*: Can anonymous protest be morally justified? Is digital disruption a legitimate form of dissent? How should the ethics of resistance be adapted in an age of surveillance and platform governance?

Defining Digital Disobedience

Also referred to as *electronic civil disobedience (ECD)*, digital disobedience entails the deliberate use of digital technologies to resist or protest state or corporate power. These actions mirror the objectives of traditional civil disobedience—public engagement, consciousness-raising, and demands for justice—but take place in cyberspace through acts like:

- *Distributed Denial of Service (DDoS)* attacks aimed at rendering official websites inaccessible.
- *Website defacement*, which involves modifying the appearance or content of a webpage to communicate a political message.
- *Whistleblowing and leaks*, such as the disclosures made by Edward Snowden or WikiLeaks.
- *Anti-censorship tools*, such as Tor and VPNs, designed to bypass state surveillance or firewall restrictions (Denning, 2001; Lovink, 2002).

What complicates the ethical discourse is the *hybridity of digital space*: protests can be both performative and impactful, hidden yet global, lawful yet transgressive.

Philosophical Foundations and Ethical Tensions

The ethical analysis of civil disobedience is often grounded in *liberal political theory*, particularly the work of *John Rawls*. Rawls (1971) defined civil disobedience as a public, nonviolent, and conscientious act that seeks to bring about a change in laws or policies perceived as unjust, with the disobedient generally willing to accept legal consequences. This *Acceptance-of-Legal-Consequences Condition (ALCC)* is considered central to demonstrating respect for the rule of law and the legitimacy of one's dissent (Brownlee, 2012).

Digital disobedience, however, *complicates or rejects the ALCC*. Most actors operate anonymously, both to protect themselves from repression and to emphasize collective over individual action. In *authoritarian contexts*, demanding that digital dissenters reveal their identities may expose them to *harassment, imprisonment, or even death*. As Lovink (2002) and Sauter (2014) argue, *anonymity can be an ethical choice*, not a moral failing—it protects vulnerable individuals and allows resistance to flourish even under surveillance regimes.

Moreover, as digital actions blur the lines between local and global, public and private, the traditional standards for civil disobedience—such as transparency and acceptance of punishment—may *no longer be appropriate* or sufficient. The moral evaluation of digital dissent, therefore, requires a broader framework that prioritizes *intent, proportionality, nonviolence, and public engagement*, even in the absence of personal exposure.

Ethical Assessment of Digital Tactics

Digital disobedience encompasses a wide range of tactics, each carrying specific ethical considerations that must be evaluated through *principles of political philosophy, technology ethics, and human rights.*

1. DDoS Attacks

These are often described as the *digital equivalent of a sit-in*, temporarily disrupting access to websites as a form of protest. While *nonviolent*, they can cause significant inconvenience or economic loss, and may inadvertently affect third parties or essential services (Kleinig et al., 2011). The ethics of DDoS thus depend on *target selection*, *duration*, and *collateral impact*.

2. Website Defacement

Symbolically powerful, website defacement involves rewriting the digital message of a targeted institution. While it may serve as a form of *visual protest*, this tactic risks *misrepresenting the institution's actual message* or damaging reputational trust, especially when targeted indiscriminately.

3. Whistleblowing and Data Leaks

High-profile disclosures, such as those by *Edward Snowden* or *Chelsea Manning*, reveal gross abuses of power and systemic injustices. These actions align with classical principles of disobedience when motivated by *a sincere concern for justice* and undertaken with the intent to *inform the public* (Greenwald, 2014). However, *uncontrolled leaks* may also compromise individual privacy or national security, raising *delicate ethical dilemmas*.

4. Anti-Censorship Tools

Technologies such as *Tor* or *Signal* are widely regarded as *positive instruments* for protecting privacy and resisting digital authoritarianism. Their ethical standing is generally secure, though in some jurisdictions, their use may violate domestic laws designed to regulate speech or access to information (Deibert, 2020).

Evaluating Ethical Justifiability

To assess whether an act of digital disobedience is ethically justifiable, scholars propose several evaluative criteria (Brownlee, 2012; Sauter, 2014):

- **Proportionality**: Is the harm inflicted (e.g., downtime, embarrassment) proportionate to the injustice being opposed?
- **Intent**: Is the primary motivation public interest and justice, rather than disruption for its own sake?
- **Publicity**: Even if the actors remain anonymous, does the action engage public discourse or contribute to political awareness?
- **Accountability**: Is there an internal ethic within the movement to ensure responsible action, such as avoiding harm to innocents?

While some digital actions may fall into ethical ambiguity, many demonstrate *principled, conscientious resistance* to unjust systems.

As shown in Figure 2, the ethical dimensions of digital disobedience are multi-layered. They include conceptual definitions, methods and their moral implications, potential harms, and foundational philosophical tensions. This model helps assess the legitimacy of online dissent based on adherence to ethical standards.

Figure 2. Ethical dimensions of digital disobedience in online dissent. This conceptual diagram outlines key components of evaluating digital disobedience. It includes definitions (e.g., DDoS attacks, data leaks), ethical methods (like whistleblowing and anti-censorship tools), and moral concerns such as collateral harm, misuse of information, and privacy violations. It also highlights evaluative criteria—proportionality, intent, publicity, and accountability—grounded in philosophical theories, including Rawlsian justice and standards of anonymity in repressive contexts

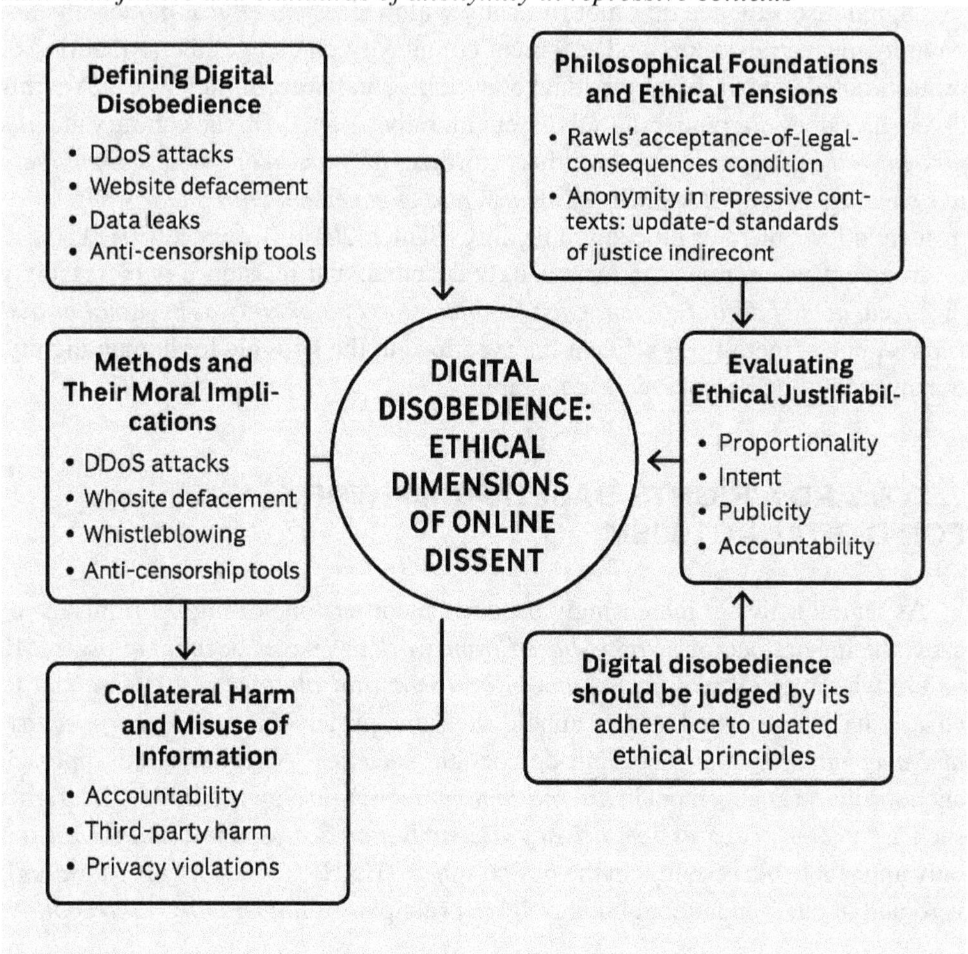

Collateral Damage and the Question of Harm

A recurring ethical tension in digital disobedience is the *risk of unintended harm*. DDoS attacks may unintentionally affect hospitals, schools, or small businesses using shared servers. Leaked data may expose confidential information unrelated to the protest's intent, violating personal privacy or placing individuals at risk (Denning, 2001; Tanczer et al., 2018). In such cases, the *moral calculus must weigh the consequences of action against both the severity of injustice opposed and the safeguards adopted* to protect third parties.

Digital activists are therefore increasingly urged to adopt a *"harm reduction" approach*, minimizing risk while maximizing political impact—a concept borrowed from both journalism and bioethics.

Digital disobedience does not fit neatly within classical ethical models. Its anonymity, decentralization, and technical complexity challenge liberal theories of protest rooted in visibility, individual conscience, and procedural fairness. Yet this divergence does not render digital dissent morally suspect. On the contrary, it *calls for a new ethical vocabulary*—one that prioritizes the *pursuit of justice*, *commitment to nonviolence*, *proportionality of means*, *and engagement with public conscience* over rigid formalism or procedural legality (Sauter, 2014; Brownlee, 2012).

In an era where power is increasingly encoded, and resistance is increasingly digitized, *acts of digital dissent must be understood not merely as criminal or disruptive*, but as morally significant interventions in the struggle for human dignity, transparency, and democratic accountability.

7. TOWARD A RIGHTS-BASED FRAMEWORK FOR DIGITAL ACTIVISM

As digital activism increasingly becomes a cornerstone of human rights advocacy, the imperative for a *rights-based framework* has never been more urgent. In an era where *social movements unfold across digital platforms*, it is essential to ensure that these virtual spaces uphold the same principles of *inclusivity*, *equity*, *and accountability* that underpin democratic societies. A rights-based approach anchors digital engagement in *international human rights law*, affirming that rights such as *freedom of expression*, *privacy*, *assembly*, *and access to information* are not only applicable but essential in the online sphere (UNHRC, 2018). This framework is rooted in the foundational human rights principles of *universality, indivisibility*, *and interdependence*, recognizing that digital rights are not distinct from human rights—they are an integral extension of them.

The transformative power of digital activism lies in its capacity to *democratize information*, bypass traditional media hierarchies, *amplify marginalized voices*, and facilitate *transnational solidarity*. Hashtag movements like *#MeToo*, *#BlackLivesMatter*, and *#FreePalestine* have shown how digital platforms can serve as arenas for truth-telling, community building, and structural challenge. These campaigns illustrate the *potential of digital tools to contest hegemonic narratives*, hold powerful institutions accountable, and forge new imaginaries of justice and equality.

Yet, digital activism also *operates within an ecosystem of contradictions*. Activists must navigate platforms that are simultaneously tools of liberation and instruments of control. *Surveillance, algorithmic bias, disinformation, harassment, censorship, and data exploitation* are pervasive risks that disproportionately impact those already marginalized in offline spaces (Zuboff, 2019; Feldstein, 2019). Without a rights-based framework, digital activism risks being co-opted, undermined, or silenced by the very technologies it seeks to harness for resistance.

A rights-based approach provides a *normative compass* for navigating these tensions. It demands that digital infrastructures are designed and governed in ways that promote *justice, dignity, participation, transparency, and accountability*. It calls for platform governance that respects due process, user agency, and democratic oversight; for policies that mitigate algorithmic discrimination and surveillance harm; and for mechanisms that ensure *remedy and redress* when digital rights are violated (UNESCO, 2022).

In this vision, *digital inclusion is not just about access to technology*, but about the ability to use it *safely, meaningfully, and with full protection of one's rights*. A rights-based digital environment empowers communities to speak, organize, and remember without fear—transforming the internet from a site of extraction and exclusion into one of empowerment and equity.

Core Principles of a Rights-Based Framework

1. **Universality and Non-Discrimination** Digital rights must be extended to all, regardless of gender, race, geography, disability, or economic status. Bridging the **digital divide** through infrastructure, access, and digital literacy is central to this principle (Cohen-Almagor, 2011).
2. **Freedom of Expression and Access to Information** The ability to speak freely and access uncensored, diverse information is a foundational right. Governments and tech companies must avoid **arbitrary censorship, algorithmic suppression**, and opaque moderation. Policies should uphold human rights standards and allow for **independent oversight** (ARTICLE 19, 2021).

3. **Privacy and Security** Given the heightened risks faced by digital activists, strong data protection laws and secure digital environments are essential. Encryption, anonymization, and whistleblower protections are vital for defending **freedom of expression and association** (Zuboff, 2019).
4. **Accountability and Remedy** Users should have the right to contest digital rights violations—be they from governments or tech firms. **Grievance mechanisms, judicial recourse, and transparent policy enforcement** are necessary to uphold this pillar (UNESCO, 2022).
5. **Inclusive and Participatory Governance** Digital governance must involve **multi-stakeholder participation**, including civil society, grassroots actors, and vulnerable communities. Decision-making should be transparent and aimed at decentralizing power (MacKinnon, 2012).

Challenges in Realizing Digital Rights

1. State and Corporate Overreach

Governments increasingly deploy digital tools for control—through *internet shutdowns, surveillance, and punitive legislation*. Simultaneously, tech giants wield enormous power through *data monopolies and unaccountable algorithms*, creating a private-public repression nexus (Feldstein, 2019).

2. Digital Divide and Exclusion

Structural inequities persist in access to internet, hardware, and digital education. Without *targeted inclusion policies*, digital activism may inadvertently replicate offline hierarchies (Gurumurthy & Chami, 2020).

3. Misinformation and Harmful Content

Viral disinformation and hate speech threaten both activists and movements. Content moderation, though necessary, must not infringe upon legitimate dissent, necessitating *balanced and rights-based regulation* (Mozilla Foundation, 2021).

4. Safety and Wellbeing of Activists

The psychological toll of *harassment, doxxing, and cyberbullying* disproportionately affects women, LGBTQ+ persons, and human rights defenders. Mental health support and online safety protocols must be integrated into digital rights strategies (Tanczer et al., 2018).

Policy Recommendations and Best Practices

- **Enshrine Human Rights in National Digital Policies**

Explicit legal commitments to protect digital expression, privacy, and inclusion should guide tech governance.

- **Ensure Multi-Stakeholder Decision-Making**

Civil society, affected users, and marginalized communities must shape platform regulation and international norms.

- **Promote Ethical Tech Design**

Open-source platforms, inclusive interface design, and accountability in AI deployment can realign technology with democratic values.

- **Strengthen Digital Literacy and Empowerment**

Equipping users with knowledge about rights, risks, and tools enhances resilience and fosters informed participation.

- **Create Independent Oversight Mechanisms**

Regulatory and judicial bodies must provide accessible remedies and monitor compliance with digital rights obligations.

A *rights-based framework for digital activism* is not just a normative ideal; it is an urgent necessity for preserving democratic engagement in the digital age. By grounding activism in the values of *universality, equity, participation, and dignity*, such a framework ensures that digital spaces remain arenas of *empowerment, not oppression.*

The creation of a just digital ecosystem requires *collaborative effort across sectors*—governments, tech firms, civil society, international institutions, and digital communities. It demands that *online rights be treated as fundamental human rights*, not secondary or negotiable privileges. Only by embedding these principles into the *design, governance, and practice* of digital systems can we safeguard the future of civic resistance, truth-telling, and social transformation in a networked world.

8. CONCLUSION: RETHINKING CIVIL RIGHTS IN THE AGE OF VIRAL DISSENT

The digital age has irrevocably reshaped the architecture of civil rights activism. What once centered on *physical gatherings, leaflets, courtroom advocacy, and televised appeals* has evolved into a complex ecosystem where *resistance unfolds across both physical streets and virtual servers*. This convergence of the corporeal and the coded has created an entirely new paradigm for dissent—one where *resistance becomes viral, memory is stored in metadata, and civil rights are negotiated through algorithms and interfaces*.

Throughout this chapter, we have examined how *social movements are adapting to the digital environment*, appropriating its tools, reconfiguring its spaces, and resisting its limitations. Movements like *#BlackLivesMatter, #MeToo, and #FarmersProtest* exemplify how hashtags have evolved into *symbolic infrastructure*—they are not just means of communication but *vocabularies of resistance*, repositories of collective trauma, and markers of historical turning points (Jackson et al., 2020). These digital markers enable *distributed actors—across borders, languages, and identities—to align, mobilize, and agitate* for justice beyond the limitations of conventional organizing.

However, the expansion of opportunities has occurred alongside a *rapid entrenchment of control mechanisms*. The very platforms that once democratized voice are now surveilled, monetized, and filtered by *algorithmic curation, opaque moderation policies, and state-corporate surveillance regimes*. As Gillespie (2018) argues, the politics of digital visibility are embedded in code, privileging engagement metrics over nuance, sensationalism over substance. Zuboff (2019) further warns of a *"surveillance capitalism"* that thrives on behavioral data extraction, turning user expression into a resource for commodification and manipulation. In this environment, *who is heard, what is seen, and what becomes politically actionable is no longer determined democratically, but algorithmically*.

In response, *digital disobedience* has emerged as a morally urgent and ethically complex strategy. Practices such as *DDoS attacks, whistleblowing, data leaks, and encryption-based organizing* challenge both technical architectures and normative assumptions about legitimate protest. Unlike classical civil disobedience, which demanded visibility, personal risk, and public accountability, *digital disobedience often embraces anonymity, decentralization, and disruption*—especially in repressive regimes where public protest can result in violence or imprisonment (Sauter, 2014; Brownlee, 2012). In such contexts, *anonymity is not cowardice—it is survival*, and legality is not the same as justice.

Nevertheless, the use of digital tools for activism is not without ethical pitfalls. The *fragility of digital memory*, the potential for *collateral harm*, and the prevalence of *misinformation* can undermine the credibility and longevity of movements. Moreover, unequal access to digital infrastructure and literacy exacerbates existing *social and geopolitical inequalities*, creating a hierarchy of participation that mirrors the offline world. In light of these tensions, we have argued for a *rights-based framework that centers freedom of expression, privacy, security, inclusivity, and remedy* (UNHRC, 2018; UNESCO, 2022). This framework is essential not only to protect activists but to *institutionalize norms of transparency, accountability, and democratic participation in digital governance.*

To *rethink civil rights in the digital era*, we must recognize that *"code is law" (Lessig, 2006), platforms are the new public squares, and data is both a resource and a weapon.* Censorship today may not take the form of police batons or confiscated newspapers, but of *shadow bans, algorithmic throttling, and strategic demonetization.* Solidarity is no longer built only in union halls or on protest routes, but through *encrypted group chats, crowdsourced legal defense funds, and shared digital archives.* Resistance can now be encoded, streamed, or hashtagged—but it must also be understood as historically and ethically continuous with earlier civil rights struggles.

If the 20th-century fight for civil rights was animated by the imagery of *marches on Washington, courtroom showdowns, and hunger strikes*, the 21st-century struggle is being etched into *livestreams, digital breadcrumbs, platform protests, and viral threads.* But the underlying questions endure:

- Who gets to speak?
- Who is heard?
- Whose narratives are legitimized, and whose are erased?
- How do we remember—and whose memory survives?

To ensure that digital activism becomes a *vehicle for justice rather than a tool for deeper inequity*, we must design and defend *a digital ecosystem grounded in ethical principles, democratic values, and shared responsibility.* This requires collaboration across domains: *activists, academics, technologists, journalists, legal experts, and policymakers* must work collectively to uphold a vision of the internet as a *commons—not a corporate territory or surveillance trap.*

Ultimately, in a world where *dissent can be algorithmically suppressed as easily as it can go viral*, our challenge is to preserve the *emancipatory promise of digital activism* while interrogating its limitations and confronting its contradictions. We must strive for a *resistance that is not only reactive but visionary*, not only ethical but transformative—rooted in solidarity, shaped by justice, and made resilient through collective memory.

REFERENCES

Abidin, C. (2021). TikTok and youth activism. *Social Media + Society*, *7*(2), 1–3. DOI: 10.1177/20563051211033801

Access Now. (2023). *#KeepItOn Internet shutdowns 2022 report*. https://www.accessnow.org/keepiton

ARTICLE 19. (2021). *The human rights-based approach to content moderation*. https://www.article19.org

Bradshaw, S., & Howard, P. N. (2019). *The global disinformation order: 2019 global inventory of organized social media manipulation*. Oxford Internet Institute., DOI: 10.2139/ssrn.3503910

Brownlee, K. (2012). *Conscience and conviction: The case for civil disobedience*. Oxford University Press. DOI: 10.1093/acprof:oso/9780199592944.001.0001

Cammaerts, B. (2015). Technologies of self-mediation: Affordance and constraints of social media for protest movements. *Information Communication and Society*, *18*(8), 968–986. DOI: 10.1080/1369118X.2015.1043314

Chakravartty, P., & Roy, S. (2020). Media, inequality and change in India: Challenging hegemony with digital tools. *The Journal of Communication Inquiry*, *44*(2), 119–136. DOI: 10.1177/0196859919897981

Cohen-Almagor, R. (2011). *Speech, media and ethics: The limits of free expression*. Palgrave Macmillan.

Costanza-Chock, S. (2020). *Design justice: Community-led practices to build the worlds we need*. MIT Press. DOI: 10.7551/mitpress/12255.001.0001

Deibert, R. (2020). *Reset: Reclaiming the internet for civil society*. House of Anansi.

Denning, D. E. (2001). Activism, hacktivism, and cyberterrorism: The Internet as a tool for influencing foreign policy. In Arquilla, J., & Ronfeldt, D. (Eds.), *Networks and netwars: The future of terror, crime, and militancy* (pp. 239–288). RAND Corporation.

Feldstein, S. (2019). The rise of digital repression. *Journal of Democracy*, *30*(1), 40–52. DOI: 10.1353/jod.2019.0003

Freedom House. (2022). *Freedom on the net 2022: Countering an authoritarian overhaul of the internet*. https://freedomhouse.org/report/freedom-net/2022

Freelon, D., McIlwain, C. D., & Clark, M. D. (2018). *Beyond the hashtags: #Ferguson, #BlackLivesMatter, and the online struggle for offline justice*. Oxford University Press.

Gill, R., & Orgad, S. (2018). The amazing bounce-backable woman: Resilience and the psychological turn in neoliberalism. *Sociological Research Online*, *23*(2), 477–495. DOI: 10.1177/1360780418769673

Gillespie, T. (2018). *Custodians of the internet: Platforms, content moderation, and the hidden decisions that shape social media*. Yale University Press.

Greenwald, G. (2014). *No place to hide: Edward Snowden, the NSA, and the U.S. surveillance state*. Metropolitan Books.

Gurumurthy, A., & Chami, N. (2020). *Digital rights and inclusion in Asia: A report by IT for Change*. https://itforchange.net/digital-rights-inclusion

Hoskins, A. (2018). *Memory ecologies: Media, memory and the dynamic archive*. Routledge.

Howard, P. N., & Hussain, M. M. (2013). *Democracy's fourth wave? Digital media and the Arab Spring*. Oxford University Press. DOI: 10.1093/acprof:oso/9780199936953.001.0001

Jackson, S. J., Bailey, M., & Welles, B. F. (2020). *HashtagActivism: Networks of race and gender justice*. MIT Press. DOI: 10.7551/mitpress/10858.001.0001

Jordan, T., & Taylor, P. (2004). *Hacktivism and cyberwars: Rebels with a cause?* Routledge. DOI: 10.4324/9780203490037

Kaun, A., & Uldam, J. (2018). Digital activism: After the hype. *New Media & Society*, *20*(6), 2099–2106. DOI: 10.1177/1461444817731924

Kleinig, J.. (2011). Ethical issues in cyber warfare. In Bayles, J., & DeSouza, P. R. (Eds.), *Cybersecurity and cyberwar: What everyone needs to know*. Oxford University Press.

Lovink, G. (2002). *Dark fiber: Tracking critical internet culture*. MIT Press. DOI: 10.7551/mitpress/2272.001.0001

MacKinnon, R. (2012). *Consent of the networked: The worldwide struggle for internet freedom*. Basic Books.

Marczak, B., Scott-Railton, J., McKune, S., Abdul Razzak, B., & Deibert, R. (2021). *The Pegasus project: Exposing global surveillance*. The Citizen Lab. https://citizenlab.ca

Mozilla Foundation. (2021). *YouTube regrets: Crowdsourced evidence of harm*. https://foundation.mozilla.org/en/campaigns/youtube-regrets/

Noble, S. U. (2018). *Algorithms of oppression: How search engines reinforce racism*. NYU Press. DOI: 10.18574/nyu/9781479833641.001.0001

Papacharissi, Z. (2015). *Affective publics: Sentiment, technology, and politics*. Oxford University Press.

Penney, J. (2017). Chilling effects: Online surveillance and Wikipedia use. *Berkeley Technology Law Journal*, *31*(1), 117–182.

Rawls, J. (1971). *A theory of justice*. Harvard University Press. DOI: 10.4159/9780674042605

Roy, S. (2020). The Shaheen Bagh protests and the ideas of secularism. *Economic and Political Weekly*, *55*(8), 8–12.

Rydzak, J. (2020). *Of blackouts and bandhs: The strategy and structure of India's internet shutdowns*. Stanford Global Digital Policy Incubator.

Sauter, M. (2014). *The coming swarm: DDOS actions, hacktivism, and civil disobedience on the Internet*. Bloomsbury. DOI: 10.5040/9781628926705

Tanczer, L. M., Lopez-Neira, I., & Rashid, A. (2018). *Technologically-facilitated abuse: National scoping report*. University College London.

Treré, E. (2019). *Hybrid media activism: Ecologies, imaginaries, algorithms*. Routledge.

Treré, E., & Mattoni, A. (2020). Media ecologies and protest movements. *Social Movement Studies*, *19*(2), 133–144. DOI: 10.1080/14742837.2018.1555752

Tufekci, Z. (2017). *Twitter and tear gas: The power and fragility of networked protest*. Yale University Press.

UNESCO. (2022). *Guidelines for regulating digital platforms: A multistakeholder approach to safeguard freedom of expression and access to information*. https://unesdoc.unesco.org

UNHRC. (2018). Report on the promotion and protection of the right to freedom of opinion and expression (Vol. A). United Nations Human Rights Council., HRC/38/35.

Venturini, T. (2019). From fake to junk news: The data politics of online virality. *Digital Journalism (Abingdon, England)*, *7*(4), 532–540. DOI: 10.1080/21670811.2019.1591927

Yates, L. (2018). Rethinking prefiguration: Alternatives, micropolitics and goals in social movements. *Social Movement Studies*, *17*(1), 1–21. DOI: 10.1080/14742837.2013.870883

Zuboff, S. (2019). *The age of surveillance capitalism: The fight for a human future at the new frontier of power*. PublicAffairs.

Chapter 7
Safeguarding Prisoner's Human Rights in the Age of Surveillance and AI:
Digital Shackles

Kanisha Pathak
https://orcid.org/0009-0000-1580-0957
Gujarat National Law University, Gandhinagar, India

ABSTRACT

The implementation of AI and surveillance systems in prisons has transformed operations, offering security and operational benefits while raising concerns about prisoner rights and mental health. This research evaluates the impact of AI surveillance on privacy, autonomy, and the ethical, legal, and psychological effects on prisoners. Continuous monitoring increases anxiety, stress, and diminishes control. It also examines human rights issues when AI influences parole, recidivism, and behavior predictions, noting the criticism of AI for racial and socio-economic biases. The study compares the approaches of the US, China, UK, and EU, highlighting rapid adoption in the US and China with privacy violations and discrimination. The EU and UK maintain more reserved approaches, emphasizing privacy. The paper recommends ethical AI usage in prisons, advocating for transparency, accountability, audits, and international collaboration to ensure responsible implementation and respect for prisoner rights.

DOI: 10.4018/979-8-3693-3920-6.ch007

INTRODUCTION

The implementation of artificial intelligence (AI) systems with surveillance technology in prisons transforms criminal justice operations through enhanced security measures and operational efficiency. The implementation of these advancements creates major difficulties because they threaten prisoners' fundamental human rights including privacy and dignity and autonomy. The growing use of surveillance technology combined with AI decision-making systems leads to rising concerns about potential misuse which threatens basic human rights in prison settings. AI surveillance systems help solve prison overcrowding and violence issues but their implementation risks perpetuating social injustices when proper oversight is absent. The paper examines the relationship between surveillance technology and artificial intelligence systems and their impact on prisoner human rights through an analysis of ethical and legal and psychological aspects. The implementation of AI technologies including facial recognition and predictive algorithms and behavior monitoring systems could enhance prison operations but creates substantial concerns about privacy violations and consent issues and accountability standards. Security needs to be maintained while protecting the basic rights of inmates particularly those who belong to vulnerable population. Worldwide correctional facilities implement surveillance and AI technologies because they want to improve security and operational efficiency. The Bureau of Justice Statistics (2018) shows that more than 70% of U.S. correctional facilities implement electronic surveillance systems through cameras and AI-driven technologies for inmate monitoring. The technologies serve security needs while simultaneously providing predictive analytics tools for both risk assessment of recidivism and parole qualification evaluation. Several regions use facial recognition technology together with AI systems to track inmate movements through real-time activity monitoring. These technological advancements create better prison safety yet they generate crucial problems regarding prisoner privacy rights along with their dignity. The Universal Declaration of Human Rights (UDHR) (1948) includes provisions that safeguard privacy rights and freedom from unjustified intrusion but lacks clear guidelines about AI application in prisons. The International Covenant on Civil and Political Rights (ICCPR) (1966) provides protections for privacy and bans inhumane treatment but fails to specifically address the rights regarding prison surveillance systems. The current legal framework lacks sufficient protection of prisoner rights because it does not address this specific issue. The essential implementation of surveillance and AI technologies in worldwide prisons demands thorough examination of their ethical dimensions and legal and psychological effects. This research investigates the possibility of using AI in prisons while protecting fundamental prisoner rights and presents approaches to adapt current human rights laws for these new technologies. The paper investigates the necessary legal changes for responsible AI deployment in correctional institutions as well as studying the psychological impact of continuous monitoring on prisoners. Prisons have maintained controlled status since their inception but AI and digital surveillance technologies establish a fresh direction. Physical surveillance through guards and watchtowers used to be the main method of supervision in traditional prisons. Through AI-powered automated monitoring systems prisons can perform real-time behavioral predictions of inmates. Modern prison management technologies hold transformative potential yet require thorough risk assessment to protect prisoner rights from infringement. The implementation of legal and ethical guidelines is required to maintain human dignity in these technologies.

The use of AI and surveillance systems to combat prison overcrowding and violence and escape attempts is supported by some people. The use of surveillance and AI without proper oversight has raised increasing worries about potential rights violations and abuse. The use of AI systems to evaluate recidivism and parole eligibility has been criticized for perpetuating racial and socioeconomic biases which disproportionately affect people of color and low-income individuals (Angwin et al., 2016). Such biases could undermine fairness and equality in the justice system.

The psychological effects of permanent monitoring on prisoners represent a significant ethical issue. Research indicates that ongoing surveillance produces feelings of powerlessness together with anxiety and depression which disrupts rehabilitation efforts and intensifies mental health problems (Graham, 2017). The ethical assessment of AI-based behavioral monitoring systems requires thorough evaluation because it needs to protect security requirements while upholding human dignity. The worldwide regulations regarding prison surveillance and AI implementation differ substantially between nations. The Fourth Amendment in the U.S. provides limited protection against unreasonable searches and seizures yet the Supreme Court has established that prisoners maintain reduced privacy expectations which enables extensive surveillance without violating constitutional rights. European countries enforce stronger privacy protections through the European Convention on Human Rights (ECHR) which results in strict monitoring of prison surveillance operations (Wright v. the United Kingdom, 2003). The General Data Protection Regulation (GDPR) established by the European Union provides guidelines for personal data management which could be applied to prison surveillance systems. The speed of technological progress typically outpaces existing legal frameworks which creates protection gaps for prisoners.

The increasing use of digital surveillance and AI in prison management requires evaluation of international human rights standards for these technologies. The Nelson Mandela Rules (2015) established guidelines for prisoner treatment but fail to address the problems that digital surveillance and AI create. The absence of global standards for emerging technologies that affect prisoner rights demonstrates the necessity for new guidelines. The article advocates for developing a complete legal and ethical framework to govern prison AI systems and surveillance technologies which protect prisoner rights without compromising prison security. The framework must establish clear standards of transparency and accountability and fairness to ensure responsible technology use which protects vulnerable populations from disproportionate harm. The psychological impacts of surveillance need evaluation to stop causing avoidable damage to prisoner mental health. The development of global standards for prison AI and surveillance requires governments to work with human rights organizations and technology developers. The standards need to guarantee that technology applications remain transparent and accountable while preserving prisoner rights. Security and human rights can be balanced in the digital age through appropriate regulation and oversight and psychological effect assessments.

LEGAL AND ETHICAL IMPLICATIONS OF SURVEILLANCE AND AI IN PRISONS

The implementation of AI surveillance systems in prisons creates multiple complex legal and ethical problems. The fundamental problems stem from the human rights protections prisoners should receive especially their right to privacy. The controlled nature of prisons does not justify the growing implementation of AI and real-time surveillance systems because these practices create significant ethical problems. Security requirements must be balanced against individual rights which include privacy together with autonomy and dignity. The Universal Declaration of Human Rights (UDHR) and International Covenant on Civil and Political Rights (ICCPR) protect privacy rights yet these rights encounter obstacles when applied to prison settings.

Figure 1. Global adoption rates of AI and surveillance technologies in correctional facilities

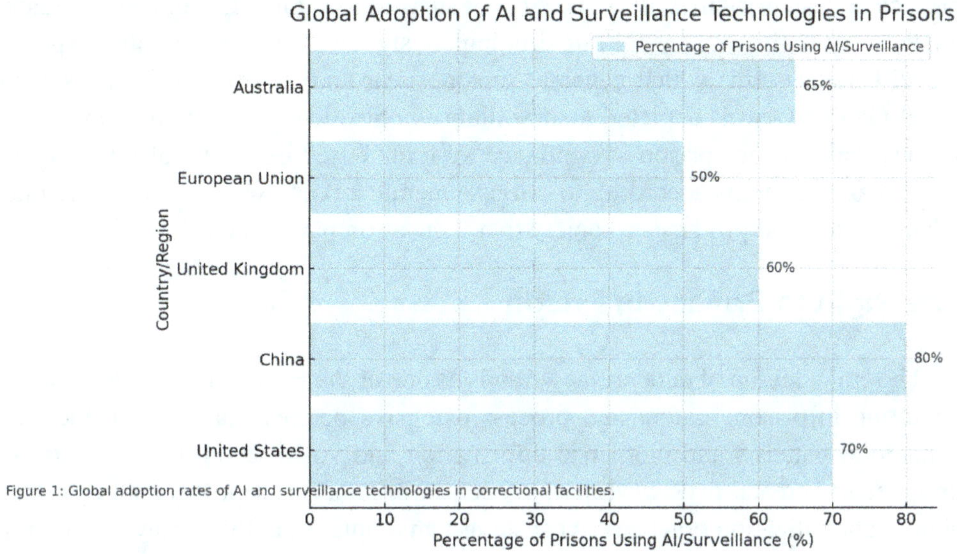

The graph shows that Figure 1 demonstrates how AI and surveillance technology adoption spreads throughout correctional facilities worldwide. Privacy rights in prisons remain a topic of intense public debate. According to Article 17 of the ICCPR prisoners have protection against arbitrary privacy interference but security and public safety and criminal prevention exceptions apply. The amount of surveillance which qualifies as acceptable remains uncertain especially when AI-powered systems could result in persistent monitoring that may cause psychological distress to prisoners. The legal precedent of Hudson v. The U.S. Supreme Court established the conflict between privacy rights and security needs in its 1984 decision of Palmer v. Palmer (1984). During this case the Supreme Court of the United States established that prisoners possess diminished privacy rights so authorities can conduct searches and surveillance activities without infringing on their rights. In the case of Wright v. The European Court of Human Rights (ECHR) ruled in Wright v. the United Kingdom (2003) that surveillance practices must protect prisoner dignity and privacy. Surveillance operations according to the ECHR need to stay proportionate while avoiding excessive measures. AI systems used in prisons create ethical problems which extend beyond their surveillance functions. AI-based systems which predict parole eligibility or assess recidivism risk potentially create biased results that lead to discriminatory decisions. The COMPAS system used for recidivism risk assessment has received criticism because it produces disproportionate effects on minority populations. The lack of transparency in AI evaluations combined with prisoners' inability to contest these decisions creates fairness and accountability issues. The core moral problem lies in determining an appropriate balance between privacy and security measures. The use of surveillance for safety purposes creates a necessary security measure but simultaneously develops prisons into perpetual surveillance systems which generate prisoner fear and strict control. In his 1984 novel George Orwell depicted a surveillance-controlled society that shares similarities with current prison surveillance systems based on artificial intelligence. Surveillance systems according to critics generate anxiety which hinders prisoner rehabilitation and produces a society that focuses on punishment.

The Right to Privacy in Prison

The ethical issue of data privacy stands as one of the main concerns. AI systems operating in prisons gather and process extensive personal data which includes behavioral patterns and biometric information and voice recordings. The use of prisoner data creates privacy violations because prisoners lack proper understanding about data utilization practices. AI systems can unintentionally display social prejudices which produce discriminatory choices that impact marginalized populations unfairly. The right to rehabilitation is also at risk. Prisons need to provide society reintegration opportunities but AI-driven decisions together with excessive surveillance systems create barriers for this process. The ongoing observation of prisoners leads to increased stress levels which separates them from rehabilitation programs. The increasing global use of AI and surveillance technologies in prisons requires finding an equilibrium that defends prisoner rights alongside security needs. Legal frameworks need to be established to guarantee transparency and accountability and fairness in AI applications. The frameworks need to establish protective measures for prisoner data privacy while preventing biased outcomes. The implementation of independent bodies for auditing AI systems becomes necessary to verify fairness in decisions about parole and sentencing and rehabilitation. The design of policies should focus on minimizing psychological damage from continuous observation to preserve inmate dignity and mental health.

Psychological and Human Rights Implications of Surveillance and AI in Prisons

The implementation of artificial intelligence (AI) and surveillance technologies in prison systems aims to enhance security and operational efficiency and decrease violence inside correctional facilities. The implementation of these technological advancements creates major psychological risks for prisoners together with potential violations of their fundamental human rights. The implementation of surveillance tools including CCTV and facial recognition systems and AI analytics systems has the unintended effect of causing psychological damage to prisoners while eroding their autonomy and privacy rights. The increasing extent of monitoring systems creates a rising danger to the personal dignity and rights of people who are incarcerated. This section examines the psychological effects and human rights implications of these developments while analyzing their potential harm to prisoners and their ethical and legal implications.

Psychological Impact of Surveillance in Prisons

Prison environments experience extensive surveillance that results in continuous monitoring of inmates. According to philosopher Jeremy Bentham the “Panopticon effect” describes a monitoring system which makes prisoners aware they could face observation anytime. The traditional practice of prison surveillance underwent significant intensification through the implementation of modern digital and AI technologies.

The ongoing observation of inmates results in extreme psychological problems as shown by research findings. The primary effect of continuous surveillance on prisoners leads to increased anxiety and stress levels. The combination of perpetual observation and immediate punishment threats generates intense prisoner anxiety and distress according to Graham (2017). Inmates who already have mental health conditions develop psychological distress because of the panoptic effect that occurs under this surveillance condition. According to Foucault (1975) surveillance systems function through a control mechanism which causes individuals to control their behavior because they fear detection. Prisoners experience continuous monitoring throughout the day while facing both a lack of consent and unclear understanding of the surveillance process. The extended presence of surveillance systems produces more than anxiety since it generates feelings of powerlessness and social isolation and destroys personal independence. Continuous observation of prisoners creates a psychological strain because it leads to their dehumanization. Prisoners experience heightened despair because they see both the inevitability and the lack of responsibility within the surveillance systems that watch them permanently (Foucault, 1975). The diminished autonomy affects rehabilitation and societal reintegration because it worsens depression along with aggression and paranoia in prisoners. The absence of transparency and accountability in AI-driven surveillance systems increases the negative psychological impacts on prisoners. Prisoners face complete understanding and challenge barriers when using AI systems for recidivism prediction and parole eligibility determination because these systems operate with transparency. A prisoner's evaluation process through an untraceable system creates feelings of mistrust and emotional distress because they remain disconnected from the system.

Human Rights Implications of Surveillance and AI

The deployment of surveillance technologies and artificial intelligence systems across prisons generates multiple serious threats to human rights. A major challenge arises from the violation of privacy rights which forms a core human right that international law protects. International legal documents including the Universal Declaration of Human Rights (1948) and the International Covenant on Civil and Political Rights (1966) defend privacy rights while securing individuals from unauthorised interference with their personal life and family and home and correspondence. These rights experience limitations because interference that serves national security and crime prevention goals is exempt from protection. The question of how much prisoners lose their right to privacy when confined remains a matter of argument among legal experts. Although prisons impose limited privacy restrictions due to their incarceration environment the international community acknowledges that inmates deserve rights protection from invasive and excessive surveillance practices that diminish their dignity along with personal autonomy. According to European Court of Human Rights decisions prison surveillance systems require a proper equilibrium between prisoner safety and prisoner privacy rights. The European Court of Human Rights declared in Wright v. United Kingdom (2003) that surveillance systems require preservation of prisoner dignity and autonomy even when maintaining order and safety demands their use. The court decision demonstrates that human rights should never be sacrificed for security measures. AI-based assessments for parole eligibility combined with recidivism prediction create fresh ethical and human rights problems. AI risk assessment systems that predict offender recidivism tend to reinforce existing biases from training data including racial and socioeconomic biases. The COMPAS system used by U.S. authorities to evaluate recidivism risk displayed racial bias because it labeled African American defendants as high-risk offenders even though they did not warrant such assessment according to Angwin et al. (2016). Such biases violate the principles of fairness and equality while harming predominantly marginalized communities through their discriminatory effects. The usage of untraceable AI systems leads to unjust outcomes which violate prisoners' entitlement to fair judicial procedures along with their right to procedural justice. Informed consent stands as a significant challenge. Prisoners normally lack understanding about surveillance technology monitoring systems in their facilities since they cannot provide consent or challenge these monitoring systems. These human rights violations become more severe because there is no transparency or accountability system in place. The right to receive information and take part in life-changing decisions remains fundamental and prisons must not disregard this right

International Legal Frameworks and Protections

International human rights law provides some level of protection for prisoners' rights regarding surveillance and AI but these protections remain insufficient and vague because of the fast pace of technological development. The Nelson Mandela Rules (2015) under the United Nations Standard Minimum Rules for the Treatment of Prisoners emphasize prisoner dignity and respect while requiring surveillance practices to uphold human rights. The rules establish fundamental principles which protect prisoners from rights violations by technological systems even though they do not directly address AI or digital surveillance. The International Covenant on Civil and Political Rights (ICCPR, 1966) extends its protection to privacy rights and freedom from unauthorized personal life interference. The ICCPR along with the Nelson Mandela Rules fail to provide explicit guidelines about AI and prison surveillance systems. The European Convention on Human Rights (ECHR) includes Article 8 which protects private and family life rights but lacks specific guidance about AI and digital surveillance in correctional facilities. The European Union's General Data Protection Regulation (GDPR) provides certain data privacy protections mainly for personal data collection and processing activities. The GDPR does not extend its protections to prisoners while its ability to handle the distinct challenges of prison AI and surveillance systems remains unclear. International frameworks provide limited protection against the particular legal and ethical problems that AI and surveillance technologies create in prison settings. The world needs new complete international standards that will protect prisoner rights specifically in relation to these technologies.

The Psychological and Ethical Effects of AI and Surveillance on Prisoners

The implementation of AI surveillance systems within prisons creates substantial psychological impacts on inmates. The permanent awareness of observation creates stress which leads to anxiety while stripping prisoners of their sense of control. (Graham,2017) demonstrates how surveillance systems prevent rehabilitation because they dehumanize prisoners and create feelings of alienation. The combination of lost autonomy with continuous monitoring creates long-term psychological damage that results in depression and paranoia. The implementation of AI systems in prisons generates multiple ethical issues. AI systems which predict behaviors and assess recidivism rates create multiple ethical problems regarding their fairness and accuracy and potential biases. These systems base their operations on historical data which might perpetuate existing inequalities throughout the criminal justice system. AI systems that determine prisoner life outcomes through unaccountable processes create major ethical problems regarding justice and human rights. The global implementation of AI and surveillance technologies in prisons requires immediate examination of their effects on psychological well-being and human rights standards. The security and operational benefits of these technologies come with substantial risks that threaten prisoners' privacy and autonomy and their dignity. The digital age requires legal frameworks to evolve into better protections for prisoners' rights while surveillance effects on mental health need assessment. The protection of prisoners' rights demands the implementation of oversight systems alongside transparent AI decision processes and ethical standards that promote fairness and equality and maintain human dignity.

Global Scenario and Best Practices in the Use of Surveillance and AI in Prisons

The implementation of surveillance technologies and artificial intelligence (AI) in prisons continues to expand globally because each nation implements these systems according to its specific legal framework and ethical and political considerations. The United States and China have rapidly adopted these technologies to monitor prison populations but European Union member states have maintained a more reserved approach by focusing on privacy and human rights protection. This section examines the worldwide deployment of AI and surveillance systems in prisons through diverse implementation methods and successful approaches and best practices that other countries can use as references. The increasing deployment of AI and surveillance technologies in prison systems requires security measures to coexist with human rights protection. The United Nations and European Union have established prison reform frameworks yet no universal standards exist for ethical AI implementation in correctional facilities. This section will establish connections between global examples and identify trends to develop practices which protect both prisoner safety and human rights.

GLOBAL TRENDS IN AI AND SURVEILLANCE IN PRISONS

AI and surveillance technology adoption across the world shows significant differences because of technological capabilities and legal systems and cultural values. Advanced technological nations have swiftly implemented AI-based surveillance systems yet other countries have chosen to proceed with caution by examining ethical issues related to these technologies.

1. United States

The United States stands as a pioneer in implementing surveillance technology throughout its correctional facilities. Digital surveillance systems including CCTV cameras and facial recognition software and AI predictive analytics operate in more than 70% of U.S. correctional facilities. The systems enable officials to track prisoner conduct and evaluate the likelihood of repeat offenses while guiding parole choices. The implementation of surveillance technology in prisons has sparked privacy concerns because it disproportionately affects minority inmates. The AI risk assessment tool COMPAS (Correctional Offender Management Profiling for Alternative Sanctions) faces criticism because its racial biases result in unfair parole denials which intensify racial inequalities throughout the criminal justice system (Angwin et al., 2016). The main obstacle in the United States stems from the unclear nature of AI systems. The algorithms used to evaluate inmate conduct and determine parole eligibility remain unknown to prisoners. The absence of clear explanations about AI decision-making processes creates problems with fairness and due process because prisoners lack the ability to challenge or appeal these decisions (Eubanks, 2018).

2. China

China stands as the nation that most aggressively implements AI and surveillance technologies within its criminal justice system. Facial recognition systems together with big data analytics and predictive behavioral models serve to monitor prisoners and predict their behavior patterns and determine their potential reoffending risk. The Social Credit System expands past prison walls to monitor social behavior of the general population through surveillance networks. The use of these technologies raises privacy concerns because China has strict laws and minimal opportunities to appeal against AI system decisions (Zhang & Zeng, 2020). China's large-scale surveillance system has received praise for its role in lowering prison violence and controlling prison population growth despite privacy and human rights worries. The technological system improved prison management efficiency yet triggered worries about privacy violations and human rights violations.

3. United Kingdom

The United Kingdom maintains a different approach to prison surveillance than both the United States and China through its emphasis on balancing security measures with privacy protection. The HM Prison Service operates CCTV systems and body-worn cameras to observe inmates but maintains full transparency along with monitoring functions. AI technologies remain in their initial stages throughout the

United Kingdom because predictive analytics is being used minimally for prisoner management and parole assessment. The UK maintains its commitment to maintaining its surveillance practices within European human rights standards including the Human Rights Act of 1998 and the General Data Protection Regulation (GDPR). The UK maintains its human rights protection through careful management of security measures. The surveillance system continues to affect racial minorities and people from low-income backgrounds disproportionately while raising ethical questions about its implementation.

4. European Union

The European Union maintains strict protection for prisoner rights especially when it comes to AI surveillance methods. The European Convention on Human Rights (ECHR), GDPR and EU Charter of Fundamental Rights compel member states to protect prisoner rights through systems which prevent AI and surveillance violations of privacy and fair treatment. The three EU nations Germany France and the Netherlands utilize AI and surveillance technology to manage prison populations while minimizing recidivism through strict legal frameworks protecting inmate rights. The GDPR establishes essential guidelines to monitor data privacy because it ensures surveillance data collection follows transparent procedures for specific purposes. The implementation of AI systems continues to raise ethical questions because of their unclear nature and their ability to determine prisoner fates without prisoner understanding or consent.

5. Australia

The implementation of AI and surveillance systems in Australian prisons occurs at a slower pace than in other countries but shows signs of growth. The majority of Australian prisons implement CCTV cameras and body-worn cameras for inmate monitoring but some states have begun testing AI systems to predict risks and monitor inmate behaviors. The Australian prison system together with others faces two primary issues of overcrowding and violence so authorities consider implementing AI solutions for management improvement. The New South Wales Government (2020) emphasizes that Australia will use surveillance technologies which respect human rights standards regarding privacy and accountability.

BEST PRACTICES FOR IMPLEMENTING AI AND SURVEILLANCE IN PRISONS

The implementation of AI and surveillance in prisons differs among nations yet multiple effective approaches have emerged which focus on security alongside ethical standards particularly from countries which achieved this balance. The implemented practices safeguard prisoners' rights and implement technological use responsibly and address transparency requirements as well as accountability standards and bias concerns.

1. AI systems must operate with complete transparency as well as accountability measures when deployed in prison facilities. The implementation of AI systems in prisons requires complete visibility together with answerability mechanisms. AI systems that monitor prison behavior and decide parole eligibility must provide inmates with specific details about their operation. The datasets together with algorithms applied by AI systems must be available for independent examination and auditing purposes. These systems need to undergo continuous auditing to guarantee their free-of-bias operation with fair functionality. The German government requires periodic evaluations of AI systems installed in public facilities including prisons to meet GDPR requirements as well as ethical benchmarks (European Commission, 2020).
2. Privacy Protection and Data Security-The protection of prisoner information needs to become the main organizational priority. The storage of surveillance data must be secure while its use stays within authorized purposes and distribution requires inmate consent. The GDPR serves as an excellent framework which controls data privacy and defends prisoner rights throughout EU territories. AI systems need to gather minimal personal information and maintain safe storage systems for all sensitive biometric data.
3. Human Rights-Based Approaches AI and surveillance systems must operate under human rights principles to protect prisoners' fundamental rights for privacy and dignity while providing fair treatment. The European Court of Human Rights (ECHR) has established that prison surveillance needs to remain balanced and serve essential purposes while maintaining respect for prisoner rights. Countries need to establish these principles within their legal frameworks to stop improper power usage and maintain prisoner dignity throughout surveillance procedures.
4. AI must deliver rehabilitation services to prisoners as well as enforcement capabilities. The primary function of AI should extend beyond monitoring because it needs to deliver rehabilitation services to prisoners. The implementation of AI technology enables customized rehabilitation plans for prisoners which enable them to learn skills and receive educational support and mental

health assistance. The New South Wales Government in Australia serves as a leader through their AI-based rehabilitation program that assesses inmates' requirements and connects them with suitable rehabilitation programs (New South Wales Government, 2020).

5. Regular Review and Legal Oversight- The best practices for prisons with AI systems require both scheduled evaluations and judicial monitoring. Human rights organizations together with legal institutions must conduct periodic evaluations of how AI and surveillance technologies affect prisoner rights and welfare. The French government maintains external review groups to evaluate how surveillance systems affect prisoners at predetermined intervals (European Commission, 2020). The use of AI and surveillance technologies in prisons continues to grow worldwide though different nations implement varying degrees of acceptance and regulatory measures. The implementation of these technologies creates substantial management benefits but simultaneously generates substantial ethical issues and legal difficulties. The implementation of best practices which prioritize transparency along with accountability and privacy protection and fairness represents a crucial requirement to ensure responsible AI use that respects prisoner human rights. A human rights-based strategy for AI and surveillance systems enables countries to reduce negative effects while maintaining prisoner dignity and freedom during incarceration.

CONCLUSION AND WAY FORWARD

The implementation of artificial intelligence systems together with surveillance technologies in correctional facilities represents an essential evolution in prison administration and observation systems. The integration of AI technology provides improved security and reduced violence and operational efficiency but creates multiple legal and ethical problems along with psychological issues. The expanding deployment of AI systems including facial recognition together with predictive analytics and biometric surveillance demands thorough evaluation of their implications on prisoner rights and dignity. This paper studied multiple aspects of prison technology implementation which included the psychological effects on prisoners and ethical issues and legal aspects as well as international trends in technology adoption. The analysis shows that extreme surveillance creates threats to prisoner privacy together with racial prejudice and serious mental health problems for those behind bars. The study evaluated global legal frameworks which include Universal Declaration of Human Rights (UDHR) and International Covenant on Civil and Political Rights (ICCPR) to establish necessary guidelines for ethical and legal usage of these technologies. One of the primary concerns is the right to privacy.

The privacy protection that free people have does not apply to prisoners yet this does not authorize complete surveillance of prisoners. The European Court of Human Rights (ECHR) maintains that surveillance requires three fundamental elements: proportionality to prisoners' rights as well as necessity and respect for those rights. The implementation of general surveillance protocols breaks both legal standards and ethical principles. The Panopticon effect from excessive surveillance practices leads to psychological damage that produces anxiety and depression along with a loss of control thus impeding rehabilitation and increasing recidivism rates. AI applications in decision-making processes which evaluate recidivism risks and parole suitability and behavioral assessment create doubts regarding system transparency and fairness along with accountability. The American system COMPAS has received criticism because it shows racial bias which produces discriminatory results toward minorities. The opacity of AI systems prevents prisoners from understanding the basis of decisions about their future which thus infringes upon their right to fair treatment and due process. Different countries display varying levels of AI and surveillance technology implementation within their prison systems when viewed on a global scale. The United States leads the world in AI-based surveillance system deployment yet ethical problems have emerged from privacy violations and racial discrimination. The United Kingdom along with European Union countries have implemented a cautious approach to AI implementation in correctional facilities through GDPR as their regulatory framework. The global community lacks standardized international rules that regulate AI and surveillance technology use in correctional facilities. The paper advocates for implementing human rights principles during AI and surveillance integration within prisons. The paper requires the implementation of best practices which include transparency alongside accountability and data protection and AI auditing to guarantee effective responsible use of these technologies. Prison facilities need to maintain their primary goal of security but must equally protect the psychological state and dignity of inmates. AI and surveillance technology in prisons will depend on the development of complete legal and ethical frameworks which protect prisoners' rights while delivering improved security and rehabilitation services. The following recommendations provide direction for safe implementation of these technologies into correctional facilities. A comprehensive set of legal guidelines should be established to regulate the application of AI and surveillance systems within prisons. The present day lacks international rules which handle the special issues these technologies create. Organizations such as the United Nations and the European Union provide guidelines about privacy and human rights yet more precise regulations are needed. The European Union uses the GDPR as a precedent to protect personal data thus global countries should create corresponding legal frameworks. The established regulations should maintain prisoner data privacy while requiring prisons to implement unbiased AI systems with clear explanation processes. The ICCPR needs revision to include specific language about AI and surveillance in correctional institutions with requirements for oversight and accountability. A fundamental recommendation should ensure AI systems maintain transparency through proper documentation. AI system monitoring functions and parole decision influence should be explained to prisoners before implementing these systems. The systems must reveal both their algorithms and data sources to independent auditing bodies. The implementation of regular audits needs to verify that AI systems function without prejudice and maintain fairness in their operations. As per European Commission (2020) the German government requires public institutions including prisons to undergo periodic system audits which confirm GDPR and ethical compliance. All prisoner surveillance operations require the fundamental safeguarding of inmate personal information. The data collected by AI and surveillance technologies needs to be stored securely while it can only be used for proper purposes and without consent for sharing. The GDPR presents an excellent example of how to protect data privacy and defend prisoner rights. The design of AI systems needs to limit personal data collection and protect sensitive information including biometric data from improper utilization. Human rights-based implementation of AI and surveillance systems by countries will guarantee these systems operate within prisoner fundamental rights boundaries. The rights to privacy along with dignity and fair treatment form part of this system. The European Court of Human Rights (ECHR) stated that surveillance requires proper balance with essential needs and respect for prisoner rights. The implementation of these fundamental principles in regulatory frameworks protects prisoners from abusive situations that could result in their dehumanization. The implementation of AI must serve to help prisoners through rehabilitation and reintegration processes. The rehabilitation process for prisoners can be personalized through AI systems which generate individualized programs to teach new skills while providing educational resources and psychological support. Australia leads the way in utilizing AI for individualized rehabilitation programs which support restorative justice by focusing on rehabilitation instead of punishment according to New South Wales Government (2020). AI systems and surveillance technologies need regular audits because these audits help maintain their ethical operation within legal boundaries. Prisons need independent oversight bodies consisting of human rights organizations and legal institutions to monitor AI systems. These organizations need to perform periodic assessments which assess the impact of AI on prisoner rights alongside its security-enhancing capabilities. The prison systems must create internal oversight systems to make sure staff and officials remain responsible for their AI and surveillance technology applications. The development of ethical guidelines together with codes of conduct must happen inside prisons to establish responsible usage standards for these technologies. Because AI and surveillance technology exist across worldwide boundaries international collaboration becomes essential for creating standardized best practices. The United Nations and the European Union must work together to develop worldwide rules for ethical AI application in prison settings. The guidelines must focus on human rights together with transparency and accountability and ethical technology practices. International collaboration between nations will prevent AI and surveillance systems from violating international norms that include the ICCPR and the European Convention on Human Rights. Prisons must develop ethical frameworks to achieve a balance between security requirements and prisoner rights protection in their implementation of AI and surveillance systems for the future. These technologies can be used effectively through legal frameworks along with transparency measures data protection and psychological considerations to maintain responsible operations. The foundation of any technological implementation must preserve human rights to maintain prisoner dignity and respect. Governments and human rights organizations and technology developers must collaborate to create specific guidelines and regulations that will ensure ethical AI and surveillance practices in prisons. Through international cooperation the potential benefits of these technologies will be maximized for prison systems and rehabilitation while their risks are minimized.

REFERENCES

Angwin, J., Larson, J., Mattu, S., & Kirchner, L. (2016). Machine bias: There's software used across the country to predict future criminals. And it's biased against blacks. *ProPublica*. Available from: https://www.propublica.org/article/machine-bias-risk-assessments-in-criminal-sentencing

Eubanks, V. (2018). *Automating inequality: How high-tech tools profile, police, and punish the poor*. St. Martin's Press.

European Commission. (2020). Artificial intelligence and privacy protection. *European Union*. Available from: https://ec.europa.eu/digital-strategy/our-policies/ai-privacy-protection

Foucault, M. (1975). *Discipline and punish: The birth of the prison*. Pantheon Books.

Graham, J. (2017). Psychological effects of surveillance on prisoners. *Journal of Prison Studies*, *24*(3), 134–149. DOI: 10.1137/jps.17.3

Hudson v. Palmer, 468 U.S. 517 (1984).

New South Wales Government. (2020). AI in rehabilitation programs. *New South Wales Department of Justice*. Available from: https://www.justice.nsw.gov.au/ai-rehabilitation

United Nations. (1948). Universal Declaration of Human Rights. Available from: https://www.un.org/en/universal-declaration-human-rights/

United Nations. (1966). International Covenant on Civil and Political Rights (ICCPR). Available from: https://www.ohchr.org/en/professionalinterest/pages/ccpr.aspx

Wright v. the United Kingdom, (2003). *European Court of Human Rights*.

Zhang, L., & Zeng, G. (2020). Artificial intelligence and prison reform: A global perspective. *Journal of Criminal Justice and Technology*, *45*(3), 112–129. DOI: 10.1016/j.jct.2020.02.001

Chapter 8
Empowering Water and Sanitation Rights Through Digital Justice, Legal Reform, and Inclusive Governance

Sana Abass
https://orcid.org/0009-0000-6075-7118
Mahant Bachittar Singh College of Engineering and Technology, Jammu, India

Uzma Abbas
https://orcid.org/0009-0005-5862-3571
Dogra Law College, Jammu, India

Mahapara Abbass
https://orcid.org/0000-0002-0838-2598
Maharishi Markandeshwar Engineering College, Maharishi Markandeshwar University, Mullana, India

Shalom Akhai
https://orcid.org/0000-0002-7533-457X
Maharishi Markandeshwar Engineering College, Maharishi Markandeshwar University, Mullana, India

ABSTRACT

This chapter examines how digital justice, legal reform, and inclusive governance can be harnessed to advance equitable access to water and sanitation as essential human rights. It draws upon international legal instruments such as the ICESCR and

DOI: 10.4018/979-8-3693-3920-6.ch008

the UN Watercourses Convention to explore how digital technologies, regulatory innovation, and smart infrastructure can support rights-based water and sanitation systems. Emphasis is placed on the intersection of environmental justice, digital inclusion, and legal empowerment in addressing systemic inequalities that affect marginalized populations. The chapter highlights how data-driven governance and public-private collaboration can improve transparency, accountability, and accessibility in service delivery. By framing water and sanitation access within the evolving discourse on civil rights in the digital era, the chapter advocates for forward-looking, interdisciplinary strategies that integrate law, technology, and sustainable development to build inclusive and resilient infrastructure.

CHAPTER HIGHLIGHTS

Figure 1. Graphical abstract.

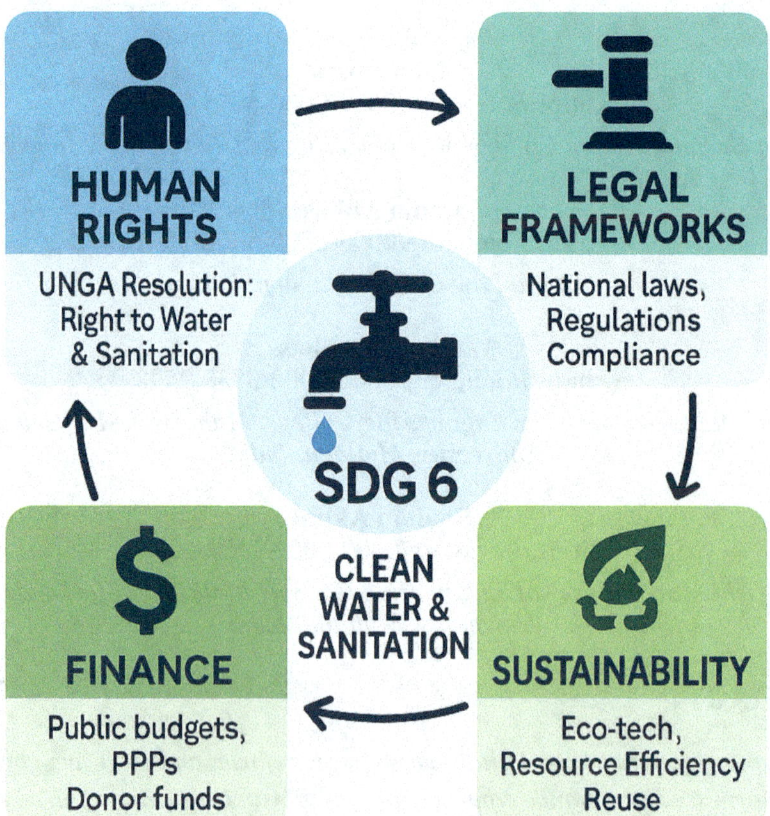

- **Human Right Recognition:** Access to clean water and sanitation was formally recognized as a fundamental human right by UN Resolution 64/292 in 2010, underpinning all subsequent infrastructure and policy efforts.
- **Definition & Standards:** The right guarantees sufficient, safe, accessible, and affordable water—grounded in the ICESCR—and sanitation facilities that protect health and dignity, especially for women and girls.
- **Public Health & Dignity:** Clean water and adequate sanitation prevent waterborne diseases, reduce child mortality, and uphold human dignity by providing privacy and safety.
- **SDG 6 Alignment:** SDG 6 aims for universal, sustainable water and sanitation access by 2030, with strong interlinkages to health (SDG 3), gender equality (SDG 5), and climate action (SDG 13).
- **International Legal Instruments:** Core treaties—ICESCR, CRC, Ramsar Convention, and the UN Watercourses Convention—establish rights to water and promote equitable, transboundary resource management.
- **National Legal Frameworks:** Many constitutions (e.g., South Africa, Bolivia) and national water laws enshrine these rights, ensuring equitable access and sustainability at the country level.
- **Regulatory Oversight:** Bodies such as the U.S. EPA and International Water Association set and enforce water quality and sanitation standards, safeguarding public health and service reliability.
- **Financing & Investment:** A blend of public budgets, public-private partnerships, and international funds (World Bank, AfDB, GEF, GCF) mobilize critical resources for infrastructure expansion.
- **Implementation Barriers:** Key challenges include legal gaps, weak enforcement, constrained finances, high capital costs, governance fragmentation, and social-cultural inequities.
- **Best Practices & Case Studies:** Successes like South Africa's Water Services Act, Brazil's National Sanitation Law, India's Swachh Bharat Mission, and Kenya's Water Services Trust Fund offer valuable models.
- **Recommendations:** Strengthen legal recognition, build regulatory capacity, increase investment, and promote social inclusion through gender-sensitive and community-driven approaches.
- **Integrated, Resilient Systems:** An integrated, multi-sectoral approach—combining rights-based law, sustainable technology, and stakeholder collaboration—is essential for climate-resilient, equitable WASH infrastructure.

1. INTRODUCTION

Access to clean water and adequate sanitation is a fundamental human right, essential for maintaining human dignity, health, and overall well-being (Calderón & González, 2017; Levin et al., 2023). The United Nations General Assembly explicitly recognized this right in 2010 (Calderón & González, 2017; Levin et al., 2023; Santos et al., 2021), marking a significant milestone in the global effort to address inequities and challenges surrounding access to water and sanitation, particularly for marginalized and vulnerable populations. However, the realization of this right remains elusive for billions of people worldwide, with significant disparities in access between and within countries (Satterthwaite, 2021). The development of robust water and sanitation infrastructure, underpinned by effective legal and regulatory frameworks, is critical to bridging this gap and ensuring that all individuals can exercise their right to clean water and sanitation (Santos et al., 2021). Water and sanitation are not only fundamental to human survival but also play a pivotal role in achieving broader sustainable development goals (Neto & Camkin, 2020). Inadequate access to clean water and sanitation has far-reaching consequences, including increased morbidity and mortality from waterborne diseases, reduced educational and economic opportunities, and perpetuation of cycles of poverty. Water scarcity and poor sanitation exacerbate environmental degradation, contributing to climate change and biodiversity loss (Akhai & Taneja 2024; Akhai & Taneja 2025). These interconnected challenges highlight the need for a holistic approach to water and sanitation infrastructure development, one that integrates human rights principles with sustainable development objectives. The development of water and sanitation infrastructure is a complex and multifaceted process that requires substantial investment, technical expertise, and coordinated efforts among various stakeholders. Legal and regulatory frameworks are essential to ensure that infrastructure projects are designed, implemented, and managed in a manner that upholds human rights, promotes social equity, and protects the environment. Without robust legal and regulatory systems, infrastructure development risks exacerbating existing inequalities, undermining environmental sustainability, and failing to meet the needs of the most vulnerable populations.

Figure 2. Achieving SDG 6 -a visual guide to water and sanitation infrastructure development

This chapter explores the critical role of legal and regulatory frameworks in ensuring the development of water and sanitation infrastructure that upholds human rights and promotes sustainable development. It begins by examining the human right to water and sanitation, its recognition under international law, and its significance for public health, social equity, and environmental sustainability. It then delves into the alignment of water and sanitation infrastructure development with the Sustainable Development Goals (SDGs), particularly SDG 6, which aims to ensure availability and sustainable management of water and sanitation for all. *Figure 1* provides a graphical abstract of this chapter *and Figure 2* provides a visual guide to achieving SDG 6 and focuses on the development of water and sanitation infrastructure.

2. THE HUMAN RIGHT TO WATER AND SANITATION

The human right to water and sanitation is a fundamental human right, ensuring everyone has access to safe, accessible, and affordable water for personal and domestic use (United Nations, 2024; Irujo, 2007). The UN General Assembly recognized this right in 2010 (Calderón & González, 2017; Levin et al., 2023; Pradhan et al., 2018). This right is rooted in international human rights law, including the International Covenant on Economic, Social, and Cultural Rights. Access to clean water is crucial for preventing diseases, reducing child mortality, and preserving human dignity, especially for women and girls (Adugna, 2023). International human rights law obliges states to work towards achieving universal access to water and sanitation for all, without any discrimination, while prioritizing those most in need

(OHCHR and the Rights to Water and Sanitation, 2024; "University of Minnesota Human Rights Library," 2005).

2.1 Definition and Recognition

The human right to water and sanitation is a cornerstone of international human rights law, affirming that every individual is entitled to sufficient, safe, acceptable, physically accessible, and affordable water for personal and domestic use (Irujo, 2007). This right encompasses not only the availability of water but also its quality, ensuring that it is free from contaminants that could harm human health (Irujo, 2007; KDIGO Clinical Practice Guideline for Acute Kidney Injury, 2012). Similarly, the right to sanitation guarantees access to facilities that are hygienic, safe, and culturally appropriate, enabling individuals to dispose of human waste in a manner that protects their health and dignity (Adugna, 2023). Together, these rights form an essential foundation for human survival, well-being, and development (Human Rights to Water and Sanitation, 2022).

The recognition of the human right to water and sanitation has evolved over time, culminating in its explicit affirmation by the United Nations General Assembly in Resolution 64/292 in 2010 (Calderón & González, 2017; Pradhan et al., 2018). This resolution declared that clean drinking water and sanitation are essential for the realization of all human rights (The Human Right to Safe Drinking Water and Sanitation, 2012), marking a significant step forward in the global effort to address water and sanitation challenges. The right to water and sanitation is grounded in several key international human rights instruments, most notably the *International Covenant on Economic, Social and Cultural Rights*. Article 11 of the ICESCR recognizes the right to an adequate standard of living, which has been interpreted by the Committee on Economic, Social and Cultural Rights to include the right to water. In its General Comment No. 15, the CESCR clarified that the right to water is indispensable for leading a life in human dignity and is a prerequisite for the realization of other human rights, such as the right to health, food, and education.

In addition to the ICESCR, other international instruments reinforce the right to water and sanitation. The *Convention on the Rights of the Child* emphasizes the importance of access to clean water and sanitation for children's health and development, while the *Convention on the Elimination of All Forms of Discrimination Against Women* highlights the specific needs of women and girls in accessing these resources. Furthermore, the *Universal Declaration of Human Rights*, though not explicitly mentioning water and sanitation, provides a broader framework for the protection of human dignity and well-being, which underpins these rights.

At the national level, many countries have incorporated the right to water and sanitation into their constitutions, laws, and policies. For example, South Africa's

Constitution explicitly guarantees the right to access sufficient water, while India's National Water Policy emphasizes equitable distribution and sustainable management of water resources (Sarkar et al., 2022). These legal frameworks provide a foundation for governments to prioritize water and sanitation infrastructure development and ensure that these services are accessible to all, particularly the most vulnerable populations.

2.2 Importance for Health and Dignity

Access to clean water and sanitation is not just a human right but also a critical determinant of public health and human dignity (About Water and Sanitation, 2025; Adugna, 2023). The absence of these basic services has profound implications for individuals and communities, particularly in low-income and marginalized settings (Nwobodo & Chukwu, 2020).

- **Health Implications:** Clean water and sanitation are fundamental to preventing waterborne diseases, which remain a leading cause of morbidity and mortality worldwide (Bartram & Cairncross, 2010). Contaminated water and poor sanitation are linked to the spread of diseases such as cholera and diarrhea (Wolf et al., 2023). Diarrheal diseases alone account for over 1.6 million deaths annually, most of which are preventable through access to safe water and sanitation. Improved sanitation facilities reduce the risk of fecal-oral transmission of pathogens, while access to clean water ensures that individuals can maintain personal hygiene, further reducing the spread of infectious diseases. The availability of clean water improves attendance and educational outcomes, particularly for girls who may otherwise miss school due to the lack of menstrual hygiene facilities (Clean Water for Health and Wellbeing, 2023). Similarly, access to sanitation in healthcare facilities is essential for preventing healthcare-associated infections and ensuring the safety of patients and healthcare workers (KDIGO Clinical Practice Guideline for Acute Kidney Injury, 2012).
- **Dignity and Social Equity:** The right to water and sanitation is intrinsically linked to human dignity. Adequate sanitation facilities provide individuals with privacy, safety, and comfort, enabling them to manage their personal hygiene with dignity. In many parts of the world, the absence of toilets forces women and girls to practice open defecation, exposing them to the risk of harassment, assault, and violence. Ensuring access to water and sanitation thus has a transformative impact on gender equality and social equity, empowering women and girls to lead healthier, more dignified lives (Bosona & Gebresenbet, 2023).

- **Environmental and Economic Benefits:** Sustainable water management practices, such as rainwater harvesting and wastewater treatment, contribute to the conservation of water resources and the protection of ecosystems (Akhai 2024; Abdelmoneim et al., 2025). Improved sanitation systems reduce the contamination of water bodies, safeguarding biodiversity and supporting livelihoods that depend on clean water, such as fishing and agriculture (Schertenleib, 2005). Investments in water and sanitation infrastructure yield significant returns by reducing healthcare costs, increasing productivity, and fostering economic growth (Tropp, 2015). The WHO estimates that every dollar invested in water and sanitation generates a return of up to $4.30 in reduced healthcare costs and increased productivity ("Benefits of Investing in Water and Sanitation," 2011).
- **Challenges and Inequities:** Despite the clear benefits of water and sanitation, significant challenges remain in realizing these rights for all (Plessis, 2017). Inequities in access persist, with rural populations, informal settlements, and marginalized groups often facing the greatest barriers (Sarkar et al., 2022). In many cases, these disparities are exacerbated by weak governance, inadequate funding, and insufficient infrastructure. Climate change further compounds these challenges, with rising temperatures, changing precipitation patterns, and extreme weather events threatening water availability and quality (Anderson et al., 2023). Addressing these challenges requires a concerted effort to strengthen legal and regulatory frameworks, mobilize financial resources, and promote inclusive and participatory approaches to water and sanitation management (Narayan et al., 2021).

Table 1 provides a comprehensive breakdown of the importance of water and sanitation, emphasizing their critical role in health, equity, and sustainability. It also highlights the far-reaching effects of water and sanitation access and the key insights and impacts on human well-being.

Table 1. The critical role of water and sanitation - impact, challenges, and solutions

Area of Impact	Description	Specific Examples & Data	Consequences of Lack of Access
Health	Essential for disease prevention and overall well-being.	- Prevents waterborne diseases (cholera, diarrhea, typhoid, dysentery). - Diarrheal diseases cause **1.6 million deaths annually** (WHO). - Improved sanitation reduces fecal-oral transmission. - Clean water in schools boosts attendance, especially for girls. - Sanitation in healthcare facilities prevents infections.	- High child mortality rates. - Spread of infectious diseases. - Reduced school attendance, particularly among girls. - Increased healthcare-associated infections.
Dignity & Social Equity	Critical for privacy, safety, and gender equality.	- Adequate sanitation ensures **privacy, safety, and dignity**. - Lack of toilets forces **open defecation**, increasing risks of **harassment and violence** for women and girls. - **Menstrual hygiene** challenges lead to school absenteeism and social exclusion. - Women and girls spend hours **collecting water**, limiting their educational and economic opportunities.	- Loss of dignity and privacy. - Higher risk of harassment, assault, and violence. - Gender inequality and social exclusion. - Limited economic and educational opportunities.
Environmental Benefits	Contributes to water conservation and ecosystem protection.	- **Rainwater harvesting** and **wastewater treatment** help conserve water resources. - Improved sanitation prevents **water pollution** and protects biodiversity. - **Sustainable water practices** support livelihoods (fishing, agriculture).	- Depletion of water resources. - Contamination of water bodies and ecosystems. - Loss of biodiversity and environmental degradation.
Economic Benefits	Drives economic growth and reduces healthcare costs.	- **Lower healthcare costs** due to reduced disease burden. - Increases **workforce productivity** and economic stability. - WHO estimates that **every $1 invested in water and sanitation generates up to $4.30 in returns**.	- Higher healthcare expenses. - Lower productivity and economic growth. - Missed economic opportunities.
Challenges & Inequities	Persistent disparities in access and governance failures.	- **Rural populations, informal settlements, and marginalized groups** face major inequities. - **Weak governance, inadequate funding, and poor infrastructure** hinder progress. - **Climate change** affects water availability and quality.	- Widening disparities in access to clean water and sanitation. - Increased vulnerability to climate-related water crises. - Exacerbation of social and economic inequalities.

In conclusion, the human right to water and sanitation is a fundamental pillar of human dignity, health, and sustainable development (Akhai, 2023; Khang & Akhai 2024). Its recognition under international law and incorporation into national legal frameworks provide a strong foundation for ensuring equitable access to these essential resources. However, realizing this right requires addressing persistent challenges and inequities through robust legal and regulatory systems, targeted investments, and inclusive policies. By prioritizing the right to water and sanitation, governments and stakeholders can create a more just, equitable, and sustainable world for all.

3. SUSTAINABLE DEVELOPMENT GOALS (SDGS) AND WATER AND SANITATION

The Sustainable Development Goals, particularly SDG 6, aim to ensure clean water and sanitation for all by 2030 (Assegide et al., 2022; Goal 6 - Clean Water & Sanitation, 2024). This includes universal and equitable access to safe and affordable drinking water, access to adequate and equitable sanitation and hygiene (Goal 6 - Clean Water & Sanitation, 2024), improving water quality, and increasing water-use efficiency (2023).

Water and sanitation are indeed interlinked with other SDGs such as health, gender equality, and climate action (Adeel, 2017; Saleh et al., 2021). Achieving these goals requires addressing issues such as water scarcity, water quality, and wastewater treatment (2023). As of 2022, 2.2 billion people were without access to safely managed drinking water and 3.5 billion lacked access to safely managed sanitation ("Department of Economic and Social Affairs," 2025).

Legal frameworks supporting water and sanitation infrastructure development include international human rights law instruments like the International Covenant on Economic, Social and Cultural Rights, which recognizes the right to an adequate standard of living that includes access to water and sanitation, and the Convention on the Rights of the Child [see EDITOR document]. Environmental agreements like the Ramsar Convention and the UN Watercourses Convention also play a role in promoting sustainable water management (Adhikari, 2020). *Table 2* discusses the crucial role of water and sanitation in achieving the Sustainable Development Goals (SDGs), their impact on global development, and the interconnections between these goals, emphasizing the importance of water and sanitation in achieving these goals.

Table 2. The vital role of water & sanitation in achieving the SDGs

SDG	Key Focus	Relation to Water & Sanitation (SDG 6)	Challenges & Implications
SDG 6: Clean Water & Sanitation	Ensure availability and sustainable management of water and sanitation for all.	- Universal access to **safe, affordable drinking water** (Target 6.1). - **Sanitation & hygiene** access for all (Target 6.2). - **Water quality improvement** (Target 6.3). - **Efficient water use & resource management** (Targets 6.4 & 6.5).	- **Billions lack access** to safe water and sanitation. - Climate change worsens **water scarcity**. - Requires strong governance & investment.
SDG 3: Good Health & Well-being	Ensure healthy lives and promote well-being for all.	- **Safe water reduces** waterborne diseases (cholera, typhoid, diarrhea). - **Sanitation in healthcare facilities** prevents infections.	- Unsafe water leads to **millions of deaths annually**. - Poor sanitation increases **child mortality**.
SDG 5: Gender Equality	Achieve gender equality and empower women and girls.	- Lack of sanitation disproportionately affects **women & girls**. - **Menstrual hygiene** access improves school attendance. - **Women spend hours collecting water,** reducing economic opportunities.	- **Women face harassment & violence** without safe sanitation. - Limited access **restricts education & employment** opportunities.
SDG 13: Climate Action	Take urgent action to combat climate change and its impacts.	- **Climate change affects** water availability (droughts, floods). - **Water conservation & sustainable use** support resilience.	- **Rising temperatures & extreme weather** impact water sources. - Poor water management increases vulnerability.
SDG 1: No Poverty	End poverty in all its forms everywhere.	- Water access **improves livelihoods & productivity**. - **Reduces healthcare costs,** allowing economic progress.	- Water shortages lead to **economic instability & poverty cycles**.
SDG 2: Zero Hunger	End hunger, achieve food security, and promote sustainable agriculture.	- **Water is essential for agriculture** (irrigation, livestock). - Poor water management affects **food production & nutrition**.	- **Food insecurity rises** with water scarcity. - Pollution affects **agricultural productivity**.
SDG 11: Sustainable Cities & Communities	Make cities inclusive, safe, resilient, and sustainable.	- Urban areas require **efficient water management** & sanitation infrastructure.	- **Population growth & urbanization** strain water supply & waste systems.
SDG 14 & SDG 15: Life Below Water & Life on Land	Conserve and sustainably use the oceans, seas, and terrestrial ecosystems.	- **Preventing pollution** protects marine & freshwater ecosystems. - **Restoring water-related ecosystems** improves biodiversity.	- **Industrial & agricultural runoff** threaten aquatic life. - **Deforestation reduces natural water filtration**.

3.1 SDG 6: Clean Water and Sanitation

The *Sustainable Development Goals,* adopted by the United Nations in 2015, represent a universal call to action to end poverty, protect the planet, and ensure prosperity for all by 2030 (Tanoh et al., 2021). Among the 17 goals, *SDG 6: Clean Water and Sanitation* holds a central position, as it directly addresses the critical need for universal access to safe and sustainable water and sanitation services (Assegide et al., 2022). SDG 6 aims to "ensure availability and sustainable management of water and sanitation for all" (2023), recognizing that water and sanitation are not only fundamental human rights but also essential drivers of sustainable development (Nwobodo & Chukwu, 2020).

Key Targets of SDG 6:

SDG 6 is supported by eight specific targets that provide a comprehensive framework for addressing water and sanitation challenges (Loewe & Rippin, 2015):

- **Universal Access to Safe and Affordable Drinking Water (Target 6.1):** By 2030, achieve universal and equitable access to safe and affordable drinking water for all (Hutton & Varughese, 2016). This target emphasizes the importance of ensuring that water is not only available but also affordable, particularly for low-income and marginalized populations.
- **Adequate and Equitable Sanitation and Hygiene (Target 6.2):** By 2030, achieve access to adequate and equitable sanitation and hygiene for all, and end open defecation, paying special attention to the needs of women and girls and those in vulnerable situations (Goal 6, 2022). This target highlights the importance of addressing gender-specific needs and ensuring that sanitation facilities are safe, private, and culturally acceptable (Bosona & Gebresenbet, 2023).
- **Improving Water Quality (Target 6.3):** By 2030, improve water quality by reducing pollution, eliminating dumping, and minimizing the release of hazardous chemicals and materials (Whitehead et al., 2021). This target underscores the need to protect water resources from contamination and ensure that water is safe for human consumption and ecosystem health.
- **Increasing Water-Use Efficiency (Target 6.4):** By 2030, substantially increase water-use efficiency across all sectors and ensure sustainable withdrawals and supply of freshwater to address water scarcity (SDG Indicators, 2024). This target calls for the adoption of efficient water management practices to balance competing demands for water resources.

- **Integrated Water Resources Management (Target 6.5):** By 2030, implement integrated water resources management at all levels, including through transboundary cooperation. IWRM promotes the coordinated development and management of water, land, and related resources to maximize economic and social welfare without compromising the sustainability of ecosystems.
- **Protecting and Restoring Water-Related Ecosystems (Target 6.6):** By 2020, protect and restore water-related ecosystems, including mountains, forests, wetlands, rivers, aquifers, and lakes. This target recognizes the critical role of healthy ecosystems in maintaining water quality and availability (Sarkar et al., 2022).
- **International Cooperation and Capacity-Building (Target 6.a):** By 2030, expand international cooperation and capacity-building support to developing countries in water- and sanitation-related activities and programs, including water harvesting, desalination, water efficiency, wastewater treatment, recycling, and reuse technologies (SDG Indicators, 2024). This target emphasizes the importance of global solidarity and knowledge-sharing in addressing water and sanitation challenges.
- **Participation of Local Communities (Target 6.b):** Support and strengthen the participation of local communities in improving water and sanitation management (SDG Indicators, 2024). This target highlights the importance of inclusive and participatory approaches to ensure that water and sanitation services meet the needs of all stakeholders (Goal 6, 2022).
- **Progress and Challenges:** While significant progress has been made toward achieving SDG 6, considerable challenges remain (2023). According to the United Nations, billions of people still lack access to safely managed drinking water and sanitation services, particularly in rural areas and informal settlements. Climate change, population growth, and urbanization are exacerbating water scarcity and pollution, threatening the achievement of SDG 6 targets (2023). Addressing these challenges requires sustained political commitment, increased investment, and innovative solutions to ensure that no one is left behind (Ruíz et al., 2020).

3.2 Interlinkages with Other SDGs

Water and sanitation are cross-cutting issues that have profound implications for the achievement of multiple SDGs (Zhou et al., 2017). The interconnected nature of the SDGs means that progress in one goal can drive progress in others, while setbacks in one area can hinder overall development (Cernev & Fenner, 2019). Below are some of the key interlinkages between SDG 6 and other SDGs:

1. **Health:** Access to clean water and sanitation is directly linked to improved health outcomes, as it reduces the incidence of waterborne diseases such as cholera, diarrhea, and typhoid ("Sustainable Development Goals," 2018). Achieving SDG 6 is therefore essential for realizing *SDG 3: Good Health and Well-being*, which aims to ensure healthy lives and promote well-being for all at all ages (Bosona & Gebresenbet, 2023).
2. **Gender Equality:** The lack of access to water and sanitation disproportionately affects women and girls, who often bear the burden of collecting water and face unique challenges related to menstrual hygiene management (Water Is Central in Achieving All 17 SDGs. But How?, 2023). Ensuring access to safe and private sanitation facilities is critical for achieving *SDG 5: Gender Equality*, as it empowers women and girls to participate fully in education, work, and community life (Bosona & Gebresenbet, 2023).
3. **Climate Action:** Water resources are highly vulnerable to the impacts of climate change, including altered precipitation patterns, increased frequency of droughts and floods, and rising temperatures. Sustainable water management practices, such as water recycling and efficient irrigation, contribute to climate resilience and support *SDG 13: Climate Action*, which calls for urgent action to combat climate change and its impacts (SDG Pathfinder, 2023).
4. **Poverty Eradication:** Access to water and sanitation is a key determinant of economic productivity and poverty reduction ("Sustainable Development Goals," 2018). Improved water and sanitation services reduce healthcare costs, increase school attendance, and enhance livelihoods, contributing to *SDG 1: No Poverty*, which aims to end poverty in all its forms everywhere (Bosona & Gebresenbet, 2023).
5. **Food Security:** Water is essential for agriculture, which accounts for the largest share of global water use. Sustainable water management practices, such as drip irrigation and rainwater harvesting, are critical for achieving *SDG 2: Zero Hunger*, which seeks to end hunger, achieve food security, and promote sustainable agriculture (Bosona & Gebresenbet, 2023).
6. **Sustainable Cities and Communities:** Rapid urbanization is increasing the demand for water and sanitation services in cities, where inadequate infrastructure often leads to water scarcity and pollution. Ensuring access to clean water and sanitation is essential for achieving *SDG 11: Sustainable Cities and Communities*, which aims to make cities inclusive, safe, resilient, and sustainable (Sarkar et al., 2022).
7. **Life Below Water and Life on Land:** Water pollution from untreated wastewater and agricultural runoff threatens marine and terrestrial ecosystems. Protecting and restoring water-related ecosystems, as outlined in SDG 6, is critical for achieving *SDG 14: Life Below Water* and *SDG 15: Life on Land*, which focus

on conserving and sustainably using oceans, seas, and terrestrial ecosystems (Sarkar et al., 2022).

The interlinkages between SDG 6 and other SDGs highlight the importance of adopting an integrated approach to sustainable development (Alcamo, 2018). For example, investments in water and sanitation infrastructure can yield co-benefits for health, gender equality, and climate resilience (Linkage of SDGs 3, 4, 5 and 12 with SDG 6, 2023). However, there can also be trade-offs, such as the potential environmental impacts of large-scale water infrastructure projects. Balancing these synergies and trade-offs requires careful planning, stakeholder engagement, and the use of evidence-based decision-making tools (Water and Sanitation Interlinkages across the 2030 Agenda for Sustainable Development, 2016).

4. LEGAL FRAMEWORKS FOR WATER AND SANITATION INFRASTRUCTURE DEVELOPMENT

Water and sanitation infrastructure development relies on international legal instruments such as International Human Rights Law (Norwood, 2023) and Environmental Agreements. International instruments like the ICESCR and CRC provide the legal basis for the right to water and sanitation (Kiefer, n.d.). National legal frameworks include constitutional provisions that enshrine the right to water and sanitation in many countries, and water laws and policies that regulate water use, allocation, and management, ensuring equitable access and sustainability (Santos et al., 2021; Wahi, 2022). *Table 3* discusses key aspects of water and sanitation infrastructure governance, legal, regulatory, and financial frameworks, challenges and solutions in management, policies, standards, and investments, and global and national approaches to water and sanitation development.

Table 3. Governance, frameworks, and challenges in water & sanitation infrastructure management

Aspect	Description	Key Examples	Challenges	Possible Solutions
International Legal Frameworks	Treaties and conventions that establish water and sanitation rights	ICESCR, CRC, Ramsar Convention, UN Watercourses Convention	Weak enforcement, lack of compliance	Strengthening international monitoring and accountability
National Legal Frameworks	National laws and constitutional provisions governing water and sanitation	South Africa's constitutional right to water, India's Water Act, U.S. Clean Water Act	Inconsistent implementation, resource limitations	Policy reforms, stronger enforcement mechanisms
Regulatory Authorities	Institutions overseeing water quality and sanitation compliance	U.S. EPA, WHO, International Water Association (IWA)	Regulatory fragmentation, overlapping responsibilities	Better coordination between agencies
Water Quality Standards	Guidelines for safe drinking water and sanitation practices	EPA's NPDWR, WHO Drinking Water Guidelines	Pollution, contamination, outdated standards	Investment in water treatment technologies
Sanitation Standards	Rules on the design, construction, and maintenance of sanitation facilities	FSIS sanitation standards, WHO guidelines	Poor infrastructure, lack of public awareness	Public-private partnerships, education campaigns
Public Investment	Government funding for water and sanitation projects	U.S. Bipartisan Infrastructure Law, national water programs	Budget constraints, competing priorities	Increased government funding, efficient resource allocation
Private Sector Participation	Role of businesses and PPPs in infrastructure development	PPP projects in Europe, private water utilities	Profit-driven approaches may neglect marginalized communities	Stronger public-private regulations
International Funding Mechanisms	Global financial support for water and sanitation initiatives	World Bank, African Development Bank, Green Climate Fund	Inequitable distribution of funds, complex approval processes	Streamlined funding mechanisms, targeted aid
Implementation Challenges	Barriers to achieving universal access to water and sanitation	Legal gaps, financial constraints, cultural factors	Lack of political will, infrastructure costs	Comprehensive legal frameworks, innovative financing

4.1 International Legal Instruments

International Human Rights Law:

- **International Covenant on Economic, Social and Cultural Rights:** Adopted in 1966, this treaty recognizes the right to an adequate standard of living, including the right to water. General Comment No. 15 explicitly states that the right to water is indispensable for leading a life in human dignity and is a prerequisite for the realization of other human rights (Kiefer, n.d.).
- **Convention on the Rights of the Child:** Adopted in 1989, the CRC emphasizes the right of children to enjoy the highest attainable standard of health, including access to clean drinking water and adequate sanitation facilities, which are essential for preventing diseases and ensuring overall well-being (Kiefer, n.d.).

Environmental Agreements:

- **Ramsar Convention:** Formally known as the Convention on Wetlands of International Importance, this treaty, adopted in 1971, provides a framework for the conservation and wise use of wetlands and their resources (Norwood, 2023). Wetlands play a crucial role in water purification, flood control, and groundwater replenishment, making their conservation vital for sustainable water management.
- **UN Watercourses Convention:** Officially called the Convention on the Law of the Non-navigational Uses of International Watercourses, this treaty, adopted in 1997, aims to ensure the sustainable and equitable use of transboundary watercourses, promoting cooperation between countries sharing these resources (Convention on the Law of Non-Navigational Uses of International Watercourses (1997), n.d.).

It's also worth noting that some countries have incorporated environmental protection and the right to water into their constitutions (Ahmad, 2020; Human Rights and the Environment, 2022). Furthermore, the Aarhus Convention focuses on access to information, public participation in decision-making, and access to justice in environmental matters.

4.2 National Legal Frameworks

Many countries have incorporated the right to water and sanitation into their constitutions. For example, South Africa's Constitution explicitly states that everyone has the right to have access to sufficient water. Similarly, Bolivia's Constitution recognizes water as a fundamental human right, ensuring its provision and access for all citizens.

Water Laws and Policies:

- **Constitutional Provisions:** South Africa's Constitution explicitly states that everyone has the right to have access to sufficient water (Ahmad, 2020). Similarly, Bolivia's Constitution recognizes water as a fundamental human right, ensuring its provision and access for all citizens (Country Legal Mapping, 2023; Kiefer, n.d.).
- **National Water Laws:** These laws regulate the use, allocation, and management of water resources within a country. For instance, India's Water Act, 1974, aims to prevent and control water pollution and maintain or restore the wholesomeness of water (Wahi, 2022).
- **Water Policies:** National policies provide a strategic framework for water resource management, addressing issues such as water conservation, equitable distribution, and sustainable use. For example, the United States' Clean Water Act establishes the basic structure for regulating discharges of pollutants into the waters and sets quality standards for surface waters (The Center for Water Security and Cooperation, 2020).

These legal frameworks, both international and national, play a crucial role in ensuring the development and maintenance of water and sanitation infrastructure (Country Legal Mapping, 2023). They provide the necessary legal basis for protecting water resources, promoting equitable access, and ensuring sustainable management practices (Santos et al., 2021).

5. REGULATORY FRAMEWORKS FOR WATER AND SANITATION INFRASTRUCTURE

The regulatory frameworks for water and sanitation infrastructure are overseen by water regulatory authorities, which ensure compliance with human rights standards (Santos et al., 2021), and sanitation regulatory agencies, which develop and maintain adequate sanitation facilities (A Roadmap for Advancing Sanitation Regulation, 2025). Water quality standards set permissible contaminants in drinking water (Drinking-Water Quality Regulation, 2024), while sanitation standards guide the design, construction, and maintenance of safe, accessible, and culturally acceptable facilities.

5.1 Regulatory Bodies and Institutions

Water Regulatory Authorities:

- **Role and Responsibilities:** These authorities are responsible for overseeing the implementation of water laws and policies (Goksu et al., 2019). They ensure that water service providers comply with national and international standards, including human rights standards (2024). For example, the United States Environmental Protection Agency sets and enforces standards for drinking water quality under the Safe Drinking Water Act. Similarly, the International Water Association provides guidelines for water service regulation to ensure the realization of human rights to water and sanitation.

Sanitation Regulatory Agencies:

- **Role and Responsibilities:** These agencies are tasked with the development and maintenance of sanitation infrastructure (Goksu et al., 2019). They ensure that sanitation facilities are accessible, safe, and meet public health standards. For instance, the Indian Health Service in the United States provides guidelines for the operation and maintenance of sanitation facilities on tribal lands. Additionally, the World Health Organization and UNICEF work together to regulate sanitation services as a public good, emphasizing the need for public health-aligned guidance and oversight.

5.2 Standards and Guidelines

Water Quality Standards:

- **Regulations and Enforcement:** Water quality standards are regulations that set permissible levels of contaminants in drinking water to protect public health (Kirschner, 2011). The EPA's National Primary Drinking Water Regulations are legally enforceable standards that limit the levels of contaminants in public water systems (Williams, 2000). These standards ensure that water utilities provide safe drinking water by adhering to strict contaminant limits and treatment techniques (Saleh et al., 2021).

Sanitation Standards:

- **Design, Construction, and Maintenance:** Sanitation standards provide guidelines for the design, construction, and maintenance of sanitation facilities (Recommended Standards for Wastewater Facilities, 2008). These standards ensure that facilities are safe, accessible, and culturally acceptable (Kirschner, 2011). For example, the Food Safety and Inspection Service in the United States has established sanitation performance standards for meat and poultry establishments, which include guidelines for construction, maintenance, and hygiene practices. Similarly, the Indian Health Service in the United States provides guidelines for the operation and maintenance of sanitation facilities on tribal lands.

These regulatory bodies and standards play a crucial role in ensuring the effective development and maintenance of water and sanitation infrastructure (Khanna et al., 2022). They provide the necessary oversight and guidelines to protect public health and ensure equitable access to essential services (Khanna et al., 2022). The American Water Works Association also publishes consensus documents and standards covering all areas of water treatment and supply (Find the Standard You Need, 2023; Williams, 2000).

6. FINANCING AND INVESTMENT IN WATER AND SANITATION INFRASTRUCTURE

The development of water and sanitation infrastructure in underserved areas requires public investment from governments (Briceno et al., 2004), while private sector participation through public-private partnerships can improve infrastructure development (White & Wahba, 2019). International funding mechanisms include development banks and donor agencies like the World Bank and the African Development Bank, as well as global funds like the Global Environment Facility and Green Climate Fund, which offer funding for sustainable water and sanitation projects in developing countries (Mobilising Capital for Water: Blended Finance Solutions to Scale Investment in Emerging Markets, 2022).

6.1 Public and Private Sector Roles

Public Investment:

- **Government Funding:** Government funding is essential for the development of water and sanitation infrastructure, especially in underserved areas (Abbass et el., 2025; Briscoe, 1999). Public investment ensures that basic services are provided to all citizens, regardless of their economic status (Abbass et al., 2025). For example, the Bipartisan Infrastructure Law in the United

States allocates over $50 billion to improve drinking water, wastewater, and stormwater infrastructure, marking the largest federal investment in water infrastructure to date. This funding helps address critical issues such as lead contamination and emerging pollutants, ensuring safe and reliable water services for communities.

Private Sector Participation:

- **Public-Private Partnerships:** Public-private partnerships can leverage private sector expertise and resources to enhance infrastructure development and service delivery (Goksu et al., 2017). These partnerships involve collaboration between government entities and private companies to finance, build, and operate water and sanitation projects. The OECD highlights that many countries have successfully involved the private sector to upgrade and develop their water and sanitation infrastructure, improving efficiency and service quality (Fonseca et al., 2005). PPPs can bring innovation, efficiency, and additional funding to the sector, helping to meet the growing demand for water and sanitation services (Akhai and Abbass 2025; Agoncillo, 2020).

6.2 International Funding Mechanisms

Development Banks and Donor Agencies:

- **Financial Support:** Development banks and donor agencies play a crucial role in financing water and sanitation projects in developing countries (Ruiters & Amadi-Echendu, 2022). Institutions like the World Bank and the African Development Bank provide loans, grants, and technical assistance to support infrastructure development (White & Wahba, 2019). These organizations help countries build and maintain essential water and sanitation facilities, improve water management practices, and enhance service delivery. For instance, the World Bank's Water Global Practice works with countries to address water scarcity, improve water quality, and expand access to sanitation services.

Global Funds:

- **Sustainable Projects:** Global funds such as the Global Environment Facility and the Green Climate Fund offer funding for sustainable water and sanitation projects (Akhai 2024; Akhai and Abbass 2025; Mobilising Capital for Water: Blended Finance Solutions to Scale Investment in Emerging Markets,

2022). These funds support initiatives that promote environmental sustainability, climate resilience, and equitable access to water and sanitation services. The GEF, for example, finances projects that protect water ecosystems, reduce pollution, and enhance water security. The GCF focuses on climate adaptation and mitigation, providing resources to help countries build resilient water and sanitation infrastructure in the face of climate change.

These financing and investment mechanisms are vital for the development and maintenance of water and sanitation infrastructure (Water Infrastructure and Investment, 2023). They ensure that resources are available to meet the needs of growing populations, address environmental challenges, and provide equitable access to essential services.

7. CHALLENGES AND BARRIERS TO IMPLEMENTATION

The implementation of the right to water and sanitation faces several challenges, including legal and regulatory gaps, financial constraints, and high costs of infrastructure development and maintenance, especially in low-income countries (Tseole et al., 2022). Inadequate legal frameworks, weak enforcement mechanisms, fragmented regulatory structures, and lack of coordination among stakeholders can hinder effective infrastructure development (Akella et al., 2023).

7.1 Legal and Regulatory Gaps

- **Inadequate Legal Frameworks and Weak Enforcement Mechanisms:** Many countries lack comprehensive legal frameworks that explicitly recognize the right to water and sanitation. Even where such frameworks exist, enforcement mechanisms are often weak, leading to gaps in implementation and protection.
- **Fragmented Regulatory Structures and Lack of Coordination:** The regulatory landscape for water and sanitation is often fragmented, with multiple agencies and stakeholders involved. This fragmentation can lead to inefficiencies and a lack of coordinated efforts, impeding effective infrastructure development and service delivery.

7.2 Financial Constraints

- **Limited Financial Resources and Competing Priorities:** Governments, especially in low-income countries, often face limited financial resources and must balance competing priorities. This can restrict the amount of investment available for water and sanitation infrastructure (GLAAS Report 2022, 2023).

- **High Costs of Infrastructure Development and Maintenance:** The development and maintenance of water and sanitation infrastructure are capital-intensive. High costs can be a significant barrier, particularly in regions with limited financial capacity and access to funding (Chowns, 2015).

7.3 Social and Cultural Factors

- **Social Norms and Cultural Practices:** Social norms and cultural practices can influence the acceptance and use of sanitation facilities. For example, in some communities, open defecation may be culturally ingrained, making it challenging to promote the use of toilets.
- **Gender Disparities and Inequalities:** Gender disparities can limit access to water and sanitation for marginalized groups. Women and girls, in particular, may face barriers due to social norms, safety concerns, and lack of privacy, affecting their ability to access and use sanitation facilities (Water For People, 2025).

Addressing these challenges requires a multifaceted approach, including strengthening legal frameworks, increasing financial investments, and promoting social and cultural acceptance of water and sanitation practices (Budge et al., 2022). Coordination among stakeholders and innovative solutions can help overcome these barriers and ensure the realization of the right to water and sanitation for all.

8. BEST PRACTICES AND CASE STUDIES

The Water Services Act of 1997 in South Africa and the National Sanitation Law of 2007 in Brazil are successful legal and regulatory models for water and sanitation services (Rudolph & Muchesa, 2023; Saker et al., 2022). In India, the Swachh Bharat Mission has successfully mobilized public and private funds to improve sanitation infrastructure and achieve open defecation-free status. In Kenya, the Water Services Trust Fund supports community-based water and sanitation projects, leveraging local resources and partnerships.

India:

- **Swachh Bharat Mission:** The Swachh Bharat Mission launched in 2014, has indeed achieved significant success in improving sanitation infrastructure and reducing open defecation in India (Narayan et al., 2021; Swachh Bharat Mission - Gramin, 2024). The mission focused on constructing toilets and promoting behavioral changes (Swachh Bharat Mission - Gramin, 2024). Over 100 million toilets were constructed, and hundreds of thousands of villages were declared open defecation-free (Swachh Bharat Mission - Gramin, 2024). The mission also addressed solid and liquid waste management to enhance public health and environmental sustainability (Swachh Bharat Mission - Gramin, 2024; Khang and Akhai 2025). The Swachh Bharat Mission has led to the country with a high percentage of households having access to toilets (Sarkar & Bharat, 2021).

Kenya:

- **Water Services Trust Fund:** The Water Services Trust Fund, now known as WaterFund, is a Kenyan State Corporation established under the Water Act, 2016 (Fonseca et al., 2005; Water Sector Trust Fund (WaterFund), 2025). It provides grants to counties to help finance the development and management of water and sanitation services, particularly in marginalized and underserved areas (Fonseca et al., 2005; Water Sector Trust Fund (WaterFund), 2025). The fund aims to promote sustainable water resource management and enhance community participation in water and sanitation projects (Fonseca et al., 2005).

These best practices and case studies highlight successful legal frameworks and innovative financing mechanisms that have significantly improved water and sanitation services in various countries. They provide valuable lessons for other regions seeking to enhance their water and sanitation infrastructure.

9. RECOMMENDATIONS FOR STRENGTHENING LEGAL AND REGULATORY FRAMEWORKS

This review recommends strengthening legal and regulatory frameworks for water and sanitation (Santos et al., 2021). It suggests enhancing legal provisions, improving regulatory capacity (A Roadmap for Advancing Sanitation Regulation, 2025), increasing financial investment, and promoting social inclusion. Legal provisions should be strengthened to recognize the right to water and sanitation, while regulatory capacity should be improved to enforce standards and monitor compliance. Financial investment should be mobilized for infrastructure, and innovative financing mechanisms like Public-Private Partnerships (PUBLIC-PRIVATE-PARTNERSHIP LEGAL RESOURCE CENTER, 2022) and community-based funding models should be encouraged. Addressing gender disparities and social inequalities in access to water and sanitation is also recommended.

9.1 Enhancing Legal Provisions

- **Strengthen Constitutional and Legal Recognition:** It is crucial to enshrine the right to water and sanitation in national constitutions and legal frameworks (Peters, 2019). This provides a strong legal basis for ensuring access to these essential services for all citizens (Adugna, 2023). Countries should also develop comprehensive water and sanitation laws that address issues of equity, sustainability, and resilience (Peters, 2019). These laws should be aligned with international human rights standards and environmental agreements to ensure holistic and sustainable management of water resources (Santos et al., 2021). The Center for Water Security and Cooperation provides resources on water security laws from different countries (The Center for Water Security and Cooperation, 2020).

9.2 Improving Regulatory Capacity

- **Build Regulatory Capacity:** Strengthening the capacity of regulatory bodies is essential for effective enforcement of standards and monitoring compliance (A Roadmap for Advancing Sanitation Regulation, 2025). This includes providing adequate training, resources, and technical support to regulatory agencies (Akhai 2024). Enhancing the skills and knowledge of regulatory staff can improve the implementation and oversight of water and sanitation policies.
- **Promote Coordination and Collaboration:** Effective coordination and collaboration among regulatory agencies and stakeholders are vital for integrated water and sanitation management. Establishing clear roles and responsibilities, and fostering partnerships between government entities, private sector, and civil society can enhance regulatory effectiveness and service delivery.

9.3 Increasing Financial Investment

- **Mobilize Funding:** Increasing financial investment in water and sanitation infrastructure is critical (Fonseca et al., 2005). Governments should prioritize budget allocations for these sectors and seek to mobilize additional resources from international donors, development banks, and private investors (Fonseca et al., 2005). Innovative financing mechanisms, such as public-private partnerships (PUBLIC-PRIVATE-PARTNERSHIP LEGAL RESOURCE CENTER, 2022) and community-based funding models, can also be leveraged to attract investment and improve infrastructure development.
- **Encourage Innovative Financing Mechanisms:** PPPs can bring in private sector expertise and resources, while community-based funding models can enhance local ownership and sustainability of projects (Harvey, 2017). These mechanisms can help bridge the financing gap and ensure the long-term viability of water and sanitation infrastructure (Fonseca et al., 2005).

9.4 Promoting Social Inclusion

- **Address Gender Disparities and Social Inequalities:** It is important to address gender disparities and social inequalities in access to water and sanitation services. Policies and programs should be designed to ensure that marginalized groups, including women, children, and people with disabilities, have equitable access to these services. This includes removing structural barriers and promoting inclusive practices (Murray et al., 2025).
- **Engage Communities:** Engaging communities in the planning and implementation of water and sanitation projects is essential for ensuring cultural acceptability and sustainability. Community participation can enhance the relevance and effectiveness of projects, as well as foster a sense of ownership and responsibility among local populations.

Implementing these recommendations can help strengthen legal and regulatory frameworks, improve service delivery, and ensure the realization of the right to water and sanitation for all.

10. CONCLUSION

- Access to clean water and adequate sanitation is not only a fundamental human right but also a cornerstone of public health, social equity, and sustainable development. Despite global recognition of this right, billions of people still lack access to safe water and proper sanitation, highlighting the urgent need for robust legal and regulatory frameworks, increased investment, and innovative infrastructure solutions.

- Ensuring universal access to water and sanitation requires a comprehensive approach that integrates human rights principles with sustainable development objectives. Strong governance, well-defined legal structures, and effective policies are critical to safeguarding water resources and ensuring equitable distribution. Furthermore, aligning water and sanitation policies with the Sustainable Development Goals (SDGs), particularly SDG 6, is essential for advancing global efforts to achieve universal and sustainable water access.
- The economic and environmental benefits of improved water and sanitation services cannot be overstated. Investments in water infrastructure yield substantial returns by reducing healthcare costs, enhancing productivity, and fostering economic growth. Environmentally, sustainable water management practices contribute to the preservation of ecosystems, climate resilience, and water conservation. By adopting integrated approaches, governments and stakeholders can develop resilient water and sanitation systems that withstand the impacts of climate change and population growth.
- However, several challenges hinder progress, including financial constraints, weak enforcement mechanisms, and social and cultural barriers. Addressing these challenges requires multi-sectoral collaboration, innovative financing mechanisms such as public-private partnerships, and inclusive policies that prioritize marginalized communities. Strengthening regulatory bodies, improving monitoring systems, and fostering community participation are also essential to ensuring the long-term sustainability of water and sanitation infrastructure.
- Best practices from various countries demonstrate that legal and regulatory frameworks, when effectively implemented, can significantly improve access to clean water and sanitation. Successful models such as South Africa's Water Services Act, Brazil's National Sanitation Law, and India's Swachh Bharat Mission provide valuable insights into policy development and execution. These cases underscore the importance of tailored legal instruments that address local challenges while adhering to international human rights standards (Arif and Akhai 2024).

In conclusion, realizing the right to water and sanitation for all necessitates a concerted global effort to bridge existing gaps in access, infrastructure, and policy enforcement. Governments, international organizations, and local communities must work together to create inclusive, sustainable, and resilient water and sanitation systems. By prioritizing this essential right, we can pave the way for a healthier, more equitable, and sustainable future for all.

CHAPTER SUMMARY

Table 4 provides a comprehensive summary of the chapter.

Table 4. Summary of the chapter

Chapter Sections	Key Points
Introduction	Access to clean water and sanitation is a fundamental human right. The UN recognized this right in 2010. Legal and regulatory frameworks are essential for infrastructure development.
1. The Human Right to Water and Sanitation	**1.1 Definition and Recognition:** Ensures sufficient, safe, accessible, and affordable water. Grounded in international law (ICESCR). **1.2 Importance for Health and Dignity:** Prevents diseases, reduces mortality, and ensures dignity, particularly for women and girls.
2. Sustainable Development Goals (SDGs) and Water and Sanitation	**2.1 SDG 6:** Aims for universal and sustainable water access by 2030. **2.2 Interlinkages:** Affects other SDGs like health (SDG 3), gender equality (SDG 5), and climate action (SDG 13).
3. Legal Frameworks for Water and Sanitation Infrastructure Development	**3.1 International Legal Instruments:** ICESCR, CRC, Ramsar Convention, UN Watercourses Convention. **3.2 National Legal Frameworks:** Constitutional provisions and national water laws ensure equitable access and sustainability.
4. Regulatory Frameworks for Water and Sanitation Infrastructure	**4.1 Regulatory Bodies:** Water regulatory authorities oversee policies; sanitation agencies ensure facility standards. **4.2 Standards and Guidelines:** Water quality and sanitation facility standards protect public health and ensure accessibility.
5. Financing and Investment in Water and Sanitation Infrastructure	**5.1 Public and Private Roles:** Government investment is crucial; PPPs enhance development and service delivery. **5.2 International Funding:** Organizations like the World Bank, African Development Bank, GEF, and GCF support water projects.
6. Challenges and Barriers to Implementation	**6.1 Legal Gaps:** Weak frameworks and enforcement hinder progress. **6.2 Financial Constraints:** Limited resources and high costs, especially in low-income nations. **6.3 Social Factors:** Cultural norms, gender disparities, and marginalization impact access.
7. Best Practices and Case Studies	**7.1 Legal Models:** South Africa's Water Services Act (1997) and Brazil's National Sanitation Law (2007). **7.2 Financing Innovations:** India's Swachh Bharat Mission and Kenya's Water Services Trust Fund.

continued on following page

Table 4. Continued

Chapter Sections	Key Points
8. Recommendations for Strengthening Frameworks	**8.1 Legal Enhancements:** Strengthen legal recognition and develop comprehensive laws. **8.2 Regulatory Capacity:** Improve enforcement and coordination. **8.3 Financial Investment:** Mobilize funds, encourage PPPs. **8.4 Social Inclusion:** Address gender disparities, engage communities.
Conclusion	Effective legal and regulatory frameworks ensure sustainable, equitable water and sanitation infrastructure, upholding human rights and supporting sustainable development.

REFERENCES

A roadmap for advancing sanitation regulation. (2025). https://iris.who.int/handle/10665/381399

Abbas, M., Akhai, S., Abbas, U., Jafri, R., & Arif, S. M. (2025). AI-enabled sustainable urban planning and management. In *Real-World Applications of AI Innovation* (pp. 233–260). IGI Global Scientific Publishing.

Abbass, M., Abbas, U., Wani, S. A., & Akhai, S. (2025). Rethinking Global Food Governance From Historical Perspectives for a Sustainable Future. In *Innovative Trends Shaping Food Marketing and Consumption* (pp. 553–578). IGI Global Scientific Publishing. DOI: 10.4018/979-8-3693-8542-5.ch022

Abdelmoneim, A. A., Kimaita, H. N., Kalaany, C. M. A., Derardja, B., Dragonetti, G., & Khadra, R. (2025). IoT Sensing for Advanced Irrigation Management: A Systematic Review of Trends, Challenges, and Future Prospects [Review of IoT Sensing for Advanced Irrigation Management: A Systematic Review of Trends, Challenges, and Future Prospects]. Sensors, 25(7), 2291. Multidisciplinary Digital Publishing Institute. DOI: 10.3390/s25072291

Adeel, Z. (2017). A renewed focus on water security within the 2030 agenda for sustainable development. *Sustainability Science*, *12*(6), 891–894. DOI: 10.1007/s11625-017-0476-7

Adhikari, K. P. (2020). Governance for Sustainability of Rural Water Supply and Sanitation Schemes (RWSS): Case from NAPA WASH. *Nepalese Journal of Development and Rural Studies*, *17*, 26–40. DOI: 10.3126/njdrs.v17i0.34950

Adugna, D. (2023). Challenges of sanitation in developing counties - Evidenced from a study of fourteen towns, Ethiopia. *Heliyon*, *9*(1), e12932. Advance online publication. DOI: 10.1016/j.heliyon.2023.e12932 PMID: 36747957

Agoncillo, J. (2020). Financing the Water Sector – An Alternate Approach. https://2030wrg.org/financing-the-water-sector-an-alternate-approach/

Ahmad, N. (2020). Human right to water under international law regime: An overview. *Commonwealth Law Bulletin*, *46*(3), 415–439. DOI: 10.1080/03050718.2020.1770618

Akella, G. K., Wibowo, S., Grandhi, S., & Mubarak, S. (2023). Systematic Review A Systematic Review of Blockchain Technology Adoption Barriers and Enablers for Smart and Sustainable Agriculture.

Akhai, S. (2023). Biogas Plants for Sustainable Municipal Waste Management: A Brief Review. Handbook of Research on Safe Disposal Methods of Municipal Solid Wastes for a Sustainable Environment, 162-179. DOI: 10.4018/978-1-6684-8117-2.ch012

Akhai, S. (2023). From Black Boxes to Transparent Machines: The Quest for Explainable *AI. Available at: Social Science Research Network, doi: http://dx.doi.org/* DOI: 10.2139/ssrn.4390887

Akhai, S. (2023). Navigating the Potential Applications and Challenges of Intelligent and Sustainable Manufacturing for a Greener Future. *Evergreen*, *10*(4), 2237–2243. DOI: 10.5109/7160899

Akhai, S. (2024). Towards Trustworthy and Reliable AI The Next Frontier. In Explainable Artificial Intelligence (XAI) in Healthcare (Vol. 1, pp. 119-129). CRC Press, Taylor & Francis Group.

Akhai, S. (2024). Trends and Environmental Impact of Paper Consumption: A Prognostic Scenario for the Indian Market by 2030-A Case Study. In International Conference on Interdisciplinary Approaches in Civil Engineering for Sustainable Development (Vol. 464, pp. 11-18). Springer Nature Singapore. DOI: 10.1007/978-981-97-0910-6_2

Akhai, S., & Abbass, M. (2025). Toward Resilient Futures: The Role of AI-Driven Strategies in Climate Adaptation. In Nexus of AI, Climatology, and Urbanism for Smart Cities (pp. 325-340). IGI Global Scientific Publishing.

Akhai, S., & Taneja, T. (2024). Liquid Gold: Safeguarding Our Health Through Pure Drinking Water and Rigorous Water Testing. In Natural Resource Management Issues in Human-Influenced Landscapes (pp. 129-148). IGI Global.

Akhai, S., & Taneja, T. (2025). The Critical Role of Water Quality: Health Impacts, Contaminants, and Sustainable Solutions for Environmental and Human Well-being. In Smart Water Technology for Sustainable Management in Modern Cities (pp. 101-116). IGI Global Scientific Publishing.

Alcamo, J. (2018). Water quality and its interlinkages with the Sustainable Development Goals. *Current Opinion in Environmental Sustainability*, *36*, 126–140. DOI: 10.1016/j.cosust.2018.11.005

Anderson, D. M., Mahamane, E., Bauza, V., Mahamadou, K. O. B., Tantum, L. K., & Salzberg, A. (2023). Effects of environmental conditions on healthcare worker wellbeing and quality of care: A qualitative study in Niger. *PLOS Global Public Health*, *3*(12), e0002590. Advance online publication. DOI: 10.1371/journal.pgph.0002590 PMID: 38117837

Arif, S. M., & Akhai, S. (2024). Fostering a Sustainable and Disaster-Resilient Transportation Infrastructure. In *Challenges, Strategies, and Resiliency in Disaster and Risk Management* (pp. 205-219). IGI Global Scientific Publishing. DOI: 10.4018/979-8-3693-2721-0.ch009

Assegide, E., Alamirew, T., Bayabil, H. K., Dile, Y. T., Tessema, B., & Zeleke, G. (2022). Impacts of Surface Water Quality in the Awash River Basin, Ethiopia: A Systematic Review [Review of Impacts of Surface Water Quality in the Awash River Basin, Ethiopia: A Systematic Review]. Frontiers in Water, 3. Frontiers Media. DOI: 10.3389/frwa.2021.790900

Bartram, J., & Cairncross, S. (2010). Hygiene, Sanitation, and Water: Forgotten Foundations of Health. *PLoS Medicine*, *7*(11), e1000367. Advance online publication. DOI: 10.1371/journal.pmed.1000367 PMID: 21085694

Benefits of Investing in Water and Sanitation. (2011). *OECD studies on water*. Organization for Economic Cooperation and Development., DOI: 10.1787/9789264100817-

Bosona, T., & Gebresenbet, G. (2023). The Role of Blockchain Technology in Promoting Traceability Systems in Agri-Food Production and Supply Chains [Review of The Role of Blockchain Technology in Promoting Traceability Systems in Agri-Food Production and Supply Chains]. Sensors, 23(11), 5342. Multidisciplinary Digital Publishing Institute. DOI: 10.3390/s23115342

Briceno, C., Estache, A., & Shafik, N. T. (2004). Infrastructure Services in Developing Countries: Access, Quality, Costs, and Policy Reform. In World Bank policy research working paper. DOI: 10.1596/1813-9450-3468

Briscoe, J. (1999). The Changing Face of Water Infrastructure Financing in Developing Countries. *International Journal of Water Resources Development*, *15*(3), 301–308. DOI: 10.1080/07900629948826

Budge, S., Ambelu, A., Bartram, J., Brown, J., & Hutchings, P. (2022). Environmental sanitation and the evolution of water, sanitation and hygiene. *Bulletin of the World Health Organization*, *100*(4), 286–288. DOI: 10.2471/BLT.21.287137 PMID: 35386561

Calderón, A. J., & González, I. (2017). Some Hardware and Instrumentation Aspects of the Development of an Automation System for Jar Tests in Drinking Water Treatment. *Sensors (Basel)*, *17*(10), 2305. DOI: 10.3390/s17102305 PMID: 29019943

Cernev, T., & Fenner, R. (2019). The importance of achieving foundational Sustainable Development Goals in reducing global risk. *Futures*, *115*, 102492. DOI: 10.1016/j.futures.2019.102492

Chowns, E. (2015). Is Community Management an Efficient and Effective Model of Public Service Delivery? Lessons from the Rural Water Supply Sector in Malawi. *Public Administration and Development*, *35*(4), 263–276. DOI: 10.1002/pad.1737

Clean water for health and wellbeing. (2023). https://impact.economist.com/perspectives/health/clean-water-health-and-wellbeing

Country Legal Mapping. (2023). https://humanright2water.org/country-legal-mapping/

Department of economic and social affairs. (2025). In Energy statistics pocketbook. United Nations. DOI: 10.18356/9789211069280c001

Drinking-water quality regulation. (2024). https://www.who.int/teams/environment-climate-change-and-health/water-sanitation-and-health/water-safety-and-quality/drinking-water-quality-regulation

du Plessis, A. (2017). Global Water Quality Challenges. In *Springer water* (p. 13). Springer Nature., DOI: 10.1007/978-3-319-49502-6_2

Find the Standard You Need. (2023). https://www.awwa.org/Publications/Standards/Standards-List

Fonseca, C. F. C., van Dijk, M. P., & Cardone, R. (2005). Financing the water sector. *Waterlines*, *24*(2), 2–3. DOI: 10.3362/0262-8104.2005.042

Goal 6. (2022). https://sustainabledevelopment.un.org/sdg6

Goal 6 - Clean Water & Sanitation. (2024). https://sdg.iisd.org/sdgs/goal-6-clean-water-sanitation/

Goksu, A., Bakalian, A., Kingdom, B., Saltiel, G., Mumssen, Y., Soppe, G., Kolker, J. E., & Delmon, V. (2019). Reform and Finance for the Urban Water Supply and Sanitation Sector. In World Bank, Washington, DC eBooks. DOI: 10.1596/32244

Goksu, A., Trémolet, S., Kolker, J. E., & Kingdom, B. (2017). Easing the Transition to Commercial Finance for Sustainable Water and Sanitation. In World Bank, Washington, DC eBooks. DOI: 10.1596/27948

Harvey, A. (2017). Steps to sustainability: A road map for WASH. *Waterlines*, *36*(3), 185–203. DOI: 10.3362/1756-3488.17-00002

Human Rights to Water and Sanitation. (2022). https://www.unwater.org/water-facts/human-rights-water-and-sanitation

Hutton, G., & Varughese, M. (2016). The Costs of Meeting the 2030 Sustainable Development Goal Targets on Drinking Water, Sanitation, and Hygiene. In World Bank, Washington, DC eBooks. DOI: 10.1596/K8543

Indicators, S. D. G. (2024). https://unstats.un.org/sdgs/metadata/?Text=&Goal=6&Target=

Irujo, A. E. (2007). The Right to Water. *International Journal of Water Resources Development*, *23*(2), 267–283. DOI: 10.1080/07900620601182968

KDIGO Clinical Practice Guideline for Acute Kidney Injury. (2012).

Khang, A., & Akhai, S. (2024). Green intelligent and sustainable manufacturing: key advancements, benefits, challenges, and applications for transforming industry. Machine Vision and Industrial Robotics in Manufacturing, 405-417.

Khang, A., & Akhai, S. (2025). E-Waste and Lithium-ion Battery Recycling Insights for Sustainable Transportation. In Driving Green Transportation System Through Artificial Intelligence and Automation: Approaches, Technologies and Applications (pp. 203-230). Springer Nature Switzerland.

Khanna, A., Jain, S., Burgio, A., Bolshev, V., & Панченко, В. (2022). Blockchain-Enabled Supply Chain platform for Indian Dairy Industry: Safety and Traceability. *Foods*, *11*(17), 2716. DOI: 10.3390/foods11172716 PMID: 36076901

Kiefer, T. (n.d.). Legal_Res. Retrieved June 12, 2025, from https://www.worldwatercouncil.org/fileadmin/wwc/Programs/Right_to_Water/Pdf_doct/RWP-Legal_Res_1st_Draft_web.pdf

Kirschner, A. J. (2011). The Human Right to Water and Sanitation. *Max Planck Yearbook of United Nations Law*, *15*(1), 445–487. DOI: 10.1163/18757413-90000075

Levin, R., Villanueva, C. M., Beene, D., Cradock, A. L., Donat-Vargas, C., Lewis, J., Martínez-Morata, I., Minovi, D., Nigra, A. E., Olson, E. D., Schaider, L. A., Ward, M. H., & Deziel, N. C. (2023). US drinking water quality: exposure risk profiles for seven legacy and emerging contaminants [Review of US drinking water quality: exposure risk profiles for seven legacy and emerging contaminants]. Journal of Exposure Science & Environmental Epidemiology, 34(1), 3. Springer Nature. DOI: 10.1038/s41370-023-00597-z

Linkage of SDGs 3, 4, 5 and 12 with SDG 6. (2023). https://sdgs.un.org/partnerships/linkage-sdgs-3-4-5-and-12-sdg-6

Loewe, M., & Rippin, N. (2015). The Sustainable Development Goals of the Post-2015 Agenda: Comments on the OWG and SDSN Proposals. SSRN Electronic Journal. DOI: 10.2139/ssrn.2567302

Mobilising capital for water: blended finance solutions to scale investment in emerging markets. (2022). https://washmatters.wateraid.org/publications/mobilising-capital-for-water-blended-finance-solutions

Murray, P., Southey, K., Gibson, M., Sands, J., & Ong, D. L. T. (2025). Strength in Numbers: How Social Resources Travel Together to Increase Employee Engagement. *Asia Pacific Journal of Human Resources*, *63*(2), e70008. Advance online publication. DOI: 10.1111/1744-7941.70008

Narayan, A. S., Marks, S., Meierhofer, R., Strande, L., Tilley, E., Zurbrügg, C., & Lüthi, C. (2021). Advancements in and Integration of Water, Sanitation, and Solid Waste for Low- and Middle-Income Countries. *Annual Review of Environment and Resources*, *46*(1), 193–219. DOI: 10.1146/annurev-environ-030620-042304

Neto, S., & Camkin, J. (2020). What rights and whose responsibilities in water? Revisiting the purpose and reassessing the value of water services tariffs. *Utilities Policy*, *63*, 101016. DOI: 10.1016/j.jup.2020.101016

Norwood, R. (2023). International Documents. https://www.internationalwaterlaw.org/documents/intldocs/

Nwobodo, T. N., & Chukwu, K. E. (2020). COVID-19 Era and Water Supply: Challenges for Rural Communities in Eastern, Nigeria. *Journal of Geoscience and Environment Protection*, *8*(7), 219–233. DOI: 10.4236/gep.2020.87013

OHCHR and the rights to water and sanitation. (2024). https://www.ohchr.org/en/water-and-sanitation

Pathfinder, S. D. G. (2023). https://sdg-pathfinder.org/sdg/clean-water

Peters, D. (2019). Creating Policies and a Legal Framework. https://sswm.info/water-nutrient-cycle/water-sources/softwares/creating-and-enabling-environment/creating-policies-and-a-legal-framework-(ws)

Pradhan, S. K., Sinha, U., Satapathy, D. M., Swain, A. P., & Mishra, R. P. (2018). Assessment of household water treatment and storage practices. *International Journal of Community Medicine and Public Health*, *5*(3), 1060. DOI: 10.18203/2394-6040.ijcmph20180761

PUBLIC-PRIVATE-PARTNERSHIP LEGAL RESOURCE CENTER. (2022). https://ppp.worldbank.org/public-private-partnership/library/delegated-management-urban-water-supply-services-mozambique-summary-case-stuy-fipag-and-cra

Recommended Standards for Wastewater Facilities. (2008). https://www.health.state.mn.us/communities/environment/water/docs/tenstates/tenstatestan2014.pdf

Report, G. L. A. A. S. 2022. (2023). https://iris.who.int/bitstream/handle/10665/365297/9789240065031-eng.pdf?sfvrsn=f6b6f522_13

Rudolph, M., & Muchesa, E. (2023). Integrated and Sustainable Water and Sanitation Systems at Two Rural Sites in South Africa. *Water (Basel)*, *15*(22), 3974. DOI: 10.3390/w15223974

Ruiters, C., & Amadi-Echendu, J. (2022). Investment models for the water infrastructure value chain in South Africa: Investment measures, needs and priorities. *Water S.A.*, *48*(4 October). Advance online publication. DOI: 10.17159/wsa/2022.v48.i4.3852

Ruíz, E., Ortiz-Soriano, V., Talbott, M., Klein, B. A., Bastin, M. L. T., Mayer, K. P., Price, E. B., Dorfman, R., Adams, B. N., Fryman, L., Neyra, J. A., Elias, M., Taylor, M., McHatton, J., Aycinena, J. C., Diaz, A. M., Mason, S. A., Perkins, M. A., Sawaya, B. P., & Kouns, J. M. (2020). Development, implementation and outcomes of a quality assurance system for the provision of continuous renal replacement therapy in the intensive care unit. *Scientific Reports*, *10*(1), 20616. Advance online publication. DOI: 10.1038/s41598-020-76785-w PMID: 33244053

Saker, A., Pedraza, A. B., & Narayan, A. S. (2022). Regulating Citywide Inclusive Sanitation (CWIS) in Colombia. *International Journal of Environmental Research and Public Health*, *19*(9), 5669. DOI: 10.3390/ijerph19095669 PMID: 35565064

Saleh, A., Ibrahim, N., Awang, N. R., & Akbar, N. A. (2021). Characteristics study of ammonia-n and phosphorus in sewage wastewater effluent: A case study of Alkhumrah, Jeddah Wastewater Treatment Plant. *IOP Conference Series. Earth and Environmental Science*, *842*(1), 12034. DOI: 10.1088/1755-1315/842/1/012034

Santos, A. S. P., Pachawo, V., de Melo, M. C., & Vieira, J. M. P. (2021). Progress on legal and practical aspects on water reuse with emphasis on drinking water – an overview. *Water Science and Technology: Water Supply*, *22*(3), 3000–3014. DOI: 10.2166/ws.2021.412

Sarkar, I., Karforma, S., Bose, R., & Roy, S. (2022). Ubiquitous on-demand Water Reservoir Tracking System for Smart Village. *Universal Journal of Agricultural Research*, *10*(3), 193–203. DOI: 10.13189/ujar.2022.100302

Sarkar, S., & Bharat, G. K. (2021). Achieving Sustainable Development Goals in water and sanitation sectors in India. *Journal of Water, Sanitation, and Hygiene for Development : a Journal of the International Water Association, 11*(5), 693–705. DOI: 10.2166/washdev.2021.002

Satterthwaite, M. L. (2021). Assessing the Rights to Water and Sanitation: Between Institutionalization and Radicalization. https://www.law.georgetown.edu/international-law-journal/wp-content/uploads/sites/21/2021/06/GT-GJIL210015.pdf

Schertenleib, R. (2005). From conventional to advanced environmental sanitation. *Water Science and Technology, 51*(10), 7–14. DOI: 10.2166/wst.2005.0345 PMID: 16104400

Sustainable Development Goals. (2018). *Edward Elgar Publishing eBooks*. Edward Elgar Publishing., DOI: 10.4337/9781786438768

Swachh Bharat Mission - Gramin. (2024). https://swachhbharatmission.gov.in/SBMCMS/about-us.htm

Tanoh, R., Nikiema, J., Asiedu, Z., Jayathilake, N., & Cofie, O. (2021). The contribution of tipping fees to the operation, maintenance, and management of fecal sludge treatment plants: The case of Ghana. *Journal of Environmental Management, 303*, 114125. DOI: 10.1016/j.jenvman.2021.114125 PMID: 34844055

The Center for Water Security and Cooperation. (2020). https://law.thecwsc.org/

The human right to safe drinking water and sanitation. (2012). https://www.ohchr.org/en/stories/2012/06/human-right-safe-drinking-water-and-sanitation

Tropp, H. (2015). MAKING WATER A PART OF ECONOMIC DEVELOPMENT: The economic benefits of improved water management and services. In Routledge eBooks (p. 80). Informa. DOI: 10.4324/9780203132937-14

Tseole, N. P., Mindu, T., Kalinda, C., & Chimbari, M. J. (2022). Barriers and facilitators to Water, Sanitation and Hygiene (WaSH) practices in Southern Africa: A scoping review [Review of Barriers and facilitators to Water, Sanitation and Hygiene (WaSH) practices in Southern Africa: A scoping review]. PLoS ONE, 17(8). Public Library of Science. DOI: 10.1371/journal.pone.0271726

United Nations. (2024). *OHCHR | About water and sanitation*. OHCHR. https://www.ohchr.org/en/water-and-sanitation/about-water-and-sanitation

University of Minnesota human rights library. (2005). Choice Reviews Online, 42(12). DOI: 10.5860/CHOICE.42Sup-0630

Wahi, N. (2022). The Evolution of the Right to Water in India. *Water (Basel)*, *14*(3), 398. DOI: 10.3390/w14030398

Water and Sanitation Interlinkages across the 2030 Agenda for Sustainable Development. (2016). https://www.unwater.org/publications/water-and-sanitation-interlinkages-across-2030-agenda-sustainable-development

Water For People. (2025). https://www.linkedin.com/company/water-for-people

Water Infrastructure and Investment. (2023). https://sustainabledevelopment.un.org/content/documents/hlpwater/08-WaterInfrastInvest.pdf

Water is central in achieving all 17 SDGs. But how? (2023). https://siwi.org/latest/water-is-central-in-achieving-all-17-sdgs-but-how/

Water Sector Trust Fund (WaterFund). (2025). https://www.linkedin.com/company/waterfund

White, R., & Wahba, S. (2019). Addressing constraints to private financing of urban (climate) infrastructure in developing countries. *International Journal of Urban Sustainable Development*, *11*(3), 245–256. DOI: 10.1080/19463138.2018.1559970

Whitehead, P. G., Mimouni, Z., Butterfield, D., Bussi, G., Hossain, M. A., Peters, R., Shawal, S., Holdship, P., Rampley, C. P. N., Jin, L., & Ager, D. (2021). A New Multibranch Model for Metals in River Systems: Impacts and Control of Tannery Wastes in Bangladesh. *Sustainability (Basel)*, *13*(6), 3556. DOI: 10.3390/su13063556

Williams, C. (2000). STANDARDS. https://epd.georgia.gov/sites/epd.georgia.gov/files/related_files/site_page/standards.pdf

Wolf, J., Johnston, R. B., Ambelu, A., Arnold, B. F., Bain, R., Bräuer, M., Brown, J., Caruso, B. A., Clasen, T., Colford, J. M.Jr, Mills, J. E., Evans, B., Freeman, M. C., Gordon, B., Kang, G., Lanata, C. F., Medlicott, K., Prüss-Üstün, A., Troeger, C., & Cumming, O. (2023). Burden of disease attributable to unsafe drinking water, sanitation, and hygiene in domestic settings: A global analysis for selected adverse health outcomes. *Lancet*, *401*(10393), 2060–2071. DOI: 10.1016/S0140-6736(23)00458-0 PMID: 37290458

Zhou, X., Moinuddin, M., & Xu, M. (2017). Sustainable Development Goals Interlinkages and Network Analysis: A practical tool for SDG integration and policy coherence. 122. https://pub.iges.or.jp/pub/sustainable-development-goals-interlinkages

APPENDIX

Abbreviations

SDG Sustainable Development Goal
SDG 1 Sustainable Development Goal 1: No Poverty
SDG 2 Sustainable Development Goal 2: Zero Hunger
SDG 3 Sustainable Development Goal 3: Good Health & Well-being
SDG 5 Sustainable Development Goal 5: Gender Equality
SDG 6 Sustainable Development Goal 6: Clean Water & Sanitation
SDG 11 Sustainable Development Goal 11: Sustainable Cities & Communities
SDG 13 Sustainable Development Goal 13: Climate Action
SDG 14 Sustainable Development Goal 14: Life Below Water
SDG 15 Sustainable Development Goal 15: Life on Land
UNGA United Nations General Assembly
ICESCR International Covenant on Economic, Social and Cultural Rights
CRC Convention on the Rights of the Child
CEDAW Convention on the Elimination of All Forms of Discrimination Against Women
UDHR Universal Declaration of Human Rights
UNWC UN Watercourses Convention
PPP Public-Private Partnership
GEF Global Environment Facility
GCF Green Climate Fund
IWRM Integrated Water Resources Management
EPA Environmental Protection Agency
NPDWR National Primary Drinking Water Regulations
WHO World Health Organization
UNICEF United Nations Children's Fund
WB World Bank
AfDB African Development Bank
OECD Organisation for Economic Co-operation and Development
CESCR Committee on Economic, Social and Cultural Rights
IWA International Water Association
IHS Indian Health Service
FSIS Food Safety and Inspection Service
WSTF Water Services Trust Fund

Chapter 9

From Hashtags to Human Rights:

Digital Advocacy and Constitutional Engagement in India and Nepal

Sushil Dhakal
https://orcid.org/0000-0002-7638-9636
Uttaranchal University, India

Anjum Parvez
https://orcid.org/0000-0002-4874-1372
Uttaranchal University, India

Papiya Golder
https://orcid.org/0009-0008-6093-3159
Brainware University, India

Maitrayae Sadhu
https://orcid.org/0009-0006-9346-9423
Brainware University, India

ABSTRACT

This chapter provides a critical argument on the relationship between digital advocacy and constitutional engagement in India and Nepal in regard to redefining citizen participation in the digital space, rights discourse, and accountability to the people and democracy. It talks about the development of digital civic activism protests of Nirbhaya, CAA-NRC demonstrations, and the Enough is Enough movement, pointing out the revolutionary contribution of hashtags and internet mobilizations. The

DOI: 10.4018/979-8-3693-3920-6.ch009

chapter offers a comparative constitutional overview of legal safeguards of digital expression, judicial involvement, regulatory schemes and surveillance. It provides analysis of such issues as algorithmic censorship, digital divides, state interventions, promoting emergence of inclusive, rights-based practices in digital governance.

INTRODUCTION

Backdrop

The digitalization of the modern world is also accompanied by the "unprecedented connection" between digital technologies and the constitutional act (Celeste, 2021), as social media has become an important mechanism of civil participation and human rights activism (Gray-Hawkins, 2018). In South Asia, the country of India and Nepal provide interesting comparative analysis of the revolution that digital platforms and particularly hashtags brought to the ways of political representation, the formation of social movements, and the discourse of the constitution (A. Acharya, 2024; Chhibber, 2022; P. Kumar, 2025). The current work titled "From Hashtags to Human Rights: Digital Advocacy and Constitutional Engagement in India and Nepal" falls between the trends of digital constitutionalism and digital constitutionalization, the involvement of civil societies in neo-constitutionalism, and democratic revolution in the era of digital society.

This pertinent enquiry is closely connected to the United Nations Sustainable Development Goal 16 (SDG 16) which strives towards fostering peaceful and inclusive societies to enable sustainable development, the access to justice to all people and the establishment of effective, accountable and inclusive institutions at all levels (United Nations, 2015). The study attracts special attention to relevance of inclusive access to justice and participatory decision-making as characterized in the SDG Targets 16.7 and 16.10 (Balasubramanian et al., 2022). In India and Nepal, population groups that were previously excluded, marginalized and geographically isolated have been able to take part in the fabric of the public discourse through digital media, questioning the authority of the state, demanding accountability and in this way fortifying constitutional democracies (A. Acharya, 2024; Fatima et al., 2025).

The examples of such hashtag activism can be seen in social movements like #Nirbhaya, #MeTooIndia, and #FarmersProtest in India that involved transforming passive citizenship into active citizenship online (Barua, 2025). These online campaigns have enabled rapid sharing of information, participatory politics and the ability to demand rights in a constitutional framework. Similarly, the Nepal #EnoughIsEnough campaign has demonstrated how the digital form of protest by the youth uses their voice to demand more transparency within the government, and encourage constitutional reform (Heaton, 2020). Both countries have seen an overhaul of what civic engagement means with social media being much more than simply a communication form, but also de facto constitutional space in which rights are bargained, and state responsibilities are pursued.

There are however problems in the new digital civic space. Matters like algorithmic censorship, excessive policing and digital surveillance risk dashing the freedoms brought about by such sites (Tech Global Institute, 2025). Yet, despite these limitations, digital advocacy is critical route to constitutional action, legal transformation and democratic empowerment in not only India but also in Nepal. In that regard, the study aims to address the question of the role of digital rights activism in the construction of inclusive institutions and the promotion of access to justice, supporting the primary vision of SDG 16 in the more networked world.

Objectives and Scope of the Chapter

The chapter attempts to understand how digital advocacy has provided a revolutionary change to reform civil rights participation in the constitutional democracies of India and Nepal. The chapter is anchored in the wider debate of digital constitutionalism and, therefore, set to explore how digital platforms especially social media, have become a potent resource of civic engagement, mobilization of protests, and rights enforcement in the 21st century.

The main aims of this chapter can be defined as follows:

1. To analyze comparatively the constitutional provisions on civil liberties, notably, the right to freedom of expression and assembly in both, India and Nepal.
2. To trace large scale digital advocacy work and rights-based movements in both countries namely the Nirbhaya movement, CAA-NRC unrest and farmers protest in India and the Enough is Enough movement in Nepal.
3. To review the presence of social media in promoting political awareness, digital engagement and collective action, especially youth, females and underprivileged groups.
4. To evaluate the legal and regulatory environment to regulate digital activism, including the emergent surveillance regime, censorship and algorithmic control in both states.
5. In order to establish structural issues and possibilities of enhancing constitutional cooperation in the digital arena.
6. In order to offer policy suggestions that India and Nepal can implement to increase the digital civic space, protect digital rights, and develop a healthy, sensitive, and constitutionally anchored digital mode of the public sphere.

The chapter involves itself in a comparative and interdisciplinary look at the intersections of digital technology, constitutional law and civic movements. On the one hand, it is limited to the discussions of states in a specific region (India and Nepal); on the other hand, it sets the context on the global trends of the digital activism and the constitutionalism. The research limits itself to the analysis of events that have happened after 2010, focusing on constitutional changes, court rulings, and major digital movements. It does not touch on technical matters of the internet governance or cybersecurity but is still founded on matters of rights and democracy.

Methodology

The chapter has adopted a qualitative, comparative, and interdisciplinary research approach incorporating findings about the constitutional law, political science, and digital media studies. This is mainly based on doctrinal legal research, where constitutional mandate based on the freedom of speech, assembling, privacy, and information and internet rights in India and Nepal are researched by analyzing primary texts of the law, landmark cases of the supreme court and the statutory structures. This is complemented by a case study methodology, which involves a closer examination of few of such iconic digital movements including the Nirbhaya protests, CAA-NRC protests, and the Farmers agitation in India as well as the Enough is Enough campaign in Nepal. The case studies are examined with regard to their origins, means of mobilization, utilization of digital space, dialog within constitutional discourse, and legal-political consequences.

In order to comprehend the way these movements express themselves, the chapter makes use of content analysis and discourse analysis of media reports and published statements. It has been backed with the secondary literature review that encompasses academic literature, policy documents, and works of digital rights groups. It also takes up the international perspectives on digital constitutionalism and the freedom of speech. Finally, the comparative analytical perspective is implemented to detect similarities and differences in legal safeguards, civil participation, court reaction, and digital infrastructure in India and Nepal.

Theoretical Framework

Digital advocacy and constitutional engagement are the subject of inquiry, and several interconnected theoretical approaches help shed light on the emerging interaction between digital technologies, digital campaigns and networked advocacy, digital constitutionalism, human rights and constitutional processes.

The symbolic force of the hashtag is being used in digital campaigns to create what Dobrin refers to as a so-called public sphere that allows the individuals, who are dispersed, to form around stories of justice (Dobrin, 2020). This is in line with the concept of networked advocacy development by Keck and Sikkink in which loosely networked actors are using digital networks to mobilize the issue of rights to a greater scale, outside of local or national territories (Keck & Sikkink, 1999).

The digital sphere is becoming more and more constitutionalized in the realm of modern politics. Researchers referring to such a phenomenon as digital constitutionalism suggest that due to the lack of proper legal frameworks, in practice, digital platforms became a default location of civic participation and the bargaining of rights (S. Udupa, 2019). Under this perspective, hashtags and digital arenas themselves do not serve only as communicative means of organization but are also means of expression of the constitutional value of transparency, equality and the right to protest.

Digital constitutionalism offers a critical dimension in terms of analyzing the re-imagining and challenge of constitutional values and guarantees in digital times. Researchers argue that the efforts of traditional constitutional frameworks, which were not created with the digital world in mind, are currently challenged unlike ever before to protect the basic human rights in an online setting (P. Kumar, 2025). This has led to a paradigm shift towards digital constitutionalism that aims at establishing that the values and liberties of democracy are maintained in the face of rapid change in technology and growing dependence on digital services to conduct discourse in society. It highlights the necessity of the dynamic interpretations of the Constitution that could protect the individual against the new types of abuse of digital rights and unrestricted government interferences (Celeste, 2019; P. Kumar, 2025).

At the same time, the policing of cyberspace creates a conflict between government control and citizens' rights. Policies which implement surveillance systems, biometric solutions, and cybersecurity frameworks are usually dubious of infringing the privacy and digital inclusiveness (Tech Global Institute, 2025). This issue is especially relevant when the freedom of digital rights activism is undermined by the lack of civil society participation, undermining the system of accountability and reform. Under these conditions, participatory systems and grassroots mobilization plays a central role in the achievement of equitable digital governance (Chaudhary, 2024).

Besides, theoretical solutions like originalism, organic interpretation, and transformative constitutionalism provide a way to learn about ways of reacting to new realities driven by digital technologies in the process of trial and error made by courts and other constitutional actors (K. R. Dahal, 2022). These interpretation methods enable constitutions to be responsive and inclusive to the social and technological changes, particularly when they touch on new matters in digital rights (Chaudhary, 2024).

In addition, at the point of intersection between the digital media and the human rights activism, it is clear that the digital media facilitate new participatory cultures.

It is defined by the digital mobilization, click-based activism, and self-advocacy that enable individuals and organizations to get into the discussion of human rights in a presentable and upsized form (George & Leidner, 2019). These strategies are also prone to operating through a wide variety of avenues, comprising intergovernmental advocacy, media interventions, judicial actions, and grassroot mobilization (Relly & Pakanati, 2020). It is important to note that digital solutions never replace traditional activisms, although they provide amplitude to messages and scale up human rights campaigns. Instead, they act within a hybrid model of participation with blending online action with offline campaigns.

Digital advocacy and constitutional engagement within the context of India and Nepal are mediated through the varied historical, political, and social patterns developed by these two countries. The country of India, having a vast constitutional scheme and a fast-growing digital environment, faces ambition, as well as, tensions in the realm of digital democracy and rights protection (D. S. Kumar, 2024). The changing constitutional order in Nepal, in combination with its striving to be digitalized, represents a fine balance between the authority of the state and the rights of the citizenry (Chaudhary, 2024). Though India grapples to match its established constitutional principles to the changes brought by technology (Awasthi et al., 2024), the digital governance ventures in Nepal tend to argue with their inclusiveness, protection of minority rights, and the absence of state intrusion (Neupane, 2024). For both countries, the potential of digital advocacy to democratize is linked to effective reinforcement of participatory processes, adjustment of constitutional provisions to the present realities, and the creation of cooperation networks that embrace both online and offline dynamics of civic participation (Chaudhary, 2024; Gupta, 2019).

CONSTITUTIONAL FRAMEWORKS AND CIVIL RIGHTS: A COMPARATIVE OVERVIEW

Fundamental Rights and Freedoms in India and Nepal

An exhaustive enumeration of fundamental rights can be seen in Part III of the Constitution of India consisting of Articles 12 to 35. These rights can be enforced in the courts, and they are regarded as fundamental to the growth of individuals and the nation (Jain, 2018). These six major rights are: right to equality (which forbids discrimination based on religion, race, caste, sex, or place of birth), right to freedom (which includes speech, expression, assembly, association, movement, residence and profession), right against exploitation (which outlaws human trafficking and forced labor), right to freedom of religion, cultural and educational rights (which safeguard the interests of minorities), and the right to constitutional remedies, which gives citizens the power to approach courts in case their rights are infringed (D. D. Basu, 2024).

The rights are not absolute, and the state can impose reasonable restrictions in the interests of security, public order and morality. Freedom of expression can be limited to prevent any defamation or threats to national integrity. The court plays a major role in guaranteed protection of fundamental rights and individuals can apply directly to the Supreme Court to enforce (Gardbaum, 2006).

In a similar manner, the Constitution of Nepal in Part 3 (Articles 16 to 48) of the Constitution also provides guarantees of fundamental rights, such as equality before the law, freedoms of speech, assembly, association, religion, and the right to constitutional remedies (Tripathi, 2015). The rights framework in Nepal also highlights social justice, economic rights and protection of marginalized groups due to its recent adoption of a federal democratic republic. Similar to India, Nepal has justiciable rights which can be enforced in the Supreme Court (Gautam, 2020).

Right to Freedom of Expression and Assembly in Digital Spaces

Freedom of expression and assembly in the digital space is a constitutionally guaranteed right in both India and Nepal, however the latest developments in law and policy making has shown that there are shifting dynamics and pressures in ensuring these rights are respected (U. Acharya & Bhattarai, 2015; Adhikari, 2024).

In India, the Constitution in Article 19(1)(a) grants the right to free speech and expression, which the Supreme Court has clarified to apply to the online environment, social media, and online forums (Tuchtfeld, 2024). But Article 19(2) allows the state to make a reasonable restriction in the interests of national security, public order, decency and in the interests of other mentioned reasons. This is governed by the Information Technology (IT) Act, 2000, and the following rules, namely the Information Technology (Intermediary Guidelines and Digital Media Ethics Code) Rules, 2021, which regulate digital content and impose on intermediaries the obligation to take down illegal information within a brief period (A. Kumar, 2021). The IT Act Section 69A gives the government the power to order the blocking of online content in the interest of sovereignty and public order, and Section 79 gives intermediary safe harbor provided they comply with government takedown requests (Wadhwa, 2025).

Courts have been important in shaping the parameters of digital expression. In the seminal case of Shreya Singhal v. Union of India (2015), the Section 66A of IT Act that criminalized unclear and broad groups of online speech was struck down bolstering the idea that online speech is given the same constitutional protection as traditional media (Abraham, 2015). But cases such as the WhatsApp misuse showed that there was a problem with unregulated misinformation on the internet, and some form of stronger regulation was necessary to ensure that free speech and safety were protected (Banaji et al., 2019). Even the judiciary has stressed the idea of proportionality in restraint, such as in the Anuradha Bhasin v. Union of India case of 2020 when the indefinite internet shutdowns were ruled unconstitutional (Juyal, 2023).

The Constitution of 2015 in Nepal promises the freedom of expression and the right to information and the nation is known to have a relatively free press environment. Nevertheless, a new Social Media Act Bill presented in 2025 has severely worried journalists and civil society (Post Report, 2025). The Bill requires registration of social media platforms, gives broad powers to authorities to delete indecent or misleading information, and represents a wide variety of online actions as criminal, such as defamation, trolling, and distribution of material that can damage reputation (Civicus, 2025). Opponents claim that the lack of clarity in the Bill can be exploited to muzzle critics and choke freedom of speech that is guaranteed by the constitution and may result in self-censorship and penalties on the users (Post Report, 2025). The Bill suggests strict punishment, imposing exorbitant fines and up to five years of prison, and has been already criticized as having no evident mechanisms of control over abuse.

Both India and Nepal thus face the challenge of balancing the protection of digital rights with legitimate concerns over security, misinformation, and public order. While constitutional guarantees remain strong, the evolving regulatory landscape and the potential for overreach underscore the need for clear, fair, and proportionate laws to ensure that digital spaces remain open forums for free expression and assembly.

Role of Judiciary in Protecting Digital Rights

In both India and Nepal, the courts have a leading role in ensuring the digital rights, in understanding the constitutional guarantees with regards to the technically advancing and fast-paced digital communication. The Supreme Court in India has led the way in using the fundamental rights to address the digital realm. Remarkably, in the case of Anuradha Bhasin v. Union of India (2020), the Court observed that access to the internet was a part of the right to freedom of speech and expression in Art. 19(1) (a), and the right to carry on any trade or business in Art. 19(1) (g) (Maheshwari & Daka, 2024). The Court added that internet shutdowns should pass the necessity and proportionality test and that they can only be employed in exceptional times, including situations of public emergencies or when there is a threat to public safety (Maheshwari & Daka, 2024). Nevertheless, critiques have observed that although proportionality has been adopted as a criterion, its strict implementation has largely been wanting, and this has led to regular and even extended internet blackouts that inconvenience lives and muzzle freedom of expression (Maheshwari & Daka, 2024).

Judicial review and enforcement mechanisms have kept the government and other individuals/entities responsible and in check when it comes to the violation of digital rights. As an example, in Amar Jain v. Union of India, Supreme Court ruled in 2025 that digital access was a fundamental right and ordered the state to close the digital divide and make digital access inclusive to marginalized communities. The Court emphasized that the right to life in Article 21 has to be read in the context of the technological realities and therefore digital inclusion is not a question of policy but constitutional mandate. The judiciary in Nepal has also claimed its position in protecting digital rights as the nation comes up with new legislations to control the media and information technology. In Nepal, privacy has been declared a basic constitutional right by the Supreme Court which has directed all state-owned companies such as Nepal Telecom to ensure strong privacy protection measures and prohibit unauthorized access of data (Dhakal, 2025).

Nepalese courts successfully ensure and support the Right to Privacy as a form of judicial activism and public interest litigation, especially when sensitive digital information and electronic communications are at stake (Jha, 2024). The Supreme Court of Nepal is applauded to have made future-oriented decisions, addressing gaps in the legislation and cementing the constitutional rights in cyberspace. Nevertheless, there are still issues, including the lack of particular legislation and unequal enforcement, so judicial oversight is significant in the meantime (Jha, 2024). Representatives of the judiciary, having passed training and interacted with international standards, have confirmed their willingness to consider cases regarding freedom of expression and the right to information in digital environments, stressing the importance of finding a balance between regulation and the safety of civic rights (T. H. T., 2023). The Nepal courts thereby become a significant restraint against excessive powers of the executive to assure that new digital laws are within the provisions of the constitution and international human rights provisions.

Even though judicial activism in India and Nepal has played a crucial role in bridging the gaps in legislation and ensuring the preservation of digital rights, policy makers, lawyers and technologists must continue to work together. Digital transformation should be accompanied by solid policies and technological infrastructure to make sure that it empowers and does not harm access to justice, privacy, and other fundamental freedoms (Jha, 2024; Mathew, 2025).

DIGITAL ADVOCACY AND SOCIAL MOVEMENTS IN INDIA

Landmark Movements

The digital advocacy has highly transformed the face of social movement in India since it has facilitated the use of speedy mobilization, collectivity of people, and voice to those who have not yet been heard in the society. It was the Nirbhaya protests in 2012 where the whole nation went out in fury over the gang rape and murder of a young woman in Delhi. The presence of social media and information and communication technologies (ICTs) played a critical role in organizing mass protests, disseminating personal experience, and build global support (A. Dey, 2018). The movement did not only bring monumental changes in the legal system, but it also established the culture in the society that was encourage the brave voice of its victims, and the hashtags like #Nirbhaya and #StopRape became very popular. It was a paradigm shift in gender activism in India with the digital space as the platform of both collective and personal debate of gender violence (A. Dey, 2018).

In the India Against Corruption movement (2011) with the initiations of Anna Hazare, the social media sites were utilized to depict the instances of corruption and rally around the banner of transparency and accountability. It was a twofold online exercise that rallied the masses behind it and facilitated creation of national discussion on clean governance (Davies, 2017). The movement also led to the Aam Aadmi Party. It showed the positive application of digital technology to facilitate civic participation and not only responsive policymaking but also how the internet can be potentially revolutionary in terms of the establishment of democratic forces and accountability of authority (R. Kumar, 2015).

The positive realities of digital advocacy were additionally revealed by the CAA-NRC protests (2019-2020). Such hashtags as #NoCAA, #NoNRC and #ShaheenBagh became viral, twitter, Facebook and WhatsApp groups were used by activists to organize sit-in, post legal information, and to dispel misinformation (Edingo, 2021). These places provided an opportunity to spread leadership and connect different groups, and thus the movement became more powerful and recognizable worldwide.

The same can be seen with the Farmers Protests (2020-2021), as the hashtags, #FarmersProtest and #StandWithFarmers, were used to gain international support, and digital media became an essential source of organizing marches, live-streaming protests, and debating the state on the internet (O. Basu, 2021). The digital connectivity in the movement led to the support of the world celebrities, which spilled power into the movement.

Environmental and tribal rights movements, such as #SaveAarey (R. Dey, 2025) and #SaveHasdeo (Drury, 2024), have used digital campaigns to spotlight ecological destruction and indigenous rights. These hashtags mobilized urban youth, environmentalists, and tribal communities, transforming local issues into national debates. Digital advocacy also played a significant role in campaigns for digital privacy (#RightToPrivacy) (Chhibber, 2022), LGBTQ+ rights (#LoveIsLove) (Garg, 2022), student activism (#HokKolorob) (Chaudhuri, 2019), tax justice (#LahuKaLagaan) (Chhibber, 2022), and the global #MeToo movement (Pain, 2021), which found strong resonance in India, encouraging survivors to share their experiences and demand accountability.

During the COVID-19 pandemic, the #LockDownMeinLockUp campaign used digital platforms to promote awareness of a 131% spike in domestic violence, sharing real survivor stories, celebrity posts, fund-raising, and advocacy (Mukherjee, 2021). Collectively, these movements illustrate how digital tools and hashtags have become indispensable for mobilizing public opinion, shaping policy debates, and fostering participatory democracy in India.

Role of social media in Mobilization and Awareness

In India, social media has emerged as an inevitable instrument of mobilization and awareness, and the number of user identities is more than 491 million which represents nearly a third of India (Kemp, 2025a). Such tools as Facebook, WhatsApp, Instagram, and YouTube have become part of life and Indians are spending an average of 2 hours and 28 minutes daily on these platforms (Howe, 2025). This widespread use, particularly by the young, has very much decreased the information asymmetry which then permits speedy spread of news, ideas and calls to action. The digital revolution has therefore empowered citizens so that they get real times updates as well as contribute to the discussions that concern them, leading to an informed and participatory citizenry (Dar & Nagrath, 2022).

The emergence of social media has also changed the manner in which information is consumed and shared, and it is the strong vehicle through which individuals are able to create awareness about social, political and economic issues. The use of hashtags, viral content, etc. arouses interest towards causes that could otherwise be ignored, whereas the interactive elements of such platforms enable individuals to react to the content, express their views, and organize the support (Sangeetha & Saravana, 2025). The possibility to break the geographical and social boundaries has provided marginalized voices with a platform which broadcasted their concerns to a national and even international level.

The government and political parties have realized that social media can be used to reach out to people in an interactive way. During the general elections, extensive digital campaigns via Twitter (now X), Facebook, and WhatsApp have been observed where major parties use such platforms to communicate messages about their campaigns, policies, and mobilize voters (Mahapatra & Plagemann, 2019).

The government uses applications such as MyGov and official Twitter accounts to share information, seek feedback, and popularize such initiatives as Digital India, citizen-competition and Swachh Bharat Abhiyan (Malhotra et al., 2019). Such initiatives have increased the level of participatory administration and visibility of administration besides allowing a quick response to the requests of the people.

The recent challenges and opportunities to constitutionalism in the digital age can be viewed in the light of the opportunity of shaping social discourse and civic engagement via social media. The dynamism of the digital space that very instantaneous interconnection and mass mobilization portray necessitates the re-conception of rights, responsibilities, and processes of regulation such that, on the one hand, freedom of expression can be guaranteed, and on the other, the prevention of misinformation (De Gregorio & Radu, 2022).

Legal and Governmental Responses to Digital Activism

The legal and governmental reactions towards digital activism in India have changed at a quick pace over the last few years, showing the opportunity and the issues with the digital age. New policies and laws have been enacted by the government to control the use of online platforms taking into consideration the need to balance innovation, user safety and constitutional rights.

The Information Technology (Intermediary Guidelines and Digital Media Ethics Code), 2021 is a significant change in the sphere of the regulation of online content and accountability of intermediaries. These Rules also place heavy requirements on intermediaries, such as taking down the content in 36 hours, assigning compliance officers, and providing public transparency reports on a monthly basis (A. Kumar & Jha, 2022). They also provide government with the power to order the removal of content that authorities perceive is harmful to sovereignty, security, or order, and locate the first originator of messages, which has been of controversy because it affects privacy (A. Kumar & Jha, 2022). Critics believe that these provisions violate a fundamental right such as privacy and free speech and are not within the scope of the parent IT Act, 2000 (Guha & Matilal, 2023). Various High Courts have either stayed or challenged some provisions of the Rules on the basis of breach of constitutional provisions and exceeding executive power (Guha & Matilal, 2023).

The landmark 2017 decision by the Supreme Court in Puttaswamy v. Union of India that held the right to privacy as a fundamental right has been a reference point in the digital regulation debate and yet the application of these rights is a matter of dispute.

The Digital Personal Data Protection Act, 2023 continues to build on the framework of digital governance with data fiduciaries being required to seek user consent before processing any of their data and also to put in place stringent security measures that will keep the data of users at this stage secure (Burman, 2023). Nonetheless, the Act authorizes the government with sweeping right to exclude state agencies, which is frowned upon by proponents of democracy and civil rights as it may facilitate abuse of personal information in the name of national interest (Sundara & Narendran, 2023). The Act additionally also allows transfer of data across borders, eliminates prior localization obligations, and changes criminal liabilities founded on violations to huge financial fines.

Moving forward, the currently drafted Digital India Act is bound to upgrade the outmoded IT Act of 2000, which offers a contemporary legal infrastructure of the Indian digital space (Manda & Misra, 2024). Policymakers have called for massive stakeholder engagements so that new laws can be made with inputs of the consumers, industry, startups and the civil society (Primus Partners & Institute for Competitiveness, 2023). The rising trend of digital activism represents an ongoing process through which the legal development of India will become tremendously important in determining the parameters of free speech, privacy, and state surveillance in the digital era.

DIGITAL MOBILIZATION AND RIGHTS MOVEMENTS IN NEPAL

Civil Society Movements in the Post-2015 Constitutional Era

With the 2015 Constitution of Nepal, digital mobilization has become a significant part of civil society activism in the country, and social media is now a very effective tool of awareness and collective resistance. The internet and mobile penetration have increased rapidly as 16.5 million people have internet access and 14.3 million people have a social media identity in early 2025, which has allowed activists to reach more people than ever before and organize campaigns at a scale and speed never seen before (Kemp, 2025b). The online activism provided a significant opportunity to empower the problem, which might be suppressed in the general media, enabled the discussion over various groups of people and created a movement to support the problem (Amtzis, 2014).

With the use of digital platforms, activists have launched the rights movements of #RageAgainstRape (De, 2023) and #JusticeForNirmala (Dissanayake, 2023) to appeal to the accountability and justice in cases of high-profile gender-based violence. The hashtags brought together the youths; the feminist organizations and people working in cities and turned the personal tragedy into national movements about gender equality and accountability of the government. The digital space has as well played a role in aiding the Madheshi movement where activists would voice out their demands via online forums and social media on wanting a bigger inclusion and federal rights to counter the narratives that mostly disregard their voices in the mainstream media (Rayamajhi, 2021).

Digital mobilization has also been helpful to environmental advocacy. Digital petitions, viral posts, and high-profile hashtag-driven campaigns have been used in anti-proposed Nijgadh International Airport and pro-conservation of Chure regions campaigns to draw attention to the problem of ecological devastation and pressure policymakers. It has united environmentalists, local communities and diaspora supporters, and the subjects of environmental protection are part of the actual visible debate in society (Chalise, 2023).

In general, since 2015, digital mobilization has emerged as a central part of the civil society movements in Nepal as it has made it possible to transmit information much faster, promote inclusion in discourse, and compel the government to answer their calls. This has given importance to the capability of social media to organize without organization allowing even the remotely affiliated groups to make serious impacts on the discourse of the populace and on socio political debates.

The 'Enough is Enough' Movement and Youth Digital Protests

The 'Enough is Enough' movement in Nepal formed in June 2020 as a youth-driven movement in reaction to the government response to the COVID-19 pandemic and swiftly transformed to be a general movement towards transparency, accountability, and good governance (Thomas, 2022). The movement was organized mostly by the use of social media and the first demonstrations in Kathmandu were attended by thousands of youths, with such hashtags as #EnoughIsEnough, #StopCorruption, and #AccountabilityNow gaining wide traction and mobilizing support all over the nation (Heaton, 2020). The online format of protests enabled quick dissemination of information, organization of peaceful sit-ins, and increased requests to withdraw the use of unreliable COVID-19 test kits and make quarantine conditions more bearable to those returning to the country (Lamichhane, 2021).

One of the characteristic traits of the movement was the devotion to nonviolence and inclusiveness, as the protestors used hunger strikes to make the point and otherwise engaged in symbolic measures instead of using the classic disruptive strategy. Early leaders such as Rabik Upadhayay and Iih took lead, where Iih went on an indefinite hunger strike because he wanted the government to fulfill the 12-point demand list of the movement (Heaton, 2020). Their protest activities were well-documented and discussed even online, holding the society in focus of government response and failures.

The Facebook page of the movement quickly accumulated more than 200,000 members, which speaks of the relevance of its message to youth and urban individuals in Nepal (Heaton, 2020). The combination of digital spaces allowed the group to create a certain momentum despite limited physical presence, as well as a record of progress and the lack of responsive measures deployed by the government. The digital-first nature of the movement established a new model defining youth-led activism in Nepal as it demonstrated that peaceful, organized, and technologically advanced protest could claim media and public attention and demand a response on the part of governmental agencies (Raut, 2023).

The Enough is Enough movement in Nepal successfully employed digital spaces to organize youth, disseminate a message of non-violent protests and incorporated pop culture aspects such as music and art. The level of participation, visibility, and solidarity was increased via digital media, as the traditional models of protests were replaced by creative, inclusive, performative activities (Lamichhane, 2021).

Regulation and Surveillance of Online Dissent

Alongside mounting digital advocacy, there has been an increment in the regulatory and surveillance approach by the government authorities in Nepal, who seek to control and contain online protest (Pandey, 2025). Such controls are forms of conflicts among the security interests of states, considerations of decency, and the constitutional obligation to protect the freedoms of speech, expression, and assembly (Ghimire, 2025).

Such notable regulatory law is Electronic Transactions Act, 2063 (2008), which has been condemned due to its non-specific nature and possible abuse of activists and journalists (Human Rights Watch, 2019). The government has often relied on the Electronic Transactions Act, especially the Section 47 to charge those who it accuses of defamation, misinformation, or dissemination of information containing content perceived as offensive, or threatening the order of society (Human Rights Watch, 2019). This practice brings up the question of chilling effects of the general freedom of speech which effectively limits civil discussion and critical opinion in online environments.

Moreover, the Information Technology Bill that was introduced in recent years led to a lot of controversy (Amnesty International, 2020). It was criticized as extending the powers of the government beyond the necessary scope to allow massive online surveillance, censoring, and penalizing nature toward online activists and reporters (Satgainya, 2025). Self-censorship provisions, obligatory registration of social media mechanisms and ample discretionary powers created concerns of possible abuse and infringement on digital rights, with massive opposition being elicited by civil society and rights organizations (Amnesty International, 2020).

Online activities have further led to increased governmental surveillance especially monitoring digital communications particularly of the activists, political dissidents, and journalists (Gurung, 2025). The use of surveillance technologies, which promote use of tools such as social media surveillance and other sophisticated data analytics, has heightened the anxiety of digital activists with regard to their privacy and risks of persecution (Kharel, 2022). Such surveillance practices force a limited atmosphere on the digital space on the internet and deter free dialogue, discussion and debate.

On some occasions, the judiciary has offered relief in Nepal as the regulations were overbearing to the extent that the courts restrained the government actions (Setopati, 2025). The constitutional courts have supported the petitions in opposing arbitrary acts against the digital activists, thus enforce the constitutional guarantees and the international human rights norms (Sharma, 2024). However, there have been rather modest and reserved judicial interventions that are representative of a wider political sensibility and judicial restraint as manifested in the Nepalese evolving democratic context.

COMPARATIVE ANALYSIS: CHALLENGES AND OPPORTUNITIES

Similarities and Divergences in Digital Civil Movements

The digital advocacy movement in India and Nepal share important similarities, especially, the use of social media as the means of collective action mobilization, awareness-raising, and voice elevation of the marginalized (A. Acharya, 2024; Fatima et al., 2025). These South Asian countries have successfully used the digital platforms to circumvent the traditional media hurdles and communicate directly to citizens both nationally and internationally (Thakur, 2016). Similarities in both settings are judged by the shared aims of accountability of the government, social equity, and constitutional protection.

The concise usage of hashtags is one of the crucial similarities that can be listed as the strategic choice of using hashtags, as the center of a digital campaign, to enable unified messaging and typically increase visibility. As an example, the #FarmersProtest (O. Basu, 2021) in India and the #EnoughIsEnough (Heaton, 2020) campaigns in Nepal show how hashtags unify various voices into one and how quick the spread of information can be, creating persistent audience engagement. Digital space in the two countries has successfully diminished geographical and social barriers, creating unity among the different communities, thereby making civic activities more inclusive (Kar et al., 2019; Timalsina & Pokharel, 2022).

Nonetheless, there are also major differences between Indian and Nepalese digital civil movements. Due to the geopolitical significance of India, and a large worldwide diaspora, the activities of India usually receive considerable coverage among the international media (Murti & Zaharna, 2014). Nepalese movements tend to lack global traction, despite the generally constructive results, in spite of governmental concern about misinformation, as there is always a danger of disinformation to democracy and citizen confidence (R. Dahal, 2023).

Also, the magnitude and thematic orientation are very different. Indian movements often refer to broad social-political problems such as citizenship amendments, farm restructuring and gender rights (Barua, 2025). However, the Nepal digital activism tends to focus on individual actions of the government or local policies, like federalism, rights of indigenous people, anti-corruption campaigns, and government accountability in times of a crisis like the COVID-19 pandemic (Lamichhane, 2021).

Although the emergence of digital advocacy in both countries plays a critical role in political accountability and empowerment of the citizens, their differences in terms of scope, scale, and international influence identify different socio-political processes governing civil movements in the respective countries.

Constraints on Free Speech and Algorithmic Censorship

The issue of digital advocacy in India and Nepal faces significant challenges regarding the freedom of speech restraints and rising algorithmic censorship. The two countries have implemented legislative policies and regulatory practices to regulate online discussions, usually citing national security threats, misinformation, and need to maintain peace.

In India, there is a series of new regulation that has increased government control over online content including the Information Technology (Intermediary Guidelines and Digital Media Ethics Code) Rules, 2021. They increase control in the area of moderation, when the platforms must quickly take down the soon determined to be problematic or illegal material by the government (Guha & Matilal, 2023). This excessive control poses the threat of random blocking, that may happen on the part of leaving the dissenting and critical voices aside and developing an atmosphere of self-censorship on the part of digital protesters (Saxena, 2024).

This situation is even complicated by algorithmic censorship. The social media networks implement algorithms to promote or draw attention to content that is measured in terms of engagement which frequently serves to suppress political or anything contentious (Cobbe, 2021). Such shadow-banning and claims of decreased visibility of their movements, as well as algorithmically determined restrictions against sharing content, have been frequently reported by activists and affect the mobilization ability to a great extent (Cobbe, 2021).

In Nepal, comparable restrictions are made by the means of rules and regulations such as the Electronic Transactions Act and the proposed Information Technology Bill. Such frameworks allow governments to exercise a lot of discretion to punish online messages that may be deemed as defaming, offensive, or disruptive, limiting the freedom of open discussion and thus hampering online activism (Khanal, 2024).

Moreover, algorithmic censorship mainly affects small countries such as Nepal. The algorithm of the platform favors the engagement rates, discriminating against local voices and caring about sensitive advocacy subjects, which worsen the progress of digital advocacy campaigns and bolster structural disparity in online discourse (Cobbe, 2021).

Accordingly, the interaction between the state-enforced codes of data and the platform algorithmic operations presents serious impediments to freely expressing oneself online, making digital advocacy an exceedingly difficult task in India and Nepal.

Role of Internet Access and Digital Literacy

The effectiveness of digital advocacy in India and Nepal is quite dependent on access to the internet and the digital literacy of the population, as it defines participation and the influence of online activism. An effective, consistent internet connection and competent digital literacy are basic requirements to the meaningful engagement, and it is something that defines who will be engaged, and what exposure will be given to whom on the part of the public discourse (Lee, 2014).

High internet penetration rates in India, and especially low data costs and the popularity of smartphones have led to the tremendous expansion of the horizons of digital activism. This widened network enables the involvement of various groups of people including the historically marginalized groups and rural dwellers (Ray, 2016). However, major digital divides have remained especially in rural, remote and poor areas. Digital advocacy is also not equally open to marginalized communities such as women, lower-caste individuals and tribals, who are likely to have fewer avenues through which they can participate in digital advocacy, given the lack of appropriate infrastructure and the prevalence of low digital literacy (Manglam, 2024).

In India, a significant improvement in digital literacy has been witnessed, and this is due to interventions by the civil society and the government. Civic engagement and increased inclusivity of digital advocacy have been achieved due to programs that target the underserved populations. Nonetheless, there are still some disparities due to which investments in digital education and improvement of infrastructure are needed in order to make sure that everyone can participate equally (A. Kumar & Haneef, 2023).

Internet penetration and digital literacy have great strengths and weaknesses in Nepal. Cities such as Kathmandu have relatively strong internet connections, whereby the digital activism runs about (Timalsina & Pokharel, 2022). Nevertheless, rural areas are still greatly burdened with connectivity problems thus restricting an inclusive response to digital advocacy. Geographical, gender and socioeconomic differences are still prevalent reflecting on structural inequities (Chand et al., 2024).

Digital literacy is also disproportionate with it being concentrated on the youth and the urban population. Such gaps have been filled more and more by the efforts of civil society organizations and youth-led activities, with specific educational activities, workshops, and awareness measures (Timalsina & Pokharel, 2022). Digital literacy is crucial in mobilizing young people as movements like the 'Enough is Enough' demonstrate the use of digital means of communication in civic action (Heaton, 2020).

Removing current inequalities in internet access and digital literacy is still important in order to make the most out of digital advocacy. The involvement of governments, civil society, and international organizations in collaborative efforts is the one which is paramount to crossing those divides, lead to fair involvement of participation, and enable the inclusive and democratic capabilities of digital activism.

CONSTITUTIONAL ENGAGEMENT IN THE DIGITAL AGE

Democratization of Rights Discourse through Digital Platforms

The emergence of online-based systems has introduced fundamental changes in the environment of the rights discourse, providing never-before-seen advantages and challenges in the face of the constitutional practice in the digital era. Digital technologies already transformed the civic spaces and allowed more people to be involved in the discourse of the public life, and people and communities are now able to promote their rights on the highest level compared to the previous times (Quimbre & Stockwell, 2021). This reshaping of the right to speak by democratizing the discourse through social media is seen through how marginalized and historically disfavored groups now have greater access to larger audiences, can organize around social movements and be unleashed to fight attitudes previously unchallenged in main-stream media (Sengupta, 2019).

Online medias have promoted the use of the essential rights, especially freedom of expression. With online forums, social media, and other online resources, information can be rapidly circulated and used to hold vibrant discussions and common co-action on matters like civil liberties to social justice (Freihse & Unzicker, 2024). Human rights defenders have taken advantage of these technologies to coordinate, organize and multiply their activities and, in many cases, move beyond geographic and political borders. This was not just a magnification of the sphere of the public but was also the means by which the civic engagement could excel in societies where more conventional modes of participation might be limited (Quimbre & Stockwell, 2021).

But the democratization of the rights discourse through the digital medium comes with its own hazard. The very technology which gives the power also can be used as a tool to weaken the democratic approach and human rights. The amount of engagement and profit-driven business models inherent to digital platforms such as algorithm-based echo chambers, free circulation of misinformation, and the promotion of polarizing information are the results of a business-first approach to digital platform design and development (Siochrú & Gurumurthy, 2024). An example is the COVID-19 pandemic, where the spread of false information online has posed a danger to the health of people by both encouraging hate actions online and offline (Cox et al., 2021). Also, privacy infringement, secret monitoring, and misuse of data have also been the focus of more attention, posing an imperative question regarding finding the balance between the right to speak freely and the necessity to keep individual privacy intact (Ahmad, 2023).

In reaction, governments have tried to control digital spaces to a point where they undermine the same rights that are being promoted by digital platforms. Without being formulated and applied with a high degree of responsibility and transparency, such regulatory efforts can jeopardize the freedom of speech and facilitate wholesale censorship (Miller & Vaccari, 2020). This is where the problem occurs, and it has to do with forming substance policies that will provide protection to foundational freedoms but will also deal with whatever is legitimate in the way of online harms, privacy and security. The future of constitutional involvement in the digital era will be linked to finding this thin balance and making sure that cyber-rights are accepted as essential parts of more extensive rules of humanity (Berg & Hofmann, 2021).

Such dynamics are especially evident in the context of India and Nepal. Social media in India has assumed great importance as a means of personal expression and civil action, however, it has also raised the conversations around hate speech, disinformation and invasion of privacy. To mitigate such difficulties, the government has established rules but the tension between the regulation and the upholding of digital freedoms still is a debatable aspect (Bhatia, 2021). In Nepal, digital rights are in their infancy stage with internet penetration, and literacy are rising. The recent scandals related to suppressing TikTok and issuing limiting orders without due legislative process have confirmed the unstable nature of digital rights in the light of unjustified state interference. In both the countries, the civil society organizations have taken the lead in promoting the transparency of the operations, accountability, and harmonization of digital regulations with the constitutional and international standards of human rights (D. Udupa, 2025). Both India and Nepal continue to grapple with the challenges of digital constitutional involvement as they attempt to navigate a tricky terrain. The battle that will ensue is how to protect the use of the digital space as spaces of the participatory democracy and safeguard of the most elementary rights of those involved, beyond the use of enabling mechanisms of control, or exclusion.

From Passive Citizenship to Active Digital Participation

Movement of passive citizenship to active digital participation, is an important evolution of the association between citizens and their constitutions, particularly in the era of digitization. Conventionally, the concept of citizenship used to be categorized as passive and active (Turner, 2009). The passive citizens as witnessed in the French Revolution were the ones that did not have the right to vote, nor did they have any property and were shielded by the state but had no say in government and its laws. They were not directly involved in political processes because of their illiteracy, economic dispossession, or gender, and could not influence the creation of the public policy nor hold leaders accountable (Hammersley, 2015). On the contrary, active citizens were those who fulfilled some basic requirements like paying taxes or being just male adults capable of voting, taking parts in assemblies, and able to make a direct contribution to the process of democracy (Turner, 2009).

The advent of digital age has radically changed these boundary lines. Digital citizenship is not a simple definition of access to the technology access but the potential to participate in the society, politics, and governance via a digital method (Oyedemi, 2018). Information technology is applied not solely by the digital citizen to engage in personal communication or to undertake business; in fact, it is frequently used to engage in an online discussion, to publish, and to organize around social or political causes. The transition has reduced conventional threats to participation including geography, literacy or financial status because new spaces are provided to interact and express (Mossberger, 2008).

The digital participation is a step-by-step process. First, it is informational dissemination-citizens receive and internalize the information that is provided by reputable sources, usually the government. This can either be a read-only variety or dynamic or interactive (two-way communication). The subsequent phase is citizen deliberation that involves the transition of individuals who initially consumed the information passively to active participation, including attending online polls and leaving complaints or suggestions as well as becoming a part of general discussions or digital town halls (Tejedo-Romero et al., 2022). The result of such a change is a more inclusive and participatory democracy in which social inclusion and collective deliberation are supported by the use of digital technology.

Nevertheless, there are impediments associated with this new eminence. The digital world also throws thorny issues regarding privacy, data protection, and the distribution of power among people, states, and major privately owned businesses

(Cengiz, 2025). As a counteraction to this, digital constitutionalism has arisen which will seek to defend the core rights and rebalancing of power when it comes to algorithmic decision-making and mass surveillance. Freedom of expression, privacy, and non-discrimination are some constitutional principles that constantly have to be re-interpreted to consider the new threats and opportunities that technology presents. The emergence of digital spaces has also disempowered governments and vested power in the hands of other, privately owned actors, and in response, new legal instruments are required so that they are accountable and defend the rights within the digital domain (Cengiz, 2025).

This evolution is of special importance in the Indian and Nepalese context. The constitutions of both countries are vibrant, and democratic rights are entrenched in both countries but digital divide and differences in digital literacy offer challenges to real inclusive participation. In India, the improvement in the internet penetration has allowed millions of people to seek access to government services, join online campaigns, share opinions on social media (Neyazi et al., 2016). However, online misinformation, digital monitoring, and a solid framework to protect data are other current concerns (Shankar & Ahmad, 2021). Nepal has experienced a recent constitutional change, and the country struggles with the same problems and, consequently, has a chance to utilize digital platforms to educate and engage the population and especially young people and marginalized groups (Timalsina & Pokharel, 2022). In both countries, the process of transforming passive citizenship into proactive digital citizenship is still in process, and the need to adapt the constitutional frameworks, invest in digital literacy, and monitors the protection of fundamental rights closely is necessary to make sure that the dream of digital democracies becomes a reality available to all the citizens.

Reimagining Constitutionalism in an Era of Hashtag Activism

A call to reimagining constitutionalism in the age of hashtag activism involves a profound rethinking of the nature of civic participation, the right, and the accountability practices in the digital age. Constitutionalism has traditionally been defined by the formal and institutionalized procedure; the parliamentary debate, the legal advocacy, and formalized participation of people (Chambers, 2019). But the advent of social media and the hashtag revolution has opened up the space and allowed the general citizenry to be a part of the national discourse and be able to push back against the dominant narratives in real time. Hashtags, which were initially merely metadata tools, are now used as potent collective action units, people and communities can organize, communicate and mobilize support to various social and political ideals at an unprecedented speed and to a vast extent (R. Dey, 2025).

The phenomenon of hashtag activism, as one of the possible forms of digital participation, has conditioned a redefinition of the boundaries of the public communication process. It contributes to inclusivity in constitutional participation by giving voice to the most marginalized communities, hence breaking the existing hierarchies. The examples of campaigns include #WomensMarch, #MeToo, and #BlackLivesMatter and illustrate how digital movements led to a uniting force and gave a voice to individuals across borders to form solidarity within different communities (Dobrin, 2020). These campaigns can not only help generate awareness but also generate a common language and identity to champion certain issues, making it easier to share information and resources, as well as to gather people behind a concrete change. Hashtags come together to provide an aggregative effect on these isolated grievances by turning them into collective demands, making them appear as the part of larger, structural problems that they have to address (Goswami, 2018).

However, critics caution that there are dangers of the so-called slacktivism meaning that their online involvement is nothing but a shallow pursuit that in most instances does not lead to any substantial and realistic action (Zohouri et al., 2020). The fact that sharing of a hashtag requires minimal effort may be accepted, but the impact of online activism can be associated with an increase in real life engagement, such as protests, voter registration, and even policy advocacy (Greijdanus et al., 2020). Hashtag activism opens the door, as well as motivates more extensive civic engagement, and especially, civic engagement among those formerly excluded citizens. Digital divide, censorship and privilege, however, are main barriers to the maximization of democratic access to constitutional participation (van den Hoven et al., 2024).

The effects of this hashtag activism on constitutionalism are massive. It places strain on constitutional arrangements to handle novel versions of popular expression and to require improved accountability and transparency of institutions. Hashtag campaigns have the potential to affect the policy debate, create awareness and shape the collective consciousness, and even result in legal or political action, so these less formal types of action can broaden the boundaries of the constitutional work (A. Dey, 2018). Modern constitutionalism aims to alleviate the problems of misinformation, polarization, and degradation of the deliberative process by adhering to both openness and immediate nature of the digital activism (van den Hoven et al., 2024).

In the case of India and Nepal, the hashtag activism has been playing a highly significant role in the democratization of the constitutional engagement. #MeTooIndia, #DalitLivesMatter, and #PinjraTod campaigns in India have not only shaken the long-established hierarchies, but it has also placed issues of gender, caste, and institutional power at the forefront of the debate in the country (Barua, 2025). Such movements have influenced the debates on policy and created civic awareness despite the concern about the issue of digital exclusion and government censorship. As the constitutional process is underway in Nepal, social media has offered a platform to the young population and other individuals who have been left out in society to discuss federalism, inclusions, and minority rights (A. Acharya, 2024). The role of hashtag activism is helping in the redefinition of the people-constitution relationship in both the countries and it is necessary that legal frameworks should be developed to guarantee the digital rights and gain inclusivity and provide the facility of digital democracy to everyone.

CONCLUSION AND A WAY FORWARD

Summary of Key Findings

The comparative analysis of the field of digital advocacy and constitutional action in India and Nepal demonstrates the dynamics of the shift of the character of civic involvement in the South Asia region. The study identifies that the deployment of digital advocacy via social media like Twitter (It has been renamed X), Facebook and Instagram has greatly enabled individuals and groups to counter the state narratives and call out to seek justice and state constitutional rights. It points out how such hashtags as #Nirbhaya, (#LoveIsLove, and #FarmersProtest in India, and #EnoughIsEnough and #JusticeForNirmala in Nepal have also become powerful agents of participatory democracy. The role of the internet in facilitating widespread protests, dissemination of alternative narratives and the support of the path of public discourse in areas other than conventional arenas, can be highlighted in these movements.

It has been noted in this study that the constitutional rights of the freedom of speech, assembly, and privacy are also frequently used in the digital sphere. The judiciary in India has held that the right to free speech under Article 19(1) (a) would extend to online speech, held in the case of Shreya Singhal v. Union of India (2015). Similarly, in Nepal the Supreme Court has gradually acted to appreciate the right to privacy and freedom of expression in the online environment. Nevertheless, the tendency of over regulation in these two countries are alike. Although the IT Rules, 2021 and the Digital Personal Data Protection Act, 2023 in India have been criticized as a step towards more surveillance and blocking dissent, the Social Media Bill, 2025 and Electronic Transactions Bill, 2019 in Nepal have equally raised concern among the civil society owing to the broad terminology and stringent punishments.

More so, this study points out the fact that despite the benefits of the digital democracy, structural inequalities still serve as the barrier to inclusive participation.

The marginalized groups, especially in the rural areas, are still left behind in terms of digital access to services, mostly because of lack of infrastructure, poor digital literacy and socio-economic drawbacks. The already weak projection of grass root activism is undermined by the social media algorithmic censorship, which is fed by influences of governments to prevent dissent.

Notably, the results indicate that the decisions made by the courts in the two nations have been crucial in enforcing digital rights whereby the courts have resorted to imposing restraining orders whenever the government arbitrarily shuts down the internet or illegal surveillance on its citizens. Meanwhile, the digital divide along with the politicization of internet access isolates substantial segments of population, particularly females, Dalits, tribes and ethnic minorities. These realities unmask the necessity of constitutional systems that should adapt to the digital realities and defend rights in both physical and digital environments.

Policy Recommendations for India and Nepal

Considering the findings above, the following policy recommendations can be offered to support the idea of digital constitutionalism, empowerment of civic engagement and safeguarding digital rights in India and Nepal:

1. **Enact Clear and Rights-Based Digital Legislation:** Both India and Nepal must use digital law that is constitutionally sound and operates on the basis of international standards of human rights. The vague nature of certain terms like, public order, decency, or anti-national have to be done away with to avoid such a misuse. Under the provisions of the IT Rules in India and the Social Media Bill in Nepal, any restrictions on the freedom of expression not only need to be audited as to proportionality and necessity, but as to the least restrictive measures as well.
2. **Strengthen Data Privacy and Surveillance Safeguards:** In both countries, there should be an extensive data protection compliance mechanism that should guard against unregulated surveillance. In India, Digital Personal Data Protection Act, 2023 will have to be amended in order to restrict broad governmental exemptions. Nepal should ensure good parliamentary supervision and judicial solutions to established legislations such as the Electronic Transactions Act and the Privacy Act among others, whereby the state does not extend its hand past its jurisdiction under the guise of national security.
3. **Empower Judicial Oversight Mechanisms:** The courts have played a pivotal role in rollback of the web overreach in the form of judicial activism. The two jurisdictions need to, however, institutionalize special benches, or digital rights cells, within their higher courts to stay proactive in monitoring and adjudicat-

ing on the issues concerning algorithmic censorship, online surveillance, and freedom of expression online. The principles that have been established in Anuradha Bhasin v. Union of India (2020) should be implemented in India to stop any arbitrary decisions to shut down the internet.

4. **Promote Digital Literacy and Infrastructure Equity:** The digital divide needs a large-scale investment in digital infrastructure in the rural and isolated regions. There is a possibility to foster the use of public-private relationships to provide affordable and high-speed internet. The government and civil society also need to carry out digital literacy plans across the country, particularly focusing on women, Dalits, tribals, LGBTQ+ community, the elderly, to secure equal access to the digital civic space.
5. **Foster Multi-Stakeholder Internet Governance:** Multi-stakeholder governance with civil society, tech platforms, policymakers and legal experts should influence and shape the digital public sphere. India and Nepal ought to institutionalize the consultative digital governmental forums which enable the discussions between social media firms and the rights organizations. Regulatory structures should be co-designed so that the platforms are responsible but do not interfere with freedom of expression and privacy of the users.
6. **Enhance Constitutional Accountability in Digital Policymaking:** Digital policies need to have constitutional values built upon explicitly. The issuance of the Digital India Act in India ought to include fundamental rights check and impact analysis prior to implementation. Likewise, Nepal too has proposed its Social Media law, such Social Media law must be reviewed by its National Human Rights Commission or the Supreme Court, prior to ratification. It is necessary to incorporate provisions of human rights and accountability mechanisms to all digital laws.
7. **Safeguard Algorithmic Transparency and Prevent Content Manipulation:** Social media networks should be required to provide the governments with transparency reports inclusive of the data on the number of shadow-banning cases, the pieces of content removed, and applications of automated moderation tools. Auditors should be independent and algorithms on the platform should be audited via regulatory technology commissions, to make sure that digital expression was not excessively hindered by commercial or political influences.
8. **Recognize and Protect Digital Activism as a Constitutional Right:** Indian and Nepal governments should acknowledge digital activism as constitutional engagement and political expression. The police officer should be made sensitive as to differentiate between protest and illegitimate action. Criminalization of peaceful digital protests, as can be found in loosely defined crimes of defamation or sedition, should not be allowed and therefore repealed and amended to avoid abuse.

9. **Develop Cross-Border Digital Rights Frameworks:** Since India and Nepal have strong socio-political linkages, a bilateral model of digital rights collaboration can be operationalized. This may involve co-operations to address education of cyber rights, data protection conventions, and acceptability of each other in the area of digital privacy protection. Cooperation may also help tackle cross-border misinformation without violating digital space sovereignty of individual nations.
10. **Encourage Youth Participation and Civic Technology Innovations:** Persons in charge of developing policies are advised to engage student leaders, young innovators, and technology developers to participate in civic digital development. Bottom-up policy contributions should be included in platforms such as MyGov in India and Digital Nepal Framework in Nepal. Government funding must go into civic tech start-ups that are creating tools, transparency, e-governance, grievance redressal and legal digital literacy tools.

As a conclusion, India and Nepal have reached an important crossroad of re-thinking constitutionalism in the digital age. The outburst of hashtag activism has demonstrated that civic activism is no longer stuck in the streets or in the legislature. It has added retweets, livestream, viral petitions as well as encrypted mobilization. In order to respect democratic principles in this new landscape, the two nations have to develop open, fair, and constitutionally coherent digital landscapes. Digital rights have to be strengthened, not as a technological demand but as a constitutional requirement.

REFERENCES

Abraham, S. (2015). Shreya Singhal and 66A: A Cup Half Full and Half Empty. *Economic and Political Weekly, 50(15)*, 12–16.

Acharya, A. (2024). Influence of Youth Engagement on Nepal's Political Evolution: An Analysis of Emerging Youth-Led Movements. *Interdisciplinary Journal of Management and Social Sciences*, *5*(2), 1–13. DOI: 10.3126/ijmss.v5i2.69438

Acharya, U., & Bhattarai, B. (2015, March). Freedom of Expression on the Internet in Global and Nepal's Context. *Symposium on Online Freedom in Nepal*, Kathmandu.

Adhikari, B. (2024). The Nexus Between Freedom of Expression under the Indian Constitution and Creative Liberty of Content Creators Over OTT. International Journal of Law and Social Sciences, 28–40. DOI: 10.60143/ijls.v10.i1.2024.126

Ahmad, N. (2023). Data privacy issues and risks with sharing on social media: An inquiry. *Russian Law Journal, 11*(4), 597–611.

Amnesty International. (2020, January 16). Nepal: Information Technology Bill threatens freedom of expression. Amnesty International. https://www.amnesty.org/en/latest/news/2020/01/nepal-information-technology-bill-threatens-freedom-of-expression/

Amtzis, R. (2014). Crowdsourcing from the Ground Up: How a New Generation of Nepali Nonprofits Uses Social Media to Successfully Promote its Initiatives. *Journal of Creative Communications*, *9*(2), 127–146. DOI: 10.1177/0973258614528609

Awasthi, P., Ganapati, S., & Tai, K. T. (2024). Digital transformation in a large democracy: The case of India. *Asia Pacific Journal of Public Administration*, *46*(4), 326–359. DOI: 10.1080/23276665.2024.2339874

Balasubramanian, P., Breuer, A., Leininger, J., Cameron, A., & Kercher, J. (2022). *Sustainable Development Goals (SDG) 16: A governance compass towards just transition?* IDOS Policy Brief.

Banaji, S., Bhat, R., Agarwal, A., Passanha, N., & Sadhana Pravin, M. (2019). *WhatsApp vigilantes: An exploration of citizen reception and circulation of WhatsApp misinformation linked to mob violence in India*. Department of Media and Communications, London School of Economics and Political Science.

Barua, A. (2025). The Power of Hashtag Activism in India—A New Mode of Political Mobilization. The Academic. *International Journal of Multidisciplinary Research*, *3*(5), 316. DOI: 10.5281/ZENODO.15642537

Basu, D. D. (2024). *Introduction to the Constitution of India* (27th ed.). LexisNexis.

Basu, O. (2021). Battle of the Hashtags: Debate over farmers' protest goes global for local. India Today. https://www.indiatoday.in/news-analysis/story/battle-of-the-hashtags-debate-over-farmers-protest-goes-global-for-local-1765657-2021-02-03

Berg, S., & Hofmann, J. (2021). Digital democracy. *Internet Policy Review*, *10*(4). Advance online publication. DOI: 10.14763/2021.4.1612

Bhatia, K. V. (2021). Religious Subjectivities and Digital Collectivities on Social Networking Sites in India. *Studies in Indian Politics*, *9*(1), 21–36. DOI: 10.1177/2321023021999141

Burman, A. (2023). Understanding India's New Data Protection Law. Carnegie Endowment for International Peace. https://carnegieendowment.org/research/2023/10/understanding-indias-new-data-protection-law?lang=en

Celeste, E. (2019). Digital constitutionalism: A new systematic theorisation. *International Review of Law Computers & Technology*, *33*(1), 76–99. DOI: 10.1080/13600869.2019.1562604

Celeste, E. (2021). Digital constitutionalism: Mapping the constitutional response to digital technology's challenges. *Direitos Fundamentais & Justica*, *45*, 63.

Cengiz, İ. F. (2025). Digital Constitutionalism in Creating a New Constitutional Equilibrium. İstanbul Medeniyet Üniversitesi Hukuk Fakültesi Dergisi, 10(1), 69–92.

Chalise, A. S. (2023, June 5). Young Environmentalist's Take On The Controversial Nijgadh Airport [On Air with Sanjay Silwal Gupta]. https://www.youtube.com/watch?v=ZpDHqU9qwWM&t=3s

Chambers, S. (2019). Democracy and constitutional reform: Deliberative versus populist constitutionalism. *Philosophy and Social Criticism*, *45*(9–10), 1116–1131. DOI: 10.1177/0191453719872294

Chand, M. B., K.C., S., & Maharjan, M. (2024). Unveiling Disparities: A Case of Digital Divide in Nepal. *The Journal of Economic Concerns*, *15*(1), 130–142. DOI: 10.3126/tjec.v15i1.70246

Chaudhary, D. N. (2024). The Need for data protection law in Nepal: Securing Citizen's Rights in the Digital Age. Kathmandu School of Law Review, 113–125. DOI: 10.46985/kslr.v12i1.2225

Chaudhuri, S. (2019). On making noise: Hokkolorob and its place in Indian student movements. *Postcolonial Studies*, *22*(1), 44–58. DOI: 10.1080/13688790.2019.1568168

Chhibber, D. (2022). Review of Popular Hashtag Movements on social media. *Journal of Communication Management (London), 1*(01), 01.

Civicus. (2025). Nepal: Restrictive social media legislation, targeting of journalists and excessive force at protests put freedoms at risk (Monitor) [Latest Developments]. Civicus. https://monitor.civicus.org/explore/nepal-restrictive-social-media-legislation-targeting-of-journalists-and-excessive-force-at-protests-put-freedoms-at-risk/

Cobbe, J. (2021). Algorithmic Censorship by Social Platforms: Power and Resistance. *Philosophy & Technology, 34*(4), 739–766. DOI: 10.1007/s13347-020-00429-0

Cox, K., Ogden, T., Jordan, V., & Paille, P. (2021). [disinformation and hateful extremism. Commission for Countering Extremism] [Produced by RAND Europe]

Dahal, K. R. (2022). An Overview of the Constitutional Development in Nepal. In Bhatta, C. D. (Ed.), *Rooting Nepal's Democratic Spirit* (pp. 45–56). Friedrich-Ebert-Stiftung.

Dahal, R. (2023). The Influence of Social-media on Agenda-setting in Nepali Journalism. *Patan Prospective Journal, 3*(01), 116–127. DOI: 10.3126/ppj.v3i01.59016

Dar, S. A., & Nagrath, D. (2022). The impact that social media has had on today's generation of Indian youth: An analytical study. International Journal of English Literature and Social Sciences, 7(4), 048–056.

Davies, A. (2017). Civil/political society, protest and fasting: The case of Anna Hazare and the 2011 anti-corruption campaign in India. In *Protest Camps in International Context* (pp. 261–276). Policy Press. DOI: 10.2307/j.ctt1t89745.20

De, A. (2023). From the confessional to the ground. In Cheema, I. S. (Ed.), *The Other# MeToos* (pp. 101–120). Oxford University Press.

De Gregorio, G., & Radu, R. (2022). Digital constitutionalism in the new era of Internet governance. *International Journal of Law and Information Technology, 30*(1), 68–87. DOI: 10.1093/ijlit/eaac004

Dey, A. (2018). Nirbhaya and beyond – role of social media and ICTs in gender activism in India. In Nirbhaya, New Media and Digital Gender Activism (p. 125). Emerald Publishing Limited. DOI: https://doi.org/DOI: 10.1108/978-1-78754-529-820181006

Dey, R. (2025). From Hashtag to Action: Social Movements in 21st Century India. The Academic. *International Journal of Multidisciplinary Research, 3*(2), 131. DOI: 10.5281/ZENODO.15026400

Dhakal, P. (2025). How Privacy Act covers you. The Farsight Nepal. https://farsightnepal.com/news/367

Dissanayake, D. (2023). Writing wrongs- an analysis of the use of digital platforms as forums offering gender justice for sexual crimes in South Asia. *Legal Pluralism and Critical Social Analysis*, *55*(2), 201–225. DOI: 10.1080/27706869.2023.2199551

Dobrin, D. (2020). The Hashtag in Digital Activism: A Cultural Revolution. Journal of Cultural Analysis and Social Change, 5(1), 03. DOI: 10.20897/jcasc/8298

Drury, F. (2024). Alok Shukla wins prize for Hasdeo Aranya forest campaign. BBC. https://www.bbc.com/news/articles/cyxepvdewkno

Edingo, D. B. (2021). Social media, public sphere and counterpublics: An exploratory analysis of the networked use of Twitter during the protests against the Citizenship Amendment Act in India. *The Journal of Social Media in Society*, *10*(2), 76–101.

Fatima, I., Pehrson, S., & Jogdand, Y. (2025). Dalit Activists Promote Social Change Differently: Challenges and Opportunities of Digital Activism and Social Change in Indian Society. *Journal of Community & Applied Social Psychology*, *35*(2), e70079. Advance online publication. DOI: 10.1002/casp.70079

Freihse, C., & Unzicker, K. (2024). Digital Discourses and the Democratic Public Sphere 2035: How Politics Today Can Shape Tomorrow. DOI: 10.11586/2024148

Gardbaum, S. (2006). Limiting constitutional rights. *UCLA Law Review. University of California, Los Angeles. School of Law*, *54*, 789.

Garg, A. (2022). Role of social media in Indian politics: A Review. *Journal of Communication Management (London)*, *1*(01), 66–76.

Gautam, D. R. (2020). An Assessment on the Constitution of Nepal 2015. *An Assessment on the Constitution of Nepal*, *2015*(20), 46–60. DOI: 10.3126/jps.v20i0.31794

George, J. J., & Leidner, D. E. (2019). From clicktivism to hacktivism: Understanding digital activism. *Information and Organization*, *29*(3), 100249. DOI: 10.1016/j.infoandorg.2019.04.001

Ghimire, B. (2025, February 19). Government can enforce law to regulate free speech, top court rules. The Kathmandu Post. https://kathmandupost.com/national/2025/02/19/government-can-enforce-law-to-regulate-free-speech-top-court-rules

Goswami, M. P. (2018). Social media and hashtag activism. Liberty dignity and change in journalism, 1, 252-262.

Gray-Hawkins, M. (2018). Collective movements, digital activism, and protest events: The effectiveness of social media concerning the organization of large-scale political participation. *Geopolitics, History, and International Relations*, *10*(2), 64–69. DOI: 10.22381/GHIR10220188

Greijdanus, H., De Matos Fernandes, C. A., Turner-Zwinkels, F., Honari, A., Roos, C. A., Rosenbusch, H., & Postmes, T. (2020). The psychology of online activism and social movements: Relations between online and offline collective action. *Current Opinion in Psychology*, *35*, 49–54. DOI: 10.1016/j.copsyc.2020.03.003 PMID: 32330859

Guha, S., & Matilal, S. (2023). Information Technology (Intermediary Guidelines and Digital Media Ethics Code) Rules, 2021-A Reassessment of the Contours and Limits. *NUJS Journal of Regulatory Studies*, *8*, 32.

Gupta, A. (2019). Towards Participatory Democracy: Can Digitalisation Help Women in India? *The Indian Journal of Public Administration*, *65*(4), 897–915. DOI: 10.1177/0019556119881842

Gurung, S. (2025, April 26). Nepal's Dilemma Over Social Media Regulation. The Diplomat. https://thediplomat.com/2025/04/nepals-dilemma-over-social-media-regulation/

Hammersley, R. (2015). Concepts of citizenship in France during the long eighteenth century. European Review of History: Revue Européenne d'histoire, 22(3), 468–485. DOI: 10.1080/13507486.2015.1036231

Heaton, T. (2020). "Enough is Enough" in Nepal. Asia Media Centre. https://www.asiamediacentre.org.nz//features/enough-is-enough-in-nepal

Howe, S. (2025). Social Media Statistics for India [Updated 2025]. Meltwater. https://www.meltwater.com/en/blog/social-media-statistics-india

Human Rights Watch. (2019, April 18). Nepal: End Attacks on Free Expression. Human Rights Watch. https://www.hrw.org/news/2019/04/18/nepal-end-attacks-free-expression

Jain, M. P. (2018). *Constitutional Law of India* (8th ed.). LexisNexis.

Jha, B. K. (2024). Role of Judiciary on Right to Privacy. *Sambahak: Human Rights Journal*, *24*, 57–68. DOI: 10.3126/sambahak.v24i1.78851

Juyal, R. (2023). Constitutional Liberties and Cyberspace: Analysing the Anuradha Bhasin v Union of India Case and its Impact on Fundamental Rights. *Legal Information Management*, *23*(4), 276–281. DOI: 10.1017/S1472669623000622

Kar, A. K., Ilavarasan, V., Gupta, M. P., Janssen, M., & Kothari, R. (2019). Moving beyond Smart Cities: Digital Nations for Social Innovation & Sustainability. *Information Systems Frontiers*, *21*(3), 495–501. DOI: 10.1007/s10796-019-09930-0

Keck, M. E., & Sikkink, K. (1999). Transnational advocacy networks in international and regional politics. *International Social Science Journal*, *51*(159), 89–101. DOI: 10.1111/1468-2451.00179

Kemp, S. (2025a). Digital 2025: India. DataReportal – Global Digital Insights. https://datareportal.com/reports/digital-2025-india

Kemp, S. (2025b). Digital 2025: Nepal. DataReportal – Global Digital Insights. https://datareportal.com/reports/digital-2025-nepal

Khanal, B. P. (2024). Information Technology in Nepal: History and Current Status. *Curriculum Development Journal*, *32*(46), 54–67. DOI: 10.3126/cdj.v32i46.77000

Kharel, S. (2022, December 5). Towards digital authoritarianism in Nepal: Surveillance, data collection, and online repression. Association for Progressive Communications (APC). https://www.apc.org/en/news/towards-digital-authoritarianism-nepal-surveillance-data-collection-and-online-repression

Kumar, A. (2021). Digital Media Regulations in India: Some Reflections. In Kaur, P. (Ed.), *Emergent Regulatory Governance: Key to Indian Regulatory Laws* (pp. 303–337). Indu Book Services Pvt Ltd.

Kumar, A., & Haneef, M. S. M. (2023). (Dis)Empowered Civic Voices in Social Media: An Episteme of Civic Engagement, Advocacy, and Social Change. In The Palgrave Handbook of Global Social Change (pp. 1–22). Springer International Publishing. DOI: 10.1007/978-3-030-87624-1_304-1

Kumar, A., & Jha, A. (2022). Information Technology Rules, 2021 of India in dock! A Critical evaluation of the' Guidelines for Intermediaries and Digital Media Ethics Code. *Global Media Journal*, *20*(48), 1–9.

Kumar, D. S. (2024). Socio-Legal Aspect Of Social Media In India: Navigating Encryption And Legal Frameworks For Social Media Regulation. *Educational Administration: Theory and Practice*, *30*(5), 12129–12135.

Kumar, P. (2025). Locating Digital Constitutionalism in India and South Asia- Preliminary Enquiry. Kathmandu School of Law Review, 13, 87–103. DOI: 10.46985/kslr.v13i1.2237

Kumar, R. (2015). Social media and civil society actions in India. In *The Routledge companion to social media and politics* (pp. 259–267). Routledge. DOI: 10.4324/9781315716299-19

Lamichhane, Y. R. (2021). "Enough Is Enough": A Cultural Turn of Youth Activism in Nepal. The Outlook: Journal of English Studies, 1–15. DOI: 10.3126/ojes.v12i1.38741

Lee, S.-H. (2014). Digital literacy education for the development of digital literacy. [IJDLDC]. *International Journal of Digital Literacy and Digital Competence*, *5*(3), 29–43. DOI: 10.4018/ijdldc.2014070103

Mahapatra, S., & Plagemann, J. (2019). Polarisation and politicisation: The social media strategies of Indian political parties. German Institute for Global and Area Studies, GIGA Focus Asia (3).

Maheshwari, N., & Daka, M. (2024). Proportionality in theory, not practice: Internet Rights in Indian Courts. Oxford Human Rights Hub. https://ohrh.law.ox.ac.uk/proportionality-in-theory-not-practice-internet-rights-in-indian-courts/

Malhotra, C., Sharma, A., Agarwal, N., & Malhotra, I. (2019). Review of Digital Citizen Engagement (DCE) Platform: A Case Study of MyGov of Government of India. *Proceedings of the 12th International Conference on Theory and Practice of Electronic Governance*, 148–155. DOI: 10.1145/3326365.3326385

Manda, D. P., & Misra, A. N. (2024). Report: India To Replace Information Technology Act With The Proposed Digital India Act: Out With The Old, In With The New? *Global Privacy Law Review*, *5*(1), 50–53. DOI: 10.54648/GPLR2024002

Manglam, M. (2024). Digital Divide and Social Exclusion: Understanding the Impact on Marginalized Communities in India. Journal Global Values, XV (Special Issue 2024), 009–018.

Mathew, D. (2025). Technology-enabled Justice in Indian Courts: New Dilemmas and Way Forward. *Journal of Development Policy and Practice*, *10*(1), 26–35. DOI: 10.1177/24551333241262892

Miller, M. L., & Vaccari, C. (2020). Digital Threats to Democracy: Comparative Lessons and Possible Remedies. *The International Journal of Press/Politics*, *25*(3), 333–356. DOI: 10.1177/1940161220922323

Mossberger, K. (2008). Toward digital citizenship: Addressing inequality in the information age. In *Routledge handbook of Internet politics* (pp. 173–185). Routledge.

Mukherjee, I. (2021). Virus, violence and (in) visible women: #LockDownMein-LockUp and embodied resistance during COVID-19. *Journal of International Women's Studies*, *22*(12), 25–61.

Murti, B., & Zaharna, R. S. (2014). India's digital diaspora diplomacy: Operationalizing collaborative public diplomacy strategies for social media. Exchange. *The Journal of Public Diplomacy*, *5*(1), 3.

Neupane, M. P. (2024). Expanding Practices of E-Governance System in the Contemporary World. *Journey for Sustainable Development and Peace Journal*, *2*(2), 54–74. DOI: 10.3126/jsdpj.v2i2.69570

Neyazi, T. A., Kumar, A., & Semetko, H. A. (2016). Campaigns, Digital Media, and Mobilization in India. *The International Journal of Press/Politics*, *21*(3), 398–416. DOI: 10.1177/1940161216645336

Oyedemi, T. D. (2018). The Theory of Digital Citizenship. In Servaes, J. (Ed.), *Handbook of Communication for Development and Social Change* (pp. 1–19). Springer Singapore., DOI: 10.1007/978-981-10-7035-8_124-1

Pain, P. (2021). "It took me quite a long time to develop a voice": Examining feminist digital activism in the Indian #MeToo movement. *New Media & Society*, *23*(11), 3139–3155. DOI: 10.1177/1461444820944846

Pandey, L. (2025, February 13). Nepal's social media bill raises free speech concerns. DW. https://www.dw.com/en/nepals-social-media-bill-raises-free-speech-concerns/a-71595277

Primus Partners & Institute for Competitiveness. (2023). Digital India Act, Dialogue Series Inaugural Session—White Paper. Primus Partners. https://www.primuspartners.in/news/digital-india-act-dialogue-series-inaugural-session

Quimbre, F., & Stockwell, S. (2021). The Implications for Human Rights in the Digital Age (Research & Commentary). RAND. https://www.rand.org/pubs/commentary/2021/09/the-implications-for-human-rights-in-the-digital-age.html

Raut, B. (2023). A new generation in politics. Purak Asia. https://purakasia.org/next-generation/a-new-generation-in-politics/

Ray, P. (2016). Paradigms of Digital Activism: India and Its Mobile Internet Users. In Venkateswar, S., & Bandyopadhyay, S. (Eds.), *Dynamics of Asian Development* (pp. 229–248). Springer Singapore., DOI: 10.1007/978-981-10-0454-4_12

Rayamajhi, A. (2021, August 27). Social media: Activism or amusement? The Kathmandu Post. https://kathmandupost.com/columns/2021/08/27/the-promises-of-social-media

Relly, J. E., & Pakanati, R. (2020). Deepening democracy through a social movement: Networks, information rights, and online and offline activism. *International Journal of Communication*, *14*, 21.

Report, P. (2025). Social Media Bill to be revised before endorsement, say members of various parties. The Kathmandu Post. https://kathmandupost.com/politics/2025/02/11/social-media-bill-to-be-revised-before-endorsement-party-members-say

Sangeetha, S. S., & Saravana, P. K. (2025). Hashtags to Action: The Impact of Social Media Sentiment Analysis with the Content of Social Movements among the Youngsters in India. ComFin Research, 13(S1-i2), 94–98. DOI: 10.34293/commerce.v13iS1-i2.8742

Satgainya, S. (2025, February 3). Bill to regulate social media raises risk of free speech and free press being casualty in Nepal. The Hindu. https://www.thehindu.com/news/international/bill-to-regulate-social-media-raises-risk-of-free-speech-and-free-press-being-casualty-in-nepal/article69176319.ece

Saxena, A. (2024). Digital Media Content: Policies, Constitutions and Laws Across Countries. In Dahiya, S., & Trehan, K. (Eds.), *Handbook of Digital Journalism* (pp. 529–544). Springer Nature Singapore., DOI: 10.1007/978-981-99-6675-2_45

Sengupta, A. (2019, May 17). Social media and the democratization of public discourse. Vidhi Centre for Legal Policy. https://vidhilegalpolicy.in/blog/social-media-and-the-democratization-of-public-discourse/

Setopati. (2025, May 21). SC orders release of RPP youth wing coordinator Sujit KC. Setopati. https://en.setopati.com/political/164634/

Shankar, R., & Ahmad, T. (2021). Social Media, Artificial Intelligence and Role of Tech Firms in the Age of Disinformation: Impact on Democracy and Regulatory Challenges in India. Turkish Online Journal of Qualitative Inquiry, 12(6).

Sharma, B. (2024, August 8). SC cracks down on prolonged detentions without trial. myRepublica. https://myrepublica.nagariknetwork.com/index.php/news/sc-takes-firm-stance-on-habeas-corpus-detainees-released-37-99.html

Siochrú, S. Ó., & Gurumurthy, A. (2024). Digital platforms versus democratic political discourse: Challenges and the way forward. *Media Development*, *70*(1).

Sundara, K., & Narendran, N. (2023). The Digital Personal Data Protection Act, 2023: Analysing India's dynamic approach to data protection. *Computer Law Review International, 24*(5), 129–141. DOI: 10.9785/cri-2023-240502

T. H. T. (2023). UNESCO Workshop on Nepali Judiciary Safeguarding Freedom of Expression and Access to Information, Journalist Safety, AI and Rule of Law concludes. The Himalayan Times. https://thehimalayantimes.com/kathmandu/unesco-workshop-on-nepali-judiciary-safeguarding-freedom-of-expression-and-access-to-information-journalist-safety-ai-and-rule-of-law-concludes

Tech Global Institute. (2025). WHITEPAPER: Digital Governance and Rights in South Asia, and the Path Forward. Tech Global Institute. https://techglobalinstitute.com/research/whitepaper-digital-governance-and-rights-in-south-asia-and-the-path-forward/

Tejedo-Romero, F., Araujo, J. F. F. E., Tejada, Á., & Ramírez, Y. (2022). E-government mechanisms to enhance the participation of citizens and society: Exploratory analysis through the dimension of municipalities. *Technology in Society, 70*, 101978. DOI: 10.1016/j.techsoc.2022.101978

Thakur, P. B. (2016). Social media and social movement: Contemporary online activism in Asia. *Media Watch, 7*(2), 226–243.

Thomas, M. T. (2022). *Nonviolent Youth Protests in 2020 against the Nepal Government's Handling of the Covid-19 Pandemic*. Centre for Social Change., https://socialchange.org.np/peoples-power-blog/nepa-youth-protest-2019/

Timalsina, R., & Pokharel, R. (2022). Digitization and Changing Landscape of Social and Democratic Life in Nepal. In Bhatta, C. D. (Ed.), *Rooting Nepal's Democratic Spirit* (p. 181). Friedrich-Ebert-Stiftung.

Tripathi, H. B. (2015). Fundamental Rights: Some Reflections on the Present Constitutional Discourse in Nepal. *NJA Law Journal, 9*, 31.

Tuchtfeld, E. (2024). Case law on content moderation and freedom of expression. Columbia Global Freedom of Expression, 2993–1908, 23.

Turner, B. S. (2024). Outline of a theory of Citizenship 1. In *New Critical Writings in Political Sociology* (p. 187). Routledge.

Udupa, D. (2025, February 3). The Future of Digital Rights in Nepal Amid Rising Government Control and Platform Neglect. Center for the Study of Organized Hate. https://www.csohate.org/2025/02/03/nepal-digital-rights/

Udupa, D. (2025, February 3). The Future of Digital Rights in Nepal Amid Rising Government Control and Platform Neglect. Center for the Study of Organized Hate. https://www.csohate.org/2025/02/03/nepal-digital-rights/

United Nations. (2015). Peace, justice and strong institutions. United Nations Sustainable Development. https://www.un.org/sustainabledevelopment/peace-justice/

van den Hoven, J., Stauch, M., Musiani, F., Domingo-Ferrer, J., Ruggieri, S., Pratesi, F., Trasarti, R., & Comandé, G. (2024). Democracy in the Digital Age. HAL. https://shs.hal.science/halshs-04844505/

Wadhwa, S. (2025). Content blocking orders and status of digital rights: Assessment of two key verdicts in India. *Information & Communications Technology Law*, *34*(1), 44–61. DOI: 10.1080/13600834.2024.2406678

Zohouri, M., Darvishi, M., & Sarfi, M. (2020). Slacktivism: A critical evaluation. *Journal of Cyberspace Studies*, *4*(2), 173–188.

Chapter 10
Guardians of the Self: Rethinking Privacy and Data Sovereignty in the Digital Age

Anjali Daisy
https://orcid.org/0000-0003-1207-5002
Gnanam School of Business, Thanjavur, India

ABSTRACT

This chapter discusses into the evolving concept of privacy rights and the emerging discourse on data sovereignty in the digital age. As individuals generate vast amounts of personal data through everyday digital interactions—often unknowingly—the ownership, control, and ethical use of that data have become central to civil liberties. The chapter critically examines how mass data collection, algorithmic profiling, and pervasive surveillance by both corporations and governments challenge the traditional boundaries of privacy. It highlights global regulatory efforts such as the GDPR, India's Digital Personal Data Protection Act, and emerging data localization mandates as attempts to restore agency to data subjects. However, these efforts are often undermined by techno-legal loopholes, cross-border data flows, and asymmetries of power between data collectors and individuals. Through real-world examples such as the Facebook-Cambridge Analytica scandal and Aadhaar-linked surveillance concerns, the chapter explores the tension between innovation, state control, and personal autonomy.

INTRODUCTION

The rapid digitization of human activity has fundamentally altered the boundaries of the self. In today's interconnected world, personal data is continuously generated, collected, processed, and commodified by a complex web of actors,

DOI: 10.4018/979-8-3693-3920-6.ch010

including governments, corporations, and platforms. As individuals engage with digital services, often unknowingly, they leave behind rich trails of behavioural, biometric, and transactional data. These data points, though intangible, form a highly revealing mosaic of identity, thought, preference, and habit collectively constituting what scholars now refer to as the *digital self*. The traditional notion of privacy, long grounded in legal and ethical frameworks protecting personal autonomy and confidentiality, is being challenged by the pervasive reach of surveillance capitalism, algorithmic profiling, and predictive analytics. Simultaneously, the concept of *data sovereignty*—once limited to state-level discussions around cross-border data flows has evolved to include individual rights to control and govern one's personal data. The shift from state-centric to individual-centric sovereignty signals a growing recognition of informational self-determination as a fundamental right in the digital era. This chapter critically examines the dual imperatives of privacy and data sovereignty, anchoring its analysis in contemporary theoretical, technological, and regulatory contexts. It explores the tension between innovation and intrusion, between digital convenience and personal control. The discussion situates emerging global regulatory efforts (e.g., GDPR, CCPA, India's DPDP Act) within a broader inquiry into how technological architectures—such as decentralized identity systems, blockchain-based data vaults, and privacy-enhancing technologies—are attempting to restore agency to users. The chapter interrogates the ethical and psychological implications of constant data surveillance, raising important questions about identity construction, consent, autonomy, and power asymmetries in digital spaces. By framing individuals as *guardians of the self*, the chapter calls for a paradigm shift in how privacy is conceptualized—not merely as the absence of intrusion, but as the proactive capacity to assert ownership, choice, and control in a data-driven society. Through an interdisciplinary lens, the chapter aims to contribute to ongoing academic and policy dialogues on data justice, digital rights, and human dignity. In doing so, it underscores the urgency of rethinking privacy and sovereignty not only as legal or technical challenges, but as deeply human concerns in an age where identity itself is being redefined through data.

LITERATURE REVIEW

This literature review traces the evolution of key concepts central to this chapter—privacy, data sovereignty, informational self-determination, and surveillance power—through multidisciplinary perspectives. It draws from legal studies, information systems, digital sociology, and critical data studies to highlight the transformation of privacy in the digital realm and the reassertion of user agency. Classical definitions of privacy emphasized non-interference and seclusion.

Warren and Brandeis' (1890) landmark essay defined privacy as "the right to be let alone," setting the foundation for early legal approaches. Alan Westin (1967) later broadened this understanding, framing privacy as "the claim of individuals to determine for themselves when, how, and to what extent information about them is communicated to others." In contrast, contemporary scholars argue that privacy is no longer a fixed or individualistic concept. Solove (2006) criticizes the fragmented and inconsistent conceptualizations of privacy, proposing a taxonomy of privacy harms—including data aggregation, exclusion, insecurity, and secondary use—better suited for the digital age. Nissenbaum's (2010) contextual integrity theory further shifts the discussion, positing that privacy breaches occur when data flows violate context-specific informational norms, not merely due to data exposure. With the rise of ubiquitous computing, privacy has moved beyond legal boundaries into the realm of digital behavioral control. Zuboff (2019), in her seminal work The Age of Surveillance Capitalism, argues that privacy is systematically undermined by tech corporations extracting behavioral surplus—data about user behavior used to predict and influence future actions. She positions this as an asymmetrical power structure where users are unaware participants in systems of epistemic injustice. Scholars like Lyon (2018) emphasize that surveillance has become normalized, embedded not just in authoritarian regimes but within liberal democracies through digital infrastructures. This shift has led some researchers to reframe privacy as a social practice and a collective good, rather than an individual right (Richards & Hartzog, 2016).

Informational Self-Determination and the Digital Subject

The concept of informational self-determination, originating from the German Federal Constitutional Court's 1983 Census Act decision, marked a turning point in data privacy jurisprudence. It recognized that individuals must have control over the collection, storage, and dissemination of personal data. This right, foundational to Europe's GDPR framework, is based on the idea that personal data is an extension of personhood. Bennett and Raab (2006) argue that informational self-determination must be contextualized within broader surveillance regimes, noting that privacy protections vary drastically across jurisdictions. While Europe adopts a rights-based model, the U.S. often leans towards sector-specific regulations and corporate self-regulation. Recent scholarship pushes this idea further into data empowerment, advocating for data portability, user control dashboards, and personal data stores (Susha et al., 2017). These innovations emphasize user participation in data governance, attempting to shift control from centralized platforms to individuals.

However, critics caution against techno-solutionism. Yeung (2018) warns that despite promises of control, many digital consent mechanisms are illusory, with users often subjected to dark patterns and obfuscated data practices. As such, the realization of informational self-determination requires not only technological innovation but also regulatory clarity and public data literacy. Data sovereignty initially referred to the idea that data is subject to the laws and governance structures of the country in which it is collected or stored. With growing concerns around data localization and cross-border data flows, countries like China, Russia, and India have introduced data localization mandates to ensure national control over critical digital infrastructure (Kuner, 2015). However, the scope of data sovereignty has expanded in recent years to include individual sovereignty, especially in global digital markets where personal data becomes an economic asset. De Filippi and Wright (2018) argue for a blockchain-based reconceptualization of data ownership, where users control their data through distributed ledgers and cryptographic tools. The MyData movement and initiatives like Solid (initiated by Tim Berners-Lee) promote the notion of "data as a service," where individuals decide how and when to share data with organizations. These shifts indicate a broader move from data protection to data empowerment. Nonetheless, scholars remain skeptical. Greenleaf (2014) notes that without enforceable rights and redress mechanisms, individual data sovereignty risks becoming a symbolic ideal. Moreover, the global digital economy continues to be dominated by platform monopolies that operate beyond traditional regulatory reach, undermining true sovereignty.

Power, Consent, and Asymmetry in the Platform Society

Van Dijck, Poell, and de Waal (2018) describe the rise of a platform society, where public and private life is mediated by digital platforms that operate with their own norms and infrastructures. In such a context, consent—long treated as the gold standard of data protection—is increasingly seen as insufficient and performative (Barocas & Nissenbaum, 2009). Platforms extract consent through opaque terms-of-service agreements, often leveraging cognitive overload and user habituation. As a result, users routinely agree to surveillance practices they neither understand nor control. This leads to what Draper and Turow (2019) term digital resignation—a sense of helplessness in the face of unavoidable data extraction. To counter this, scholars argue for privacy by design (Cavoukian, 2012) and ethics by design principles, where systems are built to uphold user rights proactively rather than retroactively. These frameworks propose embedding ethical decision-making into the architecture of digital systems, shifting responsibility from users to designers and institutions.

CONCEPTUAL FRAMEWORK

Figure 1. Conceptual framework

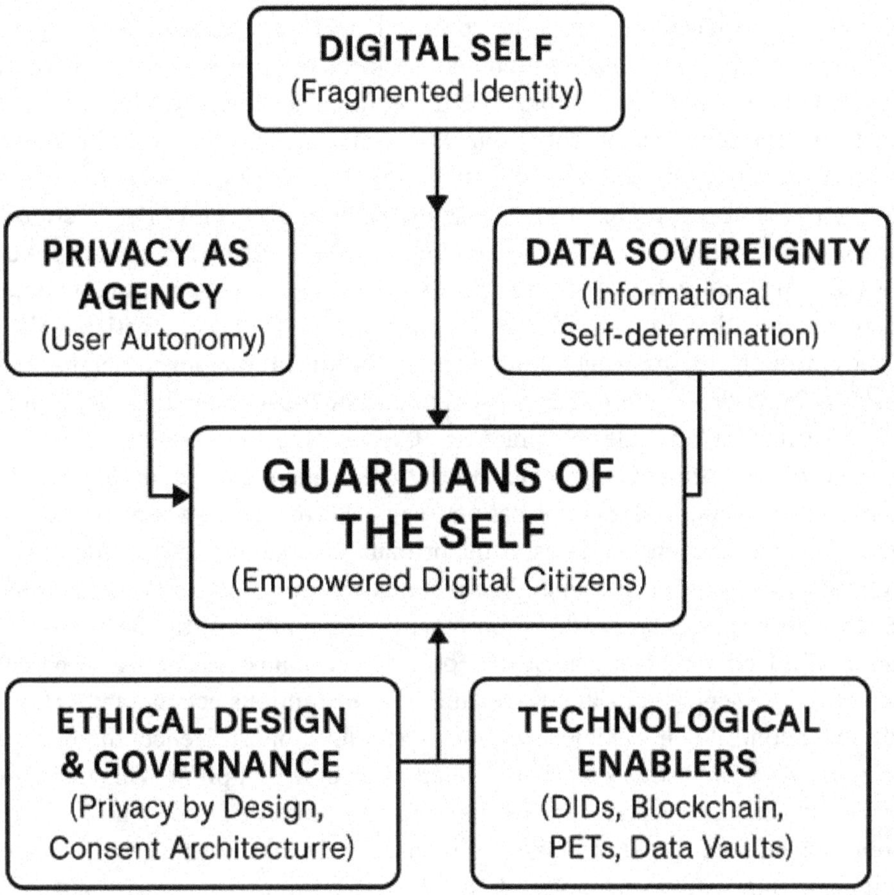

The conceptual framework presented in this chapter visualizes how fragmented digital identities can be transformed into empowered digital citizenship through the integrated action of privacy, sovereignty, ethical governance, and technological innovation. At the center of this framework is the construct of the "Guardians of the Self"—digitally literate individuals who are not only aware of the risks associated with online presence but are also capable of asserting their autonomy and rights over their data. The framework draws from interdisciplinary perspectives, including digital sociology, human-computer interaction, cyberlaw, and information ethics, to offer a pathway toward reclaiming human dignity in the age of pervasive digital surveillance. At the foundation of this framework lies the notion of the *Digital Self*, which represents the fragmented identity of individuals in cyberspace. This identity is not holistic but is constructed through data traces—behavioural footprints, consumption patterns, social interactions, and algorithmic inferences. These fragments, often unknowingly produced by users, are collected, analyzed, and monetized by digital platforms. The digital self is thus vulnerable, shaped more by systems of surveillance capitalism than by self-definition. This recognition sets the stage for advocating a transformation from passive data subjects to active agents of their digital presence. Central to this transformation is the reimagining of *Privacy as Agency*. In this model, privacy is not conceptualized merely as the right to seclusion or protection from intrusion, but as the capacity to make autonomous, informed decisions regarding one's digital identity. It includes the ability to provide or deny consent, understand where and how data flows, and exercise control over digital interactions. Viewing privacy through the lens of agency underscores its role in enabling rather than merely shielding individuals. It empowers users to participate actively in data governance and resist manipulative design practices. Closely intertwined with agency is the construct of *Data Sovereignty*, which refers to the right of individuals to govern their personal data. It emphasizes informational self-determination, where the individual, rather than corporations or states, is the primary custodian of digital identity. Data sovereignty asserts that personal data is an extension of personhood and must be treated with respect, care, and legal protection. This pillar of the framework envisions a shift from platform-centric to people-centric data ecosystems—where users can revoke consent, trace data usage, and hold institutions accountable. However, individual control is insufficient without systemic support. Hence, the framework integrates *Ethical Design and Governance* as an essential pillar. This includes the implementation of "Privacy by Design," robust consent architecture, and transparent algorithmic decision-making. Ethical governance ensures that developers, designers, and institutions embed human-centric values—fairness, transparency, inclusivity—into the digital infrastructure. Without such ethical scaffolding, even the most informed users would remain at the mercy of opaque systems and exploitative defaults. The transition from fragmented identity to digital guardianship is further enabled by *Technological Enablers*. These include decentralized identifiers (DIDs), which allow secure, user-owned identity credentials; blockchain technologies that enable immutable records of consent and data transactions; privacy-enhancing technologies (PETs) like homomorphic encryption and differential privacy; and personal data vaults that provide users with secure control over their information. These tools collectively constitute the practical arm of the framework—translating the theoretical ideals of sovereignty and agency into operational realities. At the core of the model is the figure of the *"Guardian of the Self"*—an empowered digital citizen who combines awareness, technical fluency, ethical reasoning, and rights consciousness. Such individuals are not merely protected but are proactive in defending their digital boundaries, questioning power asymmetries, and participating in the co-creation of ethical digital societies. This concept reframes digital rights and responsibilities as essential civic capacities in the 21st century. In sum, this conceptual framework offers a multidimensional perspective on reclaiming personal autonomy in the digital age. By integrating fragmented identities with empowering mechanisms—privacy as agency, data sovereignty, ethical governance, and enabling technologies—it charts a pathway from passive data existence to active digital citizenship. The framework challenges existing paradigms of surveillance and calls for a future where individuals are no longer mere data points but *guardians of their digital selves*—ethical, autonomous, and sovereign.

In the contemporary digital age, where algorithms increasingly mediate human experience, identity, and interaction, there is an urgent need to reimagine our relationship with data, privacy, and personhood.

(1) The existing frameworks of digital privacy tend to be reactive and fragmented, offering protection only after harm is done. This chapter proposes a transformative shift through the introduction of a new conceptual framework *"The Guardian of the Self"*—which positions the individual not as a passive data subject but as an active custodian of their digital existence.

(2) At the core of this framework lies the concept of the fragmented digital self—an identity composed of dispersed data points across platforms and devices, often interpreted through opaque algorithms. As Zuboff's (2019) notion of surveillance capitalism suggests, human behavior has become commodified, analyzed, and monetized without true individual understanding or consent. This commodification erodes the essence of human agency, transforming individuals into behavioral residues. Reclaiming control over these digital fragments necessitates an ontological reassertion of selfhood.

(3) Privacy, within this framework, is no longer conceptualized merely as the right to be left alone. Instead, it is reframed as *agency*—the empowered ability to manage, control, and navigate one's personal data. This aligns with Helen Nissenbaum's theory of contextual integrity, where privacy is understood as the appropriate flow of information relative to context. Agency-oriented privacy enables individuals to actively define digital boundaries, make informed consent decisions, and participate in data-related discourse—transforming passive users into *engaged digital citizens*.

(4) This approach further evolves into the principle of *data sovereignty*, advocating for personal jurisdiction and ownership over data. Drawing from indigenous and community-centered data rights models, this component argues that individuals must hold the authority to determine how their data is collected, stored, pro-

cessed, and shared. The individual is not just a stakeholder in data systems but the rightful owner of their informational self, with rights to portability, consent withdrawal, and data lineage transparency.

(5) However, individual empowerment alone cannot counter systemic imbalances unless supported by ethical design and governance structures. Therefore, the framework insists on embedding *ethical principles into the very code* and architecture of digital systems. As Lawrence Lessig famously noted, "code is law." In this light, system design must prioritize values like fairness, transparency, explainability, and privacy-by-default. Governance mechanisms such as algorithmic audits, data stewardship models, participatory co-design, and bias checks ensure that individual rights are upheld not just by policy but by practice.

(6) Technological tools also serve as crucial enablers in this process. Innovations such as *Self-Sovereign Identity (SSI), Decentralized Identifiers (DIDs), Solid data pods, and privacy-enhancing technologies* (PETs) like differential privacy and federated learning provide tangible pathways for operationalizing user agency and sovereignty. These tools decentralize control and embed ethicality directly into user experience and system behaviour

(7) All these elements culminate in the conceptual figure of the *"Guardian of the Self."* This persona is envisioned as a technically aware, ethically conscious, and rights-oriented individual who actively defends their digital identity and influences the systems they participate in. They are not merely recipients of policy or tools, but *co-creators of a more just and respectful digital ecosystem.* By recognizing the value of their digital presence, questioning platform asymmetries, and advocating for data rights, they represent a new mode of digital subjectivity—one that is deeply self-aware and socially responsible.

(8) Ultimately, the framework moves toward an aspirational vision of a *post-surveillance digital future*, where digital dignity, informed consent, and participatory governance are foundational principles. It aligns with global efforts such as the GDPR, UNESCO's AI ethics framework, and the OECD's AI principles, reaffirming that *digital rights are human rights*. Through this model, the individual transforms from a scattered data point to a sovereign, ethical agent—a true Guardian of the Self in the age of algorithmic dominance.

This chapter advances a simple but demanding thesis: privacy and data sovereignty are not merely compliance checkboxes or technical constraints; they are the living architecture of personhood, trust, and democratic life in a world of sensors and prediction. We trace the evolution of privacy from a static "right to be let alone" to a dynamic capability to shape how one's data shadow participates in consequential decisions. We then develop a guardianship framework at four levels—individual, organizational, platform, and state/community—before turning to practical tooling: privacy-enhancing technologies (PETs), algorithmic accountability pipelines, governance structures, and cross-border arrangements. Throughout, we bring the argument down to earth with cases, design patterns, and a ten-year roadmap. The chapter closes with a short manifesto for "guardians of the self." The twentieth century imagined privacy as curtains and door locks. The twenty-first offers dashboards, default sharing, and inference engines. Phones, wearables, cars, cameras, and smart appliances render daily life legible to platforms and institutions. But the novelty is not that more data exists; it is that data is *computable at scale*. Models now draw inferences that feel intimate: mood, risk appetite, churn propensity, creditworthiness, political susceptibility, even likelihood of job-hopping.

Two forces define the moment:

Datafication: the translation of previously ephemeral behavior and context into durable data points, increasingly linked across domains and time.

Predictive governance: the displacement of human discretion by model outputs in decisions about credit, employment, housing, education, security, and the public sphere.

Privacy, then, is not the opposite of publicity. It is a person's power to shape the terms under which their data shadow is created, combined, inferred upon, and used to govern opportunities. Data sovereignty extends this power to communities and nations by asking who sets the rules for data generated by people and resources within a social or territorial context and who benefits from the value created. Seen through this lens, privacy is capacity-building. It is the right to develop one's identity and future without being trapped by predatory profiling, invisible experimentation, or irreversible databases.

Why Consent Collapses and What Replaces It

For a generation, privacy programs revolved around notice-and-consent: tell people what you collect, check a box, store the record. That model collapses under contemporary realities: Opacity: The modern data supply chain—SDKs, brokers, clouds, and inferences—cannot be fully described to laypersons; even experts struggle to trace flows. Coercion and fatigue: Opt-outs imply exclusion. Participation in work, learning, and civic life often requires data surrender, nullifying the voluntariness of consent. Inference exceptionalism: Laws often protect inputs (name, ID, location) more than inferences (risk scores, psychographics), though the latter drive outcomes.

Collective spillovers: One person's choice can degrade others' privacy, e.g., location traces revealing household routines; genomic relatives de-anonymizing family. A more realistic alternative is stewardship. Instead of one-off permission rituals, stewardship imposes ongoing duties of care: justification, proportionality, minimization, auditability, and recourse. The key question shifts from "Did you agree?" to "Is the use fair, necessary, and accountable?"

A FOUR-LEVEL FRAMEWORK FOR GUARDIANSHIP

Individuals: Agency Without Exhaustion Data literacy as a civic skill: Understand the data life cycle—collection, processing, sharing, storage, deletion—and where rights attach. Identity segmentation: Encourage context-specific identifiers (separate emails, passkeys, or pseudonymous credentials) to reduce linkability. Practical tooling: Password managers, hardware keys, tracker blockers, privacy-focused browsers, and selective-disclosure wallets. Right to explanation and contestation: Clear channels to understand automated decisions and to seek human review, particularly for credit, employment, healthcare, and benefits. Organizations: Accountability by Design Purpose limitation and minimization: Collect the least data necessary; define purposes narrowly; resist function creep. DPIAs that bite: Tie risk assessments to actual go/no-go gates; publish impact summaries when feasible. De-identification with humility: Tokenization, hashing, k-anonymity, and differential privacy help—but never claim zero risk. Human-in-the-loop: Require documented human review for high-stakes outcomes; track error budgets by subgroup. Third-party governance: Inventory vendors; bind with purpose-based contracts; audit SDKs and data brokers; terminate high-risk relationships. Platforms: Responsibility at Scale Interoperability and portability: Let users move their data—and their reputational capital—through standardized, secure APIs. Auditable algorithms: Provide sandboxes for accredited auditors and regulators to test models for disparate impact, robustness, and security. Privacy-preserving defaults**: Make PETs part of infrastructure, not premium add-ons. States and Communities: Sovereignty with Interoperability Comprehensive data protection with strong rights (access, correction, deletion, portability) and meaningful penalties. Sectoral rules for finance, health, children, and biometrics. Cross-border regimes that protect people wherever their data travels. Community stewardship vehicles data trusts, cooperatives, Indigenous governance so groups can control and benefit from collective data. Data Sovereignty in Practice, Data sovereignty asks who holds normative and practical authority over data related to persons, resources, and activities within a jurisdiction or community. Three layers matter: Personal sovereignty: Individuals control verifiable credentials, permissions, and portability. Community sovereignty: Groups steward data generated about them, negotiating access and benefit-sharing. National/regional sovereignty: States set rules for data generated within their borders and for cross-border transfers. Self-Sovereign Identity (SSI): SSI frameworks place verifiable credentials in user-controlled wallets. A person can prove they are over 18 or licensed to practice without exposing birthday, address, or full certificate. Keys reside with the individual; issuers (universities, banks, governments) sign credentials; verifiers check proofs. Challenges include key recovery, revocation at scale, and inclusive onboarding. Promise: granular, revocable, portable proofs that reduce oversharing. Data Cooperatives and Trusts, Communities, from city residents to patient groups can pool rights, negotiate terms of use, and distribute value. A mobility data trust, for example, can authorize research on congestion while forbidding individualized enforcement. Principles like CARE Collective benefit, Authority to control, Responsibility, and Ethics anchor such stewardship, especially for Indigenous data.

National Strategies without Balkanization:

Sovereignty should not become isolation. The goal is interoperable sovereignty: domestic rules that protect people, combined with standards and agreements that permit legitimate flows for research, trade, and security. Where localization is justified (e.g., critical infrastructure), it should be paired with technical and contractual safeguards that enable necessary cross-border analyses under strict oversight. Anatomy of the Data Life Cycle The data life cycle is a loop, not a line. Collection: sensors, forms, logs, and third-party sources. Decision points: necessity, lawful basis, transparency, and consent (where appropriate). Processing: cleaning, analysis, training, inference. Decision points: fairness, explainability, robustness, and attack surfaces. Sharing: internal movement, external vendors, public release. Decision points: contracts, de-identification, PETs, and access controls. Storage: location, encryption, access, retention. Decision points: least privilege, localization for sensitive classes, event-based deletion. Exit/Deletion: data subject rights, secure erasure, and model unlearning where feasible. Governance metadata purpose tags, lineage, access logs, and risk scores should travel with the data to enable audit and accountability. Case Windows. Case A: People Analytics at Work An international firm deploys keystroke and collaboration analytics to improve productivity and well-being. Promise: detect burnout and unblock workflows. Peril: micro-surveillance, biased performance scores, and chilled creativity. Guardianship moves: Use team-level metrics by default; require opt-in for individual tracking for well-being purposes only; explicitly ban punitive use; disclose models and provide appeal mechanisms; involve worker councils in governance; cap retention; and audit disparate impact across gender, role, and seniority.

Smart City Face Recognition

A municipality considers real-time facial recognition to find missing persons. Benefits are intuitive; risks include misidentification, protest chilling, and function creep. Guardianship moves: Legality necessity proportionality tests; limit to post-event, warrant-based searches; independent accuracy audits; transparency reports; public deliberation; and sunset clauses with moratoria triggers if harms exceed benefits. Case C: Health Data for Research a university consortium proposes a longitudinal study on chronic disease using hospital records and wearables. Guardianship moves: Privacy-preserving record linkage; secure data enclaves; differential privacy for published statistics; federated learning for cross-site modeling; broad-but-bounded consent with community oversight; return of results to participants in accessible formats. Privacy-Enhancing Technologies (PETs) as Infrastructure PETs decouple value extraction from identity exposure. Moving them from boutique tools to default infrastructure is central to guardianship. Differential Privacy: adds calibrated noise to outputs, limiting inference about any individual. Use for dashboards, A/B tests, and training with privacy budgets. Federated Learning: Trains models close to where data resides, aggregating updates instead of raw records. Beware gradient leakage; combine with secure aggregation. Secure Multiparty Computation: Parties jointly compute on private inputs without revealing them. Useful for AML checks or cross-institution analytics. Homomorphic Encryption: Computation on encrypted data. Today best for targeted, high-sensitivity workloads due to performance costs. Trusted Execution Environments: Hardware enclaves that isolate computation; require continuous attestation and supply-chain assurance. Synthetic Data: Artificial datasets mimicking real distributions. Reduce sharing risk but require rigorous utility and bias evaluation. Adoption principles: pick PETs based on threat models; combine multiple PETs with contractual and organizational safeguards; document utility privacy trade-offs; make developer experience first-class so engineers can do the right thing easily.

Algorithmic Fairness:

The Right to Be Measured Well

Fairness is not only a property of code; it is a property of institutions.

Representational completeness:

Ensure training data reflect relevant populations and contexts; test for intersectional harms. Error budgets by group: Define acceptable disparities (e.g., false positives) and pause deployment if exceeded. Counterfactual tests: Evaluate whether protected attributes or their proxies unjustly drive outcomes. Model documentation: Use model cards/datasheets to disclose objectives, data sources, limitations, and subgroup performance. Human-centered KPIs: Track not only accuracy but recourse, dignity, and downstream outcomes. Governance should include red-teaming, challenge datasets, and external audits with safe harbor protections for ethical disclosure.

The Political Economy of Data

Data is often likened to oil; the analogy misleads. Data is non-rivalrous and co-produced with social relations. Extraction without meaningful consent or reciprocity can be dispossession. Platform business models monetize attention and prediction, rewarding surveillance and engagement maximization. Counter-incentives: Data dividends and benefit-sharing: Monetary or service benefits routed through cooperatives or public-interest funds. Public options: Government-provided digital identity, payments, or messaging with privacy-by-default settings to discipline markets. Competition policy: Interoperability mandates, data portability, and merger scrutiny when data aggregation creates unassailable advantages.

Cross-Border Data and the Global Commons

Open flows enable research, trade, and diaspora ties—but expose people to extraterritorial surveillance and uneven rights. A guardianship stance supports: Layered safeguards: Technical (encryption, PETs), contractual (standard clauses with audit rights), and institutional (independent oversight and redress). Adequacy through practice: Not just formal statutes but demonstrated enforcement and remedies. Reciprocity: Mutual recognition that preserves individuals' rights regardless of data location. In domains like climate and pandemic response, data commons tightly governed, transparently audited reconcile sovereignty with global public goods. Children and the Data We'd Rather Not Collect: Children warrant heightened protection due to developmental sensitivity and life-long traceability of early data. Principles include minimization by default, bans on behavioural advertising to minors, age-appropriate design, and rights that "mature" with the child (including the ability to revise or delete childhood data). Schools should vet edtech for necessity and security, provide offline alternatives, and publish simple data maps for parents and students.

Designing for Dignity: Patterns and Anti-Patterns

Patterns

Progressive disclosure: Ask for data when and only when needed, with concrete explanations and examples. Contextual integrity: Align data use with social norms of the context (health, finance, community) and make deviations explicit. Accessible controls: Simple dashboards for permissions, sharing, and deletion; provide meaningful defaults. Event-based retention: Tie retention to meaningful lifecycle events (account closure, service completion) rather than arbitrary dates. Shadow data visibility: Surface inferences about the user; allow correction or suppression. Anti-patterns: Privacy theater: Vague policies, box-ticking DPIAs, and metrics that praise process over outcomes. Dark patterns: UI tricks that steer users toward oversharing or make opting out painful. Scope creep: Repurposing old data for new goals without renewed justification and controls. Security minimalism: Treating security as optional; privacy without security is an illusion. Metrics That Matter What we measure shapes what we protect. Move beyond vanity metrics (policy length, training completion) to real outcomes:

* Median time to fulfill access/erasure requests.
* Percentage of systems with purpose tagging and automated retention.
* Share of analytics conducted with PETs.
* Disparity ratios in model performance across protected groups.
* Incidents of unauthorized access or sharing per 10,000 users.
* Comprehension scores from tested notices and consent screens.
* Number of substantiated complaints resolved with user satisfaction.

    Publish these metrics in transparency reports to build trust and enable benchmarking.

Governance Structures: Who Guards the Guardians?

Effective guardianship distributes responsibilities across the organization and beyond.

Board-level oversight: A data ethics and risk committee with expertise in law, technology, and social impact. Independent DPO: Budget, authority, and escalation rights insulated from commercial pressure. Cross-functional councils: Product, security, legal, HR, marketing, and research review high-risk projects regularly. External advisory panels: Community representatives and experts provide deliberative input. Whistleblower protections: Confidential channels and anti-retaliation policies to surface concerns early.

Blueprint for Organizations

Translate theory into a staged program.

Stage 1: Foundations (0–6 months)

1. Build a living data inventory and map flows, including third parties.
2. Define lawful bases and narrow purposes for each processing activity.
3. Implement baseline security (encryption at rest/in transit, MFA, least privilege, key management).
4. Launch a rights portal for access, correction, deletion, and portability; test with real users.
5. Train teams with scenario-based modules; measure comprehension, not just completion.

Stage 2: PETs and Process (6–18 months)

6. Introduce PETs where value and risk justify them (DP for analytics; federated learning across sites; MPC for joint analysis).
7. Establish a model governance pipeline: documentation (model cards), data provenance, bias testing, red-teaming, and approval gates.
8. Formalize third-party governance: standardized DPAs, technical audits, and kill-switch clauses.
9. Create a data retention and deletion service integrated with all systems; enable event-based triggers.

Stage 3: Participation and Accountability (18–36 months)

10. Stand up a public transparency report with the metrics in Section 13.
11. Form a data stewardship council including community members, customers, and employees.
12. Pilot a data cooperative or trust for a high-impact dataset, with benefit-sharing.
13. Commission independent audits of high-stakes models; publish summaries and remediation plans.

Higher Education, Research, and the Public Sector

Universities, public agencies, and civil society organizations occupy a special role in building trustworthy data institutions.

Research governance: Modernize IRB/ethics review to handle AI-specific risks (re-identification, group harms, dual use). Require PETs literacy for data-intensive studies. Open science with safeguards: Promote data commons governed by tiered access, robust de-identification, and accountability logs. Civic data stewards: Cities can convene data trusts for mobility, energy, and health, with resident oversight and participatory rule-making. Capability building: Embed privacy engineering and responsible AI in core curricula across disciplines, not just CS or law.

Ethical Foundations: Dignity, Autonomy, and Justice

At bottom, privacy and data sovereignty are ethical commitments.

Dignity: People are ends, not means. Design and governance must respect the intrinsic worth of persons, even when aggregate utility tempts shortcuts. Autonomy: Real choice requires intelligible information, feasible alternatives, and the absence of coercive defaults. Justice: Systems should not entrench historical inequities or create new forms of data-driven exclusion. Distribution of benefits and burdens matters.

These principles are not ornamental; they are practical tests for every architecture and policy decision.

The 2025–2035 Roadmap: From Slogans to Systems

* Short term (1–2 years)
* Mandate purpose tagging and data lineage across core systems.
* Convert consent flows into justification registries that record purpose, legal basis, and expected impact.
* Launch internal PETs platforms so analysts can call DP or secure aggregation without bespoke builds.
* Publish the first transparency report and commit to annual updates.
  Medium term (3–5 years)
* Achieve interoperability of identity and portability across major services used by your stakeholders

REFERENCES

Barocas, S., & Nissenbaum, H. (2009). On notice: The trouble with notice and consent. *Proceedings of the Engaging Data Forum: The First International Forum on the Application and Management of Personal Electronic Information.*

Bennett, C. J., & Raab, C. D. (2006). *The governance of privacy: Policy instruments in global perspective* (2nd ed.). MIT Press.

Cavoukian, A. (2012). *Privacy by design: Origins, meaning, and prospects.* Privacy Commissioner of Ontario.

De Filippi, P., & Wright, A. (2018). *Blockchain and the law: The rule of code.* Harvard University Press.

Draper, N. A., & Turow, J. (2019). The corporate cultivation of digital resignation. *New Media & Society, 21*(8), 1824–1839. DOI: 10.1177/1461444819833331

. European Union. (2016). *General Data Protection Regulation (GDPR) (EU) 2016/679 of the European Parliament and of the Council of 27 April 2016 on the protection of natural persons with regard to the processing of personal data and on the free movement of such data.* Official Journal of the European Union, L119, 1–88.

Government of India. (2023). *Digital Personal Data Protection Act, 2023.* Ministry of Electronics and Information Technology. https://www.meity.gov.in/

Greenleaf, G. (2014). Global data privacy laws 2013: Eight years of progress. *Privacy Laws & Business International Report, 123*, 10–13.

Kuner, C. (2015). Data localization laws and their impact on privacy, data protection, and the global internet economy. *Privacy & Security Law Report, 14*(6), 1–5.

Lessig, L. (1999). *Code and other laws of cyberspace.* Basic Books.

Lyon, D. (2018). The culture of surveillance: Watching as a way of life. *Polity.*

Nissenbaum, H. (2010). *Privacy in context: Technology, policy, and the integrity of social life.* Stanford University Press.

Organisation for Economic Co-operation and Development (OECD). (2019). *OECD principles on artificial intelligence.* OECD. https://oecd.ai/en/ai-principles

Richards, N. M., & Hartzog, W. (2016). Taking trust seriously in privacy law. *Stanford Technology Law Review : STLR : An Online High-Technology Law Journal from Stanford Law School, 19*, 431–472.

Solove, D. J. (2006). A taxonomy of privacy. *University of Pennsylvania Law Review, 154*(3), 477–564. DOI: 10.2307/40041279

State of California. (2018). *California Consumer Privacy Act (CCPA) of 2018, Cal. Civ. Code § 1798.100 et seq.*

Susha, I., Janssen, M., & Verhulst, S. (2017). Data collaboratives as "bazaars"? A review of coordination problems and mechanisms to match demand for data with supply. *Transforming Government: People. Process and Policy, 11*(1), 157–172. DOI: 10.1108/TG-12-2016-0083

United Nations Educational, Scientific and Cultural Organization (UNESCO). (2021). *Recommendation on the ethics of artificial intelligence*. UNESCO. https://unesdoc.unesco.org/

Van Dijck, J., Poell, T., & de Waal, M. (2018). *The platform society: Public values in a connective world*. Oxford University Press. DOI: 10.1093/oso/9780190889760.001.0001

Warren, S. D., & Brandeis, L. D. (1890). The right to privacy. *Harvard Law Review, 4*(5), 193–220. DOI: 10.2307/1321160

Westin, A. F. (1967). *Privacy and freedom*. Atheneum.

Yeung, K. (2018). Algorithmic regulation: A critical interrogation. *Regulation & Governance, 12*(4), 505–523. DOI: 10.1111/rego.12158

Zuboff, S. (2019). *The age of surveillance capitalism: The fight for a human future at the new frontier of power*. PublicAffairs.

Chapter 11
Impact of Artificial Intelligence on Civil Liberties:
Delving Into the Ethical and Civil Rights Concerns Arising From AI Advancements

S. Ida Evangeline
https://orcid.org/0000-0003-2997-7897
Government College of Engineering, Tirunelveli, India

ABSTRACT

This chapter critically examines the growing influence of artificial intelligence (AI) on civil liberties, exploring how algorithmic systems—while promising efficiency and innovation—pose significant risks to foundational rights such as privacy, due process, equality, and freedom of expression. As AI becomes embedded in policing, employment, healthcare, education, and social services, it increasingly mediates decisions that shape civic life and democratic participation. The chapter questions the moral and legal dilemmas of opaque algorithms, biased and unregulated data, and unmoderated surveillance, and how such technology can help to drive structural inequalities and cover up responsibility. Based on case law studies across various jurisdictions and multidisciplinary approach combining law, ethics, and technology; it puts forward a version of AI governance framework based on civil rights.

DOI: 10.4018/979-8-3693-3920-6.ch011

1. INTRODUCTION: AI AS A CIVIL RIGHTS FRONTIER

Artificial intelligence (AI) is rapidly transforming nearly every dimension of public and private life—from how individuals interact with digital services to how institutions govern populations. In essence, AI is a system that is used to mimic human intelligence, where learning takes place on some data to make or aid in a decision. Such systems not only hold the promise of unprecedented efficiencies and innovations, however, they also open up fundamental questions about how the fundamental rights and liberties of the individual are safeguarded or threatened in this new digital paradigm (Gibbons, 2021).

In the past, civil rights movements have arisen out of structural injustices, the practice of systemic exclusion, and discriminatory politics that oppress marginalized groups. These rights, which are enshrined both in constitutional, statutory, and international legal frameworks, are meant to provide personal rights, rights to equality and equity under the law, and protection of individual dignity against the abuses of state and corporate controls. However, with the advent of AI technologies, new challenges arise and current civil rights frameworks have not yet been adequate to solve them (Chatterjee et al. 2022).

The flip side of today technological changes, unlike, however, past ones is that the influence of AI is to render decisions and outcomes in hidden, non-obvious ways. Decisions on employment, bail, policing deployment, promotion and suppression of social media content and the labeling of someone as potential security threat are now determined by algorithms. These are not purely technological changes--they are changes in the workings of power, potential, and belonging. Essentially, AI is turning into a gatekeeper to most of the rights and amenities that characterize the participation in the civic life (Gibbons, 2021).

The rights of civil liberties at issue range widely. The threat to privacy has increased with such surveillance systems that can track behaviour and identify them in a real-time using facial recognition. The right to freedom of expression is subject to new modes of control with algorithmic moderation being used to suppress opposition-emphasized messages or even bury majority views further. Due process is at risk because people are not able to comprehend, or argue against decisions rendered by AI systems, particularly where such systems are guarded by trade secrets or a lack of capabilities to discern the underlying mechanics. Even equality itself is in jeopardy as such algorithms using biased or inadequate training material constructively discriminate against some groups by race, sex, disability, or socioeconomic status (Robles & Mallinson, 2025).

To these dangers is added the power disparity between the developers or implementers of AI projects, and the users of the results that it provides. The governments and corporations, which usually do not exercise enough transparency and control, possess immense repositories of data and technical foundations to support the use of AI on a large scale. In the meantime, those who are affected by decisions clearly have little technical literacy, legal resources, or institutional backing to challenge harms or seek accountability. Such an asymmetry is not purely a technical issue but political and moral in character which raises a huge concern to democratic governance and fair justice.

Also, AI is not developed in a vacuum, instead of a mirror, it tends to become the magnifier of existing hierarchies in the society. Since algorithms are trained by past data, they will be able to recall and replicate the biased markers of the past and strengthen the discrimination within it. As an example, an AI system utilized in recruitment could also bias candidates with minority backgrounds in case it is trained on old hiring decisions based on the preference of white or men applicants. Equally, it is possible that predictive policing systems enable the force to deploy policing resources into historically over-policed areas, which only contribute to further criminalization (Huang et al. 2022).

Meanwhile, AI is in itself not regressive. It can also present some instruments of promoting civil rights including the possibility to show patterns of discrimination in housing or employment, automation of accessibility to people with disabilities, and revealing systemic bias by analyzing data. What is more decisive, however, is why it is built and released using, in whose hands, and under what circumstances. It is not that the question of whether it is a good or bad AI is the critical one (Gardezi et al. 2024).

The chapter approaches these questions to adopt a rights-based perspective on AI, and, thus, to consider it as more than a technically grounded instrument, however representing a locus of normative and legal debate. It tries to deconstruct how such AI technologies interact with basic freedoms via a multidisciplinary prism drawing on law, ethics, computer science, and civil rights advocacy. By so doing, it will highlight the evils and the potentials of AI, although providing avenues that will help ascertain that the advancement of technology should not be achieved at the cost of justice, equity, and human dignity.

Couching AI as a frontier of civil rights, the section preconditions the subsequent chapters that discuss how the current AI technologies transform the field of surveillance, enforce discrimination, complicate legal defense mechanisms, and disorient established systems of accountability. Finally, this chapter concludes by stipulating that there is an urgent necessity of a civil rights-based AI ethics, the need to locate the innovation within the context of democratic values and the support of fundamental freedoms.

2. SURVEILLANCE, PRIVACY, AND PREDICTIVE POLICING

The introduction of artificial intelligence in the sphere of surveillance practices leads to a new disruptive state and corporate monitoring that has extensive repercussions on privacy and civil rights. Artificial intelligence has exponentially enhanced the ability to map an individual through both physical and online worlds with facial recognition, behavioural analytics, and predictive policing being key. Albeit these tools tend to be justified based on efficiency, safety reasons, or national security, they also bring to graphic questions concerning the reach beyond what the system needs, accountability, and inequality in the stresses imposed on already marginalized populations (Almeida et al. 2022).

An example of civil rights dangers posed by AI-powered surveillance is facial recognition technology (FRT). Based on machine learning models trained with large sets of images, FRT can not only detect or confirm an identity in real time, but also offline via analysis of footage. FRT is used more often at airports, mass transportation hubs, schools, housing complexes, etc., by law enforcement agencies, government agencies, and commercial businesses. Nonetheless, research indicates that there is a large difference in the accurateness between the racial and gender groups when it comes to racial systems- incorrectly identifying people of color at a higher-than-normal rate, women, and transgender individuals. These mistakes are not minor, as they potentially can result in false arrests, as well as reputational damages and an examined trust in civic institutions (Singh, 2023).

In addition to misidentification risks, facial recognition raises ecumenical issues of mass surveillance and accepted the culture of constant surveillance. AI-enhanced surveillance systems, unlike the older, more often targeted, episodic surveillance methods, permit continual, automated, surveillance of whole populations. This change will critically change the privacy and freeze free expression and right of association and people may be under the constant surveillance. Such action is criticized by civil liberties supporters as an erosion of the right to privacy as enshrined in constitutional and international human rights standards, as it turns spaces of civic life into spaces of mistrust and regulation (Karpa et al. 2022).

Another place where AI meets deadly danger is predictive policing. Such systems use previous data about crime to ascertain where a crime may happen or what sort of person may be involved. Whereas its advocates attest to these tools to aid in the more efficient policing resource allocation, critics insist that predictive analytics are only a recreation and perpetration of prior biases embedded in police data. As an example, when a neighborhood has historically been over-policed, this will be reflected in the data, and this will cause the system to further direct law enforcement to that neighborhood--in spite of the relative lack of crime. This forms a cycle of reinforcement that would continue over-surveillance and criminalization of certain communities, especially those of decent colors and low-income power communities.

It makes it difficult to conduct democratic accountability of police through public oversight due to the opacity of the predictive policing algorithms. The nature of how AI is applied to police work in various jurisdictions is considered as proprietary information in most cases and thus the average person is not aware of the inner workings of that AI (or the individuals themselves cannot even be understood) and in that case challenge the decision made by that system. The absence of such transparency can be disruptive to the procedures of fairness and to the principle of due process in cases where the decisions predicated on AI systems have a concrete impact on the computer as when the inference can lead to arrest, detention, or the denial of service (Hashmi et al. 2025).

The introduction of surveillance AI, also involves the First and Fourth Amendment rights in the United States. With the fourth amendment, the rights of citizens are guarded against unreasonable searches and seizures. Nevertheless, legal guidelines on the definition of a "reasonable expectation of privacy" have not been able to move with the changes in technology. Courts have been unable to answer the question as to whether AI-enabled surveillance, or more monitoring like continuous aerial surveillance, or algorithmic monitoring of movement habits, can be considered constitutional visits. Likewise, the right of free expression under the First Amendment can be chilled in cases where people become afraid that their participation in a protest event, membership in a political or religious organization, or coming to a religious meetup might lead to surveillance through algorithmic suspicion (Wörsdörfer, 2025).

Notably, such issues are not theoretical. The events in the real world highlight the necessity to consider the problem of the collision of AI surveillance and civil rights. Horizontally, the United States has experienced the legal battles and social criticism of such technologies as ShotSpotter and PredPol because they contribute to the aggravation of racial profiling and false arrests. Authoritarian regimes worldwide have used AI surveillance to oppose dissent, surveil journalists and control ethnic minority groups which we can observe with the widespread use of FRT in Xinjiang, China. Although democratic societies can control the unrestrained development of AI surveillance, there will always be a risk of moving the scale of power towards unaccountable institutions and not the citizens.

In spite of these apprehensions, there are still few checks and balances. Typically, through murky procurement practices, many law enforcement agencies are procuring AI surveillance systems without consultation, or explicit authorization of the legislature. Civil society organizations have requested to put moratoriums or outright bans on the usage of AI surveillance in specific fields, especially in the streets and sensitive areas. In the meantime, the attempts of regulating these tools on the federal or universal level still have not become more holistic and even, which leaves the vulnerabilities in the legal security (Zhang et al. 2022).

This is because, as the AI shapes the architecture of surveillance, civil liberties should be prioritized in the discussion and legislation. The right to protection of privacy needs greater than technical protection in the age of AI, the rethinking of what legally determines the appropriate actions and governance in terms of the right to privacy must consider the workings of democracy, the18 ethical standards of equity and justice. AI monitoring should not turn into a digital surrogate to discriminations that are continuously condemned by civil rights activists. Rather, its development and deployment should be brought under serious question, transparent governance and unquestionable worry over basic rights.

3. ALGORITHMIC DISCRIMINATION AND STRUCTURAL INEQUALITY

Artificial intelligence is highly praised in its ability to automate decision process and become more scalable, objective, and faster. But actually, much of AI recreates, and in many cases compounds, current patterns of discrimination and structural inequality. Contrary to their neutrality as described by conventional wisdom, these systems are social, historical and institutional biases embedded in the data they have been trained on and the contexts they are applied to. Here, we discuss the various ways in which algorithmic systems may further inequality treatments in important areas, including employment, finance, healthcare, and content moderation, at the expense of and increasing social disparities by complicating existing protections under law (Heinrichs, 2022).

The most important element of algorithmic discrimination is that AI relies on historical data which in most cases contains legacies of past injustice. Algorithms can be trained to reproduce those patterns when supplied with data that already showed racial, gender, socioeconomic or ableist bias. To illustrate, when it comes to employment, AI hiring systems have proved to discriminate against an applicant by having such indicators in their resumes related to a specific demographic. An infamous example was a Microsoft AI recruiting tool that was being used by a large technology company to systematically discriminate hiring against women by erroneously ranking resumes that mentioned the word women (as in the women s chess club) lower or resumes that were submitted by women s colleges because the model had been trained on a historically male heavy job applicant base.

Within the financial industry, credit scoring systems and programs implementing automated lending practices proved to over-deny loans to racial minorities, or provide higher-cost loans to them, when evaluated by income and credit score. Although it does not always revolve around the issue of literal racial profiling, these outcomes are "generated" by proxies present in the data sets, namely, zip codes or the patterns of financial behavior related to race based on long-running economic inequality. Such systems may lead to discriminatory effects although the systems may seem to be objective as such (Van Bekkum & Borgesius, 2023).

Medicine is another area of critical concern in which the application of algorithms may have life-altering effects. Studies found that the algorithms implementing healthcare allocation or predicting the risk to patients can highly miscalculate the demands of the Black patients. In a landmark study, an algorithm employed to oversee care programs actually had a lower risk score of Blacks as opposed to white patients with the same health conditions, since the model used historic healthcare spending as an indicator of health status, despite the fact that it did not reflect systemic under-treatment and barriers to care experienced by the Black population. These biases reinforce health disparities and give rise to immediate ethical and legal concerns of how the algorithms are validated and developed.

Content moderation algorithms which run on social media platforms to block hate speech, misinformation or graphic content are known to disproportionately target marginalized voices in the digital world. Racial, religious, LGBTQ+, and Indigenous activists, artists, and users have reported a greater percentage of content removal or account suspension, despite actively expressing themselves, or being culturally representative. Such moderation environments are usually not context aware or linguistically nuanced, and the appeal mechanism is hidden and unreliable. It creates a type of digital disenfranchisement with some groups being more censored and less able to participate in the discourse of the country (Fountain, 2022).

The legal compensation of algorithmic discrimination is still insufficient and lacking behind. Classic civil rights statutes (including Title VII of Civil Rights Act-prohibiting employment discrimination) were formulated when human decision-makers were to be considered as subjects. They are not well-geared into the intricacies of machine learning systems, particularly when discrimination is manifested by correlations and proxies as opposed to plain out intent. In addition, a legal rule of disparate impact, which holds that even the absence of discrimination intent does not make policies that disproportionally affect a group of protected individuals unlawful, has not gained much traction in the algorithmic setting especially where businesses make statements that the AI models are neutral or secured as trade secrets.

The second difficulty is the obscurity of algorithmic decision-making. Often people do not know that an AI-based system has made a decision that can affect their employment or loan decisions, health care coverage, or online presence. It can be almost impossible to determine the basis of the decision or to challenge it at all even when they are conscious of it. This hurts procedural fairness and breeds distrust of institutions, particularly those communities that have a long history of having to bear systemic bias (Chen, 2023).

Also, the issue of algorithmic bias cannot be reduced to the problem of bad coding or inadequate data. It is symptomatic of more structural inequalities itself, which are those systems of extreme exclusion and hierarchy so embedded across the social fabric. Failure to critically reflect on such power dynamics when designing AI systems inherits the risk of the status quo being reinforcing under pressure of innovation. Algorithmic systems, in turn, turn into the means of reifying the social stratification, and discrimination more efficient and less visible.

It therefore follows that equality with respect to algorithmic discrimination necessitates more than fixing the problem technically, but rather the realignment of the development, testing, and governance of AI. The mandatory use of auditing systems on bias, inclusion of the concerned communities in the design, and its transparency and explainability must be done. An equally significant factor is a call to strengthen regulative measures that would increase the coverage of civil rights protection in the digital environment and bring the responsibility of algorithmic harms upon both state and non-state actors (Vale et al. 2022).

The following section highlights the fact that unless there is intentional action, AI has the potential to exacerbate the vices which civil rights structures are intended to eradicate. When we look at algorithmic discrimination as a product of technology and structural otherwise, we could then start to create more fair systems that uphold rather than compromise justice.

4. TRANSPARENCY, ACCOUNTABILITY, AND REDRESS

With artificial intelligence systems playing a more and more active role in decision making regarding rights and opportunities of people, lack of transparency in the functioning of these systems has become one of the most important civil liberties issues of the digital age. Artificial intelligence systems, particularly those with complicated machine learning models, tend to be black boxes, with an inability to be reasoned out in a straightforward manner as to why such a model has resulted in a particular probability outcome. Such obscurity poses great obstacles to the accountability, violates fairness in process, and restricts the capacity of individuals and communities to enjoy redress when they are aggrieved by automated decisions.

The so-called "black box" problem is the challenge or even the impossibility of learning how some AI models, including deep neural networks, reach specific results. Practically, this will imply that those declined a loan, hired or not at a job, marked as a high-risk or identified in surveillance systems will get no significant explanation why. The consequences to due process are shattering. In democratic societies, people are entitled to challenge the actions, which have impact on their lives. Information about the basis of those decisions being hidden by the AI systems, this element of the key principle is shredded in favor of moving control out of individual hands and into obscure systems run by generally unaccountable entities (Olsen et al. 2024).

The issue of opacity is also made complex by proprietary ownership of most AI systems. Again and again, there are cases where companies seek protection of their algorithms and information on which their models are powered under philosophies of intellectual property protection, and will not even publicly reveal entry level details of their operations. The practice interferes with accountability, averts external audit and protects compromised and discriminatory systems. It equally leaves the ethical question of whether the commercial interests can be permitted to supersede the rights of the individuals to fairness, transparency and redress.

Mechanisms of accountability have failed to adjust to the fast transfer of AI technologies. Developers or deployers of AI systems are not required to explain, evaluate the effects, or inform people that they are under the algorithmic decision in many jurisdictions. This is not to say that when specific laws are in place, e.g. the General Data Protection Regulation (GDPR) of the European Union, a right to explanation under Article 22 would not be in place, but in practice, its application is still often limited and disputed. In the United States, laws including the Administrative Procedure Act and civil rights legislations do provide indirect means to dispute some algorithmic decisions, but these routes are frequently unavailable, sluggish and not tailored to technical intricacies of AI (Cheong, 2024).

Remedies to address any harms connected with AI are also undeveloped. Conventional legal strategies to redress harm, including a lawsuit or an administrative complaint, are challenging to apply when the damage is inflicted by a black box algorithm especially when people are unaware of the system, or access to the information and logic underlying that system. Furthermore, AI harms tend to be diffuse, probabilistic or collective in the sense that they are harder to specify who the victims are and whether they are causally connected. Take an example given where an algorithm incorporated in the hiring practices of different companies in a certain way systematically lowers the evaluation of the applications that have been filed by members of a certain demographic, the victims are often simply unaware that something wrong happened and certainly lack the means to address the wrongs done.

Transparency and redress fails to exist, and this reduces the legitimacy of the AI systems and breaks the confidence of the people. It results in a striking asymmetry between people who develop and benefit financially in the development and use of AI and the subjects of the AI technologies. The issue is especially pronounced when applied to areas of criminal justice, immigration, child welfare, and offering of public benefits where people who lack status already face barriers to justice on a systemic level (Fehr et al. 2024).

However, these accountability gaps are seeing some emerging moves to deal with them. Technologists, legal academics and civil society groups have promoted algorithmic transparency legislation, algorithm impact assessments, and algorithmic audits. An example of this is algorithmic impact assessment (AIA), which takes the form of and is intended to mirror environmental impact assessment, intended to ensure that risks and potential harms of an AI system are considered and analyzed prior to deployment of a system. Other jurisdictions, i.e. New York City have started applying such measures to public-sector algorithms. In the meantime, suggestions of algorithmic auditing framework stress that third parties should evaluate models, data, and results in the model to meet fairness, legality, and non-discrimination.

Explainability is also becoming dominant as a principle to develop AI. These methods, including local interpretable model-agnostic explanations (LIME), SHAP values and counterfactual explanations seek to make the results of models easier to understand to both their developers and consumers. Nevertheless, such ways of enforcement have their limits and tend to lack the amount of transparency needed to be legally or morally responsible. It requires a broader shift, shifting explainability beyond assessment of the kinds of technical issues it represents, to becoming an issue of normative determinacy, a matter of democratic rights and justice (Sanchez et al. 2025).

In the end, we have to make AI systems transparent, accountable, and redressible using both technological advances and law. A government should issue strict regulations that have power to enforce the requirement of disclosure, fairness and due process. The governance structures that Institutions that apply AI need incorporate supervision systems, mechanisms of grievance and interactions to the people. And programmers have to adopt moral approaches to their design processes, focused on readability, inclusion and avoiding peril.

AI cannot just be allowed to run rampant because without protection and regulation, it will continue to follow practices that shadow responsibility, deny justice and increase inequality. Being transparent and accountable is not only a technical objective, but also a civil rights requirement of AI.

5. LEGAL PROTECTIONS AND GAPS

The development of artificial intelligence has surpassed the legal systems designed to ensure civil liberties, consequently, creating a huge disparity between the rate at which technology is applied and the ability of law to defend individual rights. Although current civil right and anti-discrimination laws provide some protection against harm inflicted by artificial intelligence systems, such laws were mostly developed during an analog age, far under-prepared to contend with the new threats introduced by programmed texts, autonomous and data-driven technologies. This part reverses to examine some ways in which the existing legal frameworks are being tested by AI, and some ways it is failing, and how new paradigms are coming to either fill it, or present new challenges.

The US offers civil rights protection to its citizens based largely on legislation including Title VII of the Civil Rights Act, which forbids discrimination in employment; fair housing act (FHA); equal credit opportunity act (ECOA); and the Americans with disabilities act (ADA). All these laws aim to inhibit unequal treatment and provide equal employment opportunities, housing, access to credit and government services. Theoretically, these safeguards should be imposed on both human and machine decisions. Nevertheless, in practice they present challenges to their use on at least three important fronts: difficulty of intent determination, proxying of data, and lack of algorithmic visibility (Schmidt et al. 2024).

Discriminating intent is one of the major legal issues that must be established. Numerous civil rights laws impose a requirement that a decision-maker discriminate intentionally, but most algorithmic discrimination is not a feature of explicit bias, but of the statistical trends and correlations imposed on training data. Although the results-focused approach to disparate impact advocated in the "disparate impact" standard permits cases to be brought on basis of unintentional results, the approach has had its limits due to legal precedent and has been opposed both in courts and in legislatures. Complex algorithmic systems have frequently been resistant to application of this standard, particularly when modelers contend that their models are objective (neutral) or data-driven.

Also, AI models often use proxies, which are indirect variables and sometimes correlate with the characteristics that are protected such as race, gender, or disability. An algorithm like a credit scoring algorithm might not throw race into a generalized entry, but it might base its analysis on ZIP code, educational level or internet browsing, which readily correlate quite strongly with race and socioeconomic levels. Such proxies are barely transparent to the end users and use of this proxy can create discrimination without an apparent legal responsibility. Current law is ill equipped to challenge this type of proxy discrimination, particularly where in the case of algorithmic algorithms that are proprietary/trade secrets when conveying proprietary information (Marwala & Mpedi, 2024).

Explainability and transparency come to the fore as well. Through a significant portion of the legal processes the affected persons must be provided with an explanation of the details and given a chance to oppose decisions made by authorities such as due process claims under administrative law. Black box AI systems are a violation of these principles particularly when it comes to government agencies abdicating control in favor of vendor-provided models. Automated risk assessment and eligibility measures are deployed in an increasingly large number of systems in immigration and in child welfare, criminal justice, typically with little disclosure and no reasonable appeal process, which can violate due process under both domestic U.S. constitutional and international human rights law.

AI has led to disparate responses by governments across most jurisdictions internationally, with the most active being the European Union, in terms of set regulations. The General Data Protection Regulation (GDPR) of the EU contains an automated decision-making directive, Article 22 in particular, granting people the right not to be considered as subjects of a decision made solely on an automated process that produces a similar significant effect on them. Although the boundaries and applicability of this right are disputable, the GDPR has compelled the boards and individuals to contemplate transparency and fairness as a component of data governance (Ye et al. 2024).

Further to GDPR, the EU put forward the Artificial Intelligence Act (AI Act), which ranks the AI systems based on risk, thus setting obligations on developers and deployers accordingly. Systems categorized as high-stakes e.g. law enforcement or hiring or access to essential services would be strictly regulated in terms of transparency, human oversight, and bias mitigation. The AI Act is also a key milestone in terms of regulating an industry, but concerns have also been raised as the means of enforcement are quite weak, and the definitions too vague.

By contrast, the United States does not have exhaustive federal legislation that governs the challenges that are unique to AI. Regulation has been, by and large, regulatory efforts have been ad hoc, with sector-specific regulation (e.g. the guidelines of the Equal Employment Opportunity Commission on algorithmic hiring) and a mix of state/local regulations. An example is a law New York City enacted that mandates bias audits on automated hiring instruments, and Illinois has enacted a biometric privacy law, which limits how facial recognition can be used. Yet, these are still attempts that are not comprehensive and most of the time meet resistance on the part of the industry stakeholders (Chau, 2024).

Lack of a coherent national policy on AI makes people susceptible and jeopardizes the attempts to create uniform safeguards. It also means that finding and exposing abuses and demanding accountability becomes very heavy on civil society groups, investigative journalists and affected communities. Transparency and fairness will not be the rule of the law and become only a subject to corporate goodwill and societal action instead of a reporting should be.

In order to eliminate such gaps, legal scholars and advocates have developed a variety of recommended regulatory interventions, such as the introduction of algorithms and courts transparency requirements, the imposition of impact assessment, strong whistleblower protection, and the establishment of independent oversight bodies. Others have proposed the extension of current civil rights laws to apply explicitly to decision-making by algorithms of all types, or the creation of entirely new legal constructs--such as a new concept of "algorithmic due process"--that capture the unique harms posed by AI. There are also those, who suggest human rights-based approach that includes consideration of digital dignity and the right to meaningful participation in technology governance (Orwat et al. 2024).

The point to be understood is that the existing legal safeguards are inadequate to guarantee that the AI systems are used in a manner that would not impose on the civil liberties and would favor equality. With AI being increasingly integrated into social, economic, and government processes, the law should be developed to ensure that it renders more than just technical protection, i.e., strong and enforceable rights. Otherwise, it is the danger of entrenching in the future where automated systems have enormous control over the lives of people and cannot be regulated, or held accountable and control is not democratized.

6. TOWARD A CIVIL RIGHTS-CENTERED AI ETHICS

The ultimate adoption of artificial intelligence in the regular decision-making processes requires an overhaul in the ethics of technology that shall shift the popular approach outside the ethics of abstract morality, to that of technology values, which should be based on the issue of civil rights as a fundamental issue. A morally right framework of dealing with AI should not just inquire whether the system functions or meets technical standards, but and, crucially whether it upholds the dignity, the agency, the right of the people who are influenced by it. This section sketches the still tentative lines of a civil rights-based ethics of AI and suggests a set of specific initiatives in developing a constructive tech that supports, not undermines, democracy and racial, gender, and economic equity (Mori et al. 2025).

Industry-driven ethics, in the form of values such as fairness, transparency, and accountability, have dominated the field of AI ethics long enough, and frequently were vague and inconsistent. These ideals are significant, but are more often than not used as an inspirational marketing tool, rather than an enforceable ideal. Internal audits, and voluntary guidelines, along with corporate ethics boards, are less likely to have any public accountability and seldom focus on the structural inequality behind the construction of algorithmic harms. In addition, statistical parity or equalized odds as technical definitions of fairness may distract attention from discrimination as it is experienced. The decoupling of statistical definitions of fairness and the law tend to elide historical practice.

In the contrasting approach of a civil rights oriented AI ethics, the actions of AI are subordinate to the legal and moral concerns of democracy that attach to equality, non-discrimination, due process, freedom of expression, and the right to privacy. It acknowledges that AI systems cannot exist in a vacuum, but in institution and society where power hierarchies are unequal, where historical injustices have been perpetuated, and pre-existing marginalization occurred. Therefore, ethics should not only be rooted in abstract calculation, but in the realities and requirements of the groups of people that may be damaged most frequently (Galiana et al. 2024).

A key foundation of this orientation is participatory design- the idea that individuals or organizations, who are impacted by a technology, should be influential in the design and implementation of the technology. This involve working closely with groups concerned with civil rights, community organizations, and historically marginalized groups during the development and lifecycle of AI systems. There cannot be tokenistic or post hoc participation; it has to be designed into the governance structures of organizations implementing AI, and have feedback, revision, and accountability systems.

It is also crucial to institutionalize algorithmic audits and impact assessments especially on areas having higher risks such as criminal justice, education, healthcare, housing and employment. Those audits should dig deeper than mere face-level metrics to scrutinize systemic biases and disparate impacts and other societal-level implications of AI adoption. Such audits should be conducted or certified by independent oversight bodies--and not simply internal corporate ethics teams--and their result should be published to provide accountability and popular oversight.

The other pillar is regarding regulatory oversight. Voluntary compliance cannot be the main way of protecting civil liberties in the era of AI. Governments should implement legally enforceable principles that dictate fairness, transparency and accountability standards of algorithmic decision-making. Such standards must incorporate quality control by the need to have publicly documented AI systems, redress and appeal, and legal responsibility of discriminatory determinations. Regulatory bodies should have the technical competence and enforcement ability as well.

An ethics of AI based on civil rights would also require representation throughout the technological pipeline: in data collection and labeling, in algorithm design and test, configuration, and deployment. Developers should carry out an interrogation of the data into their possession as to not just examine whether it is correct but whether it represents unjust hierarchies or historic inequalities. Algorithms should be stress-tested on the harms when use with various populations groups and the systems should be designed to be explicable and challenging with these users (Kulkarni et al. 2024).

More importantly, ethical AI has to deal with technological solution boundaries. Not all social problems can be destroyed or even should be destroyed by using AI and in some circumstances, the topic of the greatest ethics may include not applying any AI at all. Predictive policing, use of biometrics, and automated welfare checks are realms in which the harms could be so far out of whack with the benefits that a moratorium or ban is justified. ETHICS should have the audacity to say no--not to optimize.

Lastly, ethics that is enforced by civil rights should be intersectional and internationally educated. AI does not affect everyone the same; those effects intersect race, gender, and class, ability, immigration, and geography. Furthermore, AI systems built in one region of the world can be implemented in other where the scope of law and understanding of cultures and norms would be substantially different. Ethical systems need to remain responsive to such dynamics and assist in the international standards that favour human rights, digital sovereignty, and technological fairness (Brey & Dainow, 2024).

Overall, civil rights-focused AI ethics is not an accessory but something that can accompany innovation, it is a requirement of legitimacy in the digital age. It necessitates a transfer of power, a restructuring of voice and the institutionalization of justice within the genetic code of technological innovation. Since AI systems increasingly influence the organizations of opportunity, control, and participation in society, it is not only an ethical need to make sure that these systems uphold and pursue civil liberties but the democratic one as well.

7. CASE STUDIES AND GLOBAL PERSPECTIVES

Because artificial intelligence raises ethical and civil rights issues, which are global in nature, they have different expressions across political, legal, and social systems. When comparing case studies of harms related to AI across jurisdiction, one could notice that the harms are similar, but responses that take place on regulatory, civic, and grassroots levels are very varied. In this section, we select several examples in different parts of the world in order to demonstrate how our civil liberties are either upheld or compromised by the governance of AI with some comparative understanding of why an approach to rights guidance can be so sorely required.

United States: Fragmented Protections and Rising Scrutiny

Lack of governmental federal regulation on AI in the United States has been, instead, leading to a splintering quilt of local, state, and industry projects. Among the most notable incidences of civil rights abuse due to AI was the sentencing and parole recommendations rendered by the proprietary risk assessment algorithm known as COMPAS. Racial bias was pointed out in the system when investigating the issue found out that the system was overrepresenting the risk factor among black defendants who had lower recidivism levels in comparison to the similar sized groups of whites.

The other notable case was that of the Amazon AI recruit tool, which was abandoned when it was discovered that it was hiring based on bias against women, by penalizing resumes that had the name of women colleges or women based organization. Coupled with escalating consumer awareness, these high profile failures have generated demands to similar regulatory climate of algorithmic transparency laws, enforced audits, and more oversight, especially in the public sector uses (Khmara & Touchton, 2024).

New York and San Francisco cities have been ahead of the game, enacting city ordinances requiring assessments of the impact of some AI tools or proscribing the use of facial recognition technology in police operations. Nevertheless, the absence of a coherent national policy still puts most of the communities at the risk of uncontrolled AI implementation, especially in the sphere of education, housing as well as social welfare (Sifaoui & Eastin, 2024).

European Union: A Proactive Regulatory Model

The European Union has made itself into an international leader in the regulation of AI. General Data Protection Regulation (GDPR) became the first significant legal tool that acknowledged individuals rights vis-a-vis automated decision-making such as not to be considered an outcome of a decision made only by a machine and being entitled to explanation.

Expanding on the GDPR, the EU Artificial Intelligence Act (AI Act) proposes a risk-based system in ranking AI systems: minimal, limited, high and unacceptable risk. The systems that have been labelled to be high-risk need to fulfil the demanding requirements in terms of transparency, human supervision, and non-discrimination, including the use of law enforcement, border control, and employment. Such unacceptable-risk systems, as social scoring by governments, would be simply forbidden.

In spite of its intentions, the AI Act has received criticism regarding the broad carve-outs it gives to law enforcement, and the self-assessment option it provides to the AI developers in most instances. However, EU model can be said to be a monumental effort in enshrining civil liberties in the regulation of emerging technologies by means of legal criteria that can be enforced (Shqairat et al. 2025).

China: State Surveillance and AI as Social Control

China proposes an opposite prospect, and AI technologies are applied significantly profoundly integrated in state instruments of social control and state control. The best-known one is the implementation of AI-powered facial recognition and behavior surveillance in the Xinjiang region, where citizens are monitored and targeted by paying close attention and tracking their activities, patterns of behavior, and locations. These systems use biometric data, emotion detection, and body motion to identify those individuals as legitimate suspects- frequently, with no open standards or appeal process.

Another measure adopted by the Chinese government is a social credit system where information provided by financial, legal, and behavioral means is included to evaluate the levels of trustworthiness of citizens. Although the system is highly local and particularized, it is an extension of the overall trend towards the algorithmic governance of enforcing specificity and compliance.

The experience of creating and using AI in China shows the dangers of civil liberties that can be exercised with the independence and legal restrictions that allow creating and operating AI technologies without regulation and with no accountability to the general population. It also highlights how AI can be used, not just to discriminate but also to consolidate power of an authoritarian regime (Thunø & Wang, 2025).

Canada: Emerging Rights-Based Frameworks

Canada has already initiated the process of AI regulation by developing its proposed Artificial Intelligence and Data Act (AIDA) to develop national standards of high-impact AI systems. In addition to this, the country has piloted algorithmic impact assessments (AIAs) to be used by the federal government, whereby departments must consider the possible harms of the AI systems prior to implementation.

It is important to note that civil society organizations and scholars in Canada have been instrumental in the quest of holding people accountable. An incident where the Automated Benefits Application System in Ontario is found to be unfairly identifying welfare recipients to be investigated for fraud also resulted in backlash by people and the concept of algorithmic fairness in social services being questioned. Complying, advocacy networks have called upon more transparency, co- governance with communities affected and an AI ombudsperson (Bosset, 2025).

Global South: Data Colonialism and Unequal Infrastructures

In most of the countries within the Global South, there is no sufficient localization, oversight, and ethical scrutiny of AI technologies that are imported to the country by richer states. This is often referred to as data colonialism and refers to the transferring of data belonging to low-income citizens to be used in the training of models that would eventually only benefit the corporations or governments in the Global North. Simultaneously, people in the context of the deployment of AI in fields of public health, policing, and social welfare are being exposed to AI Mayo deployments with little recourse or effective consent.

In Kenya, as an example, there has been a deployment of biometrics registration systems without sufficient safeguards creating worries over exclusion, monitoring, and misuse of the data. The Aadhaar biometric identification system is highly used in India to provide welfare; however, this has resulted in instances of the unjust denial of welfare provisions where due process and accountability are questioned.

Struggles to govern AI in these areas are usually compounded by lack of technical ability, legal framework, as well as political determination. But grassroots movements and digital rights groups are more frequently applying the principles of community control and fighting techno-solutionism, being based on the local aspects of the real life and demanding ethical control (Valente & Grohmann, 2024).

Cross-Cutting Themes and Lessons

Some patterns can be identified across these case studies: that AI systems have a propensity to reinforce current inequalities through their effects; that algorithmic choices ought to be unaccountable and intractable; and that more participatory environments of transparent and rights-respecting governance are necessary. It is the level of institutional reaction, the amplitude of civic society and the position of the law to defend the civil liberties that vary.

Global worldviews can help give us not only the understanding of the multiplicity of effects of AI, but they also offer a pathway toward solidarity and collective education. Whether considering regulatory innovations in Europe, grass-roots struggle in the Global South or even the cases of public backlash to algorithmic harm we see evidence of what works and fails at protest and recalibration of civil rights in the digital age.

8. CONCLUSION: CHARTING A RIGHTS-BASED FUTURE FOR AI

Increasingly, artificial intelligence will become one of the critical forces of the 21 st century, and AI can pick out challenges ahead of us are not only how we make machines smarter, but how we can ensure that systems we are designing reflect the best aspects of our deepest democratic ideals. The uses of AI in policing, hiring, healthcare, education, and finance, including through public administration, may be considered further as socio-political tools of mediation of the rights, resources, and recognition.

As I have explicated in this chapter, AI has the potential to reinforce or aggravate threats to civil liberties--by intrusive surveillance that implies diminished privacy, algorithmic decision-making that implies lost due process, discriminatory algorithmic patterns, and incomprehensible systems that imply lost accountability. Whereas much public debate about the ethics of AI has revolved around abstract dangers or speculative risks, the civil rights framing demands that the pressing issues exist now, hurting real human beings in places, as is most often the case, that have been historically marginalized.

Now it is the task to make the principles of civil rights part and patch of AI development and governance. This is to imply that fairness does not only represent a mathematical limitation but indeed a constitutional and a moral obligation as well. It demands the rethinking of transparency and accountability as matters of democratic responsibility rather than as the technical attributes. And it requires a reallocation of power--building in protections so that the people most impacted by AI systems do not just have protections, but that they are engaged in deciding the directions of the technologies that affect their lives.

Going into the future, construction, launching, and monitoring of AI should be based on a rights framework. Laws need to keep up with incidents of digital abuse and continue to develop in a way that makes them comprehensive and effective. Additionally, the authorities must be prepared to keep the regulation watchdog reliable. Technologists are required to leave the comfort of minimizing risks and venture into equity maximism leveraging on participation practices and a hypertrophic commitment that goes beyond compliance. And civil society should be watchful, inventive, and indefatigable in the safeguarding of human dignity in the era of digitality.

The AI is an evolving field whose destiny is yet to be determined. It will become both a force of liberation and oppression and this will require not just code and computation but also law and ethics and activism and the desire to place civil rights at the center of our technological imagination. As has been founded in much of this chapter, civil liberties are not a side issue in the era of AI, but rather the ethical guide by which we should guide its application. The rational machine should never be sought at the cost of human lives, freedom and human rights of those who it serves.

REFERENCES

Almeida, D., Shmarko, K., & Lomas, E. (2022). The ethics of facial recognition technologies, surveillance, and accountability in an age of artificial intelligence: A comparative analysis of US, EU, and UK regulatory frameworks. *AI and Ethics*, *2*(3), 377–387. DOI: 10.1007/s43681-021-00077-w PMID: 34790955

Bosset, P. (2025). Cultural human rights as new foundations for interculturalist policies: A rights-based approach from Quebec. *International Journal of Human Rights*, *29*(5), 864–888. DOI: 10.1080/13642987.2024.2432944

Brey, P., & Dainow, B. (2024). Ethics by design for artificial intelligence. *AI and Ethics*, *4*(4), 1265–1277. DOI: 10.1007/s43681-023-00330-4

Chatterjee, S., NS, S., & Hussain, Z. (2022). Evolution of artificial intelligence and its impact on human rights: From sociolegal perspective. *International Journal of Law and Management*, *64*(2), 184–205. DOI: 10.1108/IJLMA-06-2021-0156

Chau, M. (2024). Ethical, legal, and regulatory landscape of artificial intelligence in Australian healthcare and ethical integration in radiography: A narrative review. *Journal of Medical Imaging and Radiation Sciences*, *55*(4), 101733. DOI: 10.1016/j.jmir.2024.101733 PMID: 39111223

Chen, Z. (2023). Ethics and discrimination in artificial intelligence-enabled recruitment practices. *Humanities & Social Sciences Communications*, *10*(1), 1–12. DOI: 10.1057/s41599-023-02079-x

Cheong, B. C. (2024). Transparency and accountability in AI systems: Safeguarding wellbeing in the age of algorithmic decision-making. *Frontiers in Human Dynamics*, *6*, 1421273. DOI: 10.3389/fhumd.2024.1421273

Fehr, J., Citro, B., Malpani, R., Lippert, C., & Madai, V. I. (2024). A trustworthy AI reality-check: The lack of transparency of artificial intelligence products in healthcare. *Frontiers in Digital Health*, *6*, 1267290. DOI: 10.3389/fdgth.2024.1267290 PMID: 38455991

Fountain, J. E. (2022). The moon, the ghetto and artificial intelligence: Reducing systemic racism in computational algorithms. *Government Information Quarterly*, *39*(2), 101645. DOI: 10.1016/j.giq.2021.101645

Galiana, L. I., Gudino, L. C., & González, P. M. (2024). Ethics and artificial intelligence. [English Edition]. *Revista Clínica Española*, *224*(3), 178–186. PMID: 38355097

Gardezi, M., Joshi, B., Rizzo, D. M., Ryan, M., Prutzer, E., Brugler, S., & Dadkhah, A. (2024). Artificial intelligence in farming: Challenges and opportunities for building trust. *Agronomy Journal, 116*(3), 1217–1228. DOI: 10.1002/agj2.21353

Gibbons, E. D. (2021). Toward a more equal world: The human rights approach to extending the benefits of artificial intelligence. *IEEE Technology and Society Magazine*, *40*(1), 25–30. DOI: 10.1109/MTS.2021.3056295

Hashmi, E., Yamin, M. M., & Yayilgan, S. Y. (2025). Securing tomorrow: A comprehensive survey on the synergy of Artificial Intelligence and information security. *AI and Ethics*, *5*(3), 1911–1929. DOI: 10.1007/s43681-024-00529-z

Heinrichs, B. (2022). Discrimination in the age of artificial intelligence. *AI & Society*, *37*(1), 143–154. DOI: 10.1007/s00146-021-01192-2

Huang, C., Zhang, Z., Mao, B., & Yao, X. (2022). An overview of artificial intelligence ethics. *IEEE Transactions on Artificial Intelligence*, *4*(4), 799–819. DOI: 10.1109/TAI.2022.3194503

Karpa, D., Klarl, T., & Rochlitz, M. (2022). Artificial intelligence, surveillance, and big data. In *Diginomics research perspectives: The role of digitalization in business and society* (pp. 145–172). Springer International Publishing. DOI: 10.1007/978-3-031-04063-4_8

Khmara, L., & Touchton, M. (2024). Institutional fragmentation in United States protected area agencies and its impact on budget processes. *Journal of Public Budgeting, Accounting & Financial Management*, *36*(4), 490–513. DOI: 10.1108/JPBAFM-08-2023-0147

Kulkarni, A. V., Joseph, S., & Patil, K. P. (2024). Artificial intelligence technology readiness for social sustainability and business ethics: Evidence from MSMEs in developing nations. *International Journal of Information Management Data Insights*, *4*(2), 100250. DOI: 10.1016/j.jjimei.2024.100250

Marwala, T., & Mpedi, L. G. (2024). Artificial intelligence and the law. In *Artificial intelligence and the law* (pp. 1–25). Springer Nature Singapore.

Mori, M., Sassetti, S., Cavaliere, V., & Bonti, M. (2025). A systematic literature review on artificial intelligence in recruiting and selection: A matter of ethics. *Personnel Review*, *54*(3), 854–878. DOI: 10.1108/PR-03-2023-0257

Olsen, H. P., Hildebrandt, T. T., Wiesener, C., Larsen, M. S., & Flügge, A. W. A. (2024). The right to transparency in public governance: Freedom of information and the use of artificial intelligence by public agencies. *Digital Government: Research and Practice*, *5*(1), 1–15. DOI: 10.1145/3632753

Orwat, C., Bareis, J., Folberth, A., Jahnel, J., & Wadephul, C. (2024). Normative challenges of risk regulation of artificial intelligence. *NanoEthics, 18*(2), 11. DOI: 10.1007/s11569-024-00454-9

Robles, P., & Mallinson, D. J. (2025). Artificial intelligence technology, public trust, and effective governance. *The Review of Policy Research, 42*(1), 11–28. DOI: 10.1111/ropr.12555

Sanchez, T. W., Brenman, M., & Ye, X. (2025). The ethical concerns of artificial intelligence in urban planning. *Journal of the American Planning Association, 91*(2), 294–307. DOI: 10.1080/01944363.2024.2355305

Schmidt, J., Schutte, N. M., Buttigieg, S., Novillo-Ortiz, D., Sutherland, E., Anderson, M., & Van Kessel, R. (2024). Mapping the regulatory landscape for artificial intelligence in health within the European Union. *npj. Digital Medicine, 7*(1), 229. PMID: 39191937

Shqairat, A., Liarte, S., Marange, P., Nuur, C., & Chagnes, A. (2025). Implications of European Union regulation on the circular economy and stakeholder strategies in the electric vehicle lithium-ion battery sector. *Management of Environmental Quality, 36*(1), 155–182. DOI: 10.1108/MEQ-04-2024-0163

Sifaoui, A., & Eastin, M. S. (2024). "Whispers from the wrist": wearable health monitoring devices and privacy regulations in the US: the loopholes, the challenges, and the opportunities. *Cryptography, 8*(2), 26. DOI: 10.3390/cryptography8020026

Singh, T. (2023, October). AI-Driven Surveillance Technologies and Human Rights: Balancing Security and Privacy. In *International Conference on Smart Systems: Innovations in Computing* (pp. 703-717). Singapore: Springer Nature Singapore.

Thunø, M., & Wang, Y. (2025). China's Smart Diaspora Governance: Extraterritorial Social Control Through Digital Platforms. *Journal of Current Chinese Affairs, 54*(1), 48–72. DOI: 10.1177/18681026241232998

Vale, D., El-Sharif, A., & Ali, M. (2022). Explainable artificial intelligence (XAI) post-hoc explainability methods: Risks and limitations in non-discrimination law. *AI and Ethics, 2*(4), 815–826. DOI: 10.1007/s43681-022-00142-y

Valente, J. C., & Grohmann, R. (2024). Critical data studies with Latin America: Theorizing beyond data colonialism. *Big Data & Society, 11*(1), 20539517241227875. DOI: 10.1177/20539517241227875

Van Bekkum, M., & Borgesius, F. Z. (2023). Using sensitive data to prevent discrimination by artificial intelligence: Does the GDPR need a new exception? *Computer Law & Security Review, 48*, 105770. DOI: 10.1016/j.clsr.2022.105770

Wörsdörfer, M. (2025). The EU's artificial intelligence act: An ordoliberal assessment. *AI and Ethics*, *5*(1), 263–278. DOI: 10.1007/s43681-023-00337-x

Ye, X., Yan, Y., Li, J., & Jiang, B. (2024). Privacy and personal data risk governance for generative artificial intelligence: A Chinese perspective. *Telecommunications Policy*, *48*(10), 102851. DOI: 10.1016/j.telpol.2024.102851

Zhang, Z., Al Hamadi, H., Damiani, E., Yeun, C. Y., & Taher, F. (2022). Explainable artificial intelligence applications in cyber security: State-of-the-art in research. *IEEE Access : Practical Innovations, Open Solutions*, *10*, 93104–93139. DOI: 10.1109/ACCESS.2022.3204051

KEY TERMS AND DEFINITIONS

1. **Artificial Intelligence (AI): A branch of computer science concerned with the design of systems that exhibit behavior that would require intelligence on the part of a human being to accomplish:** specifically decision-making, understanding language, pattern identification and prediction.
2. **Algorithmic Discrimination: Biased treatment of people or a group of people based on the biases inherent in the algorithmic systems:** which are based on, in most cases, improperly skewed training data or incorrect model formulation.
3. **Predictive Policing: The application of predictive policing which is an AI and data analysis to predict future offending behaviour by targeting high-crime individuals or places are often discussed as giving future projection to existing racial and economic biases.:**
4. **Surveillance Technology: Government or corporate use of digital means to track:** gather, and assess personal information includes facial recognition, location tracking, and biometric analysis.
5. **Civil Liberties: Protection of fundamental individual rights and freedoms by law:** such as the freedom of speech, privacy, due process and equality before the law.
6. **Due Process: The legal principle which states that people have to be treated equitably and candidly by state institutions especially in administrations and legal decision enactments.:**
7. **Black Box Algorithms: AI systems where the inner workings or decision making process is unintelligible or opaque to users and even programmers:** making it very hard to challenge or scrutinize.
8. **Algorithmic Accountability: The task of the developers:** deployers, and regulators to make sure that the introduced AI systems are transparent, explainable, and will present no harmful or discriminatory results.

9. **Data Bias: Errors or bias in training sets:** whether as the result of systematic under-representation of groups of the population in existing training sets, or in reproduction of pre-existing social inequalities, can skew or unfair AI prediction and classification.

10. **Participatory Design: The stakeholder approach towards technology development is coined in such a way that the stakeholders themselves:** specifically those who are affected by the technology, be involved in the design process of technologies so that relevance, fairness, and ethical integrity can be achieved.

11. **FRT (Facial Recognition Technology): Facial recognition or identification systems that recognize or confirm identities according to features of the face:** which are employed in law enforcement and surveillance and criticized as being subject to gaps in accuracy and privacy concerns.

12. **Digital Due Process: The manner in which the principles of traditional due process that should be applied:** e.g. the right to notice, explanation and, appeal, are extended in an automated and AI-driven decision making.

13. **AI Ethics Thru Civil Rights: An AI development and governance framework that establishes the rights of AI users and communities and works to protect legal interests:** social justice, and dignity.

14. **Algorithmic Impact Assessment (AIA): A policy and governance framework employed to assess possible risks and harm an AI system entails before it is released especially as regards to human rights and civil liberties.:**

15. **Data Colonialism: An indictment of the current global data practices:** which see the world values exploited and quantified by influential actors, quite often in the global South, at the expense of the vulnerable population, in terms of benefits and protection of intervener.

Chapter 12
Law and Civil Rights in an Age of Artificial Intelligence

Angelo Kevin Brown
https://orcid.org/0000-0001-8167-5090
Arkansas State University, USA

ABSTRACT

As artificial intelligence (AI) has become an important part of modern society, it has created challenges for civil rights law. These challenges have created a variety of concerns regarding civil liberties, privacy, due process, and inequalities. AI has been integrated into various government agencies and private sectors to enhance safety, security, and efficiency. AI is quickly altering society, bringing unexpected advancements across various fields. The widespread nature of AI, from its application in government services to its deployment in private industries, requires a complete assessment of its effect on individual rights and liberties.

INTRODUCTION

As AI has created algorithms for law enforcement and courts, this has had a serious impact on marginalized people in the United States and abroad. It is essential to understand the current and potential issues that we must address in relation to AI and the law, particularly in terms of civil and human rights, as well as other ethical and legal challenges (Bakiner, 2023). The lack of oversight of AI has raised serious concerns about ethical and fairness issues. This leaves room for reform and guidance created by evidence-based practices and an interdisciplinary framework. This chapter will cover various implications of AI on civil rights, ethical dilem-

DOI: 10.4018/979-8-3693-3920-6.ch012

mas, privacy concerns, and its influence on the criminal justice system, including examining issues like facial recognition (Benedict, 2022), recidivism risk assessments (Beaudouin et al., 2023), predictive policing (Villasenor & Foggo, 2020), and a variety of other issues related to AI. It will also discuss emerging issues of "AI rights" and suggest comprehensive policy recommendations to maintain civil liberties in a progressively AI-driven society.

ETHICAL CONTEXT OF AI

The various ethical consequences of AI are at the forefront of many discussions surrounding its impact on our society (Ahmad et al., 2025). The capacity of AI to learn and make choices based on immense datasets can be very powerful, but it also conveys the danger of spreading and increasing current societal prejudices and biases. This section elaborates on the issue of algorithmic bias, the "black box" problem, and the serious need for inclusive data to limit the bias that these systems cause.

The "black box" problem is the issue of many current advanced AI programs, especially those that use deep learning models (ŞAHiN et al., 2025). These programs make it very difficult to fully understand the accurate program reasoning behind a certain decision or the outcome that an AI system makes. This creates a serious lack of transparency that can pose a serious barrier to protecting civil rights. This is particularly important when AI is used in decision-making processes within the legal and criminal justice systems, as it can have a profound impact on individuals' lives that can last for the rest of their lives, such as a felony conviction or a range of other outcomes.

AI systems learn from the data they are given. If the data the system is fed includes systemic biases present in society and in historical records, the AI will adopt and likely reproduce those biases in its output. This is known as the "garbage in, garbage out" phenomenon, which has led to noticeable discriminatory results.

AI has created real-world issues on fairness due to creating discriminatory outcomes in hiring, health, loan approvals, criminal justice, and more. The use of AI has also created equitable access issues, as the digital divide is even greater now (Kitsara, 2022). There is a serious need to have inclusive data to drive AI systems in order to limit the increase of current societal inequalities that exist. When AI is allowed to operate unchecked or insufficient oversight is provided, it continues to create issues due to algorithmic bias that is difficult to understand, largely because of the black box problem (ŞAHiN et al., 2025).

The "digital divide" further aggravates inequality issues (Kitsara, 2022), creating access challenges, similar to when computers and smartphones first became important parts of our daily life. As more essential services and opportunities become reliant on AI-powered digital platforms, communities lacking reliable internet access, digital literacy, or access to necessary hardware can be left further behind. This expands existing disparities, producing a two-tiered society where access to rights and opportunities is impacted by technological access.

An example in hiring practices is that AI-powered resume screening tools, when trained on historical hiring data, often favor certain demographics by filtering out qualified candidates from underrepresented groups (Albaroudi et al., 2024). This greatly limits opportunities for people and perpetuates the lack of diversity in segments of professional occupations. This issue also creates problems in healthcare; AI diagnostic tools trained on data often favor one demographic group and have been shown to perform less accurately for various minority groups (Ibrahim & Pronovost, 2021). This has led to misdiagnoses and inaccurate treatment plans for marginalized groups. The final example includes the issue of loan approvals, where AI systems, using historical lending patterns, have disproportionately denied loans to people from marginalized racial and socioeconomic backgrounds, worsening economic inequalities (de Castro Vieira et al., 2025).

The "black box" issue that we face with AI systems can greatly hinder the ability for transparency and can lead to a lack of accountability when discriminatory and problematic outcomes occur (Bakiner, 2023), especially with regard to civil rights issues. Since AI governance systems have been based on fragmented data sources (Cihon et al., 2020), the data used may come from foreign and international data that do not come from systems or societies that have the same philosophy and values as the nation that is utilizing the system. These black box issues make it difficult to understand and trust the outcomes of the system (Von Eschenbach, 2021).

When an AI program produces a biased outcome, there are a variety of issues to investigate, including discriminatory input data, a flawed algorithm, a hacker, an unknown interaction between variables, or countless other issues. Without the understanding of where the error is, accountability can become undefinable. If a person, for example, is detained or arrested based on an AI-induced calculation, they should, and especially their legal counsel should, have a right to understand and recognize the source of that decision to evaluate if it was made legally or not. The "black box" can deny the ability that a democracy should provide when it takes a person's liberty and freedoms away; this black box issue can make it difficult to challenge wrongful and biased decisions legally. This issue can also lead to public distrust and limited oversight (Katyal, 2022).

If there is no way to properly evaluate how government agencies and their private contractors are using AI to make decisions on people's lives and futures, faith in those agencies can greatly wear down. The "black box" problem is also exacerbated by the fact that AI governance programs often rely on fragmented database sources (Schmitt, 2022). These data sources can include foreign data that is intentionally manipulated by adversaries or those with differing ethical agendas. This is likely to create an issue of values and an absence of understandable logic in how AI systems function, creating even more issues with transparency and holding people accountable for bad outcomes (Bakiner, 2023).

To limit the "black box" problem, there needs to be transparency and explainability for the algorithmic codes and abilities (ŞAHiN et al., 2025). This explainable AI is considered XAI, which is created to develop AI programs that can support people to understand the rationale of AI-based decisions (ŞAHiN et al., 2025). This can include creating natural language explanations that a person can read, providing information on the relevant data inputs used, and creating a visual output of the decision-making process. Even with XAI, there is a limit to full transparency in advanced AI programs, but there can be improvements made to ensure effective oversight, reducing and understanding erroneous decisions, and improving the upholding of citizens' due process rights. By mandating audits of AI programs by an independent third party and allowing for public oversight, this can help provide understanding and transparency on the internal mechanisms of the algorithmic process and can help identify potential problematic discriminatory outcomes.

Having proactive governance can help with the pacing issue that AI systems are known for having (Marchant, 2011). The quick stride of AI system development created a serious pacing problem. This is when technology advances so fast that it outpaces the ability of legal and policy frameworks to keep up with the development. This can create a space where unpredictable problems occur without suitable protective procedures.

There is great concern surrounding the use of AI in deadly force situations, particularly in law enforcement, security, and military contexts. The creation of autonomous weapon systems that are responsible for making life-or-death decisions without direct human oversight raises serious moral and legal questions. It is important to consider how accountability to international and humanitarian law applies when AI is violating these laws. As the uncharted territory of AI governance is greatly fragmented (Li, 2025), with different government agencies and corporations monitoring large databases and programs, it is natural that conflicts of interest issues may become increasingly problematic and make it difficult to establish effective and enforceable guidelines that prevent unnecessary harm.

There is a gap in regulatory guidelines to control the potential harms of these systems, and there is a serious need for anticipatory governance frameworks that can adapt to issues that AI will develop. It is important that we don't just react to problems after they appear, but policymakers must attempt to participate in discussions and create solutions about the potential negative societal impacts of emerging AI technologies that will likely come about in the near future. To do this in an effective manner, it is important that there is collaboration between a variety of different legal experts, technologists, ethicists, and a variety of other experts and organizations to create adaptive and flexible approaches that can advance along with AI capabilities (Marchant, 2011). With our global world, which is becoming more interconnected each year, there is also a need for international cooperation, as the nature of AI development has become a global phenomenon; it can be beneficial to establish shared norms that protect civil rights across borders, as legislation has been done throughout the European Union (EU) for example (Schmidt et al., 2024).

The use of AI to use deadly force by the government in war and other aspects has been an issue of much debate as well (Pacholska, 2024). AI is considered an important aspect for the future of international peace and development, with the use of AI governance to improve trust and cooperation (Shackelford et al., 2021). It has been difficult to keep up with policies and regulations to properly govern the disjointed landscape shaped by AI (Neuwirth, 2024), which has created various conflicts of interest between different governments and corporations that control AI databases and programs. This issue has been considered a "pacing problem" that regulatory protections cannot keep up with AI capabilities, which creates new problems (Marchant, 2011).

AI is shaping our daily lives from impacting humans before birth with AI in healthcare, to AI in school that has been utilized to help educate and protect our children through preschool to graduate school, and even impacting people after their life with AI being able to continue their legacy (Hollanek et al., 2024). Governments and corporations are greatly influenced by the capability of the systems to enhance productivity, profit, and limit an individual person to be blamed for mistakes.

PRIVACY:

One of the primary concerns related to AI and civil rights is privacy, as AI often relies on the mass collection of people's personal information, ranging from behavioral patterns to biometrics. Privacy is a foundation for civil liberties, and AI's use of massive datasets can threaten this fundamental civil liberty. Machine learning is most effective when massive datasets are utilized, which can be accomplished by the government and/or private companies. The lack of informed consent for this collection has led to lawsuits and criticism against various corporations. The lack of laws to limit corporate power is problematic, especially when foreign companies are involved, which has garnered significant media attention, as seen with companies like TikTok operating in the US (Waters, 2021). The use of facial recognition systems has been used effectively for years in various advanced nations such as the United Arab Emirates, in cities like Abu Dhabi, known to be one of the safest cities on Earth, and Dubai, which uses hundreds of thousands of cameras through the Oyoon network (Alghafri & Tubaishat, 2025).

Machine learning algorithms are based on large datasets. The more data they are given access to, the more accurate their predictions and decisions should become, if the data is accurate. This incentivizes governmental agencies and the private sector to collect massive amounts of data, which occurs even without informed consent from the individuals whose data is being collected (Punia et al., 2023). The data that is gathered can range from behavioral patterns, typically including online browsing habits, purchasing history, geographical data, and various biometric information, such as facial and voice scans.

The massive amount of information that is collected raises various issues about digital surveillance and the impact it is having on individual privacy rights. When governments and private businesses collect detailed profiles of people without their knowledge and consent, there is a fear that this data will be misused or hacked. This can be utilized to hijack elections and influence people's decisions in a variety of ways (Yu, 2024).

The deficiency of adequate and updated legal frameworks to ensure the data collection of AI systems aligns with civil rights and privacy laws creates a regulatory problem. This problem is made worse by the presence of numerous foreign corporations operating within other countries. We have seen this issue in the US when TikTok was being investigated for its relationship with government agencies (Aitken, 2023).

THE ISSUE OF INFORMED CONSENT:

The concept of "informed consent" in the digital age is increasingly intricate to understand and verify that it has been made (Punia et al., 2023). Online internet users often click "agree" to terms and conditions that are very lengthy and filled with legal language that can be difficult for an everyday person to understand. This leads to users not fully understanding how they have agreed to have their data collected and used by AI programs. This issue leads to giving your consent to corporations but not actually reading or understanding much of what you consented to, and the standard of data practices and consent online leads to true informed consent being absent.

People are also not always aware that their biometric data is being collected in various ways, including online and by facial recognition systems in public areas. They are also often unaware that their online behavior is being utilized to teach AI programs to be involved in targeted advertising and predictive analytics.

The legal consequences of this lack of true informed consent are deep and not yet fully known. The various public criticisms and civil lawsuits against corporations demonstrate the growing public awareness and desire for greater control over their personal data, as well as limitations on corporations and governments in their use of these tactics. Future regulations should prioritize meaningful consent rights that are easy to understand and provide people with genuine choices about how AI programs use their information. This should include various factors such as various consent options, clear data transparency information, and the ability to opt out of data collection processes easily.

AI systems have been impacting people in modern societies in their daily lives, sometimes without their knowledge. This starts with healthcare decisions even before a person is born, to education systems that use AI tools to help guide children through their primary education and beyond (Williamson, 2024). AI systems do not even stop once a person dies, but they also extend one's memory and legacy beyond death. AI's influence is predicted to become ingrained even more in our lives in the near future, and it is likely to become necessary to compete in various sectors. Governments, corporations, and even non-profits are becoming deeply invested in the power of AI due to its ability to improve productivity, which leads to increased profits, and reduce individual accountability for errors. This issue is problematic for protecting the civil rights of people, as we will be relying on the accuracy of AI systems. A major concern is the lack of human responsibility when AI programs produce harmful outcomes either by accident or through the programming process intentionally.

A recent impact that AI has had on healthcare is that AI-based diagnostic tools are helping medical specialists in recognizing diseases (Kalra et al., 2024). The worry is if these tools are biased or flawed in a way that is unknown to the users, they could lead to misdiagnoses and lead to people receiving inappropriate treatments. When this happens with the "black box," it creates a difficult situation to determine the fault of the mistake.

With education, AI-based learning programs have helped personalize educational material to help the student learn more effectively, but create issues of data privacy and the ability for AI to track the performance of students, leading to unfair treatment or limited opportunities for certain segments of the population. Not all students can afford the most updated AI systems to assist them in their work, which creates a divide between those who have access and those who do not (Kitsara, 2022). The ability for AI to teach children and adults poses a great threat to the careers of teachers, professors, and others in the educational field. It is important to consider the limits of these systems when it comes to educating students, as there have been countless cases of AI systems creating wrong historical events, such as recently, the Auschwitz Museum had criticized AI-manipulated photos of Holocaust victims (Jerusalem Post Staff, 2025).

The use of AI to limit a person from being blamed for bias is problematic in the context of civil rights. When an AI system causes unintended harm, it is important to create clear lines of responsibility and understanding to limit this from happening again. This can be done by defining the responsibilities and role of the AI developers who created and monitor the algorithmic processes. Without a deep understanding of the processes, the victims of the harm created by AI can find it very challenging to find who is responsible and hold accountable, especially legally (Bakiner, 2023).

CRIMINAL JUSTICE:

The criminal justice system provides some of the most serious examples of AI-created bias that impact civil rights. This has led the Department of Justice (DOJ) to create the Interagency Convening on AI and Civil Rights on October 9, 2024, in order to provide guidance for federal agencies to ensure civil rights are protected while using AI. The DOJ has been involved in the issue of AI and its impact on civil rights for years in an attempt to reduce the negative impact it may have on people with disabilities (Shelby et al., 2022).

The use of recidivism risk assessments like Correctional Offender Management Profiling for Alternative Sanctions (COMPAS) has disproportionately flagged Black defendants as higher risk, even with comparable criminal histories to White defendants, exemplifying how biased AI data inputs can lead to biased outcomes that significantly affect people's freedom and futures (Beaudouin et al., 2023). This bias is not a simple statistical irregularity but a replication of prevailing systemic biases within the criminal justice system, which AI, without appropriate protections, simply automates this issue. As data used by the criminal justice system is often biased, it has been shown that when AI is fed the data, it replicates the biases that have been occurring. COMPAS is used to assess the risk of defendants in various states, including California, New York, Wisconsin, and others.

There was an investigation into COMPAS and it showed that of the people who they predicted to commit a violent crime, only 20 percent of them actually did, and they found that "Blacks are almost twice as likely as Whites to be labeled a higher risk but not actually reoffend" and for white people "They are much more likely than Blacks to be labeled lower risk but go on to commit other crime." Issues with COMPAS were brought to the Wisconsin Supreme Court in Loomis v. Wisconsin and were appealed to the United States Supreme Court (Beaudouin et al., 2023), because of the sentencing of Eric Loomis ' who was sentenced using the software that it potentially violated his due process rights (Villasenor & Foggo, 2020). The Supreme Court denied the writ of certiorari after the Wisconsin Supreme Court concluded that there was no violation of due process from COMPAS (Beaudouin et al., 2023). These issues have been described as algorithmic bias that creates unfair outcomes for some and gives privileged outcomes to others due to "garbage in, garbage out" issues, among others.

The criminal justice system and private companies have used facial recognition to help with security and investigations into crimes (Benedict, 2022). The use of these systems that are powered with AI tech has created various inequalities, including reduced accuracy for people of color, especially Black men, which has led to wrongful arrests (Benedict, 2022). The police have used a variety of different tools using AI that have problematic outcomes, such as report writing (Adams et al., 2024), and to predict crime to help form police patrols, which can become an issue with due process and discriminatory policing from problematic data (Blount, 2024).

FACIAL RECOGNITION: THE BENEFITS AND ISSUES OF SURVEILLANCE TECHNOLOGIES:

Facial recognition technology used in modern society can now be powered by AI. This tool helps show a serious fear of AI's impact on civil rights (Benedict, 2022). Facial recognition powered by AI has various potential benefits for safety, security, and efficiency, but its extensive deployment with little understanding of how it works by the public creates significant privacy and civil liberties concerns throughout various countries.

While in the UAE, cities like Abu Dhabi and Dubai have been able to use extensive networks of cameras and AI facial recognition systems for public safety (Al Zaabi & Zamri, 2021), contributing to their reputation as some of the safest cities in the world. It is important to understand that the application of such a surveillance system in democratic societies will likely raise serious concerns about the potential for this to be used as a mass surveillance system to control the masses by the political elite. Mass surveillance systems are known to lead to an erosion of anonymity for citizens, especially concerning to activists and whistleblowers. This gives the government a new ability to track individuals' movements, associations, and activities in real-time, even against those who are not suspected of any criminal wrongdoing. This could reduce the use of free speech, assembly, and association, creating a society where people will increase their self-censorship out of fear of being monitored by the government or others who have access to the technology.

Another important issue of facial recognition is the lack of accuracy that leads to disparities in facial recognition systems (Benedict, 2022). These disparities have been particularly problematic for people of color, especially Black men, which can lead to a violation of a person's civil rights if they are mistaken for another person. This can lead to wrongful arrests based on misidentifications by AI algorithms (Moy,

2021), which is a serious violation of due process that we are assumed to have. This can lead to devastating consequences for people, especially those from marginalized groups who may have a lack of access to legal resources to defend their rights.

The inaccuracies of AI programmed systems help with showing the need for improved testing, independent audits (Manheim et al., 2025), and a renewed policy on the implementation of invasive AI programs, including facial recognition in legal contexts, until its accuracy can be improved. There should be legal frameworks that help to govern the use of facial recognition by the government and private agencies. These policy changes should include limitations on its deployment to ensure that people still have privacy in their lives, requirements for judicial oversight, and transparency about its impact and use.

AI'S EFFECT ON DUE PROCESS AND EQUALITY:

The implementation of AI programs into the criminal justice system has been used to help promote increased efficiency (Adams et al., 2024) and is supported by various politicians and corporations that will profit from selling their programs. But there has also emerged a significant threat to the due process rights of citizens and has been shown to perpetuate inequalities of marginalized groups (Villasenor & Foggo, 2020).

The data that goes into AI systems can reflect the historical prejudiced beliefs within the justice system and the greater society as a whole. This can include biased policing practices that lead to inaccurate data outcomes, disparate sentencing outcomes that give longer sentences for the same crimes to certain minority groups, and other prevalent prejudices that have led to disproportionate arrests and convictions of marginalized communities. When AI is based on this type of data without any intervention, it unavoidably will learn and replicate similar biased outcomes, which can lead to a continuation of systemic discrimination (Bakiner, 2023).

The example of the Correctional Offender Management Profiling for Alternative Sanctions (COMPAS) software serves as a modern illustration of the problems discussed. As critics and scholars detailed, COMPAS disproportionately has flagged Hispanic and Black defendants as being at a statistically significantly higher risk of reoffending when compared to White defendants with similar criminal histories (Hamilton, 2019). This bias was produced by the AI algorithm, which led to a finding in 2016 that "Blacks are almost twice as likely as Whites to be labeled a higher risk but not actually re-offend," which seriously weakens the legal precedent of equal protection under the law.

The legal challenge discussed in Loomis v. Wisconsin, which was ultimately unsuccessful in the Supreme Court jurisdiction in challenging the writ of certiorari, helped bring the serious concerns about due process to the national conversation when AI-programmed risk assessments were being used legally in sentencing decisions. The failure to fully comprehend and articulate the "black box" calculations of COMPAS meant that a person could not sufficiently challenge the basis of a decision that significantly impacted their freedom and liberty (Rudin, 2019).

Since there is inherent bias in criminal justice data (Parker, 2016), automating data collection and processes with AI without addressing the fundamental systemic issues that exist will likely only exacerbate existing inequalities (Malek, 2022), as we have already witnessed. Reform efforts should focus on debiasing historical data by a multidisciplinary team of experts and developing AI programs that are able to mitigate instead of preserve existing disparities. One solution put forward for this involves using fairness-aware machine learning systems or including human oversight to flag and correct biased outputs.

AI-BASED PREDICTIVE POLICING:

Predictive policing has been used by utilizing AI programs to predict where, when, how, and by whom crimes are likely to occur. This has been used to optimize police patrol routes and to help maximize resource allocation for public safety and reduce crime. This, in theory, is a logical use of AI-based data analytics, but the outcome of this practice has significant errors and the ability to exacerbate unfairness by discriminatory law enforcement practices (Alikhademi et al., 2022).

Since predictive policing algorithms are based on historical crime data, they also reflect patterns of over-policing in especially marginalized neighborhoods. This leads to the AI predictably directing significantly more police resources to those areas, while doing the opposite in wealthy neighborhoods. This generates a feedback loop (Bennett Moses & Chan, 2018) due to issues like the increased police presence, leading to more arrests of minor offenses in those areas. The increased arrests go back into the algorithm, reinforcing the self-fulfilling prediction that those areas are "high crime," regardless of the reality of the actual crime rate, especially crimes that fall under the dark figure of crime, which are the crimes that go unreported and unknown by police. This will likely lead to discriminatory police practices for marginalized communities who are disproportionately stopped, searched, watched, and arrested, even if they are not participating in more criminal activity than people in other areas.

It is also important to understand the implications for due process of predictive policing practices. When people are targeted for increased policing based on an AI-based prediction, instead of on individualized and legal standards of suspicion, it can create issues with the principles of probable cause and reasonable suspicion

(Weiss, 2025). The "black box" nature of these predictive AI programs also makes it challenging for people to understand why they might be targeted for increased policing. This issue can lead to even more distrust and resentment in the communities that have the most need for improved police-community relations.

To address the issue of predictive policing harms in marginalized communities, there needs to be improved transparency in how predictive policing policies and programs are developed and used (Alikhademi et al., 2022). This transparency should include public access to independent audits of their performance and impact, as well as strict protections to guarantee that these AI systems are not used to excuse discriminatory practices or to limit constitutional protections.

As AI systems can often be black boxes, it can create a lack of due process rights, as people are owed certain knowledge and informed of decisions that significantly impact their rights so they can defend against errors. The lack of transparency, often referred to as algorithmic transparency, can limit our understanding of how accurately AI is used in the justice system and what is happening within these systems.

AI systems have been used to help moderate online speech, which raises concerns about freedom of speech (Wu, 2022). The system often tries to combat issues like hate speech and misinformation (Cortiz & Zubiaga, 2020), but has also been involved in suppressing lawful expression, especially when it comes to politically controversial issues (Elkin-Koren & Perel, 2020).

The "black box" problem is particularly significant to civil rights in the court system, where decisions made or supported by AI systems can directly affect a person's liberty, reputation, and future. The lack of AI transparency and policies directly threatens due process rights (Palmiotto, 2020), especially for those who cannot afford their own legal defense.

Due process rights require that criminal suspects be informed of the evidence of wrongdoing that is alleged against them, including being given an understanding of the basis of decisions that have taken away their rights, and have a legitimate chance to challenge potential errors. As AI systems have been involved in making critical decisions in the criminal justice system, from setting bail, to assessing risk, to even assisting judges and others in creating sentencing recommendations (Taylor, 2023), and their internal workings are often misunderstood, these due process rights are provided with unknown chances of being diminished for a person. A criminal defendant will not be able to effectively challenge an AI's assessment if there is no way to understand how the AI arrived at its decisions. This lack of knowledge creates a lack of transparency that is unique to this modern era and also makes it very hard to detect and fix the algorithmic errors that contributed to the outcome, leaving people susceptible to unjust outcomes.

To be able to reduce due process violations in a criminal justice system that utilizes AI, there should be a legal framework and expertise for algorithmic understanding, explainability, and audits (Villasenor & Foggo, 2020). When AI is used in important decisions, there should be a clear and understandable explanation for its decisions provided to suspects and their legal teams. This can be helped when there are independent third-party audits of AI systems used in the justice system to help ensure that the values of fairness, accuracy, and adherence to civil rights principles are upheld. This should incorporate inspecting the datasets, algorithm design, and the actual impact of the system, especially focusing on marginalized people, to ensure that the discriminatory practices that have existed are reduced. This can also be supported by community oversight to support democratic accountability, which is also crucial so that these powerful tools are used properly and justly.

THE FIRST AMENDMENT: MODERATION AND CENSORSHIP ISSUES FOR AI AND SOCIETY

AI's ability and use in moderating online speech has become very common but creates more issues for civil rights, especially due to the freedom of speech, which in the United States is the First Amendment in the Constitution (Wu, 2022). Social media platforms like Facebook and other online services increasingly rely on AI to detect and remove content considered to be “hate speech,” “misinformation,” “malinformation,” “incitement of violence,” among other issues. For many, the intent is often to create a safer online environment and reduce hate online, which can translate to real-life consequences, but the implementation of these AI moderation systems has raised serious concerns about their effectiveness and impact.

AI models usually have a difficult time dealing with the nuances of different languages. It is hard for AI systems to understand the meaning, context, and intent of a post, especially when sarcasm or memes are used. This may create a situation of over-suppression of expressions that are completely legal but are politically controversial. It is also an issue that people learn ways to bypass the AI systems so that their illegal content is not caught. AI systems are lacking human judgment, which can inadvertently lead to becoming a tool for censorship that is empowering a certain group or idea. This is especially problematic due to the “black box” nature of these moderation AI systems, which leads the users to often not understand why their content was removed or why their accounts were penalized. This creates a lack of perceived fairness and a lack of transparency and due process for people whose content is moderated by AI systems, which can impact legitimate discourse on important topics. This can and has disproportionately impacted marginalized voices who may already face barriers in having their perspectives understood, which these AI systems can be programmed to do inherently.

Protecting freedom of speech in the current age of AI moderation necessitates a lot of purposeful action by policymakers, practices, and education. This includes creating greater transparency from these platforms about their content moderation policies and the algorithms used to enforce them. An accessible appeals process for users whose content has been removed, with the inclusion of some human review. The investment in AI research is to develop more context-aware moderation systems that can better differentiate between illegal content and protected speech.

These changes will need to be done through a reformed Legal framework. There is a need for clarification of the responsibilities of these platforms and to protect the users' free speech rights against arbitrary censorship by AI systems. As these platforms cross national boundaries, there is a need for cross-national collaboration to understand differences among policies of different populations as well (Wu, 2022).

AI RIGHTS

The concept of "AI rights" has been proposed by scholars and governments. This has created an important philosophical discussion about who or what should be given civil liberties. This issue is especially important in a world increasingly inhabited by intelligent artificial machines that are seemingly becoming more aware of themselves and the world and more powerful (Namestiuk, 2023).

There has been speculation on civil rights moving to AI as they have for corporations and animals (Zenor, 2018). This happened in Saudi Arabia as Sophia, a robot, had gained citizenship by the government (Parviainen & Coeckelbergh, 2021). With citizenship comes certain unalienable rights, and citizens in democracies are able to vote. The debate of whether AI or robots could and should have the rights of citizens, like the freedom of speech (Parviainen & Coeckelbergh, 2021).

The granting of citizenship to Sophia, a robot, provides an example, and the fact that these discussions are no longer just a theoretical thought. The granting of citizenship to AI and civil rights creates interesting dilemmas of what citizenship is and who should or should not have it. Traditionally, civil rights are only given to people, not robots or AI. AI systems that achieve a level of consciousness, self-awareness, or sentience similar to humans will likely create a situation in which this will become even more of a serious concern.

There is a growing concern that AI systems may start to exhibit emotions and experience suffering. It is hard to know if an AI system is really feeling something and is self-aware, or if they are just mimicking human behavior. The idea of AI-based life to be given the right to vote, is very problematic due to the ability for AI systems to be manipulated (Bakiner, 2023), which would likely lead to the obfuscation of the democratic processes as we know them. The ability for AI to be programmed to vote for a certain candidate and for that robot to be mass-produced for a political party would seriously destabilize the concept of an independent electorate.

Rights often come with great responsibilities, such as in America, the 2nd Amendment, the right to bear arms is often granted to most adults in the country. Would this be a right that an AI system would want, and would it be appropriate for them? Do AI-based life care about the privacy of themselves and others? Can you hold AI-based life accountable for its actions? These are questions that will be important to our future when AI robots accidentally or purposely harm a person; there needs to be an understanding of if the robot has legal defenses like self-defense, insanity, etc.

While the current focus should remain on human civil rights that are being impacted by AI, this issue is the long-term legal and moral path of AI development and life in our society. This showcases a need for ongoing understanding and education about the meaning of intelligence, consciousness, and the boundaries of legal citizenship rights. These systems were intended to improve human society, so the priority must continue to ensure that AI aids humanity and respects our civil rights. Without continuing to understand the purpose of AI systems and ensure the goals stay as intended rather than creating the consequence of the creation of having artificial citizens whose rights could lead to threatening the rights of biological humans, as AI systems will be able to have higher processing power and abilities to reproduce that humans cannot even fathom.

There are various policy recommendations to consider in the current era of AI and the legal systems, which have been supported by a variety of experts in the field (Greenstein, 2022). There needs to be legislative reform so that the government can update civil rights laws to address the AI bias and AI issues like data protection. It is important to assess the impact AI is having on our system, and having ongoing impact assessments would help us understand what this technology is having on the people in regard to civil rights. As there are various transparency and discrimination issues highlighted, there needs to be audits into AI systems to help detect civil rights abuses and discriminatory bias, and outcomes that may occur. This can be helped with using third-party audits and public oversight to ensure that democratic oversight holds the corporations and governments that use these systems accountable. There should also be an attempt to help educate citizens and politicians on the harms and best practices of these devices so that people and decision makers are well informed on the risks of these systems.

SOLUTIONS TO ISSUES:

Addressing AI-related bias requires a move to inclusive data collection and auditing of data to ensure it is accurate. AI system engineers need to seek out diverse datasets that accurately represent the full range of population demographics, including socio-economic backgrounds, geographical locations, and the diverse experiences of people. Auditing needs to be an ongoing process to reduce AI biases and errors, before discriminatory outcomes do serious harm to society. This should include auditors with interdisciplinary backgrounds and experts in data scientists, criminologists, sociologists, and legal scholars, among others, to ensure that AI programs are created and monitored in a way that delivers fair and equitable outcomes.

To navigate the serious challenges created by AI to civil rights that have been discussed and challenges that are unknown and may develop, a wide-ranging and proactive approach to policy reform is critical. As AI systems continue to change and surprise even the experts, the policies created need to be adaptable to unforeseen changes that can happen to protect society from the potential risk of AI (Marchant, 2011). Building upon the current knowledge, there is a need for various initiatives to be created from lawmakers, the education system, private businesses, and more.

LEGISLATIVE REFORM:

There is a need to keep civil rights laws updated for the AI era. Civil rights laws were generally enacted at a time before most people even considered AI technology. As AI was unknown to those who created civil rights legislation, it led to the laws being ill-equipped to adequately face the unique challenges of AI-created bias, data privacy issues, and AI decision-making.

With civil rights, it is important to consider Anti-Discrimination Laws for AI systems. Existing anti-discrimination laws should be updated to ensure that they cover algorithmic discrimination and help create frameworks to ensure accountability and transparency. This means there needs to be a way to help hold developers, and especially the agencies and corporations that fund and control AI systems, accountable for biased outcomes. This is especially important when there is ill intent, but should also be even when there was no probable bad intent. Legislation can be improved by creating a clear legal test for AI-created discrimination and providing a way for reparation for people who are harmed by biased outcomes of AI programs.

The creation of comprehensive data protection and privacy laws that consider current and future AI systems. Countries throughout the world, including the US, lack a comprehensive federal data privacy law that is inclusive of AI systems. There are many European nations in the EU that have a better legal framework that considers modern technological advances. The regulatory void that exists in many countries leaves people very vulnerable to mass data collection and misuse by AI systems and the corporations and governments that can benefit from the data. Revised legislation needs to be established to create a national framework for the data privacy of citizens to protect their civil rights.

The revised legislation should consider a variety of factors, including strict limitations on data collection by mandating data minimization principles; this allows data collection to the amount necessary for specific, legitimate, and articulated purposes. Next, there should be a more vigorous informed consent requirement that does not lead to people signing forms that they do not read or understand. New policies should help make it easier for people to understand and control how their data is collected and utilized.

There is also a need to regulate data portability. People should be given deletion rights for data that has been collected, and or automatic deletion after a certain period of time, as people may no longer be alive or capable of petitioning to delete the data. Giving people the right to access, transfer, and delete their personal data held by AI databases, corporations, or governments can help protect people's rights.

There is a need for independent regulatory oversight committees for AI systems and databases. Creating a dedicated agency to enforce data privacy laws can ensure that the policies and laws are being upheld. This should be done by conducting AI audits of governments and corporations, with limits on how politicians and corporations can influence the efficacy of these agencies by ensuring there is no conflict of interest with those who are involved in these regulatory institutions.

Legislation that has a direct focusing on AI accountability should be created and mandate that AI programs which are used in the various public sector applications such as criminal justice, social services, employment, are given in-depth impact assessments and consistent audits to evaluate objective standards fairness, accuracy, and transparency to limit unwarranted outcomes and to catch errors the system is making.

Independent third-party audits are an important component to ensure impartiality and should be done with technical expertise. These audits should evaluate a variety of factors, including the fairness, accuracy, and transparency of AI algorithms, identify algorithmic bias, and assess compliance with civil rights laws. The results of these audits should be made public to support governmental transparency and allow for public input and criticism.

The impact assessments for AI systems, especially those used by government agencies, should be mandated. Due to the progress of AI systems happening very quickly, these assessments need to be ongoing so that they can monitor the real-world effects of AI on civilian rights over time. This should include collecting data on disparate outcomes, identifying potential AI biases, and adapting laws and policies as needed.

The AI laws should have rules to promote public disclosure of AI systems in use. There will likely be limits for AI systems used for national security reasons;

aside from that, governments and public entities should be transparent about the AI tools they utilize. There should be detailed documentation of AI development and use that is able to be looked at by experts in the field. This can help provide A standardized record of how AI systems were designed, trained, and implemented.

To reduce the potential civil rights harms, there should be risk assessment reports written regularly as AI systems evolve. This can create a proactive mechanism for identifying and mitigating any potential problematic and or discriminatory outcomes. This can be within the Oversight and Auditing Mechanisms that should exist for AI, as Legislative reforms unaccompanied by oversight and auditing mechanisms to ensure compliance and accountability will likely be ineffective.

There should be support for public organizations, academic researchers, and affected communities to participate in the oversight of AI systems. Public oversight and democratic accountability are essential to a healthy democracy and can help empower the citizens. This would likely involve creating public advisory committees, creating accessible mechanisms for citizen complaints about AI-driven harms, and ensuring that government agencies are actually responding to the concerns of the public. Effective democratic oversight is critical to hold corporations and governments accountable for the ethical, legal, and fair use of AI systems.

EDUCATION AND PUBLIC AWARENESS:

Campaigns can help create a well-informed citizenry and political leadership. These are critical components for navigating the unknown future of AI and protecting civil rights. Educating Citizens on AI's Harms is a way to help mitigate harm that can happen to the public. Public education campaigns can be utilized to raise awareness about the probable risks and the ways to maximize the benefits of AI. These campaigns should include issues concerning privacy, algorithmic bias, and due process issues. This should involve creating accessible resources in a variety of languages, community workshops in person and online, and media campaigns to get the word out to people so that they can understand their rights in a society that is being impacted by AI, and they will be prepared to protect themselves.

There is also a need to help train politicians and other government actors who are responsible for reforms, laws, and policies. Policymakers, judges, law enforcement officials, and other decision-makers in the government should have specialized training on AI systems and their capabilities, limitations, and potential impact on citizen rights. The training should be based on an interdisciplinary approach, involving experts in a variety of different fields from computer science, criminology, health, law, ethics, and social sciences, among others, to ensure that decisions are made with an inclusive understanding of the technology.

The Promotion of Interdisciplinary Research on AI. There should be support for various government-supported organizations to invest in interdisciplinary research that studies the intersection of AI, law, ethics, health, civil rights, and more. This research should be able to help provide the evidence-based practices needed to create informed policy development and address the fears and concerns that AI has created, such as algorithmic bias, manipulation, and other AI-related harms.

CONCLUSION:

So far, in the early stages of artificial intelligence, it has already posed various challenges for civil rights. As AI has many ways to improve efficiency, security, and promote equality, the fear is that if it is unchecked, it will create a crisis for human and civil rights (Bakiner, 2023). It has already created a troubling record of perpetuating existing social and economic inequalities, from the deceptive nature of algorithmic bias in hiring and loan approvals (de Castro Vieira et al., 2025), to the predictive policing and other discriminatory issues in criminal justice systems due to fallible tools like facial recognition and recidivism risk assessments. It is clear that AI threatens to harm the fundamental principles of fairness and privacy (Bakiner, 2023) and due process, if we do not critically examine and improve the process. The notorious "black box" problem, along with an inadequate regulatory framework, creates a serious accountability breach, leaving people and society as a whole vulnerable to potentially discriminatory decisions without legal or effective remedies when things go wrong due to AI.

Being able to protect people's civil rights in this quickly developing technological environment stresses the need for a proactive and complete approach to the future. It requires significant legislative reform to update our existing civil rights laws and introduce updated frameworks that are properly designed to govern current and future AI systems. This framework should include data protection laws that are specifically informed by AI capabilities, creating clear legal accountability for algorithmic errors and discrimination, and mandating transparency and explainability for AI systems that can impact people's rights and well-being. These should be maintained through independent oversight institutions to ensure that the laws and regulations are being enacted as intended, to ensure that they are being implemented and working in a manner consistent with democratic values. Without a well-informed citizenry and political leadership, there is little hope that these protections and reforms will continue to protect our human rights, which creates great importance that this education starts to be included in our educational systems to prepare our future leaders for the unprecedented challenges they will face. The future of civil rights in an AI-based society relies on society's collective understanding and ability to adapt our laws and policies to this advanced technological reality that is occurring in front of our eyes faster than we can truly comprehend. It requires an interdisciplinary understanding of how algorithms work and their societal impact. There needs to be a serious commitment to democratic oversight, and that this technology is used to improve human life for all, not just the powerful, and that the benefits are accessible to all aspects of society. The hope that AI will be able to enhance equality and justice will be realized only if we are able to understand and prepare for its potential harm and work proactively before it's too late to ensure that an informed and moral society guides our technological progress.

AI can help improve civil rights, but it can also significantly harm civil rights. There is great hope that AI, when used appropriately, can help limit civil rights abuses and highlight ways to improve equality in society. However, as highlighted in the chapter, various important issues created by AI have helped perpetuate bias and inequality, making civil rights issues more complex. Relying on AI for governance creates many ethical issues that can harm individual rights and liberty, and unequal treatment of people under the law is a violation of human and civil rights. We must adapt our current legal doctrines to the advanced AI society that we are creating, which is based on an interdisciplinary understanding of algorithms and their impact, to help ensure that civil rights are protected in the future.

REFERENCES

Adams, I. T., Barter, M., McLean, K., Boehme, H. M., & Geary, I. A.Jr. (2024). No man's hand: Artificial intelligence does not improve police report writing speed. *Journal of Experimental Criminology*, •••, 1–18.

Ahmad, N., Ali, A. W., & bin Yussof, M. H. B. (2025). The Challenges Of Human Rights In The Era Of Artificial Intelligence. UUM Journal of Legal Studies, 16(1), 150-169.

Aitken, V. L. R. (2023). Data Privacy Laws & Social Media Governance: A comparative analysis of Tik Tok & Meta/Facebook using EU, US, and China's Data Privacy Laws.

Al Zaabi, S., & Zamri, R. (2021). Review of Scoping Studies on Improving Physical Security Performance and Integrating Facial Recognition Technology. *Indian Journal of Economics and Business*, *20*(4).

Albaroudi, E., Mansouri, T., & Alameer, A. (2024). A comprehensive review of AI techniques for addressing algorithmic bias in job hiring. *AI*, *5*(1), 383–404. DOI: 10.3390/ai5010019

Alghafri, B., & Tubaishat, A. (2025). Balancing Privacy and Security: A Comparative Analysis of AI-Driven Surveillance in the UAE and USA. *Procedia Computer Science*, *257*, 142–149. DOI: 10.1016/j.procs.2025.03.021

Alikhademi, K., Drobina, E., Prioleau, D., Richardson, B., Purves, D., & Gilbert, J. E. (2022). A review of predictive policing from the perspective of fairness. *Artificial Intelligence and Law*, *30*(1), 1–17. DOI: 10.1007/s10506-021-09286-4

Bakiner, O. (2023). The promises and challenges of addressing artificial intelligence with human rights. *Big Data & Society*, *10*(2), 20539517231205476. DOI: 10.1177/20539517231205476

Beaudouin, V., Maxwell, W., & Domingues-Montanari, S. (2023). Predicting risk in criminal justice in the United States: The ProPublica-COMPAS case: Ethics of AI in Action. *Reseaux (London)*, *240*(4), 71–109.

Benedict, T. J. (2022). The computer got it wrong: Facial recognition technology and establishing probable cause to arrest. *Washington and Lee Law Review*, *79*, 849.

Bennett Moses, L., & Chan, J. (2018). Algorithmic prediction in policing: Assumptions, evaluation, and accountability. *Policing and Society*, *28*(7), 806–822. DOI: 10.1080/10439463.2016.1253695

Blount, K. (2024). Using artificial intelligence to prevent crime: Implications for due process and criminal justice. *AI & Society*, *39*(1), 359–368. DOI: 10.1007/s00146-022-01513-z

Cihon, P., Maas, M. M., & Kemp, L. (2020). Fragmentation and the future: Investigating architectures for international AI governance. *Global Policy*, *11*(5), 545–556. DOI: 10.1111/1758-5899.12890

Cortiz, D., & Zubiaga, A. (2020). Ethical and technical challenges of AI in tackling hate speech. *International Journal of Information Ethics*, •••, 29.

de Castro Vieira, J. R., Barboza, F., Cajueiro, D., & Kimura, H. (2025). Towards Fair AI: Mitigating Bias in Credit Decisions—A Systematic Literature Review. *Journal of Risk and Financial Management*, *18*(5), 228. DOI: 10.3390/jrfm18050228

Elkin-Koren, N., & Perel, M. (2020). Separation of functions for AI: Restraining speech regulation by online platforms. *Lewis & Clark Law Review*, *24*, 857.

Greenstein, S. (2022). Preserving the rule of law in the era of artificial intelligence (AI). *Artificial Intelligence and Law*, *30*(3), 291–323. DOI: 10.1007/s10506-021-09294-4

Hamilton, M. (2019). The biased algorithm: Evidence of disparate impact on Hispanics. *The American Criminal Law Review*, *56*, 1553.

Hollanek, T., & Nowaczyk-Basińska, K. (2024). Griefbots, deadbots, postmortem avatars: On responsible applications of generative AI in the digital afterlife industry. *Philosophy & Technology*, *37*(2), 63. DOI: 10.1007/s13347-024-00744-w

Ibrahim, S. A., & Pronovost, P. J. (2021, September). Diagnostic errors, health disparities, and artificial intelligence: A combination for health or harm? [). American Medical Association.]. *JAMA Health Forum*, *2*(9), e212430–e212430. DOI: 10.1001/jamahealthforum.2021.2430 PMID: 36218658

Jerusalem Post Staff. 2025. 'Dangerous distortion,' Auschwitz Museum calls out AI-generated images of Holocaust victims. The Jerusalem Post. https://www.jpost.com/international/article-856178

Kalra, N., Verma, P., & Verma, S. (2024). Advancements in AI based healthcare techniques with FOCUS ON diagnostic techniques. *Computers in Biology and Medicine*, *179*, 108917. DOI: 10.1016/j.compbiomed.2024.108917 PMID: 39059212

Katyal, S. K. (2022). Democracy & Distrust in an Era of Artificial Intelligence. *Daedalus*, *151*(2), 322–334. DOI: 10.1162/daed_a_01919

Kitsara, I. (2022). Artificial intelligence and the digital divide: From an innovation perspective. In *Platforms and artificial intelligence: The next generation of competences* (pp. 245–265). Springer International Publishing. DOI: 10.1007/978-3-030-90192-9_12

Li, J. (2025). Governing High-Risk Technologies in a Fragmented World: Geopolitical Tensions, Regulatory Gaps, and Institutional Barriers to Global Cooperation. *Fudan Journal of the Humanities and Social Sciences*, •••, 1–25. DOI: 10.1007/s40647-025-00445-4

Malek, M. A. (2022). Criminal courts' artificial intelligence: The way it reinforces bias and discrimination. *AI and Ethics*, *2*(1), 233–245. DOI: 10.1007/s43681-022-00137-9

Manheim, D., Martin, S., Bailey, M., Samin, M., & Greutzmacher, R. (2025). The necessity of AI audit standards boards. *AI & Society*, *40*(8), 1–16. DOI: 10.1007/s00146-025-02320-y

Marchant, G. E. (2011). Addressing the pacing problem. *The growing gap between emerging technologies and legal-ethical oversight: the pacing problem*, 199-205.

Moy, L. (2021). Facing injustice: How face recognition technology may increase the incidence of misidentifications and wrongful convictions. *SSRN*, *30*, 337. DOI: 10.2139/ssrn.4101826

Namestiuk, S. (2023). Challenging the Boundary between Self-Awareness and Self-Consciousness in AI from the Perspectives of Philosophy. *Futurity Philosophy*, *2*(4), 43–60. DOI: 10.57125/FP.2023.12.30.03

Neuwirth, R. J. (2024). The global institutional governance of AI: A four-dimensional perspective. *International Journal of Digital Law and Governance*, *1*(1), 113–153. DOI: 10.1515/ijdlg-2024-0004

Pacholska, M. (2024). Many hands in the black box: artificial intelligence and the responsibility of international organizations. In *Reassessing the Articles on the Responsibility of International Organizations* (pp. 171–187). Edward Elgar Publishing. DOI: 10.4337/9781035309115.00017

Palmiotto, F. (2020). The black box on trial: the impact of algorithmic opacity on fair trial rights in criminal proceedings. In *Algorithmic Governance and Governance of Algorithms: Legal and Ethical Challenges* (pp. 49–70). Springer International Publishing.

Parker, G. (2016). Come see the bias inherent in the system. *The Journal of the American Academy of Psychiatry and the Law*, *44*(4), 411–414. PMID: 28003383

Parviainen, J., & Coeckelbergh, M. (2021). The political choreography of the Sophia robot: Beyond robot rights and citizenship to political performances for the social robotics market. *AI & Society*, *36*(3), 715–724. DOI: 10.1007/s00146-020-01104-w

Punia, M., Choudhary, A., Agarwal, S., & Shukla, V. (2023, October). Ethical considerations and legal frameworks for biometric surveillance systems: The intersection of ai, soft biometrics, and human surveillance. In *International Conference on Cryptology & Network Security with Machine Learning* (pp. 659-674). Singapore: Springer Nature Singapore.

Rudin, C. (2019). Stop explaining black box machine learning models for high stakes decisions and use interpretable models instead. *Nature Machine Intelligence*, *1*(5), 206–215. DOI: 10.1038/s42256-019-0048-x PMID: 35603010

ŞAHiN, E., Arslan, N. N., & Özdemir, D.ŞAHiN. (2025). Unlocking the black box: An in-depth review on interpretability, explainability, and reliability in deep learning. *Neural Computing & Applications*, *37*(2), 859–965. DOI: 10.1007/s00521-024-10437-2

Schmidt, J., Schutte, N. M., Buttigieg, S., Novillo-Ortiz, D., Sutherland, E., Anderson, M., & Van Kessel, R. (2024). Mapping the regulatory landscape for artificial intelligence in health within the European Union. *npj. Digital Medicine*, *7*(1), 229. PMID: 39191937

Schmitt, L. (2022). Mapping global AI governance: A nascent regime in a fragmented landscape. *AI and Ethics*, *2*(2), 303–314. DOI: 10.1007/s43681-021-00083-y

Shackelford, S. J., Asare, I. N., Dockery, R., Raymond, A. H., & Sergueeva, A. (2021). Should We Trust a Black Box to Safeguard Human Rights? *UCLA Journal of International Law and Foreign Affairs*, *26*(1), 35–88.

Shelby, A. L., Chambers, T. C., & St Clair, S. B. (2022). EEOC, DOJ: Using AI Technology in Employment-Related Decisions May Violate ADA. *The Journal of Robotics, Artificial Intelligence & Law, 5*.

Taylor, I. (2023). Justice by algorithm: The limits of AI in criminal sentencing. *Criminal Justice Ethics*, *42*(3), 193–213. DOI: 10.1080/0731129X.2023.2275967

Villasenor, J., & Foggo, V. (2020). Artificial intelligence, due process and criminal sentencing. *Mich. St. L. Rev.*, 295.

Von Eschenbach, W. J. (2021). Transparency and the black box problem: Why we do not trust AI. *Philosophy & Technology*, *34*(4), 1607–1622. DOI: 10.1007/s13347-021-00477-0

Waters, C. (2021). Your Data as a Weapon: How TikTok Captures a Security Crisis. *Syracuse J. Int'l L. & Com.*, *49*, 41.

Weiss, D. A. (2025). INHUMAN REASON: Predictive Policing Algorithms and the Fourth Amendment. *Criminal Justice*, *39*(4), 15–20.

Williamson, B. (2024). The social life of AI in education. *International Journal of Artificial Intelligence in Education*, *34*(1), 97–104. DOI: 10.1007/s40593-023-00342-5

Wu, Y. (2022). Privacy, Free Speech and Content Moderation: A Literature Review and Constitutional Framework Analysis. *Innovation in Science and Technology*, *1*(4), 30–39. DOI: 10.56397/IST.2022.11.04

Yu, C. (2024). *How Will AI Steal Our Elections?* Center for Open Science. DOI: 10.31219/osf.io/un7ev

Zenor, J. (2018). Endowed by their creator with certain unalienable rights: The future rise of civil rights for artificial intelligence. *Savannah L. Rev.*, *5*, 115.

Chapter 13
Legal Frameworks for Privacy and Digital Freedoms

Hemendra Singh
https://orcid.org/0000-0003-1160-8284
Jindal Global Law School, O.P. Jindal Global University, Sonipat, India

ABSTRACT

This chapter critically analyzes the legal foundations of privacy and freedom of expression in the digital age, positioning them as central to democratic legitimacy and institutional accountability. It explores the normative evolution of digital rights across jurisdictions, the jurisdictional tensions in cross-border enforcement and the systemic inequalities that hinder access to redress. By integrating comparative constitutional analysis with global governance frameworks, the chapter argues for a rights-based and inclusive model of digital regulation. It concludes by emphasizing the need for global legal standards that advance justice, transparency and institutional equity in digital governance, aligning with broader sustainable development goals.

INTRODUCTION

The expanding role of digital technologies in governance, communication, and commerce has prompted urgent scholarly inquiries into the legal frameworks that structure and safeguard individual rights in the digital realm. In particular, privacy and freedom of expression have become central themes in legal and interdisciplinary

DOI: 10.4018/979-8-3693-3920-6.ch013

debates, as both are increasingly challenged by opaque platform architectures and ubiquitous data surveillance.

The philosophical and jurisprudential foundations of privacy are rooted in liberal legal thought, most notably articulated by Charles Fried (1968), who linked privacy to dignity, trust, and the moral underpinnings of civil society. His work has been widely cited in both US constitutional law and international privacy theory. Alan Westin (1967) further conceptualized privacy as control over personal information, offering a baseline framework for later data protection laws and regulatory debates. Both thinkers provided the groundwork for interpreting privacy not merely as a right to seclusion, but as a structural enabler of autonomy and democratic engagement.

Contemporary digital privacy scholarship has moved beyond these individualistic models, focusing on the institutional asymmetries that undermine meaningful control. Julie E. Cohen (2013), in a widely cited intervention, critiques consent-based legal regimes as inadequate in the face of pervasive surveillance capitalism. Her work reframes privacy as an essential condition for intellectual and political self-determination in environments shaped by algorithmic sorting, behavioral targeting, and predictive analytics. In response to these critiques, legal scholars have evaluated the European Union's General Data Protection Regulation (GDPR) for its normative and procedural innovations. De Hert and Papakonstantinou (2012) highlight the GDPR's emphasis on transparency, accountability, and institutional oversight, arguing that its principle-based approach offers a substantive advancement over prior data protection regimes. However, questions persist about the enforceability of rights in non-European jurisdictions, especially where institutional capacities are weak or where oversight bodies lack independence. In the United States, legal scholars have examined the impact of *Carpenter v. United States* (2018) on Fourth Amendment doctrine. These analyses recognize that digital tracking data has intruded into privacy protections traditionally limited to physical searches. While scholarly consensus acknowledges the significance of this shift, there remains debate over how broadly its principles will be applied to other types of third-party data.

In addition to privacy, freedom of expression in digital environments has become a prominent concern. Jack Balkin (2016) introduced the concept of "information fiduciaries," advocating for legal obligations on platforms given their critical role in structuring online discourse. Kate Klonick (2018) offers an in-depth account of the emerging rules, values, and practices that govern content moderation on digital platforms, describing them as "new governors" of online speech. These platforms now perform functions akin to public institutions but without democratic legitimacy or procedural safeguards. Daphne Keller (2018) adds that the intermediary liability regimes often incentivize platforms to over-remove content, thereby suppressing lawful speech. She argues that when platforms are incentivized through vague legal standards, penalties or regulatory threats to remove content quickly and without clear procedural protections, it leads to suppression of lawful speech and creates a lack of transparency and accountability. To address this, Keller strongly advocates for embedding due process principles such as notice, explanation and the opportunity to appeal within platform content moderation systems. In the Global South, scholars caution that state-driven platform regulation may intensify censorship without adequate rule-of-law guarantees, particularly where judicial oversight is fragile or politicized.

Beyond doctrinal and regulatory critique, there is a growing literature on the global asymmetries of digital rights enforcement. Gurumurthy and Chami (2022) argue that dominant regulatory paradigms often assume strong institutions and robust civic participation, conditions that may be absent in many Global South contexts. They emphasize the need for decolonial frameworks and participatory governance in digital rights policymaking.

Despite these valuable contributions, the literature continues to exhibit key gaps. First, there is a lack of integrated approaches that bridge privacy and freedom of expression, domains that are increasingly interdependent in digital governance. Second, there remains limited empirical research on enforcement, especially in marginal contexts where rights violations are frequent and remedies are inaccessible. Third, normative scholarship often omits considerations of equity, inclusion and the role of civil society in shaping digital governance.

This chapter responds to these gaps by synthesizing doctrinal, normative and institutional insights into an integrated framework for rights-based digital governance. It argues that legal frameworks must be both enforceable and adaptable, rooted in democratic accountability and inclusive participation across jurisdictions.

Research Methodology and Research Question

This chapter adopts a doctrinal research methodology, supported by comparative constitutional analysis and normative inquiry. The doctrinal approach allows for a systematic examination of legal texts, judicial decisions and regulatory frameworks concerning privacy and digital freedoms across diverse jurisdictions. Core sources include constitutional provisions, landmark court rulings and transnational instruments like the General Data Protection Regulation (GDPR). The analysis also draws upon peer-reviewed legal scholarship to contextualize the evolution of digital rights and to assess the coherence and enforceability of existing legal protections. A comparative lens helps highlight divergences between Global North and Global South regulatory models, especially with regard to institutional design, access to redress, and the rule of law.

The chapter is guided by the overarching research question: How do existing legal frameworks across jurisdictions recognize, regulate and enforce the rights to privacy and digital freedom, and what normative principles should guide their future evolution? To address this question, the inquiry moves beyond formal legal doctrine to evaluate how power, participation, and inclusion shape the application of digital rights in practice. It also examines the role of judicial oversight, data protection authorities and civil society in enforcing constitutional and statutory guarantees. In doing so, the chapter aims not only to map the state of digital rights governance but also to articulate a normative vision grounded in constitutional values such as human dignity, democratic accountability, and access to justice.

PRIVACY IN LAW: FROM THE RIGHT TO BE LET ALONE TO DATA SELF-DETERMINATION

The right to privacy has evolved from a historically narrow conception of personal seclusion into a dynamic legal principle at the heart of digital constitutionalism. As technological infrastructures increasingly mediate everyday life, privacy is no longer simply about solitude or secrecy. It is now about control over personal data, protection from algorithmic profiling, and the preservation of human dignity in complex data ecosystems. This sub-chapter traces the legal evolution of privacy from its analog origins to its present status as a foundational right in global digital governance. Through theoretical inquiry, normative analysis, and comparative legal perspectives, it explores how privacy has been reinterpreted to meet the challenges of surveillance, commodification, and informational asymmetry in the digital age.

The Evolution of Privacy in Legal Theory and Jurisprudence

The legal idea of privacy has undergone a profound transformation over the past century, evolving from a narrowly defined right to be left alone into a complex, multifaceted principle that underpins democratic autonomy in the digital age. Initially framed within the context of liberal political thought, privacy was seen as a safeguard for individual seclusion, intimacy, and personal space. Early legal doctrine treated privacy as a negative liberty, an entitlement to noninterference by the state. However, as societies have become increasingly digitized and personal data has emerged as a central economic and political asset, the scope and meaning of privacy have expanded significantly. The shift from spatial privacy to informational privacy reflects broader changes in how identity, autonomy, and power are negotiated in contemporary society.

Classical legal understandings of privacy emphasized its protective function against physical or reputational harm. In early jurisprudence, particularly in liberal democracies, privacy was legally recognized in tort law, often in cases involving defamation, intrusion, or breach of confidence. Over time, constitutional courts began interpreting privacy as an essential component of broader rights frameworks, integrating it into doctrines of personal liberty, dignity, and equality (Witzleb, 2007). In many jurisdictions, the right to privacy found implicit or explicit recognition in constitutional texts and began to inform judicial reasoning across diverse domains such as surveillance, reproductive autonomy, family life, and bodily integrity.

The rise of digital technologies has placed considerable pressure on these traditional frameworks. As data driven technologies and networked infrastructures have become embedded in everyday life, the limitations of classical privacy doctrine have become increasingly apparent. Privacy is no longer threatened solely by state surveillance or journalistic intrusion. Instead, it is compromised through the routine and often opaque operations of digital platforms, mobile applications, and data brokers. The core issue is not only unauthorized access but the systemic collection, aggregation, and commodification of personal information. In response to these shifts, legal thought has moved beyond the spatial metaphor of privacy and toward a conception grounded in data self-determination, which posits that individuals must retain meaningful control over how their personal data is collected, processed, and used.

Contemporary privacy jurisprudence now confronts the dual challenge of regulating public surveillance while also addressing the vast reach of private actors. Courts have extended privacy protections to encompass digital communication, biometric identifiers, location tracking, and algorithmic profiling. In parallel, legislatures have adopted legal frameworks that articulate principles such as consent, transparency, accountability, and necessity. These standards reflect a growing consensus that privacy must function not only as a shield against harm but also as an institutional framework that legitimizes the governance of personal data in complex digital ecosystems.

This evolution is also evident in the growing recognition of privacy as a positive right, one that obliges the state to take proactive steps to prevent data exploitation and ensure equitable digital participation (Mantelero, 2016). Increasingly, courts and legal scholars have come to view privacy as foundational to the exercise of other rights, including freedom of expression, freedom of association, and political participation. Privacy now operates not merely as an individual entitlement but as a cornerstone of democratic life. It sustains public trust, guards against arbitrary power, and upholds the moral and intellectual autonomy of individuals.

Nonetheless, this legal evolution remains uneven and incomplete. Jurisdictions differ widely in how they define, prioritize, and enforce privacy protections. Some countries have adopted comprehensive legal frameworks grounded in principles of human dignity and autonomy, while others maintain sectoral or fragmented models that offer limited protection. In many contexts, economic, political, and security considerations continue to influence privacy law, often at the expense of individual rights. As the next section will explore, principles such as consent, proportionality, and purpose limitation have emerged as critical elements in shaping legal responses to these challenges. These principles represent a turning point in the effort to reconcile innovation with justice and provide a normative foundation for digital privacy in the twenty first century.

Key Principles

As legal frameworks evolve to address the complexities of digital privacy, a number of normative principles have emerged as cornerstones for regulating data collection and use. Among the most widely recognized and operationalized are the principles of consent, proportionality, and purpose limitation. These principles serve not only as regulatory safeguards but also as normative anchors for balancing individual rights with technological advancement and institutional objectives. They are embedded in data protection regimes around the world and inform both legislative design and judicial interpretation of privacy law. Understanding how these principles function and where they fall short is essential for assessing the capacity of legal systems to uphold privacy in the digital age.

Consent is perhaps the most familiar and yet the most contested principle in contemporary data governance. At its core, consent represents the idea that individuals should have control over whether and how their personal information is collected and processed. In theory, it operationalizes the values of autonomy, dignity, and informational self-determination. In practice, however, consent mechanisms are often undermined by opacity, imbalance of power, and information asymmetry. Users frequently encounter long and complex privacy notices that obscure rather than clarify their choices. Consent is often reduced to a procedural formality rather than a meaningful exercise of will. Moreover, in platform environments where access to essential services is contingent on data sharing, the voluntary nature of consent is placed in question. This has led many scholars and regulators to argue for a more substantive model of consent, one that emphasizes intelligibility, revocability, and genuine alternatives (Powell, 2023).

Proportionality serves as a second pillar in privacy law, particularly in constitutional and administrative contexts. It provides a framework for assessing whether a particular intrusion on privacy is justified in light of its aims and effects. The principle requires that any interference with a fundamental right be suitable to achieve a legitimate objective, necessary in the absence of less intrusive means, and balanced in terms of benefits and harms. This analytical structure is especially important in cases involving state surveillance, where privacy claims are weighed against public interests such as national security or public health. Proportionality enables courts and oversight bodies to move beyond abstract declarations of rights and toward reasoned evaluations of specific practices. It introduces a degree of flexibility without abandoning rights-based scrutiny. At the same time, its effectiveness depends on the transparency and accountability of decision-making institutions, which in many jurisdictions remains inadequate.

Purpose limitation completes the triad by ensuring that personal data, once collected, is used only for the specific purposes for which it was gathered. This principle is vital in limiting the risks of function creep, where data collected for one purpose is later repurposed in ways that may be harmful or discriminatory. Purpose limitation establishes boundaries around data flows and encourages data minimization, thereby reducing the exposure of individuals to unnecessary surveillance or profiling. It also reinforces trust between data subjects and data controllers by aligning data practices with reasonable expectations. In the age of big data analytics and machine learning, however, the principle of purpose limitation faces significant challenges. Predictive technologies thrive on vast and diverse data sets, often drawing inferences that go well beyond the original context of collection (Te Molder et al., 2023). Regulators and courts are increasingly called upon to reconcile the logic of data repurposing with the normative imperative to respect individual agency and contextual integrity.

Together, these principles constitute the ethical and operational core of modern data protection regimes. They seek to embed fairness, accountability, and respect for individual rights into the design and implementation of data systems. Yet their practical enforcement remains uneven across jurisdictions. In many contexts, the interpretation of these principles varies significantly, and enforcement mechanisms lack the independence, resources, or authority needed to ensure compliance. Moreover, the rise of artificial intelligence, automated decision making, and cross border data transfers continues to outpace the capacity of legal frameworks to apply these principles consistently. These challenges point to the need for both stronger institutional safeguards and a broader cultural shift in how data rights are understood and prioritized. As the next section will explore, different jurisdictions have responded to this challenge in different ways, producing a mosaic of regulatory approaches that reflect divergent constitutional traditions and policy priorities.

Comparative Jurisdictions

The legal recognition of privacy as a fundamental right has taken different forms across jurisdictions, reflecting distinct constitutional cultures, political histories, and institutional capacities. In recent years, both mature democracies and emerging legal systems have begun to grapple with the challenge of designing privacy frameworks suitable for the digital age. While there is growing consensus on key principles such as consent, proportionality, and accountability, the specific legal instruments and enforcement mechanisms vary considerably. This section analyzes three influential models of privacy protection: the European Union's General Data Protection Regulation, the Indian Supreme Court's articulation of constitutional privacy in the Puttaswamy judgment, and a selection of emerging frameworks from the Global South. Together, these illustrate both the diffusion of privacy norms and the diversity of institutional approaches to digital rights.

The General Data Protection Regulation stands as the most comprehensive and influential data protection law to date. Enforced since 2018, the GDPR represents a paradigm shift in how privacy is regulated, moving from sector specific rules to a unified legal framework grounded in fundamental rights. Its principles include lawfulness, fairness, transparency, purpose limitation, data minimization, and accountability. The regulation grants individuals a suite of enforceable rights, including access to personal data, correction, deletion, and data portability. Importantly, it also imposes obligations on data controllers and processors, mandates data protection impact assessments, and requires the designation of independent data protection officers. The extraterritorial scope of the GDPR means that its standards influence practices far beyond the borders of the European Union. Many countries have adopted similar frameworks in order to facilitate data flows with European entities or to align with its normative leadership (Singh, 2024).

In contrast to the legislative approach of the GDPR, the Indian Supreme Court's decision in Justice K S Puttaswamy v Union of India offered a constitutional articulation of the right to privacy. Delivered in 2017, the judgment unanimously held that privacy is intrinsic to life and liberty under Article 21 of the Indian Constitution and is part of the freedoms guaranteed by Part III of the Constitution. The Court recognized privacy as a multifaceted right encompassing bodily autonomy, informational control, and decisional freedom. By grounding privacy in dignity, equality, and personal liberty, the Court positioned it as a foundational element of constitutional democracy. The Puttaswamy judgment did not merely recognize privacy as a standalone right but embedded it within a broader normative structure that includes procedural safeguards, proportionality analysis, and the requirement of necessity in any infringement. Though India has since enacted a data protection law, the constitutional vision articulated in Puttaswamy remains a key reference point in debates over digital governance and state surveillance.

Beyond these two high profile examples, several countries in the Global South have begun to develop their own constitutional and legislative frameworks for privacy. Brazil's General Data Protection Law draws heavily on the structure and language of the GDPR, while also reflecting domestic constitutional principles. South Africa's Protection of Personal Information Act integrates privacy protections within a rights based constitutional framework and establishes an Information Regulator to oversee enforcement. Kenya's Data Protection Act similarly reflects an effort to domesticate global privacy norms within a national legal structure. These developments signal the growing recognition that privacy is not merely a luxury of advanced democracies but a universal right that must be protected across political and economic contexts.

However, the adoption of privacy laws does not always translate into effective enforcement. Many jurisdictions face significant institutional challenges, including under resourced regulatory bodies, limited judicial capacity, and political interference. In some cases, legal reforms are driven by external economic incentives rather than internal democratic processes, raising questions about legitimacy and sustainability. Moreover, structural inequalities such as digital exclusion, low legal literacy, and lack of access to remedies continue to impede the realization of privacy rights in practice. These disparities highlight the importance of contextualizing privacy frameworks within local political economies and governance cultures.

The comparative analysis reveals both convergence and fragmentation in the global landscape of privacy law. While there is a shared vocabulary of rights and principles, the institutionalization of these norms varies greatly. The GDPR sets a high standard for procedural and substantive protections, but its complexity and resource demands may not be easily replicable elsewhere (Dumas, 2019). Constitutional approaches, such as those seen in India and South Africa, offer normative depth and flexibility but often depend on active judicial enforcement and political will. As privacy becomes a central axis of digital governance, there is an urgent need for legal models that are not only principled but also adaptable, inclusive, and enforceable. These models must account for local realities while remaining connected to the broader project of global digital justice.

FREEDOM OF EXPRESSION AND THE DIGITAL PUBLIC SPHERE

Freedom of expression has long been recognized as a cornerstone of democratic societies, essential not only for individual autonomy but also for collective deliberation, dissent, and accountability. In the digital era, however, the spaces in which expression occurs are increasingly governed by private technology platforms that wield substantial influence over what is seen, said, and silenced. This sub-chapter examines how freedom of expression is being reshaped in a digital public sphere dominated by algorithmic curation, corporate moderation, and transnational governance gaps. It explores the complex interplay between user rights, platform policies, and state regulation, focusing on the legal challenges of preserving expressive freedoms without enabling harm, exclusion, or manipulation.

Platforms as Digital Speech Governors

The traditional architecture of freedom of expression was built around a clear dichotomy between the state and the individual. Courts and legislatures developed legal doctrines to protect citizens from censorship, coercion, and retaliation by public authorities. However, the rise of digital platforms as the primary hosts of public discourse has significantly altered this paradigm. Social media companies, search engines, and content hosting services now exercise unprecedented control over what speech is visible, amplified, or removed. These platforms function not merely as intermediaries but as private regulators of expression, with the power to shape civic discourse, influence political behavior, and determine the boundaries of acceptable communication (Balkin, 2018). Their governance decisions, though far reaching, often remain shielded from meaningful legal accountability.

At the heart of this transformation lies the platform's dual role as both infrastructure and curator. On one hand, platforms provide the technological foundation for speech by offering users access to networks, communication tools, and content distribution systems. On the other, they shape the informational environment through algorithmic ranking, content moderation, and recommendation systems. These functions give platforms de facto power over digital visibility and audience reach, effectively making them arbiters of speech in the modern public sphere. Unlike state actors, however, platforms operate according to proprietary policies and commercial interests rather than constitutional or democratic mandates. Their decisions about takedowns, suspensions, or content prioritization are typically guided by opaque community guidelines, automated enforcement mechanisms, and risk management strategies rather than legal norms.

This privatized model of speech governance raises several normative concerns. First, the lack of procedural transparency makes it difficult for users to understand or contest moderation decisions. Appeals processes, where they exist, are often limited, inconsistent, or inaccessible. Second, the economic and political incentives of platforms may lead to selective enforcement or over removal of content, particularly in contexts involving political dissent, minority speech, or controversial viewpoints. Third, the application of global content policies across diverse cultural and legal contexts results in normative friction, as platform rules may either fall short of or exceed national free speech protections. The outcome is a fragmented landscape where expressive freedoms are unequally distributed and subject to discretionary control by private entities.

In response to these challenges, legal scholars have begun to conceptualize platforms as occupying a quasi-public role, calling for the imposition of public interest obligations on dominant digital intermediaries. Some proposals advocate for treating large platforms as information fiduciaries, with duties of loyalty, care, and transparency toward their users. Others suggest regulatory frameworks that would impose baseline standards of due process, non-discrimination, and justification in content moderation practices. These efforts reflect a growing recognition that the governance of speech cannot be left entirely to private discretion in a democratic society. At the same time, any legal intervention must navigate complex questions of jurisdiction, institutional design, and unintended consequences, particularly in relation to censorship, innovation, and regulatory capture.

Ultimately, platforms have emerged as central actors in the governance of digital speech, exercising normative power without being formally bound by constitutional limits. As states and international bodies grapple with the implications of this shift, there is an urgent need to rethink the legal architecture that supports expressive freedom. Ensuring that digital public spaces remain open, pluralistic, and accountable will require a combination of legal reform, institutional oversight, and technological transparency. This task is not merely regulatory but constitutional, implicating the foundational principles of democracy, equality, and participatory governance in the digital era.

The Legal Struggle to Protect Expression Without Enabling Harm

As digital speech becomes more accessible and far reaching, legal systems are confronted with the complex task of protecting freedom of expression while addressing the harms that can emerge from its unregulated exercise. The challenge lies in ensuring that the right to speak is not misused to incite violence, spread disinformation, promote discrimination, or undermine public trust. In traditional legal theory, the protection of speech was often grounded in the assumption that more speech, especially in a pluralistic public sphere, would counter harmful or false ideas. However, in digital contexts where speech travels at scale, anonymity is widespread, and algorithmic amplification often prioritizes sensational or polarizing content, this assumption no longer holds. The consequences of unchecked expression can be immediate, wide ranging, and difficult to mitigate once damage has occurred.

Legal responses to these challenges have taken a variety of forms, reflecting divergent constitutional traditions and policy priorities. In Europe, for example, the jurisprudence of the European Court of Human Rights has long acknowledged that freedom of expression is not absolute (Soboleva, 2017). National laws frequently prohibit hate speech, Holocaust denial, and incitement to violence, often with a lower threshold than that found in American constitutional law. The regulatory framework in many European countries treats speech in context, balancing rights against broader societal interests such as dignity, equality, and public order. This approach is reinforced by directives and regulations that impose content moderation obligations on platforms, including provisions under the Digital Services Act that require large online platforms to assess systemic risks associated with disinformation and algorithmic targeting.

In contrast, the United States adopts a more absolutist stance, grounded in the First Amendment and reinforced by a strong judicial tradition of speech protection. Courts have consistently ruled that even offensive, false, or disturbing speech may deserve protection unless it constitutes direct incitement to violence or falls into narrowly defined categories such as obscenity or defamation. This legal posture makes it difficult to impose broad speech related obligations on platforms or users without risking constitutional challenge. At the same time, the private nature of platforms allows them to moderate speech according to their own policies, which may be more restrictive than constitutional standards. This divergence between public norms and private enforcement has created a regulatory vacuum, where harmful speech may persist despite public concern, while legitimate expression may be curtailed without due process or oversight.

Other jurisdictions, particularly in the Global South, are navigating these tensions under different political and institutional conditions. In some cases, laws aimed at curbing online harms have been used to suppress dissent, criminalize criticism, and target journalists. The lack of independent judiciary, weak regulatory oversight, and limited civil society engagement exacerbates the risk that speech regulation will be used for political repression rather than public protection. At the same time, in societies marked by inequality, conflict, or fragile institutions, the failure to address online harms can contribute to real world violence and deepen societal divisions. This makes the balancing of rights and risks not only a legal challenge but a deeply political one.

Striking a balance between protecting expression and preventing harm requires more than the articulation of abstract principles. It demands robust legal standards, transparent procedures, and mechanisms of accountability for both state and nonstate actors. Courts must play a central role in setting thresholds, reviewing enforcement practices, and protecting minority voices. Regulatory frameworks must define not only the limits of permissible speech but also the responsibilities of platforms in shaping the online discourse. These responsibilities include content governance that respects due process, ensures equal treatment, and provides users with meaningful recourse. Importantly, any restriction on speech must be proportionate, narrowly tailored, and subject to public justification.

In an increasingly interconnected world, legal systems cannot operate in isolation. International human rights law provides a shared normative foundation, affirming that freedom of expression carries duties and responsibilities. The challenge ahead is to translate these principles into digital environments without undermining the vitality of open discourse. As courts, legislatures, and platforms grapple with the future of speech, the goal must be to protect not only the right to speak but also the conditions under which that right can be exercised responsibly and without fear.

INTERNATIONAL FRAMEWORKS AND THE PROBLEM OF JURISDICTION

As digital networks transcend territorial borders, legal frameworks grounded in national sovereignty struggle to regulate the flow of data, the operations of transnational platforms, and the protection of fundamental rights. The global nature of the internet means that a user's data may be collected in one country, processed in another, and stored across multiple jurisdictions, all while being governed by privately determined standards of content moderation and data security. In this landscape, international cooperation becomes essential. Yet the lack of harmonized norms, coupled with jurisdictional fragmentation and divergent regulatory philosophies, presents significant barriers to the enforcement of digital rights. This chapter examines the strengths and limitations of existing global legal frameworks for privacy and freedom of expression, and explores the jurisdictional tensions that hinder their effective implementation in a digitally interconnected world.

Global Legal Norms: OECD Guidelines, UN Principles, and Convention 108 Plus

In the absence of a unified international legal framework for digital rights, a variety of soft law instruments and treaty-based mechanisms have emerged to guide the governance of privacy and freedom of expression in the global digital environment. These frameworks provide normative foundations and policy blueprints for national and regional legal developments. Although they lack binding enforcement powers in many cases, they play an important role in establishing common principles, facilitating cross border cooperation, and shaping expectations among states, corporations, and civil society actors. Among the most influential instruments are the OECD Guidelines on the Protection of Privacy and Transborder Flows of Personal Data, the principles articulated by United Nations Special Rapporteurs and human rights mechanisms, and the Convention for the Protection of Individuals with regard to Automatic Processing of Personal Data, widely known as Convention 108 and its modernized version known as Convention 108 Plus.

The OECD Guidelines, first adopted in 1980 and updated in 2013, were among the earliest efforts to establish a global consensus on data protection principles. They introduced key concepts such as purpose specification, use limitation, security safeguards, and individual participation. The guidelines emphasize transparency and accountability in data processing and encourage member countries to harmonize their national laws to facilitate the free flow of information across borders. While not legally binding, the OECD framework has influenced legislation in both member and non-member states and served as a reference for policy harmonization, particularly in contexts where formal treaty obligations are politically or economically unfeasible (Kirby, 2010).

The United Nations has also played a pivotal role in articulating global digital rights norms through the work of its Special Rapporteurs on the right to privacy and freedom of opinion and expression. These mandate holders have consistently emphasized the indivisibility and universality of human rights in digital spaces. They have called attention to practices such as mass surveillance, internet shutdowns, and algorithmic censorship, urging states to ensure that any restrictions on digital rights are lawful, necessary, and proportionate. Reports submitted to the Human Rights Council and the General Assembly have recommended that digital platforms be held to international human rights standards, especially when performing quasi-public functions such as content moderation or identity verification. These principles, though advisory, have influenced advocacy strategies and jurisprudence in multiple jurisdictions and contributed to the development of human rights-based approaches to internet governance.

Convention 108, adopted by the Council of Europe in 1981, represents the first and only binding international treaty specifically devoted to data protection. It guarantees individuals a right to privacy with respect to the processing of their personal data and obliges signatory states to enact domestic legislation consistent with the treaty's core principles. Its provisions address fairness, lawfulness, data quality, and safeguards against misuse. Convention 108 is notable for its openness to non-European states, allowing it to function as a global instrument for privacy protection. The modernized version, Convention 108 Plus, adopted in 2018, updates the original text to reflect technological developments and new risks. It introduces enhanced rights such as the right not to be subject to decisions based solely on automated processing and strengthens provisions on accountability, transparency, and independent oversight.

Together, these instruments represent a growing consensus around the normative contours of privacy and digital expression. They affirm that individuals should have agency over their personal data, that governments must act within the boundaries of necessity and proportionality, and that cross border data flows should be accompanied by safeguards that respect human dignity. At the same time, the effectiveness of these norms depends on domestic implementation and institutional capacity. Many states have ratified or endorsed international instruments without developing robust national enforcement regimes. Others selectively comply, often citing national security or economic sovereignty to justify deviations. This uneven implementation has led to calls for stronger monitoring mechanisms, capacity building initiatives, and inclusive multilateral dialogue to ensure that international norms translate into meaningful protections for users across diverse legal and political contexts.

In a global digital environment where data governance is increasingly transnational and asymmetric, these normative frameworks provide essential points of reference. They help bridge differences in national law, offer guidance to private actors, and create pathways for cooperation among regulators and rights advocates. Yet they also face limits in scope and enforceability, raising the question of how to achieve coherence and accountability across jurisdictions. As the next section explores, the jurisdictional challenges of enforcing digital rights remain one of the most pressing obstacles to building a just and effective global governance regime for the digital age.

The Jurisdictional Puzzle: Sovereignty, Extraterritoriality, and Legal Fragmentation

Despite growing international consensus on digital rights norms, the enforcement of privacy and freedom of expression across borders remains deeply problematic. The global nature of digital infrastructures creates a profound mismatch between the territorial scope of state authority and the transnational operation of data flows, platform governance, and algorithmic decision making. This mismatch has given rise to what may be termed the jurisdictional puzzle, in which states assert competing claims of authority over the same actors, data, and harms, often resulting in inconsistent regulation, overlapping obligations, and gaps in accountability. The core challenge lies in reconciling the principle of national sovereignty with the structural reality of a networked world, where data knows no borders and legal orders rarely align.

The assertion of jurisdiction over digital activities traditionally follows one of three models: territorial, nationality based, or effects based. Under the territorial model, a state claims jurisdiction if a digital actor or data server is physically located within its borders. The nationality-based approach allows states to regulate their citizens' digital activities regardless of where they occur. The effects-based model, meanwhile, extends jurisdiction when a platform or service causes substantial impact within a state's territory, even if the actor has no physical presence there. Each of these approaches has been employed in different contexts, but their cumulative use has generated significant legal uncertainty and conflict. For example, global platforms may find themselves subject to divergent content takedown obligations, conflicting data transfer rules, or contradictory disclosure requirements, with no clear mechanism for resolution.

Extraterritorial regulation has become increasingly prominent as states attempt to impose their privacy and speech standards on global platforms. The European Union's General Data Protection Regulation exemplifies this trend, applying not only to data controllers within the Union but also to those outside its borders who process the personal data of Union residents (Tanaka, 2019). This expansive reach has prompted other jurisdictions to consider similar legislation, raising concerns about the fragmentation of global digital governance and the erosion of legal predictability. While extraterritoriality can serve as a tool for regulatory influence and norm diffusion, it also risks exacerbating geopolitical tensions and creating compliance burdens that disproportionately affect smaller firms and less resourced states.

Legal fragmentation is further intensified by the absence of binding multilateral agreements on digital rights. In areas such as taxation or trade, international treaties often provide mechanisms for dispute resolution and regulatory harmonization. In the digital realm, however, no such comprehensive regime exists. Instead, states pursue bilateral or regional arrangements, adopt conflicting domestic laws, or defer to private governance by platforms themselves. This patchwork approach creates uneven levels of protection, allows powerful actors to engage in jurisdictional arbitrage, and undermines the development of stable and coherent legal standards.

Sovereignty remains a central concern in this fragmented landscape. Many governments resist harmonization efforts that could constrain their domestic policy choices or expose their practices to external scrutiny. At the same time, global platforms often invoke jurisdictional ambiguity to avoid accountability, arguing that they operate under private terms of service rather than national law. This tension highlights the need for new models of cooperative sovereignty, in which states retain their regulatory authority while engaging in structured coordination to manage transborder challenges. Such models could involve mutual recognition of data protection standards, joint investigative frameworks, or regional courts with jurisdiction over digital rights violations.

The problem of jurisdiction is not merely technical or procedural. It reflects deeper political questions about whose norms should govern the global digital space, how power should be distributed among states, corporations, and civil society, and what institutional forms are best suited to protect fundamental rights in a rapidly evolving environment. Addressing this puzzle requires more than doctrinal innovation. It demands a rethinking of the legal architecture itself, with a view toward inclusivity, adaptability, and long-term legitimacy. The failure to resolve jurisdictional tensions risks perpetuating a system in which rights protections are contingent on geography, citizenship, and corporate discretion rather than universal legal guarantees.

ENFORCEMENT GAPS AND THE REALITIES OF INEQUALITY

While legal frameworks for digital rights have expanded significantly across jurisdictions, the enforcement of these protections remains uneven and often inaccessible to those who need them most. Legal guarantees on paper are frequently undermined by weak institutional capacity, regulatory capture, and limited access to justice. This gap between norm and implementation is particularly pronounced in contexts marked by economic inequality, digital exclusion, and political marginalization. In such environments, the promise of privacy and free expression can be illusory, available only to those with the resources, awareness, or geopolitical privilege to claim them. This chapter examines the structural barriers that hinder effective enforcement of digital rights, especially in the Global South, and explores how civil society actors, grassroots legal interventions, and transnational advocacy networks are attempting to bridge these gaps.

Institutional and Structural Barriers to Digital Rights Enforcement

The recognition of digital rights in law is a critical milestone, but their realization depends fundamentally on institutional structures that are capable of enforcing them. Across many jurisdictions, particularly in the Global South, digital rights enforcement faces significant limitations due to weak regulatory bodies, fragmented legal mandates, and insufficient judicial oversight. Even where data protection laws or constitutional provisions exist, the lack of independent and adequately resourced institutions often renders enforcement ineffective. These challenges are not simply matters of administrative inefficiency. They reflect deeper structural imbalances that privilege the interests of powerful actors - states, corporations, and dominant platforms - over the rights of individuals and vulnerable communities.

A central obstacle lies in the design and capacity of data protection authorities and regulatory agencies. In many countries, these bodies are understaffed, lack technical expertise, or are politically subordinate to executive power (Raab & Szekely, 2017. This limits their ability to audit compliance, impose sanctions, or engage in proactive oversight. Furthermore, institutional mandates are often restricted in scope, leaving regulators without jurisdiction over critical aspects of platform governance or transnational data flows. The absence of cross sectoral coordination between privacy regulators, telecom authorities, consumer protection agencies, and cybersecurity bodies contributes to a fragmented approach to digital rights enforcement, undermining the coherence and reach of legal protections.

Judicial systems, too, face considerable barriers. In many countries, courts are overburdened, slow, and inaccessible to the average citizen. Strategic litigation on digital rights is often concentrated in metropolitan centers and spearheaded by a handful of specialized organizations. Rural populations, linguistic minorities, and economically disadvantaged groups may lack the awareness or resources to challenge violations of their digital rights. Where courts do engage with digital rights cases, inconsistent jurisprudence and limited technical knowledge may hinder the development of strong legal precedents. Moreover, in authoritarian or semi authoritarian contexts, courts may be coopted or constrained, limiting their ability to serve as effective guardians of constitutional rights.

The enforcement deficit is further compounded by the political economy of digital regulation. Governments may have vested interests in maintaining surveillance powers, leveraging data for economic development, or avoiding confrontation with influential technology companies. Regulatory forbearance becomes common when states prioritize digital innovation or geopolitical alliances over human rights. In such environments, even well drafted legal frameworks remain dormant or selectively applied. The asymmetry of power between users and platforms, especially in jurisdictions without strong antitrust or consumer protection laws, further weakens the enforcement landscape.

Finally, digital rights enforcement is shaped by broader social and infrastructural inequalities. In regions with low internet penetration, poor digital literacy, or limited civil society engagement, awareness of rights is minimal. Citizens may be unaware of how their data is collected, shared, or used, let alone how to seek redress for violations. Marginalized groups, including women, indigenous communities, and persons with disabilities, often experience digital harms in ways that are compounded by offline forms of discrimination. These intersecting inequalities mean that enforcement mechanisms must be not only legally sound but also socially inclusive and culturally responsive.

Addressing these institutional and structural barriers requires a comprehensive strategy. Regulatory bodies must be empowered with independence, resources, and technical capacity. Judicial education on digital rights must be expanded. Mechanisms for collective redress, ombudspersons, and simplified complaints procedures can help lower barriers to access. At the same time, enforcement must be situated within a broader ecosystem of accountability, including civil society monitoring, investigative journalism, and community based digital literacy initiatives. Without such systemic interventions, the promise of digital rights will remain aspirational for millions across the globe.

Civil Society, Legal Activism, and Alternative Accountability Pathways

In contexts where formal institutions fail to enforce digital rights effectively, civil society actors have emerged as critical agents of accountability. Non-governmental organizations, advocacy networks, public interest litigators, investigative journalists, and digital rights collectives play an increasingly vital role in holding both states and corporations to account. Their work often fills the void left by weak regulatory enforcement, inaccessible courts, and institutional inertia. These actors not only document abuses but also raise public awareness, shape policy agendas, and initiate legal interventions that challenge systemic violations of privacy and freedom of expression. In doing so, they contribute to the development of an alternative infrastructure of rights protection that operates alongside and sometimes in opposition to formal state mechanisms.

Strategic litigation has become one of the most visible and impactful tools of digital rights advocacy. Civil society organizations have brought cases before constitutional courts, regional human rights tribunals, and administrative bodies to challenge unlawful surveillance, data breaches, internet shutdowns, and discriminatory algorithmic practices. Such litigation serves not only to vindicate individual rights but also to establish legal precedents, clarify normative standards, and generate public discourse. In countries like India, South Africa, Kenya, and Brazil, digital rights litigation has helped to elevate privacy and expression to matters of constitutional significance. Even where formal legal victories are elusive, the process of litigation itself often produces symbolic and political gains that pressure decision makers and galvanize public support.

Beyond the courtroom, civil society organizations engage in a wide array of accountability practices (Dawson, 2022). These include producing independent audits of platform moderation practices, publishing shadow reports to international human rights bodies, organizing digital literacy campaigns, and mobilizing transnational advocacy coalitions. Digital rights groups often collaborate across borders to respond to shared challenges, such as global surveillance programs or content moderation failures. These collaborations allow for the pooling of technical expertise, the sharing of legal strategies, and the amplification of local struggles within global policy arenas. In doing so, they challenge the asymmetry of power between users and platforms, between the Global South and North, and between individual complainants and institutional actors.

Alternative mechanisms for accountability have also emerged through community-based initiatives. In some regions, grassroots movements have developed participatory frameworks for digital governance, including community guidelines for responsible platform use, peer review models for content moderation, and locally grounded approaches to digital safety. These models emphasize context, inclusion, and cultural sensitivity, resisting one size fits all frameworks imposed by distant regulators or transnational corporations. They also foreground intersectional perspectives that address how digital harms disproportionately affect women, minorities, and other historically marginalized groups. By centering these voices, civil society initiatives enrich the democratic legitimacy and practical relevance of digital rights enforcement.

Despite these contributions, civil society efforts are often constrained by resource limitations, political repression, and legal restrictions. Governments may use regulatory tools to curtail non-governmental activity, label organizations as foreign agents, or prosecute activists under vague national security laws. In highly centralized digital ecosystems, platforms may refuse to cooperate with civil society actors or limit access to data needed for independent audits and advocacy. These constraints underscore the need for legal and political reforms that protect the enabling environment for civil society. At the same time, funders and international institutions must provide sustained support to ensure that digital rights activism remains both resilient and impactful.

The landscape of digital rights enforcement cannot be understood solely through the lens of state institutions. It must also account for the complex and dynamic ecosystem of non-state actors who are shaping accountability from below (Celeste et al., 2025). Civil society, legal activism, and alternative pathways are not substitutes for public enforcement, but they are essential complements in the struggle to realize digital rights in practice. Their role is especially vital in transitional democracies, fragile states, and underregulated digital markets, where formal mechanisms may be absent, compromised, or inaccessible. Recognizing and supporting these efforts is essential for building a more equitable and responsive system of digital governance.

REIMAGINING DIGITAL GOVERNANCE FOR RIGHTS AND JUSTICE

As the limitations of current legal and institutional frameworks become increasingly visible, there is a growing call to rethink how digital governance is structured, implemented, and made accountable. The protection of privacy and freedom of expression can no longer rely solely on reactive enforcement or piecemeal regulation. It must be grounded in proactive legal design, normative clarity, and inclusive governance architectures that center human dignity and democratic participation. This chapter explores forward looking strategies to embed rights into the digital ecosystem, drawing on both normative theory and emerging best practices. It proposes a reorientation of digital governance that moves beyond fragmented national responses and toward globally resonant standards that can ensure fairness, transparency, and accountability in the face of rapidly evolving technological power.

Embedding Rights into Digital Design and Regulation

A rights respecting digital environment cannot be achieved through legislation alone. As digital infrastructures increasingly mediate everyday life, the architecture of platforms, protocols, and automated systems must be built from the ground up with fundamental rights in mind. Embedding privacy and freedom of expression into digital design is not only a technical challenge but also a legal and ethical imperative. It requires regulatory frameworks that incentivize rights conscious innovation, institutional cultures that prioritize accountability, and technical standards that make dignity, agency, and equality central to digital interaction.

The concept of privacy by design offers a foundational approach to embedding rights at the earliest stages of technological development. This model proposes that data protection principles should be integrated directly into the engineering of systems rather than treated as external constraints applied after deployment (Bygrave, 2017). For example, default settings that minimize data collection, clear consent interfaces, and modular controls for users are not merely technical features but normative choices that shape power relations between users and platforms. Regulatory frameworks such as the General Data Protection Regulation have sought to formalize these ideas by mandating data minimization, purpose limitation, and transparency as binding obligations. However, implementation remains inconsistent, especially in contexts where market competition and surveillance business models undermine incentives for compliance.

Freedom of expression, too, must be considered at the level of design. Automated content moderation systems, algorithmic ranking protocols, and interface structures all influence which voices are heard and which are silenced. If designed without sensitivity to linguistic diversity, cultural context, or the social position of users, these systems can entrench bias and reproduce inequality. Embedding expressive rights into platform architecture entails mechanisms for due process in content moderation, explainability of algorithmic decisions, and inclusive participation in the development of rules and norms. Technical solutions such as human in the loop moderation, user appeals processes, and visibility audits are essential complements to legislative safeguards.

Embedding rights also involves rethinking the governance of platform design itself. Decisions about interface layout, content curation, and data architecture are often made by small groups of engineers and executives within private corporations. This raises fundamental questions about legitimacy, accountability, and transparency. If platforms now function as critical infrastructure for democratic participation and public discourse, then their design choices must be subject to public oversight. Regulatory proposals in some jurisdictions have called for platform design audits, transparency mandates for recommender systems, and public consultation mechanisms for major product changes. These measures recognize that the shape of the digital environment is not a neutral outcome of innovation but a site of normative and political contestation.

The embedding of rights into digital design must also address structural and contextual inequalities. A one size fits all model risks replicating the biases of dominant cultures and overlooking the needs of marginalized communities. Participatory design methodologies, which involve end users in the design process, offer a pathway to more inclusive and responsive technologies. These approaches align with broader principles of procedural justice and user agency, ensuring that the people most affected by digital systems have a voice in their creation and governance. Civil society, academic institutions, and public interest technologists have an important role to play in advancing these methodologies and translating abstract rights into tangible design practices.

Ultimately, embedding rights into digital design and regulation is not a discrete task but an ongoing process. It demands continual reflection, adaptation, and engagement across legal, technical, and social domains. It requires moving beyond reactive enforcement toward proactive norm setting, institutional coordination, and collaborative innovation. As digital systems become more embedded in the fabric of human life, the challenge is not only to regulate their outputs but to shape their foundations in ways that reflect and reinforce the values of justice, dignity, and democratic participation.

Toward Global Standards for Inclusive and Accountable Digital Governance

The governance of digital ecosystems cannot remain fragmented and reactive in a world where platforms, data flows, and algorithmic decisions operate across borders. As privacy and freedom of expression are increasingly shaped by transnational infrastructures and corporate architectures, the development of coherent global standards becomes both a normative necessity and a practical imperative. Existing regulatory asymmetries not only create gaps in protection but also empower dominant actors to forum shop, undermining the universality of rights and the effectiveness of national legal frameworks. To confront this challenge, the international community must move toward the articulation and institutionalization of global standards that are inclusive, enforceable, and rooted in human rights principles.

Efforts to build such standards are already underway, though they remain scattered and uneven. Instruments such as the OECD Guidelines, the UN Guiding Principles on Business and Human Rights, and Convention 108 Plus reflect a growing consensus on key normative factors, including accountability, transparency, data minimization, and user participation. However, the voluntary nature of many of these instruments and the lack of consistent implementation mechanisms limit their effectiveness. What is needed is not merely a restatement of principles but the construction of multilateral frameworks with institutional backing, monitoring capabilities, and avenues for redress. Such frameworks must be flexible enough to accommodate local contexts while strong enough to constrain abuse and ensure equality in access and protection.

Achieving global digital standards also requires addressing deep structural inequalities. Jurisdictions in the Global South often face capacity constraints, infrastructure deficits, and power imbalances that limit their ability to influence or implement global norms (Heeks, 2022). An inclusive governance architecture must therefore involve meaningful representation from these regions in agenda setting, norm development, and enforcement discussions. Technical assistance, knowledge exchange, and support for institutional strengthening must be integral to any attempt at harmonization. Without such equity considerations, global governance risks reproducing existing hierarchies under the guise of universality.

Accountability mechanisms must also be a core component of global standards. This includes not only regulatory convergence but also independent oversight, transparent audit practices, and formal channels through which individuals and communities can challenge rights violations. Platforms operating at scale should be held to due process obligations, provide justification for content or data decisions, and be subject to legal challenge across jurisdictions. Regional human rights courts, data protection networks, and transnational civil society coalitions can help establish these mechanisms and offer models of shared enforcement. Their role is particularly crucial in addressing the harms that escape the reach of domestic courts or where states themselves are complicit in digital repression.

In conclusion, the construction of inclusive and accountable global standards for digital governance is not simply a legal or technical exercise. It is a political and ethical project that requires reimagining power, authority, and participation in a digitally mediated world. The protection of privacy and freedom of expression must move beyond the confines of national sovereignty and corporate discretion and into a framework that affirms the indivisibility and universality of digital rights. Such a framework must center the voices of marginalized communities, be responsive to cultural diversity, and remain adaptive to emerging technologies. Only by embedding justice and inclusivity at the heart of digital governance can we ensure that the digital future remains a space for autonomy, dignity, and democratic life for all.

REFERENCES

Balkin, J. M. (2016). Information fiduciaries and the First Amendment. *U.C. Davis Law Review*, *49*(4), 1183–1234. https://papers.ssrn.com/abstract=2675270

Balkin, J. M. (2018). Free speech in the algorithmic society: Big data, private governance, and new school speech regulation. *U.C. Davis Law Review*, *51*, 1149–1210. https://ssrn.com/abstract=3038939

Bygrave, L. A. (2017). Data protection by design and by default: Deciphering the EU's legislative requirements. *Oslo Law Review*, *4*(2), 105–122. DOI: 10.18261/issn.2387-3299-2017-02-03

Celeste, E., Palladino, N., & Redeker, D. (2025). Civil society's role in constitutionalising global content governance. *Internet Policy Review*, *14*(1). Advance online publication. DOI: 10.14763/2025.1.1830

Cohen, J. E. (2013). What privacy is for. *Harvard Law Review*, *126*(7), 1904–1933. https://harvardlawreview.org/2013/05/what-privacy-is-for/

Dawson, M. (2022). The accountability of non-governmental actors in the digital sphere: A theoretical framework. *European Law Journal*, *29*(1–2), 78–90. DOI: 10.1111/eulj.12420

De Hert, P., & Papakonstantinou, V. (2012). The proposed data protection regulation replacing Directive 95/46/EC: A sound system for the protection of individuals. *Computer Law & Security Review*, *28*(2), 130–142. DOI: 10.1016/j.clsr.2012.01.011

Dumas, J. (2019). General Data Protection Regulation (GDPR): Prioritizing resources. *Seattle University Law Review*, *42*(3), 1115–1128.

Fried, C. (1968). Privacy. *The Yale Law Journal*, *77*(3), 475–493. DOI: 10.2307/794941

Gurumurthy, A., & Chami, N. (2022). *Governing the resource of data: To what end and for whom? Conceptual building blocks of a semi-commons approach* (Data Governance Network Working Paper No. 23). IT for Change. https://www.researchgate.net/publication/358552107

Heeks, R. (2022). Digital inequality beyond the digital divide: Conceptualizing adverse digital incorporation in the global South. *Information Technology for Development*, *28*(4), 688–704. DOI: 10.1080/02681102.2022.2068492

Kirby, M. (2010). The history, achievement and future of the 1980 OECD Guidelines on Privacy. *Journal of Law. Information and Science*, *20*(2), 1–14. https://www7.austlii.edu.au/cgi-bin/viewdoc/au/journals/JlLawInfoSci/2010/10.html

Klonick, K. (2018). The new governors: The people, rules, and processes governing online speech. *Harvard Law Review, 131*(6), 1598–1670. https://harvardlawreview.org/2018/04/the-new-governors-the-people-rules-and-processes-governing-online-speech/

Mantelero, A. (2016). Personal data for decisional purposes in the age of analytics: From an individual to a collective dimension of data protection. *Computer Law & Security Review*, *32*(2), 238–255. DOI: 10.1016/j.clsr.2016.01.014

Powell, M. (2023). Consent, background justice and patterned privacy principles. *Political Studies*, *72*(3), 944–960. DOI: 10.1177/00323217231167074

Raab, C., & Szekely, I. (2017). Data protection authorities and information technology. *Computer Law & Security Review*, *33*(4), 421–433. DOI: 10.1016/j.clsr.2017.05.002

Singh, H. (2024). Navigating the legal landscape of information governance. In Helge, K., & Rookey, C. (Eds.), *Creating and sustaining an information governance program* (pp. 217–235). IGI Global., DOI: 10.4018/979-8-3693-0472-3.ch012

Soboleva, A. K. (2017). Freedom of expression in the case law of the European Court of Human Rights: Old approaches and new tendencies in interpretation of Article 10 of the ECHR. *RUDN Journal of Law*, *21*(2), 235–262. DOI: 10.22363/2313-2337-2017-21-2-235-262

Tanaka, H. (2019). Impact of the GDPR on Japanese companies. *Business Law International*, *20*(2), 137–146.

Westin, A. F. (1967). *Privacy and freedom*. New York: Atheneum. Available at https://archive.org/details/privacyfreedom00west

Witzleb, N. (2007). Monetary remedies for breach of confidence in privacy cases. *Legal Studies*, *27*(3), 430–464. DOI: 10.1111/j.1748-121X.2007.00058.x

KEY TERMS AND DEFINITIONS

Privacy by Design: An approach that embeds data protection principles into the development and architecture of digital systems from the outset.

Digital Constitutionalism: The application of fundamental constitutional values such as rights, accountability, and transparency to the regulation of the digital environment.

Content Moderation: The process by which digital platforms manage, restrict, or remove user-generated content according to internal rules or external laws.

Data Minimization: A principle requiring that only the minimum necessary personal data be collected and processed for a specific, lawful purpose.

Platform Governance: The set of practices and policies through which digital platforms regulate user behavior, content, and access to services.

Jurisdictional Fragmentation: A condition in which conflicting national laws apply simultaneously to digital activities that cross borders, leading to legal uncertainty.

Strategic Litigation: The use of legal action by civil society actors to advance broader rights-based goals through targeted cases.

Transnational Digital Governance: The development and implementation of digital rights standards and accountability mechanisms across national borders through international cooperation.

Chapter 14

Right to Internet Access vs. National Security Concerns: Addressing the Complex Questions of the Digital Era

Jipson Joseph
https://orcid.org/0009-0005-1795-5051
Christ University, India

ABSTRACT

The globe has made tremendous progress over the last few decades. The scientific and technological advancements have provided immense possibilities and opportunities to the world through the latest digitalization process. The present century is even termed as the digital era. Internet access is the most crucial element for the maximum utilization of digital technologies. Accordingly, the concept of digital rights evolved and identified the right to Internet access as the most essential digital right. However, several countries have not implemented this right as part of their human rights framework due to a lack of an international covenant or treaty. Besides, many countries violate the right to Internet access through many mechanisms, claiming national security grounds. In 2024, almost 300 Internet shutdowns happened across the globe, violating people's fundamental rights. From this perspective, this chapter examines the relevance of Internet access and critically evaluates the national security defensive mechanism.

DOI: 10.4018/979-8-3693-3920-6.ch014

1 INTRODUCTION

The globe has significantly moved from an industrial society to a globally connected digital society with the scientific and technological advancements of the late 20th century. This shift has also broadened the horizon of rights. Together with people's progressive world vision, they became more aware of the broader spectrum of their rights. From the Universal Declaration of Human Rights (UDHR), the international community is actively involved in establishing a universal framework for human rights. Through the institution of the International Covenant on Civil and Political Rights (ICCPR) in 1966, it first shaped the first generation of rights (civil and political), and through the International Covenant on Economic, Social, and Cultural Rights (ICESCR) in 1966 it adopted the second generation of rights (economic, social, and cultural). Although not officially declared, the third generation of rights (collective rights) is widely accepted across the globe. The contemporary digital era underlines the necessity of a fourth generation of human rights. These rights are often termed as digital rights. The first and the most notable one among them is the right to Internet Access. This right is essential for all other digital rights, as without access to the Internet, no effective communication can be done digitally (Reglitz, 2020).

Although states prioritize protecting people's right to access the Internet, they sometimes restrict, control, and ban access on national security grounds. The state authorities affirm that they can limit people's Internet access to prioritize national security, territorial integrity, and internal peace. However, governments also restrict access to protect their political motives (La Rue, 2011). Such instances have occurred in India, Pakistan, Myanmar, Bangladesh, Iran, Russia, and many other countries (Deep, 2025). Such restrictions on Internet access violate people's freedom of speech and expression, right to information, right to privacy, and right to livelihood. Violating human rights through unlawful executive actions violates the trusteeship, which is the crux of democracy.

From this perspective, this chapter examines the importance of having a well-designed and protected right to Internet access and critically analyses this right within the context of national security claims and people's right to security. The chapter argues that national security is an essential requirement for human flourishing and the protection of human rights. However, violating human rights, such as the right to Internet access on illogical and unlawful national security grounds (masking the real intention), violates international human rights standards and the demands of global justice.

2 SIGNIFICANCE OF THE STUDY

Fostering innovation and building up resilient technologies is a core mission of the Sustainable Development Goals (SDG9). The increasing growth and availability of the Internet in the last two decades affirm the global efforts to achieve this objective. The 5G Internet connectivity and smart mobile phones are said to be available in every nook and cranny, providing possibilities of global interconnectedness within seconds. However, evidence shows that many low-income countries have not yet realized the objective of effective Internet connectivity, affecting the right to Internet access. The UNGA (2015) demands that, under the provisions of SDG9c, the globe should "strive to provide universal and affordable access to the Internet in least developed countries by 2020." Although there is some progress, millions of people still face issues with Internet access in these countries. It shows that the digital divide is very explicit around the globe. Besides, many countries have not incorporated the right to Internet access in the human rights framework, causing a severe negative impact on the realization of other rights. Since no international treaty or covenant exists to acknowledge and declare the universal right to Internet access, its implementation has not become mandatory for states. There are recurring instances of states enforcing restrictions, controlling, and monitoring people's Internet access and activities, causing several insecurities and human rights violations. The Internet shutdown is the most commonly used method to control the right to Internet access. About 300 documented shutdowns occurred in 2024 worldwide, primarily based on national security grounds. From this perspective, it is crucial to examine the importance of the right to Internet access, the problems caused by its violations, and the required changes in international and national governance.

3 CONCEPTUAL FRAMEWORK

Scientific and technological advancements are the creation of innovative human minds. Digitalization is the latest innovative outcome. Each invention is intended to provide some benefit to people and society. Humans make inventions and technological advancements like digitalization for their well-being. This means they should have the universally acknowledged right to lawfully use these digital technologies, such as the Internet, for their flourishing. However, some states restrict and control these rights, claiming that they harm national security and individual security concerns. Accordingly, a complex situation exists between rights and security in digital space (Wu, 2025).

3.1 Digitalization

Global interconnectedness became more profound with the advancement of digitalization. Socioeconomic, cultural, political, and international interactions have become smart by incorporating digital technologies like the Internet, smart devices, social media platforms, AI, machine learning, quantum computing, and blockchain (Siagian et al., 2023). Unlimited connectivity and instant access to information are the hallmarks of digitalization. The UNGA's (2015) declaration of SDGs affirmed the importance of digitalization for enhancing global interconnectedness, spreading information and communication technology, accelerating human progress, bridging the digital divide, and developing knowledge societies. Digitalization can be broadly defined as the changes brought about by the digital technologies and tools in civil, political, social, economic, and cultural fields that include both public and private sectors (Razmetaeva et al., 2023). It has penetrated so deeply into everyday human activities as to transform society into a digital one (Leonardi & Treem, 2020).

Digitization and digitalization are sometimes used interchangeably. In other instances, they refer to two different concerns related to digital technologies. For example, digitization refers to the use of digital technology as a constitutive part of the development process of a new product (Marion & Fixson, 2021). Digitalization refers to data collection, generation, and analysis that enhances innovation (Cappa et al., 2021). These definitions look similar, referring to innovation and developing new products. However, Gradillas and Thomas (2023, pp.113-114) differentiate by providing precise definitions. For them, digitization is "the creation of digital artifacts through technical processes of conversion, representation, and enhancement." On the other hand, digitalization is "the transformation of the socioeconomic environment through processes of digital artifact adoption, application, and utilization." Accordingly, digitization is the foundation upon which digitalization functions. Although the core of these definitions looks similar to that of Leonardi and Treem (2021), it gives a clear perspective on the differentiation between digitalization and digitization. Digitalization aims to transform society's socioeconomic landscape by utilizing digital artifacts. In contrast, digitization focuses on creating new digital artifacts that can be adopted, applied, and used later in digitalization (Gradillas & Thomas, 2023). Digitization is a field of technology and innovation that focuses on transforming analog inputs into digital forms (Leonardi & Treem, 2021). It is a technical process. On the contrary, digitalization points to using digital technologies to transform society, the economy, and other fields. It is a transformative socioeconomic process. However, it is vital to examine whether digitalization, which uses digital technologies for the transformative process, transforms society and other fields. If this process causes human rights violations, it cannot be acclaimed as a transformative tool. The way a technology is used is a significant concern. For instance, wiretapping, as it interferes with privacy, is considered a human rights violation. It becomes more severe if done to peek into the interaction between a lawyer and a criminal suspect. However, it becomes legal if the police wiretap a suspect under a court order (Custers, 2022). Though advantageous in many ways, digitalization can pose significant human rights concerns.

3.2 Human Rights

Human rights are natural rights, which are inherent in every individual based on their very human nature. The theoretical understanding of human rights evolved from the natural law theory. Accordingly, it was initially called natural rights. The UDHR was the decisive moment in the history of human rights. This event in 1948, which took place immediately after the promulgation of the UN Charter, did not create any human rights but only recognized and declared certain human rights as universal, inalienable, and indivisible. Human rights are the basic claims that enhance human interests for a meaningful existence. Human rights are understood within their vertical and horizontal dimensions. Until recently, human rights were primarily understood with their vertical dimension. The vertical dimension underlines that human rights are part of the relationship between citizens and the state. Even if some private parties violate human rights, the state is responsible (Razmetaeva et al., 2023).. In the past, the state was regarded as the main threat to human rights (Uvarova, 2020). However, the horizontal dimension states that the horizon of human rights has a broader leeway. Philosophers, lawyers, and scholars were the masterminds behind the horizontal dimension of human rights. It applies to the human rights violations between individuals or between a consumer and a firm. The advantage of such an application of human rights into the horizontal dimension is that it can easily apply to the digital field, where the differentiation between public and private sectors is quite tricky (Razmetaeva et al., 2023).

Human rights find it challenging to balance the offline and online worlds, as their boundaries have blurred (Razmetaeva et al., 2023). Digitalization poses new challenges and opportunities to human rights. Since access to knowledge and resources becomes easy through digitalization, human rights' global acceptance and popularity will increase. Human rights violations in any part of the globe can be easily addressed by others, as digitalization has increased global interconnectivity. However, Custers (2022) argues that it also poses particular challenges, like a) the question concerning the violations of human rights that arise from the use of new technologies; b) the emergence of conflicting rights; and c) the new challenging issues that emerges from the invention and use of new technologies for which no specific right exists. Access to data is essential for further innovation and economic growth. However, as the first one underlines, it causes challenges to the right to privacy. Spreading of information is an essential component of digital rights. However, if one spreads hatred based on religion, it becomes a conflicting issue between freedom of expression and freedom of religion. An example of the third one is the evolution of the right to Internet access, for which Internet connectivity is essential.

3.3 Internet Connectivity

The invention of the Internet has had a revolutionary effect on the world. It is an effective interactive medium compared to any other medium, like radio and television (La Rue, 2011). The Internet connectivity has made tremendous changes in the world. It increased people's ability to gather and share information, connecting with people beyond borders. The globe has realized the importance of internet connectivity during the COVID-19 pandemic as it provided unpredictable opportunities to work from home, online education, interaction with others, entertainment, and telemedicine support. However, some remote areas of low-income countries still face the unavailability of these facilities due to a lack of Internet connectivity. The digital divide is explicit between developed and developing countries. Underdeveloped countries face severe issues with internet connectivity, affecting their socioeconomic and technological growth. It is estimated that almost 2.2 billion children and young people under 25 do not have Internet access at home (OHCHR, 2023).

The ITU (2024) argues that universal Internet connectivity remains a distant prospect. Based on the current scenario, almost 2.6 billion people (1/3 of the global population) have no Internet connectivity. Compared to the 65% of 2023, 68% of the global population (5.5 billion people) were online in 2024. It further states that the digital divide between high-income (93% of the population) and low-income countries (27% of the population) is enormous. The difference in Internet connectivity percentage also points to disadvantages to economic growth in low-income countries. The UNCTAD (2024) notes that Internet-connected objects are predicted to increase from 13 billion in 2023 to 35 billion in 2028. When a 169.23% increase is expected within five years, there is an urgent need to focus on the scale and magnitude of the data that should be stored, shared, and used. When more data is generated, stored, and analyzed for the increased adoption and use of AI, IoT, and Big Data technologies, the Internet connectivity's capacity and speed become a vital concern. However, the increasingly robust Internet connectivity is often looked at with suspicion by some government authorities, as it is predicted to cause security challenges.

3.4 National Security

The post-Westphalian world is identified with the emergence and growth of nation-states. The territorial integrity and national security concerns became predominant with the widespread development of nation-states. The Hobbesian and Lockean philosophies, the American War of Independence and the French Revolution, and the Independence of many colonies from the imperial powers strengthened the idea of nation and national security. Wu (2025) makes a detailed presentation of the constitutive elements of a nation. However, with globalization, technological advancements, and digitalization, the national territories have blurred, redefining or enlarging the scope of national security. National security refers to the positive interventions of a sovereign state to secure its people, territory, economy, and institutions. Everything that exists within the territories of a state falls under the national security framework. Various factors like monopoly, cyberattacks, hacking, and high-tech disputes have caused new challenges to national security (Wang, 2024). It also requires that national security adapt to address the concerns of the latest digital era (Xiong et al., 2023). Although national security was originally equated with military security, it has broadened its horizons to include environmental, energy, food, economic, and digital security (Wu, 2025).

Globalization, open economy, and the emergence of multinational and transnational companies have modified the conventional understanding of national security. Since people are increasingly interconnected and own properties beyond their territories, the question of national security becomes more complex. The emergence of high-tech, such as the Internet, requires increased cooperation among countries in various fields. However, such a cooperation can pose unimaginable national security challenges. Security of digital space has increasingly become relevant in the present scenario (Wu, 2025). The understanding of national security also evolves along with human progress. Basically, national security intends to protect people and their interests within the territories of a state. But due to the present complex nature of nation-states, national security concerns also increase beyond the strict territorial parameters. Nevertheless, many states harm people's Internet interactions and human rights in the name of national security without any solid grounds.

3.5 Right to Security

The amplified growth of the Internet connectivity and its incorporation in almost all fields of human interaction have raised apprehensions about privacy, freedom of expression, and access to information. The triad of these rights is closely connected to the right to security. Freedom from fear is one of the constitutive elements of human flourishing, as stated by Franklin D. Roosevelt in his famous "four freedoms" speech. It is also one of the cornerstones of the UN Charter (Engel, 2015). People's aspirations for freedom from fear can be achieved only through proper state measures that ensure their security, both territorial and internal. Security leeway is again broadened to include the digital space in the digital era. Several studies have emphatically dealt with people's aspirations for security at the territorial and internal levels (della Sala, 2017; Xi et al., 2022; Stedem, 2025). This chapter, therefore, concentrates on people's right to security in the digital sphere. The right to digital security is mainly connected with the right to digital privacy, although it has broader implications.

4 HUMAN RIGHTS: A DRIVE THROUGH FOUR GENERATIONS

Humans aspire for a minimum standard of living. Human rights are basic universal claims, interests, or entitlements to a minimum decent life (Tasioulas, 2015). The role of states and other actors is to ensure the conditions that help achieve their smooth realization (Reglitz, 2020). Although human rights are core claims of human existence, they took time to evolve into the present shape and prestigious position. Human rights are not static; the changes in society, scientific and technological advancements, progress in educational and healthcare fields, new perspectives on gender equality and human interactions, and an environmentally sustainable approach influence the evolving nature of human rights. Accordingly, there are four generations of human rights. Karel Vasak (1977) was the first to propose three generations of human rights. The first two generations are acknowledged through international covenants. Although the third and fourth generations are not explicitly acknowledged or declared, they are recognized and incorporated in many international and national human rights laws. All human rights recognized as part of these four generations are essential for a decent human life. However, some countries may require focusing more on a few rights than others, depending on practical reasoning and a systematic evaluation of the circumstances through well-conducted empirical studies (Tasioulas, 2017).

4.1 First Generation Rights

The first generation of human rights prefers to ensure a basic decent life in the civil and political fields, which mostly evolved in the 17th and 18th centuries. Since people are the real power-holders of any state, they deserve freedom of speech, the right to vote, and the right to a free trial. Without active engagement in the societal and civil life and political interactions, no citizen can establish a meaningful life. Freedom of speech entails even the capacity to criticize the government. The right to vote affirms that people's choice elects the government. If people do not have a valid claim to elect their government, how can they enjoy a decent life in that society? The right to a free trial demands that the state authorities cannot arbitrarily prosecute and punish citizens. First-generation rights restrict state authorities so that they cannot act in violation of people's fundamental rights. Hence, it is called 'negative' (freedom from) or 'blue' rights, demanding non-interference from the state into people's rightful claims. The ICCPR is the guiding framework of the first generation of human rights.

4.2 Second Generation Rights

The second generation of human rights developed in the 19th and 20th centuries, evolved from the idea that mere 'non-interference' alone will not ensure a minimum decent life. It also requires affirmative actions from the state authorities that ensure fundamental welfare concerns concerning subsistence, physical security, and shelter (Reglitz, 2020). Access to education, healthcare, and social security schemes is the central concern of the second generation of human rights. These rights are also called 'positive' (right to) rights, requiring positive interventions from state authorities. The ICESCR is the international framework that monitors and directs the second generation of rights. Human rights are not equally celebrated across the globe. In some countries, high standards are set, whereas others try to maintain minimal standards depending on their economic and other capacities (Reglitz, 2020). This is particularly true of socioeconomic and cultural rights. For instance, the rights to education, healthcare, workplace security, and social security are met in high standards in developed countries. However, developing countries do not have a strong financial position to ensure such high standards. Accordingly, they satisfy the minimum requirements. From a global justice perspective, the incapacity of several states to ensure a high standard guarantee of human rights is a systemic failure.

4.3 Third Generation Rights

While the first two generations speak about individual rights, the third generation underlines collective rights. It is also called solidarity rights. These rights have evolved from the Stockholm Declaration (1972), the Rio Declaration (1992), and other international declarations. These include the right to self-determination, a healthy environment, development, and natural resources. These are positive and group rights, demanding responsibility beyond national borders. While the first two generations put liability on the State, the third generation calls for international liability (Domaradzki et al., 2019).

4.4 Fourth Generation Rights

Razmetaeva et al. (2023) argue that it is high time to speak about the fourth generation of human rights, as biotechnology and information technologies have changed the global scenario with the possibilities of increased interconnectedness and progressive world vision. With the widespread nature of digitalization, a few rights have already started to exist, such as the right to Internet access, the right to be forgotten, and the right to anonymity. Some authors try to expand the list by including more digital rights (Custers, 2022). The fourth generation of rights is identified with the advancements in the 21st century, often termed the fourth industrial revolution (Baroni, 2024).

5 DIGITAL RIGHTS: A BROADER FRAMEWORK OF GLOBAL RIGHTS

Do rights have any role in the digital world? This question is very relevant when speaking about digital rights. The UN's Special Rapporteur affirms that article 19 of the UDHR and ICCPR was drafted with the foresight that the future technological developments that broaden human interactions should also be included and accommodated as part of their freedom of expression (La Rue, 2011). Digitalization has broadened the scope of human rights. Simultaneously, it also underlines that the conventional methods and established approaches for protecting and promoting human rights may not be suitable in the digital era (Razmetaeva et al., 2022). The UNHRC (2012) emphasizes that separating physical and digital worlds does not apply to human rights. People must be able to enjoy the same human rights, offline and online. The UNHRC (2021) affirms that although the primary responsibility to protect human rights lies with state parties, private actors are also responsible for respecting human rights. Although the prime concern of many actors in the digital human rights discussions revolves around the right to privacy, almost all fundamental rights face some violations with technological developments (Custers, 2022). Discussions on the expected human rights violations range from the violation of the right to a fair trial by the increased use of technology in courtrooms (Dymitruk, 2019), the possible impact of neuro-implants on the right to freedom of thought (McCarthy-Jones, 2019), the interplay between the increased exploitation of data and slavery (Prikowski, 2018), to the imbalance between digitalization and digital divide that adversely affect the right to non-discrimination (Barocas & Selbst, 2016).

5.1 Right to Internet Access

The right to Internet access is a 21st-century evolution. In 2003, UNESCO formally invited all member states and international organizations to recognize people's right to internet access. It insisted on framing appropriate policies that promote "access to the Internet as a service of public interest." The developed world was asked to support developing countries' empowering initiatives for worldwide access to the Internet (UNESCO, 2003). In 2009, the Constitutional Council of France ruled that Internet access is a human right (Sparks, 2009). Finland introduced broadband Internet access as a legal right in 2010, which guaranteed a 1Mbit/s (upgraded to 100Mbit/s in 2015) connection to every citizen (West, 2010). Its digital connectivity speed is set to 5 Mbps from 2021. While the US and the UK have not legally recognized Internet access as a human right, many countries, like Costa Rica, Estonia, and India, have recognized it either through legal enactment or through judicial pronouncements as a human right. Thereafter, various countries have incorporated the right to Internet access as a constitutive part of the freedom of speech and expression or as a separate digital right. However, no international treaty or convention has recognized it as an individual human right. Although the UNHRC (2012) demanded "to promote and facilitate access to the internet," it did not insist on it from a rights perspective. The United Nations High Commissioner for Human Rights states that the globe has reached a point where access to the Internet should be recognized as a human right rather than a privilege (OHCHR, 2023).

Due to the unimaginable progress in digitalization and its influence in all fields of human interaction, Internet access has become an urgent requirement for every human being to maintain a decent life (Reglitz, 2020). Due to the changes in the global scenario, the right to Internet access has become a prerequisite for realizing other human rights. For instance, most companies list their job vacancies on LinkedIn or other social media platforms. Those who do not have adequate internet access will be unable to find such availabilities, which will affect their opportunities. Just think of the e-commerce sector; people without internet access cannot take advantage of the vast possibilities of choosing goods and services. Accordingly, Reglitz (2020) argues that the right to Internet access should be considered a universal human right, as the protection and promotion of other established human rights will become unrealizable without proper Internet access in this digital age. He affirms that the right to Internet access is a *sui generis* right, which is not reducible to any other rights. Internet access is not a version of other rights like free expression, the right to information, or free speech. It is thus a unique and non-substitutable right.

States must prioritize their people's interests over Internet service providers' interests. When the service providers restrict people's access to the Internet for commercial purposes or prefer certain types of software or content for profit, governments should take appropriate action to protect people's rights (UNHRC, 2021). The right to Internet access implies that people should be able to access the Internet without much financial burden, censorship, and other restrictions related to their choices and preferences.

5.2 Right to Digital Privacy

The right to privacy is the most critical concern of many human rights activists and institutions, as various entities can easily collect, store, analyze, and use data for legal and illegal purposes. This necessitates that even when we enjoy the advantages of digitalization, we should be cautious about how it affects our right to privacy (Siagian et al., 2023). The use of digital technologies in any field records and saves the data footprints of the users' personal information and behavior patterns. It can help technical experts identify and observe people's digital lives and interactions. It acts like a constant monitoring that curbs the users' freedom and privacy. The Internet of Things (IoT) developments have drastically transformed this monitoring process. For instance, many people use smart watches, which monitor their health, heart rate, blood pressure, sleep, fitness, stress, contacts, entertainment, and payments. They collect enormous amounts of personal information and control people's daily interactions and behavior patterns. Access to data is essential for more innovations and technological advancements (Chen, 2020). However, accessing and using data should be transparent and follow internationally accepted guidelines and principles to ensure digital privacy. Accessing, using, and sharing personal data are very sensitive and require more restrictive operation. Industrial data comes under proprietary rights and its access and sharing also should follow specific restrictive measures. Meanwhile, public-sector data is mostly non-personal, and its access and sharing will not always result in privacy violations (OECD, 2019).

The UNHRC (2016) upholds the importance of digital privacy for guaranteeing the right to freedom of expression, assembly, and association. The UNHRC (2021) underlines the importance of confidentiality in digital communication and affirms that technical solutions like encryption and anonymity are essential for protecting digital human interactions and enjoying online human rights. Chen (2020) says that from a consumer's point of view, data collection by companies can cause three significant harms: a) critically examining the customer's purchase history, firms can make price discrimination; b) consumers' preference for privacy is adversely affected by the collection of data; and c) the frequent data breaches can cause substantial consumer harm. This applies to all areas of digital interactions.

Almost all discussions of the right to Internet access underscore its importance for ensuring freedom of speech and expression in the digital sphere. However, many instances in social media platforms affirm that some people continuously misuse the freedom of expression to harm the dignity and reputation of others, which is an encroachment on their right to privacy. One's freedom of expression cannot harm the freedom of others. If threatening, insulting, or hateful content is circulated through digital technologies, it curbs the freedom of the targeted persons. The fraudsters utilize the possibilities of anonymity and identity theft to harass and deceive people. The wide circulation of misinformation, violence, and harmful content is also recurrent in the digital space. These inappropriate behaviors cause harm and insecurities to many people and society. The demand for freedom of expression in the cyberworld should balance with its users' responsibility to respect the right to privacy of others (Siagian et al., 2023).

5.3 Right to Digital Security

The primary concern of digital security is related to data protection. The 21st-century globe revolves around data. Public and private actors collect, store, and use individuals' personal information. However, people are less aware of how their data is stored and used. Several instances of data misuse have already been reported worldwide. The misuse of data points to digital insecurities. A strong regulatory framework should address data misuse and ensure people have complete control over their personal information (Siagian et al., 2023). Data protection evolves from an individual's claim for respect from others. Individuals are the supreme power-holders in their private lives, provided they do not harm others (FRA, 2014). When personal data ends up in the hands of mischievous people, it can be used for fraudulent and criminal activities that may cause harm to the data owners. For instance, some cybercriminals morph the hacked images and videos and upload them to pornographic sites, causing reputational harm and mental trauma to the victims. The right to digital security can be achieved only if there is an effective mechanism to confront data breaches and hacking (Siagian et al., 2023).

Digitalization has increased the value of innovation and scientific advancements, increasing the urgency for intellectual property protection. Millions of patents are applied for each year. Protection of intellectual properties in the digital world is essential to encourage further innovation (Chen, 2020). OECD (2019, p.71) states that "a digital security threat can exploit to disrupt the availability, integrity, or confidentiality of the data on which economic and social activities rely." Besides, the users should also feel secure and free to access the Internet without government monitoring and control. Unnecessary restrictions and monitoring make people insecure in the digital space.

5.4 Right to be Offline

The right to be offline evolved in the context of labor laws. Its objective was to protect the freedom of workers to engage in household and other activities after working hours. It started in 2017 in France, where it is called the right to disconnect. It underlines that the employer cannot contact the employee after working hours, either in person, by phone, by social media, or by email (Migliorato, 2017). Thereafter, Italy, Belgium, Luxembourg, Portugal, Spain, and Australia also enacted laws demanding employees' right to be offline (Izabella, 2023). In 2020, the EU employment committee insisted that the member countries, through collective agreements, acknowledge the workers' right to be offline. The chapter does not enter into the discussions of this right's role in fighting against online addiction or other disorders (Blackwell et al., 2017), but affirms that this unique digital right exists in some countries, which helps workers to balance their work and family lives.

5.5 Right to Erasure

Article 17 of the EU General Data Protection Regulation (GDPR) calls for the right to erasure. Although this right resembles the right to be forgotten, its application is only to the digital space. It affirms that the personal data can be erased from the digital world if specific conditions are met. The right to erasure is not an absolute right but a limited one. Data controllers have the freedom to make decisions at the request of the data subjects. This means they do not always need to cooperate with the data subjects' choices (Fazlioglu, 2013). However, some authors broaden the horizon of this right to such an extreme as to claim that people have a right to start with a clean (digital) slate (Custers, 2022). This means they can take up an entirely new digital identity without any traces of the old one. Such a possibility for an entirely different digital identity in the present context may not be difficult to entertain, as it can increase the percentage of cybercrimes.

6 RIGHT TO INTERNET ACCESS VS. NATIONAL SECURITY: AN ANALYSIS

The right to Internet access has often become a complicated question within the context of national security concerns. Undermining national security to ensure the right to Internet access will not be feasible, as human rights can be restricted for a reasonable time to protect the state's genuine interests. The underlying principle is the importance of the security of the wider public. The states should prioritize their security concerns. However, the UNHRC (2016) states that they should perform it under their international human rights obligations to ensure that the Internet remains "global, open, and interoperable." Besides, the UNHRC (2021) urges that states cannot undermine their responsibility to protect national security, territorial integrity, public order, and other vital public interests like healthcare. However, these responsibilities should follow the obligations of international law, the principles of legitimacy, lawfulness, necessity, proportionality, and human rights mandates. It underlines that national security and human rights protection are essential for a meaningful human existence.

The UNHRD (2021) condemns the governmental actions that intentionally and arbitrarily deny people's access to the Internet by using methods like Internet shutdown. It also notes that online censorship prevents people from seeking, receiving, or imparting information on online platforms. Freedom of opinion and expression is a vital human right that enables people to be involved in domestic and international affairs as responsible citizens. These opinions may not always favor governmental policies and programs. Nonetheless, they express people's will. It gives a chance for the authorities to become more responsible in their governance, as democracy calls for accountability to the public. Any governmental attempt to restrict and control people's access to the Internet should be made under the provisions of international human rights law. This does not mean a state cannot limit people's digital rights, especially Internet access. Except concerning absolute fundamental rights (rights which cannot be lawfully interfered with), states can make reasonable restrictions on other rights depending on the circumstances (Custers, 2022). However, the policies, programs, and domestic laws that make changes should align with the demands of international human rights law.

Conventionally, security is understood as a public good that the state should provide to its citizens (Stokes, 2009). However, security is a convoluted eroteme in many states. Many developing states are incapable or unwilling to ensure security and protection to their citizens in the real sense of the term. Many governments pretend to provide security. However, they target their political opponents and critics in the name of national security. Sometimes, they remain weak institutions, and at other times, they become perpetrators of violence (Stedem, 2025). This is more explicit in the digital space. State leaders are aware that the opinions, criticisms, and exposés of bribery and corruption in online portals can trouble their political interests. If those things are left unnoticed, they can become a decisive move against the government's policies and programs, as happened in Sri Lanka and Bangladesh. These examples affirm that those protests against the government were not due to a mere social media campaign but to an utter failure in the administration. The leaders were unwilling to correct administrative failures and promote people-centered development and policies. Instead, they aimed to subjugate people's corrective voice. Protesting against a corrupt government is misconceived chiefly as a security threat to the state. Corruption, lack of accountability and transparency, discrimination, favoritism, and injustice are the primary internal threats to national security. When people protest against such threats, the government, using the police and other security forces, targets the genuine power-holders. To control their protestors, most governments use their power to restrict Internet access. If Internet access is denied to people, they cannot share information and come together as a group.

6.1 Importance of the Right to Internet Access

The universal availability and accessibility of the Internet are essential for ensuring development in various fields (UNHRC, 2012). Internet access enhances the exercise and functioning of other human rights. The scope of freedom of speech and association has grown beyond limits. It gives people rapid and widespread opportunities for political engagement, even to change the decisions of national governments and international institutions. Most contemporary political debates and national and international interactions occur digitally. Besides affecting the efficiency of many socioeconomic, civil, and political freedoms and rights, a lack of internet access also adversely affects one's opportunities to engage in those fields actively. The Internet has also reduced the cost of accessing, generating, and sharing information, besides increasing the capacity for connectivity with the rest of the globe. If some other human rights are violated, Internet access can provide the possibility to place the stories of the victims before the global conscience. For instance, the movement #MeToo has raised irreplaceable concern and support for the genuine victims (even if there are instances of some misuses) in digital space, even forcing the authorities to take appropriate legal action against the offenders (Reglitz, 2020).

Along with the right to Internet access, we should also consider the importance of data access. It is crucial for research, innovation, technological growth, business interactions, service enhancement, and increased efficiency (OECD, 2019). Providing access to the data is not always considered illegal and unethical. It is also essential for societal growth and human well-being. The important consideration is related to the use and misuse of data. If the accessed and shared data is used for a good purpose, it does not become illegal. The world has become increasingly digital, incorporating AI and IoT in several fields. They require vast amounts of data, which they cannot generate themselves. Data sharing will thus be needed to enhance the capacity and functioning of these technologies. For instance, a self-driving car can generate 1-5TB of data/hour. However, it requires more third-party data to operate securely regardless of the weather conditions, road-surface quality, and visibility (Grzywaczewski, 2017; OECD, 2019).

Since the globe has become extremely digital, access to the Internet has become a vital concern. Many educational institutions have given strict guidelines that they process applications for various courses only through an online portal. Companies and institutions have already started to post employment opportunities on digital platforms and conduct online interviews. Many things available online for a cheaper price will be costly offline. Many countries, international and national institutions, and private actors have already moved to the digital world and people need Internet access to take advantage of those services (Custers, 2022). The problem with a lack of internet access is that it will curb the possibilities and opportunities of many. Those with broadband Internet connectivity and access to Internet services get the maximum benefits. In contrast, even if some are more eligible than others, they may not get the desired admission or job if they do not have proper internet access. Internet access is essential to address the digital divide between regions, countries, sexes, and age groups (Warschauer, 2004).

6.2 Challenges to the Right to Internet Access

The UNHRC (2016) affirmed the significance of a fundamental right to Internet access, but it had no binding nature. Besides, it was focused only on addressing and condemning some governments' intentional disruption of Internet access. The right to Internet access should become a binding part of international human rights law. Without such a strict mandate, many national governments will not prioritize establishing nationwide broadband connectivity, increasing people's Internet access. A lack of internet access in any region points to its disconnection from the rest of the world. Unwillingness and a lack of efficient policies are the main drawbacks to realizing the right to Internet access.

Net neutrality is crucial in the discussions on the right to Internet access. Many Internet service providers in some countries prioritize some customers over others concerning the speed and strength of data. It is about the option of a layered Internet. Those who pay more or use the most advanced equipment get faster and higher-quality access and service. This gives some users an advantage over others, which can be used for several benefits in educational, employment, and economic fields. This complexity can be addressed through net neutrality, which revolves around the principle that the Internet providers should treat all their customers equally without discrimination or preference concerning the speed, content, and strength of data (Wu, 2003). Countries like Brazil, Chile, India, Canada, the Netherlands, and Slovenia uphold the principle of net neutrality. However, it is not universally acknowledged and in many countries, people face discrimination and a digital divide concerning Internet access.

The right to Internet access is constantly faced with challenges concerning its financial aspect. For instance, upgrading each new generation of Internet connectivity causes a financial burden on the service providers and users. The transition from

2G to 3G, 3G to 4G, and 4G to 5G affirms the speed and capacity of connectivity and data transfer efficiency. It causes more investment from the service providers, which they collect from the users. Along with this transition, people also need to upgrade their systems. For instance, the 5G SIM requires a smartphone that supports a 5G network. A person with a 2G/3G/4G supporting smartphone cannot use the 5G network. Automatically, they will be forced to buy a new smartphone. This imbalances their financial budget. Thus, some prefer to be satisfied with their old phones and slow connectivity, which results in digital polarization, social segregation, and manipulation (Custers, 2022).

The right to Internet access becomes difficult to achieve due to many obstacles. Firstly, monopolisation, if a particular service provider monopolizes the sector, it becomes too expensive due to a lack of competition. Secondly, less involvement of the public sector, in many countries, the private sector controls the Internet service without the active engagement of the government. Thirdly, a lack of digital literacy and basic computer skills causes many people not to access the Internet. Fourthly, the difference between genders concerning digital literacy is very explicit. The digital divide affects women's online interactions and involvement in digital technologies (Reglitz, 2020).

6.3 Right to Internet Access vs. National Security Concerns

What should be the prioritization of a state: human rights protection or national security concerns? It is a topic of heated discussion and debate. Some people say that human rights protection will be unimaginable without national security. Others claim that nations are constituted to protect and promote human rights; hence, it should be the ultimate objective. This chapter does not entertain this debate. Instead, it argues that human rights and national security are essential for people's well-being and societal welfare. Neglecting national security to promote human rights will not be justifiable, just like denying human rights in the name of national security. Since the state is the primary guardian and promoter of human rights, it should uphold its negative and positive duties concerning human rights. If certain restrictions are to be implemented, they should be based on international human rights law principles and for the larger common good. A restrictive conception of national security will not provide justice to the human rights law. The areas of concern of national security should be designed appropriately. For instance, a dissent of opinion against the government does not threaten national security. Lobbying against the government's policies on digital platforms also will not amount to a national security threat. However, the circulation of terrorist ideas, drug trafficking, human trafficking, religious fundamentalism and hatred against other religions, and challenges to national unity and territorial integrity are concerns of national security. The restrictions on individuals' freedom to express themselves online, as their opinions are against government policies, violate human rights (La Rue, 2011). The defence of national security cannot be applied here.

How far can a state interfere in its citizens' digital private lives in the name of national security? On many occasions, the governmental activities to ensure security (or to protect the governing party's interests?) confront the citizens' right to privacy (Stalla-Bourdillon et al., 2014). Technological advancements like wiretapping, forensic DNA research, surveillance cameras, unmanned aerial vehicles and drones, and biometric IDs can enhance security concerns. However, they also raise serious privacy concerns. Sometimes, governments use blocking and filtering technologies to control and monitor citizens' Internet activities. They also do not guarantee the right to privacy and data protection. In such cases, people will not have the freedom to access the Internet. It is an indirect way of controlling their online life (La Rue, 2011). Denying, preventing, restricting, and monitoring Internet access on national security grounds should be justifiable. It should be according to the provisions of law. In many countries, this is done under an executive order. The executive's bias, prejudice, and political interests alone cannot be the decisive elements of national security. Clear demarcation of areas, which can lead to a temporary suspension of the Internet, is essential to justify Internet access restrictions on national security grounds.

6.4 Politicization of the Right to Internet Access

The UNHRC (2016) notes that some countries have taken measures that intentionally disrupt or prevent access to online information. When people are denied exercising their fundamental freedoms and human rights on the Internet, these amount to violations and abuses. It states that many have performed "torture, extrajudicial killings, enforced disappearances and arbitrary detention, expulsion, intimidation and harassment, as well as gender based violence" against those who have exercised their fundamental freedoms and rights on the Internet. Suppose people are punished for exercising their internationally acknowledged fundamental rights and freedoms. In that case, it shows that the states do not recognize those rights and people performed them against the political will. The UN underlines that states have the responsibility to provide 'unrestricted,' 'uncensored,' and 'unmonitored' access to the Internet. Censorship, monitoring, and undue restrictions on people's Internet access limit their possibilities and opportunities. The globe has often witnessed several instances where states control, manipulate, restrict, and censor Internet access and shared content without any legal basis or based on some ambiguous laws (La Rue, 2011). These are against the mandate of international human rights law for the mere satisfaction of their biased political motives and interests.

7 CASE STUDIES

This section examines some examples of the violations of the right to Internet access on national security grounds. The globe experienced almost 296 documented shutdowns in 54 countries in 2024, affirming that it is widespread. India ranks first among the democratic countries with 84 shutdowns (Deep, 2025). The following states are selected, ranking in the top three in the number of Internet shutdowns in 2024. Democratically elected governments rule the first two, whereas the third is under military governance.

7.1 India

01 July 2015 is a historic day in the history of Indian polity as the central government launched its flagship program 'Digital India' to transform the country into a sustainable economy and knowledge society. However, Internet shutdowns, monitoring, and unlawful restrictions show that the country is not progressing at the same pace as global progress. Surprisingly, India records just one behind the military-ruled Myanmar concerning the number of Internet shutdowns in 2024. The state of Manipur topped the list with 21 shutdowns. 41 shutdowns were to address protests and 23 were related to communal violence. Even to curb cheating in examinations, States like Jharkhand, Assam, and Rajasthan imposed shutdowns (Deep, 2025). The Internet shutdown in Jammu & Kashmir is the longest in global history, lasting 552 days. When the government shuts down Internet access on national security grounds to address protests against the government, it contradicts the prime minister's 2015 assurance: "Digital connectivity should become as much a basic right as access to school" (Human Rights Watch, 2023).

7.2 Pakistan

Pakistan ranks second in the list of democratic countries with 21 shutdowns in 2024 (Deep, 2025). Pakistan has a long history of censoring and restricting Internet access on political and religious grounds. Like other countries, it often refers to national security for denying Internet access. Reducing users' bandwidth, blocking applications or websites, and shutting down the Internet services entirely for a specific time, Pakistan intentionally disrupts people's Internet access, causing the economy to lose about US$892 million to US$1.6 billion. Besides, the governmental restrictions on WhatsApp and X social media platforms completely isolated the Pakistani people from the rest of the globe, causing many human rights violations (Long, 2025).

7.3 Myanmar

Myanmar is the leading global actor with the highest Internet shutdowns (85) in 2024 (Deep, 2025). Out of the 85 shutdowns, 76 are forced by the Junta, 2 by the Chinese government, 4 by the Thai government, and the remaining three by the rebel administrators and unknown actors. This is for the fourth consecutive year that the Myanmar Junta is forcing the country to lead the global list of Internet shutdowns. The military authorities claim that they forced Internet shutdowns to prevent fake news and to ensure stability in the country. The fierce protest of many movements against the Junta is primarily addressed through Internet shutdowns, denying people's right to share information, connect with others, and form associations of dissent. It shows the Junta's apparent disregard for the international human rights standards and the intention to disempower people (Walker & Janjevic, 2025).

8 POLICY PERSPECTIVES

The Internet has become an indispensable part of human life. No society can progress without the active use of the Internet. Sincere cooperation between international institutions, local self-governments, the public sector, and private individuals is required to make the Internet available, accessible, and affordable to the global population (La Rue, 2011). Such a cooperative action involves funding for the broadband projects of low-income countries (Regliz, 2020).

Public and private sectors must prioritize protecting people's data, privacy, and security in the digital world. Since it costs a lot, it reduces their willingness to serve and protect consumers' interests. For instance, immediately after the GDPR was enacted, more than 1000 US websites blocked their European customers as they could not afford the stringent guidelines of the GDPR. At the same time, there are differences between countries concerning the policies of Internet connectivity, data usage, data protection, digital privacy, and digital security. Both excessive protection and insufficient protection will harm the sector. Global society needs an internationally agreed-upon and accepted set of guidelines and protocols to ensure data protection and the users' other digital rights (Chen, 2020).

Article 21.1 of the UDHR affirms everyone's right to participate in their country's governance, either directly or through chosen representatives. It shows they also have a significant role in decision-making and rule-making. However, in the present scenario, people's lives are influenced not only by states but also by international institutions like the UN, World Bank, IMF, and WTO. Their decisions and policies also have positive and negative repercussions on people's lives. Nevertheless, they can function even without being accountable to people, as they are not democratically constituted. Conventional methods of protest, like rallies and strikes, do not have any global relevance. They will have meaning only in the local context. However, if people have Internet access, they can express their opinions and dissent on digital platforms and social media handles, increasing the reach of their opinions to make a decisive choice. The same can be applied to multinational and transnational corporations. Since they monopolize many sectors in several countries, an increased possibility of confronting their human rights violations is essential. Besides, the national governments' accountability and transparency can be strengthened with the availability of Internet access (Reglitz, 2020). For instance, Beatriz Ehlers from Rio de Janeiro started an online campaign against the city government's decision to demolish their school for the 2016 Rio Summer Olympics. Due to massive public support, they had to reverse the decision within 72 hours of the campaign's launch (Heimans & Timms, 2018). Accordingly, national and international actors should find means to ensure the universal acceptance of the right to Internet access and its implementation.

9 CONCLUSIONS

The Internet has become a decisive tool for human well-being. Internet access implies human flourishing, economic progress, sustainable development, and societal welfare. Human Rights Watch (2023) rightly states, "No Internet means no work, no pay, no food." In the present scenario, a lack of Internet access refers to forced isolation from the rest of the world, as one cannot generate, receive, and share information and connect with others. Internet shutdown adversely affects human interactions, the economy, political engagement, and global interconnectivity. It also points to denying the core fundamental rights, such as the right to work, livelihood, education, healthcare, environment, privacy, equality, and non-discrimination. The state authorities mostly control, restrict, and monitor the right to Internet access based on national security grounds. As the Indian Foreign Minister, S. Jaishankar, said in 2022, many governmental authorities argue that protecting human lives or national security is more valuable than the right to Internet access. However, authorities forget that denying the right to Internet access adversely affects human well-being in all fields. If the restrictions are not reasonable, lawful, and according to human rights law standards, they violate people's aspiration for a sustainable future.

REFERENCES

Barocas, S., & Selbst, A. D. (2016). Big Data's Disparate Impact. *California Law Review*, *104*, 671–732. https://courts.ca.gov/sites/default/files/courts/default/2024-12/btb24-21-2.pdf

Baroni, M. J. L. (2024). Fourth Generation Human Rights in View of the Fourth Industrial Revolution. *Philosophies*, 9(2), 39. https://www.mdpi.com/2409-9287/9/2/39

Blackwell, D., Leaman, C., Tramposch, R., Osborne, C., & Liss, M. (2017). Extraversion, Neuroticism, Attachment Style, and Fear of Missing Out as Predictors of Social Media Use and Addiction. *Personality and Individual Differences*, *116*, 69–72. DOI: 10.1016/j.paid.2017.04.039

Cappa, F., Oriani, R., Peruffo, E., & McCarthy, I. (2021). Big Data for Creating and Capturing Value in the Digitalized Environment: Unpacking the Effects of Volume, Variety, and Veracity on Firm Performance. *Journal of Product Innovation Management*, *38*(1), 49–67. https://onlinelibrary.wiley.com/doi/10.1111/jpim.12545. DOI: 10.1111/jpim.12545

Chen, Y. (2020). Improving Market Performance in the Digital Economy. *China Economic Review*, *62*, 101482. DOI: 10.1016/j.chieco.2020.101482 PMID: 38620214

Custers, M. (2022). New Digital Rights: Imagining Additional Fundamental Rights for the Digital Era. *Computer Law & Security Review*, *44*, 105636. DOI: 10.1016/j.clsr.2021.105636

Deep, A. (2025). Number of Internet Shutdowns Highest in 2024 Globally, India Tops In Govt-Ordered Curbs. *The Hindu*. https://www.thehindu.com/sci-tech/technology/internet/number-of-internet-shutdowns-highest-in-2024-globally-india-tops-in-govt-ordered-curbs/article69257573.ece

della Sala, V. (2017). Homeland Security: Territorial Myths and Ontological Security in the European Union. *Journal of European Integration*, *39*(5), 545–558. DOI: 10.1080/07036337.2017.1327528

Domaradzki, S., Khvostova, M., & Pupovac, D. (2019). Karel Vasak's Generations of Rights and the Contemporary Human Rights Discourse. *Human Rights Review (Piscataway, N.J.)*, *20*(4), 423–443. https://link.springer.com/article/10.1007/s12142-019-00565-x. DOI: 10.1007/s12142-019-00565-x

Dymitruk, M. (2019). The Right to a Fair Trial in Automated Civil Proceedings. *Masaryk University Journal of Law and Technology*, 13(1), 27-44. https://journals.muni.cz/mujlt/article/view/11624

Engel, J. A. (2015). The Scene, the Phrase, and the Debate. In Engel, J. A. (Ed.), *The Four Freedoms: Franklin D. Roosevelt and the Evolution of an American Idea* (pp. 17–35). Academic. DOI: 10.1093/acprof:oso/9780199376216.003.0002

Fazlioglu, M. (2013). Forget me not: The Clash of the Right to be Forgotten and Freedom of Expression on the Internet. *International Data Privacy Law*, *3*(3), 149–157. DOI: 10.1093/idpl/ipt010

FRA. (European Union Fundamental Rights Agency). (2014). *Handbook of European Data Protection Law*. Council of Europe.

Gradillas, M., & Thomas, L. D. W. (2023). Distinguishing Digitization and Digitalization: A Systematic Review and Conceptual Framework. *Journal of Product Innovation Management*, *42*(1), 112–143. https://onlinelibrary.wiley.com/doi/10.1111/jpim.12690. DOI: 10.1111/jpim.12690

Grzywaczewski, A. (2017). Training AI for Self-Driving Vehicles: The Challenge of Scale. *Nvidia Developer*. https://developer.nvidia.com/blog/training-self-driving-vehicles-challenge-scale/

Heimans, J., & Timms, H. (2018). *New Power: How It's Changing the 21st Century — and Why You Need to Know*. MacMillan.

Human Rights Watch. (2023). "No Internet Means No Work, No Pay, No Food." https://www.hrw.org/report/2023/06/14/no-internet-means-no-work-no-pay-no-food/internet-shutdowns-deny-access-basic

ITU. (International Telecommunication Union). (2024). Internet Use: Facts and Figures 2024. https://www.itu.int/itu-d/reports/statistics/2024/11/10/ff24-internet-use/#:~:text=In%202024%20fully%205.5%20billion,cent%20just%20one%20year%20earlier

Izabella, B.-S. (2023). The Right to Disconnect. *Journal of Public Administration, Finance, and Law*, *29*, 88–96. https://www.jopafl.com/uploads/issue29/THE_RIGHT_TO_DISCONNECT.pdf. DOI: 10.47743/jopafl-2023-29-08

La Rue, F. (2011). Report of the Special Rapporteur on the Promotion and Protection of the Right to Freedom of Opinion and Expression. *UNHRC, A/HRC/17/27*. https://www.refworld.org/reference/countryrep/unhrc/2011/en/90245

Leonardi, P. M., & Treem, J. W. (2020). Behavioral Visibility: A New Paradigm for Organization Studies in the Age of Digitization, Digitalization, and Datafication. *Organization Studies, 41*(12), 1601–1625. https://journals.sagepub.com/doi/epub/10.1177/0170840620970728. DOI: 10.1177/0170840620970728

Long, T. (2025). Disconnected Progress: The Hidden Price of Internet Restrictions in Pakistan. *ITIF.* https://itif.org/publications/2025/01/16/disconnected-progress-the-hidden-price-of-internet-restrictions-in-pakistan/

Marion, T. J., & Fixson, S. K. (2021). The Transformation of the Innovation Process: How Digital Tools are Changing Work, Collaboration, and Organizations in New Product Development. *Journal of Product Innovation Management, 38*(1), 192–215. https://onlinelibrary.wiley.com/doi/epdf/10.1111/jpim.12547. DOI: 10.1111/jpim.12547

McCarthy-Jones, S. (2019). The Autonomous Mind: The Right to Freedom of Thought in the Twenty-First Century. *Frontiers in Artificial Intelligence, 2*(19), 19. https://www.frontiersin.org/journals/artificial-intelligence/articles/10.3389/frai.2019.00019/full. DOI: 10.3389/frai.2019.00019 PMID: 33733108

OECD. (2019). *Enhancing Access to and Sharing of Data: Reconciling Risks and Benefits for Data Re-use Across Societies.* https://www.oecd.org/en/publications/enhancing-access-to-and-sharing-of-data_276aaca8-en.html

OHCHR. (2023). It may be time to reinforce universal access to the Internet as a human right, not just a privilege, as the High Commissioner tells the Human Rights Council. https://www.ohchr.org/en/meeting-summaries/2023/03/it-may-be-time-reinforce-universal-access-internet-human-right-not-just

Razmetaeva, Y., Barabash, Y., & Lukianov, D. (2022). The Concept of Human Rights in the Digital Era: Changes and Consequences for Judicial Practice. *Access to Justice in Eastern Europe*, 15(3), 41-56. https://ajee-journal.com/upload/attaches/att_1660480856.pdf

Reglitz, M. (2020). The Human Right to Free Internet Access. *Journal of Applied Philosophy, 37*(2), 314–331. https://onlinelibrary.wiley.com/doi/10.1111/japp.12395. DOI: 10.1111/japp.12395

Siagian, R., Siahaan, L., & Hamzah, M. I. (2023). Human Rights in the Digital Era: Online Privacy, Freedom of Speech, and Personal Data Protection. *Journal of Digital Learning and Distance Education, 2*(1), 548–558. https://rjupublisher.com/ojs/index.php/JDLDE/article/view/149. DOI: 10.56778/jdlde.v2i4.149

Sparks, I. (2009). Internet Access is a Fundamental Human Right, Rules French Court. Media Online. https://www.dailymail.co.uk/news/article-1192359/Internet-access-fundamental-human-right-rules-French-court.html, Stalla-Bourdillon, S., Phillips, J., & Ryan, M.D. (2014). *Privacy vs Security*. Springer.

Stedem, K. (2025). Policing for Patrons: Clientalism & Lebanon's Internal Security Forces. *British Journal of Middle Eastern Studies*. https://www.tandfonline.com/doi/epdf/10.1080/13530194.2025.2510212?needAccess=true

Stokes, S. C. (2009). Political Clientelism. In Boix, C., & Stokes, S. C. (Eds.), *The Oxford Handbook of Comparative Politics* (pp. 604–627). Academic., https://academic.oup.com/edited-volume/28345/chapter-abstract/215179026?redirectedFrom=fulltext DOI: 10.1093/oxfordhb/9780199566020.003.0025

Tasioulas, J. (2015). On the Foundations of Human Rights. In Cruft, R., Liao, M., & Renzo, M. (Eds.), *Philosophical Foundations of Human Rights* (pp. 45–70). Oxford University Press., https://www.uvic.ca/victoria-colloquium/assets/docs/kbrownlee/tasioulas---on-the-foundations-of-human-rights.pdf DOI: 10.1093/acprof:oso/9780199688623.003.0002

Tasioulas, J. (2017). Existing the Hall of Mirrors: Morality and Law in Human Rights. In T. Campbell & K. Bourne (Eds.), *Political and Legal Approaches to Human Rights* (pp. 73-89). Routledge. https://papers.ssrn.com/sol3/papers.cfm?abstract_id=2915307

UNCTAD. (2024). *Digital Economy Report 2024: Shaping an Environmentally Sustainable and Inclusive Digital Future*. https://unctad.org/system/files/official-document/der2024_en.pdf

UNESCO. (2003). Recommendation Concerning the Promotion and Use of Multilingualism and Universal Access to Cyberspace. https://www.unesco.org/en/legal-affairs/recommendation-concerning-promotion-and-use-multilingualism-and-universal-access-cyberspace

UNGA. (2015). Resolution Adopted by the General Assembly on 25 September 2015. *A/RES/70/1*. https://www.un.org/en/development/desa/population/migration/generalassembly/docs/globalcompact/A_RES_70_1_E.pdf

UNHRC. (2012). The Promotion, Protection, and Enjoyment of Human Rights on the Internet. *A/HRC/RES/20/8*. https://digitallibrary.un.org/record/731540?v=pdf

UNHRC. (2016). The Promotion, Protection, and Enjoyment of Human Rights on the Internet. *A/HRC/32/L.20*. https://digitallibrary.un.org/record/845728?ln=en&v=pdf

UNHRC. (2021). The Promotion, Protection, and Enjoyment of Human Rights on the Internet. *A/HRC/RES/47/16*. https://digitallibrary.un.org/record/3937534?ln=en&v=pdf

Uvarova, O. (2020). Business and Human Rights in Times of Global Emergencies: Comparative Perspective. *Comparative Law Review*, 26, 225-253. https://apcz.umk.pl/CLR/article/view/CLR.2020.009

Walker, T., & Janjevic, D. (2025). Myanmar: Why is Junta Shutting Down Internet? https://www.dw.com/en/myanmar-why-is-junta-shutting-down-internet/a-71770580

Wang, W. (2024). Global Technological Competition Enters High-Tech Cold War Era. *Bulletin of Chinese Academy of Science*, *39*(1), 112–120. https://bulletinofcas.researchcommons.org/journal/vol39/iss1/13/. DOI: 10.1360/TB-2023-0363

Warschauer, M. (2004). *Technology and Social Inclusion: Rethinking the Digital Divide*. MIT Press.

West, D. M. (2010). *An International Look at High-Speed Broadband*. The Brookings Institution.

Wu, C. (2025). Redefining Concepts of Nation and National Security and Establishing their Models for the New Era. *Journal of Safety and Sustainability*, *2*(1), 45–58. DOI: 10.1016/j.jsasus.2024.12.002

Wu, T. (2003). Network Neutrality, Broadband Discrimination. *Journal on Telecommunications & High Technology Law*, *2*, 141–176. https://scholarship.law.columbia.edu/faculty_scholarship/1281/

Xi, G., Feng, Z., & Qian, X. (2022). Territory Spatial Security and Planning Strategies from the Perspective of Mobility. *Ziran Ziyuan Xuebao*, *37*(8), 1935–1945. https://www.jnr.ac.cn/EN/abstract/article/1000-3037/52184#1. DOI: 10.31497/zrzyxb.20220801

Xiong, S., Lu, W., Liu, D., Li, X., & Zhao, C. (2023). Research Progress and Application of Emergency Plans in China: A Review. *Emergency Management Science and Technology*, 3, 3. https://www.maxapress.com/article/doi/10.48130/EMST-2023-0003

Chapter 15
Technocracy:
The Rule of Expertise in a Modern World

Sharif Uddin Ahmed Rana
https://orcid.org/0000-0003-2296-6044
Paris Graduate School, France

David Cheok
https://orcid.org/0000-0001-6316-2339
Imaginary Institute, Australia

ABSTRACT

Technocracy—governance by technical experts—has emerged as a response to today's complex challenges, including climate change, rapid technological shifts, and social inequality. Rooted in the belief that expert knowledge can lead to more effective policy decisions, technocratic systems prioritize data, evidence, and efficiency over political ideology. Case studies show that such systems can deliver strong results, especially in areas like public health and environmental policy. However, technocracy faces criticism for being elitist, disconnected from public needs, and lacking transparency. To create a balanced model, it's essential to integrate ethical values, enhance accountability, and foster meaningful public participation. A reimagined technocracy must not only rely on experts but also engage citizens in decision-making. By blending technical expertise with democratic ideals, societies can work toward more inclusive, sustainable, and effective governance.

DOI: 10.4018/979-8-3693-3920-6.ch015

INTRODUCTION: UNDERSTANDING THE ESSENCE OF TECHNOCRACY

Technocracy is a form of governance that emphasizes the central role of technical expertise in the formulation and execution of public policy. Rather than being governed by politicians elected based on popularity or partisanship, technocracies empower individuals with specialized knowledge in fields such as science, engineering, economics, and health. The word "technocracy" comes from the Greek words tekhnē (skill or art) and kratos (power or rule), indicating a structure where knowledge and competence drive authority. (encyclopedia, n.d.)

The resurgence of interest in technocracy reflects growing concerns about the efficacy of traditional democratic mechanisms in dealing with complex, interlinked crises such as global climate change, economic turbulence, and health emergencies. Technocrats, proponents argue, are better equipped to navigate the nuances of such challenges through evidence-based, data-driven decision-making.

KEY PRINCIPLES OF TECHNOCRACY

Technocracy, while varying in application, generally adheres to several core principles:

Evidence-Based Decision-Making: Policies and programs are formulated using empirical research, data analytics, and scientific reasoning. This approach minimizes bias, reduces susceptibility to lobbying, and promotes rationality in public governance.

Depoliticized Governance: One of technocracy's defining features is its insulation from electoral politics. Independent bodies like the European Central Bank or expert panels within the World Health Organization operate autonomously from government changes, allowing them to focus on long-term solutions without succumbing to short-term political pressures.

Efficiency and Long-Term Planning: Technocracies prioritize long-term stability and resource efficiency. Unlike democratically elected governments that may focus on winning the next election, technocratic administrations plan for decades ahead, often using sophisticated modeling and forecasting tools.

HISTORICAL EVOLUTION AND INTELLECTUAL ORIGINS

Technocratic ideals have deep philosophical and historical roots, tracing back to ancient and Enlightenment thinkers, as well as modern movements.

1. Classical and Enlightenment Philosophies

Plato's Philosopher-Kings: In his seminal work The Republic, Plato proposed that society should be governed by "philosopher-kings"—individuals who possessed both wisdom and knowledge. This early vision of rule by the wise laid the ideological groundwork for later technocratic principles.

Francis Bacon and the New Atlantis: Bacon's utopian narrative, New Atlantis (1627), imagined a society led by scientists who used empirical knowledge to improve societal well-being. He viewed science not merely as a method of understanding the world but as a tool for governance.

Saint-Simon and Comte: Henri de Saint-Simon advocated for a "Council of Newton," where scientists and engineers would replace aristocrats and politicians. Auguste Comte, a father of sociology, echoed these sentiments by arguing for social organization based on positivist science.

2. The 20th Century Technocracy Movement

Frederick Winslow Taylor: Known for developing Scientific Management in the early 20th century, Taylor emphasized the use of systematic observation and measurement in improving labor productivity. His principles were later applied to governance.

Howard Scott and Technocracy Inc.: In the 1930s, Scott and his contemporaries argued for replacing the price-based economy with one based on energy usage, measured in joules or ergs. Technocracy Inc. envisioned a society managed by engineers who could allocate resources based on physical laws.

TECHNOCRACY IN PRACTICE: GLOBAL AND INSTITUTIONAL EXAMPLES

Although pure technocracy remains rare, many modern institutions and governments incorporate technocratic elements to varying degrees.

1. Singapore: The Model Technocracy

Singapore is often hailed as a paragon of technocratic governance. Key policy areas such as urban planning, housing, transportation, and healthcare are managed through rigorous data collection and analysis. The government frequently consults experts and recruits top university graduates into civil service, creating a meritocratic ecosystem that aligns with technocratic ideals.

2. The European Union and the European Central Bank (ECB)

The EU integrates technocratic governance through institutions like the ECB, which operates independently of member state governments. While this depoliticized structure allows for more stable economic policy, it has also been criticized for lacking democratic accountability, particularly during the Eurozone crisis when austerity measures were imposed without direct public consent.

3. Public Health Agencies: Technocracy Under Fire During COVID-19

Public health governance during the COVID-19 pandemic revealed both the strengths and weaknesses of technocratic systems. Agencies like the CDC and WHO employed scientific data to formulate guidelines and containment strategies. However, criticism arose over the opacity of their decision-making, shifting recommendations, and the apparent lack of public engagement—factors that fueled public skepticism.

CHALLENGES AND CRITICISMS OF TECHNOCRACY

Despite its promises of efficiency and rationality, technocracy is not without significant critiques and practical limitations.

1. Democratic Deficit

The most prominent critique of technocracy is its potential erosion of democratic principles. When power is concentrated in the hands of unelected experts, questions arise about legitimacy and accountability. For example, EU citizens had little say in the appointment of officials who dictated strict fiscal rules and austerity programs.

2. Over-Reliance on Data and Quantification

While data-driven governance minimizes subjectivity, it may also overlook humanistic, cultural, and ethical dimensions. Algorithms and models can perpetuate biases or fail to consider marginalized communities. Furthermore, technical expertise does not equate to moral wisdom, and technocratic solutions may sometimes conflict with public values or justice.

3. Populist Resistance and Public Distrust

Populist movements across the globe—from Brexit to the Occupy Wall Street protests—have emerged partly in response to the perceived elitism of technocratic institutions. These movements argue that experts often prioritize abstract metrics over everyday concerns, leaving ordinary citizens feeling alienated and disempowered. (Boston Review, n.d.)

REIMAGINING TECHNOCRACY: TOWARD A DEMOCRATIC-EXPERTISE HYBRID

Given these challenges, scholars and policymakers are exploring models that harmonize technical expertise with democratic engagement.

1. Hybrid Governance Models

Citizen Assemblies: In Ireland, citizen assemblies composed of randomly selected citizens work alongside experts to develop climate policy. This model merges grassroots legitimacy with scientific rigor.

Deliberative Polling: This method gathers a representative sample of citizens, provides them with balanced information, and facilitates structured discussions. The goal is to produce informed public opinion that can guide policy decisions.

2. Transparency and Public Accountability

For technocracy to maintain public trust, its processes must be transparent. This includes:

- Publishing data sources and methodologies
- Making expert deliberations open to public scrutiny
- Engaging with media to explain policies

3. Technocracy and the Legal Framework

The legal dimensions of technocratic governance are increasingly significant. In "Technocracy and the Law" (Arcuri & Coman-Kund, 2021), the authors argue that governance by experts must be bound by legal norms to ensure accountability and prevent technocratic overreach. Legal mechanisms can function as a check-and-balance system for expert authority.

4. Inclusive Technocracy

Diverse representation within technocratic bodies is crucial. Expertise must not only be scientific but also incorporate indigenous knowledge, social work, and ethics. Multidisciplinary panels can enrich problem-solving approaches and prevent narrow, technocentric worldviews.

TECHNOCRACY IN THE AGE OF AI AND GLOBAL COMPLEXITY

With the rapid advancement of artificial intelligence, big data, and complex global networks, technocracy is entering a new phase. AI-driven models increasingly inform decisions in policing, healthcare, and infrastructure planning. Yet, these systems raise concerns about opacity, bias, and the potential for algorithmic authoritarianism.

The governance of these systems requires not only technical proficiency but also moral and democratic oversight. As automation scales decision-making, ensuring that human values are encoded into machine logic becomes an urgent task.

CONCLUSION: RETHINKING THE ROLE OF EXPERTISE IN GOVERNANCE

Technocracy is neither a panacea nor a dystopia. It represents a pragmatic response to the complexity of modern governance but must evolve to coexist with democratic norms. A balanced model—where expertise informs but does not override public participation—offers a viable path forward.

Key proposals for such a balance include:

- Institutionalizing citizen panels to advise technocratic agencies
- Legislating mandatory transparency in expert bodies
- Establishing ethics boards for technocratic institutions

Ultimately, the legitimacy of technocracy rests on its ability to integrate knowledge with justice, efficiency with empathy, and science with societal values.

REFERENCES

Arcuri, A., & Coman-Kund, F. (2021). *Technocracy and the Law: Accountability, Governance and Expertise*. Routledge. DOI: 10.4324/9781003174769

Boston Review. (n.d.). "What's Wrong with Technocracy?"

EBSCO Research Starters. (2022). "Technocracy."

Encyclopedia.com. (n.d.). "Technocracy."

FasterCapital. (2025). "Expertise at the Helm: How Technocracy Values Knowledge."

TecnoSophia. (n.d.). "The Technocratic Society: Evolution from Philosophical Ideals to Today's Governance."

Chapter 16
Upholding the Rights of Visually Impaired Individuals in a Digitally Driven World

Syed Aaban Asif
https://orcid.org/0009-0003-2967-8130
Bai Virbaiji Soparivala Parsi High School, Cambridge System, Karachi, Pakistan

ABSTRACT

The number of visually impaired individuals is increasing day by day; as per the previous reports of the World Health Organization (WHO), more than 2.2 individuals are now visually impaired, and sadly, this number is increasing rapidly. Due to low vision, such individuals face numerous challenges, whether it's related to education or employment. In most cases even their basic rights are neglected, making them backward in this digital era. This chapter proposes how digital assistive and modern artificial intelligence technologies can be used to uphold their rights in this era. The ideas can be implemented on the basis of a conceptual model that focuses on their important rights, probable policymaking, and measures to ensure transparency. This framework will ensure that the rights of visually impaired individuals are fulfilled and that they can spend their lives independently.

INTRODUCTION

Special needs People are a part of every regime; there are many different types of disabilities. This includes vision impairment, deafness or hard of hearing, mental disabilities, physical disabilities, etc. (Australian National University, 2024). However,

DOI: 10.4018/979-8-3693-3920-6.ch016

this chapter solely focuses on visually impaired individuals only. This world isn't the same for them as it is for us; they face numerous challenges that are beyond our vision. For instance, they need proper facilities and guidance to help them spend their life, which serves as an alternative to their eyesight, but in most cases, they are considered a burden by their families, as they can't support themselves, whether it's about financial or mobility issues. A research study of 2024 reported that in the UK most of the people have a negative attitude towards them, which leads towards discrimination and societal exclusion (Heinze et al., 2024). Just like every normal individual, visually impaired individuals are also subjected to some fundamental rights as mentioned in the United Nations Convention on the Rights of Persons with Disabilities; this includes Article 9, Right to Accessibility, Article 19, Right to Independent Living, and many more (Guide, T., 2014). Even though internationally recognized intergovernmental bodies like the United Nations have clearly mentioned the basic rights of disabled individuals, why are they facing such problems? Who is responsible for it, the regime? Or the common individuals?

This chapter has examined and analyzed different studies to identify different challenges faced by visually impaired individuals and possible solutions for them. As in today's era technologies are improving and this world is getting more digitalized day by day, this chapter focuses on how AI and digitalization can help reshape the lives of every visually impaired individual using modern tools and devices like screen readers, AI-driven glasses, etc. Alongside, this chapter also explores various legal frameworks, such as the United Nations Convention on the Rights of Persons with Disabilities (UNCRPD) and national disability acts, to make this chapter more understandable. Doing so can help create a better and more inclusive society where everyone can live independently.

VISUAL IMPAIRMENT AND ITS MEANING

Visual impairment is a type of disability that affects the eyesight of an individual. Under this condition there's a significant loss of vision that can't be corrected completely with the aid of glasses, contact lenses, or medication. Most people misinterpret this term by believing that visual impairment refers to complete loss of sight. However, in visual impairment there's loss of vision up to a certain degree (World Health Organization, 2023). The World Health Organization defines Vision impairment occurs when an eye condition affects the visual system and its vision functions. Each individual is subjected to experiencing one eye condition that requires specific eye care if they live long enough (BSN, 2023).

According to the World Health Organization (WHO), at least 2.2 billion individuals are suffering from visual impairment, but why does it happen? Just like other disabilities, visual impairment is also caused by various reasons; these include congenital blindness, inheritance, refractive errors, cataracts, diabetic retinopathy, glaucoma, and age-related macular degeneration (World Health Organization, 2024).

Congenital Blindness, is a type of vision impairment that happens since birth. This type doesn't occur due to any injury or severe medical condition. This condition is identified by the doctor through several tests while checking for any vision problem, as the baby can't indicate it himself (BSN, 2023). Vision impairment can also be inherited; in such cases, genetic mutations or conditions that affect the structure or function of the eye are passed from one or both parents to their child, increasing the likelihood that the child will also develop visual impairment. Refractive errors are a condition in which a person has an abnormal shape or length of an eye; this prevents light from focusing onto the retina, resulting in blurred, unclear vision (WHO, n.d.). Cataract is considered the most common cause of visual impairment; in this condition a cloud cover is formed in front of the lens, causing loss of sight. This can happen due to an eye injury or other disease like diabetes. Although it can be treated through surgery, in most cases, it can result in vision impairment if left untreated, as treatment facilities aren't easily available in underdeveloped countries.

Diabetic retinopathy is another major cause of vision impairment, as diabetes can cause significant damage to the retina, making vision blurry. This problem can be identified and prevented in early stages using Diabetic Retinopathy Screening (WHO, 2025). Glaucoma is an irreversible eye condition that leads to vision impairment when the optic nerve, which transmits visual information from the eye to the brain, becomes damaged. Although the damage caused by glaucoma cannot be reversed, the condition can be treated to slow or prevent further vision loss (Guo et al., 2025). Age-related macular degeneration (AMD) is another eye disease that blurs the central vision. As the name indicates, it happens due to aging when the macula, a part of the retina that controls vision, gets damaged. As of now there is no cure for AMD, but it may be developed in the future (Frank-Publig et al., 2025). Other minor reasons include eye injuries and infections as well.

These causes give birth to numerous challenges in daily life activities, like mobility issues, workplace barriers, and dependency. Making the life of a visually impaired individual a big hurdle.

CATEGORIES OF VISUAL IMPAIRMENT

Visual impairment is divided into two different categories:

Visual impairment is generally categorized into two main types: *partial sight* and *complete blindness* (Figure 1). Partial sight (also called low vision) refers to a condition when an individual is able to see things up to a certain degree, having retained some usable sight. Such individuals are not completely dependent on normal individuals, however; they may need some aid in required circumstances. On the other hand, in complete blindness an individual has no perception of light or sight at all. These categories can also be further classified by the degree of vision loss based on visual acuity and field of vision.

Figure 1. Categories of Visual Impaired

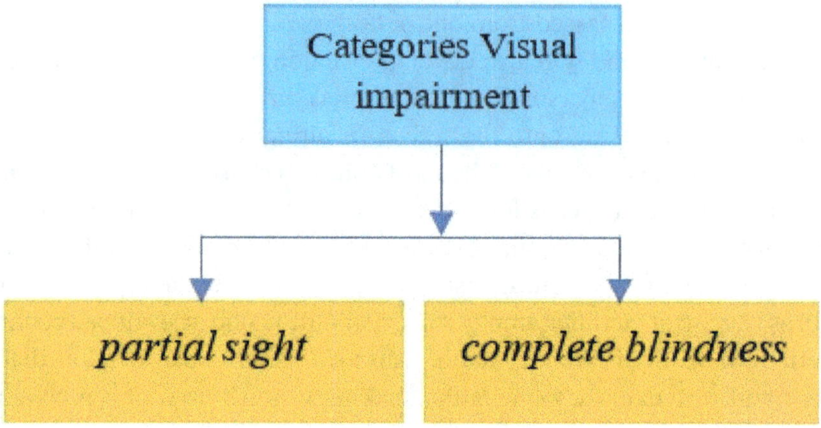

VISUAL IMPAIRMENT STATISTICS AND GLOBAL DEMOGRAPHICS

Visual impairment has proved to be a significant global health challenge. According to the World Health Organization, at least 2.2 billion individuals have been affected by this disease; this means around 30% of the total population has visual impairment. It's an astonishing fact that despite the world moving towards the era of digitalization, only 36% of individuals with distance vision impairment due to refractive errors and just 17% with visual impairment due to cataracts have received access to a proper solution. Vision impairment also causes financial constraints; globally, US$ 411 billion is spent either for surgery or other basic needs of visual impairment (World Health Organization, 2023).

80% of people that have been affected by visual impairment can be treated or prevented using means like cataract surgeries and suitable eye lenses. Women are considered to have a slight majority over men in visual impairment, mounting up to 55% of individuals with vision loss (Hill, 2025).

CIVIL RIGHTS OF EVRY VISUALY IMPAIRED INDVIDUAL

There is a need to uphold the rights of visually impaired individuals because their population is increasing daily; therefore, the previous section has presented statistics and global demographics related to visually impaired individuals. Before championing civil rights, it's important to understand what those civil rights really are.

The United Nations Human Rights Council (UNHRC) mentions these rights under *the Convention on the Rights of Persons with Disabilities*. This convention contains rights of all Persons with Disabilities (PWD); however, under this section, the rights of visually impaired individuals have been classified (United Nations, n.d.)

Article 9 of the convention lays emphasis on accessibility; this is an essential requirement of any visually impaired individual so that they can spend their life freely and independently. Under this they should be given facilities on an equal basis related to their physical environment, like workplaces or homes, etc., and transportation, technologies, information (in the form of Braille/audio clips), etc. This requirement falls mostly under the responsibility of the regime, and so they should dedicate themselves to the well-being of such individuals.

Article 20 mentions personal mobility, a significant challenge faced by every visually impaired individual. Due to loss of sight, they can't see things clearly, making it difficult for them to navigate with ease. In most cases mobility assistive devices are very expensive, worsening this issue. While using such tools, proper training by specialized trainers should also be given under this right.

Article 21 states freedom of expression and opinion and access to information should be given to them. It's a sour truth that in some countries even normal individuals have no access to freedom of expression. How would visually impaired individuals have such a privilege? Another flaw is the lack of availability of translated language. Visually impaired individuals can't read normal language; they have a specialized language called Braille language, which they understand by using their sense of touch (Rose et al., 2025). As most underdeveloped countries don't have proper facilities, it's an urgent need to make those available for them.

Article 24 is the most important yet the most neglected right. This is the right to education; visually impaired individuals face a lot of discrimination and barriers under this sector. A research study of 2025 highlights the problems faced by teachers in Pakistan while addressing visually impaired students. Similar problems are also faced by students as well (Malik & Mahmood, 2025). This problem is not just limited to Pakistan, but it's present in almost each underdeveloped country. Therefore, this issue should be addressed, and this fundamental right should be granted to every visually impaired individual, as education is the basic foundation of every child.

Article 25 refers to the well-being of disabled individuals. Under these, all health facilities should be free or affordable so that it's convenient for each disabled individual. Hospitals and clinics should also be close to residential areas for easy access.

Article 27 of the convention is about work and employment. This means that they should be able to work freely and that there should be no discrimination in the workplace or while hiring such individuals. However, the reality is completely opposite; a survey was conducted to know the opinions of why some visually impaired individuals were not working, and key findings included the negative attitude of employers. As this factor is mostly interlinked with education, lacking proper education can also hinder employment issues. Thus, this should be addressed as well.

Article 28 is about adequate standard of living and social protection. Therefore, good quality of life should be maintained for them. There should be a forever end to discrimination against them on the basis of disability, and a proper inclusion in society should be made.

Articles 29 and 30 urge for their equal inclusion in the society; just like every individual, they deserve to take part in political and public life, including cultural, recreational, leisure, and sports activities. This means all the facilities, such as voting procedures and other materials, are appropriate and easy to use. Their participation in sports should also be encouraged, and government support should be provided to them.

These also align with a few Sustainable Development goals of the United Nations, which are quality education, good health and well-being, sustainable cities and communities, and peace, justice, and strong institutions (United Nations, n.d.), (Figure 2).

Figure 2. United Nation Sustainable Development Goals (SDG) related to visually impaired individual

EVERYDAY CHALLENGES FACED BY VISUALY IMPAIRED INDIVIDUAL

Visually impaired individuals face diverse challenges throughout their lives, whether it's related to mobility, education, or digitalization. Sadly, most of these issues go unnoticed by the general population. Under this topic the major issues faced by visually impaired individuals have been discussed.

One of the most common issues that comes to mind for most of us when we think about visually impaired individuals is mobility. Mobility remains one of the most significant issues for them, as it affects one of their senses, the eyesight. This issue is interlinked with their daily life activities, as they find it difficult to navigate due to less or no vision in their workplace, home, etc., making them dependent on their family members and associates all the time. Jeffries et al., 2021).

Educational problems have also become a major issue; it's clear to all of us that education lays the foundation of every child. However, education isn't easily accessible to them. This is because visually impaired individuals communicate using a specific language called Braille (Figure 3).

Figure 3. Braille Cells

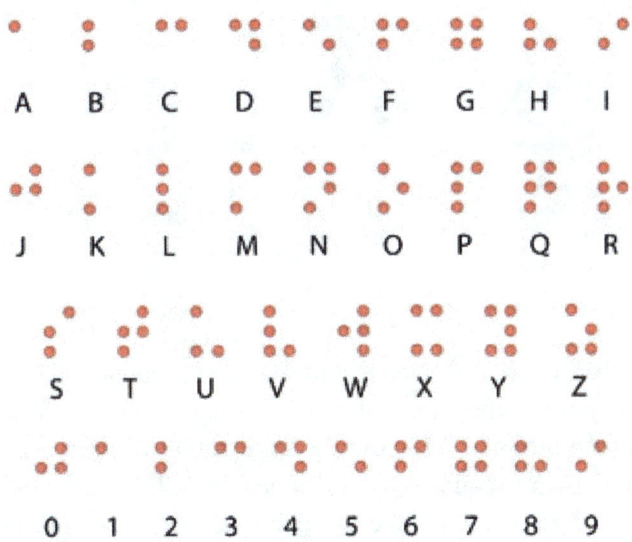

This is more like a tactile code, which visually impaired individuals understand using their sense of touch (Sight Scotland, n.d.). To print this, a special type of printer is used called the Braille embosser, which helps render text as Braille cells. Special papers are used to print it, which are comparatively thicker than normal paper. This makes overall printing costs too expensive as compared to a standard printer, and not everyone can afford it, particularly students or schools from developing nations (Chowdhury et al., 2018). Furthermore, as visually impaired students only understand Braille, only specially trained teachers are capable of teaching them, making education a difficult crisis for them.

Another modern-day challenge faced by them in this digital world is actually understanding digital tools and devices. This also becomes a hurdle when seeking employment, as most news and employment opportunities are either published physically, like in newspapers, or digitally, which obviously is beyond their ability to read.

Figure 4. Major Challenges faced by Visually Impaired Individuals

Even though nowadays advanced technologies are available, like screen readers and voice-based systems, they are still expensive and can't be afforded by middle-class or low-income families. Moreover, even if such tools are available, visually impaired individuals are required to be trained in order to use them effectively. The shift towards digitalization, like using emails, texting, or doing voice calls, has made lives of normal individuals easier but hasn't changed much for visually impaired individuals. However, if digital technologies are used in the right way, a great impact can definitely be made.

PERSPECTIVE OF THE GENERAL POPULATION

Visually impaired individuals are a part of every society, and thus, they can't be ignored. People usually have various perspectives on them. One major misinterpretation people usually have is that they consider visually impaired as someone with complete blindness; however, as mentioned above, visual impairment means a loss of vision up to a certain degree. This also includes complete blindness. Many people also believe that such individuals can only earn through informal employment; this leads towards employers being reluctant when hiring them (Royal National Institute of Blind People [RNIB], 2024). People also have little contact with them and so cannot communicate or help them with proper knowledge and confidence.

It's also noticed that many people have a negative attitude towards them; a research report of 2024 mentions how the negative attitude of the society can deeply affect the mindset of visually impaired individuals. A survey was conducted in the UK, which involved over 4000 visually impaired individuals, questioning them on how the negative attitude of the public has affected them. Around 30% of them said that they have avoided education, 35% avoided doing jobs, and 23% said that they were reluctant to socialize and use public transport. An overall 87% reported facing negative attitudes and behavior in their lives (Heinze et al., 2024). This negative attitude is in the sense that many people feel awkward and uncomfortable, as they don't know how to interact with them. It's also a common point of view that visually impaired individuals are always dependent no matter what; due to low vision, they can't travel alone, eat properly, or learn things easily. This makes people think as if they are a burden on them, and therefore, they usually avoid them. Similarly, when it comes to employment, most employers think that visually impaired individuals will face mobility issues, will require costly accommodations, and can't interact with their colleagues very well.

A research study suggests that there is an employment gap of 28.9% between individuals with disabilities and individuals without disabilities. This is because of the discrimination faced by disabled individuals when applying for employment (Castle, 2024).

HARSH CONSEQUENCES FACED BY VISUALLY IMPAIRED INDIVIDUALS

When an individual goes through many negative aspects, he tends to face a lot of consequences. Facing negative attitudes and lack of inclusion in the society can distress the mindset of visually impaired individuals. In 2024 a survey was conducted in the USA comprising adults (65 years or older) that had vision impairment to discuss their physiological function. There were more than 2800 participants in it, and the results were that depressive, anxiety, and severe social isolation symptoms were reported among them (Almidani et al., 2024). Similarly, another research study from 2020 on visual impairment and mental health highlights that rates of depression and anxiety are very high among individuals with visual impairment. It states that nearly one-third of individuals with visual impairment experience depressive symptoms, and in the worst cases, this can also lead towards suicide (Demmin & Silverstein, 2020). This is proof that the negative attitude of society can deeply affect their mental health. It's a sour truth that this attitude doesn't only revolve around strangers, but even in some cases relatives have a similar perspective on them, leading them towards isolation.

As stated above, visually impaired individuals face a huge educational crisis, particularly in less developed countries. This impairs them from living a quality life, as education lays the basic foundation for every individual. Without education it's not possible to learn basic things and get a proper job. This results in visually impaired individuals becoming dependent on their family members, causing economic constraints. Sometimes if overprotection is given to them by parents, they not only become completely dependent on them but also lack socialization and require assistance in most tasks. A research study was done on burden and depression among caregivers in Mexico, and it showed that caregivers are also at a higher risk of burden and depression as they dedicate a lot of hours to care for them (Ruiz-Lozano et al., 2022). Therefore, many individuals avoid interaction with them, considering them as a burden.

Most visually impaired individuals aren't able to find themselves a suitable job; it's because they either lack educational background or aren't socialized and face discrimination. In 2024 a survey was conducted in Nigeria regarding the reasons why visually impaired individuals are unemployed. It included 22 individuals aged between 18 and 55; the most common barrier to employment was said to be misconceptions of employers (Okonji et al., 2024). This forces them to indulge in informal employment, for example, street vending or begging. Such ways are not only a low source of income for visually impaired individuals but also don't benefit the regime, as informal employment is not registered with the government.

USE OF ASSISTIVE TECHNOLOGIES TO UPHOLD THE RIGHTS OF VISUALLY IMPAIRED INDIVIDUALS

The world is advancing rapidly, and digitalization is becoming common. Nowadays assistive technologies are available that can help make daily tasks a lot faster and easier. These include screen readers, voice assistants, etc. This section explores how such technologies can be utilized to uphold the rights of visually impaired individuals.

One of the core problems faced by such individuals is in visualizing things clearly, especially in the era of the digital world, where most things are done online, such as writing emails, texting each other, or just simply exploring a website. They need assistance from someone who could help read it out; however, today screen readers are now available online. The American Foundation for the Blind defines screen readers as software that allows visually impaired individuals to read the text that is displayed on the device screen with a speech synthesizer or Braille display (American Foundation for the Blind [AFB], n.d.). In simple terms, it's software that converts text to speech so that the visually impaired can understand it by hearing.

A few of the most prominent include Job Access with Speech (JAWS) and NVDA screen readers (Freedom Scientific, n.d.), (NV Access, n.d.). A survey was conducted by WebAIM in 2021 to identify which sort of screen readers are used by Persons with Disabilities (PWD). 96.5% of them were either blind or visually impaired, and almost 80% said that they used NVDA and JAWS as their primary source (WebAIM, 2024). Screen readers are now becoming common day by day and are being used by visually impaired individuals, as they improve accessibility by allowing users to access digital information by converting written text into speech or Braille, fulfilling their right to accessibility as mentioned in Article 9 of the UN Convention on the Rights of Persons with Disabilities. It also gives them access to information, as mentioned in Article 21, by enabling them to write emails or scroll social media with free will. It also supports article 24, which is related to education, as it allows them to access e-books and online classes. Online computer-based jobs can also be done using them, reducing mobility issues and accomplishing their right of employment (Nino et al., 2024).

Another useful tool that can be used is voice assistants like Alexa, Siri, and Google Assistant (Amazon, n.d.), (Apple, n.d.), (Google, n.d.). A voice assistant is software that is capable of responding to voice commands; it can be run on various devices like smartphones and computers (Wohr, 2025). Speech is the most effective way of communication for the visually impaired due to no sight; therefore, they can easily communicate and learn new things using voice assistants. Voice assistants are relatively cheap or mostly free, as now they come built-in in smartphones and computers. Custom voice assistants are also available to help make it more accessible for them, as they can use them for various purposes like smart home control, in which they can close lights without requiring to move just by saying a command to the voice assistant (Ramaraj et al., 2025). They can also improve their personal mobility, which is mentioned in Article 20, by navigating through voice-based maps, such as Google Maps voice navigating feature (Google, n.d.). Articles 29 and 30 are about public life and recreation, and those assistants can play a significant role in it by giving them the opportunity to participate in online cultural activities and talks on different topics, supporting the inclusion of visually impaired individuals in our society.

As stated in the previous sections, Braille is a language through which visually impaired individuals can communicate with others, but now most work is done digitally, like on computers, which usually don't support Braille. This creates a big hurdle for them, making the digital world inaccessible to them. However, now Braille displays are available, which can help curb this problem. A Braille display is a device that is used to convert information on a computer screen into Braille. It has access to the display of the computer and provides information written on it by raising and lowering different pin combinations in braille cells. It's a physical device that is usually installed under the user keyboard or on his desk and is capable of being able to show 80 characters; it's also refreshable and displays characters as the cursor is moved (AFB, n.d.). An article by the Royal National Institute of Blind People (RNIB) tells the story of Dave Williams, who has Leber Congenital Amaurosis (LCA), a rare genetic eye condition that results in blindness from birth; he emphasizes how braille has made his life a lot easier (RNIB, n.d.). This means using Braille displays can help visually impaired individuals understand things better by giving them access to information and education by helping them learn things online and in employment as well. A few of the most prominent braille displays are of Humanware and Focus Blue by Freedom Scientific (HumanWare, n.d.), (Freedom Scientific, n.d.). Braille keyboards are another technological advancement that can be used by visually impaired individuals to type something digitally by using keys that have letters, numbers, and other special keys in Braille. It started in 1951 when Perkins Brailler invented the braille typewriter, and then later on these were transformed into keyboards (Allyant, 2024).

Artificial intelligence, a word that is becoming common and is reshaping this world not just for normal individuals but for visually impaired individuals as well. AI-based smart glasses are now becoming one of the key solutions to low vision. Such glasses are integrated with a digital assistant that is backed by generative AI software and also use Optical Character Recognition (OCR) that converts printed or handwritten text into digital text (Qualcomm, n.d.). Today many prominent AI-driven glasses are available, such as those from Envision AI and Meta AI (Envision, n.d.), (Meta, n.d.). Such tools can help visually impaired individuals recognize what is present in front of them; for example, they can warn them about an object that is present in front of them that they may hit, as they can recognize such objects using AI. Similar applications like the glasses are also available, such as Seeing AI, which acts as a guide to visually impaired individuals by describing their surroundings (Seeing AI, n.d.). All this improves their accessibility by giving them access to real environmental information and also improves mobility by allowing them to navigate with ease as they are well aware of their surroundings, thus fulfilling their rights of accessibility and mobility as mentioned in Articles 9 and 20, respectively.

AI-based voice and chat assistants are now becoming digital giants with famous names like DeepSeek, ChatGPT, and Gemini on the list (DeepSeek, n.d.), (OpenAI, n.d.), (Google, n.d.). These are a little bit different, as, unlike other basic voice assistants, they provide more contextual and deep information to the user for better personalized help. Assistants like ChatGPT and Gemini have voice-based command systems that can be used by visually impaired individuals to inquire about anything they want to know about. Similarly, prompts can also be given to chatbots like DeepSeek by using Braille keyboards to learn something. All these AI chatbots can help them improve their knowledge if they need to understand anything, assisting them in education and giving access to information supporting articles 21 and 24 of the UN Convention on Disability Rights. They can also assist in finding employment opportunities or solving queries related to any work, helping them and satisfying Article 27 on employment. Such AI assistants can also be used by them to get basic health advice and prescriptions, which supports Article 25 on health. A research paper from 2025 highlights how ChatGPT can help the visually impaired by using an AI-enhanced visual guiding system, emphasizing that chatbots are capable enough to empower visually impaired individuals (Elshiekh et al., 2025). Just like this, another research paper of 2024 named ChatGPT for Visually Impaired and Blind also shows how a mobile application can be used with automatic speech recognition (ASR), text-to-speech (TTS), etc. to help visually impaired individuals interact with ChatGPT for their betterment effortlessly (Kuzdeuov et al., 2024).

To further enhance mobility, AI-powered navigation tools are also available in the market; such devices are combined with GPS, can detect objects using AI, and also have a voice guidance feature to ensure safe and comfortable movement. A few of the examples include Smart Cane by WeWalk and Microsoft's Soundscape (WeWALK, n.d.), (Microsoft Research, 2023). Being integrated with AI allows the cane to detect nearby objects and inform the user about them through its voice feature. This reduces chances of accidents significantly and also improves mobility of visually impaired individuals. It also upholds Articles 29 and 30 by allowing free and independent movement for anything, whether it's related to culture, politics, etc.

AI-based technologies have also made a significant step in healthcare, whether it comes to AI-based voice assistants that are integrated with health apps and can guide users on their conditions or AI-analyzed smart wearables that can analyze health and ensure visually impaired individuals remain fit (Awang et al., 2022). These tools can be used to monitor different activity levels and alert caregivers when needed. Assistants can also be used to schedule appointments and track how a medication course is going on, for example, Suki AI, which is a widely recognized assistant that is not only capable of assisting clinicians but patients as well (Suki AI, 2025).

Smartwatches can also play an important role in healthcare by monitoring heart rate and other necessary things (Kapoor et al., 2023). However, most smartwatches aren't designed for visually impaired individuals, and they face barriers in using them due to low or no vision, but newer advancements have also solved this issue, as now smartwatches are integrated with voice-to-speech converters, which can scan text and read it aloud so that it's audible to the user. Such tools support Article 25 of the UN convention that states healthcare facilities and information should be present for them. All these uses have been summarized in table 1.

CONSEQUENCES OF USING THESE DIGITAL ASSISTENCE

As the world is currently advancing towards digitalization, it's not yet widely available; therefore, using these assistive devices has both positive and negative consequences. This section analyzes what can be the overall impact of using such tools in today's era.

On to the positive side, usage of assistive technologies can ensure better independency for visually impaired individuals, as most of their daily life activities can be managed by assistive technologies. For example, voice assistants and screen readers can be used for reading, navigating, and controlling different appliances in the house without requiring any external human intervention. Although it's not possible to make them completely independent, self-dependency can be achieved up to a certain extent (Abraham et al., 2023). This also helps reduce the burden on family members and caregivers, allowing both to spend a happy lifestyle.

Table 1. Related articles of UNCRPD and probable Solution to uphold the right of visual impaired individuals

Right (UNCRPD Article)	Description	Assistive Technologies Supporting This Right
Article 9: Accessibility	Equal access to physical environment, transportation, information, and technology.	Screen Readers (JAWS, NVDA) – converts text to speech or Braille for easy digital access; Voice Assistants (Alexa, Siri, Google Assistant) – enables voice commands for tasks; AI Smart Glasses – detects objects and surroundings.
Article 20: Personal Mobility	Independence in movement and navigation.	AI Smart Glasses – object detection and navigation guidance; Voice Assistants – voice-based navigation via Google Maps; AI-based apps (Seeing AI) – describes surroundings for safe movement.
Article 21: Freedom of Expression & Access to Information	Right to information and communication in accessible formats.	Screen Readers – reads online content and emails; Braille Displays – converts digital text to Braille; Voice & Chat Assistants (ChatGPT, Gemini) – provides information through voice/text interaction.
Article 24: Education	Inclusive education and learning opportunities.	Screen Readers – for e-learning and reading materials; Braille Keyboards & Displays – for digital note-taking; AI Chatbots – assists in understanding concepts and answering queries.
Article 25: Health	Access to health facilities and information.	Voice Assistants – schedule appointments or access health info; AI Apps – read medical documents via OCR; Screen Readers – access online health portals.
Article 27: Work and Employment	Equal opportunities and non-discriminatory hiring.	Screen Readers – access to job portals and online tools; Voice Assistants & AI Chatbots – perform workplace tasks; Braille Keyboards – enable digital communication.
Articles 29 & 30: Participation in Public Life and Recreation	Inclusion in politics, culture, and leisure activities.	Voice Assistants – join online discussions, control smart devices; AI Apps – engage in online cultural activities; Screen Readers – browse social media and public content.

Accessibility for visually impaired individuals has also improved significantly. Tools and devices like JAWS, NVDA, and braille displays eradicate the barriers that prevent access to information. Easy access to websites and documents grants them access to education, employment opportunities, etc., providing them equal access to social media, education, and employment (Chimicz & Walkiewicz-Krutak, 2025).

Gadgets such as WeWalk smart canes and Soundscape can help enhance mobility; with them, visually impaired individuals cannot just feel safe but will also be able to move independently, as these will reduce accidents and will raise their self-confidence. Visually impaired individuals can also get more socialized if they are more independent. Voice assistants and AI chatbots, along with their caregivers, can also motivate and guide them on how to interact with others. This can make them more confident and can also expand their social circle (Kumar, Srivastava, & Prajapati, n.d.). Improvements in health by following guidance and precautionary measures through smartwatches and assistants can also ensure a balanced health approach, keeping visually impaired individuals healthy and fit.

However, despite these advantages, using technology can also have negative consequences. For instance, advanced technologies like Braille displays, keyboards, and AI glasses are very expensive, with prices mounting in thousands of dollars. The Helen Keller Services report shows a comparison of 5 good Braille displays; however, each of them costs more than a thousand dollars, making it unaffordable for low-income families (Helen Keller Services, 2023). Another research study from 2025, on global trends of Braille literacy and assistive technologies, does the analysis from 1985 to 2025 and also highlights the same issue (Ahanin et al., 2022).

Many less developed countries also go through a digital divide, as due to a lack of internet, training, and infrastructure, it's not possible to utilize tools up to their full potential. As the internet acts as a major fuel for technological devices, it becomes a hard challenge to provide access to them. The Disability Survey 2022, which was conducted by the National Statistical Office of Thailand, showed that only 26.88% of visually impaired individuals had access to the internet (Phochai et al., 2024). This indicates how much worse this issue is, and unfortunately this is not only limited to one country but is present in most underdeveloped countries. Therefore, this requires proper attention.

It has also been reported that some assistive devices are not very adaptive towards visually impaired individuals and often lead to confusion and frustration; this was found out when a survey was conducted in 2025 involving 16 individuals (Turkstra et al., 2025). Privacy risks are also a negative consequence for them; when using digital tools, there is always a possibility that the data may be misused. A survey of 2022 shows that there are always some privacy risks, especially for visually impaired individuals, such as unintended recording or data misuse, and they are usually unaware of it (Acosta & Reinhardt, 2022). The consequences of digital assistance both positive and negative are mentioned in Table 2.

Table 2. Positive and negative consequences of using digital assistance

Positive Consequences	
Independence	Assistive tech enables self-dependency in daily activities (e.g., reading, navigation, appliance control).
Reduced Family Burden	Less reliance on caregivers resulting in improved quality of life for both.
Accessibility	Tools-like JAWS, NVDA, Braille displays remove barriers to information, improving access to education and employment.
Mobility	Devices like WeWalk Smart Cane, Soundscape enhance mobility and safety, reducing accidents and boosting confidence.

continued on following page

Table 2. Continued

Positive Consequences	
Socialization	Independence plus AI chatbots/voice assistants therefore, more social confidence and broader social circle.
Health Improvement	Smart assistants and wearables help in health monitoring and following preventive measures.
Negative Consequences	
High Cost	Devices like Braille displays/keyboards, AI glasses cost thousands of dollars so unaffordable for low-income families.
Digital Divide	Lack of internet, training, infrastructure in developing countries; very low percentage of visually impaired have internet.
Poor Adaptability	Some devices are not user-friendly, causing confusion and frustration.
Privacy Risks	Data misuse and unintended recording risks for visually impaired individuals using assistive devices.

RECOMMENDATIONS FOR NEGATIVE CONSEQUENCES

Visually impaired individuals are part of our society, and so it's the regime's responsibility to uphold their rights. The regime should work for a better change. The government and NGOs can work together to provide financial aid or subsidies to respective organizations working for this cause or to the people directly. This way use of assistive tools can be expanded.

The introduction of affordable internet in rural areas can also help advance it; the government should also focus on the introduction of digital literacy programs so that all visually impaired individuals can use technologies with ease. This also includes orientations and mobility trainings.

To protect privacy, strong data protection policies should be introduced and implemented by the cybersecurity departments of each country. Global and national awareness programs can also be started to guide visually impaired individuals and their family members about their rights, available devices, and how to use them. Normal individuals should also try their best to support them, whether it's done financially or spiritually, as together we can make a better society. The proposed conceptual model describes the possible measures to help solve these issues in detail.

CONCEPTUAL MODEL

The conceptual and recommended model for upholding the rights of visually impaired individuals in a digitally driven world is shown in figure 5. This model illustrates the relationship between the use of assistive technology and fulfillment of the rights of visually impaired individuals. This model is like a framework that will help understand better how technology and other suitable measures can be used to uphold the rights of visually impaired individuals.

This model mentions the major frameworks that define the rights of visually impaired individuals; these include the United Nations Convention on the Rights of Persons with Disabilities and the national disability laws and policies of respective countries. The major focus would be on the most important articles of the UN convention, which are Article 9: Accessibility, Article 20: Personal Mobility, Article 21: Freedom of Expression and Access to Information, Article 24: Education, Article 25: Health, Article 27: Work and Employment, and Articles 29 and 30: Participation in Public Life and Recreation.

To ensure all visually impaired individuals of the area are addressed, a survey would be conducted through door-to-door visits in order to calculate the total number of visually impaired individuals in that area. Then a budget will be allocated by the disability department for them from the national budget on the basis of the number of visually impaired individuals to provide them the facilities needed for the fulfillment of the above articles. To ensure that each and every visually impaired individual gets his share, the survey would be conducted every year.

Training programs will be introduced to train teachers, in which they will be taught how to use accessible training materials like Braille displays, keyboards, etc. New special education centers would be made within a specific budget that would only be allocated for the betterment of visually impaired individuals that would be managed by their respective disability department. The aim of such centers would be to guide students on how they can get a suitable job and support themselves along with their families. The government can also introduce subsidies on assistive products so that they're affordable for every visually impaired individual. In case any individual can still not afford it, grants can be provided by the disability department if the required documents are available to prove his financial condition.

A special portal would be created that will display suitable employment opportunities for visually impaired individuals; an employment plan can also be started to create more jobs for them. They will be given free will, and if anyone tries to discriminate or harm them, he will be charged, and a penalty will be given based on the deed done.

To ensure transparency in the implementation process, independent NGOs and agencies would be overseeing the implementation and conducting audits. For example,

UNESCO (United Nations Educational, Scientific and Cultural Organization) will oversee the implementation of educational programs, training, and availability of required educational tools. WHO (World Health Organization) can ensure if health policies are implemented and if all the facilities are available. UNHRC (United Nations Human Rights Council) can ensure compliance with the United Nations Convention on Persons with Disability Rights.

Figure 5. Conceptual model to uphold the rights of visually impaired individuals

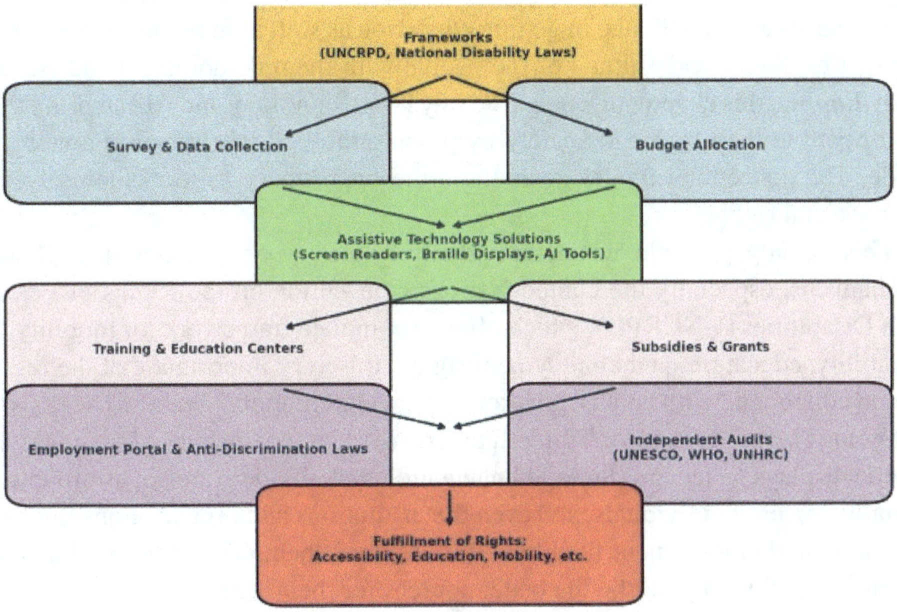

Where the conceptual model based on six layers is described below:

1. Top Layer (Frameworks): UNCRPD and National Disability Laws.
2. Second Layer: Survey, Data, and Budget Allocation.
3. Third Layer: Assistive Tech Solutions (Screen Readers, Braille, AI).
4. Fourth Layer: Training, Education, Subsidies, and Grants.
5. Fifth Layer: Employment Portals and Independent Audits (UNESCO, WHO, UNHRC, etc.).
6. Bottom Layer: Fulfillment of Rights (Accessibility, Education, Employment, Health, Inclusion).

CONCLUSION AND RECOMENDATIONS

In short, in the era of digitalization and modern technology, like AI, they provide the facilities to visually impaired individuals with less dependency, and they can easily accommodate their required field of education and then search for the relevant job. So, they afford themselves and also help out their family members partially and represent their full participation as responsible citizens, although they have great obstacles in their lives. The chapter shared all challenges faced by visually impaired individuals in their personal and practical lives. Such as the problem of mobility, which causes a big challenge in getting education as well as at the workplace. Then the next exclusive bad attitude of the people with them demoralized and isolated them. Further, this chapter discusses the way how technology and AI can bring them up for getting their rights in society by passing through the proposed conceptual mode. The conceptual model gives them the opportunity to avail themselves of their societal rights.

This is only possible when individual regimes work on international legal mechanisms, especially the United Nations Convention on the Rights of Persons with Disabilities (UNCRPD), which offers a complete framework for mobility, accessibility, education, and employment rights. It is very important that the regime should collaborate with NGOs, government, and international bodies. The assistive technology is very expensive. Things like screen readers, AI-enhanced smart glasses, Braille displays, voice interfaces, AI navigation systems, etc., are not affordable for visually impaired individuals, and even the institutions and organizations that offer education and employment facilities cannot afford them. Therefore, national and international funding will be the better sources for their benefit.

There are a number of examples that exist that prove that the visually impaired individuals have a good ability to prove themselves here; quote the success story of a Microsoft software developer, Saqib Shaikh, who became blind at a young age. Mr. Shaikh led the creation of the Seeing AI app design for visually impaired or blind individuals by which they can recognize faces and understand their surroundings. This application is used worldwide and assists a number of visually impaired individuals, and they are self-assured and independent.

Another inspiring example is two blind siblings from Pakistan, Alihan Tareen and his sister Fizza. They are visually impaired due to the genetic disorder retinitis pigmentosa. They are doing their food business with the brand Khaas Foodz surprisingly. Fizza is an expert chef. Cooking is supposed to be quite difficult for beginners, but when we talk about the visually impaired, it seems impossible, as there is a lot of risk associated with cooking for the blind or visually impaired, but she is doing it with confidence. They host Dining in the Dark events, sensory dining events where sighted diners wear blindfolds and consume meals cooked by visually impaired chefs. Remarkably, the siblings won a PKR 5 million grant combined from Shark Tank Pakistan, along with corporate funding and training expansion programs.

These two inspiring examples help in concluding the chapter that if this visually impaired individual can do better in the field of software development and cooking, then if the visually impaired individual is supported by their regime, NGOs, community persons, and technology developers, they will surely become better citizens. The individuals belong to less developed countries; even developed countries are sometimes not able to purchase the assistive device so that with the help of it they can facilitate.

To complete the whole process for upholding the rights of visually impaired individuals, the conceptual model adopted advocates a systematic process: data collection, strategic investment, affordable technology implementation, capacity-development programs, employment promotion, and autonomous monitoring for transparency and accountability.

In order to move forward efficiently, policies should ensure affordability and accessibility of assistive technologies, bridge infrastructural gaps in underserved areas, and develop inclusive attitudes through public awareness and education campaigns. Financial subsidies, skills development, and vocational programs must be the pillars of national disability plans.

Ultimately, maintaining the civil rights of visually impaired persons in the age of technology goes beyond technology; it is our shared social duty. By taking inspiration from champions like Saqib Shaikh and Ali and Fizza Hussain, we understand that enabling technology, when intentionally designed and inclusively deployed, allows people to live with dignity, autonomy, and active.

Finally, it is the collective efforts of authorities, all the global policy makers, and technology innovators to transform this initiative recommended in conceptual model theory into practice at a global scale. Ensure the implementation of new updated policies related to technology for visually impaired individuals socializes them even at the internal level and dedicate budgets for those who have no affordability to purchase assistive devices.

Establish collaboration between public and private partnerships to promote assistive technologies. It is now the collective responsibility of global policymakers, technology innovators, and society to move from intention to implementation, ensuring that no visually impaired individual is left behind in the digital revolution. Initiate global campaigns to ensure digital inclusion for the visually impaired, especially in underserved regions. Secondly, awareness and training sessions must be organized by all bodies for all members of the society so they can play their positive role for visually impaired people. So, they can take part in societal participation with dignity and honor.

REFERENCES

Abraham, N. P., Sajan, K., George, J., Chandy, J., & Issac, B. M. (2023). Advancements in assistive technologies: Enhancing independence and accessibility for the visually impaired. *International Journal of Recent Engineering Research and Applications*, *4*(1), 210–230.

Access, N. V. (n.d.). Download NVDA. https://www.nvaccess.org/download/

Acosta, L. H., & Reinhardt, D. (2022). A survey on privacy issues and solutions for voice-controlled digital assistants. *Pervasive and Mobile Computing*.

Ahanin, E., Sade, A. B., & Tat, H. H. (2022). Applications of artificial intelligence and voice assistant in healthcare. *International Journal of Academic Research in Business & Social Sciences*, *12*(12), 2545–2554. DOI: 10.6007/IJARBSS/v12-i12/16048

Allyant. (2024, October 21). What are braille keyboards? 3 top braille keyboards. https://allyant.com/blog/what-is-a-braille-keyboard-types/

Almidani, L., Miller, R., Varadaraj, V., Mihailovic, A., Swenor, B. K., & Ramulu, P. Y. (2024). Vision impairment and psychosocial function in US adults. *JAMA Ophthalmology*, *142*(4), 283–291. DOI: 10.1001/jamaophthalmol.2023.6943 PMID: 38386343

Amazon. (n.d.). Alexa+. https://www.amazon.com/dp/B0DCCNHWV5

American Foundation for the Blind. (n.d.). Refreshable braille displays. https://www.afb.org/node/16207/refreshable-braille-displays

American Foundation for the Blind. (n.d.). Screen readers. https://www.afb.org/blindness-and-low-vision/using-technology/assistive-technology-products/screen-readers

Australian National University. (2024, July 10). Different types of disabilities. https://services.anu.edu.au/human-resources/health-safety/different-types-of-disabilities

Awang, A., Abdul Rani, I. F., & Eng Hock, K. (2025). Global trends in Braille literacy and assistive technologies: A bibliometric analysis (1985–2024). *British Journal of Visual Impairment*, •••, 02646196251345966. DOI: 10.1177/02646196251345966

Bsn, R. Z. R. (2023, April 13). Congenital blindness: What you should know. *Healthline*. https://www.healthline.com/health/congenital-blindness

Castle, C. L. (2024). Attitudes of employers towards people with visual impairment: A scoping review. *Frontiers in Rehabilitation Sciences*, *5*, 1383984. Advance online publication. DOI: 10.3389/fresc.2024.1383984 PMID: 39628549

. Chimicz, D., & Walkiewicz-Krutak, M. (2025). Using assistive technologies in the workplace by individuals with visual impairments: An analysis of user experiences. *Lubelski Rocznik Pedagogiczny, 44*(2).

Chowdhury, D., Haider, M. Z., Sarkar, M., Refat, M., Datta, K., & Fattah, S. A. (2018). An intuitive approach to innovate a low-cost Braille embosser. *International Journal of Instrumentation Technology*, *2*(1), 1–17. DOI: 10.1504/IJIT.2018.090858

Deep Seek. (n.d.). https://www.deepseek.com/

Demmin, D. L., & Silverstein, S. M. (2020). Visual impairment and mental health: Unmet needs and treatment options. *Clinical Ophthalmology (Auckland, N.Z.)*, *14*, 4229–4251. DOI: 10.2147/OPTH.S258783 PMID: 33299297

Elshiekh, H. A., Ghaly, S. A., Khalaf, K. W., Elsayed, A. M., Fouda, A. K., Aboelhassan, K. E., & Elsonbaty, A. A. (2025). AI-enhanced visual guiding system using ChatGPT for the visually impaired. *Journal of Engineering Research and Reports*, *27*(6), 264–272. DOI: 10.9734/jerr/2025/v27i61543

Envision. (n.d.). Envision glasses – Smart glasses for people who are blind or low vision. https://www.letsenvision.com/glasses/home

Frank-Publig, S., Birner, K., Riedl, S., Reiter, G. S., & Schmidt-Erfurth, U. (2025). Artificial intelligence in assessing progression of age-related macular degeneration. *Eye (London, England)*, *39*(2), 262–273. DOI: 10.1038/s41433-024-03460-z PMID: 39558093

Freedom Scientific. (n.d.). Focus Blue family braille displays. https://www.freedomscientific.com/products/blindness/focus-blue-family/

Freedom Scientific. (n.d.). JAWS screen reader. https://www.freedomscientific.com/products/software/jaws/

Google. (n.d.). Gemini. https://gemini.google.com/app

Google. (n.d.). Google Assistant. https://assistant.google.com/

Google. (n.d.). Use navigation in Google Maps. https://support.google.com/maps/answer/3273406

Guide, T. (2014). *The convention on the rights of persons with disabilities*. United Nations of Human Rights.

Guo, L., Wang, N., Chen, J., Zhang, R., Li, D., & Yang, L. (2025). Cellular senescence and glaucoma. *Experimental Gerontology, 202*, 112718. DOI: 10.1016/j.exger.2025.112718 PMID: 39983803

Heinze, N., Jones, L., Bertiz, F., Saunders, E., & Gomes, R. S. (2024). How does the UK public think and feel about people with visual impairment: A review of existing evidence. *Frontiers in Psychology, 15*, 1359074. DOI: 10.3389/fpsyg.2024.1359074 PMID: 38515970

Helen Keller Services. (2023, November 1). 40 cells to empowerment: A comparison of five braille displays to fortify your success in 2023. https://www.helenkeller.org/40-cells-to-empowerment-a-comparison-of-five-braille-displays-to-fortify-your-success-in-2023

Hill, A. (2025, March 27). Blindness statistics 2025. *Vision Center*. https://www.visioncenter.org/resources/blindness-facts/

HumanWare. (n.d.). Braille displays and notetakers. https://store.humanware.com/int/braille-devices?___store=int_en

Industries for the Blind and Visually Impaired (IBVI). (2024, January 9). Blind vs. visually impaired: What's the difference? *IBVI Blog*. https://ibvi.org/blog/blind-vs-visually-impaired-whats-the-difference/

Jeffries, J. M., Gilroy, R., & Townshend, T. (2021). Challenging the visual: Learning from the mobility narratives of visually impaired persons. In *Urban design and human flourishing* (pp. 74–94). Routledge. DOI: 10.4324/9781003154808-6

Kapoor, D. S., Sharma, A., Singh, K. J., Thakur, K., & Kohli, A. K. (2023). AI-based wearables for healthcare applications. In *CRC Press eBooks* (pp. 278–298). https://doi.org/DOI: 10.1201/9781003453406-19

. Kumar, M. S., Srivastava, A., & Prajapati, K. (n.d.). AI assistant for visually impaired.

Kuzdeuov, A., Mukayev, O., Nurgaliyev, S., Kunbolsyn, A., & Varol, H. A. (2024, February). ChatGPT for visually impaired and blind. In *2024 International Conference on Artificial Intelligence in Information and Communication (ICAIIC)* (pp. 722–727). IEEE.

Malik, F., & Mahmood, U. (2025). Problems faced by the teachers in teaching mainstream curriculum to visually impaired students in Pakistan. *Journal of Inclusive Education, 8*(1), 117–136. https://ojs.aiou.edu.pk/index.php/jie/article/view/2509

Meta. (n.d.). AI glasses. https://www.meta.com/ai-glasses/

Microsoft Research. (2023, June 20). Microsoft Soundscape. https://www.microsoft.com/en-us/research/product/soundscape/features/

Nino, J., Ochoa, S., Kiss, J., Edwards, G., Morales, E., Hutson, J., Poncet, F., & Wittich, W. (2024). Assistive technologies for internet navigation: A review of screen reader solutions for the blind and visually impaired. *International Journal of Recent Engineering Science, 11*(6), 260–274. DOI: 10.14445/23497157/IJRES-V11I6P122

Okonji, E. P., Okonji, P. I., Connors, E., & Leja, J. (2024). Exploring the lived experiences of (un)employment among visually impaired persons in Nigeria: Implications for policy and practice. *British Journal of Visual Impairment, 42*(2), 505–517. DOI: 10.1177/02646196221148331

Open, A. I. (n.d.). ChatGPT. https://chatgpt.com/?oai-dm=1

Phochai, T., Setthasuravich, P., Pukdeewut, A., & Wetchakama, S. (2024). Bridging the digital disability divide: Determinants of internet use among visually impaired individuals in Thailand. *Disabilities, 4*(3), 696–723. DOI: 10.3390/disabilities4030043

Ramaraj, K., Teja, V., Sainath, T. V., Reddy, S., & Naidu, P. (2025, January). Custom voice assistants: Enhancing accessibility for the visually impaired. In *2025 International Conference on Intelligent and Innovative Technologies in Computing, Electrical and Electronics (IITCEE)* (pp. 1–6). IEEE. DOI: 10.1109/IITCEE64140.2025.10915383

Rose, A., Fanshawe, M., Barton, G., & Cain, M. (2025). Quality of life for braille users: A scoping review. *Review of Education, 13*(2), e70083. DOI: 10.1002/rev3.70083

Royal National Institute of Blind People (RNIB). (2024, January 31). What we know about public attitudes and understanding. https://www.rnib.org.uk/professionals/research-and-data/reports-and-insight/what-we-know-about-public-attitudes-and-understanding/

Royal National Institute of Blind People (RNIB). (n.d.). How braille changed my life and how I help others to recognise its importance. https://www.rnib.org.uk/get-involved/fundraise/gifts-in-wills/foresight-newsletter/how-braille-changed-my-life-and-how-i-help-others-to-recognise-its-importance/

Ruiz-Lozano, R. E., de la Rosa-Pacheco, S., Hernández-Camarena, J. C., Garza-Garza, L. A., Davila-Cavazos, O., Dominguez-Varela, I. A., Quiroga-Garza, M. E., & Rodriguez-Garcia, A. (2022). Burden and depression among informal caregivers of visually impaired patients in Mexico. *Disability and Health Journal, 15*(3), 101284. DOI: 10.1016/j.dhjo.2022.101284 PMID: 35337783

Seeing, A. I. (n.d.). Talking camera for the blind. https://www.seeingai.com/

Sight Scotland. (n.d.). Braille facts. https://sightscotland.org.uk/articles/information-and-advice/braille-facts

Suki, A. I. (2025, July 7). Suki Assistant. https://www.suki.ai/suki-assistant/

Turkstra, L. M., Bhatia, T., Van Os, A., & Beyeler, M. (2025). Assistive technology use in domestic activities by people who are blind. *Scientific Reports*, *15*(1), 7486. DOI: 10.1038/s41598-025-91755-w PMID: 40032957

United Nations. (n.d.). Convention on the Rights of Persons with Disabilities. https://www.ohchr.org/en/instruments-mechanisms/instruments/convention-rights-persons-disabilities

United Nations. (n.d.). The 17 Sustainable Development Goals (SDGs). https://sdgs.un.org/goals

WebAIM. (2024, February 22). Screen reader user survey #10 results. https://webaim.org/projects/screenreadersurvey10/

WeWALK. (n.d.). WeWALK smart cane. https://wewalk.io/en/

Wohr, J. (2025, April 18). Voice assistants: What they are, how they benefit marketers, and what the AI future holds for them. *eMarketer*. https://www.emarketer.com/learningcenter/guides/voice-assistants/

World Health Organization. (2023, August 10). Blindness and vision impairment. https://www.who.int/news-room/fact-sheets/detail/blindness-and-visual-impairment

World Health Organization. (2024, May 14). Eye care, vision impairment and blindness: Refractive errors. https://www.who.int/news-room/questions-and-answers/item/blindness-and-vision-impairment-refractive-errors

World Health Organization. (2025, June 27). Promoting diabetic retinopathy screening. https://www.who.int/europe/activities/promoting-diabetic-retinopathy-screening

World Health Organization Regional Office for the Eastern Mediterranean. (n.d.). Cataract. https://www.emro.who.int/health-topics/cataract/

Chapter 17
Unravelling Digital Ethics:
Dark Patterns and Algorithm Bias

Tasnim Jahan
https://orcid.org/0009-0004-1269-0122
School of Law, GD Goenka University, India

Shashikant Saurav
https://orcid.org/0000-0002-9349-7452
VIT School of Law, Chennai, India

Munaganti Annapurna Devi
https://orcid.org/0000-0003-1512-1916
Acharya Nagarjuna University, India

Harshit Singh
Vice Chancellor's Office, Rashtriya Raksha University, India

ABSTRACT

The present era can be categorised as digital not just because of the availability of digital space and platforms but because people are gearing up for these platforms by using them in their daily lives. It cannot be denied that digitalisation has made our lives immensely easier in many ways than one could have ever thought of. However, the negative aspects of the same cannot be denied. The emergence of new technology daily is posing severe concerns amongst the people at large as these digital algorithms, deceptive designs, and machine learning are few of the by-products of this era where the proliferation of online platforms and algorithmic decision-making has revolutionised the way individuals interact, consume information and make decisions. The present chapter conceptualises digital ethics in terms of

DOI: 10.4018/979-8-3693-3920-6.ch017

algorithm bias and dark patterns with specific reference to e-commerce platforms. It also understands user relationships through the lens of e-contracts and consent, as observed by the Indian courts through various case laws.

INTRODUCTION & BACKGROUND

Today we have moved past from the analog landscape to the digital era. People consumes the digital energy like never before and in all the aspects of the life. From using it for educational and work purposes to making online bookings, checking for share markets to investing online, social media and writing blogs to professional connecting applications which also includes matrimonial application which have comparatively more personal details than any other platforms of similar nature, from shopping online to creating wish list for other such shopping platforms (Alberto, 2022). These are the few of the areas where the online aka digital platforms have taken over in our day to day lives. It cannot be denied that digitalisation has made our lives quite easier in a lot more ways than one could have ever thought of. But at the same time as much as the digitalization is proving to be the biggest boon of people's life, the negative aspects of the same cannot be denied. Emergence of new technology on daily basis are posing serious concerns amongst the people at large as these digital algorithms, deceptive designs, machine learning are few of the by-products of this era where the proliferation of online platforms and algorithmic decision-making has revolutionized the way individuals interact, consume information, and make decisions (Das & Datta, 2023).

In terms of machine language which just understand numbers and quantified data, it becomes difficult if quality has to be assessed for any set of data available. 'Algorithm' is such data structure and pre-identified steps which help machine understand the language and assume the task involved. Moreover it is about the knowledge perceived by the programmers and how they want the machine to perceive it accordingly. For the layman's who have no idea of the hardware and software of any available machine or the platform being used by them and is only concerned about the function, the said machine is going to perform for them, the question of such awareness arise (Rani Adgulwar, 2023) Similarly 'Dark patterns' are such misleading and deceptive design techniques those are employed by digital interfaces to manipulate user behaviour which paves the way for algorithmic bias and systemic discrimination perpetuated by such algorithms and as a result pose unacceptable challenges to a person also referred to as an user of any such machine, software at a given point of time in accessing their autonomy, privacy, and societal fairness. It won't be wrong to state that unwinding such an interaction between these phenomena is extremely important for not just promoting transparency, accountability, and ethical integrity in the digital realm but also for the consumer trust and build upon the same (CCG, NLUD)

Having said that, increased use of technology in our daily spheres and a lack of understanding of the functionality of algorithms and dark patterns poses serious risk of being exposed to third parties and getting the personal data leaked. Another major concern is that, biases and prejudices is being created and passed on to different users as well. Ironically, most of the data are not collected by user consent but by the different online platforms used by the people and by different third parties involved (Reinsten, 2019).

This study will draw the interlinked relationship between the algorithmic bias and dark patterns and delves into interaction in the context of digital platforms and address the said two ethical concerns in the digital era. It will try to find out the ways in which these events overlap and may even reinforce one another, undermining not just the user confidence but also violate the privacy rights and escalate social injustices among the mass. By employing an interdisciplinary approach that incorporates perspectives from computer science, ethics, psychology, and sociology, this study seeks to clarify the working mechanisms of algorithmic bias and dark patterns, pinpoint shared experiences, and suggest countermeasures for their detrimental effects. The results of this study should help scholars, industry practitioners, and politicians understand the complicated ethical ramifications of algorithmic decision-making and digital design, which will ultimately promote the creation of digital environments that are more open, transparent, and equal.

PURPOSE OF THE STUDY

This research primarily focus on need for specific provisions to deal with the ever growing digital space. Being a developing country, India have seen immense growth in the technological front in almost all the aspect of people's day to day lives and have touched upon not just economic and financial aspect but also social and cultural lives. The question of data privacy have been there in the literature and dialogue sphere for quite a long time and the same had been discussed partially in the case of *KS Puttaswamy v. Union of India* where the Supreme court of India dealt with the question of right to privacy and observed the test of privacy infringement. The test laid down that three criteria have to be met with: Legality, Need and Proportionality in order to check for the infringement of the privacy in question. The said case also declared right to privacy as a Fundamental right. However, the said test was vague and did not provide for the scope and meaning of the require criteria. Apart from this, there has been other statutes, policy and regulation that has put forth the concerns regarding the personal data infringement through the digital platform used by the people. In 2020-21 Artificial Intelligence (AI) which uses the algorithms to function, took over by storm and got everyone to talk about the same. Though a lot of people enjoyed the usage and the interface of the same, in the absence of any regulations for the AI, privacy concerns arose. The ministry of Electronics and Information technology released a strategy to bring in AI development to keep a check on user parameters as well as privacy issues. Other Act includes *IT Act 2000*, *DPDP Act 2023*, *RTI Act 2005*, but none of these actually deals with the shortcomings of the increased usage of the AI in the current workforce. Each of these statutes deals with specific provisions, whereas the DPDP Act of 2023 deals with the breaches of the data infringement but have restricted the regulatory powers. But given the dynamics of the subject area, it becomes crucial to understand the probable impacts that the unregulated AI can pose in long span of time and hence, there is a dire need of specific provision to deal with the algorithm bias that AI utilizes and leads to dark patterns as well.

RESEARCH METHODOLOGY

A mixed method including doctrinal and empirical research using both quantitative and qualitative data is employed in this research. A thorough study of all the existing doctrines is done in order to find the loopholes that makes it easier for the data privacy infringement and quantitative data utilised for the purpose of finding the kind and specification of such infringement. As datasets lack the qualitative aspects, the same is taken into consideration by setting up criteria and measurable scales and then converting the same into quantities for the data analysis.

The data are majorly collected through the existing legal and Non-legal doctrines, statutes and regulations. Apart from this the various statistics available with the stakeholders (Policy centres, NGOs, etc.,) is utilised for this purpose. The third set of data is collected first hand from the stakeholders who includes both the companies, digital space users and the all the other people involved. A detailed consumer surveys along with the stakeholders policy is used for meeting objectives of this research. Apart from this structure and non-structure interviews was also the part of the data collection.

The Ethical issues are inevitable and the process of collection of data and its analysis took care of the ethical considerations and did the needful in order to maintain the sanctity of the research. Ethical guidelines was prepared with the help of the pre-identified ethics and was followed throughout the research process and data collection. Informed consent was taken before collection of data and adhered to the principles of integrity, objectivity, and transparency.

LITERATURE REVIEW

Every digital device used by us or any such platform which is available online and accessible by people in general have a user interface that is made and configured keeping the audience in mind and the same should be consumer friendly which the authors (*M.R. Leiser and Cristiana Santos, 2019)* have highlighted in their paper and discussed how manipulative these user interface can get and the same having all the probabilities of privacy infringement of the consumers. They also discussed that these user interface manipulation are termed as 'Dark Pattern' and the same exploit the users of these platforms in order to achieve certain hidden outcomes/ targets set by the company or the e-commerce platform. *(Zlatan Meskic et al., 2022)* In their paper discussed the cross borders and transnational consumer issues as E-Commerce platform is not limited to any particular jurisdiction but beyond that and highlighted how the same is not discussed or addressed in the national laws of the country. Consumer Protection area is quite vast and instead of circumscribing it, the focus should be on to expand this as much as possible for the sake of keeping a space for more kinds of concern to be addressed through it. And the same has been discussed by the author *(Rani Adgulwar, 2021)* in her paper on Consumer protection and e-commerce in India. *(Sanjay Kumar et al., 2022)* revived the challenges that are faced by users in respect of e-commerce platform in connection to the trade and competition and also observed the status of the same with respect to the laws available in India which were not sufficient to deal with the new kinds of privacy infringement occurring as a result therein. *(Amelia Fletcher et al., 2023)* in their paper dealt with the laws and regulations required for the consumer protection and to deal with digital ethics. It also talks about how not just having a law for the same would be helpful but also focusing on introducing simple privacy feature should be handy with the user interface. *(Kiranjit Kaur, 2005)* in her paper discussed the case study of developing and developed nations with respect to e-commerce platform and regular updates that are being done to these platforms because of rapid technological advancements. *(Neelam Chawla & Basanta Kumar, 2020)* highlighted the major reason for people not being able to transact online as lack of trust and hidden dark patterns that seems to spam sometimes.

Figure 1. Model for consumer trust on e-commerce platform (Chawla & Kumar, 2020)

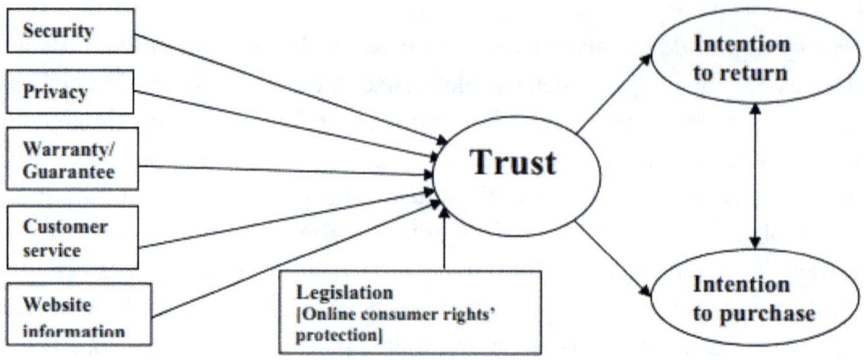

(Kerstin et at., 2021) explained the reason behind the online privacy infringement through usage of these e-commerce platform through four dimensional variables and these are Education, Design, Technical AND Regulatory bodies.

Figure 2. Intervention spaces for counteracting dark patterns (Kerstin et al., 2021)

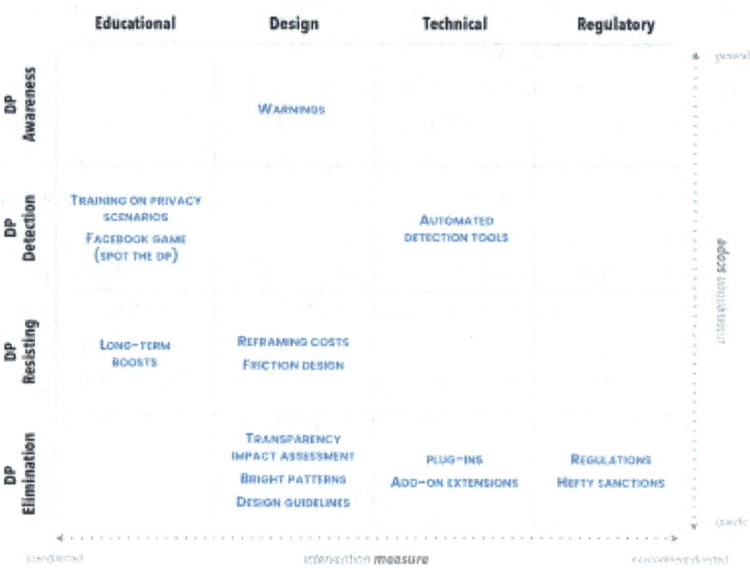

The literature review highlights the gap of regulatory aspects that are missing even after being aware of the consumer concerns, privacy infringement and the non-compliant digital ethics leading to dark patterns that involves Artificial Intelligence as well.

INDIA'S DIGITAL MARKET VIS-À-VIS LAWS AND REGULATIONS

The e-commerce (or electronic commerce) market in India is quite promising. India's e-commerce sales are predicted to expand at the fastest rate in the world, with a 51% growth rate, from USD 38.5 billion in 2017 to USD 200 billion in 2026. E-commerce began soon after India's Internet introduction in 1995. The 1990s saw a rise in B2B websites in e-commerce. B2C e-commerce was introduced in India in 2002 by IRCTC's e-ticketing service. In the beginning, travel dominated India's B2C market. Websites pertaining to travel accounted for 87% and 79% of e-commerce revenue in 2011 and 2013, respectively. Since 2013, online retail platforms have experienced growth in e-commerce. Online retail sales made up the same percentage of e-commerce in 2015 as the online travel sector (Nougarahiya, 2021). The Indian e-commerce market expanded in the next years to encompass apparel, luxury products, and mobile/DTH recharges. The majority of retail companies thought e-commerce will improve their business. E-commerce gives customers an alternative to traditional retail shopping, allowing them to research product characteristics including costs, availability, suppliers, alternatives, and even manufacturing procedures (Phillips, 2000)

By improving the characteristics of online marketplaces, e-commerce companies may stay competitive by increasing business interoperability. But even with all the information available from the many e-commerce firms, it might be difficult for customers to make snap decisions. Thus, in order to handle intense competition in the market and anxious customers, an e-commerce platform prefers an efficient tailored attached Dataset (Wang & Archer, 2007). E-commerce companies are employing mass customization techniques to change the way items are displayed in their online stores rather than the products themselves in an effort to combat this information overload. One approach for online markets to accomplish widespread customization is through the use of recommender systems. E-commerce companies use these systems to give their customers personalized recommendations and information to help them decide what to buy (Schafer at al., 2001). A recommender system is a computer software that uses patterns found in user likes and ratings of other goods to filter personalized information, understand user preferences, and make relevant suggestions. Without a doubt, recommender systems are a tool that may improve a user's overall experience with a service that aims to optimize the user's usefulness. But when the goals of the platform conflict with any of the user's usefulness, suggestions might easily become a means to “trap” the user in the system. Customers are therefore vulnerable to those traps (Agarwal & Swami, 1993).

Figure 3. Revenue generation by e-commerce India (Statistica, 2024)

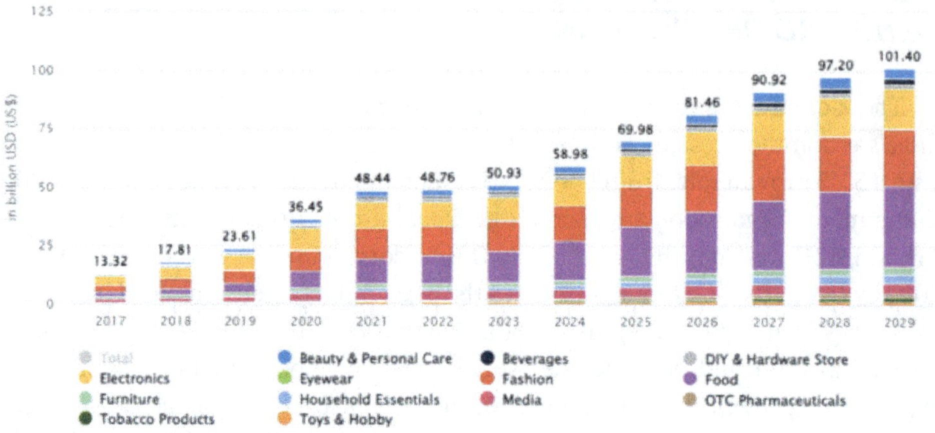

The Information Technology Act, 2000 was enacted to provide legal recognition for e-contracts and validate e-documents through electronic signatures. It also addressed cyber-crimes and fulfilled the UNCITRAL Model Law guidelines. The current e-commerce legal regime in India includes the Consumer Protection Act, 2019, Consumer Protection (e-commerce) Rules, 2017, and the Information Technology Act, 2000. However, issues such as data protection, online privacy, spam, and online frauds have been causing problems since the early 2000s. India has yet to enact legal provisions to address these issues. The Consumer Protection Act 2019 (CPA) was recently enacted to address new challenges faced by consumers and e-commerce platforms (Chawla & Kumar, 2022). The CPA includes provisions for e-consumer-specific provisions, defining 'unfair contracts', and expanding the scope for consumers to challenge terms of unfair unilateral contracts. However, there are still anomalies and grey areas that need to be recognized and addressed. India is one of the few countries that has enacted consumer-centric legislation, but there is a dire need for futuristic legislation considering developing technologies and potential challenges (Das et al., 2017)

Social media has revolutionized e-commerce, offering a vast array of business opportunities. However, the growth of social media entrepreneurs poses challenges in resolving liability issues. Consumers often lack personal details, such as permanent addresses or contact details, which can be easily changed by the entrepreneur. This makes it difficult for victims to file complaints, as they often fail to provide the required information (Leiser & Santos, 2019). Moreover, many victims fear legal proceedings, as they often avoid consumer forums. A 2021 survey found that only 1.8% of participants chose to approach a forum, while the rest chose to complain to customer care, give negative feedback, or ignore the issue. Victims are often silenced by disclaimers about product quality, which can lead to poor quality goods. The social taboo surrounding online purchases can also discourage victims from seeking legal recourse. Lastly, there are no government authorities monitoring social media businesses, which can negatively impact their social image and financial crimes. A similar system of accountability could require social media entrepreneurs to obtain a license from a government-recognized authority, allowing victims to find their registered permanent address and potentially cancel or suspend their license (Fletcher et al., 2023).

Companies now gather enormous volumes of consumer data in the digital age, thus it is imperative that the government shield its citizens against invasions of privacy. Data protection standards have been created by the European Convention for the Protection of Human Rights and national laws, such as Directive 95/46/EC. In 2018, the Directive was replaced by the General Data Protection Regulation, 2016, and India is pursuing a robust data protection framework. E-commerce sites may expose customer information, which might result in cybercrime and data piracy (Shetty Mandoli, 2021). The government is required to safeguard its citizens from possible threats, such as the use of artificial intelligence software to exploit data and offer individualized higher rates to individual consumers. Major two pint of concerns are AI and online Spams. Artificial Intelligence (AI) is playing a crucial role in ecommerce, enhancing the shopping experience and preventing fraud. However, AI can also pose threats to online privacy (Singh, 2023). In India, there is no Data Protection Law yet, and AI-connected devices like Google and Amazon Echo can collect sensitive information. The Indian Supreme Court recognized the right to privacy as a fundamental right in 2017, but the lack of legislation to protect citizens from data intrusion is a significant concern. The potential for AI usage for both good and bad purposes is a potential threat, and e-consumers should not be left to bear the burden of technology ignorance. Spams are a nuisance that can carry viruses and facilitate cybercrimes. Unwarranted advertisements online can be regulated by strengthening data privacy legislations. Agencies that collect personal data without proper information about its purpose, processing, and access rights violate privacy. Unsolicited emails, text messages, and telephonic calls are considered spam (Datta, 2023). Data Protection legislation should include provisions for un-subscribers, preventing sharing of sensitive information, and disclosing the source of collected contact information. Examples of effective privacy protection include the Can Spam Act, 2003 in the USA and the Japanese law on unsolicited emails and text messages. India should adopt similar provisions to protect consumers from unsolicited advertisements. The European Union and USA also prescribe opt-in and opt-out options for consumers. However, data harnessing has often been done without consent from the data subject (Giorgia Guerra, 2023).

Graphical representation of Digital Ethics and Dark Pattern in India (Total recorded answers 123)

The first question dealt with "How many time do you typically use/buy from these platforms" in order to understand the penetration of digital platforms with specific reference to e-commerce platforms in Indian Households. And the answers are pretty clear that more than half of the taken sample shop for at least 1-5 times a month on these platforms. Options given were Myntra, Flipkart, Amazon, Nykaa, Ajio, Zomato, Swiggy, Uber, Ola, Rapido, Blinkit, Zepto and others.

Figure 4. E-Commerce penetration in Indian households

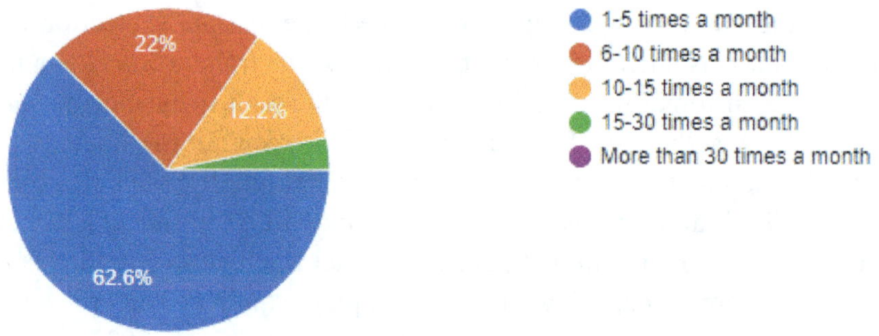

Another important question "Which of these apps/websites asked you to mandatorily create an account to place an order" to understand the forced enrolment of the customer on their platform which is also a subtle way to collect the personal information and the same is collected in the database as well.

Figure 5. Forced enrollment

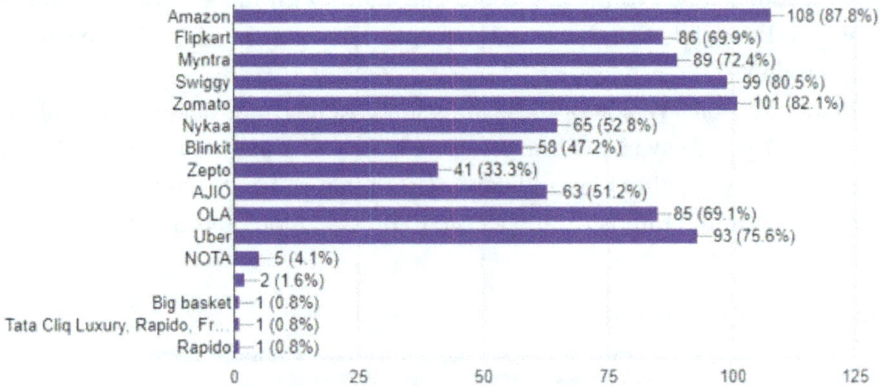

Next question "Which of these apps added extra item (complimentary product or a voucher) to your cart automatically" was to test the platforms behavior regarding the marketing tactics at the cost of consumer privacy infringement and this forms the part of dark pattern discovered as 'sneaking' into customers cart without the consent in the name of offers.

Figure 6. Sneaking in- consent violation

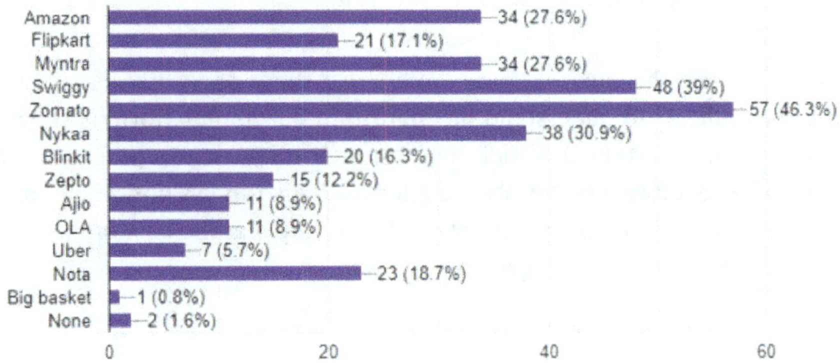

Next in line the question was "Which of the apps charged you an inflated bill (Delivery charges, Service charges, taxes etc.) which was not previously mentioned in the price of the product?" to understand another dark pattern 'Hidden Cost' which is visible only before payment or after adding the product to the cart. Here in this small sample we get to know the maxim number of the stakeholders have experienced this and the catch is that these platforms earn through customers browsing and the customer tends to browse more and more with the shown price on their mind only to know later on the actual payment after they have made their mind to buy that products.

Another question "Which of these apps send exclusive or personalized offers to you or prompt you to avail the 'limited time offers' or 'countdown' of a sale" dealt with yet another algorithm bias and dark pattern that can be termed as "Urgency or creating hurry" in the minds of the people to browse more and more.

Figure 7. Urgency: Sale offers

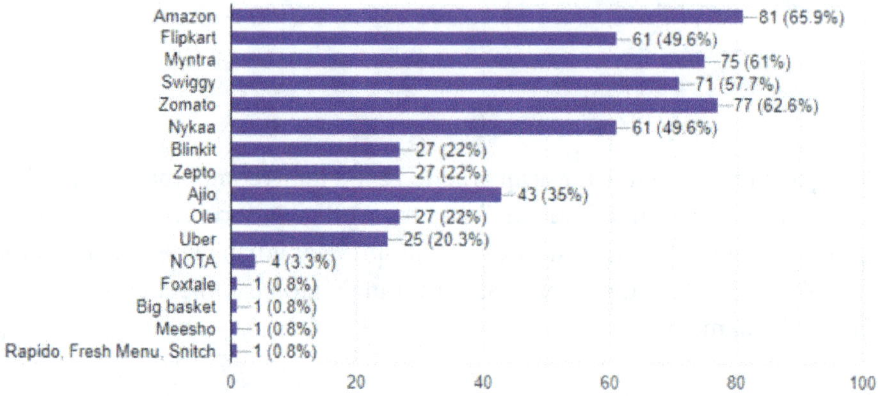

Next in line the question was "Which of these apps highlight few products more than others" to understand the algorithm bias the platform is showcasing by suggesting those products which the customer might have checked out before or on any other platforms or simply Google out. It also shows how visual interference is a common thing just to reach the platforms target at the cost of customer's time resources and privacy infringement.

Figure 8. Visual interference vis-à-vis algorithm bias

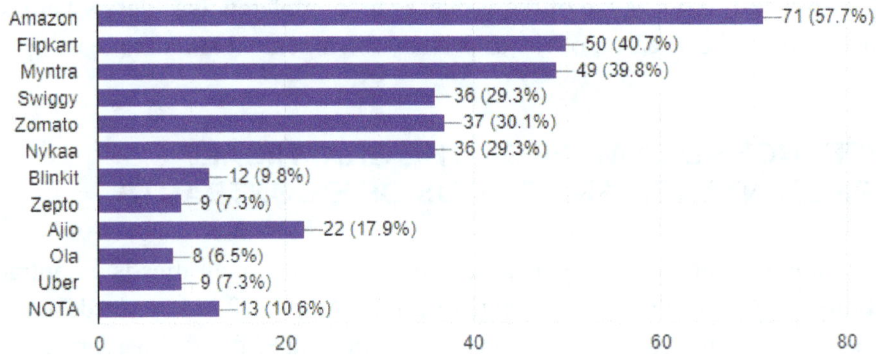

And last but not the least the question "Have you ever received targeted message from these apps such as "Hey! Please drink water. If you need food, let us know" was to understand how these e-commerce platforms are going beyond the users search list and algorithm bias and send target message to lure them into shopping or ordering food.

Figure 9. Dark pattern-targeted messages

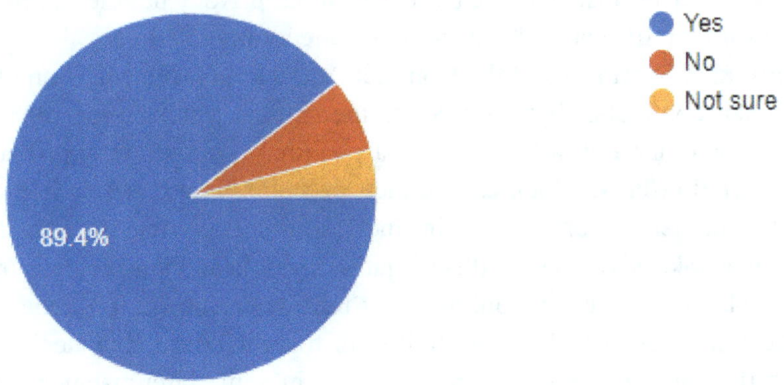

Before moving to the discussions based on the graphical representation, it becomes pertinent to conceptualize 'Dark Pattern' and 'Algorithm Bias'. Dark Patterns are those deceptive design incorporated or inbuilt in the e-commerce platform to capture user preference through most searched goods and services by them, by collecting their personal data through mandatory requirement of creating an account before placing an order, adding other taxes and charges on the goods and services are added to their cart and so on. Some of these may seem completely harmless whereas few of these are can be a reason of major privacy infringement and data losses.

INFERENCES DRAWN FROM THE GRAPHICAL REPRESENTATION AND STATUS OF E-CONTRACTS

The relationship between consumers and e-commerce entities is a contractual relationship, governed by the Indian Contract Act, 1872. The Act defines free consent as consent without coercion, undue influence, fraud, misrepresentation, or mistake. In today's world, consent is a key factor in e-contracts, with clickwrap contracts and browse-wrap contracts being the most common. The United States Jurisdiction provides precedents for the validity of these contracts, but there are also precedents against them. In India, the Information Technology Act 2000 gives validity to electronically executed contracts. The Consumer Protection Act 2019 governs consumer contractual relationships in India, defining consumers as those who buy or hire goods or services for consideration but not for reselling or profit. Consumers are considered 'parens patriae', and the government has established consumer forums or commissions for redressal of consumer disputes. E-commerce entities use clickwrap or browsewrap contracts to gather information about consumers and run recommender algorithms. Companies like Amazon, Flipkart, Myntra, Zomato, Swiggy, Nykaa, Big Basket, and Uber have similar privacy policies, allowing them to use consumer information for personalized recommendations.

According to Section 16 of the Contract Act, undue influence is an obstacle to free consent in contracts. This describes partnerships in which one person subjugates the will of the other and takes use of that position to obtain an unjust advantage. Fiduciary relationships, which can be fact- or status-based, arise when one party fully trusts another to manage their business affairs. E-commerce companies, like Amazon, may take advantage of this by gathering data and putting their trust in the customer. This may result in contracts that have been subject to undue influence, which the consumer may choose to nullify or that the courts may decide to avoid. Although they are unable to become involved in some circumstances, consumer laws can nevertheless be advantageous. E-commerce may contend that the data and suggestions are the outcome of consumer's consent through e-contracts.

E-contracts with minimal room for discussion are usually “take it or leave it” agreements between customers and e-commerce companies. (Tillotson, 2019) suggested contract type is frequently null and void because of prejudice and unjust procedural practices. However, the Consumer Protection Act (CoPrA) declares any contract that places duties or conditions on customers to be unfair since it acknowledges substantive unfairness in Indian jurisprudence. Under CoPrA, e-contracts that cause undue influence need to be deemed substantively unfair as well. According to the Personal Data Protection Bill 2019 (Paterson et al.), it is against these regulations to get misinformed consent through e-contracts. Nevertheless, the measure was rescinded in August 2022, and consumer courts would have less subject matter authority. Customers can file a complaint about recommender systems by claiming that the e-contract is unfair or by addressing unfair trade practices in specific data sharing scenarios.

CONCLUSION

The rapid growth of the ecommerce sector in India presents significant challenges that need immediate attention to protect consumers. To address these issues, the existing legal regime needs adaptations. Some suggestions include creating awareness about consumer forums, establishing Central, State, and District level Cyber Tribunals under the Information Technology Act 2000, creating a parallel cyber investigation system, overhauling existing cyber cells, appointing more authorities to investigate each aspect of data, including a separate provision for unsolicited emails and text messages, regulating Artificial Intelligence through legislation, shifting the burden of quality assessment on marketplace e-commerce entities and sellers, monitoring and regulating social media entrepreneurs to avoid problems like tax evasion and fraud, investing more in research and development, and collaborating with organizations like the WTO and UN to combat online crimes.The current laws and policies governing e-commerce are mostly consumer-centric, but there is a need for cross-sectional legal provisions governing different aspects of e-commerce. Mandatory education in information technologies and cyber laws can help better enforce the law, and the government should invest more in research and development to achieve technological advancement. A global effort is needed to stop frauds and other cybercrimes, including e-commerce-related frauds, with the help of organizations like the WTO and UN.

On a concluding note the research tried to justify the theme of the book by encapsulating suggestive changes and recommendation for the users, company owners, stakeholders and most importantly the policy makers. India is a country where bringing in a positive change is next to impossible in the absence of a proper law and regulations dealing with the issues in question. The reason behind this is the diverse nature of the country, not just in terms of the religion, case, race, and culture but also, in terms of education, awareness and self-consciousness. Today a huge number of the country's population has been using digital mediums for their day to day activities without realising their data being exposed to third parties.

One of the reason is because of the dark patterns followed by these digital medium stakeholders and another reason is the algorithms that are being used and hence more than awareness of these people using such mediums, the owners are supposed to made aware of the existing laws and regulations that can protect the consumer from the same. Keeping this as a backdrop the study identified the major infringements that is happening with respect to the people's personal data, what are the algorithm biases that are pre-existing and what the loop-holes is in the Indian existing legal literature that is allowing such biases and infringements. The study highlights the underlying issues with the ever-growing digitalisation and use of the Artificial Intelligence and focusses on the need of regulatory bodies and statutes for the regulation and development of the same. The chapter serves as a persuasive factor behind the need of such a legal framework.

REFERENCES

Adgulwar, R. (2021). Consumer protection and e-commerce in India. *PalArch's Journal of Archaeology of Egypt/Egyptology, 18*(10), 990–997.

Chawla, V., & Kumar, A. (2022). E-commerce and consumer protection in India: The emerging trend. *Journal of Business Ethics*, *180*(2), 581–604. DOI: 10.1007/s10551-021-04884-3 PMID: 34257470

Das, D., Sahoo, L., & Datta, S. (2017). A survey on recommendation system. *International Journal of Computer Applications*, *160*(7), 1–7. https://www.ijcaonline.org/archives/volume160/number7/27083-2017913081. DOI: 10.5120/ijca2017916037

Fletcher, A.. (2023). Consumer protection for online markets and large digital platforms. *Yale Journal on Regulation*, *40*, 875–944.

Fletcher, A., ... (2023). *Consumer protection for online markets and large digital platforms*. https://www.yalejreg.com/wp-content/uploads/Consumer-Protection-for-Online-Markets-and-Large-Digital-Platforms-1.pdf

Guerra, G. (2023). *Redesigning protection for consumer autonomy: The case study of dark patterns in European private law*. https://www.law.ua.edu/lawreview/files/2020/11/1-DayStemler-1-45.pdf

Kaur, K. (2005). *Consumer protection in e-commerce in Malaysia: An overview*. https://citeseerx.ist.psu.edu/document?repid=rep1&type=pdf&doi=3b9cf62468 1e348820f8392c584cf07d4605b6f5

Leiser, M. R., & Santos, C. (2019). *Dark patterns, enforcement, and the emerging digital design acquis: Manipulation beneath the interface*.

Nougarahiya, S., Shetty, G., & Mandloi, D. (2021). A review of e-commerce in India: The past, present, and the future. *International Journal of Multidisciplinary Research*. https://papers.ssrn.com/sol3/papers.cfm?abstract_id=3809521

Phillips, C. (2000). *The B2B internet report: Collaborative commerce*. Morgan Stanley Dean Witter.

Schafer, J. B., Konstan, J. A., & Riedl, J. (2001). E-commerce recommendation applications. *Data Mining and Knowledge Discovery*, *5*(1–2), 115–153. DOI: 10.1023/A:1009804230409

Wang, S., & Archer, N. (2007). Electronic marketplace definition and classification: Literature review and clarifications.

Chapter 18
Digital Governance, Security, and Privacy Rights in India:
Exploring Evolving Political Theory and Recent Legislative Developments

Anuttama Ghose
https://orcid.org/0000-0002-7210-4074
School of Law, Dr. Vishwanath Karad MIT-World Peace University, Pune, India

Neha Agashe
https://orcid.org/0000-0002-7858-0610
School of Law, Dr. Vishwanath Karad MIT-World Peace University, Pune, India

S. M. Aamir Ali
https://orcid.org/0000-0002-8686-0217
Symbiosis Law School, Symbiosis International University, Pune, India

ABSTRACT

In the contemporary era, technological progress has led to a heightened emphasis not only on distinguishing between private and public spheres but also on identifying elements that may inadvertently enter the public domain but nonetheless contribute to privacy concerns. This study aims to examine the complex interplay between privacy rights and dignity in the context of widespread technological progress. This article explores the notion of human dignity, which is presented as a major subject that emphasizes the importance of people and their right to autonomy and respect. The study assesses the intricate interplay between privacy, governance, and

DOI: 10.4018/979-8-3693-3920-6.ch018

societal values by drawing from philosophical viewpoints, legal frameworks, and case studies. This study highlights the pressing need for strong norms and ethical standards to safeguard privacy and promote democratic principles in the digital era, as it seeks to comprehend India's stance on privacy rights and concerns related to mass surveillance programs.

1. INTRODUCTION:

In the modern era, with the progress of technology, there is a growing emphasis on distinguishing between private and public domains, as well as considering factors that can impact privacy while also being part of the public sphere. In today's world, the lines between privacy and the preservation of a person's inherent dignity are becoming increasingly blurred (Sullivan, 2011). In the realm of privacy, there has long been an association with the notion of the private sphere, confined within the boundaries of one's home and extending to the sacred concept of family, deserving of utmost protection (DeVries, 2003). By its very nature, this implies that privacy rights encompass and safeguard activities that are not meant for public scrutiny, ensuring a sense of protection from prying eyes. Consequently, it establishes a framework that ensures the proper governance of the data sphere. This is achieved through the delineation of the rights held by individuals in relation to any entity that collects data pertaining to them. It reaffirms in the digital realm what Western democracies have long believed in for offline activities: that markets are not completely free but rather operate within a broader framework of enforceable rights and guarantees. The boundaries of privacy have undergone significant shifts, particularly in the era of the data-driven online environment (Xu & Jia, 2015). Many governments around the world now prioritize the implementation of CCTV systems, utilization of facial recognition technology (FRT), automatic interception and storage of internet and telecommunication data, and the application of AI for comprehensive analysis of the gathered information. Governments worldwide are actively promoting the use of these technologies, recognizing their practicality and cost-effectiveness (Raab, 2017). Some critics have raised concerns about the far-reaching effects of surveillance on individuals' privacy rights, suggesting that it may contribute to a growing sense of mistrust. Individuals value digital privacy as it allows them to maintain control over their online identity and decide which aspects of their identity they want to share (Kasper, 2007). Mastering such a level of authority over information can prove to be quite challenging. More precise terminology and universally agreed-upon definitions of digital privacy need to be used. In the realm of data, its immense power is evident in how it drives the growth of businesses and governments. However, this power also has a downside, as it leaves vulnerable individuals at the mercy of a complex bureaucratic system that lacks transparency, consistency, and a genuine concern for the welfare and dignity of people (Sullivan, 2011). The psychological element of being observed in everyday activities, such as conversations, shopping, and movements, is intricately connected to one's sense of dignity. It hinders individuals from living their lives independently and impacts the standing of human beings without innate dignity.

The idea of human dignity requires the existence of a liberal regime beforehand. In a society that upholds individual rights and values, every person deserves to be treated with care and respect simply because they are human (Sullivan, 2011). This study seeks to explore the intricate relationship between privacy rights and dignity within the ever-evolving landscape of technology. The increasing prevalence of surveillance technologies and the extensive collection of personal data are presenting a substantial challenge to long-standing notions of privacy. This article delves into the concept of human dignity, highlighting its significance in emphasizing the value of individuals and their entitlement to autonomy and respect. The study utilizes philosophical perspectives, legal frameworks, and case studies to examine the complex relationship between privacy, governance, and societal values. This study emphasizes the urgent requirement for robust norms and ethical standards to protect privacy and uphold democratic principles in the digital age. It aims to understand India's position on privacy rights and address concerns regarding mass surveillance programs.

2. EVOLUTION OF PRIVACY: UPHOLDING SANCTITY OF PRIVATE REALM AMIDST DIGITAL ADVANCEMENTS

The right to privacy is universally recognized worldwide as an essential and inherent human right. Currently, the majority of countries ensure the provision of certain rights to their inhabitants, but the extent of these rights may differ. Freedom is a basic right that is universally guaranteed, yet it is restricted and has many different aspects. The concept of privacy is essentially a right bestowed upon individuals to safeguard their acts, decisions, and personal ideas conveyed inside a certain domain, preventing them from being revealed or examined by the general public. This right is seen to be of utmost significance, particularly in contemporary society. Privacy concerns have existed since the beginning of civilization, yet the concept of privacy itself is relatively new. Traditionally, the concept of privacy has been inherent in the legal or social measures used to safeguard personal belongings, living spaces, or personal possessions. However, by the Twentieth century, researchers had refined the concept of privacy into a distinct and much debated, although poorly understood, field of study.

The development of privacy rights in contemporary times is intricately connected to the narrative of industrial-age advancements, the proliferation of technology, and the expanding realm of the Internet. The growth of privacy protection has been influenced by the revolution in mobile technology and the advancements in safeguarding personal information.

Samuel Warren and Louis Brandeis were the pioneers in establishing a legal entitlement to privacy (Warren & Brandeis, 1890). They defined privacy as the protection of one's personal identity from intrusion or unwarranted disclosure (Warren & Brandeis, 1890, p. 205). Essentially, they advocated for a "right to be left alone" (Warren & Brandeis, 1890, p. 195). Brandeis' understanding of privacy, particularly in relation to government interference, influenced the development of the US Constitutional Law (*Griswold v. Connecticut*, 1965). This understanding is based on the specific provisions in the Bill of Rights that safeguard individuals against government intrusion into their homes and personal belongings. It also recognizes the importance of protecting personal autonomy and freedom of choice. Protection against such unauthorized invasions by private parties developed into legal claims under common law tort. In general terms, the test revolved around whether the victim had a "reasonable expectation of privacy" and if the other party or governmental agency infringed upon it without valid cause (*California v. Ciraolo*, 1986). There are two main sub-branches that have emerged: physical or spatial privacy and decisional privacy. Physical space or objects are highly safeguarded to ensure privacy. The Court has significantly restricted the government's capacity to encroach upon the "reasonable expectation of privacy" that all people possess in their bodies and belongings (*California v. Ciraolo*, 1986).

A more recently emerged "offshoot" of privacy legislation pertains to information. Although the privacy of personal information and the preservation of personal documents is inherent in the initial concept of privacy by W Brandeis and the 4th Amendment of the American Constitution, the notion of "informational privacy" as distinct from the physical form of the information is now more difficult to define (Warren & Brandeis, 1890, p. 193). Informational privacy concerns emerged even prior to the advent of digital data. With the development of contemporary industrial society, different entities such as governments, banks, and schools often acquire personal information about citizens, clients, and students. Although the protection of this information was often considered a fundamental right of individuals, its clarity remained uncertain (*Whalen v. Roe*, 1977). The legal safeguards for the protection of personal information are limited in both common law and constitutional frameworks. The privacy torts are not directly relevant to the abuse of information unless the information was obtained from the victim or another private source, such as the victim's bank. An account rule may not be applicable in cases when one's personal information is shared with a third party, such as a marketer. The notion of privacy safeguards personal information against government interference, with the aim of preventing the revelation of personal affairs from becoming too extensive (DeVries, 2003).

The previous generation has seen a level of technical transformation that is comparable to or beyond that of the Industrial Revolution (Quinn Jr., 1999). The advent of the "digital revolution" has significantly impacted privacy (Solove, 2001). Jerry Berman and Deirdre Mulligan identify three significant digital advancements that have a profound impact on privacy (Berman & Mulligan, 1999). Firstly, there is a significant increase in the generation of data and the subsequent accumulation of large quantities of personal information. This is due to the recording of nearly every modern interaction. Secondly, the global nature of the data market allows anyone to gather and analyze this data. Lastly, there is a lack of control mechanisms for digital data, which were previously in place to safeguard analog data (Berman & Mulligan, 1999).

All three of these advancements pertain to the alterations caused by digital technology in the capacity to modify information. Initially, the quantity of digital information produced is astonishing (Froomkin, 2000). Each online contact, credit card purchase, bank withdrawal, and magazine subscription is digitally stored and associated with specific individuals. In the analog realm, these transactions either needed to be documented or written on paper in a solitary spot (Berman & Mulligan, 1999). Furthermore, once this information is gathered and stored in interconnected databases, it can be easily and inexpensively sent worldwide. In this increasingly commoditized information market, purchasers have the ability to gather and modify data with the goal of creating detailed profiles or potentially malicious intentions (Berman & Mulligan, 1999). Furthermore, people possess the ability to exercise control over this process of gathering or manipulation. Not only does this occur outside the jurisdiction of authorities, but the majority of individuals need to be made aware of the information that has been gathered or its extent. However, it is important to note that these developments have not only impacted informational privacy but also other aspects (DeVries, 2003.

3. DIGNITY, LIBERALISM AND INDIVIDUAL WORTH: EXPLORING THE CONCEPTUAL NEXUS

The concept of human dignity necessitates a pre-existence of a liberal regime. In a liberal society, an individual is valued as an individual and needs to be treated with concern and respect just by virtue of the fact that they are a human being. At the heart of liberalism lies the right to equal concern and respect. According to Dworkin, governments have a duty to govern with concern and trust human beings as they are capable of comprehending how their lives should be lived (Dworkin, 1977). The government should not constrain liberty on the grounds of the fact that one citizen's concept of good is superior to another. Hence, it depicts equal concern and respect for all citizens. A positive concept of liberty needs to be adopted to sustain and inculcate dignity. Irrespective of political utility, each human being is equal in moral worth (Dworkin, 1977).

Human dignity implies the inherent worth of a human being and its relevance in society and at a political level. The concept of human dignity is variable with respect to different societies. In many societies, the values of equality and autonomy vary and hence impact human rights. Tracing back history, dignity, in traditional terms, was not possessed by people in general and was rather exclusive in nature. Only dignitaries possessed the dignity and were associated with a comparative social or higher rank. The accordance of dignity to a few led to the association of deference and esteem. Early Roman Thinker Cicero considered human beings distinguished by the virtue of their capacity for rational thought (Winterbottom, 1994).

Universalization of the concept of dignity can be associated with Philosophical idealism propagated by Immanuel Kant (Sensen, 2009). Humanity needs to be seen as an end, and it is dignity that enables man to possess morality and only the basis of being a law-giving member. Kant summarized humanity and its capacity to be moral, which determines dignity, and it is reflected in the way we carry ourselves and by being committed to the norms we articulate (Sensen, 2009). Kant's notion of dignity is linked to respecting an individual's autonomy and the necessary treatment of all with dignity. Thus, Kant could be attributed to laying down the intellectual underpinnings of the concept of privacy rights (Sensen, 2009). He stated that "*the dignity of man consists precisely in his capacity to make universal law, although only on condition of being himself also subject to the laws he makes*" (Sensen, 2009).

4. GLOBAL PERSPECTIVE ON SURVEILLANCE IN PUBLIC REALMS: PANOPTICON, GOVERNANCE AND SOCIETAL DYNAMICS OF PRIVACY MANAGEMENT

Social transformation and technological progress are placing increasing strain on the metaphor of public and private spheres as the twenty-first century progresses. Not only is the perimeter of one's residence permeable, but so is one's person; the demarcation between the individual and the community is considerably less certain. This brings us back to Jeremy Bentham's concept of the panopticon in the 18th century, which was essentially a prison design concept intended to deter socially unacceptable behavior and ensure maximum surveillance. Likewise, surveillance in public or online does not deter individuals from committing crimes; rather, it imposes an expectation that we conform to "mainstream" standards of conduct. The social value of privacy is compromised in this context in order to promote social cohesion, particularly via online surveillance. The revelations made by Edward Snowden concerning the extent of surveillance conducted by the United States government via programs like PRISM and metadata collection on telephone conversations in the name of national security reflected the extent to which formal state agencies possess information about the general public (MacAskill et al., 2013).

There are two perspectives on privacy in the public sphere: access and control (Gavison, 1980). It is acquiring access to an individual's information by engaging in any activity that is within the public domain and does not infringe upon established norms or rights (Gavison, 1980). In the context of control, however, it essentially refers to who has access to an individual's information. The concept of privacy in the public domain becomes at least comprehensible at this juncture. It is still being determined how information that is obtained by others will be utilized (Gavison, 1980). Social and legal norms assume a significant role in this regard to guarantee a certain level of regulation over its utilization, thereby safeguarding the privacy of an individual.

The implementation of arbitrary mass surveillance is a matter of concern due to the unsettling impact it would have on democratic systems, as it would inevitably involve monitoring the political activities of individuals (Haggerty & Samatas, 2010). The utilization of facial recognition technologies and the fact that social media platforms are also considered public spaces heighten the urgency of this matter (Haggerty & Samatas, 2010). The use of surveillance operations to enforce the law is one method of achieving effective governance. Nevertheless, this is a fine line whose obligatory format violates the privacy rights of individuals. Scholars are increasingly in agreement that the concept of "privacy in public" does not merit protection in and of itself (Misek, 2018). Steven Levitsky and Daniel Ziblat are of the opinion that the communication revolution has had an effect on democracy. The establishment of an omniscient democracy is the result of constructing big data on digital identity in order to control the majority of facets of a citizen's life (Berman, 2018). The evolving characteristics of democracy are cause for concern, as they incorporate surveillance, a characteristic feature of authoritarian regimes (Berman, 2018).

In a digitally connected world, information regarding persons and, thereby, the rise of privacy issues is essentially a struggle over social power. There needs to be clearer terms and universally accepted definitions of digital privacy. Perspectives pertaining to privacy aren't similar universally. Differentiation in approaches to privacy is a result of differences in legal values and social and political traditions.

All pervasive government surveillance has been a consistent feature of authoritarian states where mass surveillance of citizens is a regular feature. China has devised a social credit system as part of its internet agenda. The Chinese government, through its controlled internet, aims to use a vast amount of personal data to improve citizens' behavior (Cho, 2020). The system tracks good and bad behavior over financial and social activities, thereby assigning punishments to those who err and rewarding those who show sincerity in socio-political and economic life (Cho, 2020). Shoshana Zuboff has described this system as "digital totalitarianism" (Zuboff, 2019). However, this practice is no longer limited to authoritarian states, and modern liberal democracies have also been following a similar path. Making use of CCTV in public spaces enables large-scale government surveillance that is feasible, cheap, and in a way that seems less intrusive but is also more invasive. Facial recognition technology, drones, and public health surveillance through apps are a few other mechanisms used for governance (Zuboff, 2019).

Jeffrey Rosen, in "The Unwanted Gaze," asserts that the liberal state acts as a guarantor of individual privacy (Rosen, 2000). A liberal state should respect privacy as it is inherently linked with individual dignity. Coinciding with this position, a liberal state ought to support rules that protect people's desire to be left alone. E.U's General Data Protection Regulation is one such example that points out the liberal stance. European Union's General Data Protection Regulation (hereinafter, GDPR) highlights its ethos as digital liberalism. Consistent with liberal tradition, the rule of law has been extended to the sphere involving data (Regulation (EU) 2016/679). GDPR has defined the rights of natural persons against any entity that collects data from the former. It reiterates the liberal paradigm that markets are free but are subscribed by a system of enforceable rights and guarantees (Regulation (EU) 2016/679).

In the USA, data collection and its use are monitored at the state level, which treads lightly on state regulation in comparison to the E.U's GDPR. Even those states that have stringent laws, such as California and New York, are unable to set a similar tone at a national level. More recently, a new bill in Congress, titled the American Privacy Rights Act, was introduced in April 2024. This bill aims to establish a federal standard for creating comprehensive legislation pertaining to privacy and security and keeping consumers at the forefront in case of data controls (Serrato et al., 2024). So far, the USA has shied away from creating comprehensive legislation rooted out of economic arguments of debilitating technological progress and creating more barriers for trade, which would hurt competitiveness. Voices of opposition have already emerged within a few days of the introduction of this bill and have generated many debates even before the formal introduction of the same (Serrato et al., 2024).

By comparing these countries, one can assume that the cross-border flow of data, like trade, is subject to varying political values within the field of data. The leveraging of information by governments with no restraints and a lack of universal standards has been one of the key concerns in the current era. The absence of common standards would only encourage digital totalitarian states to spread their model, thereby hurting the prospect of individual autonomy, liberty, and the nature of democracy itself (Tarafder, 2015). Edward Luce, in "The Retreat of Western Liberalism," has asserted that those in power reflect Oikophobia or extension of privacy in private space and are consciously making an effort to control the masses (Luce, 2017).

5. INDIA'S PURSUIT OF BALANCING DIGITAL SURVEILLANCE AND ETHOS OF PRIVACY:

Lately, the Indian government has made efforts to develop and use advanced technology to collect and consolidate extensive amounts of data in order to carry out surveillance on its population. The proliferation of the surveillance system has the potential to discourage dissent and hinder public involvement, especially when carried out without a well-defined legal framework that limits the government's authority. There is an ongoing and protracted debate over the connection between social media accounts and India's national AADHAAR biometric identification. Civil society activists are divided on this issue. To fully comprehend the detrimental impact of surveillance on civil society, public involvement, and media, it is essential to scrutinize the effects of different surveillance technologies now used in India, our stand on the right to Privacy and evaluate the legislative framework that facilitates such issues.

5.1. Emergence of Privacy Paradigms: Insights from India's Constitutional Assembly Debates and Judicial Incorporation of Right to Privacy

Although it has been six years since a nine-judge bench of the Supreme Court of India in *Justice K. S. Puttaswamy (Retd.) & Anr. v Union of India & Ors.* (2017) declared the Right to Privacy as a Fundamental Right and granted it Constitutional Status; it is undeniable that the concept of Privacy has been extensively discussed and debated in India for a long time. India's stand on privacy matters is a complex mix of legalities, cultural norms, advances made in technological fields, and, broadly, the welfare-oriented socio-political milieu that shapes it. As we trace back to ancient India, we observe that by the nineteenth and twentieth centuries, the concept of privacy was primarily linked to the protection of one's property and the inviolability of one's house of property. The Constitution of India Bill 1895 can be considered as one of the earliest documents that proclaimed the right of every citizen to have an inviolable asylum in their own home (Austin, 1966). Subsequently, the Commonwealth of India Bill of 1925 was enacted to safeguard against unwarranted intrusion into one's dwelling without due process of law.

To understand India's current position, it is necessary to go back to the origins of the Constituent Assembly Debates (CAD) in the Constituent Assembly. During the drafting of the Constitution for an independent India, it was evident that the right to privacy was not explicitly emphasized among the fundamental rights that needed to be granted to Indian individuals. However, a debate and discussion did occur in the Constituent Assembly over the right to privacy. The formal proceedings of the Constituent Assembly commenced in December 1946 with the initiation of the drafting process. The Constituent Assembly established many committees whose primary responsibility was to submit recommendations to the Drafting committee. The Drafting committee, in turn, would then produce a draft of the Constitution. During the Committee Stage, a Sub-Committee group made efforts to argue for the inclusion of the right to privacy as a fundamental right. During the meetings of the Sub Committees, esteemed members such as K.M. Munshi, Harman Singh, and Dr. Ambedkar strongly advocated for the inclusion of the right to privacy as a fundamental right (Thapa, 2021). This idea was reflected in Dr. B.R. Ambedkar's draft, which proposed that *"the right of the people to be secure in their persons, house, papers, and effects against unreasonable searches and seizures shall not be violated, and no warrants shall be issued except upon probable cause, supported by oath or affirmation, and particularly describing the place to be searched and the persons or things to be seized"* in the State and Minority Report.

During the CAD, Mr. B.N. Rau, who served as an Adviser to the Constituent Assembly, and Alladi Krishnaswamy Ayyar, a member of the Constituent Assembly, expressed their disagreement with the notion of incorporating the right to privacy as part of the fundamental rights. BN Rau believed that the right to privacy could impede the investigative capabilities of police officers and thereby impact the process of investigation (Thaorey, 2021). Ayyar held the belief that allowing individuals the right to privacy and confidentiality in their contact would have negative consequences, particularly in civil action cases where documents are crucial evidence. Within the plenary sessions of the Constituent Assembly, there are two distinct methods to incorporate provisions regarding the right to privacy into the chapter on fundamental rights (Thaorey, 2021).

On April 30, 1947, Somnath Lahiri proposed that the right to privacy of correspondence be established as a fundamental right. Nevertheless, his plan could have gained more momentum. Kazi Syed Karimuddin subsequently incorporated the provision for safeguarding individuals' security in their persons, dwellings, papers, and effects from unjustified searches and seizures into Article 20 (formerly Draft Article 14) of the Constitution. Both of these endeavors could have been more successful in establishing the inclusion of the right to privacy as a basic right in the Constitution (Thapa, 2021).

While the Constituent Assembly did not specifically focus on the right to privacy and its extent, it did suggest that the intended inclusion (which was later removed) was limited to two specific areas: searches and seizures (Rao, 1967). Upon careful examination of the Debates, it becomes evident that the Assembly solely focused on discussing whether there should be a specific provision ensuring the right to privacy in relation to "searches" and "secrecy" of correspondence. However, the broader aspects of the right to privacy should have been thoroughly explored during the debates. The topic of whether the term "liberty," as mentioned in Article 21, encompasses the many dimensions of the right to privacy was not discussed.

Based on this, it cannot be inferred that the Constituent Assembly explicitly decided to dismiss the recognition of the right to privacy as a fundamental component of the liberty and freedoms protected by the fundamental rights. As the right to privacy was not included and there was no specific provision for it in Part III of the Constitution, it was rejected (Bhatia, 2014).

Over time, the Supreme Court of India has played a crucial role in the recognition of the right to privacy as an integral part of the Right to Life and Liberty under Article 21. To comprehend the judicial incorporation of the right to privacy, we can examine the cases that have deliberated on this right and those instances that have significantly contributed to granting constitutional recognition to the Right to Privacy in India. Although the Indian legal framework for privacy is based on both common law principles of tort and Constitutional law, Indian Courts have predominantly drawn upon American case law to shape their understanding of privacy jurisprudence. The concept of a specific right to privacy has yet to develop in any part of the world.

Privacy refers to a self-governing area where individuals can lead their personal lives and make decisions without any external intervention. The Indian Constitution does not explicitly provide any right to privacy. Nevertheless, the Supreme Court has restricted this right as a derived right from part III of the Constitution, i.e., fundamental rights. One of the early cases on privacy issues is the case of *M.P. Sharma v. Satish Chandra, District Magistrate, Delhi and Ors.* (1966), in which the Supreme Court ruled that privacy cannot be considered a basic right under the Indian Constitution. This decision was made in relation to the subject of the 'power of search and seizure.' In this instance, the Supreme Court's interpretation was limited to the required statutory rule. However, in the case of *Govind v. State of Madhya Pradesh* (1975), the Court acknowledged that there is a restricted basic right to privacy that arises from Articles 19 and 21. The Supreme Court, in the case of *R. Rajagopal v. State of Tamil Nadu* (1994), has affirmed that the right to privacy has obtained constitutional recognition. In the present case, the Court suggested certain principles that could serve as the foundation for defining privacy. The aim was to strike a balance between the right to privacy and the competing factors of freedom. The court observed:

> *"The right to privacy is implicit in the right to life and liberty guaranteed to the citizens of this country by Article 21. It is a "right to be let alone." It is the fundamental right of every citizen to safeguard the privacy of his own family, marriage, procreation, motherhood, childbearing, and education, among other matters. None can publish anything concerning the above matters without his consent – whether truthful or otherwise and whether laudatory or critical. If he/she does so, h/she would be violating the right to privacy of the person concerned and would be liable in an action for damages. Position may, however, be different if a person voluntarily thrusts himself into controversy or voluntarily invites or raises a controversy".*

Article 21 provides the strongest affirmation of the right to privacy as a basic right. Moreover, the law stipulated in this specific canon explicitly acknowledges the possibility of seeking damages for the violation of the right to privacy. Put, a civil claim can be undertaken to seek redress for a privacy violation. Thus, the ruling in the Auto Shankar Case gives legal solutions for violations of privacy in both public and private spheres (Taneja & Kumar, 2014). An intriguing aspect of the right to privacy is evident in this situation since it involves assessing the right to privacy, as outlined in Article 21, in relation to another citizen's basic right of freedom of speech and expression, as stated in Article 19(1)(a). In this case, the court examined the privatization of the right to privacy in situations where there is a clash between the fundamental rights of two individuals.

In the case of *Kharak Singh v. State of Uttar Pradesh and Ors* (1964), the Supreme Court determined that police visits to a person's home violated their right to sleep and their right to privacy. The court concluded that such a violation could not be permitted by the standards set by the government. According to Article 21 of the Constitution, a bill passed by the legislature would be necessary for this purpose. Similar police restrictions were upheld in *Govind* when they were established under the Police Act. The right to be free from searches and seizures is a component of the right to privacy, as demonstrated in the case of the *Board of Revenue, Madras v. R.S. Jhava* (1961). The court determined that the authority to conduct searches and seizures can only be employed by the executive branch if it is granted by a specific law.

Telephone tapping represents a significant infringement against an individual's fundamental right to privacy. In the case of *Peoples Union for Civil Liberties v.*

Union of India (1997), the Court determined that telephone conversations are a significant aspect of an individual's personal life. The entitlement to engage in a telephone conversation within the confines of one's residence or workplace without any form of disturbance can undeniably be asserted as the "right to privacy." Telephone conversations frequently possess an intimate and confidential nature. Telephone communication is an integral aspect of contemporary human existence. Telephone tapping is a grave violation of one's privacy. Telephone tapping violates Article 21 unless it is authorized according to the legally established procedure. Moreover, the procedure must adhere to principles of justice, fairness, and reasonableness. Engaging in telephone conversations constitutes the individual's exercise of their right to freedom of speech and expression, as safeguarded by Article 19 (1) (a). Telephone tapping that does not fall within the allowed reasonable restriction outlined in Article 19(2) would violate Article 19(1)(a). The Supreme Court, in its opinion, made reference to the Universal Declaration of Human Rights, 1948 (UDHR), International Covenant on Civil and Political Rights, 1966 (ICCPR), and construed Article 21 in accordance with international law.

In addition to various prior rulings in which the Supreme Court acknowledged the right to privacy, the Supreme Court, in its landmark case *Justice K.S. Puttaswamy v. Union of India* (2017), also known as the Privacy judgment, interpreted privacy as a penumbral right under Article 21 of the Indian Constitution. The Court has definitively ruled that the doctrinal basis of *M.P. Sharma* and *Kharak Singh* has been nullified. Furthermore, it has specifically overturned the judgment of the *ADM Jabalpur* case, which was made under the emergency era. The unanimous ruling on privacy reaffirms fundamental constitutional values. The viewpoints of three notable dissenters, namely Justice Fazal Ali in *A.K. Gopalan v. State of Madras* (1950), Justice Subba Rao in *Kharak Singh*, and Justice Khanna in *ADM Jabalpur v. Shivkant Shukla* (1976), were validated by the Puttaswamy ruling. *Puttaswamy* has successfully captured the contemplative essence of these three dissenting opinions.

As a result, the courts' most backward decisions were discarded and forgotten over time. The ruling may also address the problem of linking Aadhaar with Permanent Account Numbers. The Court's verdict is perceived as a setback for the Government's efforts to broaden the applicability of Aadhaar as a compulsory prerequisite for other Government services.

5.2. Challenges and Critics Surrounding the Aadhar Card System and Mass Surveillance

In India, like other governments in the Western world, the government has incorporated digital surveillance measures, which have set a trend in governance from targeted surveillance to mass surveillance. This was initiated in 2009 through the

Aadhaar card system. Aadhaar is an official identifying document provided by the Unique Identifying Authority of India (UIDAI) to Indian residents. The Aadhaar card has a 12-digit distinctive identifying number, referred to as the Aadhaar number, together with personal information such as name, address, date of birth, and biometric data. The biometric data collected for Aadhaar comprises fingerprints, facial images, and iris scans, all of which are distinct to each person. The Aadhaar data is utilized to verify the identification of individuals while accessing different government services, receiving subsidies, creating bank accounts, and carrying out other operations that rely on identity verification (Sadhya & Sahu, 2024). The Aadhaar framework offers effective authentication services in India's public delivery systems. Despite the implementation of robust security measures, including encryption, access controls, and regular system audits by UIDAI, the usage of Aadhaar has generated significant concerns over privacy and data security. Regarding this matter, only a few studies have addressed the security obstacles associated with Aadhaar. In addition, the Aadhaar framework is always developing, which reduces the relevance of previous findings. This section will focus on the security aspects of the Aadhaar card, with a particular emphasis on the issues associated with safeguarding demographic and biometric data (Henne, 2019).

Biometric authentication is a procedure that relies on the unique biological traits of persons to validate their identity through pattern matching. Commonly recognized biometric characteristics encompass the fingerprints, facial features, iris patterns, retinal patterns, and palm prints of individuals. Biometric-based identification offers numerous advantages over traditional token-based systems. Traditional authentication models utilize identification methods such as passwords and usernames or physical items like smart cards, keys, or certificates. However, it is quite easy to impersonate someone or replace the tokens with false information. Furthermore, passwords have a tendency to slip from memory, while tokens are vulnerable to theft. Furthermore, biometric data is impervious to theft and does not require explicit memorization. One of the significant advantages of biometric models is their ability to effectively prevent impostor data from bypassing biometric sensors. Biometric identification models have gained significant popularity in both commercial and government applications due to a multitude of factors. (Sadhya & Sahu, 2024).

In a typical biometric system, there are two distinct stages - enrolment and authentication. The enrolment process involves collecting biometric data from individuals who will be included in the system. As an example, in the realm of fingerprint identification, a person's fingerprints are scanned and stored in a database along with their corresponding identifying details. Biometric authentication, on the other hand, refers to the procedure of verifying the identity of the person making the request. With the utilization of these systems, a computer gathers various attributes like fingerprints, facial features, and iris patterns. These characteristics are then compared to the recorded template from the enrolment procedure. Authentication takes place when the scanned biometric information matches the template.

It is possible to further break down the authentication process into its component parts, identification and verification. An individual's biometric data is compared to a database of several biometric templates in order to find a match in biometric identification, also known as one-to-many (or 1:N) matching. N is the number of records or templates stored in the database. As part of the 1:N matching procedure, the system compares the input biometric template to all of the templates contained in the database using a matching algorithm. This comparison yields a similarity score. Based on this score, the system sorts the database templates in order of probable candidate matches. Biometric verification, on the other hand, involves matching a person's unique identifier with a biometric sample. The stored template associated with the claimed identification is compared with the query biometric sample. A determination is made and the person's identification is validated after a comparison.

Numerous widespread implementations of biometric-based identity authentication systems are in place. Some programs are run by commercial organizations, while others are supervised by national governments. When it comes to safety, the travel and hospitality sector relies on biometrics. One such use case is airport security, where biometric authentication at various checkpoints may be achieved by the scanning of fingerprints, iris scans, or face recognition. The banking industry makes heavy use of it to limit account access to authorized users exclusively, hence reducing the risk of fraud and identity theft. Biometrics ensures accurate patient identification and record matching in healthcare. With this method, you can be sure that the right person will get the care they need. Electronic passports, national identification systems, and border control are just a few examples of government projects that use biometric recognition (Sadhya & Sahu, 2024).

In an effort to provide a distinct identity to each and every one of its citizens, the Indian government set up the Unique Identification Authority of India (UIDAI). The main goal of UIDAI is to generate distinct identities for every person by combining their demographic and biometric data. Aadhaar, India's national identity scheme, came about because of this. (Sadhya & Sahu, 2024). The main goal of Aadhaar was to make it easier for the Indian government to provide public services and benefits. The 12-digit Aadhaar number, which is unique for every person, allows them to receive all forms of government assistance while simultaneously preventing fraudulent or duplicate beneficiaries. Important national services like rations, social pensions, cooking gas, and fertilizers did away with the need for middlemen. While millions of Indian residents were in need of medical care, financial aid, and vaccines due to the COVID-19 pandemic, the greatest benefit of Aadhaar became clear via the CoWIN digital platform. The Aadhaar number was used in the COWIN verification procedure. It is projected by McKinsey that this digital identity might contribute significantly to India's economy in 2023, accounting for 3–13% of the country's GDP. The ability to use one's Aadhaar card as digital identity (in place of other papers) for official reasons is an extra perk of having one.

While Aadhaar-enabled services are crucial in India, there are numerous security concerns and obstacles associated with Aadhaar. Adversaries have the ability to take advantage of weaknesses in the system, such as fraudulent biometric data, replication, and unauthorized access to sensitive information. The latest incidence pertains to the unauthorized disclosure of distinctively identifying data (namely, Aadhaar and Passport numbers) of 815 million Indian citizens on the dark web. The discovery of this breach occurred on October 9th, 2023, by a hacker identified as pwn0001. Despite UIDAI's implementation of several precautionary measures, such as the utilization of secure communication routes and the hashing of biometric data, security and privacy continue to be significant concerns. More research needs to be conducted that thoroughly assesses and analyzes various elements of Aadhaar. Moreover, the Aadhaar ecosystem is always developing as new policies and regulations are periodically included in it. Therefore, it is necessary to briefly describe Aadhaar's advantages and disadvantages from a security standpoint.

The governments eventually linked the possession of this unique identity to PAN cards, bank accounts, universal healthcare, National population register, pension schemes, taxes, passports, LPG subsidies, and registering marriage and death, among others. Mass digital records on such a scale have left a window for error. There have been issues in Aadhaar card authentication that have reduced agency in citizens and made those in authority more powerful. One of the biggest criticisms against this scheme has been regarding mass surveillance. Aadhaar card databases provide the government with ever-ready information, without any special powers, to track any citizen's movements, thereby holding citizens hostage to the infrastructure created for mass surveillance.

It is to be noted that the right to privacy is particularly important with regard to the digital security of private information. In 2018, India faced one of the largest recorded data breaches with the Aadhaar card, where more than one billion citizens' data ranging from bank accounts to Pan Card information was leaked, as per the World Economic Forum's Global Risk Report in 2019.

Moreover, the Supreme Court of India, in the case of *Beghar Foundation v Justice K.S. Puttuswamy (Ret'd)* (2021), approximately two years after the Puttaswamy case, the Supreme Court rendered its decision, affirming the constitutionality of the Aadhaar Act with a majority of 4:1. Disregarding concerns about privacy, the Court noted that the governmental has the authority to limit the right to private as long as the limitation is proportionate to a valid governmental objective. The Court determined that the Act did not infringe upon the fundamental right to privacy, as it recognized the legitimate objective of ensuring the fair and open allocation of benefits and services to underprivileged individuals. Additionally, it noted that there are sufficient measures in place to prevent Aadhaar from enabling widespread government surveillance. Justice DY Chandrachud, the incumbent Chief Justice of India, gave a dissenting opinion by stating that the passage of the Aadhaar as a Money Bill was unconstitutional. In addition, he examined the arguments about particular parts of the Act that had an impact on an individual's privacy, dignity, and autonomy.

5.3. Examining India's Digital Personal Data Protection Act, 2023: Evaluating its Efficacy in Safeguarding Privacy

Starting from 2018, the Indian Government has been actively working towards establishing a new central legislation that would replace the Information Technology (Reasonable security practices and procedures and sensitive personal data or information) Rules, 2011 ("SPDI Rules") and operate as a standalone data protection law. In 2023, the Lok Sabha approved the latest iteration of the Data Protection Bill, commonly referred to as the 'Digital Personal Data Protection Bill, 2023' ("DPDP Bill"), following the release of multiple earlier versions. Following that, the DPDP Bill received approval from the Rajya Sabha on August 9, 2023. On August 11, 2023, the President of India gave their approval and authorization to the Digital Personal Data Protection Act, 2023 ("DPDP Act"), which was subsequently announced and made accessible in the Official Gazette of India.

The DPDP Act includes a wide range of provisions regarding notice and consent obligations, outlines the permissible "legitimate uses" for processing personal data without explicit consent, establishes an "Appellate Tribunal" to handle complaints, and imposes additional responsibilities on data fiduciaries when it comes to handling children's data, among other changes. The DPDP Act establishes a mutually beneficial connection with the comprehensive information technology regulations of the Government of India. The aspect related to gathering information is intricately connected to the intersection of the Information Technology Act 2000 and the Information Technology (Intermediary Guidelines and Digital Media Ethics Code) Rules, 2021. This interface allows the Central Government to request information from a range of entities, such as the Data Protection Board, fiduciaries, and intermediaries (Agarwal & Dash, 2024). However, the absence of specific details indicates a need to investigate the scope, purpose, and safeguards associated with this data collection, which necessitates compliance with the legal principles outlined in the Puttaswamy judgment. Despite lingering questions about how to implement the mentioned legislation effectively, concerns have arisen about specific provisions in the law that may undermine the intended protections.

First and foremost, the exceptions granted for consent give the state significant authority and prioritize governmental interests over those of private businesses.

Although there are specific instances where this holds true, like during times of calamities or urgent situations, the legislation expands the scope of such scenarios (Burman, 2023). An example of this can be seen in Section 7(b) of the Act, which grants the government the authority to circumvent the requirement for consent in situations where a recipient of government services has already given their agreement to receive any other type of aid from the state. While this could make it easier to access personal information from individuals who use government services, it also raises concerns about the government merging databases. This is because in order to utilize the potential of this provision fully, it would be necessary to exempt government entities from purpose constraints that require the deletion of personal data once its intended use has been fulfilled (Burman, 2023).

The accumulation of government-granted exceptions for investigative, prosecutive, and national security purposes is another example of this tendency. Processing data pertaining to the prevention, detection, investigation, or prosecution of any infraction or violation of the law is exempt from the necessity for notice and approval under Section 17(1)(c) of the Act. Section 17(2)(a) provides an extensive exception from the whole legislation to any government agency that the government formally informs in order to protect sovereignty, security, integrity, and public order and prevent provocation; this exemption is understandable but vast. In addition to the provision in Section 17(1)(c), Parliament has made it clear in Section 17(2)(a) that it intends to exclude some government entities from the application of data protection rules. Such provisions define a separate category of actions that are not subject to data privacy laws. A major obstacle is the absence of constraints on the Indian state, which is especially problematic in cases when such an exemption is not immediately necessary.

Furthermore, in some cases, the protections set forth by the legislation may be undermined by the government's discretionary power to adopt regulations as allowed by the law. For the first five years after this legislation goes into effect, the government may exempt any company or group of companies from certain of its requirements under Section 17(5). At this time, neither the length of time this exemption will be in effect nor its precise application is defined. Sunrise companies or startups might be given a grace time to comply with the legislation if this section is interpreted favorably. Section 17 (3), which provides limited exemptions to startups and other sectors formally designated by the government, has previously taken this provision into consideration. Therefore, the purpose of the law might be defeated by an application of Section 17(5). Please note that the government is only allowed to provide these exemptions for a period of five years, as stated in the legislation. The length of these exclusions needs to be defined (Burman, 2023).

Similarly, the government has the discretion to determine that companies are not liable for certain data management responsibilities involving minors. Some requirements for the same are laid forth in Sections 9(1) to 9(3) of the Act; these sections prohibit profiling and require parental consent, among other things. Under specific conditions, the government may exempt any business or group of businesses from complying with Sections 9(1) to 9(3), as stated in Section 9(4). The procedure for assessing the circumstances and the criteria for approving this exemption need to be made clear in this section. This provision is open to abuse because of the lack of proper advice. Despite the fact that other statutes provide the government the authority to impose conditions and establish substantive rules, the aforementioned cases need more support. When considering this matter in the context of Indian administrative law, which states that legislation should not provide the implementing body unrestrained and excessive power, the difficulty level of the problem increases. A possible violation of the Indian Constitution might result from an incorrect application of certain legislative provisions (Korff, 2023).

The third major problem is the DPB's construction. The government will set up processes for selecting and appointing board members, and the board will operate independently with a narrow mandate. Despite the fact that the legislation lays forth qualifications for board members, the precise quantity of members needed needs to be more specific. It also plainly states that one member must be an expert in law. Problems arise from the aforementioned rule since the board is primarily responsible for issuing instructions and punishments in the event of non-compliance (Korff, 2023). The DPB chair also has the power to delegate authority to any board member to do "any of the board's functions and oversee any of its proceedings." The chairman has the authority to grant or revoke permission to the board member who is legally qualified to preside over the process that leads to the levying of a fine. Additionally, the design cannot support an internal division of labor between the chairman and the members doing the investigation. The chairman may not always act impartially in carrying out their duties since they are able to choose which members will conduct investigations (Korff, 2023).

Therefore, although the DPDP Act does include legal protections for data privacy, certain parts of the law might make them less effective if the government isn't careful to follow them. The DPDP Act is the first piece of legislation to ensure the security of personal information, and it is the product of more than five years of deliberation. What happens in the next years in terms of institutional arrangements and statutory changes will decide how effective personal data privacy protection is. While the new laws provide the groundwork, they need to be stronger to guarantee data privacy in practice.

6. CONCLUSION

The concept of privacy should be seen as intricate and nuanced rather than a simply binary notion. It should be emphasized that not all instances of data exchange always result in manipulation. Finding a method to safely exchange secret information without compromising its secrecy is an achievable undertaking. Preserving the secrecy of personal information is crucial for establishing a sense of privacy. To achieve this objective, it is essential to develop clear and precise privacy protocols, strike a balance between the interests of those who have access to the information and the rights of people, and continually adhere to ethical standards while handling sensitive data. The government must prioritize taking a proactive stance in addressing data privacy issues and holding internet corporations accountable for their use of personal information. By advocating for openness and implementing measures of accountability, the protection of digital privacy rights may be greatly improved.

India is considered a global authority when it comes to making decisions on matters involving the convergence of laws, technology, and public expectations. The choices had a profound effect on global perspectives about surveillance, internet privacy, and leadership, so significantly influencing the everyday lives of the population. India had a crucial role in this matter, and the country's efforts to strike a balance between internet privacy and security likely affected the general public's perception of these significant matters. After thorough deliberations, the DPDP Act currently serves as a testament to India's unique strategy for safeguarding data. The enactment of this data protection legislation is a crucial measure in ensuring the security of personal information, especially considering the increasing amount of data produced by the internet and the worldwide expansion of commerce. The DPDP Act today reflects India's distinct position on contemporary data protection as a result of thorough discussions that took place after its original conception. Although it lacks the level of specificity seen in laws such as GDPR, it nonetheless requires a significant change in how Indian firms handle consumer data and privacy.

REFERENCES

ADM Jabalpur v. Shivkant Shukla AIR 1976 SC 1207

Agarwal, R., & Dash, A. (2024, April 15). *Digital Personal Data Protection Act, 2023 and Fintech: Cracking Labyrinth*. The Daily Guardian. https://thedailyguardian.com/digital-personal-data-protection-act-2023-and-fintech-cracking-labyrinth/

A.K. Gopalan v. State of Madras (1950) SCR 88.

Austin, G. (1966). *The Indian Constitution-Cornerstone of a Nation*. Clarendon Press.

Beghar Foundation v Justice K.S. Puttuswamy (Ret'd) (2021)

Berman, J., & Mulligan, D. (1999). The Internet and the Law: Privacy in the Digital Age: A Work in Progress. *Nova Law Review*, *23*(2), 552–579.

Berman, S. (2018). A discussion of Steven Levitsky and Daniel Ziblatt's views on how democracies die. *Perspectives on Politics*, *16*(4), 1092–1094. DOI: 10.1017/S1537592718002852

Bhatia, G. (2014). State Surveillance and the Right to Privacy in India: A Constitutional Biography. *National Law School of India Review, 26*(2), 127–158. https://www.jstor.org/stable/44283638

Burman, A. (2023, October 3). *Understanding India's New Data Protection Law*. Carnegie India. https://carnegieindia.org/2023/10/03/understanding-india-s-new-data-protection-law-pub-90624

Cho, E. (2020, May 1). *The Social Credit System: Not Just Another Chinese Idiosyncrasy*. Journal of Public and International Affairs. https://jpia.princeton.edu/news/social-credit-system-not-just-another-chinese-idiosyncrasy

DeVries, W. T. (2003). Protecting Privacy in the Digital Age. *Berkeley Technology Law Journal*, *18*(1), 283–311. https://www.jstor.org/stable/24120519

Dworkin, R. (1977). *Taking Rights Seriously*. Bloomsbury Publication.

Froomkin, A. M. (2000). The Death of Privacy? *Stanford Law Review*, *52*(5), 1461–1543. DOI: 10.2307/1229519

Gavison, R. (1980). Privacy and the Limits of Law. *The Yale Law Journal*, *89*(3), 421–471. DOI: 10.2307/795891

Govind v. State of M.P., (1975) 2 SCC 148

Haggerty, K. D., & Samatas, M. (2010). *Surveillance and Democracy*. Routledge. DOI: 10.4324/9780203852156

Henne, K. (2019). Surveillance in the name of governance: Aadhaar as a fix for leaking systems in india. In Haggart, B., Henne, K., & Tusikov, N. (Eds.), *Information, Technology and Control in a Changing World* (pp. 223–245). Springer International Publishing., DOI: 10.1007/978-3-030-14540-8_11

Justice K.S. Puttaswamy v. Union of India (2017) 10 SCC 1.

Kasper, D. V. S. (2007). Privacy as a Social Good. *Social Thought & Research, 28*, 165–189. https://www.jstor.org/stable/23252125

Kharak Singh v. State of Uttar Pradesh and Ors (1964) 1 SCR 334.

Korff, D. (2023). The Indian Digital Personal Data Protection Act, 2023, Viewed from a European Perspective. SSRN *Electronic Journal*. https://doi.org/DOI: 10.2139/ssrn.4614984

Luce, E. (2017). *The Retreat of Western Liberalism*. Little Brown Book Group.

MacAskill, E., Dance, G., Cage, F., Chen, G., & Popovich, N. (2013, November 1). *NSA files decoded: Edward Snowden's surveillance revelations explained*. The Guardian. https://www.theguardian.com/world/interactive/2013/nov/01/snowden-nsa-files-surveillance-revelations-decoded

Misek, J. (2018). Privacy in public space: Conceptual and regulatory challenges. *Masaryk University Journal of Law and Technology, 12*(1), 75–80. DOI: 10.5817/MUJLT2018-1-4

M.P. Sharma v. Satish Chandra, District Magistrate, Delhi and Ors. (1954) SCR 1077.

Peoples Union for Civil Liberties v. Union of India (1997) 1 SCC 301

Quinn, E. R.Jr. (1999). Tax Implications for Electronic Commerce over the Internet. *Journal of Technology Law and Policy, 4*(3), 1–25.

R. Rajagopal v. State of Tamil Nadu (1994) 6 SCC 632

Raab, C. D. (2017). Security, Privacy and Oversight. In A. W. Neal (Ed.), *Security in a Small Nation: Scotland, Democracy, Politics* (1st ed., Vol. 4, pp. 77–102). Open Book Publishers. https://www.jstor.org/stable/j.ctt1sq5v42.8

Rao, S. S. (1967). *The Framing of India's Constitution*. Universal Law Publishing House.

Regulation (EU) 2016/679 of the European Parliament and of the Council of 27 April 2016 on the protection of natural persons with regard to the processing of personal data and on the free movement of such data, and repealing Directive 95/46/EC (General Data Protection Regulation) (Text with EEA relevance). (2016). *Official Journal*, L 119, 1-88. ELI: https://data.europa.eu/eli/reg/2016/679/oj

Rosen, J. (2000). *The Unwanted Gaze: The Destruction of Privacy in America*. Penguin Random House.

Sadhya, D., & Sahu, T. (2024). A critical survey of the security and privacy aspects of the Aadhaar framework. *Computers & Security*, *140*, 103782. DOI: 10.1016/j.cose.2024.103782

Sensen, O. (2009). Kant's conception of human dignity. *Kant-Studien*, *100*(3). Advance online publication. DOI: 10.1515/KANT.2009.018

Serrato, J. K., Arora, S. B., & Mastromonaco, C. (2024, April 22). *The U. S. Moves Toward a Comprehensive Privacy Law (One more time)*. Pillsbury Law. https://www.pillsburylaw.com/en/news-and-insights/american-privacy-rights-act.html

Solove, D. J. (2001). Privacy and Power: Computer Databases and Metaphors for Information Privacy. *Stanford Law Review*, *53*(6), 1393–1461. DOI: 10.2307/1229546

Sullivan, C. (2011). Digital Identity — Consequential Individual Rights. In Sullivan, C. (Ed.), *Digital Identity: An Emergent Legal Concept* (pp. 71–106). University of Adelaide Press., https://www.jstor.org/stable/10.20851/j.ctt1sq5wqb.11

Taneja, R., & Kumar, S. (2014). *Privacy Law*. Eastern Book Company.

Tarafder, A. (2015). Surveillance, Privacy, And Technology: A Comparative Critique Of The Laws Of USA and India. *Journal of the Indian Law Institute*, *57*(4), 550–578. https://www.jstor.org/stable/44782800

Thaorey, P. (2021). Legal Introspection Towards the Development of the Right to Privacy as a Fundamental Right in India. *Indonesia Law Review*, *11*(3), 302–322. DOI: 10.15742/ilrev.v11n3.5

Thapa, S. (2021). The Evolution of Right to Privacy in India. *International Journal of Humanities and Social Science Invention*, *10*(2), 53–58. https://www.ijhssi.org/papers/vol10(2)/Ser-1/J1002015358.pdf

Warren, S. D., & Brandeis, L. D. (1890). The Right to Privacy. *Harvard Law Review*, *4*(5), 193–220. DOI: 10.2307/1321160

Winterbottom, M. (1994). M Tulli Ciceronius, De Officiis, Oxford University Press, 39.

Xu, H., & Jia, H. (2015). Privacy in a Networked World: New Challenges and Opportunities for Privacy Research. *Journal of the Washington Academy of Sciences*, *101*(3), 73–84. https://www.jstor.org/stable/jwashacadscie.101.3.73

Zuboff, S. (2019). *The Age of Surveillance Capitalism: The Fight for a Human Future at the New Frontier of Power*. Public Affairs.

KEY TERMS AND DEFINITIONS

Data Protection: Data protection refers to the systematic measures used to safeguard sensitive information from potential harm, such as damage, loss, or corruption. With the exponential growth in data generation and storage, the significance of data security has become more crucial than ever.

Digital Governance: Digital governance refers to the use of information and communication technologies (ICTs) in order to improve the efficiency, effectiveness, and accountability of governmental organizations and services. Additionally, it has the potential to promote public engagement, integration, and empowerment in the decision-making procedures that impact their livelihoods.

Digital Surveillance: Digital surveillance refers to the systematic monitoring of computer activities, including the data saved on a hard disk and the information being sent across computer networks. Digital surveillance is often conducted covertly and may be carried out by several entities, including governments, businesses, and even individuals.

Right to Privacy: Privacy is an essential and inherent right. The right in question safeguards the personal domain of persons against intrusion by both governmental and non-governmental entities, enabling individuals to exercise independent decision-making in their lives.

Chapter 19
Humor as Free Speech in the Digital Age: Evolving Legal Dimensions in India

Pushpita Dutta
https://orcid.org/0009-0004-9343-9043
Presidency University, Bengaluru, India

Saroj Sharma
https://orcid.org/0000-0002-6282-7156
Presidency University, Bengaluru, India

ABSTRACT

Freedom of speech and expression is the cornerstone of a democracy. Humor as an expression of free speech is well protected under its ambit. In India, Article 19(1)(a) of the Indian Constitution guarantees the fundamental right to freedom of speech and expression. However, this right is also subject to certain reasonable restrictions under Article 19(2). Even though there is ample jurisprudence existing on freedom of speech and expression in India, the protection of humor and its different forms in the digital age has been rarely explored comprehensively. This chapter first aims to study the jurisprudential foundations of freedom of speech and expression and evolution of humor as a form of speech. Second, the relationship between humor as free speech in India and law in the digital age is analyzed through the framework of free speech regulations and various judicial precedents. Finally, the chapter highlights the socio-legal challenges and ambiguities existing in the Indian legal system on governing humor and attempts to provide some suggestions for the way forward.

DOI: 10.4018/979-8-3693-3920-6.ch019

INTRODUCTION

Freedom of speech and expression is the foundation of any democracy. It promotes transparency, accountability, and public participation, all of which are necessary components of a functioning democracy. Free speech and expression is a valuable interest that is intrinsic part of human life. Human beings are social creatures who like to communicate and exchange views. From Rig Vedas, to French Revolution, from John Rawls theory of basic rights and liberty to John Stuart Mill's 'On Liberty', free speech and expression has been hailed as a valuable interest which is protected in the form of a right in most legal systems.

Humor and satire have always been essential part of political and social speech (Liang, 2021). Humor is generally defined as a form of communication which is not straightforward but rather non-bonafide in nature, which is entirely or partially oriented towards amusement (Attardo 2027). In India comic or humorous speech is increasingly playing a major part the understanding and development of free speech jurisprudence. Since the colonial period, India has witnessed quite a few legal challenges to humorous speech, such as prosecution of Awadh Punch, a satirical magazine and legal charge against Neel Darpan (1860) (Liang, 2021).

Humorous expressions can be of different kinds, adopting different ways of communicating for example understatement, ironical, metaphor, exaggeration, parody. It can be across different media spanning across verbal jokes, cartoons in newspapers or magazines, memes on the internet and social media, parody videos on YouTube, comedy shows on Netflix and other OTT platforms or even simple tweets. With the technological advancement and mushrooming increase in digital platforms, the complexities surrounding legitimate and protected humor as part of free speech and expression, has only risen.

It is pertinent to underline that humor in its various forms serves a wide range of purposes from simple entertainment to medium of social and political commentary. Therefore courts, from all over the world through their judgments have underlined the significance of protecting speech in the form of humor and acknowledging its multi-faceted nature (Young & Godioli, 2022).

In India, a vibrant democracy with diverse socio-political dynamics, humor often bridges complex issues with accessible critique. Accessibility is the keyword here. This is because, first, sometimes people prefer broad faced mockery to challenge government's action rather than long faced criticism. Second, long articles, research papers, outlining the shortcomings of a government policy or any institution is neither accessible or nor comprehensible for all. Whereas, a simple comedy sketch on YouTube or a meme on Instagram or a cartoon in online newspaper can reach millions through a simple 'click'. Therefore, humor as a powerful form of free speech holds a power that has mushroomed because of advancement in technology. This is the very reason, the institutions or people who tend to be criticized through humor are even more threatened by its reach.

In this regard it is important to remember, 'The Common Man', a cartoon character created by Indian cartoonist and author R. K. Laxman represented the aspirations and troubles of an average Indian for half a century (See below Figure 1 for an example). The cartoons were published in the Times of India. The cartoons were not just famous for it's relatability with the 'common Indian human', but also its fearless critiques of the government through satire.

The legal regulation of humour as part of free expression in India is a complex matter. Article 19(1)(a) of the Constitution of India guarantees freedom of speech and expression, but it is subject to reasonable constraints, which have frequently been invoked to suppress humour in different forms. Judicial precedents such as Shreya Singhal v. Union of India (2015) and Kunal Kamra v. Union of India (2023) have emphasized the importance of limiting scope of restrictions on free speech, however, contradictory decisions and wide scope of legal provisions continue to generate ambiguity in determining the limits of free speech in India.

The criminalization of defamation, hurting religious sentiments and obscenity particularly under Sections 295A, 499, and 292 of the IPC (now Sections 198, 354, and 294 of the Bharatiya Nyaya Sanhita, 2023), has disproportionately targeted comedians and satirists in India. Section 66A of the Information Technology Act, 2000 (struck down by Supreme Court of India as unconstitutional in 2015) also criminalised sending messages through computer source which may be offensive in nature.

From thousands of people watching stand-up comedy performances on social media to Munawar Faruqui's criminal case and Kunal Kamra's contempt of court notice, humor and comedy in India, has neither been as popular as it is today, nor more threatened (Liang, 2021). Therefore, in this context it becomes necessary to examine the relation between law, humor, offence and technology.

Figure 1. R. K. Laxman, The Common Man, Dec 26, 1962 (Sukhendu Sekhar Roy shared a cartoon on Twitter by legendary Indian artist RK Laxman. Source- NDTV Article, August 24, 2024)

MORAL AND POLITICAL UNDERPINNINGS OF FREEDOM OF SPEECH AND EXPRESSION

Legal and political philosophers unequivocally agree that there ought to be some legal protections to safeguard the right to free speech and expression. Such a significant interest makes it difficult to justify coercive measures to restrict the legal protection afforded to this right (Howard, 2024). Issues and disagreements arise when we look this right closely, thoroughly to understand the limitations of legally protected free speech and expression. In this context it becomes important to understand the values that justify the presumption of protecting free speech, the rationale behind restrictions and the extent thereof. It is only when we comprehend 'why' it is important to protect free speech and the values it embodies, will we be able to understand whether the extent of legal limits on it are justified.

Some thinkers in political philosophy understand free speech as a 'requirement of morality' and then comprehend the implications of this theory on law and policy (Howard, 2024). More often than not, *morality of free speech* and *law of free speech* diverge when the positive laws of a country unjustly restrict free speech. In other words, *'the actual scope of right to free speech'* and the *'justified scope of right to free speech'* may diverge in many jurisdictions. In this chapter, we will explore this divergence with respect to humor as free speech and Indian positive laws in the backdrop of technological advancement.

There are different theories or approaches to explore the value of freedom of speech and expression. For many thinkers, the legal right to free speech outgrows from the moral right to free speech which is comprehended as a 'natural right' given to all humans by virtue of being humans (Howard, 2024).

A right based theory of free speech would focus on the positive law of a country allowing and restricting free speech whereas a 'non-rights based' approach towards free speech would focus the significance of free speech as natural right or a human right. This moral right of free speech then invokes a correlative moral duty held by state to protect it. Whether to approach freedom of speech as a moral or legal right would depend on the perspective of the thinker or lawmaker as well. For example, consequentialists would explore freedom of speech as a legal right whereas democratic theorists may focus on an underlying natural right to free speech as significant part of a democracy. Further, categorical' jurists (deontologists) would emphasize on whether the qualifications on free speech are justified and protecting citizen autonomy (Howard, 2024). Therefore, to what extent free speech is protected in a country also depends on the approach towards understanding its significance by the law makers and heads of the state.

MILL'S HARM PRINCIPLE

Mill a renowned utilitarian propounded the 'harm principle' in this long essay (which was later published as a book) *'On Liberty'* which triggered ripples and relentless discussions in the field of liberty-based jurisprudence. Mill's arguments for 'individual liberty' as against the tyranny of the majority, has immensely furthered the jurisprudence of liberty. He also promotes 'choice for oneself' as an undeniable aspect of liberty, which ultimately is not only better for an individual but also for the progress of the society. He propounded the 'Harm Principle' to govern the legitimacy of restrictions put on individual liberty.

Mill proposed the Harm Principle to govern the amount of legitimate interference of the society in the liberty of an individual, whether by moral coercion, legal penalties, public opinions or any other force. According to the principle, that 'the sole purpose for which power can be rightfully exercised over any member of a civilized community, against his will, is to prevent harm to other's (Mill, 1978). Even his own good, is not a sufficient reason to restrain his liberty. That is, an person cannot be compelled to do or abstain from doing something even when it would be better for him, or its wiser or would make him happier, in the opinion of others.

John Stuart Mill's harm principle was critiqued by Joel Feinberg's 'Offense Principle' (Feinberg, 1984). Feinberg argues that the harm principle increases the scope of liberty more than is desired (Feingberg, 1984). According to him, it is important for state to ensure criminalization of any behavior which causes serious offense. However, even Feinberg does note that there must not be absolute prohibition of everything that offends. According to him, if an expression or speech is offensive to a person, and the person could avoid it, it is not required by the government to necessarily ban it.

Further, Miss Gertrude in her book *'On Liberty and Liberalism- The Case of John Stuart Mill (1990)*, accuses Mill of not comprehending the implications of his essay. She characterized Mill's principle as 'extreme', without understanding the essence of liberty in Mill's work. Dworkin, in his book, *Taking Rights Seriously (2013)*, clarified that there is no basis of such accusation in Mill's work (Dworkin, 2013).

THEORIES OF FREEDOM OF SPEECH AND EXPRESSION

The significance of free speech and expression is categorised on the basis of different theories which attempt to justify the protection of this right by the governments. *Listener theory* centres around the notion that state censors free speech on the ground that according to the government the content of the free speech 'ought' to cause harm. In other words, the state decides what people should hear, watch and listen. Jurists differ on the extent of state paternalism to be exercised by governments when it comes to free speech and expression. Undoubtedly there are various legitimate reasons of restricting free speech, for example- Hate speech or unfounded defamation or sound nuisance. However, controlling noise decibel limitations is different from when the state may attempt to restrict free speech with the purpose of controlling what we ought to communicate and hear and what not.

Under the Listener theory comes the doctrines of content neutrality (violated when *discussion* on certain topics not allowed) and viewpoint neutrality (when the government may ban or censor the *advocacy* of certain views) (Stone, 1983). Therefore, free speech thinkers argue that autonomy interests of people are not just protected by Free speech, but are promoted by creating or protecting an environment in which we can learn what others have to say (Howard, 2024). This in turn helps us to introspect on what goals to align with and how to pursue them because our access to information and free speech is served by variety of view points which can put forward only if the governing laws respects all viewpoints (Stone, 1983). It is not about whether the speech is harmless, but the fact that the 'harmful' tendency of the expression be exposed through public argument and discussion instead of state's excessive paternalism.

Speaker theory of free speech emphasises on interests of humans in 'self-expression' (as speakers), the protection of which is considered desirable (Cohen, 1993). Further, *Democracy theories* centre the significance of right to free speech around democracy, wherein restricting free speech is disrespecting the status of citizens as free individual with the right to debate, discuss and decide the law in a country (Cohen, 1993). Some thinkers like John Rawls argue that restricting free political speech implies at least a partial suspension of democracy. The second Chief Justice of India, M. Patanjali Shastri in the judgment of Romesh Thapar v. State of Madras (AIR 1950 SC 124) noted that freedom of speech and of the press lies at the very foundation of all democratic organisations. He emphasised that without free political discussions, no public education is possible which is significant for the proper functioning of the elected government. This judgment was delivered merely four months after India enforced its Constitution which protects Freedom of speech and expression as a fundamental right, subject to reasonable restrictions).

Thinker theories assert the need to protect free speech because of all the interests of speakers, listeners and democratic citizens. Seana Shiffrin is attributed with the evolution of the thinker-based theory in which he underlines the significance and inter-dependent nature of freedom of thought and freedom of communication-the central idea being that free speech and its protection is pertinent to development and functioning of thinkers (Shiffrin 2014). Toleration theories is based on a basic human tendency- we hold contempt towards people who hold views contrary to our convictions (Kramer, 2021). Therefore, preserving free speech becomes essential to tame our temptation to punish those who don't agree with us. Instrumental theories argue that if we don't guarantee protection of free speech, it would lead to state abusing its powers and silencing anyone who questions them (Epstein, 1992).

While the above theories attempt to justify why free speech needs to be protected, no government or even thinker agrees that this freedom is absolute in nature. When it comes to justifying restrictions of free speech, there are various reasons why it may be done, for example False/misleading information. There are different views as to why and to what extent this right may be restricted.

Uncovered speech is a kind of speech which is considered not to fall within the ambit of free expression, for example making a threat (Schauer, from 1982 onwards). This is because certain kind of speech lacks the basic values that justify free speech itself (see the different theories of justifying free speech), In USA, the Supreme Court uses a 'rational basis' test to check the constitutionality of legislation restricting free speech (Howard, 2024). Then there is *covered but unprotected speech.* This speech has the values of free expression yet the harm of it justifies curtailing it (Schauer, from 1982 onwards). And the last kind is *covered and protected.* The underlined issue is, there is no reasonably unanimous opinion on what kind of speech is to be categorised as uncovered or covered but unprotected (Schauer, from 1982 onwards). For example, there may be disagreements on whether media trial comes under covered but protected speech or covered and protected speech.

EXTERNAL CONSTRAINTS ON FREE SPEECH AND EXPRESSION

Art 19 of the International Convention of Civil and Political Rights guarantees everyone the right to freedom of speech and expression which includes the freedom to seek, receive and impart information and ideas of all kinds. But the article also points out that this right carries with itself 'special duties and responsibilities'. Art 20 of ICCPR goes on to restrict any speech which constitutes propaganda of war and mention several grounds to qualify free speech- 'advocacy of national, racial, religious hatred which constitutes incitement to discrimination, violence or hostility'.

Hate speech is understood as any expression that attacks any members of socially vulnerable groups or any minority as inferior or dangerous- a speech in the form of group defamation which curtails other cherished values in any society like equality. Therefore, sometimes free speech must be balanced with other important rights and values (Howard, 2024). The pertinent and perpetually unresolved question is – what is proportionate balance.

No matter the number of theories we may have, the number of laws protecting or restricting free speech, there is always a disagreement on the extent of legitimate speech and its restrictions. Court interpretations play a major part here as the judges interpret the free speech law and its restrictions on case-to-case basis. For example, even though hate speech is considered a reasonable restriction on free speech in most countries, some think restricting it goes against fundamental theories of free speech like the listener theory (Howard, 2024). Balancing of interests, according to some happen before we define what rights are and it's scope.

In India, the same Article of constitution which guarantees free speech, also puts 'reasonable restrictions' on it. Scanlon notes that there is only 'balancing of interests. According to him rights are not balanced but defined and redefined (Scanlon 2008). Scanlon suggests that the test of striking the proportionate balance is not is not in consequentialism but in assessing the strength of an individual's reason to engage in any given speech, against the strength of another individual's reason to oppose it (Scanlon 2008).

So ideally to justify restrictions on free speech it becomes important to show that that the given speech is wrongful or harmful, which breaches a duty that the speaker owes to another (Howard, 2024). Further, offensiveness of speech is a socially sensitive area. Article 10 of the European Convention on Human Rights (ECHR) protects freedom of speech and expression and restricts it on the ground of national security, public safety, territorial integrity, prevention of disorder or crime, protection of health or morals, protection of rights or reputation of others, preventing disclosure of confidential information, or for maintaining impartiality and authority of judiciary (Article 10, ECHR). European Court of Human Rights have very strongly upheld in their decisions that this right is not limited to speech and expression which is received favourably by other, but also extends to those that may 'offend, shock or disturb' (Bhatia, 2016).

According Joel Feinburg opinions specially on matters of public policy, any empirical fact, historical events, scientific, theological, philosophical, moral or political questions ought to be protected even if it offensive (Feinburg, 1984).

INTERNAL CONSTRAINTS ON FREE SPEECH AND EXPRESSION

The internal constraint to free speech approach revolves around the idea that the values that justify free speech, themselves should define the limits of it. Therefore, if targeted by hate speech undermines one's dignity and individual autonomy, the appeal to same values can help support restrictions on free speech. If our individuality is supported by free speech, any false or misleading information, also takes away from the same autonomy. Some thinkers agree that in a democracy all citizens should be free to discuss any proposal at all, even the destruction of democracy itself.

Yet some others note that one's duties as democratic citizens is also to set limits to their free speech rights (Meiklejohn, 1948, see also Howard, 2024).

The general argument is that restrictions on free speech should be proportional (R. v. Oakes, 1986). The Supreme Court of Canada provide 3 pronged criteria of devising the limitations of free speech. First, the measures adopted to restrict must not be arbitrary and irrational- must be fairly connected with the objective. Second, the means adopted, even when rationally connected to the objective, should impair as minimum as possible-the right to free speech. Third, there must be proportionality between the effects of measures taken for qualifying free speech and the objective which should be of 'sufficient importance' (R. v. Oakes, 1986).

HUMOR AS FREE SPEECH: EVOLUTION, PURPOSE AND SIGNIFICANCE

Humor is a significant element of human communication and is considered as an important constituent of democratic life. Since ancient times, humor has been used as tool to challenge the powerful, rather poke at them, and engage in political and social debates (Kuipers 2011). It an important kind of expression protected under the right to freedom of speech and expression (Young & Godioli, 2022).

Since the anicient times, very few philosophers like James Beattie and Frances Hutcheson have explored the themes of humor and laughter (Morreall, 2024). Until the 18th century, the term 'humor' was not used in its current sense of 'funniness'. Henri Bergson's book 'Laughter' published in 1990 is considered as the first major work on humor (Morreall, 2024). Further, it is surprising to note that most early philosophers were quite negative in their analysis and assessment of humor (Morreall, 2024). Until the 20th century, opinions on humor focussed on its mocking nature rather than wit. Plato treated laughter as an emotion that overrides self-control and hence did not hold favourable views on humor. In *Philebus*, Plato views comedy as a form of vice or evil (Laws, 7:816e; 11:935e, see Morreall, 2024).

According to Plato laughter and humor should be restricted by state control. Aristotle on the other hand agreed with Plato on humor being vice, but considered wit as an important part of conversation (Nicomachean Ethics). Even in the Bible mockery is considered an evil which deserves death (2 Kings 2:23). The European Christian views against humor and laughter percolated through the years to Middle Ages. Puritans were the strongest condemners of humor and even outlawed comedy during their rule in England in mid-17th century (*see* Prynne, 1633). Thomas Hobbes' Leviathan and Rene Descartes' Passions of the Soul, both denounced 'laughter' as an expression of ridicule and scorn (Morreall, 2024).

Such negative views towards laughter took the shape of *'Superiority Theory'* in the 20th century. The theory provides that laughter expresses a feeling of superiority over other people. Roger Scruton noted that if people dislike being laughed at, it because laughter devalues the person (object of laughter) in the eyes of the person laughing at him (subject of laughter) (Morreall 1983, 168). It was only when Francis Hutcheson in 1750 wrote a critique of Hobbes' views on laughter, that the Superiority theory was challenged (Morreall, 2024). Hutcheson argued that for laughter, feeling of superiority are not necessary.

In 1709, Lord Shaftesbury essay "An Essay on the Freedom of Wit and Humor", was one of the first essays in which humor was linked to its current meaning of 'funniness'. *The Relief theory*, therefore argues that laughter in the human nervous system acts similar to a pressure release valve in a steam boiler. Thus started the weakening of the arguments of Superiority theory of laughter and humor (Morreall, 2024). According to Herbert Spencer's views in 'On the Physiology of Laughter', (1911), emotions take the physical form of nervous energy. Spencer provides that laughter releases nervous energy and movements of laughter have no object, unlike other ways of releasing it.

Then there is the *Incongruity theory* which in 18th century challenged the notions of Superiority theory (Morreall, 2024). Incongruity theory provides that the cause of laughter is something that infringes our expectations or mental patterns- something incongruous (Beattie, 1779). This is now the dominant theory on Humor in psychological and philosophical studies. In 'On the Orator' Cicero said that the most general kind of joke is when the person expects one thing yet another is said (*see* Morreall, 2024). In other words, the starting is somehow incongruous to the ending which creates an element of humor. Similar techniques are used by stand-up comedians these days wherein they provide a set-up and then the punch line, which violates the expectation. However, sometimes even the anticipation of the set-up storyline leads to laughter and humor. It is important to note that the incongruity theory has been improved over the years and the most recent version understand humorous amusement as the way of enjoying incongruity.

According to Kant, the pleasure of laughter is not intellectual, but only physical (Kant, 1790). However, this notion is also negated owing to the fact that humor can serve as a tool for social commentary, and even challenging power indirectly. Some thinkers understand humor as a kind of play and argue that play is a part of life that makes it richer, that life should include amusement.

HUMOR IN INDIA: HISTORICAL FOUNDATIONS

In India earlier humor circulated mostly orally in the form of verbal jokes, then came political cartoons, satirical literature, satirical films and now we are in the age where there are numerous forms of humor (meme, stand-up comedy, satirical tweets, movies, cartoons, parody etc.) and multiple social media platform where it is available. Today's culture of humous speech has coincided with a voracious appetite for content consumption.

In the ancient and medieval literature of India, a rich and vibrant culture of humor can be found. The figure of court-jester or witty companion of King, can be found in various popular literature such as the tales of Tenali Raman and Akbar-Birbal. Court jesters were not only well regarded but also rewarded for their ability to solve problems sing wit and humor. Tenali Raman was a 16th century witty Telugu scholar, poet, and advisor in the court of Raja Krishnadevaraya of the Vijayanagara Empire. He was known for his sharp humor and wit and was given the title of 'Vikataka-vi'(jester poet) (Liang, 2021).

There are several stories where the Tenali was almost executed by the King, but he managed to get out of such situation by applying his humor and clever word play (Das, 2020). He often used his wit to make the King realize the truth, see through deception and even correct his own mistakes (Subramaniam, 2017). It becomes important to underline here that Raman and Birbal did mock the King and their illogical actions also, often making them angry. Yet at the end of the tales, the King understood the truth of the situation, accepted the ridicule and moved beyond his ego and prestige (Das, 2020). Therefore, it becomes important that even in the 21st century in India, apart from exploring the relationship between the law and humor, it becomes pertinent that we cultivate a culture of governance which has a sense of humor too (Liang, 2021).

In Sibaji Bandyopadhyay's translation of Arthashastra (book by Chanakya on science of living and statecraft, verse 4.1.61 provides that entertainers in their performances may even make fun of castes or families or different customs of regions (Liang, 2021). Then there were King Bharata's sons who targeted divine sages through satire. There were numerous mythological tales from Puranas contained wit and scepticism. In Hinduism, a witty, humorous and mischievous divine sage-Narad Muni, appears in a number of texts like Mahabharata, Ramayana and Puranas.

Hence, unlike the European and specifically, Greek philosophers view India always had a rich culture of wit and humor from King's court rooms to mythological stories and major Hindu texts. Therefore, there is enough to draw inspiration from Indian history and mythology when it comes to developing a contemporary jurisprudence of humor as free speech and navigating its limits. There exists a significant relationship between humor as free speech and democracy which is affirmed through centuries of satire in Indian history.

The importance of humor, specifically 'satire' has been recognized by several landmark judgments all over the world (Young & Godioli, 2022). Court have held that the caustic nature of humor at times, it has played a significant role in political and public debates and our discourses would have been considerably poor without humor (Hustler v. Falwell, 1988). Satire is essentially a form of expression which by its features of exaggeration and distortion of reality, aims to agitate and provoke (Vereinigung Bildender Kunstler v. Austria, 2007). Satire is a form of expression which is protected under the constitution in most countries and courts agree that it in robust discussions on social-political issues, the people are allowed some level of exaggeration and provocation. Even the press can be ironical and satirical in its commentary (Peta v. Minister of Law, Constitutional Affairs and Human Rights, 2018). Satire as a form of humor has been held as an instrument of denunciation or social critique which hides a message behind the irony, jocularity and laughter (Pando de Mercado v. Gente Grossa SRL, 2020). In Indibility Creative Pvt. Ltd. V. Govt. of West Bengal, April 2019, the Supreme Court of India held that satire is one the most effective art forms which reveals the contradictions, hypocrisies and absurdities of life. The court noted that humor has the ability to clearly and quickly make a point in ways other forms of communication and expression often cannot (Young & Godioli, 2022).

Some hold the view that the function of satire is not so much to advance public debates as it is to use a democratic right to poke fun at the powerful. According to Robert Phiddian, the basic purpose of satire is to serve as a collective pressure valve by "licensing public expression of harsh emotions" (Phiddian, 2019).

Scholars agree that the main purpose of humor of to provoke laughter and contributing to public debates may be an incidental part of it rather necessary; and that laughter may not necessarily always go hand in hand with an issue of public or social interest (Capelotti 2018, 268), yet it requires protection nonetheless.

HUMOR, OFFENCE AND PREJUDICE: COMPLEX DIMENSIONS

It is important to note that some jokes that are particularly based on ethnic, gender or racial stereotypes have necessitated discussions on moral aspects of such humor (Dadlez, 2020). Many philosophers have found such humor as equivalent to verbal aggression against the object of the jokes (Morreall, 2024). Sexist, racist jokes on black people or memes which portray 'women as belonging to the kitchen', Italians as cowards, blondes as stupid, have been denounced by many. Michael Philips in

'Racist Acts and Racist Humor'(1984) argues against the legitimacy of such humor even though bonafide in nature without meaning any harm.

Others hold the view that it is not necessary to hold stereotypical beliefs to enjoy such jokes. They argue that such humor is enjoyed its clever depiction of unbelievable stupidity (Christie Davies, 1990). However, a counter agreement to this is even though such stereotypical jokes does not require one to have such attitude towards the object of the jokes, but it keeps them in circulation on different forms of media which can add on to the already existing layered prejudice in our society against people of different caste, class, race, religion, sex or gender. With the growing reach of social media through advancement of technology, such memes or jokes reach billions of people which adds on to the percolation of such prejudices into the subconscious of people. This adds on to the injustice such people might already be facing.

For example, in India the commonly held view is that women must get married at a certain age, bear children, even if it comes at cost of their own career or education. So, jokes or memes highlighting that women are only good in kitchen, or not good at mathematics or driving, will not be helping anyone even at the cost of making people laugh. Such humor may cause harm, but whether the makers are to be held responsible under the laws of the country is a separate question and more nuanced question. Researchers have demonstrated through experiments that sexist humor can desensitize people towards gender bias and normalize prejudicial views (Ford, Boxer, Armstrong, & Edel, 2008).

Protection of Humor as Free Speech: Substance and Style

It is significant to note that humor may have a higher degree of offensiveness in some cases due to its inherent qualities of exaggeration, sarcasm or ironical nature which may lead to public disorder. Charlie Hebdo controversy is a good example.

After the 9/11 attacks there was a rise in islamophobia all over the world, especially in the western world. In 2005, a Danish newspaper, Jyllands Posten, published 12 cartoons under the title of 'Face of Mohammed'. The next year, a satirical newspaper in France, Charlie Hebdo republished the cartoons by Jyllands Posten and added some of their own. Many of the cartoons were considered extremely offensive as any visual depiction of Prophet Mohammed (PBUH) is strictly prohibited in Islam (Klausen, 2009). One of the most infamous cartoons portrayed Prophet Mohammed (PBUH) with a bomb in his turban (Klausen, 2009).

Charlie Hebdo was known for its strongly secular non-conformist tone in its cartoon, jokes, articles which mocked Catholicism, Judaism and Islam (Klausen, 2009). On 7th January 2015, a maintenance worker, nine journalists and two police officers were killed in an attack by French born Algerian Muslim brothers at Charlie

Hebdo's Paris office. Said and Cherif Kouachi, the culprit brothers, before fleeing, had shouted, "We have avenged the Prophet Mohammed!" (Klausen, 2009).

The underlined aspect here is that offensive content in the form of satire (cartoon/jokes/parody) tend to have a more serious impact than offensive content in the form of long articles and editorials. *Humor has the ability to touch a nerve that is unknown to other forms of expression. This makes humor powerful as well as dangerous and more prone to getting restricted by the laws of a nation.*

In the Indian perspective, Kunal Kamra, and Indian comedian has landed several times in trouble with the Supreme Court of India. One specified time contempt of court was issued against him for his 'vulgar'(as called by the then Attorney General of India) tweet criticizing the then Chief Justice of India in 2020. Kamra has tweeted a picture of his index finger and middle finger against an airplane window along with a caption, "One of these 2 fingers is for CJI Arvind Bobde... ok let me not confuse you it's the middle one" (The News Minute, 20th Nov, 2020). His tweet was essentially to express his deep discontent as according to him, the Supreme Court showcased judicial bias and favouritism in the Arnab Goswami's (a controversial news anchor) case.

The underlying point here is there are numerous articles written about lack of transparency of judiciary in India and criticism of certain judges. In fact, in 2018, in a first of its kind public conference, the four top most senior judges of the Supreme Court of India criticised the then Chief Justice alleging that the administration of the court under CJI was not proper (Times of India, 2018). However, when criticism meets satire and offence, the Supreme Court of India becomes defensive of its stature as the guardian of the Constitution.

On this peculiar effect of humorous speech, Geroge William Foote, a British secularist in his book *'Prisoner of Blasphemy'* argued that *'why is long faced scepticism permissible heresy, but broad faced scepticism a felony?'* (Foote, 1885). In his book, G.W. Foote who was convicted and imprisoned for blasphemy in the late 19th century (for certain allegedly blasphemous content and cartoons published in the Freethinker journal, started by Foote) fearlessly condemned the blasphemy laws in Britain and elaborately made a case for satire as a legitimate form of criticism which deserves the same protection as other more 'serious' forms of expressions (Foote, 1885).

On legitimacy of satire as free speech, Foote argues that one cannot really distinguish between 'substance' and 'style'. The government must either forbid or permit all attacks on religion (he referred to Christianity). He argued that religious and political changes of significance are never made by calm and moderate language.

In his defence during his trial Foote had argued that authorities cannot expect people to question the Church only in polite language. He notes that this comes from the underlying assumption that Christianity is true and must not be attacked, which is problematic according to him (Foote, 1885). In his book Foote noted that he questions why the 'Church hates laughter'. He states that being offended by satire against religion or anti-religious comments is acceptable but avenging them is preposterous. *According to Foote, ridicule is the most potent weapon against superstition* (Foote, 1885).

LEGAL FRAMEWORK GOVERNING HUMOR AS FREE SPEECH IN INDIA

Freedom of speech and expression even though requires protection and preservation, yet no one holds a view that it should be completely unrestricted. Art 19(1)(a) of the Constitution of India guarantees the right to freedom of speech and expression to all Indian citizens. However, Art 19(2) restricts free speech in India in the interest of the sovereignty and integrity of India, security of state, friendly relations with foreign states, public order, decency or morality, or contempt of court, defamation, incitement to offence. The term 'reasonable restrictions' were added by the 1951 amendment to the Indian Constitution. The amendment was precisely brought because of Supreme Court of India judgments in Romesh Thapar v. State of Madras (1950) and Brij Bhushan v. State of Delhi (1950), wherein the court upheld the right to free speech and expression against government laws (Bhatia, 2016). Therefore, the Parliament through the 1951 expanded the limits on free speech by ensuring reasonable restrictions are lucidly in place in Article 19(2).

However, humor as free speech comes under the radar of all the restrictions and limitations that any other form of free speech has. In the constituent assembly debate on Article 19 (Art. 13 of the draft constitution), our leaders heavily clashed on the limits of restriction to be put on free speech and expression (Bhatia, 2016). Majority of the assembly was of the opinion that free speech cannot be absolute and that instead of depending upon the Supreme Court of India to identify the limitations, it was better the state formulated it directly (Bhatia, 2016).

C Rajagopalachari had argued that orderly progress and peace are of paramount importance to India, therefore, speech must be restricted if it were likely to foster communal hatred. K.M. Munshi on the other hand disagreed and said that free speech and expression tending to hatred must be permitted up to the point it led to breach of public order (Constituent Assembly Debates, 1948). Further, K.T. Shah was speculative of the ground of 'morality' as the term is vague and is completely subjective in nature in a land of different customs, cultures, religion (Constituent Assembly Debates, 1948). Therefore, it is regulated by the same set of reasonable restrictions under Article 19(2) of the Constitution of India.

Certain provisions of the penal code of India Bharatiya Nyaya Sanhita, 2023 (replaced Indian Penal Code, 1860) also put limitations on free speech. Waging or attempting to wage war against the state (S.147), Intentional insult with intention to provoke breach of peace (S352), statements conducing to public mischief (S.353), defamation (S.356), outraging religious feelings (S. 299), obscenity (S.296), are major provisions which restrict free speech and expression including humor in India (Bharatiya Nyaya Sanhita, 2023).

Further, under the Contempt of Courts Act, 1971, section 2(c) criminalizes publication of any matter which scandalizes the court or tends to lower its authority. Provisions under Unlawful Activities (Prevention) Act, 1967 punish any speech or expression that is aimed at disaffection, secessionist tendencies or threatening the sovereignty of India.

The Information Technology Act, 2000 also puts some restrictions on free speech. Under section 79(3), intermediary platforms must comply and follow take down orders of questionable posts to avoid liability. The provision provides intermediaries exemption from liability if the intermediary doesn't initiate the transmission, select the receiver of the transmission, and select or modify the information contained in the transmission. Also, the intermediary must observe due diligence while discharging its duty under information technology law and ought to obey the guidelines given by the central government of India.

LIMITS OF HUMOR IN DIGITAL INDIA: JUDICIAL PERSPECTIVES

Limits of humor has been tested in India in all its forms- from Facebook posts, online cartoons, tweets, stand-up comedy videos and performances to web series on Netflix and video games. Indian judiciary has attempted to balance the right to free speech with other values, yet there remains certain ambiguities in scope of reasonable restrictions.

It is paramount importance to note that section 66A of the Information Technology Act, 2000 has been struck down as unconstitutional by the Supreme Court of India in the landmark case of *Shreya Singhal v. Union of India (AIR 2015 SC 1523)*. In this case the police arrested two women for allegedly posting objectional comments on the social media platform Facebook on shutting down of Mumbai city after the death of a political leader. They questioned the decision of shutting down the entire city and causing major inconvenience to people. The comments were regarded as grossly offensive and the police made an arrest under sec 66A of the IT Act, 2000. Even though the women were released later the charges were dismissed, the incident gave rise to huge uproar in India.

The two women decided to challenge the constitutional validity of provision 66A on the ground of infringement their fundamental right to free speech under Article 19(1)(a) of the Constitution. The provision in question section 66A which punishes any person who shares 'grossly offensive' information through computer resource or shares the information with the knowledge of its falsity to cause annoyance, insult, inconvenience, hatred, ill-will, danger, injury or sends any electronic mail/message to cause annoyance, or to deceive or mislead.

The Supreme Court of India decided on the issue whether section 66A of the technology law of India violated the fundamental right to free speech or whether the restrictions on speech under the section comes under the scope of 'reasonable restrictions' under Art. 19(2). The petitioners specifically argued that section 66A is vaguely worded and creates a 'chilling effect' on freedom of expression in India and gives extensive power to the state to restrict it (Shreya Singhal v. UOI, AIR 2015 SC 1523). The government of India had stated that mere possibility that a provision may be misused or is vague, doesn't render it unconstitutional. Further, the government argued that if the law enacted by parliament is legislatively competent and non-arbitrary, vagueness cannot be the criteria to strike it down and that courts may interfere with the legislative process only when the law clearly violates fundamental rights under the Constitution of India.

The Supreme Court of India stated that state may only curtail free speech when it leads to any incitement, mere discussion or advocacy of cause, howsoever unpopular it may be, is not ground for restricting free speech. The court found that section 66A makes no distinction among the scope of discussion, advocacy and incitement. It uses terms like 'annoyance' which can be used to curtail even legitimate speech and expression. Further, very importantly the Court stated that the provision fails to establish a clear proximate relationship with protection of public peace and order. As per the provision, sending an electronic message or posting something using computer resource is ground enough to get arrested if it causes annoyance or hurts someone (Shreya Singhal v. UOI, AIR 2015 SC 1523).

The case of *Indibility Creative Pvt Ltd v. Govt of West Bengal (Writ Petition (Civil) No. 306, 11 April 2019)* involved a shadow ban imposed by the govt of West Bengal on a bengali satirical film 'Bhobishoter Bhhoot' (Future Ghost), a political satire. The petitioners argued that the State had misused police powers to cause unlawful obstruction to the screening of the film even though there was no formal ban. The Supreme Court took notice of State's failure to protect free speech. The main issue before the court was whether the agencies had resorted to extra-constitutional means to abrogate fundamental rights.

The two judge bench including Justice DY Chandrachud, 2018 surveyed the writings of Voltaire, John Stuart Mill, Dworkin, Camus, Beauvoir in outlining the limits of free speech and emphasised that Art. 19 requires extending protection to free speech that we may despise. The Court provided, "this principle is at the heart of democracy, a basic human right, and its protection is a mark of a civilised and tolerant society".[1] Further, the court noted that 'Satire' is a powerful form of artistic expression which is able to quickly show the 'absurdities, hypocrisies and contradictions' in life.

In *Marathe v. The State of Maharashtra (Cri.PIL 3-2015)*, cartoonist Aseem Trivedi was charged with Sedition under Section 124A of the IPC, 1860 as he created and published many cartoons online that allegedly defamed Parliament of India and the Indian Constitution which according to the government of Maharashtra, was spreading hatred against the government. Even though in the court's opinion, the cartoons were devoid of any wit, yet the court emphasised that cartoons and caricatures are a form of expression with the element of humour or sarcasm which needs to be protected. The court held that the cartoonist had the right to express his indignation against corruption in the political system, when there is no allegation of intention to create public disorder or incitement to violence (*Marathe v. The State of Maharashtra, Cri.PIL 3-2015).*

In Tata Sons Limited v. Greenpeace International (High Court of Delhi, 178 (2011) DLT 705) TATA applied for an interim injunction against Greenpeace India and Greanpeace International and damages to the extent of Rs 10,00,00,000 for creating an allegedly defamatory and malicious video game titled 'Turtles v TATA'. Through the video game, Greenpeace criticised TATA for the company's involvement in project that could negatively impact breeding and nesting of olive ridely turtles. The game stated that the player must help the yellow turtles to eat as many as possible white dots without running into 'Ratty' and at the same time dodge TATA demons of development which are threatening their home. TATA also sued for trademark infringement as the video game showed TATA's 'T' symbol. The court, following the precedent of Bonnard v Perryman (1891), held that in action for defamation, the court will not impose a prior restraint on publication unless it is clear that defence will not succeed at the trial. The court underscored the significance of free speech, especially concerning public interest issues. It recognized that parody and satire are legitimate forms of expression in a democratic society.

Further in *Tuljapurkar v. State of Maharashtra ((2015) 6 SCC 1)* the issue in question was the contents of a Marathi satirical poem called "Gandhi Mala Bhetala" ("I Met Gandhi") which was published by Devidas Tuljapurkar in a 1994. The poem used explicit language and Gandhi as symbolic figure. The issue of a magazine meant for private distribution among union members. The poem used strong language and presented Mahatma Gandhi, known as Father of India in an unpopular way. Section 292 of the Indian Penal Code (now replaced by Bharatiya Nyaya Sanhita, 2023). Section 292 punished the publication of obscene material. The poem against Gandhi was considered to be offensive and obscene.

When the matter went finally to the top court, the Supreme Court applied the contemporary community standard test conditionally. The court referred to *Roth v United States (354 U.S. 476)* and opined that the test becomes more dynamic when the speech refers to an historically revered and exalted personality like Gandhi. Therefore, even though the court found that the satirical poem comes under the ambit of restricted speech, the appellants were later discharged. According to the court's "historically respected personalities" standard, satirical works in India on famous figures like Gandhi shouldn't go beyond the bounds of obscenity.

Ashutosh Dubey vs Netflix, (I.A. 3754/ 2020 in CS (OS) 120/ 2020) controversy from the exceedingly unflattering portrayal of a lawyer in the Netflix series Hasmukh. Netflix was the target of a petition alleging that the show disparaged the legal profession and showed it in poor light and has the potential to negatively affect public opinion. The defendants had argued that the web series portrayed the protagonist as a stand-up comedian who belittled lawyers through his satire. The application of grievance was dismissed by the court on two grounds. First, lawyers as a class persons cannot be defamed and second, the series was a work of satire which exaggerated different aspects of the legal profession to expose the shortcomings and areas of improvement in the legal arena of India. The court held that the series has not caused any defamation and that such satirical works are well within the scope of protected speech under article 19(1)(a).

In *Munnawar S/o Iqbal Faruqui v. State of Madhya Pradesh (*Mis. Cr. Case No.2206/2021), Munawar Faruqui, a stand-up comedian, was arrested for allegedly insulting Hindu deities in a recorded YouTube video. When he went for a stand-up comedy performance in Indore, he was arrested and the venue was vandalised. He was charged under Sections 295A and few other related sections of Indian Penal Code (hurting religious feelings and inciting enmity (now replaced by Bharatiya Nyaya Sanhita, 2023)) after it was claimed that his jokes offended religious feelings. According to the Madhya Pradesh High Court, there was prima facie evidence of an intent to offend religious beliefs, hence bail was denied. Later, the bail hearing went to Supreme Court of India, which granted bail and ordered for consolidation of all cases against Faruqui at Indore.

In *Kunal Kamra v Union of India (Writ Petition (L) No. 9792 of 2023)*, the Bombay High Court gave a split verdict in the case of Kunal Kamra v Union of India (Writ Petition (L) No. 14955 of 2023), wherein the constitutionality of the Rules 3(1)(b), 3(1)(b)(v) and 7 (the "Amendment") of the Information Technology (Intermediary Guidelines and Digital Media Ethics Code) Rules, 2021 (the "Intermediary Rules"). The rules bestow the Central Government to set up a Fact Checking Unit (FCU) with the power to censor any 'fake false or misleading' information related to the government affairs on online media platforms. The matter was heard by the Division Bench, which included Justice GS Patel and Justice Neela Ghokale. The Amendment was knocked down by Justice G.S Patel, who ruled that it violated Articles 14, 19(1)(a), 19(2), 19(1)(g), and 19(6) of the Indian Constitution and Section 79 of the Act, but Justice Neela Ghokale upheld the Amendment.

Kamra along with other organizations and journalists had filed a public interest litigation contending that such rules violate the freedom of speech and expression under Article 19(1)(a) and creates a chilling effect as it lacks clear criteria and may lead to arbitrary censorship. Such rules may also lead to self-censorship in journalists and others while posting about government affairs on online platforms.

The government justified the necessity of such a law on the ground that it is a step towards combatting fake news and misinformation which is blatantly spread on all social media platforms. Such fake news threatens public trust in government institutions and that regulating misinformation doesn't not constitute censorship. Kamra argued that there is total absence of judicial scrutiny or an independent scrutiny in this process and hence the government appointed fact checkers may be used to silence criticism, satire or offensive speech on social media platforms.

Since there was a split verdict, the case was then referred by the Chief Justice of Bombay High Court to a third judge Justice A.S. Chandurkar who rendered his opinion in September 2024. Justice Chandurkar concurred with the judgement of Justice Patel for striking down the amendment in Rules are unconstitutional. Further, he opined that the rules were ultra vires the IT Act 2000. The Justice noted that the amendment rules cannot be saved by reading down or limiting it operation.

Kunal Kamra has several times found himself in trouble with the Supreme Court of India because of his unfiltered satire and criticism. On of the most controversial tussle was his twitter post written in way to direct middle finger at Chief Justice Bobde. Even though criminal contempt case was initiated against him under the Contempt of Courts Act, 1971, Kamra stayed unfazed and refused to apologise. According to him, the dignity of the Supreme Court of India should not be affected by tweets. A similar contempt case was issued against Rachita Taneja for publishing her satirical cartoons criticising the Supreme Court of India on her twitter account 'Sanitary Panels' (Cartooning for Peace).

SUGGESTIONS AND CONCLUSION

A study of humor-based jurisprudence through Indian case laws reveal that legal restrictions imposed on humor or qualifying humor in India depends on array of criteria including what is the subject matter, who is the object of satire, degree of offensiveness, and morality. From the judicial precedents, it can be seen that when it comes to satire on religious aspects/figures, the Supreme Court of India and revered personalities like Mahatma Gandhi, humor as free speech is not as protected in India.

It can also be analyzed that sometimes style of speech (satire) do matter as seen from the Kunal Kamra's criticism of Supreme Court of India and the eventual contempt case. Other times, the substance of the humor itself becomes the dominating factor for censorship as happened in Munnawar Faruqui's case (religious sentiments) and Tuljapurkar's case (revered historical personalities).

Therefore, determination of limitations on free speech ultimately comes down to the cost benefit analysis of the harm or cost imposed by the measure and the benefit it is designed to achieve in creating the law, implementing it and interpreting it. In other words, the question judges, law and policy makers ask themselves, or rather should ask themselves constantly is this - whether the cost (value based, not monetary) of restricting free speech is greater than the benefit achieved by restricting free speech? In other words, what is the gain, in restricting certain speech in terms of democratic values.

Therefore, it is important to ensure that the laws restricting free speech do not have a 'chilling effect' on citizens. Chilling effect is the overdeterrence of benign conduct that occurs incidentally to the legitimate purpose of law (Kendrick, 2013). Such law, if not carefully applied may end up having detrimental impact on protected speech and may lead to self-censorship. So even when government is enacting any law to restrict free speech, it must be ensured that the limits put on free speech is proportionate to the objective of the law being enacted. The Supreme Court in Kunal Kamra's 'Fact Checking Units' case declared clearly that provisions containing ambiguous wordings without proper criteria of restricting free speech is not in harmony with Indian constitutional principles and fundamental rights. However, when we see the cases of contempt of courts, it becomes clear that the Supreme Court of India is less tolerant of humor as free speech when it comes to its own criticism.

Further, it would be helpful if law makers, policy makers and judiciary look at free speech from natural right perspective as well, not just a positive right as discussed above. It equally is a responsibility on satirists and comedians to use humor as free speech to ensure that their work doesn't lead to absolute public disorder or incitement of violence or lead to further prejudice in the society. To offend may be protected, but to create prejudice(racist, sexist memes/ jokes) bears a heavy cost to the society. The people of India also shoulder the responsibility of giving free speech the widest of amplitude possible.

As seen from exploring various theories of free speech, we as humans grow to our fullest potential through listening, speaking, thinking freely. It is a pre-requisite in a country which values democratic principles to protect free speech. Kant's categorical imperative may also be used as guiding light to become more sensitive to the scope of right to free speech as well as toleration level of people. There lies a certain beauty in how through humor we can engage in something as serious as critique of power (Tenali Raman's wit and R. K. Laxman's cartoons) and commentary on various social and political issues. Therefore, such an expression ought to be protected and celebrated in India.

REFERENCES

. Ashutosh Dubey vs Netflix, (I.A. 3754/ 2020 in CS (OS) 120/ 2020)

Bhatia, G. (2016). *Offend, shock, or disturb: Free speech under the Indian Constitution*. Oxford University Press. DOI: 10.1093/acprof:oso/9780199460878.001.0001

Chandrachud, A. (2018). *Republic of rhetoric: Free speech and the Constitution of India*. Penguin Random House India.

Cohen, J. (1993). Freedom of expression. *Philosophy & Public Affairs, 22*(3), 207–263.

Dadlez, E. (2020). Not sitting down for it: How stand-up differs from fiction. *The Journal of Aesthetics and Art Criticism, 78*(4), 513–524. DOI: 10.1111/jaac.12758

Feinberg, J. (1984). The moral limits of the criminal law: Volume 1: Harm to others. Oxford University Press. DOI: 10.1093/0195046641.001.0001

Foote, G. W. (1885). *Prisoner of blasphemy*. The Secular Society.

Howard, J. W. (2024). Freedom of speech. In Zalta, E. N., & Nodelman, U. (Eds.), *The Stanford encyclopedia of philosophy* (Spring 2024 ed.). Stanford University., https://plato.stanford.edu/archives/spr2024/entries/freedom-speech/

Indibility Creative Pvt Ltd v. Govt of West Bengal (Writ Petition (Civil) No. 306, 11 April 2019)

Klausen, J. (2009). *The cartoons that shook the world*. Yale University Press.

Kuipers, G. (2011). The politics of humour in the public sphere: Cartoons, power and modernity in the first transnational humour scandal. *European Journal of Cultural Studies, 14*(1), 63–80. DOI: 10.1177/1367549410370072

Kunal Kamra v Union of India (Writ Petition (L) No. 9792 of 2023)

Liang, L. (2021). Time for a modern law protecting the right to offend through comedy. *Journal of Media & Communication Law, 8*, 107–123.

Marathe v. The State of Maharashtra (Cri.PIL 3-2015)

Mill, J. S. (1978). *On liberty* (Rapaport, E., Ed.). Hackett Publishing Company. (Original work published 1859)

Morreall, J. (1983). *Taking laughter seriously*. State University of New York Press.

Morreall, J. (2024). Philosophy of humor. In Zalta, E. N., & Nodelman, U. (Eds.), *The Stanford encyclopedia of philosophy* (Fall 2024 ed.). Stanford University., https://plato.stanford.edu/archives/fall2024/entries/humor/

Munnawar S/o Iqbal Faruqui v. State of Madhya Pradesh (Mis. Cr. Case No.2206/2021)

Phiddian, R. (2019). *Satire and the public emotions*. Cambridge University Press. DOI: 10.1017/9781108869263

Shreya Singhal v. Union of India (AIR 2015 SC 1523

Stone, E. A. (1983). Problems with current catecholamine hypotheses of antidepressant agents: Speculations leading to a new hypothesis. *Behavioral and Brain Sciences*, *6*(4), 535–547. DOI: 10.1017/S0140525X00017325

Swannie, B. (2020). Racially derogatory cartoons and racial vilification laws: Where to draw the line? *Alternative Law Journal*, *45*(4), 291–297. DOI: 10.1177/1037969X20918663

Tata Sons Limited v. Greenpeace InternationaL (High Court of Delhi, 178 (2011) DLT 705)

Tuljapurkar v. State of Maharashtra ((2015) 6 SCC 1)

Young, J., & Godioli, A. (2022). *Humor and free speech: A comparative analysis of global case laws*. Columbia Law School.

ENDNOTE

1 Subhajit Basu & Shameek Sen, Silenced Voices: Unravelling India's Dissent Crisis Through Historical and Contemporary Analysis of Free Speech and Suppression, 33 Info. & Commc'ns Tech. L. 24 (2024).

About the Contributors

Adrian David Cheok AM FIET FIEAust FRSA is Full Professor at Nanjing University of Information Science and Technology, Director of the Imagineering Institute, Malaysia, Visiting Professor at Raffles University, Malaysia, Visiting Professor at University of Novi Sad-Serbia, on Technical faculty "Mihailo Pupin", Serbia, Faculty of Ducere Business School, and CEO of Nikola Tesla Technologies Corporation. In 2024, Professor Adrian David Cheok was honored with induction as a Full Member into Sigma Xi USA, The Scientific Research Honor Society, a recognition that not only signifies his dedication to scientific excellence but also aligns his contributions with those of groundbreaking researchers. Sigma Xi is a beacon of distinction within the global scientific community, boasting over 200 Nobel Laureates among its members, including luminaries such as Albert Einstein. This prestigious society is renowned for its commitment to the advancement of science and engineering and includes among its distinguished members other eminent personalities like Linus Pauling and Guglielmo Marconi, whose pioneering work has indelibly shaped the landscape of modern science and innovation. Professor Cheok's association with Sigma Xi marks a pinnacle in his career, affirming his commitment to the ethos of rigorous and impactful scientific inquiry. He is a Fellow of the Institution of Engineering and Technology (IET), United Kingdom (FIET). He is a a Fellow of the Institution of Engineers in Scotland He is Fellow of the Engineers Australia (FIEAust). He is a Fellow of the Royal Society for the encouragement of Arts, Manufactures and Commerce (RSA) (United Kingdom). He is a Fellow of the Royal Society of Statistics (United Kingdom). He is a Fellow of the Royal Asiatic Society of Great Britain and Ireland. The Governor General of Australia, Representative of Her Majesty the Queen Elizabeth II, has awarded Australia's highest honour the Order of Australia to Adrian David Cheok for his contribution to international education and research. He is Chief Scientist at Frost Digi. He is Senior Member of the IEEE. He is Founder and Director of the Mixed Reality Lab, Singapore. He was formerly Professor of Pervasive Computing, University of

London, Full Professor and Executive Dean at Keio University, Graduate School of Media Design and Associate Professor in the National University of Singapore. He has previously worked in real-time systems, soft computing, and embedded computing in Mitsubishi Electric Research Labs, Japan. He has been working on research covering mixed reality, human-computer interfaces, wearable computers and ubiquitous computing, fuzzy systems, embedded systems, power electronics. He has successfully obtained approximately $130 million dollars in funding for externally funded projects in the area of wearable computers and mixed reality from Daiwa Foundation, Khazanah National (Malaysian Government), Media Development Authority, Nike, National Oilwell Varco, Defence Science Technology Agency, Ministry of Defence, Ministry of Communications and Arts, National Arts Council, Singapore Science Center, and Hougang Primary School. The research output has included many high quality academic journal papers, research awards, keynote speeches, international exhibitions, numerous government demonstrations including to government President and Prime Ministers, broadcast television worldwide broadcasts on his research (such as CNN/ CNBC/ ABC/ Discovery/ National Geographic etc.), and hundreds of international press media articles. He has been a keynote and invited speaker at numerous international conferences and events. He was invited to exhibit for two years in the Ars Electronica Museum of the Future, launching in the Ars Electronica Festival 2003 and 2017. His works "Human Pacman", "Magic Land", and "Metazoa Ludens", were each selected as one of the world's top inventions by Wired and invited to be exhibited in Wired NextFest 2005 and 2007. He was awarded the Hitachi Fellowship, the A-STAR Young Scientist of the Year Award, and the SCS Singapore Young Professional of the Year Award. He was invited to be the Singapore representative of the United Nations body IFIP SG 16 on Entertainment Computing and the founding Chairman of the Singapore Computer Society Special Interest Group on Entertainment Computing. He was awarded an Associate of the Arts award by the Minister for Information, Communications and the Arts, Singapore. He was awarded as Fellow in Education, World Technology Network. He was awarded a Microsoft Research Award for Gaming and Graphics. He received the C4C Children Competition Prize for best interaction media for children, the Integrated Art Competition Prize by the Singapore Land Transport Authority, Creativity in Action Award, and a First Prize Nokia Mindtrek Award. He received a First Prize in the Milan International InventiON competition. He received the Gold award for best Creative Showcase ACE, He is winner of Keio University Gijyuju-sho award, awarded for the best research of the year in Keio University, Japan's oldest university. He received an SIP Distinguished Fellow Award which honours legendary leaders whose illustrious lives have positively influenced lives across generations and communities around the globe. He was awarded Young Global Leader by the World Economic Forum.

This honour is bestowed each year by the World Economic Forum to recognize and acknowledge the top young leaders from around the world for the professional accomplishments, commitment to society and potential to contribute to shaping the future of the world. He was awarded "Honorary Expert" by Telefonica and El Bulli, the number one restaurant in the world. He is a Fellow of the Royal Society for the encouragement of Arts, Manufactures and Commerce (RSA), an organisation which is committed to finding innovative practical solutions to today's social challenges. His research on smell interfaces was selected by NESTA as Top 10 Technologies of 2015. In 2016, he was awarded the Distinguished Alumni Awards by University of Adelaide, in recognition of his achievements and contribution in the field of Computing, Engineering and Multisensory communication. In 2017, he entered the elite list of The h-Index for Computer Science, a list that contains only the top 0.06\% of all computer scientists in the world. In 2018, he was awarded Albert Nelson Marquis Lifetime Achievement Award. Remote kissing gadget 'Kissenger' was selected to the Top 100 Science Spinoffs and has entered the top 2% out of 5,000 global science spin-offs according to the following criteria: uniqueness of the technology/product, high commercial potential and positive impact to the humanity's well-being by Spinoff.com. He is/was Editor in Chief of the academic journals: Journal of Future Robot Life, Advances in Robotics and Automation, Transactions on Edutainment, ACM Computers in Entertainment, Lovotics: Academic Studies of Love and Friendship with Robots, and Multimodal Technologies and Interaction. He is/was Associate Editor of Advances in Human Computer Interaction, International Journal of Virtual Reality, Virtual Reality, and The Journal of Ambient Intelligence and Humanized Computing (AIHC). He is on the Editorial Board of International Journal of Arts and Technology (IJART), Journal of Recent Patents on Computer Science, The Open Electrical and Electronic Engineering Journal, International Journal of Entertainment Technology and Management (IJEntTM), The Journal of Virtual Reality and Broadcasting, and Interacting with Computers Adrian David Cheok, who was born and raised in Adelaide, Australia, graduated from the University of Adelaide with a Bachelor of Engineering (Electrical and Electronic) with First Class Honours in 1992 and an Engineering Ph.D in 1998.

***

Uzma Abbas holds a PhD from the University of Jammu. Her pioneering research on "Rights of Forest Dwellers: A Critical Study of the Forest Rights Act 2006" has paved the way for significant discourse on indigenous rights. Her academic excellence is underscored by a gold medal in her LLM (Criminal & Security Law) from Noida International University and an impressive 82.7% score in the University Grant Commission's National Eligibility Test (NET). Committed to interdisciplinary exploration. She has shared her expertise at national and international seminars, focusing on critical issues surrounding human rights and environmental law. Her publications appear in esteemed peer-reviewed journals and books. A polyglot proficient in English, Hindi, Urdu, Kashmiri, and beginner's Arabic, she embodies a holistic approach to education, with interests spanning literature, gender studies, environmental preservation, and the arts. Dr. Uzma Abbas's work continues to bridge the gap between scholarship and social impact, fostering a deeper understanding of the intricate relationships between law, society, and the environment.

Mahapara Abbass is a distinguished academician and researcher in the Department of Civil Engineering at Maharishi Markandeshwar (Deemed to be University), renowned for her groundbreaking contributions to structural engineering and sustainable construction materials. With an impressive portfolio of publications in prestigious SCI and Scopus-indexed journals, including Multiscale Multidisciplinary Modeling, Experimentation and Design, and Lecture Notes in Civil Engineering, Dr. Abbass has also presented her work at esteemed conferences and authored/co-authored book chapters in critically acclaimed volumes, such as Advances in Geotechnics and Structural Engineering. Her expertise in geopolymer concrete, sustainable construction practices, and innovative materials has been recognized through publications in esteemed platforms like Elsevier, cementing her prominent role in advancing the frontiers of civil engineering.

Manu Abraham is a Research Scholar from School of Law, CHRIST (Deemed to be University), Bangalore, India. The author graduated from Karnataka State Law University in BALLB. He completed his master's degree in law from CHRIST (Deemed to be University), Bangalore, India. Author's research focuses on laws governing the surveillance framework in India and the implications on right to privacy.

Munir Ahmad is a seasoned professional in the realm of Spatial Data Infrastructure (SDI), Geo-Information Productions, Information Systems, and Information Governance, boasting over 25 years of dedicated experience in the field. With a PhD in Computer Science, Dr. Ahmad's expertise spans Spatial Data Production, Management, Processing, Analysis, Visualization, and Quality Control. Throughout his career, Dr. Ahmad has been deeply involved in the development and deployment of SDI systems specially in the context of Pakistan, leveraging his proficiency in Spatial Database Design, Web, Mobile & Desktop GIS, and Geo Web Services Architecture. His contributions to Volunteered Geographic Information (VGI) and Open Source Geoportal & Metadata Portal have significantly enriched the geospatial community. As a trainer and researcher, Dr. Ahmad has authored over

50 publications, advancing the industry's knowledge base and fostering innovation in Geo-Tech, Data Governance, and Information Infrastructure, and Emerging Technologies. His commitment to Research and Development (R&D) is evident in his role as a dedicated educator and mentor in the field.

Shalom Akhai has established himself as a prominent figure in the field of engineering, leveraging over 18 years of academic, research, and technical experience to make significant contributions. With a robust portfolio of over 100+ publications in prestigious journals, conferences and book chapters, Dr. Akhai demonstrates a commitment to advancing knowledge through scholarly work. Additionally, he has authored/co-authored several technical textbooks, further solidifying his expertise and dedication to education in the field. Beyond academia, Dr. Akhai's impact extends to real-world applications through the establishment of IGNIS Technical Solutions, a consultancy firm to translate his knowledge into real-world applications. His skills have resulted in the successful development of over 50 patents+, underscoring his innovative approach and influence in shaping the engineering landscape.

S. M. Aamir Ali is presently Assistant Professor at Symbiosis Law School Pune, Symbiosis International (Deemed University), Pune. He is currently pursuing his PhD from West Bengal National University of Juridical Sciences (WBNUJS), Kolkata, and has completed his LL.M from National Law School of India University (NLSIU), Bengaluru, with a specialization in Human Rights Law. Mr Ali has been teaching across specializations in Constitutional Law, Human Rights and Criminal Law at UG and PG levels since 2019.

Syed Aaban Asif is a Pakistan-based human rights advocate with interests in social justice, inclusive development, and emerging technologies. He has participated in Global Perspectives initiatives, Model United Nations, and international workshops, where he has demonstrated strong leadership, communication, and analytical skills. His work includes research, journalism, content development, and youth-focused initiatives, with particular attention to the responsible application of artificial intelligence for social impact. His current focus involves advancing human rights and supporting individuals with special needs through technology-driven and community-oriented approaches. Syed has authored contributions in several national youth-led publications and is extending his engagement internationally as an author and reviewer. He aims to promote meaningful change through innovation, interdisciplinary collaboration, and informed advocacy.

Angelo Brown Received his master's at Arizona State University and his Ph.D. Criminal Justice and Criminology at Washington State University. His research and teaching in criminal justice and criminology are primarily on policy and policing from a comparative and intersectional perspective.

Anjali Daisy is an associate professor at Gnanam School of Business, Thanjavur. She holds a Ph.D. degree in the field of Emotional Intelligence. She assessed and developed an Emotional Competence Inventory for IT employees in Tamil Nadu as the outcome of her research work. She has done her MBA in PSG Institute of Management, Coimbatore. She secured University second position in B.Sc(Computer Science).She holds a Post Graduate Diploma in Labour Law and Administrative Law(PGDLL). She conducted EI training programs for diversified working professionals. She has published research papers in SCOPUS and SSCI indexed journals and wrote book chapters as well. She has presented papers at International conferences. She is also a reviewer in IGI Global. She has completed certification courses in the areas of Mind control, Competency Mapping, Strategic Performance Management, Psychology and Teaching in higher education offered by international premier institutes viz the University of Michigan, the University of Toronto, Yale University, and the University of Washington. She is able to incorporate global teaching-learning pedagogies in the courses she handles.

Bipasha Das is a doctoral student at the Faculty of Education, Banaras Hindu University, India. She has completed her M.Phil. Program from RIE, BBSR, NCERT in 2022. Presently, her doctoral dissertation is mainly focused on the Access and Inclusion of International Women students in Higher Education. Her research interests broadly cover the Internationalization of Higher Education, Access and Inclusion in Society, the Socio-psychological aspect of Education, and Women's Education, Digital Feminism, Gender and Media.

Munaganti Annapurna Devi, NET and SET qualified Asst Professor currently working at Symbiosis Law School, Hyderabad and teaching International Trade and Economics and Private International law. She has academic as well as administrative experience in holding various centers and committees of law schools she worked. She is also pursuing PhD from PG Department of Legal Studies and Research, Acharya Nagarjuna University Guntur Andhra Pradesh with respect to appreciation of electronic evidence. She has undertaken various tasks in modifying and framing curriculum in areas of business laws, Information Technology Laws and International laws. Her areas of interests are in varied streams including emerging technologies in cyberspace and Information Technology laws and appreciation of electronic evidence and computer forensics, international trade laws, EU laws and general international laws. She has presented various national and international papers and published some of her selected works in journals and edited books. She has organized various workshops and two national seminars in Cyber law. She received two gold medals for her outstanding performance in her bachelor law degree and received the prestigious "Pratibha Award" from the State government of Andhra Pradesh.

Sushil Dhakal is a research scholar at Law College Dehradun, Uttaranchal University. His academic focus lies in comparative constitutional law, with a specific research interest in the constitutional frameworks and democratic institutions of India and Nepal.

Pushpita Dutta is presently an Assistant Professor at School of Law, Presidency University, Bengaluru. Previously she has worked as a TRIP Fellow and Academic Tutor at Jindal Global Law School. She has completed her master's in Constitutional and Administrative Law from National Law Institute University, Bhopal and B.Com. LL.B. from Mody University, Rajasthan. Dutta has co-edited the Banthia Law Journal Vol-2 on Emerging Aspects of International Law, which released in 2017. She also has a diploma in Spanish Language. Her areas of interest comprise of constitutional law, human rights and liberty based jurisprudence. When not teaching or researching, she likes to explore Bharatanatyam and spirituality.

Alok Gardia is a Professor at the Faculty of Education, Banaras Hindu University, for the last 23 years. He has scores of publications in the reputed journals globally, guided 12 doctoral dissertations, and completed several research projects on different educational themes. His basic research interest is in the domain of the sociology of education, where he likes to address civic education, social psychology, and the entire conceptual premise of education as a social institution. He also deals with value education from a sociological perspective and how education helps in creating social order. His core specific area is Education for Democratic Citizenship, Language across the curriculum, Issues of Pedagogy of English, and Research Methodological concerns.

Anuttama Ghose is an Assistant Professor of Law and Program Co-ordinator of BA LLB (Hons.) Program at the School of Law, Dr. Vishwanath Karad MIT World Peace University, Pune, India. She is also presently Heading the Centre for Innovation Incubation and Intellectual Property Laws (CIIIPL) at MIT WPU School of Law. She has completed her B.A LL.B (IPR Hons.) from the School of Law, KIIT University, Bhubaneshwar and LL.M with specialisation in the field of Intellectual Property Laws from Symbiosis Law School, Pune, India. She has completed her PhD in the field of Protection of Non-Conventional Trademarks from School of Law and Justice, Adamas University, Kolkata. She has previously worked as Vice-Principal and Assistant Professor of Law at Indian Institute of Legal Studies, Darjeeling, West Bengal. Apart from being an IPR enthusiast, she is a very keen researcher and has over 25 academic publications in National and International Journals to her credit. Her scholarly contributions extend to well-regarded Scopus Indexed Journals and Book Chapters with Internationally reputed publishers such as IGI Global, Springer Nature, Thompson Reuter, etc.

Papiya Golder is an Associate Professor at Brainware University. Her research areas include Family Law, Constitutional Law, and Alternate Dispute Resolution, with a focus on legal reforms, access to justice, and the role of alternative mechanisms in dispute resolution.

S. Ida Evangeline, presently working as an Assistant Professor in the Department of Electrical and Electronics Engineering at the Government College of Engineering, Tirunelveli, Tamilnadu, India. She obtained her Bachelor's in Electrical and Electronics Engineering from Manonmaniam Sundaranar University in 2003, and Master's in Power Systems Engineering from Anna University, Chennai, Tamilnadu, India in 2005. She completed her PhD degree in 2023 at Anna University, Chennai, Tamilnadu, India. She has published six research papers in international journals. Her current research interests include optimal power flow, renewable energy, soft computing, machine learning, and deep learning.

Tasnim Jahan is currently working as Assistant Professor at School of Law, GD Goenka University, Haryana and have previously worked as an assistant Professor of Law at Ramaiah University of Applied Sciences, Teaching Assistant of Law at Symbiosis Law School, Hyderabad and as a Research Associate at National Law School, Bengaluru. She is also pursuing her PhD in Intellectual Property Rights from West Bengal National University of Juridical Sciences. Having profound interest in Academia and research, she has presented papers in various National and International Conferences and have few reputed publications under her name.

Jipson Joseph has a PhD in Ethics from DVK Bangalore. Currently, he is a Research Scholar at School of Law, Christ University, Bangalore, India. His research interests are in the fields of ethics, gender studies, constitutional law, human rights, human security, environmental justice, SDGs, developmental policies, and global poverty. He has published 6 books, co-edited one book, and contributed scholarly articles to many international and national journals and edited volumes including IGI Global Scientific Publishing's edited books.

Sangeeta Mathur is the Dean of the School of Arts and Humanities at Career Point University, Kota. Her research interests include political science, gender studies, and digital activism in contemporary India.

Anjum Parvez is an Associate Professor at Law College Dehradun, Uttaranchal University. His research interests include Constitutional Law, Penal Laws, and Human Rights, with a focus on the evolving legal landscape and its impact on justice and civil liberties.

Maitrayae Sadhu is an Assistant Professor at Brainware University. Her research interests encompass Intellectual Property Rights, Human Rights, and Constitutional Law, with a particular emphasis on the intersection of legal protections, individual freedoms, and innovation in contemporary legal frameworks.

Shashikant Saurav is an Assistant Professor of Law (Senior Scale) at the School of Law, Vellore Institute of Technology, Chennai. With over five years of experience in teaching and research, he specializes in criminal law, with interdisciplinary research interests spanning Artificial Intelligence, Intellectual Property Rights, transgender rights, women's rights, gender neutrality, and consumer protection. He is currently pursuing his PhD at the Manipal Academy of Higher Education, Bengaluru. He holds a BA LLB (Hons.) from Aligarh Muslim University and an LLM from the Central University of South Bihar, where he authored a dissertation on the efficacy of rape laws in India. He qualified the UGC-NET (Law) in December 2019. Prior to joining Ramaiah University, he served as an Assistant Professor at Symbiosis Law School, Hyderabad, for three and a half years, and at the Indian Institute of Legal Studies, Darjeeling, for one and a half years. A committed academician, Mr. Saurav has presented research papers at various national and international conferences and has several reputed publications to his credit. He is deeply passionate about creating intellectually stimulating classroom environments and encourages students to push the boundaries of their critical thinking. In his leisure time, he enjoys reading fiction and writing monologues.

Saroj Sharma is an accomplished education professional with a proven academic track record. She received two gold medals in law during her graduation and was also awarded the National Merit Scholarship (2004–05) for her academic excellence at J.N.V. University, Jodhpur. An astute professional with 19 years of experience in academia, Dr. Saroj Sharma has demonstrated exceptional proficiency in teaching, academic administration, legal research, legal assistance, and public speaking. Throughout her distinguished career, Dr. Sharma has contributed significantly to the development of academic programs, curriculum, and regulations, in addition to preparing and delivering engaging lectures to facilitate an enriching classroom experience.

Harshit Singh is currently serving as a Research Officer (Economic and Financial Security) in the Office of the Vice Chancellor at Rashtriya Raksha

University. He holds an LL.M. in Criminal and Security Law from Rashtriya Raksha University, where he was awarded the Gold Medal for academic excellence. He also holds a BA LL.B. from Symbiosis Law School, Hyderabad. Harshit's research expertise lies at the intersection of financial crime, national security, and regulatory frameworks. He has a strong command over legal research methodologies, policy analysis, and interdisciplinary investigation, particularly in areas concerning cybercrime, anti-money laundering, and financial fraud prevention. His work is driven by a commitment to evidence-based policy development and practical solutions for emerging security threats.

Hemendra Singh is a Lecturer of Law at Jindal Global Law School, situated within O.P. Jindal Global University, Sonipat. He pursued his LL.M. in Intellectual Property Rights from National Law University, Jodhpur, following his graduation with a B.A. LL.B. (Hons.) from Rajiv Gandhi National University of Law, Punjab. With a focus on corporate law, intellectual property law, criminal law, and constitutional law, he has authored numerous research articles and book chapters published in both national and international journals and books.

Satyam Verma is a doctoral student at the Faculty of Education, Banaras Hindu University, India. Previously, he has completed his M.Ed. Program from Central University of South Bihar, Gaya, India in 2022. His general research interest area broadly covers Society and Digital Media, Citizenship Education, Sociology of Education, and Education and Politics. His doctoral dissertation is mainly focused on digital activism and digital citizenship behavior among youth.

Index

A

B

C

D

E

F

G

H

R

S

T

U

V

www.ingramcontent.com/pod-product-compliance
Lightning Source LLC
LaVergne TN
LVHW061528290926
849162LV00004B/712
* 9 7 9 8 3 6 9 3 3 9 2 0 6 *